Joint Workshop on Linguistic Annotation, Multiword Expressions and Constructions (LAW-MWE-CxG 2018)

Santa Fe, New Mexico, USA
25 – 26 August 2018

ISBN: 978-1-5108-6913-4

LAW-MWE-CxG 2018

Joint Workshop on Linguistic Annotation, Multiword Expressions and Constructions

Proceedings of the Workshop

August 25-26, 2018
Santa Fe, New Mexico, USA

Introduction

The Joint Workshop on Linguistic Annotation, Multiword Expressions and Constructions (LAW-MWE-CxG-2018)[1] took place on August 25-26, 2018 in Santa Fe (USA), in conjunction with the 27th International Conference on Computational Linguistics (COLING 2018). This was simultaneously the 12th edition of the Linguistic Annotation Workshop (LAW XII) and the 14th edition of the Workshop on Multiword Expressions (MWE 2018). The event was organized and sponsored by the Special Interest Group for Annotation (SIGANN)[2] and the Special Interest Group on the Lexicon (SIGLEX)[3] of the Association for Computational Linguistics (ACL). It was also endorsed by the Special Interest Group on Computational Semantics (SIGSEM)[4].

The workshop brought together three divergent, but overlapping, research communities studying linguistic annotation, multiword expressions, and grammatical constructions. *Linguistic annotation* of natural language corpora is the backbone of supervised methods for statistical natural language processing. It is also essential for evaluation of both rule-based and supervised systems and can help formalize and study linguistic phenomena. *Multiword expressions* (MWEs) are word combinations, such as *all of a sudden*, *hot dog*, *to pay a visit* or *to pull one's leg*, which exhibit lexical, syntactic, semantic, pragmatic and/or statistical idiosyncrasies. Computational research on MWEs encompasses NLP modeling and processing, as well as annotation. *Grammatical constructions* (which include MWEs) are conventional associations of lexical, syntactic, and pragmatic information, such as *the-ComparAdjP-the-ComparAdjP* (*the more the merrier*, *the higher the better*, etc.). In the framework of Construction Grammar (CxG), linguistic knowledge about constructions is captured in an inventory of form-meaning pairings of varying degrees of internal complexity and lexical fixedness.

In order to promote synergies between these three largely complementary scientific topics, we called for papers in two tracks: the regular *research track* and the *shared task track*. The topics promoted in the research track included, but were not limited, to:

- Joint topics on constructions, annotation, and MWEs:
    - MWE and construction annotation in corpora and treebanks
    - MWE and construction representation in manually and automatically constructed lexical resources
    - Extending MWE discovery and identification methods to constructions
    - MWEs and constructions (and their annotations) in language acquisition and in non-standard language (e.g. tweets, forums, spontaneous speech)
    - Evaluation of MWE and construction annotation and processing techniques
    - Computationally-applicable theoretical studies on MWEs and constructions in psycholinguistics, corpus linguistics and grammar formalisms, and/or how such studies can impact annotation of constructions
- Annotation-specific topics:
    - Annotation procedures, whether manual or automatic, including machine learning and knowledge-based methods
    - Maintenance and interactive exploration of annotation structures and annotated data
    - Qualitative and quantitative annotation evaluation
    - Linguistic considerations, representation formats and exploration tools for merged annotations of different phenomena

---

[1] `http://multiword.sourceforge.net/lawmwecxg2018/`
[2] `https://www.cs.vassar.edu/sigann/`
[3] `http://siglex.org/`
[4] `http://www.sigsem.org`

- Standards, best practices, documentation, interoperability, and comparison of annotation schemes
- Development, evaluation and innovative use of annotation software frameworks

- MWE-specific topics:
    - Original MWE discovery and identification methods
    - MWE processing in syntactic and semantic frameworks (e.g. HPSG, LFG, TAG, Universal Dependencies, WSD, semantic parsing), and in end-user applications (e.g. summarization, machine translation)

We received 34 submissions (22 long and 12 short papers) in the research track, one of them was further withdrawn. We selected 16 long papers and 6 short ones. From those, 9 papers were presented orally and the remaining 13 as posters. The overall selectivity rate was 65%. Of the 22 presented papers, 16 concerned linguistic annotation, 14 multiword expressions, and 5 constructions. As many as 11 papers addressed at least 2 of the 3 workshop topics, which makes us believe that the intended synergy effect has been achieved.

The shared task track was the culmination of the PARSEME Shared Task on Automatic Identification of Verbal Multiword Expressions[5], preceded by a corpus annotation campaign in 20 languages, coordinated by the PARSEME[6] scientific network. The shared task attracted 12 teams, which presented 17 systems, most of them highly multilingual. Eight of those teams submitted system description papers, all were selected and presented as posters. The reviewing modalities were different in this track (notably the requirement of originality did not apply), therefore we do not count these papers in the workshop selectivity rate.

In addition to the oral and poster sessions, the workshop featured three invited talks:

- Lori Levin, Carnegie Mellon University (Pittsburgh, USA), "Annotation Schemes for Surface Construction Labeling"
- Adam Przepiórkowski, University of Warsaw and Polish Academy of Sciences (Warsaw, Poland), "From Lexical Functional Grammar to Enhanced Universal Dependencies"
- Nathan Schneider, Georgetown University (USA), "Leaving no token behind: comprehensive (and delicious) annotation of MWEs and supersenses"

We are grateful to the paper authors for their valuable contributions, the members of the Program Committee for their thorough and timely reviews, all members of the organizing committee for the fruitful collaboration, the shared task organizers, annotators, and system developers for their hard work, and all the workshop participants for their interest in this event. Our thanks also go to the COLING 2018 organizers for their support, as well as to SIGLEX, SIGANN and SIGSEM, for their endorsement.

Agata Savary, Carlos Ramisch, Nancy Ide and Adam Meyers

---

[5]`http://multiword.sourceforge.net/sharedtask2018`
[6]`http://www.parseme.eu`

Organizers

Workshop Organizers

Nancy Ide, Vassar College, USA
Adam Meyers, New York University, USA
Carlos Ramisch, Aix Marseille University, France
Agata Savary, University of Tours, France

Program Committee Chairs

Jena D. Hwang, Institute for Human and Machine Cognition, USA
Miriam R L Petruck, ICSI, USA
Sameer Pradhan, cemantix.org and Vassar College, New York, USA
Carlos Ramisch, Aix Marseille University, France
Agata Savary, University of Tours, France
Nathan Schneider, Georgetown University, USA

Publication Chairs

Melanie Andresen, Universität Hamburg, Germany
Agata Savary, University of Tours, France

Publicity Chairs

Adam Meyers, New York University, USA
Agata Savary, University of Tours, France

Programme Committee

Omri Abend, The Hebrew University of Jerusalem, Israel
Ron Artstein, Institute for Creative Technologies, USC, USA
Timothy Baldwin, University of Melbourne, Australia
Libby Barak, University of Toronto, Canada
Riyaz A. Bhat, University of Colorado Boulder, USA
Archna Bhatia, Carnegie Mellon University, USA
Ann Bies, Linguistic Data Consortium, University of Pennsylvania, USA
Francis Bond, Nanyang Technological University, Singapore
Claire Bonial, Air-Force Research Lab, USA
Antonio Branco, University of Lisbon, Portugal
Miriam Butt, Universität Konstanz, Germany
Aoife Cahill, Educational Testing Service, USA
Nicoletta Calzolari, National Research Council of Italy, Italy
Marie Candito, Paris Diderot University, France
Özlem Çetinoğlu, University of Stuttgart, Germany
Christian Chiarcos, University of Frankfurt, Germany
Anastasia Christofidou, Academy of Athens, Greece
Kathryn Conger, University of Colorado Boulder, USA
Matthieu Constant, Université de Lorraine, France
Paul Cook, University of New Brunswick, Canada
Silvio Ricardo Cordeiro, Federal University of Rio Grande do Sul, Brazil
Béatrice Daille, Nantes University, France

Haris Papageorgiou, Institute for Language and Speech Processing, Greece
Antonio Pareja-Lora, Universidad Complutense de Madrid, DMEG and ATLAS, Spain
Yannick Parmentier, Université d'Orléans, France
Carla Parra Escartín, Dublin City University, Ireland
Agnieszka Patejuk, Institute of Computer Science, Polish Academy of Sciences, Poland
Pavel Pecina, Charles University, Czech Republic
Scott Piao, Lancaster University, UK
Thierry Poibeau, CNRS and École Normale Supérieure, France
James Pustejovsky, Brandeis University, USA
Ines Rehbein, University of Heidelberg, Germany
Arndt Riester, University of Stuttgart, Germany
Josef Ruppenhofer, Heidelberg University, Germany
Manfred Sailer, Goethe-Universität Frankfurt am Main, Germany
Sabine Schulte im Walde, University of Stuttgart, Germany
Djamé Seddah, Paris-Sorbonne University, France
Michael Spranger, Sony Labs, Japan
Manfred Stede, University of Potsdam, Germany
Sara Stymne, Uppsala University, Sweden
Stan Szpakowicz, University of Ottawa, Canada
Tiago Torrent, Federal University of Juiz de Fora, Brazil
Beata Trawinski, Institut für Deutsche Sprache Mannheim, Germany
Yuancheng Tu, Microsoft, USA
Ruben Urizar, University of the Basque Country, Spain
Aline Villavicencio, Federal University of Rio Grande do Sul, Brazil
Veronika Vincze, Hungarian Academy of Sciences, Hungary
Michael Wiegand, Saarland University, Germany
Susan Windisch Brown, University of Colorado Boulder, USA
Shuly Wintner, University of Haifa, Israel
Andreas Witt, Institut fur Deutsche Sprache, Germany
Amir Zeldes, Georgetown University, USA
Heike Zinsmeister, Universität Hamburg, Germany

Invited Speakers

Lori Levin, Carnegie Mellon University, Pittsburgh, USA
Adam Przepiórkowski, University of Warsaw and Polish Academy of Sciences, Warsaw, Poland
Nathan Schneider, Georgetown University, USA

Short Papers

Shared Task Papers

Conference Program

Saturday, August 25, 2018

8:55–9:00	*Opening*

Session 1: Multiword Expressions

9:00–10:00   **Invited talk:** *Leaving no token behind: comprehensive (and delicious) annotation of MWEs and supersenses*
Nathan Schneider

10:00–10:30   *Poster boosters of research papers*

10:30–11:00   *Coffee break*

Session 2: Multiword Expressions

11:00–11:30   *Fixed Similes: Measuring aspects of the relation between MWE idiomatic semantics and syntactic flexibility*
Stella Markantonatou, Panagiotis Kouris and Yanis Maistros

11:30–12:00   *Edition 1.1 of the PARSEME Shared Task on Automatic Identification of Verbal Multiword Expressions*
Carlos Ramisch, Silvio Ricardo Cordeiro, Agata Savary, Veronika Vincze, Verginica Barbu Mititelu, Archna Bhatia, Maja Buljan, Marie Candito, Polona Gantar, Voula Giouli, Tunga Güngör, Abdelati Hawwari, Uxoa Iñurrieta, Jolanta Kovalevskaitė, Simon Krek, Timm Lichte, Chaya Liebeskind, Johanna Monti, Carla Parra Escartín, Behrang QasemiZadeh, Renata Ramisch, Nathan Schneider, Ivelina Stoyanova, Ashwini Vaidya and Abigail Walsh

12:00–12:10   *TRAVERSAL at PARSEME Shared Task 2018: Identification of Verbal Multiword Expressions Using a Discriminative Tree-Structured Model*
Jakub Waszczuk

12:10–12:20   *TRAPACC and TRAPACCS at PARSEME Shared Task 2018: Neural Transition Tagging of Verbal Multiword Expressions*
Regina Stodden, Behrang QasemiZadeh and Laura Kallmeyer

12:20–12:30   *Poster boosters of 6 other shared task papers*

12:30–13:50   *Lunch break*

13:50–15:50   **Session 3: Posters**
The RST Spanish-Chinese Treebank
Shuyuan Cao, Iria da Cunha and Mikel Iruskieta
The Other Side of the Coin: Unsupervised Disambiguation of Potentially Idiomatic Expressions by Contrasting Senses
Hessel Haagsma, Malvina Nissim and Johan Bos
Fine-Grained Termhood Prediction for German Compound Terms Using Neural Networks
Anna Hätty and Sabine Schulte im Walde
Verbal Multiword Expressions in Basque Corpora
Uxoa Iñurrieta, Itziar Aduriz, Ainara Estarrona, Itziar Gonzalez-Dios, Antton Gurrutxaga, Ruben Urizar and Iñaki Alegria
Towards a Computational Lexicon for Moroccan Darija: Words, Idioms, and Constructions
Jamal Laoudi, Claire Bonial, Lucia Donatelli, Stephen Tratz and Clare Voss

15:50–16:20   *Coffee break*

16:20–18:00   *Session 4: Posters*

Sunday, August 26, 2018

	Session 5: Constructions
9:00–10:00	**Invited talk**: *Annotation Schemes for Surface Construction Labeling* Lori Levin
10:00–10:30	*The Interplay of Form and Meaning in Complex Medical Terms: Evidence from a Clinical Corpus* Leonie Grön, Ann Bertels and Heylen Kris
10:30–11:00	*Coffee break*
	Session 6: Constructions
	Processing MWEs: Neurocognitive Bases of Verbal MWEs and Lexical Cohesiveness within MWEs Shohini Bhattasali, Murielle Fabre and John Hale
	Discourse and lexicons: lexemes, MWEs, grammatical constructions and compositional word combinations to signal discourse relations Laurence Danlos
	From Chinese word segmentation to extraction of constructions: two sides of the same algorithmic coin Jean-Pierre Colson
12:30–13:50	*Lunch break*
	Session 7: Linguistic annotation
13:50–14:50	**Invited talk**: *From Lexical Functional Grammar to Enhanced Universal Dependencies* Adam Przepiórkowski (joint work with Agnieszka Patejuk)
14:50–15:20	*Annotation of Tense and Aspect Semantics for Sentential AMR* Lucia Donatelli, Michael Regan, William Croft and Nathan Schneider
15:20–15:50	*An Annotated Corpus of Picture Stories Retold by Language Learners* Christine Köhn and Arne Köhn
15:50–16:20	*Coffee break*
	Session 8: Linguistic annotation
16:20–16:40	*Improving Domain Independent Question Parsing with Synthetic Treebanks* Halim-Antoine Boukaram, Nizar Habash, Micheline Ziadee and Majd Sakr
16:40–17:40	*Business meeting*

Annotation Schemes for Surface Construction Labeling

Lori Levin
Carnegie Mellon University
Pittsburgh, PA, USA
lsl@cs.cmu.edu

Abstract

In this talk I will describe the interaction of linguistics and language technologies in Surface Construction Labeling (SCL) from the perspective of corpus annotation tasks such as definiteness, modality, and causality. Linguistically, following Construction Grammar, SCL recognizes that meaning may be carried by morphemes, words, or arbitrary constellations of morpho-lexical elements. SCL is like Shallow Semantic Parsing in that it does not attempt a full compositional analysis of meaning, but rather identifies only the main elements of a semantic frame, where the frames may be invoked by constructions as well as lexical items. Computationally, SCL is different from tasks such as information extraction in that it deals only with meanings that are expressed in a conventional, grammaticalized way and does not address inferred meanings. I review the work of Dunietz (2018) on the labeling of causal frames including causal connectives and cause and effect arguments. I will describe how to design an annotation scheme for SCL, including isolating basic units of form and meaning and building a "constructicon". I will conclude with remarks about the nature of universal categories and universal meaning representations in language technologies. This talk describes joint work with Jaime Carbonell, Jesse Dunietz, Nathan Schneider, and Miriam Petruck.

Bio

Lori Levin received a B.A. in linguistics from the University of Pennsylvania in 1979 and a Ph.D. in linguistics from MIT in 1986. She is a Research Professor at the Language Technologies Institute at Carnegie Mellon University, specializing in language technologies for low-resource languages. She is also co-Chair of the North American Computational Linguistics Olympiad.

References

Jesse Dunietz. 2018. *Annotating and automatically tagging constructions of causal language.* Ph.D. dissertation, Carnegie Mellon University, Pittsburgh, Pennsylvania, USA.

Proceedings of the Joint Workshop on
Linguistic Annotation, Multiword Expressions and Constructions (LAW-MWE-CxG-2018), page 1
Santa Fe, New Mexico, USA, August 25-26, 2018.

From Lexical Functional Grammar to Enhanced Universal Dependencies

Adam Przepiórkowski
Institute of Philosophy
University of Warsaw *and*
Institute of Computer Science
Polish Academy of Sciences
ul. Jana Kazimierza 5
01-248 Warszawa, Poland
`adamp@ipipan.waw.pl`

Agnieszka Patejuk
Faculty of Linguistics, Philology and Phonetics
University of Oxford *and*
Institute of Computer Science
Polish Academy of Sciences
ul. Jana Kazimierza 5
01-248 Warszawa, Poland
`aep@ipipan.waw.pl`

Universal Dependencies (UD; Nivre et al. 2016) has recently become a *de facto* standard as a dependency representation used in Natural Language Processing (NLP). As perhaps most of syntactic processing in NLP involves dependency structures, it is safe to say that it is becoming a standard for syntactic processing at large. There are 122 treebanks for 71 languages in the July 2018 release 2.2 of UD, publicly available at `http://universaldependencies.org/`. New UD treebanks are often the result of converting corpora adhering to other annotation schemes – not only dependency-based, but also constituency-based.

Lexical Functional Grammar (LFG; Bresnan 1982, Dalrymple 2001, Bresnan et al. 2015) is a linguistic theory which assumes two syntactic levels of representation (in addition to other, non-syntactic levels): constituency structure (c-structure) and functional structure (f-structure). In the case of the Polish sentence (1), in which two asyndetically coordinated verbs within a clausal subject share a number of dependents, the c-structure is given in (2) and the f-structure – in (3):[1]

(1) Wydawało   się, że wojna   jednak go   przerosła,   przeraziła.
    seemed.3.SG.N RM that war.NOM.SG.F after all him.ACC overwhelmed.3.SG.F scared.3.SG.F
    'It seemed that, after all, the war overwhelmed and scared him.'

The first aim of this paper is to describe a procedure of converting such LFG structures to dependency representations following the UD standard, specifically, its enhanced version 2. Conversion of LFG structures to dependency structures is not a new task, but – with the exception of Meurer 2017 – previous attempts are only mentioned or very roughly outlined in the literature. Moreover, previous work has been limited to *dependency trees* as the output format. As is well known, simple dependency trees cannot straightforwardly represent many kinds of linguistic information, so the conversion from representations such as those assumed in LFG invariably resulted in considerable loss of information.

The current version 2 of Universal Dependencies assumes, apart from basic dependency trees, also *enhanced dependency structures*, which make it possible to represent phenomena beyond the scope of simple trees. For example, the result of converting the LFG structures (2)–(3) to UD is shown in (4) (with the basic tree displayed above the text and the enhanced structure – below the text, with the differences shown in red). The second aim of this paper is to examine to what extent rich information available in LFG structures is or may in principle be preserved in such enhanced UD representations.

The empirical basis for the conversion is a manually disambiguated LFG parsebank of Polish (Patejuk and Przepiórkowski 2014) consisting of over 17,000 sentences (almost 131,000 tokens). Since this is a parsebank, it only contains analyses successfully provided by the LFG parser of Polish (Patejuk and Przepiórkowski 2012b, 2015) and selected by human annotators as correct. While this constrains the number and kinds of constructions present in the corpus, the underlying LFG grammar of Polish is currently one of the largest implemented LFG grammars, and it includes a comprehensive analysis of various kinds of coordination and its interaction with other phenomena (Patejuk and Przepiórkowski 2012a), so there is no shortage of sentences which pose potential difficulties for the conversion.

[1] RM in (1) stands for 'reflexive marker', which in this case is an inherent part of the verb *wydawało się* 'seemed'; other abbreviations are standard. LFG structures shown in (2)–(3) are visualisations produced by the INESS system (`http://clarino.uib.no/iness/`; Rosén et al. 2012), which hosts the Polish LFG structure bank, among other treebanks.

*Proceedings of the Joint Workshop on
Linguistic Annotation, Multiword Expressions and Constructions (LAW-MWE-CxG-2018)*, pages 2–4
Santa Fe, New Mexico, USA, August 25-26, 2018.

(2)

(3)

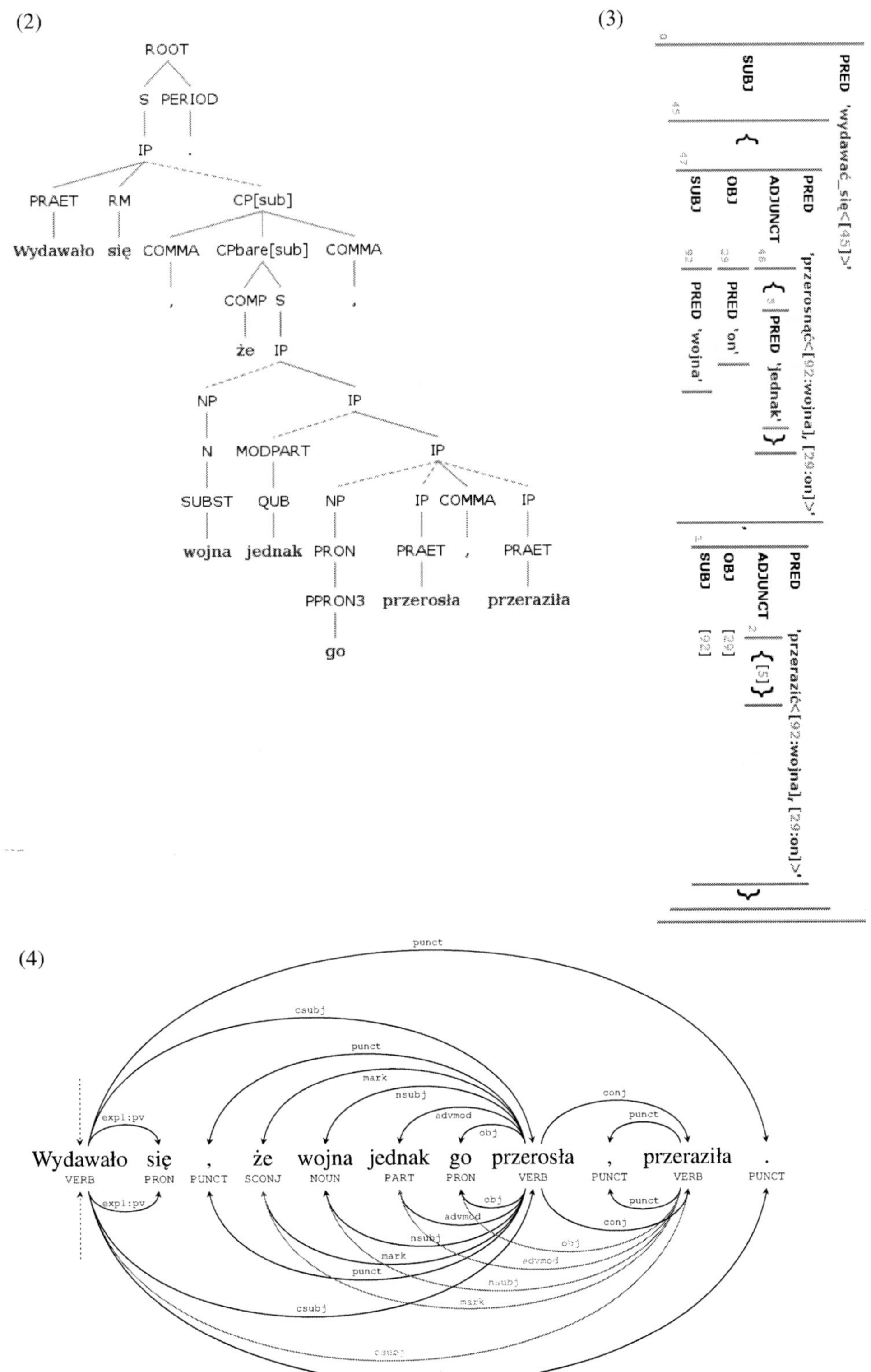

(4)

References

Joan Bresnan, Ash Asudeh, Ida Toivonen, and Stephen Wechsler. 2015. *Lexical-Functional Syntax*. Blackwell Textbooks in Linguistics. Wiley-Blackwell, 2nd edition.

Joan Bresnan, editor. 1982. *The Mental Representation of Grammatical Relations*. The MIT Press, Cambridge, MA.

Mary Dalrymple. 2001. *Lexical Functional Grammar*. Academic Press, San Diego, CA.

Paul Meurer. 2017. From LFG structures to dependency relations. In Victoria Rosén and Koenraad De Smedt, editors, *The Very Model of a Modern Linguist*, volume 8 of *Bergen Language and Linguistics Studies*, pages 183–201. University of Bergen Library, Bergen.

Joakim Nivre, Marie-Catherine de Marneffe, Filip Ginter, Yoav Goldberg, Jan Hajič, Christopher D. Manning, Ryan McDonald, Slav Petrov, Sampo Pyysalo, Natalia Silveira, Reut Tsarfaty, and Daniel Zeman. 2016. Universal Dependencies v1: A multilingual treebank collection. In Nicoletta Calzolari, Khalid Choukri, Thierry Declerck, Marko Grobelnik, Bente Maegaard, Joseph Mariani, Asuncion Moreno, Jan Odijk, and Stelios Piperidis, editors, *Proceedings of the Tenth International Conference on Language Resources and Evaluation, LREC 2016*, pages 1659–1666, Portorož, Slovenia. ELRA, European Language Resources Association (ELRA).

Agnieszka Patejuk and Adam Przepiórkowski. 2012a. A comprehensive analysis of constituent coordination for grammar engineering. In *Proceedings of the 24th International Conference on Computational Linguistics (COLING 2012)*, pages 2191–2207, Mumbai, India.

Agnieszka Patejuk and Adam Przepiórkowski. 2012b. Towards an LFG parser for Polish: An exercise in parasitic grammar development. In *Proceedings of the Eighth International Conference on Language Resources and Evaluation, LREC 2012*, pages 3849–3852, Istanbul, Turkey. ELRA.

Agnieszka Patejuk and Adam Przepiórkowski. 2014. Synergistic development of grammatical resources: A valence dictionary, an LFG grammar, and an LFG structure bank for Polish. In Verena Henrich, Erhard Hinrichs, Daniël de Kok, Petya Osenova, and Adam Przepiórkowski, editors, *Proceedings of the Thirteenth International Workshop on Treebanks and Linguistic Theories (TLT 13)*, pages 113–126, Tübingen. Department of Linguistics (SfS), University of Tübingen.

Agnieszka Patejuk and Adam Przepiórkowski. 2015. Parallel development of linguistic resources: Towards a structure bank of Polish. *Prace Filologiczne*, LXV:255–270.

Victoria Rosén, Koenraad De Smedt, Paul Meurer, and Helge Dyvik. 2012. An open infrastructure for advanced treebanking. In *LREC 2012 META-RESEARCH Workshop on Advanced Treebanking*, pages 22–29, Istanbul, Turkey. ELRA.

Leaving no token behind: comprehensive (and delicious) annotation of MWEs and supersenses

Nathan Schneider
Georgetown University
Washington, DC, USA
`nathan.schneider@georgetown.edu`

Abstract

I will describe an unorthodox approach to lexical semantic annotation that prioritizes corpus coverage, democratizing analysis of a wide range of expression types. I argue that a lexicon-free lexical semantics—defined in terms of units and supersense tags—is an appetizing direction for NLP, as it is robust, cost-effective, easily understood, not too language-specific, and can serve as a foundation for richer semantic structure. Linguistic delicacies from the STREUSLE and DiMSUM corpora, which have been multiword- and supersense-annotated, attest to the veritable smörgåsbord of noncanonical constructions in English, including various flavors of prepositions, MWEs, and other curiosities.

Bio

Nathan Schneider is an annotation schemer and computational modeler for natural language. As Assistant Professor of Linguistics and Computer Science at Georgetown University, he looks for synergies between practical language technologies and the scientific study of language. He specializes in broad-coverage semantic analysis: designing linguistic meaning representations, annotating them in corpora, and automating them with statistical natural language processing techniques. A central focus in this research is the nexus between grammar and lexicon as manifested in multiword expressions and adpositions/case markers. He has inhabited UC Berkeley (BA in Computer Science and Linguistics), Carnegie Mellon University (Ph.D. in Language Technologies), and the University of Edinburgh (postdoc). Now a Hoya and leader of NERT, he continues to play with data and algorithms for linguistic meaning.

Proceedings of the Joint Workshop on
Linguistic Annotation, Multiword Expressions and Constructions (LAW-MWE-CxG-2018), page 5
Santa Fe, New Mexico, USA, August 25-26, 2018.

Processing MWEs: Neurocognitive Bases of Verbal MWEs and Lexical Cohesiveness within MWEs

Shohini Bhattasali
Cornell University
Ithaca, NY, USA
sb2295@cornell.edu

Murielle Fabre
Cornell University / Ithaca, NY, USA
INSERM-CEA / Paris-Saclay, France
mf684@cornell.edu

John Hale
Cornell University / Ithaca, NY, USA
DeepMind / London, UK
jthale@cornell.edu

Abstract

Multiword expressions have posed a challenge in the past for computational linguistics since they comprise a heterogeneous family of word clusters and are difficult to detect in natural language data. In this paper, we present a fMRI study based on language comprehension to provide neuroimaging evidence for processing MWEs. We investigate whether different MWEs have distinct neural bases, e.g. if verbal MWEs involve separate brain areas from non-verbal MWEs and if MWEs with varying levels of cohesiveness activate dissociable brain regions. Our study contributes neuroimaging evidence illustrating that different MWEs elicit spatially distinct patterns of activation. We also adapt an association measure, usually used to detect MWEs, as a cognitively plausible metric for language processing.

1 Introduction

This study focuses on how Multiword Expressions are processed in the brain and provides a functional localization of different facets of MWEs using neuroimaging data. If MWEs are indeed non-compositional, then perhaps their comprehension proceeds through a single, unitary retrieval operation, rather than some kind of multistep compositional process. If we assume a single retrieval operation for these MWEs, how do the differences in their grammatical category affect their processing? Are they observable on the neuronal level?

Proceeding from this general hypothesis, this paper investigates the neural substrates of different types of MWEs and MWEs with different levels of compositionality. Firstly, verbal MWEs are distinguished from non-verbal MWEs and the neural bases of each are compared. Additionally, to model lexical cohesivenss of MWEs we use Pointwise Mututal Information, PMI (Church and Hanks, 1990), which is an association measure and traditionally used to identify MWEs. This gradient metric of cohesiveness within MWEs is correlated with brain activity to illustrate whether MWEs with varying degrees of compositionality evoke different patterns of activation in the brain. In this way, we provide further insight about MWE processing during natural language comprehension.

2 Background

2.1 Previous MWE Processing studies

MWE comprehension has been shown to be distinct from other kinds of language processing. For instance, it is well-established at the behavioural level that MWEs are produced and understood faster than matched control phrases due to their frequency, familiarity, and predictability (Siyanova-Chanturia and Martinez, 2014), in accordance with incremental processing (Hale, 2006). This would follow if MWEs were remembered as chunks, in the sense of Miller (1956) that was later formalised by Laird, Rosenbloom and Newell (1986; 1987).

Proceedings of the Joint Workshop on
Linguistic Annotation, Multiword Expressions and Constructions (LAW-MWE-CxG-2018), pages 6–17
Santa Fe, New Mexico, USA, August 25-26, 2018.

Eye-tracking and EEG work further documents this processing advantage across a wide range of
MWE sub-types, e.g.

- Binomials (Siyanova-Chanturia et al., 2011b),

- Phrasal verbs (Yaneva et al., 2017),

- Complex prepositions (Molinaro et al., 2013; Molinaro et al., 2008),

- Nominal compounds (Molinaro and Carreiras, 2010; Molinaro et al., 2012),

- Lexical bundles (Tremblay and Baayen, 2010; Tremblay et al., 2011),

- Idioms (Underwood et al., 2004; Siyanova-Chanturia et al., 2011a; Strandburg et al., 1993; Laurent
  et al., 2006; Vespignani et al., 2010; Rommers et al., 2013).

For example, Siyanova-Chanturia et al. (2011b), found their eye-tracking results illustrate that bino-
mial MWEs such as *bride and groom* are processed faster that the reversed three-word phrase *groom and
bride*, due to the high-frequency nature of the former expression.

However, previous work has focused on a particular subtype of MWEs and to our knowledge, none of
them have implemented a fMRI study of MWEs within a naturalistic text to either contrast between different categories of MWEs or model the cohesiveness within them. Recent computational work (Savary
et al., 2017; Cholakov and Kordoni, 2016; Gharbieh et al., 2016; Uresova et al., 2016) has focused on
verbal MWEs in order to identify them within a corpus, rather than study how they are processed in a
naturalistic setting.

2.2   MWEs and Compositionality

The name MWE loosely groups a wide variety of linguistic phenomena including idioms, perfunc-
tory greetings, character names, and personal titles. What unifies cases of MWEs is the absence of a
wholly compositional linguistic analysis; they are "expressions for which the syntactic or semantic properties of the whole expression cannot be derived from its parts" (Sag et al., 2002). The naturalistic story
used as a stimulus in this study includes various types of MWEs and some examples from the stimulus,
The Little Prince are given below. The bold expressions were identified using a MWE analyzer, explained further in §4.2. Over half of the attestations in the text are headed by a verb and can be labelled
as VPs (see §5.2.1). These encompass verb participle constructions, light verb constructions, and verb
nominal constructions among others. The remaining attestations are a mixture of nominal compounds,
greetings, personal titles, character names, and complex prepositions.

(1)   So I thought **a lot** about the adventures of the jungle and **in turn**, I managed with a **coloured
      pencil** to make my first drawing.

(2)   My **little fellow**, I don't know how to draw anything except **boa constrictors**, closed and open.

(3)   When I drew the baobabs, I was spurred on by a **sense of urgency**.

(4)   'What are you doing there?', he said to the drinker who he found sitting **in silence** in front of **a
      number** of empty bottles and **a number** of full bottles.

(5)   You must **see to it** that you regularly **pull out** the baobabs as soon as they can be told **apart from**
      the rose bushes to which they look very similar to when they are young.

(6)   "**Good morning**", said the **little prince** politely, who then turned around, but saw nothing.

However, MWEs cannot be strictly binarized as compositional and non-compositional. These expressions fall along a graded spectrum of compositionality. To capture the varying degrees of compositionality within MWEs, we use an association measure, known as Pointwise Mutual Information (PMI). While
PMI scores are commonly used in computational linguistics to identify MWEs as ngrams with higher
scores are likely to be MWEs (Evert, 2008), in this study they are utilized as a gradient predictor to describe the the lexical cohesiveness of MWEs. Intuitively, its value is high when the word sequence under

consideration occurs more often together than one would have expected, based on the frequencies of the individual words (Manning et al., 1999). More formally, PMI is a log-ratio of observed and expected counts:

$$\text{PMI} = log_2 \frac{c(w_n^1)}{E(w_n^1)} \tag{1}$$

MWEs can receive positive or negative PMI scores which indicate cohesion or repulsion respectively between the words in a sequence (Church and Hanks, 1990). MWEs that receive a higher PMI score are seen as lexically more cohesive, which is interpreted as more noncompositional (less compositional). Thus, these scores are repurposed in this study to describe the cohesive and noncompositional aspect of MWEs and utilized to obtain a quantifiable metric to correlate with the fMRI signal. Krenn (2000) also suggests that association measures such as PMI and Dice's coeeficient (Dice, 1945; Sørensen, 1948; Smadja et al., 1996) are better-suited to identify high-frequency collocations whereas other association measures such as log-likelihood are better at detecting medium to low frequency collocations. Since MWEs are inherently high-frequency collocations, we chose PMI as a metric to describe the strength of association between these word clusters.

3 Research Questions

To summarize, this study investigates the following:

- Are the differences between the grammatical categories of MWEs observable at the cerebral level? Does processing of verbal MWEs implicate separate brain areas from non-verbal MWEs? Specifically, if the strong relationship between verbs and their arguments are encoded in different brain areas compared to non-verbal MWEs featuring no argumental structure? (c.f. Analysis 1 in §5.2.1)

- Do MWEs with varying levels of cohesiveness tap into different cognitive resources? For example, are MWEs with higher PMI scores processed differently from MWEs with lower scores? Do they activate dissociable brain regions? (c.f. Analysis 2 in §5.2.2)

4 fMRI study

4.1 Method

We follow Brennan et al., (2012) in using a spoken narrative as a stimulus. Participants hear the story over headphones while they are in the scanner. The sequence of neuroimages collected during their session becomes the dependent variable in a regression against word-by-word predictors, derived from the text of the story.

4.2 Stimuli & MWE Identification

The audio stimulus was Antoine de Saint-Exupéry's *The Little Prince*, translated by David Wilkinson and read by Nadine Eckert-Boulet. It constitutes a fairly lengthy exposure to naturalistic language, comprising 15,388 words and lasting over an hour and a half.

Within this text, 742 MWEs were identified using a transition-based MWE analyzer (Al Saied et al., 2017). Al Saied et al. use unigram and bigram features, word forms, POS tags and lemmas, in addition to features such as transition history and report an average F-score 0.524 for this analyzer across 18 different languages which reflects robust cross-linguistic performance. For an illustrated example of the MWE identification process with this analyzer, please see the Appendix. The analyzer was trained on examples from the Children's Book Test, CBT (Hill et al., 2015) from the Facebook bAbI project to keep the genre consistent with our literary stimulus. This corpus consists of text passages that are drawn from the Children's section of Project Gutenberg, a free online text repository. External lexicons were used to supplement the MWEs found with the analyzer. The external lexicons included the Unitex lexicon (Paumier et al., 2009), the SAID corpus (Kuiper et al., 2003), the Cambridge International Dictionary of Idioms (White, 1998), and the Dictionary of American Idioms (Makkai et al., 1995). While 742 MWEs might seem like a restricted sample, this data was acquired with experimental constraints since our fMRI study was almost two hours long which is on the longer end for similar neuroimaging studies.

4.3 Participants

Participants were fifty-one volunteers (32 women and 19 men, 18-37 years old) with no history of psychiatric, neurological, or other medical illness or history of drug or alcohol abuse that might compromise cognitive functions. All strictly qualified as right-handed on the Edinburgh handedness inventory (Oldfield, 1971). They self-identified as native English speakers and gave their written informed consent prior to participation, in accordance with Cornell University IRB guidelines.

4.4 Presentation

After giving their informed consent, participants were familiarized with the MRI facility and assumed a supine position on the scanner gurney. The presentation script was written in PsychoPy peirce:2007. Auditory stimuli were delivered through MRI-safe, high-fidelity headphones (Confon HP-VS01, MR Confon, Magdeburg, Germany) inside the head coil. The headphones were secured against the plastic frame of the coil using foam blocks. Using a spoken recitation of the US Constitution, an experimenter increased the volume until participants reported that they could hear clearly. Participants then listened passively to the audio storybook for 1 hour 38 minutes. The story had nine chapters and at the end of each chapter the participants were presented with a multiple-choice questionnaire with four questions (36 questions in total), concerning events and situations described in the story. These questions served to confirm participants' comprehension. They were viewed via a mirror attached to the head coil and answered through a button box. The entire session lasted around 2.5 hours.

4.5 Data Collection

Imaging was performed using a 3T MRI scanner (Discovery MR750, GE Healthcare, Milwaukee, WI) with a 32-channel head coil at the Cornell MRI Facility. Blood Oxygen Level Dependent (BOLD) signals were collected using a T2-weighted echo planar imaging (EPI) sequence (repetition time: 2000 ms, echo time: 27 ms, flip angle: 77deg, image acceleration: 2X, field of view: 216 x 216 mm, matrix size 72 x 72, and 44 oblique slices, yielding 3 mm isotropic voxels). Anatomical images were collected with a high resolution T1-weighted (1 x 1 x 1 mm^3 voxel) with a Magnetization-Prepared RApid Gradient-Echo (MP-RAGE) pulse sequence.

5 Data Analysis

5.1 Preprocessing

fMRI data is acquired with physical, biological constraints and preprocessing allows us to make adjustments to improve the signal to noise ratio. Primary preprocessing steps were carried out in AFNI version 16 (Cox, 1996) and include motion correction, coregistration, and normalization to standard MNI space. After the previous steps were completed, ME-ICA (Kundu et al., 2012) was used to further preprocess the data. ME-ICA is a denoising method which uses Independent Components Analysis to split the T2*-signal into BOLD and non-BOLD components. Removing the non-BOLD components mitigates noise due to motion, physiology, and scanner artifacts (Kundu et al., 2017).

5.2 Statistical Analysis

The General Linear Model (GLM) typically used in fMRI data analysis is a hierarchical model with two levels (Poldrack et al., 2011). At the first level, the data for each subject is modelled separately to calculate subject-specific parameter estimates and within-subject variance such that for each subject, a regression model is estimated for each voxel against the time series. The second-level model takes subject-specific parameter estimates as input. It uses the between-subject variance to make statistical inferences about the larger population.

The research questions presented above in §3 motivate two statistical analyses. The first analysis localizes verbal MWEs and non-verbal MWEs to see if they activate spatially different networks in the brain. The second analysis investigates MWEs along a quantitative gradient of lexical cohesion. Both analyses employ the GLM, and were carried out using SPM12 (Friston et al., 2007). The predictors were convolved using the canonical HRF in SPM. For both of these analyzes, the MWE candidates were taken to be the expressions from the transition-based analyzer (as described in §4.2).

5.2.1 Analysis 1: Verbal MWEs vs. Non-verbal MWEs

We regressed the word-by-word predictors described below against fMRI timecourses recorded during passive story-listening in a whole-brain analysis. For each of the 15,388 words in the story, their timestamps were estimated using Praat TextGrids (Boersma, 2002). MWEs were identified, as described in §4.2 and the presence/absence of verbal expression yielded two categories of MWEs (i.e. 56% verbal vs. 44% non-verbal). The Stanford POS tagger and the NLTK POS tagger were used to annotate the words within the MWEs with their grammatical categories (Bird and Loper, 2004; Manning et al., 2014). Additionally, we entered four regressors of non-interest into the GLM analysis (SPM12): word-offset, word frequency, pitch, intensity which serve to improve the sensitivity, specificity and validity of activation maps (Bullmore et al., 1999; Lund et al., 2006). To control for sentence-level and phrase-level compositional processes, we included a regressor formalizing syntactic structure building based on a bottom-up parsing algorithm (Hale, 2014), as determined by the Stanford parser (Klein and Manning, 2003). Controlling for structural composition allows us to isolate and focus our investigation on noncompositional processing, as in MWEs. These regressors were not orthogonalized.

5.2.2 Analysis 2: Cohesiveness within MWEs

Analysis 2 uses the same predictors as in Analysis 1, except that the categorical indicators for MWEs is replaced with the gradient predictor, PMI. All the 742 MWEs that were annotated with a 1 in Analysis 1 are in Analysis 2 marked with their PMI score. This score is based on corpus frequency counts from the Corpus of Contemporary English (Davies, 2008), and were calculated using `mwetoolkit` (Ramisch et al., 2010; Ramisch, 2012). These regressors were also not orthogonalized.

5.2.3 Group-level Analysis

In the second-level group analysis, each contrast was analyzed separately at the group-level. An 8 mm FWHM Gaussian smoothing kernel was applied on the contrast images from the first-level analysis to counteract inter-subject anatomical variation. All the group-level results reported in the next section underwent FWE voxel correction for multiple comparisons which resulted in T-scores > 5.3.

6 Results

Behavioural results of the comprehension task showed attentive listening to the auditory story presentation. Across 51 participants, average accurate responses to the comprehension questions was 90% (SD = 3.7%).

6.1 Group-level results for Verbal MWEs vs Non-verbal MWEs

The main effect for presence of MWEs elicited activation mainly in bilateral Supramarginal Gyrus, right Angular Gyrus, right MFG, and right Precuneus Cortex (Fig. 1A). Whole-brain contrasts show that these two types of MWEs activate different brain regions with no overlap. Verbal MWEs appear right-lateralized compared to non-verbal ones in IPL and in IFG triangularis (Fig.1B). The opposite contrast yielded a mostly right-lateralized and wider pattern of activation, including bilateral Supramarginal Gyrus extending to STG and right SMA together with smaller activation clusters in Pars Opercularis and MTG (Fig. 1B). Contrasts were inclusively masked with the main effect of all MWEs.

6.2 Group-level results for Lexical Cohension with MWEs

Increasing cohesiveness, as seen through positive activation with PMI (Fig. 2, in purple), elicits the Precuneus and Supplementary Motor Area, while decreasing cohesiveness, as seen through negative activation with PMI (Fig. 2, in orange), correlates with activity in well-known nodes of the language network, such as Broca's area and the posterior Temporal Gyrus.

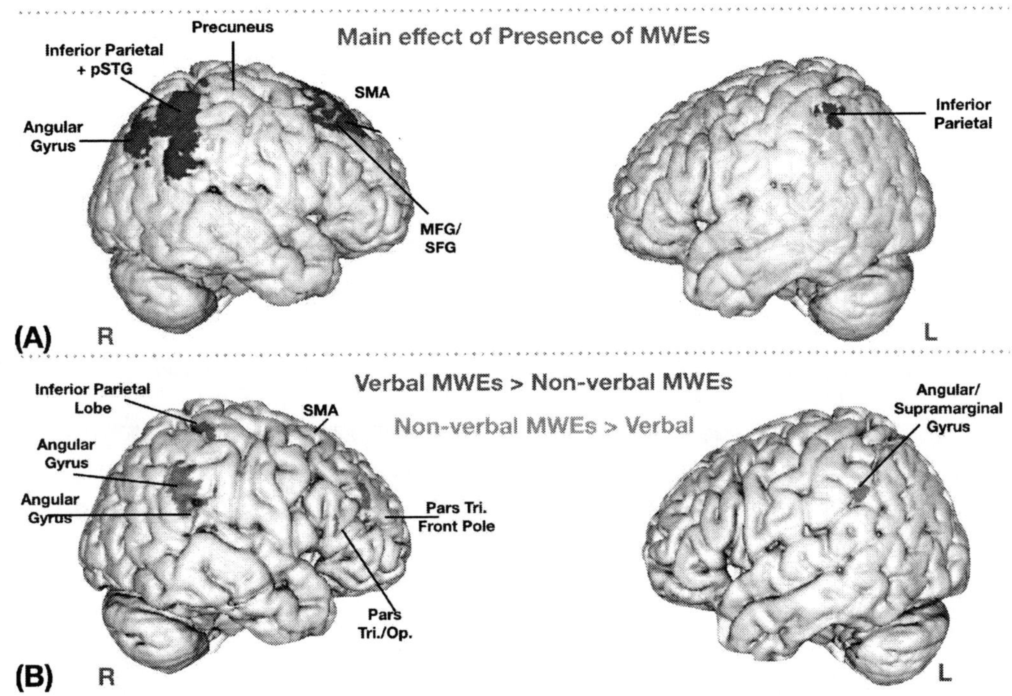

Figure 1: (A): Whole brain main effect for MWEs in blue. (B): Contrast images with significant clusters for [Verbal MWEs > Non-verbal MWEs] in pink and for [Nonverbal MWEs > Verbal MWEs] in green.

Regions	Cluster size (in voxels)	MNI Coordinates x	y	z	p-value (corrected)	T-score (peak level)
Verbal MWEs >Non-verbal MWEs						
R IFG Pars Triangularis	71	46	36	14	0.000	7.38
R Inferior Parietal Lobule	57	50	-40	52	0.002	6.38
Non-verbal MWEs >Verbal MWEs						
R Angular Gyrus	585	56	-42	14	0.000	9.43
R Supplementary Motor Area	235	12	20	60	0.000	8.91
L Cerebellum	58	-22	-72	-30	0.002	7.85
L Supramarginal Gyrus	32	-60	-50	34	0.001	6.50
R IFG Pars Triangularis/Opercularis	28	56	22	8	0.001	6.51

Table 1: Significant cluster for contrasts between verbal MWEs and non-verbal MWEs after FWE voxel correction for multiple comparisons with p < 0.05. Peak activation is given in MNI Coordinates.

7 Discussion & Further Work

The results from Analysis 1 provide evidence that MWEs activate areas consistently reported as the lexical semantic network, such as Supramarginal, Parietal areas, and SMA (Binder et al., 2009). MWEs mostly implicate a right-lateralized network while contrastively, compositional processes have been essentially linked to left lateralization (Friederici and Gierhan, 2013; Bemis and Pylkkänen, 2013; Bemis and Pylkkänen, 2011). Previous findings also show that the bilateral Supramarginal Gyrus is sensitive to co-occurence frequency of word combinations as reported previously for semantically meaningful and frequent word-pairs (Graves et al., 2010; Price et al., 2015).

Additionally, the significant clusters for verbal and non-verbal MWEs illustrate spatially distinct pat-

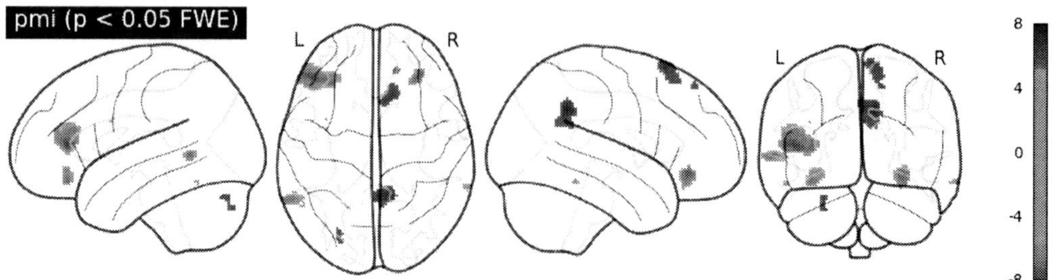

Figure 2: Significant cluster for the increasing and decreasing cohesion measure of MWEs after FWE voxel correction for multiple comparisons with p < 0.05 and cluster-extent threshold (k > 50) for display purposes. Peak activation is given in MNI Coordinates.

Regions for PMI	Cluster size (in voxels)	MNI Coordinates			p-value (corrected)	T-score (peak-level)
		x	y	z		
Correlated with increasing MWE cohesion						
R Precuneus Cortex	263	10	-50	36	0.000	7.30
R Precuneus Cortex		10	-48	24	0.000	5.84
R Superior Frontal Gyrus/Supplementary Motor Area (BA6)	154	10	22	68	0.000	6.34
Correlated with decreasing MWE cohesion						
L IFG Pars Triangularis	448	-46	36	8	0.000	8.01
R IFG Pars Orbitalis/Middle Frontal Gyrus	117	32	38	-12	0.000	7.29
L Posterior Middle Temporal Gyrus	53	-62	-52	2	0.000	6.76
L IFG Pars Orbitalis/Middle Frontal Gyrus	67	-36	38	-16	0.000	6.62

Table 2: Significant cluster for the increasing and decreasing cohesion measure of MWEs after FWE voxel correction for multiple comparisons with p < 0.05. Peak activation is given in MNI Coordinates.

terns of activation and a dorso-ventral gradient is observed in Brocas area for verbal versus non-verbal MWEs. Activation patterns for verbal MWEs suggest that verb-argument selectional relations in frequent verbal expressions exclusively involve right hemisphere activity in Brocas area and IPL.

In the case of non-verbal MWEs, we do not make a strong conclusion since it is a mixed bag of nominal compounds, complex prepositions, greetings, personal titles among other types. We did not contrast between verbal and nominal MWEs since our dataset is skewed towards verbal MWEs and we have very few attestations of nominal MWEs in the text (< 7%).

Our results from Analysis 2 show that highly cohesive MWEs implicate the Precuneus and the SMA, suggesting that only truly lexicalized linguistic expressions rely on these areas rather than traditional frontal and temporal nodes of the language network. These areas have been implicated in memory and naming tasks (Crosson, 2013; Halsband et al., 2002). Less cohesive MWEs activate core areas of the language network implicated in composition (Fedorenko et al., 2016; Friederici and Gierhan, 2013; Pallier et al., 2011; Snijders et al., 2009) which suggests that less cohesive MWEs are processed compositionally and are not retrieved as a unit.

Apart from an association measure like PMI, there are alternate approaches to describes MWEs such as word space models (based on distributional semantics) which could also serve as a metric of compositionality for these noncompositional word clusters. This type of metric would utilize the distributional patterns of words collected over large text data to represent semantic similarity between words in terms of spatial proximity (Sahlgren, 2006). However, in the current study we were not trying to model the semantic opacity of these expressions but that could be an area to explore in the future to investigate another aspect of MWEs.

This study only included native speakers of English as participants and is part of a larger project investigating MWEs cross-linguistically to compare if they are processed similarly. Another future research direction would be to replicate the same experiment with non-native speakers to study how early or late acquisition of English would impact the neural bases recruited in processing these noncompositional expressions.

Another approach to illustrate this gamut of compositionality would be to compare a compositional expression like a VP against a noncompositional verbal MWE (e.g. *kick the ball* vs. *kick the bucket*. Morphosyntactically, these would be structurally similar yet they should be processed differently if our hypothesis about the neurocognitive mechanisms underlying language processing is correct. Based on our prediction, the neuroimaging data should illustrate a spatial dissociation between compositional VPs and noncompositional verbal MWEs.

8 Conclusion

Our results point to a spatial differentiation between verbal MWEs and non-verbal MWEs since they localize to different areas of the brain. Thus, this study provides neuroimaging evidence of different types of MWEs. Additionally, it also illustrates that the grammatical category of the words inside MWEs is crucial to how they are processed in the brain. For example, in the verbal MWEs scenario, the word clusters headed by a verb activate spatially different regions from non-verbal MWEs, plausibly due to the inherent argument structure present in verbal MWEs. Furthermore, this result illustrates that even within these noncompositional verbal expression, there is an aspect of argument structure composition within its subparts.

Furthermore using PMI as a gradient predictor shows that highly cohesive MWEs and less cohesive MWEs tap into different cognitive resources, as evidenced through their separate neural correlates. This suggests a difference between processing truly lexicalized MWEs in contrast to MWEs which are possibly analyzed compositionally. Lastly, one of the main contributions of this study is in repurposing PMI, an association measure to describe MWEs in terms of cohesion and thus showing that they are a cognitively informative metric to model cohesiveness and compositionality within word clusters in natural language.

Acknowledgments

This material is based upon work supported by the National Science Foundation under Grant No. 1607441.

References

Hazem Al Saied, Marie Candito, and Matthieu Constant. 2017. The ATILF-LLF system for the PARSEME Shared Task: a Transition-based Verbal Multiword Expression Tagger. In *Proceedings of the 13th Workshop on Multiword Expressions (MWE 2017)*, pages 127–132, Valencia, Spain, April. Association for Computational Linguistics.

Douglas K Bemis and Liina Pylkkänen. 2011. Simple composition: A magnetoencephalography investigation into the comprehension of minimal linguistic phrases. *The Journal of Neuroscience*, 31(8):2801–2814.

Douglas K Bemis and Liina Pylkkänen. 2013. Basic linguistic composition recruits the left anterior temporal lobe and left angular gyrus during both listening and reading. *Cerebral Cortex*, 23(8):1859–1873.

Jeffrey R Binder, Rutvik H Desai, William W Graves, and Lisa L Conant. 2009. Where is the semantic system? a critical review and meta-analysis of 120 functional neuroimaging studies. *Cerebral Cortex*, 19(12):2767–2796.

Steven Bird and Edward Loper. 2004. Nltk: the natural language toolkit. In *Proceedings of the ACL 2004 on Interactive poster and demonstration sessions*, page 31. Association for Computational Linguistics.

Paul Boersma. 2002. *Praat, a system for doing phonetics by computer.* Glot International.

ET Bullmore, MJ Brammer, S Rabe-Hesketh, VA Curtis, RG Morris, SCR Williams, T Sharma, and PK McGuire. 1999. Methods for diagnosis and treatment of stimulus-correlated motion in generic brain activation studies using fmri. *Human brain mapping*, 7(1):38–48.

Kostadin Cholakov and Valia Kordoni. 2016. Using word embeddings for improving statistical machine translation of phrasal verbs. In *Proceedings of the 12th Workshop on Multiword Expressions*, pages 56–60.

Kenneth Ward Church and Patrick Hanks. 1990. Word association norms, mutual information, and lexicography. *Computational linguistics*, 16(1):22–29.

Robert W. Cox. 1996. Afni: software for analysis and visualization of functional magnetic resonance neuroimages. *Computers and Biomedical research*, 29(3):162–173.

Bruce Crosson. 2013. Thalamic mechanisms in language: A reconsideration based on recent findings and concepts. *Brain and Language*, 126(1):73–88.

Mark Davies. 2008. *The Corpus of Contemporary American English (COCA): 560 million words, 1990–present.* BYE, Brigham Young University.

Lee R Dice. 1945. Measures of the amount of ecologic association between species. *Ecology*, 26(3):297–302.

Stefan Evert. 2008. Corpora and collocations. In Anke Lüdeling and Merja. Kytö, editors, *Corpus linguistics: an international handbook*, pages 1212–1248. W. de Gruyter, Berlin. article number 58.

Evelina Fedorenko, Terri L Scott, Peter Brunner, William G Coon, Brianna Pritchett, Gerwin Schalk, and Nancy Kanwisher. 2016. Neural correlate of the construction of sentence meaning. *Proceedings of the National Academy of Sciences*, 113(41):E6256–E6262.

Angela D Friederici and Sarah ME Gierhan. 2013. The language network. *Current Opinion in Neurobiology*, 23(2):250–254.

K.J. Friston, J. Ashburner, S.J. Kiebel, T.E. Nichols, and W.D. Penny, editors. 2007. *Statistical Parametric Mapping: The Analysis of Functional Brain Images*. Academic Press.

Waseem Gharbieh, Virendra Bhavsar, and Paul Cook. 2016. A word embedding approach to identifying verb-noun idiomatic combinations. In *Proceedings of the 12th Workshop on Multiword Expressions*, pages 112–118.

William W Graves, Jeffrey R Binder, Rutvik H Desai, Lisa L Conant, and Mark S Seidenberg. 2010. Neural correlates of implicit and explicit combinatorial semantic processing. *Neuroimage*, 53(2):638–646.

John Hale. 2006. Uncertainty about the rest of the sentence. *Cognitive Science*, 30(4):643–672.

John T Hale. 2014. *Automaton theories of human sentence comprehension*. CSLI Publications.

U Halsband, BJ Krause, H Sipilä, M Teräs, and A Laihinen. 2002. Pet studies on the memory processing of word pairs in bilingual finnish–english subjects. *Behavioural brain research*, 132(1):47–57.

Felix Hill, Antoine Bordes, Sumit Chopra, and Jason Weston. 2015. The Goldilocks principle: Reading children's books with explicit memory representations. *arXiv preprint arXiv:1511.02301*.

Dan Klein and Christopher D Manning. 2003. Accurate unlexicalized parsing. In *Proceedings of the 41st Annual Meeting on Association for Computational Linguistics-Volume 1*, pages 423–430. Association for Computational Linguistics.

Brigitte Krenn. 2000. Empirical implications on lexical association measures. In *Proceedings of The Ninth EURALEX International Congress*.

Koenraad Kuiper, Heather McCann, Heidi Quinn, Therese Aitchison, and Kees van der Veer. 2003. Syntactically Annotated Idiom Dataset (SAID) LDC2003T10. In *Linguistic Data Consortium*, Philadelphia.

Prantik Kundu, Souheil J Inati, Jennifer W Evans, Wen-Ming Luh, and Peter A Bandettini. 2012. Differentiating bold and non-bold signals in fmri time series using multi-echo epi. *Neuroimage*, 60(3):1759–1770.

Prantik Kundu, Valerie Voon, Priti Balchandani, Michael V. Lombardo, Benedikt A. Poser, and Peter A. Bandettini. 2017. Multi-echo fmri: A review of applications in fmri denoising and analysis of bold signals. *NeuroImage*, 154:59 – 80. Cleaning up the fMRI time series: Mitigating noise with advanced acquisition and correction strategies.

John Laird, Paul Rosenbloom, and Allen Newell. 1986. Chunking in Soar, anatomy of a general learning mechanism. *Machine Learning*, 1.

Jean-Paul Laurent, Guy Denhières, Christine Passerieux, Galina Iakimova, and Marie-Christine Hardy-Baylé. 2006. On understanding idiomatic language: The salience hypothesis assessed by ERPs. *Brain Research*, 1068(1):151–160.

Torben E Lund, Kristoffer H Madsen, Karam Sidaros, Wen-Lin Luo, and Thomas E Nichols. 2006. Non-white noise in fmri: does modelling have an impact? *Neuroimage*, 29(1):54–66.

Adam Makkai, M. T. Boatner, and J. E. Gates. 1995. *A Dictionary of American idioms*. ERIC.

Christopher D Manning, Hinrich Schütze, et al. 1999. *Foundations of statistical natural language processing*, volume 999. MIT Press.

Christopher Manning, Mihai Surdeanu, John Bauer, Jenny Finkel, Steven Bethard, and David McClosky. 2014. The stanford corenlp natural language processing toolkit. In *Proceedings of 52nd annual meeting of the association for computational linguistics: system demonstrations*, pages 55–60.

George A. Miller. 1956. The magical number seven, plus or minus two: Some limits on our capacity for processing information. *Psychological Review*, 63(2):81–97.

Nicola Molinaro and Manuel Carreiras. 2010. Electrophysiological evidence of interaction between contextual expectation and semantic integration during the processing of collocations. *Biological Psychology*, 83(3):176–190.

Nicola Molinaro, Francesco Vespignani, Paolo Canal, Sergio Fonda, and Cristina Cacciari. 2008. Cloze probability does not only affect N400 amplitude: The case of complex prepositions. *Psychophysiology*, 45(6):1008–1012.

Nicola Molinaro, Manuel Carreiras, and Jon Andoni Duñabeitia. 2012. Semantic combinatorial processing of non-anomalous expressions. *Neuroimage*, 59(4):3488–3501.

Nicola Molinaro, Paolo Canal, Francesco Vespignani, Francesca Pesciarelli, and Cristina Cacciari. 2013. Are complex function words processed as semantically empty strings? A reading time and ERP study of collocational complex prepositions. *Language and Cognitive Processes*, 28(6):762–788.

Richard C Oldfield. 1971. The assessment and analysis of handedness: the edinburgh inventory. *Neuropsychologia*, 9(1):97–113.

Christophe Pallier, Anne-Dominique Devauchelle, and Stanislas Dehaene. 2011. Cortical representation of the constituent structure of sentences. *Proceedings of the National Academy of Sciences*, 108(6):2522–2527.

Sébastien Paumier, Takuya Nakamura, and Stavroula Voyatzi. 2009. Unitex, a corpus processing system with multi-lingual linguistic resources. *eLEX2009*, page 173.

Russell A Poldrack, Jeanette A Mumford, and Thomas E Nichols. 2011. *Handbook of functional MRI data analysis*. Cambridge University Press.

Amy R Price, Michael F Bonner, Jonathan E Peelle, and Murray Grossman. 2015. Converging evidence for the neuroanatomic basis of combinatorial semantics in the angular gyrus. *Journal of Neuroscience*, 35(7):3276–3284.

Carlos Ramisch, Aline Villavicencio, and Christian Boitet. 2010. mwetoolkit: a Framework for Multiword Expression Identification. In *LREC*, volume 10, pages 662–669.

Carlos Ramisch. 2012. A generic framework for multiword expressions treatment: From acquisition to applications. In *Proceedings of ACL 2012 Student Research Workshop*, pages 61–66. Association for Computational Linguistics.

Joost Rommers, Ton Dijkstra, and Marcel Bastiaansen. 2013. Context-dependent Semantic Processing in the Human Brain: Evidence from Idiom Comprehension. *Journal of Cognitive Neuroscience*, 25(5):762–776.

Paul S. Rosenbloom and Allen Newell. 1987. Learning by chunking: A production-system model of practice. In *Production System Models of Learning and Development*, pages 221–286. MIT Press.

Ivan A Sag, Timothy Baldwin, Francis Bond, Ann Copestake, and Dan Flickinger. 2002. Multiword expressions: A pain in the neck for NLP. In *International Conference on Intelligent Text Processing and Computational Linguistics*, pages 1–15. Springer.

Magnus Sahlgren. 2006. *The Word-Space Model: Using distributional analysis to represent syntagmatic and paradigmatic relations between words in high-dimensional vector spaces.* Ph.D. thesis.

Agata Savary, Carlos Ramisch, Silvio Cordeiro, Federico Sangati, Veronika Vincze, Behrang QasemiZadeh, Marie Candito, Fabienne Cap, Voula Giouli, and Ivelina Stoyanova. 2017. The parseme shared task on automatic identification of verbal multiword expressions.

Anna Siyanova-Chanturia and Ron Martinez. 2014. The idiom principle revisited. *Applied Linguistics*, 36(5):549–569.

Anna Siyanova-Chanturia, Kathy Conklin, and Norbert Schmitt. 2011a. Adding more fuel to the fire: An eye-tracking study of idiom processing by native and non-native speakers. *Second Language Research*, 27(2):251–272.

Anna Siyanova-Chanturia, Kathy Conklin, and Walter JB Van Heuven. 2011b. Seeing a phrase time and again matters: The role of phrasal frequency in the processing of multiword sequences. *Journal of Experimental Psychology: Learning, Memory, and Cognition*, 37(3):776.

Frank Smadja, Kathleen R McKeown, and Vasileios Hatzivassiloglou. 1996. Translating collocations for bilingual lexicons: A statistical approach. *Computational linguistics*, 22(1):1–38.

Tineke M Snijders, Theo Vosse, Gerard Kempen, Jos JA Van Berkum, Karl Magnus Petersson, and Peter Hagoort. 2009. Retrieval and unification of syntactic structure in sentence comprehension: an fmri study using word-category ambiguity. *Cerebral cortex*, 19(7):1493–1503.

Thorvald Sørensen. 1948. A method of establishing groups of equal amplitude in plant sociology based on similarity of species and its application to analyses of the vegetation on danish commons. *Biol. Skr.*, 5:1–34.

Robert J Strandburg, James T Marsh, Warren S Brown, Robert F Asarnow, Donald Guthrie, and Jerilyn Higa. 1993. Event-related potentials in high-functioning adult autistics: Linguistic and nonlinguistic visual information processing tasks. *Neuropsychologia*, 31(5):413–434.

Antoine Tremblay and R Harald Baayen. 2010. Holistic processing of regular four-word sequences: A behavioral and ERP study of the effects of structure, frequency, and probability on immediate free recall. *Perspectives on formulaic language: Acquisition and communication*, pages 151–173.

Antoine Tremblay, Bruce Derwing, Gary Libben, and Chris Westbury. 2011. Processing advantages of lexical bundles: Evidence from self-paced reading and sentence recall tasks. *Language Learning*, 61(2):569–613.

Geoffrey Underwood, Norbert Schmitt, and Adam Galpin. 2004. The eyes have it. *Formulaic Sequences: Acquisition, Processing, and Use*, 9:153.

Zdenka Uresova, Eduard Bejček, and Jan Hajic. 2016. Inherently pronominal verbs in czech: Description and conversion based on treebank annotation. In *Proceedings of the 12th Workshop on Multiword Expressions*, pages 78–83.

Francesco Vespignani, Paolo Canal, Nicola Molinaro, Sergio Fonda, and Cristina Cacciari. 2010. Predictive Mechanisms in Idiom Comprehension. *Journal of Cognitive Neuroscience*, 22(8):1682–1700.

Victoria Yaneva, Shiva Taslimipoor, Omid Rohanian, et al. 2017. Cognitive processing of multiword expressions in native and non-native speakers of English: Evidence from gaze data. In *International Conference on Computational and Corpus-Based Phraseology*, pages 363–379. Springer.

Appendix

Overview of the MWE identification, as per Al Saied et al., (2017):

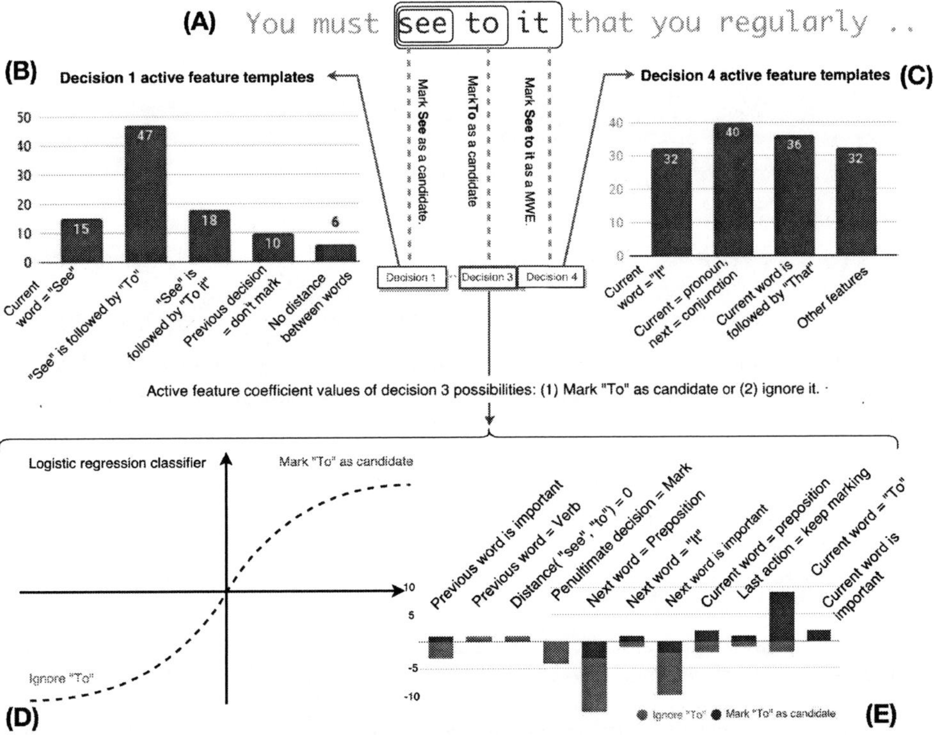

Figure 1: Identifying the multiword expression *see to it*. Panel (A) shows the context in which the MWE occurs. Identification in this case proceeds on the basis of four Decisions, numbered 1 through 4. The first three Decisions mark see , to and it respectively as candidate words. With the fourth Decision, the entire MWE is identified. The sorts of text-properties influencing Decisions 1 and 4 are shown in panels (B) and (C) respectively. These feature templates encourage the probabilistic classifier (panel D) to either mark or not. Panel (E) offers a closer look at the word to in terms of particular features that either encourage or discourage marking. Because the coefficient values are higher on the features that favour marking, the classifier chooses to mark to as a candidate for inclusion in the MWE.

The Interplay of Form and Meaning in Complex Medical Terms:
Evidence from a Clinical Corpus

Leonie Grön
KU Leuven, Belgium
`leonie.gron@kuleuven.be`

Ann Bertels
KU Leuven, Belgium
`ann.bertels@kuleuven.be`

Kris Heylen
KU Leuven, Belgium
`kris.heylen@kuleuven.be`

Abstract

We conduct a corpus study to investigate the structure of multi-word expressions (MWEs) in the clinical domain. Based on an existing medical taxonomy, we develop an annotation scheme and label a sample of MWEs from a Dutch corpus with semantic and grammatical features. The analysis of the annotated data shows that the formal structure of clinical MWEs correlates with their conceptual properties. The insights gained from this study could inform the design of Natural Language Processing (NLP) systems for clinical writing, but also for other specialized genres.

1 Introduction

Meaning, in everyday language, is created by the interaction of words in context, not simply by the words themselves. Word combinations are governed by grammatical rules and semantic constraints. However, some sequences show a distinctive *idiomaticity*: They either occur with an outstanding frequency, defy grammatical rules or convey a meaning that goes beyond the sum of their parts (Baldwin and Kim, 2010). Over the past decades, a number of frameworks has been proposed to approach such sequences from different theoretical angles. Consequently, they have been variably referred to as collocations, lexical bundles or multi-word expressions (MWEs), to name but a few terms. MWEs attract continuous scientific attention, not only due to their prevalence in the lexicon (Jackendoff, 1997), but also because they are a crucial factor in the performance of NLP: A system that cannot handle idiomatic expressions will at least miss semantic nuances, or fail to interpret the input completely.

Similarly, in specialized discourses, units of information are rarely encoded by a single term; instead, the majority of domain-specific concepts is referred to by MWEs, in particular, complex noun phrases (Daille, 1994; De Hertog & Heylen, 2012). Structured knowledge sources, which not only list the domain-specific vocabulary, but also model taxonomic relations, can serve to predict co-occurrences at the conceptual level. For instance, SNOMED CT (SNOMED International, 2018a) is a systematic medical terminology, which is primarily used to assign conceptual codes to electronic health records (EHRs). In SNOMED CT, each term is linked to a concept that belongs to a semantic category (e.g. *findings*, such as a symptom or a disease, and *procedures*, such as a method of investigation or therapy). Depending on the semantic category, each concept can be modified by a fixed set of qualifiers: A finding can be classified with regard to its severity, whereas a procedure can be specified with regard to the device used. However, this taxonomy provides little guidance about how the combination of the terms appears in practice. For instance, the MWE *obese abdomen* comprises two atomic concepts, the primary finding (*obesity*) and the anatomical site (*abdomen*). In Dutch, this observation can be expressed by a pre-modified noun phrase (*abdominale obesitas* 'abdominal obesity'), an attributive construction (*abdomen obees* 'abdomen obese'), a prepositional phrase (*obesitas thv abdomen*, which is short for *obesitas ter hoogte van abdomen* 'obesity at the abdomen'), or a reduced version thereof (*obesitas*

Proceedings of the Joint Workshop on
Linguistic Annotation, Multiword Expressions and Constructions (LAW-MWE-CxG-2018), pages 18–29
Santa Fe, New Mexico, USA, August 25-26, 2018.

abdomen 'obesity abdomen'). Given the productivity of morpho-syntactic processes, the exhaustive listing of all possible forms is obviously impractical.

According to cognitive theories of terminology, though, morpho-syntactic alternations in specialized terms are not arbitrary. Instead, variation is functional and can serve to convey different semantic nuances (Bowker & Hawkins, 2006; Faber et al., 2010). Likewise, constructional approaches to language posit that the pairing of syntactic structures with semantic components can create meaning in itself (Goldberg, 1995; Goldberg 2003). It is thus conceivable that habitual combinations of medical concepts pattern with particular structures at the formal level. If this is the case, such patterns could be leveraged to improve applications for clinical language processing, such as the automatic mapping of terms to ontological concepts.

To investigate this hypothesis, we conduct a corpus study, whereby we analyze sample of MWEs relating to different types of medical concepts. We develop an annotation scheme that captures grammatical and syntactic features of the MWE, and the semantic properties of the constituents. Using this annotation scheme, we analyze the interplay of semantic properties with the syntactic and grammatical structure of the MWEs, and their degree of lexicalization.

The remainder of this paper is structured as follows: In Section 2, we give an overview of related research to sketch the background of this work. In Section 3, we present our methodology: After introducing our dataset, we outline our approach for the identification, annotation and evaluation of the MWEs. Following the summary of the results (Section 4), we discuss the main findings of our study. Finally, in Section 5, we conclude with the implications of our work for future research on the processing of MWEs.

2   Background

As the scope of phraseological studies has widened considerably over the past decades, the names and definitions of MWEs have proliferated. In this paper, we adopt the definition proposed by Baldwin and Kim (2010), who define MWEs as expressions that consist of multiple lexical items, and that are marked by idiomaticities at the lexical, syntactic, semantic, pragmatic and/or statistical level. As Ramisch (2015) points out, this definition does not make any restrictions with regard to the granularity of the lexical items as they appear in the surface form; consequently, even orthographically joint forms, such as compound nouns can be considered MWEs. Likewise, this definition does not confine the notion of idiomatic behavior to one level of linguistic analysis. Traditionally, semantic opacity has been considered a main property of MWEs (Choueka, 1988; Fillmore et al., 1988; Smadja, 1993); conversely, this approach allows to treat compositionality as a continuum, and include semantically opaque and fully compositional MWEs alike.

With regard to languages for special purposes (LSPs), the central role of MWEs has long been acknowledged: Schulze and Römer (2008) emphasize that phraseological items are inseparably intertwined with the respective domain, as certain linguistic structures are instrumental to convey specialized meanings. The relationship between LSPs and their domain is thus dialectal in nature: While the language is a central constituent of the domain, the domain shapes the communicative needs. These needs shape syntactic and morphological patterns, which become consolidated through repeated usage.

Faber and Léon-Araùz (2016) propose a taxonomy of phraseal context factors, which is based on scope (local vs. global) and the dimension of linguistic analysis (syntactic, semantic or pragmatic). In this framework, MWEs are interpreted as a form of local context, whereby recurrent contexts can be modelled by syntagmatic grammatical patterns. Crucially, they observe a mutual attraction between syntactic and semantic structures; therefore, grammatical sequences and semantic relations should not be studied in isolation.

Similar patterns have been observed with nominal compounds. In general, the semantic relation between the constituents is indeterminable, as the underlying relation has been deleted or submerged as part of the compounding process (Levi, 1978). The full meaning can thus only be inferred through domain knowledge (Cabezas-García & San Martín, 2017). However, ten Hacken (2015) notes that, in biomedical compounds, the grammatical properties of the headword can give an indication of the relationship with the other constituent (i.e. the non-head).

Thus far, however, the analysis of medical MWEs has mostly focused on the biomedical domain, both with regard to phraseal expressions (e.g. Léon & Divasson, 2006; Laso & John, 2013; Lossio-Ventura,

Jonquet, Roche & Teisseire, 2016) and compounds (e.g. Cabezas-García & San Martín, 2017; Yadav et al., 2017). Meanwhile, the usage of MWEs in clinical practice has received relatively little attention. One obvious reason for this asymmetry is that clinical datasets are notoriously difficult to obtain. In English, a number of datasets has been labelled with medical identifiers (i.e. codes from a structured knowledge source such as SNOMED CT) and made available in the context of shared tasks, such as the i2b2 challenges (i2b2 National Center for Biomedical Computing, 2018) and the CLEF eHealth evaluation labs (CLEF eHealth, 2018). In addition, a number of corpora has also been annotated with semantic relations, PoS tags and, to varying depths, syntactic structure (e.g. Pakhomov, Coden & Chute, 2006; Roberts et al., 2009; Uzuner, Solti & Cadag, 2010; Uzuner, South, Shen & DuVall, 2011; Sum, Rumshisky & Uzuner, 2013; Albright et al., 2013; Styler et al., 2014; Savkov et al., 2016). However, for languages other than English, the distribution of clinical datasets is severely limited by the even more complex privacy regulations outside of the United States (cf. Névéol et al., 2018 for a comprehensive review). Still, an increasing number of – albeit not shareable – datasets has been annotated with both semantic and syntactic information, e.g. for Portuguese (Oleynik et al., 2010), Polish (Marciniak & Mykowiecka, 2011), Finnish (Haverinen et al., 2011; Laippala et al. 2014), Spanish (Costumero et al., 2014; Oronoz et al., 2015) and French (Deléger et al. 2017). In Dutch, clinical corpora have been labelled with features relating to negation, temporality and experiencer (Afzal et al., 2014) and codes from ICD-9 (Scheurwegs et al., 2017). However, we are not aware of any annotation projects that cover syntactic or grammatical properties of clinical Dutch; this paper thus presents a first attempt to fill this gap.

3   Methods

3.1   Corpus Structure

Our analysis is based on a corpus of Dutch EHRs provided by the department of endocrinology of a Belgian hospital. In total, this corpus consists of 14,999 documents and covers the medical history of 500 patients. All patients are diagnosed with diabetes and visit the hospital in regular intervals for a check-up. During these consultations, they report on their own assessment of their condition (e.g. the self-monitoring of the glucose level) and undergo a set of routine procedures (e.g. the screening for microalbuminuria). The EHR serves to summarize the outcome of these procedures, to give recommendations for further therapy (e.g. a change in insulin dose) or suggest additional interventions (e.g. the transplantation of beta-cells).

A selection of EHRs was manually annotated by five students with a background in biomedical sciences. During the annotation stage, they annotated the complete medical histories of individual patients with clinical codes. They were instructed to identify all medical terms, including non-standard term variants, and link them to the corresponding concept identifier from SNOMED CT (SNOMED International, 2018a). At the end of this stage, the annotation of 179 cases had been completed; 300.693 medical entities were identified, relating to 16,151 unique terms and 7,945 concepts. During the validation stage, three annotators verified the term-concept associations. They were presented with a list of unique pairs of terms and concept codes and asked to confirm the correctness of the assigned code, and rate the domain pertinence of the concept (i.e. whether it is specific to the domain of endocrinology). To estimate the consistency of their judgements, a part of the term-concept pairs was validated by all annotators; the interrater agreement, as calculated by Fleiss' kappa, was substantial (κ=0.62). After filtering out those terms that had been judged as incorrectly annotated during the second stage, we retained 7,687 concepts, corresponding to 15,025 unique terms and 274,082 entities for further analysis.

3.2   Phrase Types included for Analysis

For our study of MWEs, we include nominal phrases with external modifiers as well as compounds. In Dutch, external modifiers can precede or follow the head noun, whereby the grammatical form of the modifier constrains its relative position (Broekhuis, Keizer & den Dikken, 2012). Pre-nominal modifiers can be adjectives (e.g. *lichte hypertensie* 'light hypertension') or participles (e.g. *IgE-gemedieerde allergie* 'IgE(Immunoglobulin E)-mediated allergy'); post-nominal modifiers can be prepositional phrases (e.g. *eczeem aan de handen* 'eczema at the hands'), relative clauses (e.g. *hypertensie die hier wordt opgevolgd* 'hypertension which is followed up here'), participles (e.g. *pijn uitstralend naar schouders* 'pain radiating to shoulders') or adverbials (e.g. *hypoglycemie postprandiaal* 'postprandial hypoglycemia'). Dutch compounds are right-headed. While combinations with other grammatical types are possible (e.g. *rechterbovenbeen* 'right upper leg'), the juxtaposition of two nouns (e.g. *nierfalen* 'kidney failure') is most productive (Booij, 2007). Many medical compounds contain neoclassical elements, either in combination with each other (e.g. *pancreastransplantatie* 'pancreas transplantation'), or with Dutch lexemes (e.g. *corfalen* 'heart failure'). However, in many neoclassical compounds, the left element (i.e. the non-head) cannot be used as an independent word (e.g. *hypertensie* 'hypertension'). Depending on whether such elements occur in their full or abbreviated form, they have been defined as *confixes* (including *pseudoprefixes* and *pseudosuffixes*), or *splinters* in the literature (Meesters, 2004; Džuganová, 2013). In this study, we do not consider confixes and splinters as separate lexical elements. Consequently, a term such as *hypertensie* will be treated as a single noun, rather than a compound.

3.3   Retrieval of MWEs for Annotation

We focus on MWEs relating to concepts from 2 semantic categories, namely *procedures* and *findings*. To select a set of concepts for each category, we first rank all concepts referring to either *procedures* or *findings* by their absolute frequencies in the annotated part of the corpus. We retrieve the associated terms for the top nine concepts per category. After reviewing the variants linked to one concept, we manually compile a list of lexical stems to retrieve all occurrences of the associated terms. The generation of these stems is based on practical considerations, rather than linguistic criteria. For instance, to retrieve occurrences of the term *hypertensie* 'hypertension', we use the clipped form *hypert* rather than the lexical stem of the headword (*tensie*). The reason is that, firstly, the stem *tensie* would produce a high number of false positives, i.e. matches where the term is used in a different context than that of the target concept (e.g. *tensies thuis* 'tensions at home', which refers to the measurement of the blood pressure in the home setting); secondly, this stem would miss those instances where the clipped variant is used verbatim (e.g. *lichte hypert op rpl*, which is short for *lichte hypertensie op raadpleging* 'light hypertension during consultation').

Then, we match these stems against the entire corpus. For each match, we extract the term along with the three adjacent tokens in the left and right context. Altogether, we identify 63,559 instances of *procedures* and 59,731 of *findings*. Tables 1 and 2 provide examples of the target concepts, terms and lexical stems for both semantic categories.

Concept identifier in SNOMED CT	Preferred term in SNOMED CT	Dutch term variants	Lexical stems
SCTID 73211009	diabetes mellitus	*diabetes mellitus; dm; suikerziekte*	diabet; dm; suikerziek
SCTID 38341003	hypertensive disorder, systemic arterial	*hypertensie; bloedhoogdruk*	hypert; bloedhoogdr
SCTID 414916001	obesity	*obesitas, adipositas*	obes, adipo

Table 1. Concepts, terms and lexical stems used for the identification of MWEs relating to *findings*.

Concept identifier in SNOMED CT	Preferred term in SNOMED CT	Dutch term variants	Lexical stems
SCTID 16310003	diagnostic ultrasonography	*echografie; sonografie*	echo; sono
SCTID 3324009	laser beam photocoagulation	*fotocoagulatie; lasertherapie*	fotoco; laser
SCTID 77465005	transplantation	*transplantatie; tx*	transplant; tx

Table 2. Concepts, terms and lexical stems used for the identification of MWEs relating to *procedures*.

Next, we review the matches to identify all noun phrases where one of the target terms is the syntactic head of the phrase, and where the context conveys medically relevant information. After filtering out those instances that do not fulfill these grammatical and semantic criteria, we retain 11,354 expressions of *procedures*, and 13,537 expressions of *findings*. Finally, we sort the expressions by the relative position of the modifier (i.e. left- vs. right-branching). Among the left-branching expressions, we further distinguish between compound nouns and noun phrases with an external modifier (e.g. a pre-modifying adjective). All compound nouns are split into their constituents for further analysis. This leads to a 3-

way-distinction between phrase types. Table 3 gives an overview of the different phrase types by semantic category.

	Compounds	Phrases with external modifier in the left context	Phrases with external modifier in the right context
Findings	*ochtend hypo* 'matinal hypoglycemia'	*symptomatische hypoglycemie* 'symptomatic hypoglycemia'	*hypo met convulsies* 'hypoglycemia with convulsions'
Procedures	*YAG laser* 'Nd:YAG laser'	*panretinale laser* 'panretinal laser therapy'	*laser od* 'laser therapy of oculus dexter (right eye)'

Table 3. Overview of the different phrase types by semantic category of the headword.

3.4 Annotation of MWEs with PoS Values and Semantic Features

For the annotation of the MWEs, we use WebAnno, a web-based tool for linguistic annotations (de Castilho et al., 2016). We create two layers of annotation (grammatical and semantic), and define a custom tagset at each level.

Grammatical level: For the tagging of PoS values, we use the tagset introduced in the Penn Guidelines for the annotation of biomedical text (Warner et al., 2012). Compared to the original Penn tagset (Santorini, 1990), this extended version contains 4 additional labels, AFX (unbound affix), GW (mistranscription), HYPH (unbound hyphen) and XX (uninterpretable material). These additional tags have been introduced to handle the particular linguistic features of clinical writing, such as non-canonical spelling variants, ad-hoc abbreviations and undecipherable forms. Similar to Fan et al. (2013), we follow the tagging conventions described in these guidelines, but adjust them to the properties of our data: In the original guidelines, the distinction between common nouns and proper nouns is primarily based on the capitalization of the full form. However, we find that this is not a viable strategy in our case, as orthographic conventions are not followed strictly in our data. Instead, we reserve the tags for proper nouns (i.e. *NNP* for singular, and *NNPS* for plural forms) to eponyms (e.g. *hashimoto*, which refer to 'Hashimoto's disease') and commercial names (e.g. *NovoRapid*, which is the registered tradename of an insulin product). In addition, for abbreviations and misspellings, we used the same tag as for the canonical full form, if it can be determined; otherwise, we tag them with the label for un-interpretable material (*XX*).

Semantic level: For the annotation of conceptual properties, we create a tagset based on the attributes described in the Editorial Guide of SNOMED CT (SNOMED International, 2018b). This guide defines a set of properties that can be used in conjunction with particular semantic types. For instance, a *finding* can be modified with regard to its *clinical course* (e.g. acute, chronic) or *severity* (e.g. mild, moderate); a *procedure* can be specified by the *device* used (e.g. a catheter), or the *direct substance* (e.g. a pharmacological agent used for injection). Semantically empty tokens, such as function words, are skipped on the semantic level. Table 4 provides examples for different types of attributes combining with *findings* and *procedures* respectively.

Attribute	Example expressions for *findings*	Attribute	Example expressions for *procedures*
Cause	*diabetische retinopathie* 'diabetic retinopathy'	Component	*glycemie meting* 'measurement of blood glucose level'
Severity	*lichte hypertensie* 'mild hypertension'	Site	*schouder ingreep* 'surgery of the shoulder'
Site	*abdominale obesitas* 'abdominal obesity'	Substance	*injectie insuline* 'injection of insuline'

Table 4. Examples of different attribute types combining with *findings* and *procedures*.

3.5 Analysis of Grammatico-semantic Patterns

With our study, we aim to answer two questions: Firstly, we investigate whether there is a correlation between the semantic category of the headword and the preferred phrase types. This will also give an indication of the average degree of lexicalization of the different categories. Secondly, we examine whether fixed concept combinations pattern with particular grammatical constructions. We thus analyze the annotated MWEs in two stages.

Correlation between semantic categories, preferred phrase types and the degree of lexicalization: For both *findings* and *procedures*, we calculate the absolute and relative frequencies of the individual phrase types, as well as the average length in tokens. For each phrase type, we group the expressions by their paired tag sequences; all expressions that have identical annotations at both the semantic and PoS layer are thus associated with one *pattern*. To evaluate the degree of lexicalization, we count the unique expressions per pattern. This value thus indicates if the associated patterns serve as productive templates, which allow for paradigmatic changes of the lexical elements, or if they correspond to frozen expressions, which are fully lexicalized in usage.

Patterning of concept combinations with grammatical constructions: For a more fine-grained analysis of the grammatical structure, we focus on the five most frequent concept combinations per category. To identify these, we make an inventory of all possible constellations of semantic constituents (e.g. *procedure* and anatomical *site*; *procedure* and *substance*) and rank them by their absolute frequency. For the top five combinations, we extract all patterns (i.e. paired tag sequences) that instantiate these semantic combinations. For instance, for the semantic combination *procedure* and *site*, we identify the patterns 'procedure/NN, site/NN' and 'site/JJ, procedure/NN', whereby the tags 'NN' and 'JJ' refer nouns and adjectives respectively. For the combination of *procedure* and *substance*, we retrieve the patterns 'substance/NN, procedure/NN' and 'procedure/NN, substance/NN'. For each grammatico-semantic pattern, we calculate the frequency relative to all patterns that express the underlying semantic combination.

4   Results

Distribution of phrase types and degree of lexicalization: The distribution of phrase types varies considerably between the semantic categories. While compounds only make up a minor share of the patterns for *findings*, they are the dominant phrase type among *procedures*. Conversely, left-branching phrases with external modifiers are the preferred type for *findings*, whereas they account for a relatively small portion of the *procedures*. For right-branching phrases though, the proportions are almost equal. Regardless of the phrase type, the average length of the expressions is longer for *findings* than for *procedures*. In general, the right-branching expressions are longer than pre-modified phrases and compounds. Overall, the average number of unique expressions by pattern is higher among the *procedures,* which indicates a lower degree of lexicalization. However, even though the relative frequencies of the individual phrase types vary across semantic categories, we note similar global trends with regard to their productivity: For both *findings* and *procedures*, the left-branching phrases are the most productive phrase type, followed by the right-branching phrases. Compounds, on the other hand, appear less variable, hence more lexicalized, for both semantic categories. The full results are provided in Tables 5 and 6.

Patterning of concept combinations with PoS sequences: With both *findings* and *procedures*, we observe a highly skewed frequency distribution of the concept combinations. For both categories, the top 5 combinations of semantic constituents account for roughly two thirds of all identified MWEs. *Findings* are typically specified with regard to their *cause, clinical course, severity*, the *anatomical site* or *time*. *Procedures* co-occur mostly with modifiers relating to *components, abstract properties*, the *time* or *anatomical site*. Likewise, the individual concept combinations are strongly dominated by single PoS sequences. On average, the most frequent PoS sequence accounts for more than half of all MWEs that express a given combination (67.4% for *findings*, 58.3% for *procedures*). However, there are striking differences with regard to the preferred grammatical structure. Among the *findings*, all top patterns consist of left-branching noun phrases, whereby the headword is pre-modified by an adverb, or by one or more adjectives (e.g *veneuze pulmonale hypertensie* 'venous pulmonary hypertension'). By contrast, among the *procedures*, purely nominal sequences prevail; these take either the form of compounds (e.g. *lipiden meting* 'measurement of lipids'), or reduced prepositional phrases, where the subordinating preposition is left out (e.g. *rx thorax* 'x-ray of the chest'). Among the *procedures*, 3 of the 5 concept combinations contain plural forms, which do not appear in the PoS patterns for *findings*. Tables 7 and 8 list the most frequent concept combinations by semantic category, along with the dominant PoS sequence and example expressions.

	Compounds	Phrases with external modifier in the left context	Phrases with external modifier in the right context
Absolute frequency	187	11,001	2,349
Relative frequency	0.01	0.81	0.17
Average length in tokens	2.84	3.03	3.26
Number of unique patterns	19	383	210
Average number of expressions per pattern	1.33	3.63	2.83

Table 5. Distribution and structure of phrase types among MWEs relating to *findings*.

	Compounds	Phrases with external modifier in the left context	Phrases with external modifier in the right context
Absolute frequency	7,835	1,482	2,037
Relative frequency	0.69	0.13	0.18
Average length in tokens	2.46	2.46	2.84
Number of unique patterns	392	147	141
Average number of expressions per pattern	2.57	3.69	3.38

Table 6. Distribution and structure of phrase types among MWEs relating to *procedures*.

Concept combination	Dominant PoS sequence	Example expression	Relative frequency of the PoS sequence
finding, cause	JJ, NN	*alimentaire obesitas* 'alimentary obesity'	0.90
finding, clinical course	RB, NN	*vaak hypoglycemie* 'frequently hypoglycemia'	0.35
finding, severity	JJ, NN	*morbiede obesitas* 'morbid obesity'	0.74
finding, site	JJ, JJ, NN	*veneuze pulmonale hypertensie* 'venous pulmonary hypertension'	0.54
finding, time	JJ, NN	*matinale hypo* 'matinal hypoglycemia'	0.83

Table 7. Most frequent concept combinations and PoS patterns relating to *findings*.

In sum, both levels of analysis provide evidence for the interplay of conceptual properties with grammatical structure: The majority of MWEs referring to *findings* consists of left-branching phrases with an external modifier; the grammatical structure of the most frequent concept combinations is nearly identical. By contrast, the *procedures* show a clear preference for nominal constructions, in particular compounds and reduced prepositional phrases. In general, though, MWEs of this category are more variable, which manifests itself in both lexical and morpho-syntactic alternations.

Concept combination	Dominant PoS sequence	Example expression	Relative frequency of the PoS sequence
procedure, component	NNS, NN	*lipiden meting* 'measurement of lipids'	0.44
procedure, component, abstract property	JJ, NNS, NN	*gunstig lipidenprofiel* 'acceptable lipid profile'	0.71
procedure, component, time	NN, NN, NNS	*glycemie dag profielen* 'glycemic day profiles'	0.72
procedure, time	NN, NN	*jaar bilan* 'yearly balance'	0.59
procedure, site	NN, NN	*rx thorax* 'x-ray of the chest'	0.46

Table 8. Most frequent concept combinations and PoS patterns relating to *procedures*.

5 Discussion

Our results illustrate the interdependency of form and meaning in the expression of complex medical concepts. This finding corroborates the observation that "special and specialized information is entrenched in linguistic structures" (Schulze and Römer, 2008).

Firstly, the semantic type of the headword co-determines preferences for particular phrase types. In particular, with left-branching MWEs headed by *procedures*, nominal compounds are most frequent; with *findings*, phrases pre-modified by adjectives prevail. This tendency can be partly attributed to the predominance of a small number of fixed concept combinations. For some types of concepts, the corresponding terms are morphologically inflexible, which enforces the use of particular phrase types. For instance, *procedures* can combine with terms relating to substances, such as *injectie insuline* 'injection of insulin'. For lack of a derived adjective, the use of a nominal construction is – at least in Dutch – obligatory. On the other hand, *findings* are often specified with regard to their clinical course or severity (*morbiede obesitas* 'morbid obesity'), where no semantically equivalent noun form is available. However, this tendency prevails in cases where both grammatical types – nouns and derived adjectives – are available; thus, it cannot be explained by the lack of particular word forms alone. Instead, it seems that grammatical structures are instrumental to convey certain semantic relations. In MWEs relating to *procedures*, the headwords are typically combined with terms referring to concrete entities, which are the direct object of the act itself; this core relation seems to be strongly linked to nominal constructions. On the other hand, *findings* are characterized with regard to inherent properties as they manifest themselves to the observer; such qualities clearly pattern with attributive adjectives. The association between grammatical patterns and semantic relations also accounts for the asymmetrical distribution of reduced phrase types. For instance, the elision of function words is acceptable in some semantic constellations, but not in others. Given the default relation between two nominal constituents ('A is the object of B'), the omission of a preposition is acceptable in phrases combining a *procedure* and an anatomical site, component or substance (e.g. *echografie halsvaten* 'echography of the neck vessels'). By contrast, such an underspecified construction cannot be used for other types of relations. For example, to specify the etiological relation between a cause and a *finding*, the full phrase must be used (e.g. *nefropathie tgv diabetes*, which is short for *nefropathie ten gevolge van diabetes* 'nephropathy resulting from diabetes', but not **nefropathie diabetes* 'nephropathy diabetes').

Secondly, the semantic type influences the variability of the MWEs, both at the lexical, and at the grammatico-syntactic level. Overall, MWEs referring to *findings* are strongly lexicalized. This may be partly explained by the fact that, for the most frequent concept combinations, the set of potential modifiers is rather confined. For instance, for most *findings*, there is only a small number of medically attested causes; this limits the number of combining concepts, and consequently, that of individual expressions. However, even in combination with modifiers of time or severity, which do not underlie such rigid conceptual restrictions, the strong dominance of individual PoS patterns prevails. By contrast, MWEs relating to *procedures* are more flexible; they serve as productive templates that allow for the paradigmatic insertion of different concepts. This increases the potential for variation in the syntactic and grammatical form.

6 Conclusion

MWEs are dense units of information, which enable the concise expression of complex concepts. They play a pivotal role in specialized discourses, as they allow speakers to interact in a precise, yet economical way. Their communicative power resides both in the use of domain-specific terminology, and that of particular constructions, which support the nuanced encoding of meanings and relations. Therefore, the automatic processing of specialized texts crucially depends on their correct interpretation.

The detailed study of specialized corpora is essential to identify such constructions. In this paper, we have presented an analysis of MWEs in clinical usage. Using a structured terminology as a starting point, we have exploited the relations defined in this taxonomy to design an annotation scheme, which allowed us to capture regularities at both the grammatical and the semantic level. While our analysis was confined to a narrow selection of medical concepts, the approach could easily be expanded to a wider range of concepts, or transferred to other domains. Such analyses would lead to valuable insights about the structure of specialized MWEs, which could inform the design of more advanced applications for semantic reasoning.

Acknowledgements

This work was supported by Internal Funds KU Leuven. We are grateful to all anonymous reviewers for their detailed comments and suggestions. We would also like to thank Kristina Geeraert for her valuable input.

References

Afzal, Z., Pons, E., Kang, N., Sturkenboom, M., Schuemie, M. J., & Kors, J. A. (2014). ContextD: An Algorithm to Identify Contextual Properties of Medical Terms in a Dutch Clinical Corpus. BMC Bioinformatics, 15. http://doi.org/10.1186/s12859-014-0373-3

Albright, D., Lanfranchi, A., Fredriksen, A., Styler, W. F. I., Warner, C., Hwang, J. D., … Savova, G. K. (2013). Towards Comprehensive Syntactic and Semantic Annotations of the Clinical Narrative. J Am Med Inform Assoc, 20, 922–930. http://doi.org/10.1136/amiajnl-2012-001317

Baldwin, T., & Kim, S. N. (2010). Multiword Expressions. In N. Indurkhya & F. J. Damerau (Eds.), Handbook of Natural Language Processing (pp. 267–292). Boca Raton: CRC.

Booij, G. (2007). The Morphology of Dutch. Oxford: Oxford University Press.

Bowker, L., & Hawkins, S. (2006). Variation in the Organization of Medical Terms: Exploring some Motivations for Term Choice. Terminology, 12(2006), 79–110. http://doi.org/10.1075/term.12.1.05bow

Broekhuis, H., Keizer, E., & den Dikken, M. (2012). Syntax of Dutch: Nouns and Noun Phrases. Amsterdam: Amsterdam University Press.

Cabezas-García, M., & San Martín, A. (2017). Semantic Annotation to Characterize Contextual Variation in Terminological Noun Compounds: A Pilot Study. In Proceedings of the 13th Workshop on Multiword Expressions (MWE 2017) (pp. 108–113). Valencia: Association for Computational Linguistics.

Choueka, Y. (1988). Looking for Needles in a Haystack or Locating Interesting Collocational Expressions in Large Textual Databases. In C. Fluhr & D. Walker (Eds.), Proceedings of the 2nd international conference on computer-assisted information retrieval (Recherche d'Information et ses Applications – RIA) (pp. 609–624).

CLEF eHealth (2018). Datasets. Retrieved May 25, 2018, from https://sites.google.com/site/clefehealth/datasets

Costumero, R., Lopez, F., Gonzalo-Martín, C., Millan, M., & Menasalvas, E. (2014). An Approach to Detect Negation on Medical Documents in Spanish. In International Conference on Brain Informatics and Health (pp. 366–375). Cham: Springer.

Daille, B. (1994). Study and Implementation of Combined Techniques for Automatic Extraction of Terminology. In The Balancing Act: Combining Symbolic and Statistical Approaches to Language. Workshop at the 32nd Annual Meeting of the Association for Computational Linguistics (pp. 29–36). Stroudsburg: Association for Computational Linguistics.

de Castilho, R. E., Mujdricza-Maydt, E., Yimam, S. M., Hartmann, S., Gurevych, I., Frank, A., & Biemann, C. (2016). A Web-based Tool for the Integrated Annotation of Semantic and Syntactic Structures. In Proceedings of the LT4DH workshop at COLING 2016 (pp. 76–84). Osaka.

De Hertog, D., & Heylen, K. (2012). The Prevalence of Multiword Term Candidates in a Legal Corpus. In G. Aguado de Cea (Ed.), Proceedings of the 10th Terminology and Knowledge Engineering Conference (TKE2012): New Frontiers in the Constructive Symbiosis of Terminology and Knowledge Engineering (pp. 283–290). Madrid: Universidad Politecnica de Madrid.

Deléger, L., Campillos, L., Ligozat, A.-L., & Névéol, A. (2017). Design of an Extensive Information Representation Scheme for Clinical Narratives. J Biomed Inform, 8(37), 1–18. http://doi.org/10.1186/s13326-017-0135-z

Džuganová, B. (2013). English Medical Terminology – Different Ways of Forming Medical Terms. European Journal of Bioethics, 4(7), 55–69.

Faber, P., & León-Araùz, P. (2016). Specialized Knowledge Representation and the Parameterization of Context. Frontiers in Psychology, 7. http://doi.org/10.3389/fpsyg.2016.00196

Faber, P., Tercedor, M., Sánchez, S., López, C. I., León, P., Arauz, A., … Martínez, S. M. (2010). A Cognitive Linguistics View of Terminology and Specialized Language. New York: De Gruyter Mouton.

Fan, J., Yang, E. W., Jiang, M., Prasad, R., Loomis, R. M., Zisook, D. S., … Huang, Y. (2013). Syntactic Parsing of Clinical Text: Guideline and Corpus Development with Handling Ill-Formed Sentences, 20, 1168–1177. http://doi.org/10.1136/amiajnl-2013-001810

Fillmore, C. J., Kay, P., & O'Connor, M. C. (1988). Regularity and Idiomaticity in Grammatical Constructions: The Case of Let Alone. Language, 64(3), 501–538. http://doi.org/10.2307/414531

Goldberg, A. E. (1995). Constructions. A Construction Grammar Approach to Argument Structure. Chicago: University of Chicago Press.

Goldberg, A. E. (2003). Constructions: A New Theoretical Approach to Language. TRENDS in Cognitive Science, 7(5), 219–224. http://doi.org/10.1016/S1364-6613(03)00080-9

Haverinen, K., Ginter, F., Viljanen, T., Laippala, V., & Salakoski, T. (2010). Dependency-based PropBanking of Clinical Finnish. In Proceedings of the Fourth Linguistic Annotation Workshop (pp. 137–141). Uppsala: Association for Computational Linguistics.

i2b2 National Center for Biomedical Computing (2018). NLP Research Data Sets. Retrieved May 25, 2018, from https://www.i2b2.org/NLP/DataSets/Main.php

Jackendoff, R. (1997). Twistin' the Night Away. Language, 73, 534–559.

Laippala, V., Viljanen, T., Airola, A., Kanerva, J., Salanterä, S., Salakoski, T., & Ginter, F. (2014). Statistical Parsing of Varieties of Clinical Finnish. Artif Intell Med, 61(3), 131–136.

Laso, N. J., & John, S. (2013). A Corpus-based Analysis of the Collocational Patterning of Adjectives with Abstract Nouns in Medical English. In I. Verdaguer, N. J. Laso, & D. Salazar (Eds.), Biomedical English: A Corpus-Based Approach (pp. 55–72). Amsterdam: Benjamins.

Léon, I. K., & Divasson, L. (2006). Nominal Domain in the Biomedical Research Paper: A Grammatico-rhetorical Study of Postmodification. In M. Gotti & F. Salager-Meyer (Eds.), Advances in Medical Discourse Analysis: Oral and Written Contexts (pp. 289–310). Bern: Lang.

Levi, J. (1978). The Syntax and Semantics of Complex Nominals. New York: Academic Press.

Lossio-Ventura, J. A., Jonquet, C., Roche, M., & Teisseire, M. (2016). Biomedical Term Extraction: Overview and a New Methodology. Information Retrieval Journal, 19(1), 59–99. http://doi.org/10.1007/s10791-015-9262-2

Marciniak, M., & Mykowiecka, A. (2011). Towards Morphologically Annotated Corpus of Hospital Discharge Reports in Polish. In Proceedings of BioNLP 2011 Workshop (pp. 92–100). Portland: Association for Computational Linguistics.

Meesters, G. (2004). Marginale Morfologie in het Nederlands: Paradigmatische Samenstellinge, Neoklassieke Composita en Splintercomposita. Gent: Koninklijke Academie voor Nederlandse Taal- en Letterkunde.

Névéol, A., Dalianis, H., Velupillai, S., Savova, G., & Zweigenbaum, P. (2018). Clinical Natural Language Processing in Languages Other than English: Opportunities and Challenges, 9(12).

Oleynik, M., Nohama, P., Cancian, P. S., & Schulz, S. (2010). Performance Analysis of a POS Tagger Applied to Discharge Summaries in Portuguese. Stud Health Technol Inform, 160, 959–963.

Oronoz, M., Gojenola, K., Pérez, A., & de Ilarraza, Arantza Díaz Casillas, A. (2015). On the Creation of a Clinical Gold Standard Corpus in Spanish: Mining Adverse Drug Reactions. J Biomed Inform, 56, 318–332.

Pakhomov, S. V, Coden, A., & Chute, C. G. (2006). Developing a Corpus of Clinical Notes Manually Annotated for Part-of-Speech, 75, 418–429. http://doi.org/10.1016/j.ijmedinf.2005.08.006

Ramisch, C. (2015). Multiword Expression Acquisition. A Generic and Open Framework. Cham: Springer International Publishing.

Roberts, A., Gaizauskas, R., Hepple, M., Demetriou, G., Guo, Y., Roberts, I., & Setzer, A. (2009). Building a Semantically Annotated Corpus of Clinical Texts. Journal of Biomedical Informatics, 42(5), 950–966.

Santorini, B. (1990). Part-of-Speech Tagging Guidelines for the Penn Treebank Project (3rd Revision, 2nd printing). Retrieved from http://www.cis.upenn.edu/~bies/manuals/tagguide.pdf

Savkov, A., Carroll, J., Koeling, R., & Cassell, J. (2016). Annotating Patient Clinical Records with Syntactic Chunks and Named Entities: The Harvey Corpus. Language Resources and Evaluation, 50(3), 523–548. http://doi.org/10.1007/s10579-015-9330-7

Scheurwegs, E., Luyckx, K., Luyten, L., Goethals, B., & Daelemans, W. (2017). Assigning Clinical Codes with Data-driven Concept Representation on Dutch Clinical Free Text. Journal of Biomedical Informatics, 69, 118–127. http://doi.org/10.1016/j.jbi.2017.04.007

Schulze, R., & Römer, U. (2008). Introduction. Patterns, Meaningful Units and Specialized Discourses. International Journal of Corpus Linguistics, 13(3), 265–270. http://doi.org/10.1075/ijcl.13.3.01sch

Smadja, F. (1993). Retrieving Collocations from Text: Xtract. Comput Linguist, 19(1), 143–177.

SNOMED CT. (2018a). SNOMED CT. Retrieved May 13, 2018, from https://www.snomed.org/snomed-ct

SNOMED CT (2018b). SNOMED CT Editorial Guide. Retrieved May 14, 2018, from https://confluence.ihtsdotools.org/display/DOCEG/SNOMED+CT+Editorial+Guide

Styler, W. F. I., Bethard, S., Finan, S., Palmer, M., Pradhan, S., de Groen, P. C., …Pustejovsky, J. (2014). Temporal Annotation in the Clinical Domain. Trans Assoc Comput Linguist, 2, 143–154.

Sun, W., Rumshisky, A., & Uzuner, Ö. (2013). Evaluating Temporal Relations in Clinical Text: 2012 i2b2 Challenge. J Am Med Inform Assoc, 20(5), 806–813.

ten Hacken, P. (2015). Naming Devices in Midddle-Ear Surgery: A Morphological Analysis. In P. ten Hacken & R. Panocová (Eds.), Word Formation and Transparency in Medical English (pp. 55–72). Newcastle upon Tyne: Cambridge Scholars Publishing.

Uzuner, Ö., Solti, I., & Cadag, E. (2010). Extracting Medication Information from Clinical Text. Journal of the American Medical Informatics Association, 17(5), 514–518.

Uzuner, Ö., South, B. R., Shen, S., & DuVall, S. L. (2011). 2010 i2b2/VA Challenge on Concepts, Assertions, and Relations in Clinical Text. J Am Med Inform Assoc, 18(5), 552–556.

Warner, C., Lanfranchi, A., O'Gorman, T., Howard, A., Gould, K., & Regan, M. (2012). Bracketing Biomedical Text: An Addendum to Penn Treebank II Guidelines. Retrieved May 14, 2018, from https://clear.colorado.edu/compsem/documents/treebank_guidelines.pdf

Yadav, P., Jezek, E., Bouillon, P., Callahan, T. J., Bada, M., Hunter, L. E., & Cohen, K. B. (2017). Semantic Relations in Compound Nouns: Perspectives from Inter-Annotator Agreement. In A. V Gundlapalli, M.-C. Jaulent, & D. Zhao (Eds.), MEDINFO 2017: Precision Healthcare through Informatics (pp. 644–648). Hangzou: International Medical Informatics Association and IOS Press.

Discourse and Lexicons: Lexemes, MWEs, Grammatical Constructions and Compositional Word Combinations to Signal Discourse Relations

Laurence Danlos

Université Paris Diderot, Laboratoire de Linguistique Formelle
2 Place Thomas Mann, 75013 Paris, France
Laurence.Danlos@linguist.univ-paris-diderot.fr

Abstract

Lexicons generally record a list of lexemes or non-compositional multiword expressions. We propose to build lexicons for **compositional** word combinations, namely "secondary discourse connectives". Secondary discourse connectives play the same function as "primary discourse connectives" but the latter are either lexemes or non-compositional multiword expressions. The paper defines primary and secondary connectives, and explains why it is possible to build a lexicon for the compositional ones and how it could be organized. It also puts forward the utility of such a lexicon in discourse annotation and parsing. Finally, it opens the discussion on the constructions that signal a discourse relation between two spans of text.

1 Introduction

Lexicons generally record a list of lexemes — e.g., a list of English verbs in VerbNet (Karin Kipper and Palmer, 2006) —or a list of multiword expressions (MWEs) — see (Losnegaard et al., 2016) for a survey on MWE ressources. We quote (Savary and Cordeiro, 2018): "Multiword expressions are word combinations, such as *all of a sudden, a hot dog, to pay a visit* or *to pull ones leg,* which exhibit lexical, syntactic, semantic, pragmatic and/or statistical idiosyncrasies. (…) A prominent feature of many MWEs (…) is their non-compositional semantics, i.e. the fact that their meaning cannot be deduced from the meanings of their components, and from their syntactic structure, in a way deemed regular for the given language."

   We propose to build lexicons for **compositional** word combinations, namely "secondary discourse connectives". They play the same function as "primary discourse connectives" but the latter are lexemes or non-compositional multiword expressions. Primary and secondary connectives are illustrated below in the examples in (1), which all express a causal relation between Fred's jokes and his friends' hilarity [1] In (1a), the causal relation is explicitly signalled by the primary connective (in magenta) *therefore* which is an adverb; in (1b), it is signalled by the primary connective *as a result,* which is a frozen multiword prepositional phrase. In (1c), it is signalled by *this caused*, a secondary connective (in blue) which is made of an anaphoric subject and a verb, both used with a compositional meaning; in (1d), it is signalled by *because of this*, a prepositional phrase made of a compound preposition followed by an anaphoric pronoun.

(1) a. Fred didn't stop joking. Therefore, his friends enjoyed hilarity throughout the evening.

    b. Fred didn't stop joking. As a result, his friends enjoyed hilarity throughout the evening.

    c. Fred didn't stop joking. This caused hilarity among his friends for the whole evening.

    d. Fred didn't stop joking. Because of this, his friends enjoyed hilarity throughout the evening.

[1]In this paper, either we deliberately use invented examples for purposes of succinctly illustrating particular phenomena, or we use real examples for more complex phemomena (the source of such examples is then given in footnote).

Proceedings of the Joint Workshop on
Linguistic Annotation, Multiword Expressions and Constructions (LAW-MWE-CxG-2018), pages 30–40
Santa Fe, New Mexico, USA, August 25-26, 2018.

The notion of a (primary) discourse connective was introduced a long time ago and there exist several lexicons in different languages, see Section 2. These lexicons record a list of lexemes or MWEs, as it is the case of other lexicons.

The notion of a secondary connective is more recent: it was originally introduced by (Rysová and Rysová, 2014). It is helpful both in discourse annotation and discourse parsing as explained in Section 4. Although secondary connectives are compositional word combinations, it is possible to build a lexicon for secondary connectives in a given language because they follow a limited number of templates and each template is "lexically headed" by a unique core unit, i.e. the unit that has the strongest meaning, which belongs to a closed list. For example, one of the templates in English is headed by a "discourse verb"[2] such as *cause, provoke, be due to, precede, follow . . .*, which belongs to a closed list. Moreover, a discourse verb is the lexical head of a secondary connective only if its subject is an anaphoric pronoun such as *this, that, it*, as it is the case in (1c). If the subject of a discourse verb is a definite noun phrase, as in (2a), the subject-verb combination is called a "free connecting phrase" in (Rysová and Rysová, 2014).[3] Another template is headed by a (simple or compound) preposition such as *because of*, which is the lexical head of a secondary connective only if it introduces an anaphoric pronoun, as it is the case in (1d). If it introduces a nominal phrase as in (2b), the prepositional phrase (*because of his jokes*) is a free connecting phrase.

(2) a. Fred didn't stop joking. <u>His jokes caused</u> hilarity among his friends for the whole evening.

    b. Fred didn't stop joking. <u>Because of his jokes</u>, his friends enjoyed hilarity throughout the evening.

Some templates for secondary connectives include an abstract anaphora — an anaphora which refers to an " abstract entity" (Asher, 1992), such as eventualities or facts — but this is not always the case, see Section 3. One of the basic difference between secondary connectives and free connective phrases is context dependency: the use of free connective phrases is heavily dependant on context, contrary to the use of secondary connectives. As an illustration, consider (3). The causal relation in (3a) is expressed by the free connecting phrase *because of this illness*. Its use makes sense because the left context mentions Fred's pneumonia, which is the antecedent of the anaphoric noun phrase *this illness*. On the other hand, this expression cannot be used in (3b) — which is incoherent (hence the sign #) — because there is no antecedent for the anaphoric noun phrase. It contrasts with the secondary connective *because of this*, which can be used in either context, (3c).

(3) a. Fred has pneumonia. <u>Because of this illness</u>, he will be absent from his work for two weeks.

    b. #Fred is on his honeymoon. Because of this illness, he will be absent from his work for two weeks.

    c. Fred /has pneumonia/ is on his honeymoon. Because of this, he will be absent from his work for two weeks.

In a nutshell, there exist at least three types of word combinations to signal a discourse relation between two spans of texts: (i) primary connectives, which are one-word expressions or frozen MWEs and for which several lexicons have already been built in different languages, (ii) secondary connectives, which are multi-word combinations used with a compositional meaning but with a unique lexical head, and for which we will describe how to build lexicons and how to use these lexicons in discourse annotation and parsing, and (iii) free connective phrases, which are multi-word combinations used with a compositional meaning and which cannot be recorded in a lexicon because of their productive nature due to (at least) two content words with a compositional meaning: lexical entries like *his jokes caused* ou *because of this*

---

[2]A discours verb is a verb with two arguments both referring to eventualities, such as *cause* (*An earthquake caused a tsunami*). It plays a role in discourse when one of its argument is an anaphora (*There has been an earthquake. It caused a tsunami in Japan*). The notion of discourse verb was originally introduced in (Danlos, 2006).

[3]This term is not appropriate for a word combination such as *his jokes caused*, which do not form a phrase. However, it is appropriate for *because of his jokes*, so we use it.

illness would be undesirable because of their heavy dependence on context and the absence of a lexical head.

It should be noted that some primary connectives may be considered as grammaticalized forms of secondary connectives. This idea is supported by the historical origin of the present-day primary connectives that arose from similar structures (and parts of speech) as present-day secondary connectives. See English *because* coming from combination of a preposition *bi* and noun *cause* or German *dagegen* containing the preposition *gegen* and a referential part *da*. This means that, due to language changes and possible increasing grammaticalization, secondary connectives may become primary in the future.

The paper is organized as follows. Section 2 gives a brief summary on primary connectives. Section 3 presents the main templates for English secondary connectives. Section 4 shows the usefulness of connective lexicons for both discourse annotation and parsing. Section 5 discusses on two possible ways to organize secondary connective lexicons, one is explored for French, the other one for Czeck. Finally, Section 6 opens the discussion on grammatical constructions with a discourse use.

2 Primary connectives

We define a primary discourse connective as an element which is, morpho-syntactically, a single-word unit or a frozen multiword unit, and semantically, a predicate with two arguments referring to eventualities. This characterization of primary discourse connective corresponds to the traditional notion of "connective" as used in the literature; see, e.g., (Zwicky, 1985; Hrbáček, 1994; Pasch et al., 2003; Fischer, 2006) or (Urgelles-Coll, 2010).

We follow the convention established by the PDTB (Penn Discourse Tree Bank, an English corpus annotated at the discourse level (PDTB Group, 2008)), which uses the term *Arg2* for the argument that is linked to the syntactic host clause of the connective, and *Arg1* for the other argument. To make the arguments easy to identify, the span of text corresponding to Arg2 is henceforth in italics, while Arg1 is in boldface; and we use colors for the discourse connectives — see (4).

(4) **Fred didn't go to work** because *he is sick.*

According to (Danlos et al., 2018), the main morpho-syntactic categories of primary connectives are: subordinating or coordinating conjunctions, prepositions or postpositions (in some languages such as German), suffixes (in some languages such as Turkish), adverbs and frozen prepositional phrases. On the semantic side, the PDTB distinguishes around thirty different sense tags of connectives (organized in a hierarchy), which characterize the discourse relation between the arguments of connectives. For example, the sense tag of *because* in (4) is Reason, which applies when the connective indicates that the situation specified in Arg2 is interpreted as the cause of the situation specified in Arg1.

Lexicons for (primary) connectives have first been built for French — LexConn (Roze et al., 2012; Danlos et al., 2015) — and German — DiMLex (Stede, 2002; Scheffler and Stede, 2016). As the DiMLex XML format has proven to be quite compatible with approaches to lexicons in other languages, the original format of LexConn was converted to the DiMLex format, and new lexicons for Italian (Feltracco et al., 2016), Portugese (Mendes et al., 2018) and English (Das et al., 2018) have recently been constructed following the DiMLex format.

3 Templates for secondary connectives

Secondary connectives play the same discourse function as primary connectives, but they are compositional word combinations which are lexically headed by a unique core unit. They often allow modifications and variants as it is the case of verbal MWEs for example.

We describe below four templates for secondary connectives, specifying for each one the syntactic category of its lexical head (which is underlined). These templates are illustrated with English examples, but there exist equivalents in many other languages. As the notion of a secondary connective is relatively new, we are not in a position to guarantee exhaustivity neither to give any frequency data.

3.1 Adverbial prepositional phrases

Secondary connectives in the form of prepositional phrases (PPs) are of two types according to the lexical head: the preposition or the noun. The first type is a combination of a preposition, the lexical head, and an anaphoric expression, mostly a demonstrative pronoun, like *despite/besides this, due/thanks to this, because/in spite of this*, as in (5a); no modification is possible. The second type is lexically headed by the noun, like *for this reason, under these conditions, for this purpose*, as in (5b); the noun can be modified by an adjective (*for this unbelievable reason*) and inflected (*for these reasons*).

(5) a. **I had all the necessary qualifications.** Despite this, *I didn't get the job.*

    b. **We were stuck in a traffic jam.** For this reason, *we couldn't attend the event.*

These two types of secondary PPs are schematized as PP/Prep and PP/N, respectively: in these schemes, the core unit (Prep or N) is indicated on top of the syntactic category PP.

3.2 Templates headed by a discourse verb

Other secondary connectives are lexically headed by a discourse verb (see note 2) , e.g., *cause, precede, follow, prove* or *mean*. The subject of a discourse verb in a secondary connective is an anaphoric pronoun referring to Arg1. The examples in (6) show that Arg2 can be nominal or clausal.

(6) a. **The increase in MHPG in hypothalamus and brain stem occurred as early as 1 hr postdosing;** this preceded *the earliest measurable sign of tremor and initial hypothermia.* [4]

    b. **The student feels more supported and is less afraid to ask.** This provokes that *he does not disconnect and continues to pay attention in class.*[5]

Discourse verbs can be used in the active or passive form (e.g., *this was preceded by, this was caused by*). In the passive form, they signal the "dual relation" of that signalled in the active form, e.g., *precede* in the active form signals a temporal relation in which the situation in Arg1 precedes that in Arg2, and the dual temporal relation in the passive form, i.e. Arg2 precedes Arg1. Discourse verbs can be modified by an adverb with a modal or evaluative value (*this was obviously due to, this unfortunately caused*). They are schematized as DVs.

3.3 Copula templates

Other secondary connectives contain a semantically weak verb, mostly the copula *be*. The lexical head may appear before or after the copula. First, the copula can be built with a subject whose head noun is the lexical head of the connective like *reason, condition, consequence, example, conclusion*. The examples in (7) show that Arg2 can be nominal or clausal. The copula can be omitted to yield examples such as (8).

(7) a. **The tourism industry has grown over the years.** The reason is *the arrival of international flights to the capital.*

    b. **The tourism industry has grown over the years.** The reason is that *international flights started arriving at the capital.*

(8) **International flights arrived at the capital.** Result: *the tourism industry has grown over the years.*

Second, the copula can be built with a subject which is an anaphoric pronoun referring to Arg1. The lexical head follows the copula: it can be a noun as in (9a), a subordinating conjunction as in (9b), or a preposition as in (9c).

---

[4]P.H Chen, *Toxicology and applied Pharmacology*, vol 77.

[5]Florentino Blazquez Entonado & Santiago Marin Garcia, *Co-operative learning in the teaching of mathematics in secondary education.*

(9) a. **International flights arrived at the capital.** That is the <u>reason</u> why the tourism industry has grown over the years.

  b. **Out in space, the sky looks black, instead of blue.** This is <u>because</u> *there is no atmosphere.*

  c. **Jane got pregnant.** This was <u>before</u> *her father's death.*

These copula templates are schematized as BE/SubjN when the lexical head is the head of the subject and as BE/AttN, BE/Conj or BE/Prep otherwise. When the core unit is a noun, it can be modified by an adjective (*a possible reason is that, that is the simple reason why*). The copula can be modified by an adverb (*this was probably before*).

It should be noted that the noun *reason* is the lexical head of the secondary connective both in (7) and (9a), but it expresses that Arg2 is the reason of Arg1 in the former examples and the dual relation in the latter.

3.4 Secondary subordinating conjunctions and prepositions

This set of secondary connectives includes PPs that may introduce a complement in the form of a clause, a VP or an NP, see (10). They are in the form *Prep the N that/of* where *N* is the lexical head, which can be modified (*in the vain hope that*). They can be qualified as secondary subordinating conjunctions or prepositions.[6]

(10) a. **People were trained** in the <u>hope</u> that *they would find jobs.*

  b. **Rwanda is also developing ICT** with the <u>aim</u> of *becoming a regional hub and supporting economic growth.*

  c. **He applied for a job in a new city** in the <u>hope</u> of *a positive answer.*

These PPs may appear without a complement but with an anaphoric determiner, as in *Many of its operational programmes and activities have been reoriented in line with this aim.*

4 Use of secondary connectives in discourse annotation and parsing

In discourse annotation, the first task is to identify the primary connectives in the corpus. This task generally relies on a lexicon of primary connectives which is projected into the corpus. A verification phase is needed to check that any item in the lexicon is actually used as a connective in the corpus: for example, *in short* in English is either a connective adverbial or a word sequence in the MWE *in short supply*, similarly *bref* in French is either a connective adverbial ('in short') or an adjective ('short'). Next, the sense and the arguments of the connective are annotated.

During the annotation of the PDTB (Prasad et al., 2008), it has been noted that discourse relations may be explicitly signalled by word combinations which are not primary connectives; they are called "alternative lexicalizations" (AltLex) (Prasad et al., 2010). In the PDTB-2 corpus, 624 tokens are annotated as AltLex. They correspond in our terminology either to primary connectives[7], or secondary connectives or free connecting phrases. According to (Prasad et al., 2010), word combinations are annotated as AltLex when there is no (primary) connective and when "a discourse relation is inferred, but insertion of a connective leads to redundancy". We believe that redundancy is not a clear criterion for identifying AltLex, because a discourse segment can be introduced by both a primary and a secondary connective that signal the very same discourse relation, as in the real-life examples (11) below. In (11a), the result discourse relation is signalled by both *as a result* and *this caused*; when following the PDTB annotation guidelines, *this caused* would not be annotated as an AltLex, because of the presence of the primary connective *as a result*. This leads to incoherencies and to wrong identification of arguments: the Arg2 of

---

[6]As far as we know, there are no multi-word expressions that can be qualified as secondary coordinating conjunctions.

[7]A primary connective may be annotated as an AltLex because the list of primary connectives in the PDTB-2 is made up of only 100 elements, and so several connectives are missing, like the adverb *thereafter*, as well as any preposition with a discourse use, like *in order to*. The English lexicon of (Das et al., 2018) contains 150 entries.

as a result would be wrongly identified as the rest of the sentence, i.e. *this caused families to send their children to work*, while it is rightly identified as *families to send their children to work* when *this caused* is recognized as a secondary connective.

(11) a. **Families, especially in Lebanon, have passed through different decades of wars (...).** As a result, this caused *families to send their children to work.*[8]

    b. **... the patient began to show evidence of insanity by incoherent talk, false ideas, nervousness, and outbursts of vicious excitement.** Later, this was followed by *mutism, refusal to eat, and stupor.*[9]

Moreover, a discourse segment can be introduced by both a primary and a secondary connective that signal different discourse relations, as in (12) in which *however* signals a contrastive relation and *this caused* a causal relation. Repairing these two connectives leads to the right identification of Arg2 (in italics).

(12) **The Middle Unit of the Chalk Mar was encountered in the crown of the TBM drives on the marine side of the NATM excavations.** However, this caused *only very limited delays.*[10]

In conclusion, we believe that the first task in discourse annotation should be to identify both primary and secondary connectives in the corpus, thanks to the projection of lexicons for the two types of connectives. As far as we know, no verification phase is needed after projecting the lexicon of secondary connectives into a corpus, in contrast with primary connectives (see above).[11] We underline that both primary and secondary connectives can be embedded under a report or propositional attitude verb, as in (13), which means that there is no *a priori* constraint, when projecting lexicons into a corpus, on the position of connectives in a sentence.

(13) a. **Fred will go to Peru next year.** Jane thinks on the other hand *he will go to France.*

    b. Because of this, **the bitcoin address could be well formed ... in a sense ...** I suppose this is the reason why *blockchain doesn't reject it.*[12].

So far, we have only discussed cases where discourse relations between two spans of text are explicitly signalled by lexical items (primary or secondary connectives, or free connectives phrases); such relations are called "explicit relations". However, it happens quite frequently — roughly, half of the time (Braud and Denis, 2016) — that discourse relations are not overtly marked; they are called "implicit relations". To illustrate, the causal relation between Fred's jokes and his friends' hilarity is explicit in (14a-b) — first presented in Section 1 — and implicit in (14c)

(14) a. **Fred didn't stop joking.** As a result, *his friends enjoyed hilarity throughout the evening.*

    b. **Fred didn't stop joking.** This caused *hilarity among his friends for the whole evening.*

    c. **Fred didn't stop joking.** *His friends enjoyed hilarity throughout the evening.*

Implicit relations are hard to handle both in discourse annotation and parsing. In discourse annotation, the annotators are supposed to infer the type (sense) of the implicit relations, which leads to a decrease of the inter-annotator agreement in comparison with the annotation of explicit relations. In discourse parsing, the situation is even worse: in shallow discourse parsing, which aims at automatically identifying discourse relations and their arguments in text, determining the type of relation is much more difficult

---

[8]Philippe W. Zgheib, *Business & Economics.*

[9]Bernard Glueck, *Studies in Forensic Psychiatry.*

[10]Colin S. Harris, Paul M. Varley, Colin D. Warren, *Technology & Engineering.*

[11]This also contrasts with MWEs : a MWE recorded in a lexicon may have a literal meaning in a corpus and not its idiomatic one (Savary and Cordeiro, 2018), while a secondary connective has only a literal compositional meaning.

[12]`https://bitcoin.stackexchange.com/questions/67126/is-1wh4bh-a-valid-bitcoin-address`

for implicit than for explicit relations, e.g., in the system of (Oepen et al., 2016), the difference in F1-measure is 13 points. Essentially all shallow discourse parsers (see the shared tasks at CoNLL 2015 and 2016) follow the pipeline model implemented in (Lin et al., 2014), which first identifies connectives, their arguments, and the relations they signal, and in a later stage tries to classify implicit relations using a separate module.

As both discourse annotators and parsers first identify connectives, and next try with difficulty to handle implicit relations, it is better to reduce the number of implicit relations as much as possible. This can be done if the expressions we have labeled secondary connectives are recognized as connectives. For example, if the expression *this caused* in (14b) is identified, thanks to a lexicon, as a secondary discourse connective with a causal meaning, no implicit relation between the two sentences is at stake and the causal relation can be identified as easily as in (14a).[13]

In conclusion, we believe that systematically handling secondary connectives — and having them play a similar role to that of primary connectives — can be highly beneficial both for discourse annotation and parsing.

5   Building lexicons for secondary connectives

We present two solutions to organize a lexicon for secondary connectives: the first one, which relies on the templates in which secondary connectives appear, facilitates the projection of secondary connectives into corpora — which helps both discourse annotation and parsing, as shown in the previous section — but may be hard to use for a human reader; the second one, which relies on the lexical heads of secondary connectives, is hard to use for projection into corpora but easy to read for a human user. The first solution is explored for a French lexicon, the second one for a Czech lexicon (Mírovský et al., 2017), which is under development, following annotation of the PDiT (Prague Discourse Treebank 2.0 (Rysová et al., 2016)).

The template-based solution consists in dividing the secondary connective lexicon into sub-lexicons, a sub-lexicon per template. This means creating a sub-lexicon for the template PP/Prep, another one for the template PP/N, another one for the template DV, etc. This solution can be compared to what is done for MWEs: there exist sub-lexicons for verbal, nominal, adjectival, …MWEs. In a sub-lexicon for a given template, the lexical entries are the lexical heads which are all of the same syntactic category, e.g. *Prep* in the sub-lexicon of the secondary connectives which follow the PP/Prep template or *V* in the sub-lexicon for the DV template. The properties recorded in a sub-lexicon may describe the possible variants and modifications of secondary connectives — e.g. in the DV sub-lexicon, the possibility for the verb to be used in the passive form, or in the PP/N sub-lexicon, the possibility for the noun to be modified and/or inflected. Other properties may describe the sense(s) of the secondary connective(s)[14], the existence of an equivalent primary connective if any, etc.

This organization in template-based sub-lexicons facilitates the projection of secondary connectives into a corpus since each template corresponds to one or two regular expression(s) which define search patterns to locate the secondary connectives into a corpus. However, this solution can be inconvenient for a human user, who may want to find all the secondary connectives with the same lexical head in one place, as advocated in (Danlos et al., 2018). So another solution to build a lexicon of secondary connectives is to keep all the secondary connectives with the same lexical head within a single entry. Such a lexicon is illustrated for English in (15) for the entry *reason*, which is the lexical head of secondary connectives following three templates. For each template, its scheme (e.g., PP/N) is given and followed by its specification. The following abbreviations are used in the specifications of the schemes: Ana for anaphoric, Det for determiner, Adj for adjective, Pro-Subj for a subject pronoun (referring to an eventuality); the symbol N stands for a variable whose value is given in the lexical head field; optionality is marked with parenthesis and alternatives are written within brackets. Under each scheme, the field

---

[13] In the discourse annotation/parsing of (14a-b), the question left after identification of the primary or secondary connective is to find the first argument (Arg1) of the causal relation. It boils down to find an antecedent to the anaphora in (14b).

[14] In the DV sub-lexicon, two senses (corresponding to a discourse relation and its dual relation) must be recorded if the discourse verb can be used in the passive form (Section 3.2).

Realizations gives concrete examples of the scheme, and the binary feature Inflection indicates if N can be inflected.

(15) **Lexical head: N = *reason***

> **Scheme 1 = PP/N** : for [Ana-Det (Adj)/Ana-Adj] N
> Realizations: *for this reason, for given reason*
> Inflection = 1
>
> **Scheme 2 = BE/SubjN**: Det (Adj) N BE (that)
> Realizations: *the reason is, a possible reason is that*
> Inflection = 1
>
> **Scheme 3 = BE/AttN**: Pro-Subj BE the (Adj) N why/for which
> Realizations: *that is the reason why; this is the simple reason for which*
> Inflection = 1

The information given in (15) is complemented by other fields that appear in each scheme: for example, the sense of the secondary connective, the existence of a primary connective equivalent if any, foreign language equivalents, etc. This is illustrated in (16) for the first scheme.

(16) **Lexical head: N = *reason***

> **Scheme 1 = PP/N** : for [Ana-Det (Adj)/Ana-Adj] N
> Realizations: *for this reason, for given reason*
> Inflection: 1
> Sense : Result
> Primary connective equivalent: therefore
> Foreign language equivalents:
> - Czech: z tohoto důvodu
> - French: pour cette raison
> - German: aus diesem Grund
>
> **Scheme 2 = BE/SubjN**: Det (Adj) N BE (that)
> . . .

6   What's else could lexically signal discourse relations?

So far, we have seen that discourse relations can be lexically signalled by primary connectives, secondary connectives or free connecting phrases. Are they the only word combinations used to signal a discourse relation between two spans of text? The answer is no: there are other devices, for example constructions such as the comparative correlative construction (CC) discussed *inter alia* by (Ross, 1967; McCawley, 1988; Fillmore, 2013) and illustrated in (17a), or the reversed CC illustrated in (17b) and whose interpretation is close to that of the sentence in (17c) with a primary connective.

(17)   a. The more I read, the more I understand.

> b. I understand more, the more I read.
>
> c. **I understand more** as *I read more*,

We call "discourse constructions" examples such as (reversed) CCs in (17a-b), with the aim of filling the gap between the domains of discourse studies and construction grammars. These two domains ignore each other most of the times, though not always. For example, conditional sentences with the primary connective *if* have long been studied in construction grammars (Jackendoff, 2002). On the other side, discourse studies are concerned with "parallel connectives" which are defined in (PDTB Group, 2008) as "pairs of connectives where one part presupposes the presence of the other, and where both together take the same two arguments", and are illustrated in (18); parallel connectives share the same structure as that of CCs, namely: *X1 S1 Punct X2 S2*.

(18) a. On the one hand, Mr. Front says, it would be misguided to sell into "a classic panic." On the
other hand, it's not necessarily a good time to jump in and buy.

b. If the answers to these questions are affirmative, then institutional investors are likely to be
favorably disposed toward a specific poison pill.

We wish to add that some some lexemes that usually are primary connectives, such as the subordinating conjunction *because*, should not be treated as such in (19), as discussed in construction grammars (Fillmore, 2013).

(19) Just <u>because</u> I live in Berkeley doesn't mean I'm a revolutionary.

In a nutshell, there exist grammatical constructions which should be discussed in discourse studies. This is left for future research.

7 Conclusion

We have shown that discourse relations can be lexically signalled by primary connectives, secondary connectives, free connecting phrases, and also by some discourse constructions. Primary connectives are often grammaticalized variants of secondary connectives, and there already exist primary connective lexicons in various languages, which describe the properties from 150 to 250 lexical entries (lexemes or MWEs). Secondary connectives, which are compositional, modifiable and inflectable, appear in syntactic structures that are lexically headed by a unique core unit, i.e., the unit that has the strongest meaning. It is possible to build lexicons for secondary connectives, and we have presented two ways to organize such lexicons, one primarily based on syntax, the other on lexical heads. Free connecting phrases are compositional and include at least two content words, which make it undesirable to record them in a lexicon. Discourse constructions need further work.

We explained why primary and secondary connective lexicons are quite helpful for both discourse parsing and annotation. The reasons are twofold: right identification of the Arg2 of discourse relations and decrease of number of implicit relations. These reasons are practical and not theoretical. Nevertheless, we want to emphasize the following point : in discourse theories (such as RST or SDRT (Mann and Thompson, 1988; Asher and Lascarides, 2003)), which rely on compositional semantic analyses without making use of the notion of secondary connectives, an implicit relation would be posited in (14b) for example, but what is the type of this discourse relation? It can be only a very weak relation such as "Commentary", which means that the second sentence gives a comment on/ a follow up of the first one. Such a relation doesn't give a structural analysis of discourse, which is the aim of RST and SDRT, and thus should be avoided anyway. Moreover, we have no idea on how these theories would handle discourse constructions such as those briefly discussed in Section 6.

One question is left open: we have shown that lexicons for secondary connectives can be built although these word combinations are compositional — but lexically headed. Is it envisageable to build other lexicons recording compositional lexical entries? And if it is, for which type of lexical entries?

Acknowledgements

I thank Marie Candito and the reviewers for their fruitful comments.

References

Nicholas Asher and Alex Lascarides. 2003. *Logics of Conversation*. Cambridge University Press, Cambridge.

Nicholas Asher. 1992. *Reference to Abstract Objects in Discourse*. Kluwer, Dordrecht.

Chloé Braud and Pascal Denis. 2016. Learning connective-based word representations for implicit discourse relation identification. In *Proceedings of the 2016 Conference on Empirical Methods in Natural Language Processing (EMNLP 2016)*, pages 203–213, Austin, Texas.

Laurence Danlos, Margot Colinet, and Jacques Steinlin. 2015. FDTB1 : Repérage des connecteurs de discours dans un corpus français. *Revue Discours*, 15.

Laurence Danlos, Katerina Rysov, Magdalena Rysov, and Manfred Stede. 2018. Primary and secondary discourse connectives: definitions and lexicons. *Dialogue & Discourse*, 9-1:50–78.

Laurence Danlos. 2006. Discourse verbs and discourse periphrastic links. In *Proceedings of the second workshop on Constraints in Discourse (CID 2006)*, Maynooth, Ireland.

Debopam Das, Tatjana Scheffler, Peter Bourgonje, and Manfred Stede. 2018. Constructing a lexicon of English discourse connectives. In *Proceedings of the 19th Annual SIGdial Meeting on Discourse and Dialogue (SIG-DIAL 2018)*, Melbourne, Australia.

Anna Feltracco, Elisabetta Jezek, Bernardo Magnini, and Manfred Stede. 2016. Lico: A lexicon of Italian connectives. In *Proceedings of the Third Italian Conference on Computational Linguistics (CLiC-IT 2016)*, Napoli, Italy.

Charles Fillmore. 2013. Berkeley Construction Grammar. In Thomas Hoffmann and Graeme Trousdale, editors, *The Oxford Handbook of Construction Grammar*. Oxford: Oxford University Press.

Kerstin Fischer. 2006. Towards an understanding of the spectrum of approaches to discourse particles: introduction to the volume. *Approaches to discourse particles*, pages 1–20.

Josef Hrbáček. 1994. *Nárys textové syntaxe spisovné češtiny*. Trizonia, Prague, Czechia.

Ray Jackendoff. 2002. *Foundations of Language: Brain, Meaning, Grammar, Evolution*. Oxford: Oxford University Press.

Neville Ryant Karin Kipper, Anna Korhonen and Martha Palmer. 2006. Extensive classifications of English verbs. In *Proceedings of the 12th EURALEX International Congress*, Turin, Italy.

Ziheng Lin, Hwee Tou Ng, and Min-Yen Kan. 2014. A PDTB-styled end-to-end discourse parser. *Natural Language Engineering*, 20:151–184.

Gyri Smrdal Losnegaard, Federico Sangati, Carla Parra Escartn, Agata Savary, Sascha Bargmann, and Johanna Monti. 2016. Parseme survey on mwe resources. In *Proceedings of the Tenth International Conference on Language Resources and Evaluation (LREC 2016)*.

William Mann and Sandra Thompson. 1988. Rhetorical structure theory: Towards a functional theory of text organization. *TEXT*, 8:243–281.

James McCawley. 1988. The comparative conditional construction in English, German and Chinese. In *Proceedings of the Fourteenth Annual Meeting of the Berkeley Linguistics Society*, pages 176–187.

Amalia Mendes, Iria del Rio Gayo, Manfred Stede, and Felix Dombek. 2018. A lexicon of discourse markers for Portuguese. In *Proceedings of the Tenth International Conference on Language Resources and Evaluation (LREC 2018)*, Miyazaki, Japan.

Jiří Mírovský, Pavlína Synková, Magdaléna Rysová, and Lucie Poláková. 2017. *CzeDLex 0.5*. Charles University, Prague, Czech Republic.

S. Oepen, J. Read, T. Scheffler, U. Sidarenka, M. Stede, E. Velldal, and L. vrelid. 2016. OPT: OsloPotsdamTeesside—Pipelining Rules, Rankers, and Classifier Ensembles for Shallow Discourse Parsing. In *Proceedings of the CONLL 2016 Shared Task*, Berlin, Germany.

Renate Pasch, Ursula Brauße, Eva Breindl, and Ulrich Herrmann Waßner. 2003. *Handbuch der deutschen Konnektoren*. Walter de Gruyter, Berlin/New York.

PDTB Group. 2008. The Penn Discourse Treebank 2.0 annotation manual. Technical report, Institute for Research in Cognitive Science, University of Philadelphia.

Rashmi Prasad, Nikhil Dinesh, Alan Leea, Eleni Miltsakaki, Livio Robaldo, Aravind Joshi, and Bonnie Webber. 2008. The Penn Discourse Treebank 2.0. In *Proceedings of the Sixth International Conference on Language Resources and Evaluation (LREC'08)*, Marrakech, Morocco.

Rashmi Prasad, Aravind Joshi, and Bonnie Webber. 2010. Realization of discourse relations by other means: Alternative lexicalizations. In *Proceedings of the 23rd International Conference on Computational Linguistics (COLING 2010): Poster Volume*, Beijing, China.

John Robert Ross. 1967. *Constraints on Variables in Syntax*. PhD. MIT, USA.

Charlotte Roze, Laurence Danlos, and Philippe Muller. 2012. LexConn: a French Lexicon of Discourse connectives. *Revue Discours*, 10.

Magdaléna Rysová and Kateřina Rysová. 2014. The centre and periphery of discourse connectives. In Wirote Aroonmanakun, Prachya Boonkwan, and Thepchai Supnithi, editors, *Proceedings of the 28th Pacific Asia Conference on Language, Information and Computing (PACLIC 2014)*, pages 452–459, Bangkok, Thailand.

Magdaléna Rysová, Pavlína Synková, Jiří Mírovský, Eva Hajičová, Anna Nedoluzhko, Radek Ocelák, Jiří Pergler, Lucie Poláková, Veronika Pavlíková, Jana Zdeňková, and Šárka Zikánová. 2016. *Prague Discourse Treebank 2.0*. Charles University, Prague, Czech Republic.

Agata Savary and S R. Cordeiro. 2018. Literal readings of multiword expressions: as scarce as hen's teeth. In *Proceedings of the 16th International Workshop on Treebanks and Linguistic Theories (TLT 16)*, Charles University in Prague, Czech Republic.

Tatjana Scheffler and Manfred Stede. 2016. Adding semantic relations to a large-coverage connective lexicon of German. In *Proceedings of the Ninth International Conference on Language Resources and Evaluation (LREC 2016)*, Portorož, Slovenia.

Manfred Stede. 2002. DiMLex: A lexical approach to discourse markers. In A. Lenci and V. Di Tomaso, editors, *Exploring the Lexicon - Theory and Computation*. Edizioni dell'Orso, Alessandria.

Miriam Urgelles-Coll. 2010. *The syntax and semantics of discourse markers*. Continuum Studies in Theoretical Linguistics. A&C Black, London, UK.

Arnold M. Zwicky. 1985. Clitics and particles. *Language*, 61(2):283–305.

From Chinese Word Segmentation to Extraction of Constructions:
Two Sides of the Same Algorithmic Coin

Jean-Pierre Colson
Université catholique de Louvain
Louvain-la-Neuve, Belgium
`jean-pierre.colson@uclouvain.be`

Abstract

This paper presents the results of two experiments carried out within the framework of computational construction grammar. Starting from the constructionist point of view that there are just constructions in language, including lexical ones, we tested the validity of a clustering algorithm that was primarily designed for MWE extraction, the *cpr-score* (Colson, 2017), on Chinese word segmentation. Our results indicate a striking recall rate of 75 percent without any special adaptation to Chinese or to the lexicon, which confirms that there is some similarity between extracting MWEs and CWS. Our second experiment also suggests that the same methodology might be used for extracting more schematic or abstract constructions, thereby providing evidence for the statistical foundation of construction grammar.

1 Introduction

In many respects, constructionist approaches have led to a new paradigm in the description of language structure. Building on Langacker's cognitive grammar (Langacker, 2008), the different versions of construction grammar (CxG) converge on the notion of constructions, defined as Saussurean signs, i.e. "conventional, learned form-function pairings at varying levels of complexity and abstraction" (Goldberg, 2013: 17). A construction may be a word in the traditional sense (e.g. *book*), a bound morpheme (*pre-, -ing*), an idiom (*spill the beans, take the rough with the smooth*), a partially filled idiom (*take X into account*), but also an abstract construction such as the ditransitive construction or the passive. As the famous quotation goes (Goldberg, 2006: 18), "It's constructions all the way down", i.e. language structure is made of nothing else than constructions, at various degrees of abstraction and schematicity. Schematic slots are the positions in the constructions allowing for several choices (e.g. X in *take X into account*), whereas specific (or substantive) slots are fixed (e.g. *into* and *account* in the same construction).

The continuum between lexicon and syntax plays a key role in CxG: there is no strict borderline between grammar on the one hand and the lexicon on the other, and this cline has been called the *constructicon* (Fillmore, 1988; Goldberg, 2003). Thus, the constructicon includes all types of constructions, be they of a more syntactic, morphological, phonological, phraseological, pragmatic or lexical nature.

As a general theory of language, CxG has far-reaching consequences for corpus and computational linguistics. In particular, it sheds a new light on multiword expressions (MWEs), in the general sense of all word combinations displaying lexical, syntactic, semantic, pragmatic and/or statistical idiosyncrasies. Indeed, all constructions are per definition partly *idiosyncratic* and in that sense partly *idiomatic*: "What may license referring to some constructions as idioms and not others is merely a reflection of the fact that effects of idiomatic variation are best observable in partially schematic complex constructions – however, this does not make them fundamentally different in nature from other constructions." (Wulff, 2013: 285)

It is worth noting that constructions are seen as a complex network, ranging from abstract to specific, from simple to complex and from schematic to idiomatic constructions. Crucially, this network of constructions is thought to be of a probabilistic nature (Croft, 2013; Stefanowitsch, 2013).

41

Proceedings of the Joint Workshop on
Linguistic Annotation, Multiword Expressions and Constructions (LAW-MWE-CxG-2018), pages 41–50
Santa Fe, New Mexico, USA, August 25-26, 2018.

Although there may be different ways of adhering to the constructionist approach, we think that (at least) two major theoretical claims of CxG have practical consequences for any computational analysis of MWEs:

1. As morphemes are also constructions, MWEs should rather be studied as MMEs (multimorphemic expressions). This makes it possible to apply the notion of constructions to the diversity of languages (Croft, 2001), and to be coherent with the constructicon. It indeed follows from the notion of constructicon that morphology and syntax are two sides of the same coin. For Booij (2013), exactly the same principles apply to schematic and idiomatic constructions at morphological and syntactic level. Thus, "A constructional idiom is a (syntactic or morphological) schema in which at least one position is lexically fixed, and at least one position is variable" (Booij, 2013: 258).
2. The network of constructions is of a probabilistic nature, so that statistical associations should not (only) be measured between the component parts of MWEs, but also at various levels of schematicity and abstraction.

From a practical point of view, point 1 makes it necessary to question the validity of traditional corpus analysis based on tokens (the traditional strings of letters separated by a blank). Constructionist morphology (Booij, 2013) suggests that associations between morphemes should be studied in the same way as syntactic associations between words, which means that using algorithms based on simple tokens will yield incomplete results. Besides, point 2 implies that statistical associations may exist between schematic and specific slots of constructions, which makes it necessary to adapt the corpus data by means of POS-tagging or more sophisticated representations. Some promising results have already been achieved by *collostructional analysis* (Gries and Stefanowitsch, 2004; Stefanowitsch, 2013), a methodology that makes it possible to quantify association strength in constructions, and is derived from collocational approaches used in corpus linguistics. Key findings are the statistical association between verbs and argument structure constructions, and the probabilistic relation between abstract grammatical constructions and concrete lexical constructions, the traditional words of the language. By having recourse to statistical measures and to linguistic corpora, collostructional analysis confirms that there is a cline from grammar to lexicon, and that the global network of all constructions may (largely) be governed by probabilistic principles.

For all these reasons, the implications of CxG for corpus and computational linguistics should not be underestimated, and a number of common practices of both disciplines should be adapted if we apply the principles of CxG:

- *Tokenization*: the traditional tokens should be questioned and cross-token measures should also be tested if we take morphological constructions into account
- *Lemmatization*: if morphemes are considered as constructions (Booij, 2013), lemmas should be considered as conventional units of meaning, and their concrete realizations (with different affixes) may be as important as the lemmatized form
- *Phonological features*: most corpora do not take phonological features into account (intonation, word stress), but these are an integral part of the construction. To give just one example, *not* will in most cases be treated as a simple substantive construction *inheriting* from the abstract NEG-construction (negation), but it can also be a complex idiomatic construction in cases such as *This book is excellent. Not!* (an ironical way of expressing the opposite of the preceding clause, with rising intonation). In this example, the idiomatic construction will have a rising intonation as one of its defining features, which should ideally be rendered by corpus annotation.

According to Gries (2013), the automatic extraction of collocations (in the general sense of MWEs) from corpora has been going on for over 50 years, but has produced very mixed results. If we add one level of complexity, that of constructions as defined by CxG, the situation may get even worse. Most studies dedicated to the extraction of MWEs face the problem of the validity of the gold standard. The very notion of MWEs may receive slightly different definitions, and it co-exists with other terms such as *collocations, set phrases, idioms, phraseological units*, to name just a few. Finally, *formulaic language* (Wray, 2008) has shed new light on the importance of all kinds of MWEs in the development and psychological background of language.

For the reasons set out above, improving the automatic extraction of MWEs from linguistic corpora, while integrating the fresh insights gained from CxG, appears at best as a daunting challenge. However, we will argue that CxG provides us with the following clues as to the extraction of meaningful structures in language:

1. According to CxG, the whole network of constructions is of a probabilistic nature.
2. As a consequence, the same statistical method should yield comparable results at the various levels of abstraction and specificity.
3. Improving the extraction algorithm at one point of the probabilistic network (for instance, for the extraction of MWEs) should therefore be useful as well for other types of constructions.

It is noteworthy that the continuum from syntax to lexicon, one of the tenets of CxG, poses another major problem to the extraction of MWEs. As in information retrieval, precision and recall play a central role in automatic extraction of collocations and MWEs, but these two notions can only be tested with reference to a gold standard: native speakers provide the researcher with manual results, for instance a list of the MWEs or a subcategorization of them. However, the cline from syntax to lexicon and from abstract to specific constructions implies that such a task is nigh on impossible, because of the very high number of borderline cases between all categories of constructions.

In this paper, we will argue that working from Chinese word segmentation may offer fresh insights into the organization of the probabilistic network of constructions mentioned by CxG. Mandarin Chinese is an unsegmented language (words are not separated by a blank). This offers the advantage of a linguistic material that can be analyzed along the whole continuum of constructions, from simple and complex words to idioms and proverbs.

2   Related work

The very notion of *word* remains controversial in Mandarin Chinese (Dixon and Aikhenvald, 2002). Experiments show that native speakers of Chinese not only disagree among themselves as to the exact segmentation of all sentences, but are often unable to replicate their own previous decisions (Bassetti, 2005). It is generally accepted that there is **an agreement of about 75 % among native speakers** as to the correct segmentation of a Chinese text into words (Sproat et al., 1996; Ying Xu et al., 2010). From the point of view of construction grammar, Chinese is therefore an excellent example of the continuum between syntax and lexicon, as even native speakers are sometimes confronted with the fuzzy borderline between constructions, phrases and words, which results in unclear segmentation.

In computational linguistics and information retrieval (IR), the state-of-the art method for Chinese word segmentation (CWS) is to tokenize an input text by using a monolingual supervised model trained on hand-annotated data, e.g. the Chinese treebank (Xue et al., 2005). It should be emphasized that such a method is not quite compatible with construction grammar, as it relies, for segmenting constructions, on decisions made by native speakers and dictionaries: this means that the cline from syntax to lexicon, and the description of constructions as a whole will depend on elements of linguistic representation rather than on evidence gained from corpora.

A full data-driven and statistical approach to the segmentation of Chinese has been taken by Xu et al. (2009), who propose the *Tightness Continuum Measure*. Their approach is based on document frequencies for segmentation patterns in corpora, and has been tested for 4-grams (in this case 4 Chinese characters or *hans*). Their results confirm the continuum of 'tightness and looseness' (Xu et al., 2009: 9) for Chinese strings, but the authors do not mention the fact that this actually corroborates one of the basic assumption of construction grammar, viz. the cline from syntax to lexicon. The *Tightness Continuum Measure* has been applied to Chinese information retrieval (CIR) by Xu et al. (2010). Their results show, again with the example of Chinese 4-grams, that a segmentation based on the *Tightness Continuum* performs better for CIR. It should be noted, however, that the better scores obtained with the *Tightness Continuum* were measured with scores used in IR and not against manually segmented texts.

More recent attempts to achieve or improve CWS on the basis of algorithms involve bilingual constraints in statistical machine translation (Zeng et al., 2014) or neural networks (Cai and Zhao, 2016).

It has also been pointed out that there is a high degree of similarity between CWS and MWE extraction (Xu et al., 2010). This should come as no surprise, if we take the constructionist view that language is made up of a complex and probabilistic network of constructions, in which there is no clear border between (free) syntax and MWEs. Any progress made in data-driven CWS may therefore have a positive impact on MWE extraction, and vice versa.

However, the problem with existing studies is that they are almost always of limited scope, and do not deal with both phenomena on a large scale, with recourse to huge linguistic corpora in several languages. An attempt to fill this gap has been proposed by the *IdiomSearch* project (Colson, 2017). A provisional web application has been designed[1] in order to test the automatic extraction of MWEs in the broadest sense from large linguistic corpora in English, Spanish, French and (simplified) Mandarin Chinese. The statistical score used is the *cpr-score* (Colson, 2017), an adaptation of a well-known technique used in IR, *metric clusters* (Baeza-Yates and Ribeiro-Neto, 1999). From a mathematical point of view, the *cpr-score* may be described as follows.

Let a given *n*-gram of length *n* be represented as $(w_1, w_2, ..., w_n)$, with each w_i belonging to the lexicon of a given language (for example the 3-gram "*spill the beans*"). We denote the gram appearing at position t in the corpus by the variable x_t. Thus, $x_t = w_i$ means that the gram w_i (e.g. *beans*), from the *n*-gram $(w_1, w_2, ..., w_n)$, is present at position t (represented by a long integer) in the corpus file.

We further denote as

$$n(w_1, w_2, ..., w_n) \triangleq n(x_t = w_1, x_{t+1} = w_2, ..., x_{t+n-1} = w_n) \tag{1}$$

the number of occurrences (frequency) of the **exact** *n*-gram $(w_1, w_2, ..., w_n)$, for instance the frequency of *spill the beans*, in the whole corpus, with no other token between the component grams (excluding e.g. *spill the proverbial beans*). As indicated in the right-hand side of Equation (1), it aims to count the number of occurrences of the event $(x_t = w_1, x_{t+1} = w_2, ..., x_{t+n-1} = w_n)$ in the corpus. Moreover, the expression

$$n\left(x_{t_1} = w_1, x_{t_2} = w_2, ..., x_{t_n} = w_n \mid \max(t_{i+1} - t_i) \leq W; \ i = 1, ..., n-1\right) \tag{2}$$

counts the total number of occurrences of the component grams (e.g. *spill*, *the* and *beans*), appearing sequentially at some positions $t_1 < t_2 ... < t_n$, in the corpus but with the constraint that they should be separated by a window of less than $W + 1$ positions (the maximum gap window is less or equal to W). The constant variable W (maximum window length) has been experimentally set at an integer value corresponding to a distance of 20 to 50 tokens, according to the corpus and the language. For English, it is typically set at a value representing a distance of about 20 words (as tokens).

Thus, (1) will give the exact frequency of the *n*-gram with no window between the component grams, while (2) allows for a maximal window (corresponding to up to 50 tokens) between each gram. The final expression used to measure the *cpr-score* is simply the ratio between (1) and (2):

$$cpr = \frac{n(w_1, w_2, ..., w_n)}{n\left(x_{t_1} = w_1, x_{t_2} = w_2, ..., x_{t_n} = w_n \mid \max(t_{i+1} - t_i) \leq W; \ i = 1, ..., n-1\right)}$$

Figure 1. The *cpr-score*

As in the case of metric clusters, the geometric distance between relevant elements of meaning is crucial in this approach. The implementation of the *cpr-score* can be achieved by several computational techniques, for instance by measuring the position of the strings in the whole file, by having recourse to regular expressions, or by complex indexation systems. The fastest results have been obtained by implementing a *query likelihood model* (Manning et al., 2009) such as the *Lemur Project*.[2] The *Indri Retrieval Model* included in this project can thus be parameterized to compute *cpr-scores* on pre-indexed corpora. Preliminary results obtained with the *cpr-score* indicate a level of precision higher than 95 percent if measured on a list of MWEs from dictionaries. Measuring precision and recall for MWEs of length 2 to 12 in real texts, however, poses the thorny theoretical issue of what can be objectively called a MWE or an idiomatic construction. It is also worthy of note that the *cpr-score*, deriving from metric clusters, is not fundamentally different from the above mentioned *Tightness Continuum* (Xu et al., 2010),

---

[1] http://idiomsearch.lsti.ucl.ac.be
[2] https://www.lemurproject.org/

based on document frequencies. We would argue that the use of document frequencies is precisely another way of introducing a windowing technique, which can therefore be seen as another variant of metric clusters.

3 An experiment in Chinese word segmentation (CWS) based on MWE recognition

As we have seen in section 1, construction grammar claims that there is a cline from syntax to lexicon, and that the structure of language therefore consists of a complex network of interrelated constructions. If this theoretical claim is correct, algorithms that are designed to extract MWEs should also be able to extract lexical constructions, provided that the corpus is adapted to that purpose. For European languages, it will for instance be necessary to start from morphemes instead of (conventional) words. In the case of Chinese, construction grammar predicts that looking for larger elements of meaning against the backdrop of a network of constructions will bring segmentation (CWS) and MWE recognition very close to each other.

In this paper we report the first results of an innovative experiment designed to test this general hypothesis.

3.1 Methodology

As this experiment is an extension of the *IdiomSearch Project*, we used as a reference corpus the same Mandarin Chinese corpus: a web-based general corpus, compiled by the *WebBootCat* tool provided by the *Sketch Engine*.[3] The methodology for compiling a general web corpus on the basis of *seed words* is fully described in Baroni et al. (2009). The likewise assembled corpus of (simplified) Mandarin Chinese comprises about 1 billion Chinese characters; as most Chinese *words* found in dictionaries consist of 2 characters, and some of 3 characters or more, we can estimate about 300 million words in the reference corpus. The corpus was indexed using the *Lemur toolkit* mentioned in section 2.

As we wanted to test the validity of a general purpose statistical score designed for MWE extraction at various levels (from bigrams to 12-grams), we implemented the *cpr-score* on the indexed corpus, by means of a Perl script. As there are some limitations inherent to very frequent records on a query likelihood model, all request yielding the maximum frequency of 50,000 were treated by another section of the script, in which a regular expression implemented the *cpr-score* on a non-indexed version of the same corpus. The average processing time for every request was 0.07 second on the indexed corpus, and 1.5 second on the non-indexed corpus (running on a pc with Linux).

In order to measure the performance of the *cpr-score* for CWS, we used the well-known MSR dataset, from the second *International Chinese Word Segmentation Bakeoff* (Emerson, 2005). For computing recall, precision and F-score of the segmented text, we used the standard scoring program (Perl script) provided by the Bakeoff.[4]

As in the case of the *Tightness Continuum* (Xu et al., 2010), the methodology for segmenting the input text was purely statistical, and used no list of training words or dictionaries of any kind. It should be stressed that such a methodology is purely data-driven, and rests upon the theoretical assumption that language structure itself includes recurrent patterns of meaning that can be captured by an algorithm, with no human intervention or any decision based on linguistic norm or culture.

Our computer program implementing the *cpr-score* proceeds as follows. Each Chinese character (han) is added one at a time, and the score is computed on the reference corpus. Let us take a simple example: the Chinese word[5] 高等教育 (*gāoděng jiàoyù*, higher education). Our algorithm first considers the bigram 高等 and checks its *cpr-score* on the reference corpus: 0.64. The *cpr-score* ranges from 0 to 1, and the high significance threshold has been experimentally set at 0.40 (Colson, 2017). Then, the third gram is added, 教, and the score for the trigram 高等教 is measured: 0.84. As the score is going up, the trigram is left unsegmented. Finally, the last gram 育 is added, and the score for the fourgram 高等教育 is computed, which yields 0.90. Again, the score is going up, so that the whole fourgram is left unsegmented.

---

[3] https://www.sketchengine.eu
[4] http://sighan.cs.uchicago.edu/bakeoff2005/
[5] This 4-gram is considered as two words by Google Translate (https://translate.google.com) but as one word by the MSR gold standard (http://sighan.cs.uchicago.edu/bakeoff2005/)

3.2 Results and discussion

Table 1 presents the results obtained by our experimental segmenter based on the *cpr-score* (Seg-cpr) and by a state-of-the-art segmenter, the Stanford segmenter[6], for the MSR dataset.

MSR dataset	Recall	Precision	F measure
Seg-cpr	0.749	0.658	0.700
Stanford-segmenter	0.882	0.843	0.862

Table 1: Results of CWS by means of Seg-cpr and Stanford-segmenter.

As shown in Table 1, the results obtained by our experimental segmenter based on the *cpr-score* are obviously less good than those of the Stanford segmenter, but this hardly comes as a surprise, as the *cpr-score* **was not designed for CWS** in the first place. We have also stressed in section 3.1. that our methodology, contrary to state-of-the-art segmenters such as the Stanford segmenter, does not rely on segmented corpora or on dictionaries, but only on statistical attraction as measured by the *cpr-score*. Contrary to most segmenters, it is not a mirror of how language users tend to segment the language, but of how **the language itself** contains statistically significant elements of meaning.

It is besides quite striking that the recall rate obtained by Seg-cpr (0.749) comes very close to the average rate of segmentation agreement among native speakers of Chinese (0.75, as mentioned in section 1). Contrary to manually segmented corpora, or to segmenters based on dictionary learning or segmentation pattern learning, our results are objectively measured by the algorithm on an *unsegmented* reference corpus. For this reason alone, a recall of 0.749 computed from the gold standard established by Chinese native speakers is quite high.

A fine-tuned analysis makes these results even more intriguing. In 5 to 10 percent of the cases, wrong segmentation by Seg-cpr was simply due to the fact that the n-gram was not used a single time on the reference corpus of about 250-300 million words. As the *cpr-score*, on which the tool is based, requires a frequency of at least 3 occurrences, the absence of an n-gram / word from the reference corpus inevitably leads to wrong segmentation, but this is to be blamed on the corpus size, not on the algorithm.

Taking a closer look at cases of obviously wrong segmentation by Seg-cpr raises other intriguing questions. One has to do with **discontinuous sequences**, a central issue in construction grammar as well. As a matter of fact, another 5 to 10 percent of the instances of wrong segmentation by Seg-cpr is due to discontiuous statistical association. Let us take the example of a Chinese fivegram from the MSR dataset, considered as one word by the gold standard, 个人计算机 (*gèrén jìsuànjī*, personal computer). Table 2 shows the *cpr-score* and the frequency of the different levels of grams in our reference corpus.

	Cpr-score	Frequency
个人	0.63	97,167
个人计	0.18	171
个人计算	0.55	140
个人计算机	0.73	122

Table 2: *cpr-score* and frequency of the component grams of 个人计算机 (*gèrén jìsuànjī*).

As shown in table 2, the fivegram 个人计算机 (*gèrén jìsuànjī*, personal computer), is identified as a whole as a very significant statistical association (*cpr-score* > 0.40), but working with one gram (in this case, a Chinese han) at a time reveals that the score goes down at the level of the trigram, and then up again. This is a clear example of a **discontinuous association** between successive Chinese characters, and is by no means an exception. The same situation occurs within several Chinese idioms in the source text, e.g. 付之东流 (*fùzhīdōngliú*, to lose sth irrevocably), and this also holds true of many foreign words that are transliterated into Chinese, e.g. 马克思主义 (*mǎkèsīzhǔyì*, Marxism) or 卡斯帕罗夫 (*kǎsīpàluōfū*, Kasparov). In all those cases, our experimental methodology worked gram per gram, and the *cpr-score* was therefore unable to segment correctly. A further elaboration of the methodology should

---

[6] The version used here is stanford-segmenter 3.8.0 (https://nlp.stanford.edu/software/segmenter.html)

address this complex issue. Results such as these are actually a confirmation of the global statistical association, as measured by the *cpr-score*, between elements of meaning in Chinese (words, collocations, idioms). They also mean that the results of our experimental Seg-cpr tool (with already a recall of 0.749 for the MSR dataset) could be further improved by introducing a more complex algorithm taking discontinuous cases into consideration. It should further be pointed out that similar cases of discontinuous association measured by the *cpr-score* have been noted for idiomatic constructions in English (Colson, 2017), e.g. *long time no see* or *the next thing I knew*.

All in all, the results of this experiment confirm our hypothesis that MWE extraction and CWS are closely related. The *cpr-score* was designed in the first place for MWE extraction, and yields convincing results for English, Spanish and French. In this experiment, we have used it for Chinese segmentation in a simplistic way, by adding one gram at a time. Even then, the overall recall rate is pretty high (0.749) and reaches the average rate of agreement between Chinese native speakers. Besides, a closer analysis reveals that taking discontinuous association into account would further increase recall and precision. From a theoretical point of view, such a complex network of probabilistic associations is quite compatible with construction grammar. The interesting cases of discontinuous associations may even provide us with some clues about the possible extraction of more complex constructions, as we will see in the following section.

3.3   Clues as to automatic extraction of constructions

As stated above, a statistical extraction method that is fully compatible with construction grammar should be able to deal with all constructions: lexical constructions (as in the case of Chinese word segmentation), idiomatic ones (e.g. MWEs), but also constructions with more schematic slots (e.g. *X take Y into account*), and maybe even abstract constructions such as the ditransitive construction.

Our clustering method (the *cpr-score*) already yields promising results for CWS and MWE extraction, but we may wish to test it further on more schematic or abstract constructions. This may indeed be beneficial to the improvement of grammatical material selection in language teaching, and may contribute to providing more evidence for the statistical grounding of construction grammar.

As a simple clustering algorithm, the *cpr-score* is non-parametric and can therefore be easily extended to longer sequences. Besides, it allows for complex implementations in databases using a query likelihood model, but also very simple ones in the form of regular expressions (*regexes*). The recourse to complex regexes makes it possible to check the *cpr-score* for schematic or abstract constructions, provided that the corpus annotation contains information on the construction under investigation.

The crux of the matter is indeed to extract constructions from corpora containing sufficient annotation techniques. As stated in section 1, a corpus used for the extraction of complex constructions should ideally include information related to intonation. In the meantime, using large POS-tagged corpora already provides us with a lot of testable material with respect to schematic constructions. Let us start from the fairly simple construction *the more... the more*. If construction grammar is right, corpora should be able to reveal that there is statistical association between them, even though the length of the window may vary. We may easily test it with the *cpr-score* by choosing a window of 8 words between the two parts of the construction, and by using our experimental program *Construction Extractor*, based on regexes.[7] In this case, the *cpr-score* obtained with a randomly selected portion (200 million tokens) of the ukWac corpus (Baroni et al., 2009) reaches 0.64 for a frequency of 1332: as might have been expected, there is indeed a measurable association between *the more* and *the more*, even with as many as 8 words between them.

Our aim was to test more complex constructions on a tagged corpus of about 100 million tokens. For this purpose, we used another randomly selected portion of the ukWac corpus (Baroni et al., 2009), and we had recourse to the Stanford POS tagger[8] for tagging it. According to CxG, the probabilistic network of constructions is valid at various levels of abstraction and schematicity. As a matter of fact, part of that complex interplay between morpho-syntactic features can easily be captured by considering the tagged

---

[7] The simple implementation of the *cpr-score* by means of regexes involves a division between resp. the frequency with the smaller window (in this case, 8 words) and the larger window (which we set on the basis of previous experiments at 10 times the smaller window). In Perl syntax, the regex for the frequency with the larger window may simply look like this: /the\smore\s(\S+\s){0,80}the\smore/i

[8] We used version 3.9.1 of the Stanford POS tagger (https://nlp.stanford.edu/software/tagger.shtml)

corpus as a geometrical space in which metric clustering can be measured. In other words, the statistical clustering algorithm (in this case the *cpr-score*) will just be looking for the association between parts of constructions and specific tags, as shown in table 3.

	Cpr-score	**Frequency**	**Window (*w*)**
it is *w* ADJ *w* what	0.12	428	4
it is *w* amazing *w* what	0.52	11	4

Table 3: *cpr-score* and frequency of a schematic construction and a derived MWE.[9]

Table 3 displays the *cpr-score* and the frequency for the MWE *it is amazing what* on the 100 million word part of the ukWac corpus, tagged by the Stanford POS tagger, given a maximal window of 4 words before and after the adjective *amazing*. This MWE, a specific lexical (and partly idiomatic) construction actually *inherits* (in CxG parlance) from the more schematic construction *it is ADJ what*. As shown in table 3, we can measure a weaker association at this more schematic level as well. The lowest significance threshold of the *cpr-score* has been (experimentally) set at 0.065, so that a score of 0.12 is sufficient to detect such a degree of association prevailing within more schematic constructions.

Other examples of schematic constructions that were extensively studied in the literature on CxG (Hoffmann and Trousdale, 2013) include the Ditransitive construction (e.g. *give a book to someone*) and the All-cleft /Wh-cleft construction (as in *all he had to do was to arrive on time*). As illustrated by table 4, our POS-tagged corpus also yields association scores for these constructions.

	Cpr-score	**Frequency**	**Window (*w*)**
NOUN VERB *w* NOUN *w* NOUN[10]	0.27	163979	5
all PRONOUN *w* VERBPast *w* VERBPast[11]	0.29	460	7

Table 4: *cpr-score* and frequency for the Ditransitive and All-cleft construction

Table 4 displays in the first line an approximation of the ditransitive construction in the tagged corpus, just taking into account nouns followed by a verb, followed by two nouns, with windows of 5 words in both cases. Even at this level of abstraction, it is noteworthy that the *cpr-score* implemented by a simple regex is able to measure some statistical attraction. The same holds true of the All-cleft construction in the second line of table 4. In this case, we restricted the search to the presence of two verbs in the past within a window of seven words. The regex in footnote 11 was of course checked for its validity, and it yields sentences (with the Stanford POS tags) such as *All DT he PRP did VBD the DT whole JJ time NN was VBD tell VB me PRP about IN*, or *All DT he PRP had VBD really RB expected VBN was VBD now RB propped VBN up RP on IN his PRP$ bedside NN table NN*. As predicted by CxG, there is indeed a **measurable statistical attraction in the very structure of the All-cleft itself**, as the *cpr-score* reaches a significant level of 0.29.

Our preliminary research yields similar levels of attraction for other cases of schematic constructions. For instance, the Verb Object Prep construction (as in *take a lot of effort*) yields a *cpr-score* of 0.31 for a frequency of 212 001, with a window of 3 words; similarly, the As-Noun comparison construction (e.g. *as bright as stars*) displays a score of 0.53 for a frequency of 429, with a window of 2 words.

---

[9] The output of the Stanford POS tagger was adapted by a Perl script, replacing the underscore signs by blanks, so that a simple regex could be used for measuring the *cpr-score*: /it\sPRP\sis\sVBZ\s(\S+\s){0,40}\S+\sJJ\s(\S+\s){0,40}what\sWP/i
[10] Regex used: /NN\s\S+\sV\S*\s(\S+\s){0,50}NN\s(\S+\s){0,50}NN/
[11] Regex used: /all\sDT\S+\sPRP\s(\S+\s){0,70}VBD\s(\S+\s){0,70}VBD/i

4   Conclusions

Starting from CxG's claim that there is a cline from syntax to lexicon and a complex network of constructions in language, at various levels of abstraction and schematicity, we have performed a first experiment on Chinese Word Segmentation. Algorithms used in CWS are usually trained on hand-annotated data, and are therefore a reflection of culture and tradition. However, we wanted to test to what extent an algorithm (the *cpr*-score) used for MWE extraction would yield results for CWS. For the reference text used, our algorithm reached a recall of 0.749 measured automatically from a gold standard established by native speakers. This may hardly be due to chance, as our segmentation method implied a binary choice at every single Chinese character. Besides, our recall score reaches the average degree of agreement between native speakers of Chinese. An analysis of the wrong cases of segmentation reveals that a discontinuous methodology may still improve the overall score on the basis of the same algorithm.

Our aim was not to provide a better segmenter for Chinese, because state-of-the-art tools trained on annotated data will inevitably reach higher scores measured on the same type of annotated data. We just wanted to test the hypothesis that CWS displays many similarities with MWE. The fact that a simple implementation of the *cpr-score*, designed in the first place for MWE extraction in European languages, reaches acceptable rates for CWS is a striking conclusion, that seems only compatible with one of the tenets of CxG: words are expressions and vice versa, as all language structure is just a network of constructions.

Building on these findings, we carried out a second experiment devoted to the extraction of more schematic or abstract constructions. Our preliminary results suggest that what is valid at the level of words and expressions will also be applicable to more schematic levels, so that the *cpr-score* or other clustering algorithms may be used for identifying constructions. The next application of this methodology may be the automatic extraction of the most fixed and recurrent schematic / partly schematic / idiomatic / abstract contexts of frequent verbs or nouns, based on the same algorithm.

References

Ricardo Baeza-Yates and Berthier Ribeiro-Neto. 1999. *Modern Information Retrieval*. ACM Press /Addison Wesley, New York.

Marco Baroni, Silvia Bernardini, Adriano Ferraresi and Eros Zanchetta. 2009. The WaCky Wide Web: A collection of very large linguistically processed Web-crawled corpora. *Journal of Language Resources and Evaluation*, 43: 209–226.

Benedetta Bassetti. 2005. Effects of writing systems on second language awareness: Word awareness in English learners of Chinese as a foreign language. In Vivian Cook and Benedetta Bassetti (eds.), *Second Language Writing Systems*. Multilingual Matters, Clevedon: 335–356.

Geert Booij. 2013. Morphology in Construction Grammar. In Thomas Hoffmann and Graeme Trousdale (eds.), *The Oxford Handbook of Construction Grammar*. Oxford University Press, Oxford/NewYork: 255–273.

Deng Cai and Hai Zhao. 2016. Neural Word Segmentation Learning for Chinese. In *Proceedings of the 54th Annual Meeting of the Association for Computational Linguistics*, Berlin: 409–420.

Jean-Pierre Colson. 2017. The IdiomSearch Experiment: Extracting Phraseology from a Probabilistic Network of Constructions. In Ruslan Mitkov (ed.), *Computational and Corpus-based phraseology, Lecture Notes in Artificial Intelligence 10596*. Springer International Publishing, Cham: 16–28.

William Croft. 2001. *Radical Construction Grammar: Syntactic Theory in Typological Perspective*. Oxford University Press, Oxford.

William Croft. 2013. Radical Construction Grammar. In Thomas Hoffmann and Graeme Trousdale (eds.), *The Oxford Handbook of Construction Grammar*. Oxford University Press, Oxford/NewYork: 211–232.

Robert M.W. Dixon and Aleksandra Y. Aikhenvald (eds.). 2002. *Word: A Cross-Linguistic Typology*. Cambridge University Press, Cambridge, UK.

Thomas Emerson. 2005. The second international Chinese word segmentation bakeoff. In *Proceedings of the fourth SIGHAN workshop on Chinese language Processing*: 123–133.

Charles Fillmore. 1988. The Mechanisms of Construction Grammar. *Berkeley Linguistic Society*, 14: 35–55.

Adele Goldberg. 2003. Constructions. A New Theoretical Approach to Language. *Trends in Cognitive Sciences*, 7(3): 219–224.

Adele Goldberg. 2006. *Constructions at Work*. Oxford University Press, Oxford.

Adele Goldberg. 2013. Constructionist Approaches. In Thomas Hoffmann and Graeme Trousdale (eds.), *The Oxford Handbook of Construction Grammar*. Oxford University Press, Oxford/NewYork: 15–31.

Stefan Th. Gries. 2013. 50-something years of work on collocations. What is or should be next … *International Journal of Corpus Linguistics* 18: 137–165.

Stefan Th. Gries and Anatol Stefanowitsch. 2004. Extending Collostructional Analysis: A Corpus-based Perspective on 'Alternations'. *International Journal of Corpus Linguistics* 9(1): 97–129.

Thomas Hoffmann and Graeme Trousdale (eds.). 2013. *The Oxford Handbook of Construction Grammar*. Oxford University Press, Oxford/NewYork.

Christopher D. Manning, Prabhakar Raghavan and Hinrich Schütze. 2009. *An Introduction to Information Retrieval*. Cambridge University Press, Cambridge, UK.

Diana McCarthy, Bill Keller and John Carroll. 2003. Detecting a Continuum of Compositionality in Phrasal Verbs. In *Proceedings of the ACL-SIGLEDX on Multiword Expressions*: 73-80.

Joaquim Silva, Gaël Dias, Sylvie Guilloré, and José Gabriel Pereira Lopes. 1999. Using LocalMaxs Algorithm for the Extraction of Contiguous and Noncontiguous Multiword Lexical Units. In *Proceedings of 9th Portuguese Conference in Artificial Intelligence* (EPIA 1999): 849.

Richard Sproat, Chilin Shih, William Gale and Nancy Chang. 1996. A Stochastic Finite-State Word-Segmentation Algorithm for Chinese. *Computational Linguistics* 22(3): 377–404.

Anatol Stefanowitsch. 2013. Collostructional analysis. In Thomas Hoffmann and Graeme Trousdale (eds.), *The Oxford Handbook of Construction Grammar*. Oxford University Press, Oxford/NewYork: 290–306.

Alison Wray. 2008. *Formulaic Language: Pushing the Boundaries*. Oxford University Press, Oxford.

Stefanie Wulff. 2013. Words and idioms. In Thomas Hoffmann and Graeme Trousdale (eds.), *The Oxford Handbook of Construction Grammar*. Oxford University Press, Oxford/NewYork: 274–28.

Ying Xu, Christoph Ringlstetter and Randy Goebel 2009. A Continuum-based Approach for Tightness Analysis of Chinese Semantic Units. In *Proceedings of the 23rd Pacific Asia Conference on Language, Information and Computation*: 569–578.

Ying Xu, Randy Goebel, Christoph Ringlstetter and Grzegorz Kondrak. 2010. Application of the Tightness Continuum Measure to Chinese Information Retrieval. In *Proceedings of the Workshop on Multiword Expressions: from Theory to Applications (MWE 2010)*. Coling 2010, Beijing: 54–62.

Xiaodong Zeng, Lidia S. Chao, Derek F. Wong, Isabel Trancoso and Liang Tian. 2014. Toward Better ChineseWord Segmentation for SMT via Bilingual Constraints. In *Proceedings of the 52nd Annual Meeting of the Association for Computational Linguistics*, Baltimore:1360–1369.

Fixed Similes: Measuring Aspects of the Relation between MWE Idiomatic Semantics and Syntactic Flexibility

Stella Markantonatou
Institute for Language
and Speech Processing,
Athena RIC,
Greece
stiliani.markantonatou
@gmail.com

Panagiotis Kouris
School of Electrical and
Computer Engineering,
National Technical
University of Athens,
Greece
pkouris@islab.ntua.gr

Yanis Maistros
School of Electrical and
Computer Engineering,
National Technical
University of Athens,
Greece
maistros@cs.ntua.gr

Abstract

We shed light on aspects of the relation between the semantics and the syntactic flexibility of multiword expressions (MWE) by investigating fixed adjective similes (FS), a predicative. MWE class not studied in this respect before. We work on Modern Greek data[1] and find that only a subset of the observed syntactic structures is related with idiomaticity. We identify and measure two aspects of semantic idiomaticity, one of which seems to allow to predict FS syntactic flexibility. Our research draws on a resource developed with the semantic and detailed syntactic annotation of web-retrieved material, indicating frequency of use of the individual similes.

1 Introduction

The relation between the idiomatic semantics of multiword expressions (MWE) and their syntactic flexibility, namely the ability of a MWE to occur in different syntactic configurations without loss of the idiomatic meaning, has offered a fertile field of research because it challenges the notion of compositionality, namely the derivation of the meaning of an utterance from the meaning of its components and its syntactic structure. The (predicative) free subject verb MWEs of the type verb+noun (V+N) have been one of the privileged fields of these studies. We add to the understanding of this relation by investigating a class of predicative (non-verb) MWEs that, to the best of our knowledge, has not been studied from this point of view so far, namely the class of fixed similes (FS) of the type adjective+connector+(article)+noun such as *sweet like honey*. Modern Greek, a lesser studied language in this respect, is our object language. We ask whether the occurrence of the syntactic structures considered as manifestations of syntactic flexibility is related with (idiomatic) semantics and we find that this holds only for some structures –a subset of which could be characterised as syntactic alternatives. Our results corroborate the idea that syntactic structures demonstrate varying sensitivity to the semantics of their components and that the presence of syntactic variants may not be dependent only on idiomatic semantics. Next, we investigate the notion of idiomaticity. We understand idiomaticity as the degree of similarity between the FS semantics and the semantics of their free property (i.e., the free adjective, see Table 1) and, we identify and measure two types of similarity, one of which allows us to make predictions about FS syntactic flexibility. Our results were drawn from a resource developed as part of the research presented here by extensively annotating a large amount of web-retrieved unique FS usage examples. The special feature of this resource is that it offers an as good as possible approximation of the actual FS usage in texts, both in terms of frequency and in terms of structure selection.

Table 1 shows the terminology for the parts of an FS adopted from Hanks (2005):

[1]We acknowledge support of this work by the project "Computational Sciences and Technologies for Data, Content and Interaction" (MIS 5002437) which is implemented under the Action "Reinforcement of the Research and Innovation Infrastructure", funded by the Operational Programme "Competitiveness, Entrepreneurship and Innovation" (NSRF 2014-2020) and co-financed by Greece and the European Union (European Regional Development Fund).

Proceedings of the Joint Workshop on
Linguistic Annotation, Multiword Expressions and Constructions (LAW-MWE-CxG-2018), pages 51–61
Santa Fe, New Mexico, USA, August 25-26, 2018.

entity modified by the FS	adjective	connector	(article) noun
tenor	property		vehicle

Table 1: Terminology for the parts of an FS.

In §2 we contextualise our work with respect to state-of-the-art research. In §3 we talk about data collection and annotation and the development of the resource. In §4 we describe the results we receive by quantitatively studying the resource. We present our conclusions and our plans for the future in §5.

2 Related work

Simile is a figure of speech, which, unlike metaphor, draws attention to the likeness between the tenor and the vehicle that are implied to share certain properties (Veale and Hao, 2007). Similes draw on conventional beliefs about likeness and effectively convey the speaker's superlative evaluation of the tenor (Israel et al., 2004). They follow the same structure as comparative, e.g. *Knowledge is **sweeter than honey***, equative, e.g. *Her argument was **as clear as glass*** and similative statements, e.g. *My hands were **cold like ice*** (Chila-Markopoulou, 1986; Israel et al., 2004; Niculae and Danescu-Niculescu-Mizil, 2014; Mpouli and Ganascia, 2015). Many conventional similes tend to be fixed and have idiom status (Hanks, 2005). For instance, FS6 κόκκινος σαν αστακός (kokinos san astakos) 'red as lobster' (see Table 2) applies mainly to persons or body (parts) (96,4% in our data) to denote blushing or sunburned people; this meaning can not be derived from the parts of the FS. Some English FS tend to select tenors from a small range of semantic fields (Mpouli and Ganascia, 2015); for Greek see Figure 1. FS have been found to share a good part of simile usage in English (Niculae and Danescu-Niculescu-Mizil, 2014).

Modern Greek FS assume the syntactic functions of the adjectives (Markantonatou et al., 2016). They appear as complements of the copula (1), as phrasal adjuncts controlled by the subject of the main verb (3), in verbless sentences (4), in the typical adjective position between the determiner and the noun (5) and, rarely, as subjects and objects of verbs or prepositions. In all these structures, FS can be replaced with the superlative of the adjective (exemplified only for the complement of copula (2)). They may occur with the adverb πολύ (poli) 'much' or, rarely, with some other intensifying adverb. In this case, the simile is not pronounced as a unit but as if a punctuation mark existed between the property and the σαν+vehicle part. We annotated these structures as *empp* (phrasal emphasis (Table 3)). We will treat FS as MWE adjectives.

(1)   Ήταν ο   ύπνος   γλυκός   σαν το μέλι   της κερήθρας.
Itan o   ipnos   glikos   san to meli tis kierithras.
was the sleep.nom sweet.nom like the honey the honeycomb.gen

'Sleep was as sweet as the honey of the honeycomb.'

(2)   Ήταν ο   ύπνος   πάρα πολύ γλυκός.
Itan o   ipnos   para poli glikos.
was the sleep.nom much very sweet.nom

'Sleep was extremely sweet.'

(3)   Ελαφρύς σαν πούπουλο, πήδηξε στο   μαξιλάρι.
Elafris   san pupulo, pidikse sto   maksilari.
light.nom like feather, jumped on.the pillow

'As light as the feather, he jumped on the pillow.'

(4)   Ύπνος   γλυκός   σαν μέλι.
Ipnos   glikos   san meli.
sleep.nom sweet.nom like honey

'A sleep as sweet as honey.'

(5)   Ένας γλυκός σαν μέλι ύπνος τον τύλιξε.
Enas glikos san meli ipnos ton tilikse.
a   sweet like honey sleep him wrapped

'He had a very sweet sleep.'

Computational methods distinguishing between similes and other comparisons take advantage of the attested semantic distance between the similes' tenor and vehicle and of definiteness (Niculae and Danescu-Niculescu-Mizil, 2014). However, we show that in Modern Greek, determiner distribution is independent of FS idiomaticity (§4.1).

The study of large amounts of data of V+N MWEs has shown that MWE syntactic flexibility is related to MWE idiomaticity modeled as the semantic distance between the environments where the MWE and its parts occur (Fazly et al., 2009). Our research on FS sheds more light on this attested relation.

A much debated proposal claims that MWE syntactic flexibility is related with MWE semantic analysability, namely the degree to which the idiomatic semantics of the MWE can be derived synthetically from the (idiomatic) meanings of its parts (indicatively, Nunberg et al. (1994), Kay and Sag (2012) argue in favor of the syntactic analysability approach and Laporte (2018) argues against it). Interestingly, (Kay and Sag, 2012, 4) maintain that while "meaningful idiom words can be modified and can appear in syntactic contexts that meaningless ones cannot", only those language structures that "do not entail interpretive consequences (as does, for example, English topicalization) are precisely the syntactic contexts that permit meaningless idiom words to be "displaced."" We demonstrate that the syntactic environments in which FS occur can be split into FS semantics sensitive and insensitive ones.

3 The resource

N	Greek FS	English translation	Instances	Percentage
1	άσπρος (λευκός) σαν το πανί	as white as a sheet	462	9.5%
2	στολισμένος σαν φρεγάτα	Lit. adorned like a frigate	16	0.3%
3	απαλός σαν πούπουλο	Lit. soft like feather	36	0.7%
4	απαλός σαν χάδι	Lit. soft like cuddle	174	3.6%
5	ελαφρύς (αλαφρύς) σαν πούπουλο	as light as a feather	201	4.1%
6	κόκκινος σαν αστακός	Lit.red like lobster	104	2.1%
7	οπλισμένος (αρματωμένος) σαν αστακός	Lit. armed like a lobster	388	8.0%
8	μαλακός σαν βούτυρο	as soft as butter	162	3.3%
9	γερός σαν ταύρος	as strong as a bull	102	2.1%
10	πιστός σαν σκύλος (σαν σκυλί)	as faithful as a dog	69	1.4%
11	κόκκινος σαν παπαρούνα	as red as a poppy	173	3.6%
12	ντυμένος σαν αστακός	Lit. dressed like lobster	24	0.5%
13	κόκκινος σαν παντζάρι	as red as a beetroot	122	2.5%
14	γλυκός σαν μέλι	as sweet as honey	501	10.3%
15	άσπρος (λευκός) σαν το γάλα	as white as milk	517	10.6%
16	κρύος σαν τον πάγο	as cold as ice	272	5.6%
17	γρήγορος (γοργός) σαν την αστραπή	as quick as a flash	275	5.7%
18	μαύρος σαν το σκοτάδι	as black as pitch	81	1.7%
19	μπερδεμένος σαν κουβάρι	Lit. knotted like ball	84	1.7%
20	άσπρος (λευκός) σαν το χιόνι	as white as snow	1099	22.6%

Table 2: FS distribution in the resource.

3.1 Data collection

With a tailor-made Facebook application (Mitrović and Markantonatou, 2018) we asked 260 native speakers of Modern Greek to specify which of 152 similes they would use in their everyday exc hange.[2] Krippendorff's alpha coefficient (Artstein and Poesio, 2008) was used to evaluate inter-speaker agreement. 85 similes were found to be used by a critical number of speakers. According to Baldwin and Kim

[2]The similes were collected from the Hellenic National Corpus (HNC), http://hnc.ilsp.gr/, and a corpus of 100 million words that was collected with crawlers. The corpora were searched for the pattern adjective+σαν+noun and only structures that appeared more than once were retained.

(2010), the selected similes can be considered MWEs because (i) they fulfill the statistical idiomaticity criterion; as explained in §3.2, the similes are subject to minimal lexical variation (ii) most of them fulfill the semantic idiomaticity criterion (§2). Of them, we selected 20 FS (Table 2) that represent the classes defined in two different simile classifications by the semantics of the vehicle and of the property, one of Modern Greek FS (Mpolla-Mavridou, 1996) and one of English similes (Hanks, 2005). A corpus consisting of 4900 unique usage examples (instances from now on) was collected from the web with exhaustive searches, which allowed our resource to represent instance frequency.[3] Regular expressions were used to capture the rich morphology of Modern Greek, its flexible word order as well as lexical and syntactic variation. The retrieved material was cleaned from multiple occurrences of the same instance and from machine translation outputs. Table 2 shows the distribution of instances per FS in the corpus.

3.2 Lexical and syntactic variation in the case of Modern Greek FS

Lexical variation is not attested for most FS in our data (Table 2). The adjectives άσπρος (aspros) 'white', οπλισμένος (oplismenos) 'armed' and γρήγορος (grigoros) 'fast' variate between synonyms that differ in terms of style and the variants occur in considerable frequencies. FS1 άσπρος σαν το πανί (aspros san to pani) 'as white as sheet' is exceptional because there is a small number of adjectives with the sense *pale* that variate with άσπρος: κίτρινος (kitrinos) 'yellow', ωχρός (ochros) 'ashy, ghostly', χλωμός (chlomos) 'pale'. FS10 πιστός σαν **σκύλος** (pistos san skilos.masc) 'as faithful as a dog', variates with πιστός σαν **σκυλί** (pistos san skili.neut) because the vehicle occurs in both genders.

Syntactic variation is more frequent in our data. The FS alternative with connector σαν (san) 'like, as' (6) is the most frequently used form, which we will call the normative form. The same property and vehicle may appear in a comparative structure; (7) features a morphological comparative form and (8) a phrasal one (Chila-Markopoulou, 1986). They can also appear in an equative form (9). Similar observations have been made for English (Niculae and Danescu-Niculescu-Mizil (2014); Mpouli and Ganascia (2015)). We will use the term FS alternative to refer to syntactic variations (6)-(10): we have also treated as FS alternatives the structures that contain a punctuation mark (comma, full stop, dots) between the property and the connector+vehicle part of the FS (10) provided that the parts on either side of the punctuation mark are predicated of the same entity.

(6)   Σε   παίρνει ο γνωστός μεσημεριανός ύπνος,   ο **γλυκός σαν μέλι**.
     Se   perni o gnostos mesimerianos ipnos,   o glikos san meli.
     you.acc take   the familiar noon   sleep.nom, the sweet like honey

     'The familiar nap, that is sweet like honey, comes all over you.'

(7)   Είναι **γλυκύτερος από μέλι** και δυστυχώς   δεν δείχνει σκυλί επιβίωσης.
     Ine   glikiteros apo meli kie distichos   den dichni skili epiviosis.
     is   sweeter   than honey and unfortunately not shows dog of.survival

     'It is sweeter than honey but, unfortunately, it does not seem to be a survivor dog.'

(8)   Έλεγε τραγούδια γλυκά, **πιο   γλυκά κι από το μέλι** της   μέλισσας.
     Elegie tragudia   glika, pio glika ki apo to meli tis   melisas.
     said   songs   sweet more sweet and from the honey of.the bee

     'He sang sweet songs, sweeter than the honey of the bee.'

(9)   Αλείφουν τις βρύσες με   μέλι, ώστε   ο   καινούριος χρόνος να είναι **τόσο γλυκός σαν το μέλι**.
     Alifun   tis vrises me meli, oste   o   kienurgios chrons na ine toso glikos san to meli.
     rub   the taps with honey so that the new   year   to be   as   sweet like the honey

     'They rub the taps with honey to ensure that the new year will be as sweet as honey.'

(10) Και είναι **τόσο απαλό. Σαν το στερνό σου χάδι**.
     Kie ine toso apalo. San to sterno su chadi.
     and is   so   soft   like the last   your cuddle

     'And it is so soft. Like your last cuddle.'

---

[3]The available Modern Greek corpora offered less than a hundred of instances.

3.3 Syntactic and semantic annotation

Syntactic annotation modeled FS syntactic flexibility; it captured the normative form and the deviations from it observed in the data, including FS alternatives. As Greek FS function as adjective MWEs (§2), we assume that their semantics is represented by the semantics of the NPs they select as tenors (Table 1). We used WordNet supersenses to annotate the tenors; this detailed semantic annotation allowed us to distinguish between types of idiomaticity. In the remainder, we will use the term FS semantics to denote the set of semantic annotations assigned to the tenors of a particular FS in the resource. High degrees of inter-annotator agreement were obtained as confirmed by Krippendorff's alpha coefficient.

3.3.1 Syntactic annotation

Table 3 summarises the labels used to annotate syntactic flexibility. The last four lines of Table 3 show the FS alternants. The annotators used a manual developed for this purpose.

Label	Phenomenon	Example-Litteral Translation
iwo	connector+vehicle+property	san pupulo elafris (like feather light)
ixp-w	word (not tenor) after property	elafri poli san pupulo (light much like feather)
ixp-n	tenor (only noun) after property	elafri fagito san pupulo (light food like feather)
ixp-creative	words > 1 after property	elafris san puli ochi san pupulo (light like bird not like feather)
mod	modifier of vehicle	elafris san pupulo chielidoniu (light like feather swallow.poss)
empm	morphological emphasis on property	pan-alafro san pupulo (emp-light like feather)
empp	phrasal emphasis on property	poli elafris san pupulo (very light like feather)
mwo	FS combined with other MWE	elafri san pupulo to choma pu ton skepazi[4] (light like feather the soil that him covers)
agr	vehicle agrees with plural tenor	skies elafries san pupula (shadow.pl light like feather.pl)
det	determiner before vehicle	elafris san to pupulo (light like the feather)
var	lexical variation	aspros/lefkos san pani (white like cloth)
comp	πιο adjective (και/κι) από noun	pio elafris ki apo pupulo (more light and from feather)
toso	τόσο adjective όσο/σαν det+noun	toso elafris oso/san to pupulo (as light as the feather)
ixp-punc	punctuation after property	elafris, san pupulo (light, like feather)
constr	**the determinerless normative form**	**elafris san pupulo** (light like feather)

Table 3: The labels for syntactic flexibility annotation.

To check inter-annotator agreement 630 instances (12,9% of the data), representing 6 FS (FS19, FS18, FS12, FS11, FS9, FS8), were annotated by 3 linguists. Krippendorff's alpha coefficient was equal to 0.91.

3.3.2 Semantic annotation

WordNet supersenses were used to semantically annotate the tenors (Schneider et al., 2013; Schneider and Smith, 2015). No sufficient WordNets are available for Modern Greek, so we translated Greek tenors into English. In case of pronouns or pro-drop phenomena, the tenor was induced from the context.

To check inter-annotator agreement 2400 instances (49% of the data), representing 4 FS (FS20, FS19, FS18, FS1), were annotated by 5 linguists. Krippendorff's alpha coefficient was equal to 0.95.

Figure 1 shows the distribution of semantic categories of tenors in the resource. We see that FS (at least, the ones we studied) mainly describe humans and that they select a small set of semantic categories (Mpouli and Ganascia, 2015), which partly explains the high inter-annotator agreement.

3.4 The Flat-Folia resource

To make the annotated resource[5] machine-readable, extensible and reusable, we converted it to Folia format (van Gompel and Reynaert, 2013), an XML-based format for linguistic annotation. We use the

---

[4]MWE1: elafri to choma pu ton skiepazi, lit. *light the soil that covers him* (it is said for those who have passed away), FS: elafris san pupulo 'as light as a feather'.

[5]The resource can be accessed at http://glotta.ntua.gr/Similes/.

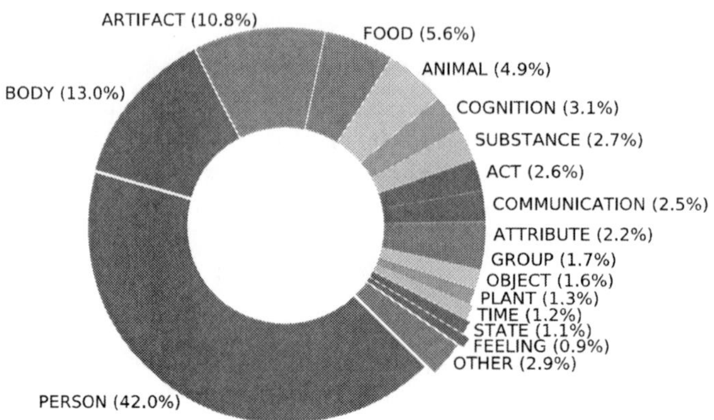

Figure 1: Distribution of semantic categories of tenors in the resource.

Flat - FoliA Linguistic Annotation Tool,[6] which allows users to view and edit Folia annotated documents.

4 Investigating the resource

4.1 The relation between syntactic flexibility and tenor semantics

Shannon entropy is used as a measure of the syntactic and semantic diversity (Manning and Schütze, 1999; Lebani et al., 2015). For the syntactic entropy, each FS instance is represented as a vector including binary values of the syntactic features defined in Table 3 (presence or absence of a feature). Thus, syntactic entropy is measured according to the distinct vectors and their frequency. Semantic entropy is measured by the number of occurrences of each semantic category (Figure 1).

Pearson correlation coefficient (Benesty et al., 2009) showed a strong positive linear relationship between the syntactic and semantic diversity (equal to 0.84 with $p - value = 3.2 \cdot 10^{-6}$), across the FS for the syntactic features *constr, comp, toso, ixp-punc, ixp-creative, ixp-n, empp, mwo*. We observe a positive relation between fixedness and semantic idiomaticity, also observed for V+N MWEs (Fazly and Stevenson, 2007). Correlation improved for the aforementioned syntactic features and deteriorated for the features *iwo, ixp-w, mod, var, det, empm* (Table 3). This result is reminiscent of the (Kay and Sag, 2012, 4) observation that syntactic contexts may or may not interfere with MWE semantics (§2). The relation between the syntactic and semantic diversity of each FS is depicted in Figure 2.

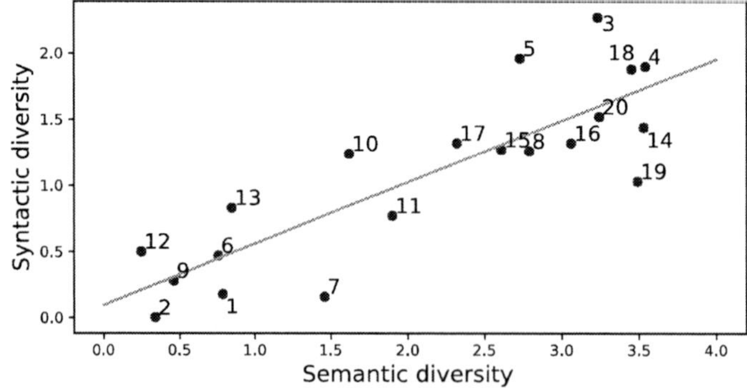

Figure 2: The linear relation between the syntactic and semantic diversity of the similes (the diversity is measured in terms of Shannon entropy).

---

[6]FLAT is an open source software developed at the Centre of Language and Speech Technology, Radboud University Nijmegen. It can be obtained from https://github.com/proycon/flat

4.2 Classification of FS by syntactic flexibility

Clustering over the vectors including binary values of the syntactic features (presence or absence of a feature) failed to produce an FS classification by syntactic flexibility (such as the one proposed for all MWEs in Sag et al. (2002)); rather, it produced interesting FS instance clusters. We applied Logistic Principal Component Analysis (LPCA) (Landgraf and Lee, 2015) to achieve dimensionality reduction and to visualize the FS instances in two dimensions. The k-Means algorithm[7] is used to separate the data in k clusters of FS instances, where the instances in each cluster are expected to have similar characteristics (Berkhin, 2006). Although the instances could be analyzed in more clusters employing more complicated clustering algorithms, in this initial approach, we identify significant knowledge in a more general separation, as we describe below.

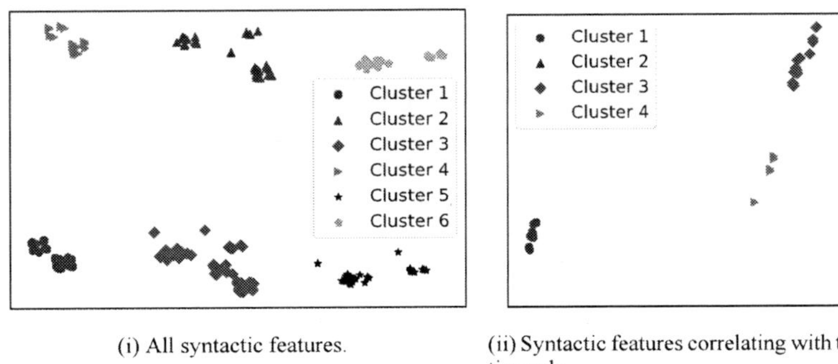

(i) All syntactic features.

(ii) Syntactic features correlating with tenor semantics only.

Figure 3: Clustering FS instances.

When all syntactic features are used, we obtain six clusters (Figure 3(i)) with prominent features *det*, *var*, *comp* and *constr*. Only *constr*'s and *comp*'s syntactic diversity correlates with tenor's semantic diversity (§4.1). The most frequent features by cluster are: cluster 1, *constr* (the normative form); cluster 2, *det*, *var*; cluster 3, *det*; cluster 4, *var*; cluster 5, *det*, *comp*, *constr*; cluster 6, *det*, *comp*, *constr*, *var*.

When only the syntactic flexibility features that contribute positively to the flexibility-idiomatic semantics correlation are used (§4.1), we obtain four clusters (Figure 3(ii)) with prominent features *constr*, *comp*, *ixp-punc* and *toso*. The most frequent features by cluster are: cluster 1, *constr* (the normative form, i.e. absence of any syntactic feature); cluster 2, *comp*, *constr*; cluster 3, *ixp-punc*, *constr*; cluster 4, *toso*, *constr*. The feature *constr* occurs in the clusters 2, 3 & 4, so these clusters can be characterized by their other features *comp*, *ixp-punc* and *toso*. The four structures are the FS alternatives (§3) that more or less partition the set of FS instances (only *ixp-punc* co-occurs with the other FS alternatives, very rarely).

Geeraert et al. (2017), using eyetracking, identified lexical variation (corresponding to our feature *var*) as one of the "easiest" MWE variations for English in terms of comprehension. This might indicate that MWE variations that are "easy" in terms of comprehension are, at the same time, independent of MWE idiomaticity and "more prominent" than other syntactic structures in the speakers' output.

4.3 Predicting syntactic flexibility

To better understand the relation between semantic and syntactic diversity, we sought a quantitative definition of idiomaticity. Intuitively, since FS function as MWE adjectives (§2), rather than defining idiomaticity as the distance of the context of the constituents of the FS from the context of the FS itself (Fazly and Stevenson, 2007), we defined it as the similarity between the tenor semantics and the semantics of the NPs selected by the free property of the FS. For instance, we calculated the similarity between the semantics of the tenors of FS1 άσπρος σαν το πανί (aspros san to pani) 'as white as a sheet' and the semantics of the NPs selected by the free occurrences of the adjective άσπρος (aspros) 'white'. We defined two measures of semantic similarity:

---

[7]The popular k-means algorithm is sufficient because the obtained clusters have clear limits.

Semantic similarity measure 1 (SSM1): Cosine similarity (Manning and Schütze, 1999) based on frequency is applied to the vectors of the two sets of supersenses described above, which include the frequency of each supersense, for instance, the frequency of the supersense person in the semantics of FS1 and in the semantics of the NPs selected by the FS's free property. To ensure comparability of the vectors, frequencies have been normalized in the range zero to one.

Semantic similarity measure 2 (SSM2): Cosine similarity based on binary vectors: the vectors of both supersence sets which include only the presence or absence (i.e. 1 or 0, respectively) of each supersense. For instance, FS1 selects 7 semantic categories and the respective free adjective selects 17; 5 semantic categories occur in both sets.

Simile	1	2	3	4	5	6	7	8	9	10	11	12	13	14	15	16	17	18	19	20
SSM 1	.09	.23	.67	.80	.74	.14	.99	.66	.61	.89	.28	.99	.16	.87	.27	.43	.51	.56	.79	.58
SSM 2	.46	.45	.72	.72	.75	.58	.68	.73	.42	.42	.78	.47	.47	.93	.86	.77	.65	.75	.77	.79

Table 4: The *Semantic Similarity Measure 1 (SSM1)* and the *Semantic Similarity Measure 2 (SSM2)* of the semantics of the 20 similes and the supersences of the respective free adjectives.

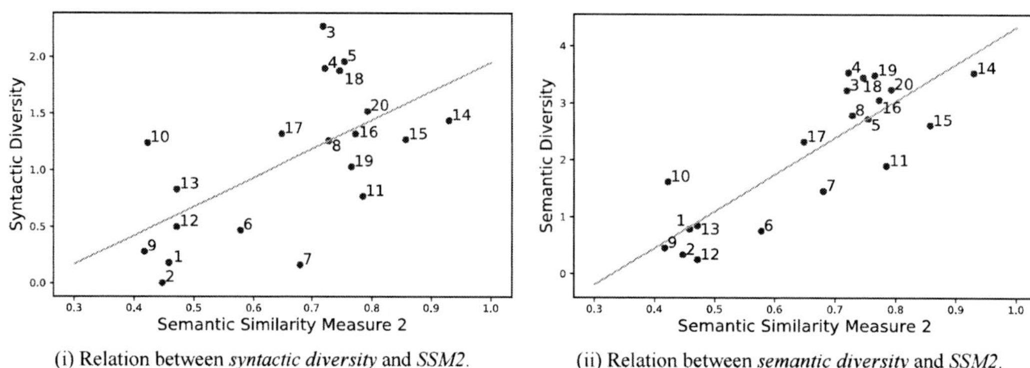

(i) Relation between *syntactic diversity* and *SSM2*.

(ii) Relation between *semantic diversity* and *SSM2*.

Figure 4: The linear relation between *syntactic diversity* or *semantic diversity* and *semantic similarity measure 2 (SSM2)*.

For each property of the 20 FS, we retrieved the first 200 unique instances from the HNC. We excluded MWEs involving the adjectives, for instance, for the property κόκκινος (kokinos) 'red' we excluded the occurrences of κόκκινη γραμμή (kokini grami) 'red line'[8]. The NPs selected by the adjectives in question were annotated semantically with the WordNet supersenses. The results of both semantic similarity measures are reported in Table 4.

We found that only $SSM2$ is correlated with syntactic diversity and semantic diversity (only syntactic flexibility features correlating with syntactic diversity were used (§4.1)). Pearson correlation coefficient between syntactic diversity and $SSM2$ is equal to 0.61 with $p - value = 4.4 \cdot 10^{-4}$ (Figure 4(i) depicts the correlation) and between *semantic diversity* and $SSM2$, it is equal to 0.85 with $p - value = 2 \cdot 10^{-6}$ (Figure 4(ii) depicts the strong linear correlation). The positive linear correlation between syntactic diversity and $SSM2$ is less strong than between semantic diversity and $SSM2$ (Figure 4). This might indicate that some similes tend to be used in particular syntactic configurations, which interfere with the semantically sensitive syntactic alternants; this is a hypothesis that will be checked with future research.

Because cosine similarity by the semantic categories selected by the FS and its free property correlates well with the syntactic and semantic diversity of FS, it could be used as a predictor of the semantic idiomaticity of FS.

---

[8]Κόκκινη γραμμή (kokini grami) denotes a boundary or limit which should not be crossed.

5   Conclusion

The quantitative study of the Modern Greek fixed simile (FS) resource adds interesting new aspects to the understanding of the relation between MWE syntactic flexibility and idiomatic semantics and paves the way to further research.

We found that cosine similarity by the semantic categories selected by the FS and its free property, but not cosine similarity by frequency, correlates well with both the syntactic and semantic diversity of FS and it could be used as a predictor of FS syntactic flexibility and idiomaticity. Furthermore, syntactic deviations from the normative form can be split in "FS semantics sensitive " and "FS semantics insensitive" ones. The latter introduce noise in the correlation of idiomaticity and syntactic flexibility and in their correlation with cosine similarity by semantic categories ($SSM2$). Finally, the clustering of FS instances as vectors of syntactic flexibility features showcases some "semantics insensitive syntactic deviations" as dominant features. The same constructions have been shown by V+N MWE comprehension studies to require less comprehension effort than other syntactic constructions. If future research shows that a correlation exists, it may be inferred that, along with idiomatic semantics, syntactic flexibility depends on certain cognitive factors/skills.

Aknowledgements

We thank Katerina Selimi, Dimitra Stasinou, Vasiliki Moutzouri and Maria Chantou for their help at the annotation phase of this work.

References

Ron Artstein and Massimo Poesio. Inter-coder agreement for Computational Linguistics. *Computational Linguistics*, 34(4):555–596, December 2008.

Timothy Baldwin and Su Nam Kim. Multiword expressions. In Nitin Indurkhya and Fred J. Damerau, editors, *Handbook of Natural Language Processing, Second edition*, pages 267–292. CRC Press, Boca Raton, 2010.

Jacob Benesty, Jingdong Chen, Yiteng Huang, and Israel Cohen. Pearson correlation coefficient. In *Noise reduction in speech processing*, pages 1–4. Springer, 2009.

Pavel Berkhin. A survey of clustering data mining techniques. In *Grouping multidimensional data*, pages 25–71. Springer, 2006.

Despina Chila-Markopoulou. *Modern Greek comparative constructions: A syntactic analysis of adjectival and adverbial comparatives*. PhD thesis, National and Kapodistrian University of Athens, 1986. (In Greek).

Afsaneh Fazly and Suzanne Stevenson. Distinguishing subtypes of multiword expressions using linguistically-motivated statistical measures. In *Proceedings of the Workshop on A Broader Perspective on Multiword Expressions*, pages 9–16. Association for Computational Linguistics, June 2007.

Afsaneh Fazly, Paul Cook, and Suzanne Stevenson. Unsupervised type and token identification of idiomatic expressions. *Computational Linguistics*, 35(1):61–103, 2009. ISSN 0891-2017. URL http://aclweb.org/anthology/J09-1005.

Kristina Geeraert, R. Harald Bayen Bayen, and John Newman. Understanding idiomatic variation. In *Proceedings of the 13th Workshop on Multiword Expressions (MWE 2017)*, page 80–90, April 2017.

Patrick Hanks. Similes and sets: The English preposition "like". In *Languages and Linguistics: Festschrift for Professor Fr. Čermák*. Philosophy Faculty of the Charles University, Prague, 2005.

Michael Israel, Jennifer Riddle Harding, and Vera Tobin. On simile. In Michel Achard and Suzanne Kemmer, editors, *Language, Culture and Mind*, pages 123–135. CSLI Publications, 2004.

Paul Kay and Ivan A. Sag. A lexical theory of phrasal idioms. Available at: www1.icsi.berkeley.edu/~kay/idioms-submitted.pdf, 2012.

Andrew J. Landgraf and Yoonkyung Lee. Dimensionality reduction for binary data through the projection of natural parameters. *arXiv preprint arXiv:1510.06112*, 2015.

Eric Laporte. Choosing features for classifying multiword expressions. In Manfred Sailer and Stella Markantonatou, editors, *Multiword expressions: Insights from a multi-lingual perspective*, Phraseology and Multiword Expressions. Language Science Press, 2018.

Gianluca E. Lebani, Marco Senaldi, and Alessandro Lenci. *Modeling idiom variability with entropy and Distributional Semantics*. Universitätsbibliothek Tübingen, 2015.

Christopher D. Manning and Hinrich Schütze. *Foundations of statistical Natural Language Processing*. MIT press, 1999.

Stella Markantonatou, Panagiotis Kouris, Katerina Selimi, Dimitra Stasinou, and Yanis Maistros. Ψυχή άσπρη σαν το χιόνι but never ψυχή άσπρη σαν το γάλα: semasio-syntactic comments on the fixed similes of modern greek. In *Proceedings of the 38th Annual Meeting of the Department of Linguistics, School of Philology, Aristotle University of Thessaloniki, (In Memoriam Michalis Setatos*, Thessaloniki, 2016.

Jelena Mitrović and Stella Markantonatou. A cross-linguistic study on greek and serbian mwes and enrichment of lexical resources via crowdsourcing. In Stella Markantonatou and Anastasia Christofidou, editors, *Multiword expressions in Greek*, volume 15 of *Deltio Epistimonikis Orologias ke Neologismon*. Language Science Press, 2018.

Vasileia Mpolla-Mavridou. *A contrastive study of the fixed similes of the Greek and English languages*. PhD thesis, Aristotle University of Thessaloniki, 1996. In Greek.

Suzanne Mpouli and Jean-Gabriel Ganascia. "pale as death" or "pâle come le mort": Frozen similes used as literary clichés. In *EUROPRHAS 2015: Computerised and Corpus-Based Approaches to Phraseology: Monolingual and Multilingual Perspectives*, 2015.

Vlad Niculae and Cristian Danescu-Niculescu-Mizil. Brighter than gold: Figurative language in user generated comparisons. In *Proceedings of the 2014 Conference on Empirical Methods in Natural Language Processing (EMNLP)*, pages 2008–2018. Association for Computational Linguistics, October 2014.

Geoffrey Nunberg, Ivan A. Sag, and Thomas Wasow. Idioms. *Language*, 70(3):491–538, 1994.

Ivan A. Sag, Timothy Baldwin, Francis Bond, Ann A. Copestake, and Dan Flickinger. Multiword expressions: A pain in the neck for NLP. In *Proceedings of the 3rd International Conference on Computational Linguistics and Intelligent Text Processing*, volume 2276/2010 of *CICLing '02*, pages 1–15, London, UK, 2002. Springer-Verlag. ISBN 3-540-43219-1.

Nathan Schneider and Noah A. Smith. A corpus and model integrating multiword expressions and supersenses. In *Proceedings of the 2015 Conference of the North American Chapter of the Association for Computational Linguistics: Human Language Technologies*, pages 1537–1547. Association for Computational Linguistics, May–June 2015. URL http://www.aclweb.org/anthology/N15-1177.

Nathan Schneider, Behrang Mohit, Kemal Oflazer, and Noah A. Smith. Coarse lexical semantic annotation with supersenses: An Arabic case study. In *Proceedings of NAACL-HLT 2013*, pages 661–667. Association for Computational Linguistics, June 2013.

Maarten van Gompel and Martin Reynaert. Folia: A practical xml format for linguistic annotation-a descriptive and comparative study. *Computational Linguistics in the Netherlands Journal*, 3:63–81, 2013.

Tony Veale and Yanfen Hao. Learning to understand figurative language: From similes to metaphor to irony. In *Proceedings of the 29th Annual Meeting of the Cognitive Science Society (CogSci 2007)*, 2007.

Fine-Grained Termhood Prediction for German Compound Terms Using Neural Networks

[††]**Anna Hätty** and [‡]**Sabine Schulte im Walde**
[†]Robert Bosch GmbH, Germany
[‡]Institute for Natural Language Processing, University of Stuttgart, Germany
`anna.haetty@de.bosch.com`, `schulte@ims.uni-stuttgart.de`

Abstract

Automatic term identification and investigating the understandability of terms in a specialized domain are often treated as two separate lines of research. We propose a combined approach for this matter, by defining fine-grained classes of termhood and framing a classification task. The classes reflect tiers of a term's association to a domain. The new setup is applied to German closed compounds as term candidates in the domain of cooking. For the prediction of the classes, we compare several neural network architectures and also take salient information about the compounds' components into account. We show that applying a similar class distinction to the compounds' components and propagating this information within the network improves the compound class prediction results.

1 Introduction

DOMAIN-SPECIFIC TERMS are linguistic expressions which characterize a domain, and the automatic recognition of terms is an important basis for further NLP tasks, such as thesaurus creation, automatic translation, and, more generally, for domain knowledge acquisition and for improving the comprehension of a domain. Automatic term recognition often comprises two steps: to evaluate a term candidate for its *unithood*, i.e. identifying boundaries of meaningful phrases, and then to evaluate its *termhood*, i.e. determining the degree of association to a specific domain (Kagueura and Umino, 1996). A related task to term recognition is the identification of domain terms unfamiliar to non-experts, i.e., identifying terms the average reader does not understand. This technology is mostly applied to the health domain, such as medical terms extracted to improve the communication between doctors and patients. The evaluated terms are mostly extracted from medical terminologies (Elhadad, 2006; Zeng-Treitler et al., 2008; Grabar and Hamon, 2014; Grabar et al., 2014). Since these terminologies are available, what constitutes a term can often be taken as a given. However, difficult terms occur in other domains as well, and huge terminologies are not always available. In this work, we make a first attempt to combine the two tasks of automatic term recognition and term difficulty identification by reformulating them as one problem considering different tiers of termhood. In our proposal, we define four classes of termhood, which range from general-language words to obscure, domain-specific terms. This replaces the concept of termhood treated as a binary problem often seen in term annotation (Arcan et al., 2014; Bernier-Colborne and Drouin, 2014; Zadeh and Handschuh, 2014a) and identification tasks (Ventura et al., 2014; Riedl and Biemann, 2015). We demonstrate the effectiveness of our tier system by first conducting an annotation task, followed by an automatic classification using neural networks tailored for our task.

In this work, we focus on the cooking domain and the German language. As a basis for the experiments, 400 German closed compounds are taken as term candidates. We focus on closed compounds for the following reasons: Closed compounds are complex expressions that consist of two or more simple words and contain no spaces or hyphens, e.g. *Meeresfrüchte* "seafood". In German, closed compounds

---

Proceedings of the Joint Workshop on
Linguistic Annotation, Multiword Expressions and Constructions (LAW-MWE-CxG-2018), pages 62–73
Santa Fe, New Mexico, USA, August 25-26, 2018.

are a common way and highly productive way of creating multi-word expressions. Since most terms are usually longer than one word – Justeson and Katz (1995) find that terms most frequently have a length of two words – closed compounds represent a large proportion of German terms. Furthermore, unithood of closed compound term candidates does not have to be evaluated, since the components are naturally agglutinated and phrase boundaries are evident (in contrast to other multi-word expressions). Instead, compound splitting is required, and the split points are relatively obvious to native speakers, while detecting unithood is not. Another advantage of taking compounds as a basis here is that by addressing complex phrases we can illustrate and exploit the interplay between the termhood tiers of the compounds and their components.

To address the fine-grained termhood prediction of German compound terms, we design a system with three steps: (i) performing compound splitting, (ii) computing features for the compounds and their components, and (iii) applying neural network classifiers to predict the termhood classes. For the neural classifiers, we first adapt the network to German compound words so that it takes information about the components into account. As a second step, we apply a corresponding termhood tier distinction to the compounds' components which further improves the compound class prediction results.

The paper is structured as following: Section 2 describes related work for terminology identification. We illustrate the problem in Section 3 and define the termhood classes. In Section 4, the model for term class prediction is introduced. Section 5 explains the data annotation and evaluation. In Section 6, results are presented and discussed. We conclude in Section 7.

2   Related Work

Approaches for automatic term identification can broadly be classified into four categories: linguistic (Justeson and Katz, 1995; Basili et al., 1997), statistical (Schäfer et al., 2015), hybrid (Frantzi et al., 1998; Maynard and Ananiadou, 1999) and machine learning approaches (Merley da Silva Conrado and Rezende, 2013). Recently, word vector and deep learning approaches (Zadeh and Handschuh, 2014b; Amjadian et al., 2016; Wang et al., 2016) have emerged.

Addressing information about components for evaluation of complex terms (multiword or compound terms) has proven to be effective and was exploited in several termhood measures. The C-value method (Frantzi et al., 1998) is commonly used, which combines linguistic and statistical information and takes nested terms into account for evaluating termhood. The FGM score (Nakagawa and Mori, 2003) computes termhood by taking the geometric mean of the number of distinct left and right neighboring words for each component of a complex term. CSvH (Basili et al., 2001) is a corpora-comparing measure that computes the termhood for a complex term by biasing the termhood score with the general-language frequency of the head. Hätty et al. (2017) combine several termhood measures with a random forest classifier to extract single and multi-word terms and apply the measures recursively to the components. Meanwhile, component information has also been used for the related task of keyphrase extraction. Erbs et al. (2015) split German compounds to enhance individual term frequencies, leading to an improved keyphrase extraction. Zhang et al. (2016) propose a new joint-layer RNN architecture for both classifying keywords and keyphrases. The prediction of the keyword influences the prediction of the keyphrase.

The task of detecting a lay reader's familiarity with certain domain terms, i.e. the terms' difficulty or understandability, is a comparably smaller research area, and a subtask of the more general areas of complex word identification and text readability assessment. It often involves steps of term substitution through simpler synonyms (Kandula et al., 2010) or providing an explanation (Elhadad, 2006).

Notably, Fukushige and Noguchi (2000) adopt an approach for term recognition that involves the concept of term difficulty; they concentrate on the recognition of terms that are both typical to the domain and cannot be easily understood. They motivate this approach by pointing out that these are the terms typically included into a domain-specific glossary.

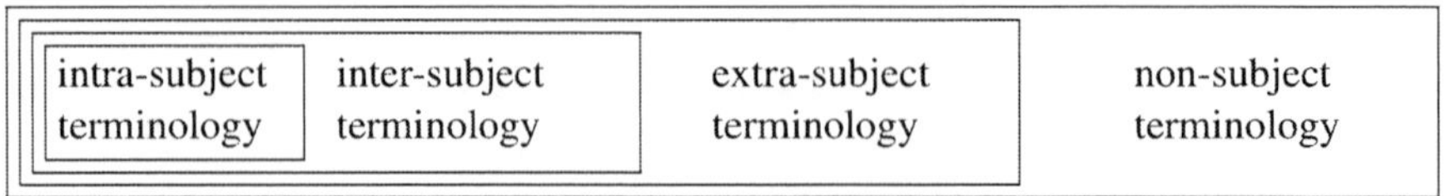

Figure 1: Tiers of terminology (Roelcke, 1999), our translation.

3   Termhood Classes and the Role of Closed Compounds

3.1   Defining Termhood Classes

Our goal is to extend the binary notion of termhood and thereby joining the two tasks of automatic term identification and evaluating term difficulty. To achieve this, we propose one task comprising several fine-grained classes of termhood.

The task of automatic term annotation and identification is typically implemented as a binary decision, i.e. recognizing terminology within non-specialized vocabulary. However, from a theoretical point of view, a term candidate can be associated to a domain to different degrees. This is reflected in the definition of *termhood*, and more explicitly in theories describing different kinds of terms (Trimble, 1985; Roelcke, 1999; Tutin, 2007). For example, the model by Roelcke (1999) separates terms into four tiers (Figure 1): *intra-subject terminology* which is specific to the domain, *inter-subject terminology* which is specific to this and other domains, *extra-subject terminology* which does not belong to the domain but is used within it and *non-subject terminology* which is shared across all specific domains. We aimed to create such a tier model with some variation due to the following considerations:

- We want to keep it simple for the annotators, as it is not easy to compare the same term across different domains. We also see no need for that because we want to characterize a domain independently of other domains.

- We consider term difficulty as part of the tier model for a term's strength of association to a domain. It should naturally align to the idea of a gradual increase of term specificity to the domain (as already pointed out in Grabar et al. (2014)): The more difficult or specialized a term is, the more distinctive it is from general language and the more it is associated to a domain. If terms are both general and understandable, it is sometimes hard to distinguish them from general-language words. Thus, the more expert knowledge is needed to understand a term, the stronger it should be associated to a domain.

Considering these points, we introduce the four tiers shown in Table 1: The first tier are the non-terms with no topical relation to the domain, which still may appear in the domain context, such as the word *Deutschland* in *Gericht aus Deutschland* "dish from Germany". The class SIMTERM includes all non-domain terms which are related to the domain to some extent, either by having received a special relevance for the domain (e.g. *Zimmertemparatur* "room temperature" as a temperature measure for dishes) or by semantic relatedness (e.g. *Tiernahrung* "pet food"). The class TERM represents terms which are highly associated to the domain but still understandable. The last class is SPECTERM, whose elements are highly associated to the domain and not understandable for the non-expert reader. With this tier model, we gradually evolve from general to specialized word senses.

3.2   Mutual Impact of Termhood Classes for Compounds and their Components

As already shown in several automatic term identification studies, components of a complex term candidate can be useful for predicting its termhood. We demonstrate in detail how this is the case for our 4-tier model.

In the ideal case, the components define the termhood of the compound:

Tomate (TERM) + Püree (TERM) → Tomatenpüree (TERM)
tomato + puree → tomato puree

Class	Description	Example
NONTERM	not a domain term	*Deutschland* "Germany"
SIMTERM	semantically related to the domain	*Vitaminbedarf* "requirement of vitamins"
TERM	prototypical and understandable term of the domain	*Schweinebraten* "roast pork"
SPECTERM	prototypical and non-understandable term of the domain	*Blausud [blue boiling]* "special kind of boiling fish by adding acid"

Table 1: Termhood classes.

Here, knowledge about the components is sufficient to predict the compound's termhood. So even if there is a lack of information about the compound due to reasons such as low frequency, its termhood can still be predicted on the basis of the components.

However, in other cases knowing the termhood of the components does not necessarily help to directly infer the termhood of the compound. Sometimes the components share the same termhood class, but the compound is a member of a different class.

Example 1:

Mittel (NONTERM) + Alter (NONTERM) → Mittelalter (NONTERM)
mean + age → Middle Ages

Bei (NONTERM) + Fuß (NONTERM) → Beifuß (SPECTERM)
with + foot → mugwort

Example 2:

Mais (TERM) + Anbau (NONTERM) → Maisanbau (SIMTERM)
maize + cultivation → cultivation of maize

Mais (TERM) + Kolben (NONTERM) → Maiskolben (TERM)
maize + cob → maize cob

In the opposite case the compound class is the same but the components' termhood class changes:

Paprika (TERM) + Salat (TERM) → Paprikasalat (TERM)
sweet pepper + salad → sweet pepper salad

Paprika (TERM) + Hälften (NONTERM) → Paprikahälften (TERM)
sweet pepper + halves → halves of sweet pepper

Nevertheless, even in these cases component information is useful because certain termhood classes can be excluded. For example, in the first case, although the component classes are the same, the options for the compound classes are narrowed down to two very different classes. In addition, we expect that a prediction system will learn the interplay between the termhood of compounds and components, and even if the information about a compound is missing, it can be transferred from similarly constructed compounds.

Since especially broad domains like cooking contain many neologisms (e.g. because of new recipe creations: *Parmesanchips* "crisps with Parmesan cheese"), and are anyway very productive, this effect is very advantageous. Many compounds will not be frequent enough to be evaluated for their termhood, and thus components are helpful in evaluating the termhood class.

4 Model for Term Class Prediction

In the following, we describe the model architecture for predicting the previously defined termhood classes (in Figure 2). As mentioned before, we expect information about the compounds' components to be helpful for predicting the termhood classes. For that reason, the compounds need to be split in a first step, to identify the components. Word embeddings and other features will then be computed for both the compound and its components. We test several neural network architectures to predict a compound's termhood class.

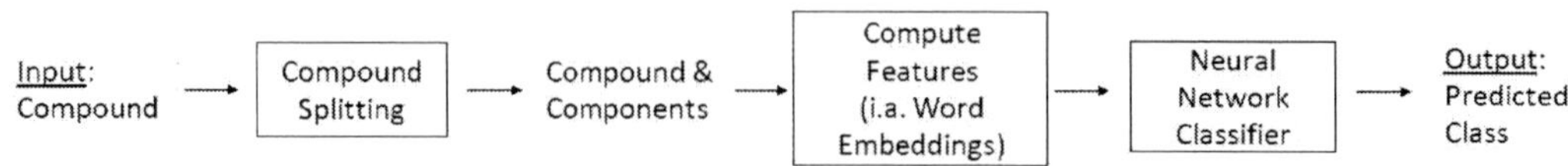

Figure 2: Model architecture.

4.1 Compound Splitting

Compounds are always split into their two main components. We use three splitters:

- *CharSplit* (Tuggener, 2016) is an n-gram-based splitter which is reported to have an accuracy of $\approx$ 95% accuracy for head detection on the GermaNet compound test set.

We further use two morphologically informed splitters.

- *CompoST* (Cap, 2014) is a compound splitter which uses both the morphological resource SMOR (Schmid et al., 2004) and frequency information about components in corpus data for finding the optimal split points. CompoST splits conservatively, leading to a high splitting precision, but many unsplit compounds.

- The *Simple Compound Splitter* (SCS) by Weller-Di Marco (2017) relies on handcrafted morphological rules and frequency information. Weller-Di Marco (2017) compared SCS to an SMOR-based splitter, a variant of CompoST. SCS exhibits higher recall and a higher F1-score.

4.2 Word Embeddings

We compute word embeddings for compounds and components. We use the Word2Vec CBOW model (Mikolov et al., 2013) with a window size of 5 and a minimum frequency of 5 to generate 200-dimensional vectors. The embeddings are pre-trained on Wikipedia, and then trained on the texts from the cooking domain. After compound splitting, 27 components cannot be found, partly because they are infrequent or do not exist as an independent word; but mostly because they are falsely split or the components cannot be lemmatized correctly. To those components we assign a random word vector.

4.3 NN Classifier: Baseline and Hyperparameters

Our basic neural network construction takes one or several concatenated words as input, for which the respective weights in the embedding layer are already set; the weights are initialized with the pre-trained word embedding weights. The final dense layer with a softmax activation predicts the four classes. The architecture is shown in Figure 3.

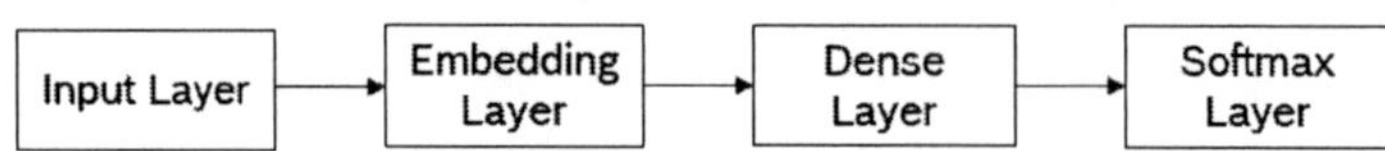

Figure 3: Basic neural network architecture.

The parameters of the neural networks are set to the same values across all network constructions and experiment implementations: the batch size is set to 32, epochs to 50. All dense layers have a dimension of 64. The word embeddings are used to initialize the word weight matrix. The weight matrix is not updated in the training process (since too many parameters would need to be trained). We do not aim for optimizing the model parameters but for comparable architectures, in order to show the effectiveness of the information gained by the input data.

4.4 NNClassifier: Incorporating Compound and Component Information

In the following, we describe the construction of classification models which incorporate both compound and component information. The models build on one another, and we show how additional information about the components leads step by step to a better prediction of the compound termhood class.

Compound and Component Vectors: CONCATVEC   In this first model, we stick with the baseline architecture and only modify the input: instead of either relying on the compounds or the component embeddings solely, the network trains on the concatenated embeddings.

Productivity and Compound Frequency: VECPRODFREQ   When only taking word embedding information as basis for the prediction, the models receive cumulated information about both the more general domain Wikipedia and the specific cooking domain. However, for the components, additional information about their occurrence in the specific domain is useful. There are two reasons: On the one hand, very specific term parts of the class SPECTERM can be distinguished better from TERM, since these are expected to be less productive and less frequent. For example, the component *blau* 'blue' in *Blausud* (Table 1) refers to a special cooking process and will only occur in this term and the related term *Blaukochen [blue cooking]*. On the other hand, very general or ambiguous components can be tested for their relevance to the domain; for example, components like in *Teigränder "rim of pastry"* or *Lorbeerblatt* "bay leaf" are NONTERM. The system can learn that they are nevertheless components which are accepted within a TERM or SPECTERM compound, if they appear in many other compound terms. Thus, we introduce two new features for components:

- Frequency: How frequently does a component appear in other words?

- Productivity: Of how many words the component is part of?

To address this information, we design a shared-layer network architecture as depicted in Figure 4 (but now without the auxiliary output layers). All features – the compound and both the component embeddings, the productivity and frequency of both components – pass through separate layers in the network first, and the information is then concatenated within the network, and compound classes are predicted with a softmax output layer.

Optimization for termhood of components: CONSTOPT   As a variant to process the compound and component embedding information more effectively, we finally use a multi-input multi-output shared-layer model, which is depicted in Figure 4. As for the previous model, this one takes five inputs and information is concatenated later on within the network. Additionally, three auxiliary output layers for each the compound and both components are introduced: For the compound, the four described termhood classes are predicted. The auxiliary output layer is a mere regularization mechanism here. For the component, optimization by the auxiliary outputs should sharpen their termhood, since we consider the components' termhood as strongly influential for the termhood of the compound (as explained in detail in section 3). We do not have information about the intrinsic termhood of the component, but we heuristically infer it from the compounds in which a component occurs. As basis, we take all the compounds in the training set and create four classes analogous to the compound classes. Since all combinations would result in too many classes, we make the following distinctions:

- *specific terms*: all components that only appear in SPECTERM compounds; the difference to TERM gets sharpened

- *term*: all components which occur in TERM compounds

- *similar terms*: shared components of SIMTERM and TERM; these SIMTERM components are especially critical, since the other component decides the class (see section 3)

- *other*: the rest of the components

We set the loss weight for the main output to 1, and the weights for the auxiliary outputs to 0.2, which reports the best experiment result.

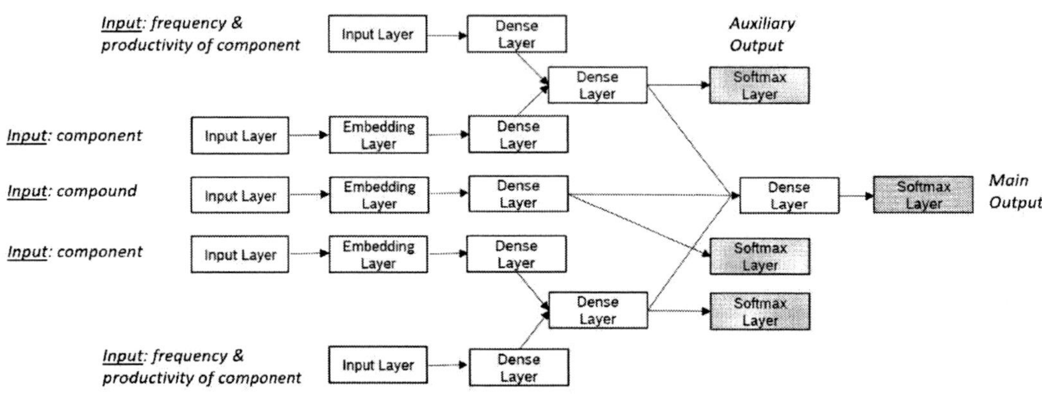

Figure 4: CONSTOPT model.

5   Data, Annotation and Evalaution

We evaluate our approach in the domain of cooking, where 34 cooking recipes are collected randomly from *kochwiki*[1] and *wikibooks*[2]. From these texts, roughly 260 cooking compound terms are identified by three annotators. After briefly reviewing the data, the portion of SPECTERM elements we find is rather low to be used for training (about 10 very specific terms). Therefore, we manually extract compound terms from cooking and cooking-related term lists from Wikipedia. For the classes NONTERM and SIMTERM, we retrieve unannotated compounds of the cooking recipes. We additionally add 15 concepts for the class SIMTERM which have some semantic similarity to the cooking domain (e.g. *Tiernahrung* "pet food", *Küchenzeile* "kitchenette").

For this experiment, the compounds are required to appear sufficiently frequently, such that a word embedding can always be created based on Wikipedia and the cooking domain texts. The reason for this is that we want to show that component information improves the prediction results; thus we want to have an optimal setting for compounds against which the new information can be compared and added to. For the same reason, there is no minimum frequency for the components, to have a realistic setting. We crawl texts from wiki pages (e.g. *kochwiki, wikibooks* and *wikihow*[3]) to attain the minimum frequencies. In total, the collection contains 404 texts from the cooking domain, consisting of roughly 150,000 words. The text collection consists mostly of recipes, but contains descriptions of ingredients or cooking methods as well.

The resulting set of 400 compounds are then prepared for the annotation process: the compound terms are provided with either a definition (from *Wikipedia, kochwiki* or *Wiktionary*[4]) or, if a definition could

---

[1] https://www.kochwiki.org/
[2] https://de.wikibooks.org/wiki/Kochbuch
[3] https://de.wikihow.com/
[4] https://de.wiktionary.org/

not be found, a context sentence from the cooking recipes. Then 5 annotators were asked to decide for one of the four classes NONTERM, SIMTERM, TERM and SPECTERM.

The final classes are selected via majority vote of the annotators. For 46% of the compounds there is a complete agreement (5 out of 5), for 29% there was a 4:1 agreement. For 4 terms, there was no majority voting; these terms are excluded from the compound set, resulting in 396 terms overall.

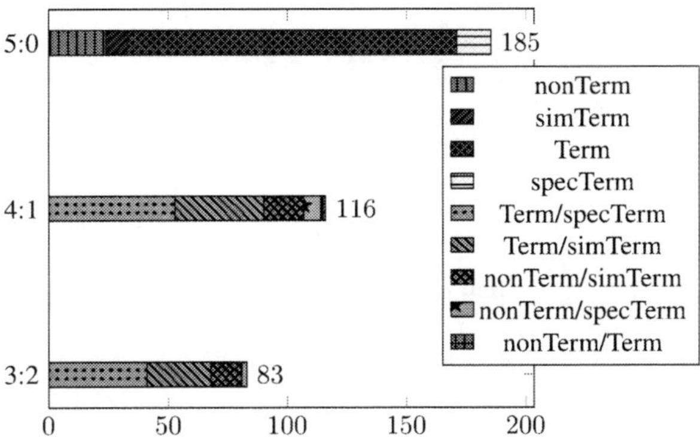

Figure 5: Agreement and disagreement for termhood class annotation.

Figure 5 shows the agreement (5:0) and the disagreement (4:1 and 3:1) for term class annotations. The 5:0-bar shows the number of elements for which the decision is with one consent. These elements are distributed over all classes. For 4:1 and 3:2 disagreements, the number of elements are shown for the two classes in favor of which the decision is made. Annotators are mostly disagreeing between TERM and SPECTERM. This is an expected result, since the knowledge level even of non-expert annotators differs to a certain degree, resulting in a different class selection. Furthermore, nearly all divergences are between neighboring classes (nonTerm/simTerm, Term/simTerm, Term/specTerm) while the divergences between other classes are negligible. This is a good indicator that the class design represents a valid scale of termhood.

After taking the majority vote we get a final distribution of elements per class, as shown in Table 2.

NONTERM	SIMTERM	TERM	SPECTERM
44	43	250	59

Table 2: Number of annotated terms per class.

6 Results and Analysis

6.1 Compound Splitting

Table 3 shows the correct compound splits for the (combinations of) the three splitters. Since CharSplit always splits, we take its splitting performance as baseline. For our specific domain and without special training, CharSplit achieves 91.4% correct splits. There are 25 completely wrong splits (e.g. *Vol|lei* "whole egg" instead of *Voll|ei*), 9 elements have splits on the wrong side (e.g. *Marzipanroh|masse [marzipan raw mass]* "marzipan paste") instead of *Marzipan|rohmasse*).

We further combine splitters to improve the results: Since CompoST splits conservatively and with a high precision, in case of a split we always rely on its output. For combining CompoST and CharSplit, this results in 94.2% correct splits.

Since there are still problems with recognizing the plural -N (*Traube|Nsaft* "grape juice" instead of *Trauben|saft*), we then add the Simple Compound Splitter (SCS), which explicitly models this phenomenon. Since SCS needs a basis of POS, lemma and frequency information, we compute this information on the cooking dataset. Then we combine the three splitters in the way that we again rely first on

CompoST, then apply SCS and finally use CharSplit for the rest of the compounds. This results in the best split score of 95.7%.

Splitters	Wrong splits	Wrong side	% correct splits
CharSplit	25	9	91.4 %
CompoST + CharSplit	14	9	94.2 %
CompoST + SCS + CharSplit	9	8	95.7 %

Table 3: Splitting performances of the three compound splitters.

6.2 Termhood Classification of the Neural Networks

In Table 4, we provide the results for the different models. We apply 5-fold cross-validation and use Precision, Recall and F1-score as evaluation measures. In brackets next to the method name, the overall F1-score is given, weighted and averaged over all classes.

For the baselines, results show that taking only compounds as input provides a better result than only taking component as input. However, note that we provide ideal conditions for compounds, by enforcing a minimum frequency. For the advanced models CONCATVEC, VECPRODFREQ and CONSTOPT, the overall F1-score continuously increases for every improvement we made to the system.

Focusing on the individual classes, NONTERM and TERM achieve a high recognition rate. We attribute this to the fact that they are the two prototypical opposing classes. SEMSIM and SPECTERM reach only decent results at first. When comparing the best model to the best baseline model, the results for the two classes experience a boost. The prediction for SEMSIM gains 17% improvement on the F1-score, SPECTERM even gains 21%.

Method	Non-Term	SimTerm	Term	SpecTerm
Component Baseline [0.69]				
Precision	0.77	0.47	0.78	0.53
Recall	0.50	0.40	0.89	0.32
F1-score	0.6	0.41	0.83	0.37
Compound Baseline [0.72]				
Precision	0.86	0.61	0.79	0.47
Recall	0.77	0.42	0.86	0.37
F1-score	0.80	0.48	0.82	0.40
CONCATVEC [0.75]				
Precision	0.83	0.54	0.82	0.61
Recall	0.68	0.40	0.89	0.54
F1-score	0.74	0.44	0.85	0.57
VECPRODFREQ [0.77]				
Precision	0.85	0.66	0.82	0.62
Recall	0.73	0.53	0.88	0.54
F1-score	0.77	0.58	0.85	0.57
CONSTOPT [0.80]				
Precision	0.88	0.69	0.85	0.64
Recall	0.75	0.63	0.9	0.59
F1-score	0.79	0.65	0.88	0.61

Table 4: Results for baselines and advanced models per class.

Finally, we analyze the predictions of the model to explore reasons for misclassification. One reason behind it could be wrong splits (e.g. *Ei|klar* "egg white", split to *Eik|lar*). However, only 4 out of 17 incorrectly split compounds are predicted incorrectly. Since no embeddings could be computed for wrong components (and a default randomly initialized embedding is taken instead), the model probably learns to rely on other features in this case. The most interesting classes for deeper analysis are SIMTERM and SPECTERM, since the other two classes are predicted well. For SIMTERM, we do not find obvious differences between the correctly classified compounds, and the ones which are predicted as TERM. For SPECTERM, we find at least two kinds of terms that seem to be classified mostly correctly: rather opaque terms (e.g. *Fetthenne [fat hen]* "sedum"), and many terms with one non-understandable, and one understandable component term (e.g. *Tonkabohnen* "tonka beans"). A lot of SPECTERM compounds are classified as TERM. One reason for this might be that a compound includes a very typical TERM component (e.g. *Blindbacken* "blind-baking").

7 Conclusion

We present an approach for combining automatic term identification and evaluation of a term's understandability. We frame it as one task by defining classes representing a fine-grained concept of termhood. As basis, 400 German compounds are selected as candidates for termhood annotation in the domain of cooking. The prediction of these classes is then carried out in a three-step process: applying compound splitting, computing features for compound and components and finally applying a neural network classifier to predict the termhood classes. For the splitting, several existing compound splitters are combined. The features include word embeddings, and productivity and frequency of the components within the specific domain. For the neural network classifier, we design several models to adequately address the information about the compound and its components. A special focus is placed on predicting heuristically approximated classes for the components' termhood, thus improving the prediction of the compound's termhood class as well. The best model achieves a 8% relative improvement on F1-score in comparison to the best baseline model.

The fine-grained notion of termhood introduced here is important for getting a better understanding of the domain. Furthermore, it may be interesting for related topics, such as Keyphrase Extraction and Named Entity Recognition.

As future work, we plan to enlarge the compound basis for both closed compounds and other kinds of multi-word expressions. We especially see potential for the CONSTOPT model, since the basis of complex terms to get evidence for the termhood of components would increase. In addition, we want to include further terminology-specific features into the classifiers, especially corpora-comparing termhood measures. Further we want to explore more deeply the effect of a network trained on complex terms and components features for predicting previously unseen complex terms.

References

Ehsan Amjadian, Diana Inkpen, Tahereh Paribakht, and Farahnaz Faez. 2016. Local-global vectors to improve unigram terminology extraction. In *Proceedings of the 5th International Workshop on Computational Terminology (Computerm)*, pages 2–11, Osaka, Japan.

Mihael Arcan, Marco Turchi, Sara Tonelli, and Paul Buitelaar. 2014. Enhancing statistical machine translation with bilingual terminology in a CAT environment. *Proceedings of the 11th Biennial Conference of the Association for Machine Translation in the Americas (AMTA)*, pages 54–68.

Roberto Basili, Gianluca De Rossi, and Maria Teresa Pazienza. 1997. Inducing terminology for lexical acquisition. In *Proceedings of the 2nd Conference on Empirical Methods in Natural Lanaguge Processing (EMNLP)*, Providence, USA.

Roberto Basili, Maria Teresa Pazienza, Alessandro Moschitti, and Fabio Massimo Zanzotto. 2001. A contrastive approach to term extraction. In *Proceedings of the 4th Terminology and Artificial Intelligence Conference*, pages 119–128.

Gabriel Bernier-Colborne and Patrick Drouin. 2014. Creating a test corpus for term extractors through term annotation. *Terminology*, 20(1):50–73.

Fabienne Cap. 2014. *Morphological Processing of Compounds for Statistical Machine Translation.* Dissertation, Institute for Natural Language Processing (IMS), University of Stuttgart.

Noemie Elhadad. 2006. Comprehending technical texts: Predicting and defining unfamiliar terms. In *AMIA annual symposium proceedings*, volume 2006, pages 239–243. American Medical Informatics Association.

Nicolai Erbs, Pedro Bispo Santos, Torsten Zesch, and Iryna Gurevych. 2015. Counting what counts: Decompounding for keyphrase extraction. In *Proceedings of the ACL 2015 Workshop on Novel Computational Approaches to Keyphrase Extraction*, pages 10 – 17, Beijing, China.

Katerina T. Frantzi, Sophia Ananiadou, and Jun-ichi Tsujii. 1998. The c-value/nc-value method of automatic recognition for multi-word terms. In *Proceedings of the 2nd European Conference on Research and Advanced Technology for Digital Libraries*, pages 585–604, London, UK.

Yoshio Fukushige and Naohiko Noguchi. 2000. Statistical and linguistic approaches to automatic term recognition: NTCIR experiments at matsushita. *Terminology*, 6(2):257–286.

Natalia Grabar and Thierry Hamon. 2014. Unsupervised method for the acquisition of general language paraphrases for medical compounds. *Proceedings of the 4th International Workshop on Computational Terminology (Computerm)*, pages 94–103.

Natalia Grabar, Thierry Hamon, and Dany Amiot. 2014. Automatic diagnosis of understanding of medical words. In *Proceedings of the 3rd Workshop on Predicting and Improving Text Readability for Target Reader Populations (PITR)*, pages 11–20.

Anna Hätty, Michael Dorna, and Sabine Schulte im Walde. 2017. Evaluating the reliability and interaction of recursively used feature classes for terminology extraction. In *Proceedings of the 15th Conference of the European Chapter of the Association for Computational Linguistics, Student Research Workshop*, pages 113–121, Valencia, Spain.

John S. Justeson and Slava M. Katz. 1995. Technical terminology: Some linguistic properties and an algorithm for identification in text. *Natural Language Engineering*, 1(1):9–27.

Kyo Kagueura and Bin Umino. 1996. Methods of automatic term recognition: A review. *Terminology*, 3(2):259–289.

Sasikiran Kandula, Dorothy Curtis, and Qing Zeng-Treitler. 2010. A semantic and syntactic text simplification tool for health content. In *AMIA annual symposium proceedings*, volume 2010, pages 366–370. American Medical Informatics Association.

Diana Maynard and Sophia Ananiadou. 1999. Identifying contextual information for multi-word term extraction. In *Proceedings of 5th International Congress on Terminology and Knowledge Engineering*, pages 212–221.

Thiago Alexandre Salgueiro Pardo Merley da Silva Conrado and Solange Oliveira Rezende. 2013. A machine learning approach to automatic term extraction using a rich feature set. In *Proceedings of the North American Chapter of the Association for Computational Linguistics - Human Language Technologies*, pages 16–23, Atlanta, Georgia, USA.

Tomas Mikolov, Ilya Sutskever, Kai Chen, Greg Corrado, and Jeffrey Dean. 2013. Distributed representations of words and phrases and their compositionality. In *Advances in Neural Information Processing Systems (NIPS)*, pages 3111–3119.

Hiroshi Nakagawa and Tatsunori Mori. 2003. Automatic term recognition based on statistics of compound nouns and their components. *Terminology*, 9(2):201–219.

Martin Riedl and Chris Biemann. 2015. A single word is not enough: Ranking multiword expressions using distributional semantics. In *Proceedings of the 2015 Conference on Empirical Methods in Natural Language Processing (EMNLP)*, Lisboa, Portugal.

Thorsten Roelcke. 1999. *Fachsprachen*. Grundlagen der Germanistik. Erich Schmidt Verlag.

Johannes Schäfer, Ina Rösiger, Ulrich Heid, and Michael Dorna. 2015. Evaluating noise reduction strategies for terminology extraction. In *Proceedings of Terminology and Artifical Intelligence*, pages 44–49, Granada, Spain.

Helmut Schmid, Arne Fitschen, and Ulrich Heid. 2004. A German computational morphology covering derivation, composition, and inflection. In *Proceedings of the 4th International Conference on Language Resources and Evaluation (LREC)*, pages 1263–1266, Lisbon, Portugal.

Louis Trimble. 1985. *English for Science and Technology: A Discourse Approach.* Cambridge Univ. Press.

Don Tuggener. 2016. *Incremental Coreference Resolution for German.* Dissertation, Faculty of Arts, University of Zurich.

Agnes Tutin. 2007. Traitement sémantique par analyse distributionelle des noms transdisciplinaires des écrits scientifiques. *In Actes de TALN*, pages 283–292.

Juan Antonio Lossio Ventura, Clement Jonquet, Mathieu Roche, and Maguelonne Teisseire. 2014. Yet another ranking function for automatic multiword term extraction. In *Advances in Natural Language Processing - 9th International Conference on NLP*, pages 52–64, Warsaw, Poland.

Rui Wang, Wei Liu, and Chris McDonald. 2016. Featureless domain-specific term extraction with minimal labelled data. In *Proceedings of the Australasian Language Technology Association Workshop 2016*, pages 103–112, Melbourne, Australia.

Marion Weller-Di Marco. 2017. Simple compound splitting for German. In *Proceedings of the 13th Workshop on Multiword Expressions (MWE)*, pages 161–166, Valencia, Spain.

Behrang Zadeh and Siegfried Handschuh. 2014a. The acl rd-tec: A dataset for benchmarking terminology extraction and classification in computational linguistics. In *Proceedings of the 4th International Workshop on Computational Terminology (Computerm)*, pages 52–63, Dublin, Ireland.

Behrang Zadeh and Siegfried Handschuh. 2014b. Evaluation of technology term recognition with random indexing. In *Proceedings of the 9th International Conference on Language Resources and Evaluation (LREC)*, pages 4027–4032, Reykjavik, Iceland.

Qing Zeng-Treitler, Sergey Goryachev, Tony Tse, Alla Keselman, and Aziz Boxwala. 2008. Estimating consumer familiarity with health terminology: A context-based approach. *Journal of the American Medical Informatics Association*, 15(3):349–356.

Qi Zhang, Yang Wang, Yeyun Gong, and Xuanjing Huang. 2016. Keyphrase extraction using deep recurrent neural networks on twitter. In *Proceedings of the 2016 Conference on Empirical Methods in Natural Language Processing (EMNLP)*, pages 836–845, Austin, TX, USA.

Towards a Computational Lexicon for Moroccan Darija:
Words, Idioms, and Constructions

Jamal Laoudi[*], Claire Bonial[†], Lucia Donatelli[‡], Stephen Tratz[†], Clare Voss[†]
[*]ARTI, Alexandria, Virginia 22030
[†]Army Research Laboratory, Adelphi, Maryland 20783
[‡]Georgetown University, Washington, DC 20057
{jamal.laoudi.ctr, claire.n.bonial.civ, stephen.c.tratz.civ,
clare.r.voss.civ}@mail.mil, led66@georgetown.edu

Abstract

We explore the challenges of building a computational lexicon for Moroccan Darija (MD), an Arabic dialect spoken by over 32 million people worldwide that only recently has begun appearing frequently in written form. We raise the question of what belongs in such a lexicon and start by describing our work building traditional word-level lexicon entries with their English translations. We then discuss challenges in translating idiomatic MD phrases and the creation of multi-word expression (MWE) lexicon entries whose meanings could not be fully derived from the individual words. Finally, we describe our preliminary exploration of constructions for inclusion in an MD *constructicon*, initially eliciting translations of established English constructions, and then shifting to document, when spontaneously offered, variant renderings of native MD counterparts.

1 Introduction

What methods exist to guide the construction of a computational lexicon for a low-resource language that is widely spoken, but for which there is little reference literature and no standard orthography? We are interested in the specific case of Moroccan Darija (MD) that is now emerging in the written, informal contexts of social media. There, we find a wide variety of multi-word expressions (MWEs), including idioms, that are characterized by semi- or non-compositionality, where their meaning cannot be derived strictly from their individual words. Such expressions therefore present a significant challenge for Natural Language Processing (NLP), language-learning, and machine translation (MT) tasks, which have traditionally assumed that the vocabulary of the relevant language is available in a (computational) lexicon so that a sentence's full meaning can be derived from the combined meanings of its individual words. For MT of under-resourced languages, and MD in particular, available methods assume that translation proceeds from the source language (SL) by way of entries in a limited bilingual dictionary, into the corresponding target language (TL). In the case of semi- and non-compositional expressions of low-resource source languages, however, well-established methods do not exist for identification and inclusion of such expressions in computational lexicons.

As a result, correctly interpreting and translating semi- and non-compositional expressions relies on first identifying MWEs that function as a unit paired with a particular meaning. Identification can be facilitated by manually tagging such expressions and incorporating them into lexical resources. However, incorporation into a lexicon can also come with a variety of challenges, as outlined by Sag et al. (2002). Fixed idiomatic expressions, such as *kick the bucket* can be added to a lexicon as a single-entry, fixed phrase allowing only for minimal morpho-syntactic variation (here, tense), so that the phrase is treated computationally as if it were a single word (an approach called 'words with spaces' (Sag et al., 2002)). However, many other flexible expressions allow for enough variation that listing all alternates in a computational lexicon can be prohibitively impractical. Similarly, fully syntactic patterns can carry meaning separate from the constituent parts and be extremely productive, or flexible, in the component words (e.g., *The X-er The Y-er: The more I read, the less I understand; The higher you fly, the harder you fall*). Such pairings of form and meaning, or constructions (Goldberg, 1995), are productive to the

74

Proceedings of the Joint Workshop on
Linguistic Annotation, Multiword Expressions and Constructions (LAW-MWE-CxG-2018), pages 74–85
Santa Fe, New Mexico, USA, August 25-26, 2018.

point that listing all possible instantiations of the expression in a static lexicon is not feasible. As an alternative, these patterns can be listed in a *constructicon*, or an inventory of constructions in which the general linguistic patterns are described without specifying all realizations with particular word forms (Fillmore et al., 2012).

In this research, we begin to address the challenges of semi- and non-compositional MWEs in MD that arise while building up a MD lexicon consisting of 1) individual MD tokens and their translations, 2) a collection of MD idioms, and 3) a preliminary constructicon listing MD constructions based on an examination of constructions found in English and their correspondents in MD. Our objective in building the MD lexicon is to facilitate translation of MD into English and vice-versa. After providing some background on MD (Section 2), we will describe each portion (1-3 above) of the lexicon in Sections 3-5. We examine translation in the order of words, idioms, then constructions as this reflects compatibility with traditional lexicons: words are traditional members of lexicons, some (more fixed) idioms are compatible with a 'words-with-spaces' lexicon entry, and constructions are the least compatible in that they require an inventory that represents grammatical patterns as opposed to fixed word forms or expressions. Of current interest is the contribution of a collection of MD idioms; thus, in Section 4 describing the MD idioms, we provide an analysis of the strategies used to translate idioms as well as a quantitative results illuminating which strategies were applicable to particular idiom types.

2 Moroccan Darija: an Arabic Dialect

The Arabic language family encompasses many varieties, including Modern Standard Arabic (MSA) and a large number of regional dialects. Despite being the standard written form of Arabic and appearing in many formal venues such as news broadcasts and parliamentary speeches, MSA is not the native language of any Arabic speaker (Bouamor et al., 2014). Instead, typical everyday conversation is conducted in Arabic dialects (or other languages) rather than MSA. Arabic dialects vary substantially from MSA and each other, with significant phonological, morphological, and syntactic differences (Brustad, 2002), as well as in their vocabularies. For example, MSA has been established as VSO, whereas MD is viewed as SVO (Simons and Fennig, 2018). The dialects have varying degrees of mutual intelligibility, with those of northwestern Africa (e.g., Morocco, Algeria, Tunisia) being particularly challenging to outsiders.

Although Arabic dialects lack orthographic standards and historically have not been written, they now appear constantly in online social media. Unfortunately, these dialects are severely under-resourced from a computational perspective, impeding the creation of NLP systems, such as machine translation engines. MT systems trained on large parallel MSA-English corpora perform substantially worse on dialectal text than when such systems are trained on significantly smaller Arabic dialect-English parallel corpora created via crowdsourcing (Zbib et al., 2012), illustrating the need for computational lexical resources specific to the individual dialects.

3 Traditional Lexicon: Words and Their Translations

The most straightforward component to include in an MD computational lexicon is a traditional word-level lexicon consisting of words and their translations. For our work, we leverage Hespress.com, a popular news portal whose reporting covers events in Morocco and other topics of interest to Moroccans. The articles span numerous domains, including politics, sports, and entertainment. Although the articles are primarily written in MSA, the commentary is mixed, with many languages/dialects represented, including MSA, MD, English, French, and Amazigh. As a first step, we collected a copy of the commentary available on the Hespress website and filtered out commentary posts that lacked content in Arabic script.[1] To isolate posts written primarily in MD, we employed an in-house token-level MD classifier[2] to label the individual tokens[3] of the remaining posts as either MD or MSA. We only considered commentary posts with at least 6 tokens identified as MD and with MD tokens outnumbering MSA tokens by a 4-to-1 or greater margin. This left us over 128,000 commentary posts identified as primarily MD. We then

---

[1] Arabic dialects such as MD also frequently appear in Latin script as "Arabizi" (Yaghan, 2008).
[2] The full details of this system are beyond the scope of this paper.
[3] We tokenized the text automatically based on whitespace and punctuation.

had a native Darija speaker translate the 2,000 shortest such commentary posts and provide in-context token-level glosses. After removing posts written in other languages (e.g., MSA, Amazigh) or containing offensive content, 1,836 translated posts remained, with a total of 17,261 tokens and 5,528 unique token types. The 5,528 types have an average of 2.32 glosses per type.

The only machine-readable lexicon for MD we are aware of currently available for comparison is published by the MADAR (Bouamor et al., 2018) project. The MADAR lexicon is structured around 1,045 *concept keys*, each of which is defined by a 3-tuple of English, French, and Modern Standard Arabic (MSA) lexical translations (e.g., {*think, penser,* ظَنّ }). For each concept key, MADAR had Arabic dialect translations produced by translators in 25 different cities spanning the Arabic-speaking world, including two Moroccan cities—Fes and Rabat.

We note substantial overlap with our lexicon. Of the 1,032 unique MD translations provided by MADAR's Fes and Rabat translators, 342 correspond to items in our lexicon. However, there are several important differences between the two lexicons. For example, the MD entries in MADAR were all generated in translation from other languages whereas ours were originally produced in MD and then translated into English. Because of this, our lexicon is likely to contain a variety of morphological and orthographic variations for the same base word, in contrast to the MADAR lexicon. Also, the MADAR concept keys were derived from the Basic Travel Expressions Corpus (Takezawa et al., 2007) and, thus, the lexicon is most relevant to the travel domain. In contrast, our lexicon spans multiple complementary domains, including politics, sports, and entertainment.

4   More than a Word: Idioms

In the process of creating the word-level lexicon described in Section 3, we encountered numerous idioms. Idioms pose an intriguing question in the development of a lexicon, as their status straddles the boundary between being compositional and non-compositional in meaning. A central challenge in identifying and translating idioms is thus pinpointing this variable idiomatic meaning and transferring the semantic, stylistic, and contextual import of the idiom in question from SL to TL. Here we review several theories for interpreting idiomatic meaning. We then present the strategies for idiom translation that our translator found consistently helpful in guiding his work in reference to other established idiom translation techniques.

4.1   Idiomatic Meaning

Nunberg et al. (1994) analyze idioms for three primary semantic properties: (i) *conventionality*, measured by the discrepancy between idiomatic phrasal meaning and the compositional meaning derived from the individual constituents; (ii) *opacity/transparency*, or the clarity of motivation for the expression given its meaning; and (iii) *compositionality*, understood as the degree to which the phrasal meaning can be gleaned from the component constituents. Fernando (1996) additionally divides idioms into three classes, each with distinct measures of these semantic properties and, in turn, distinct implications for translation. So-called "pure idioms" are opaque, non-literal MWEs that are conventionalized in use and non-compositional (cf. Sag et al. (2002) for non-decomposable idioms and their syntactic diagnostics); "semi-idioms" are semi-opaque and have one or more literal constituents and one with a non-literal sub-sense; and "literal idioms" are transparent expressions that are either invariable or allow little variation (cf. Sag et al. (2002) for decomposable idioms and their syntactic diagnostics). Facing the task of translation, these idiom types merit subtly different approaches to both capture their meaning and relate them to the SL and TL lexicons.

Idioms additionally possess pragmatic levels of meaning external to any semantic (de)composition or formal linguistic properties (Fillmore et al., 1988; Croft and Cruse, 2004). Speakers know how to use certain expressions in the correct linguistic context and social situation. This pragmatic knowledge relies on, but is not viewed, traditionally, as contributing to the semantic interpretation of the original idiomatic expression itself. Idioms thus raise the question, should this "extra-linguistic" knowledge[4] be included in a computational lexicon?

---

[4]Knowledge not included in individual words, rules of grammar, or principles of compositional semantics

4.2 Idiom Translation Strategies

In translating an idiom, the question arises as to whether the translator ought to convey directly the presence of the idiom by maintaining the original words in literal translations of the SL, while perhaps also including a historical and cultural explanation. Alternatively, a translator could choose to simply translate from their understanding of the non-literal, implied meaning, without seeking a comparable idiom in the TL—that is, in effect removing any trace of the idiom.

Our translator found the work of Baker (1992) a helpful guide in approaching this translation task. Baker's four strategies have been employed in several idiom translation studies (cf. Strakšienė, 2009 for English-Lithuanian and 2010 for English-Russian; Shojaei (2012) for English-Turkish; Akbari (2013) for English-Persian). These are characterized in the tables below with MD idiom examples, each with a Romanized, tokenized transliteration, an English token-by-token gloss, and their corresponding English translation:

1. **Translation to an idiom of similar meaning and form**. This strategy is used when the SL and TL possess idioms of the same general meaning and lexical and syntactic content. This correspondence may occur either because idioms are compositional and transparent in both languages (or "literal" (Fernando, 1996)); or because the idioms are both non-compositional and opaque, yet conventionalized (Nunberg et al., 1994), in both languages.

MD Source Text	إلى كانت دارك جاج متشيرش على الناس بالحجر
Transliteration	ila kana-t dar-ek jaj ma-t-chayar-ch a'la al-nassa bi-l-ah'jar
Gloss	if were-it house-your glass not-you-throw-(NEG) at the-people with-the-stones
English Translation	People who live in glass houses shouldn't throw stones

Table 1: Example of idiom-to-idiom translation with preservation of form and meaning

2. **Translation to an idiom of similar meaning but dissimilar form**. This strategy is used when idioms in the SL and TL possess the same meaning but utilize different lexical items to convey that meaning. This correspondence occurs if the syntax available to create idiomatic meaning in one language is unavailable in the other. Likely, the idioms in SL and TL are "semi-idioms" (Fernando, 1996).

MD Source Text	المزوق من برى كيف حاليك من داخل
Transliteration	al-mzawaq min barra kif hali-k min dakhil
Gloss	the-colorful from outside how situation-your from inside
English Translation	Looks can be deceiving

Table 2: Example of idiom-to-idiom with shared meaning but different form

3. **Translation by paraphrase**. Paraphrase, the most common method to translate idioms (Shojaei, 2012), is employed when a match between SL and TL does not exist, or when it may be infelicitous to use idiomatic language in TL when it is felicitous in SL. This method is often used when idioms are opaque and non-compositional semantically; as such the more pragmatic meaning is translated. This occurs for "pure-idioms" (Fernando, 1996).

4. **Translation omitted**. Idioms are omitted from TL although present in SL for those cases when there are no equivalent expressions between the two languages, or when the SL meaning cannot be easily paraphrased for stylistic or pragmatic reasons.

Baker's four strategies work in a successive manner with the ultimate goal of preserving idiom meaning in the TL. Ideally, translators employ strategy (1), whereby the SL and TL possess idioms similar in both

MD Source Text	الا ربحتو ها وجهي
Transliteration	ila rbah't-u ha wajh-i
Gloss	if won-you here face-my
English Translation	There is no way you are going to win

Table 3: Example of idiom-to-[non-idiom] paraphrase

MD Source Text	گالو كحاز گالو ضهر الحمار قصير
Transliteration	gal-u kh'az gal-u dhar al-h'mar qssir
Gloss	told(he)-him move_over told(he)-him back the-donkey short
English Translation	Omission (1st guy: "make room", 2nd guy: "there's no room to spare")

Table 4: Example of idiom omitted, not translated

meaning and form. Given that this is not always possible, translators are instructed to proceed down the list of strategies to accomplish their task, as our translator did.[5]

4.3 MD Idioms: Preliminary Results

MD idioms, as found in the informal texts of social media and the commentary posts of our collection, includes intentionally playful wording, rhymes, and different types of figures of speech. The sentence structure of idioms may also be uncommon or unusual, though easy to understand. The idioms identified in our collection are generally non-transparent, i.e., their meaning cannot be derived from the words they contain. The wording of these idioms also generally does not allow for vocabulary substitutions or omission. Our translator observed that it is not uncommon for MD idioms to be structured as two-part, action-reaction expressions, indicating if X happens, then Y happens, resembling the two-part English construction, The X-er the Y-er.

With our work on creating a MD Lexicon, we isolated a total of 94 sentences with idiomatic expressions. Out of these, 52 were unique or existed in a single form. Of the remaining, two idioms occurred in nine different forms, one in six different forms, two in four different forms, and five in two different forms. After removing duplicates, we ended up with 62 unique idioms. A breakdown of which of the above translation types these idioms fall into is given below.

- Type 1 Translation to an idiom of similar meaning and form: No such cases in this specific collection were found. We have however found such examples in other data we collected (see Future Work).

- Type 2 Translation to an idiom of similar meaning but dissimilar form: In our example set, nine idioms out of the set of 62 unique idioms fell into this category.[6]

- Type 3 Translation by paraphrase: This category formed the overwhelming majority with a total of 51 out of 62 idioms.

- Type 4 Translation omitted: In our example sentences, we had two such cases.

The prevalence of translation by paraphrase is not surprising, given that this is the most common strategy cited in other translation efforts and given the rather extreme typological differences between English and MD. However, translation by paraphrase likely entails that potentially subtle nuances of meaning of

---

[5]Though Baker further identifies a fifth strategy for idiom translation, compensation, whereby idiomatic meaning is recreated elsewhere in the translated text, we do not make use of this strategy as our focus is on sentence-level translation and not discourse-level translation.

[6]Occasionally two idioms in a language may be used to convey the same meaning, providing translators with further issues to consider. In MD, for example, هزك الما وضربك الضو and مشيتي فيها are used interchangeably (same underlying meaning) and would both translate adequately as *You're fresh out of luck.*, even though individual native MD speakers may differ in their use of one over the other.

the idiom are lost in translation; additionally, for MD in particular, the playfulness of wording and sound expressed through syntactic form is lost. Although it may be difficult to pinpoint precisely which elements are lost in translation, there is value in indicating which strategy is used in translation for resources. A record of a lost idiom is at least an acknowledgment of the fact that there are likely undetermined meaning differences between the SL idiom and TL paraphrase that can potentially be recovered.

5 Constructions

Another set of challenges for translation comes in the form of constructions. Under a Construction Grammar approach, a *construction* is defined as any pairing of form and meaning, and therefore includes not only traditional entries in lexicons, such as morphemes and individual words, but also more complex forms, such as partially lexically-filled or fixed as well as fully general linguistic patterns (e.g., the previously mentioned The X-er the Y-er pattern) (Goldberg, 2003). The latter linguistic patterns are of special interest in this work because these meaning-carrying forms must be first recognized in order to then be correctly interpreted or translated. Such forms have not been included in many traditional generative lexicons.[7] Translations proceeding on a word-by-word basis would fail to recognize, for example, the semantics of correlation carried by The X-er the Y-er. This is problematic because, like idioms, the constructional semantics may require translation into a different construction or compositional phrasing in another language. Although idioms can be considered one type of construction, there are additional types of constructions carrying non-compositional meaning that are generally not included in a listing of idioms because they are fully general linguistic patterns that can be flexibly and productively filled with a variety of different lexical items. *Constructicons* (inventories of constructions) have been developed in some languages as a resource to facilitate recognition, interpretation and translation of constructions (Fillmore et al., 2012; Torrent et al., 2014; Bäckström et al., 2014). Here, we provide a preliminary exploration of constructions that should be considered for an MD constructicon.

A native speaker of MD and author of this paper examined instances of particular motion and degree-related constructions drawn from the Abstract Meaning Representation (AMR) corpus (Banarescu et al., 2013; Bonial et al., 2018). We selected AMR instances of constructions because the corpus offers a data-driven (as opposed to seeking out instances of a construction; these are constructions that arose in sentence-by-sentence AMR annotation) variety of annotated examples, which also facilitates a sense of the relative frequency of particular constructions in a larger corpus. After the native speaker of MD examined these English examples, examples of what were thought to be instantiations of the same construction in MD were selected. In addition, translation was attempted of some of the English examples in order to evaluate what constructions may or may not exist in both English and MD.[8] The findings of this analysis are given below, listed by construction type.

CAUSED-MOTION Construction (English) specifies that a causer argument directly causes a theme argument to move along a path designated by a directional phrase (Goldberg, 1995):

Subject.Agent Verb Object.Theme Oblique.Path
He blinked the snow off of her eyelashes.
They booed him off the stage.
She sneezed the foam off the cappuccino.

This construction is quite productive in English, licensing a variety of different verbs that are not typically associated with motion semantics, as shown above. Precisely what constraints exist upon the compatibility of a particular verb within this construction remains under debate. This idiosyncratic semi-productivity is precisely what makes adding this construction to the lexicon—as opposed to adding on motion senses

---

[7] Recently, expanding from within a generative framework, Dorr and Voss (2018) propose multi-layered verb structures for a computational lexicon to support spatial language understanding.

[8] Ideally, an MD constructicon would be developed through a careful analysis of the language through the lens of construction grammar, thereby avoiding the inevitable bias that stems from considering correspondents to English constructions. We hope to complete such analysis in the future as we develop the needed expertise in both construction grammar and MD. It would also be fruitful to explore a semi-automatic approach to detecting constructions, like that of Forsberg et al. (2014).

to what are typically non-motion verbs (like *blink*)—an effective strategy for providing more systematic coverage for the semantics of this construction in a computational lexicon. An examination of MD shows that a version of the Caused-Motion construction[9] exists in MD, as shown in Table 5.

We noticed, however, that the productivity and constraints on the Caused-Motion construction (e.g., determining which verbs can be licensed within it), at this stage in our analysis of MD, appear to be distinct from English. In particular, while English allows for a wide variety of verbs that lexicalize how the motion is caused (e.g., *boo, sneeze, blink*), we have observed that, for the examples our translator provided from MD, the motion semantics was expressed in two parts: through a distinct motion verb and through another word expressing the manner of causation, as shown in two example sentences in Table 6.

MD	قطع الصدفة من القميجة
Transliteration	qtaa' al-sadfa min al-qamija
Gloss	cut(he) the-button from the-shirt
English Source	He cut the button off the shirt

Table 5: Example of Caused-Motion construction in MD

MD	رمش حتى حيد الثلج من شفاره	اعطس حتى طارت الكشكوشة من الكابوتشينو
Translit.	ramach h'ta h'ayad al-talj min chfar-u	a'tass h'ta tara-t al-kachkouch min al-cappuccino
Gloss	blinked(he) till removed the-snow from eyelashes-his	sneezed(he) till flew_out the-foam from the-cappuccino
English	He blinked the snow off his eyelashes	He sneezed the foam off of the cappuccino

Table 6: English Caused-Motion examples expressed in MD through a motion verb & a distinct mention of cause/manner.

MD	دخلت الماشينة للاكار تتغوت	دخلت النحلة للبيت تتزنزن
Transliteration	dakhl-t al-machina l-al-laguar ta-t-ghawat	dakhl-t al-nahla li-l-biyt ta-t-zanzan
Gloss	entered-it the-train to-the-station (PRS)-it-scream	entered-it the-bee to-the-room (PRS)-it-buzz
English Source	The train whistled into the station	The bee buzzed into the room

Table 7: Sound Emission Verbs are realized separately from Motion Verbs in MD, in contrast to English, In which the Intransitive-Motion construction can license the motion semantics of what Is typically a sound-emission verb.

INTRANSITIVE-MOTION Construction (English) carries motion and path semantics and licenses a variety of non-motion verbs, including sound emission verbs that are especially prevalent (Goldberg, 1995) :

Subject.Theme Verb Oblique.Path
The bee buzzed into the room.
The train whistled into the station.

However, MD—like many *verb-framing languages,* (Talmy, 1985; Talmy, 2000)—requires the sound emission verb be realized in surface form separately from the motion verb, as in Table 7.

COMPARATIVE construction (English) expresses the equality or non-equality of two values on a scale. For inequality, comparatives can be realized with a separate degree-word mention of what is more or

---

[9]Arguably, this could be an instantiation of a Resultative construction instead of a Caused-Motion construction. Further elicitation is needed.

less, or this can be realized in a comparative form of an adjective: [10]

    Subject.Item1   Copula (Degree word)   Adjective.Property   AdverbialPhrase.Item2
    This building is newer than the one we saw earlier.
    The orange cat is less intelligent than its grey friend.

In MD, we observe that comparatives can be expressed either using the elative form of the adjective followed by من , similar to MSA, or, instead, by using the base form of the adjective followed by على . Examples for these cases are presented in Table 8.

MD	هد الطوموبيل اغلى من الشي لاخر	هد الطوموبيل غالية على الشي لاخر
Transliteration	had al-tomobile aghla min al-chi l-akhor	had al-tomobile ghalia a'la al-chi l-akhor
Gloss	this the-car more_expensive than the-thing the-other	this the-car expensive over the-thing the-other
English Source	This car is more expensive than the rest.	This car is more expensive than the rest.

Table 8: Examples of MD Comparative construction

The Superlative construction is realized very similarly to English, as shown in Table 9.

MD	هذ هو اكبر متحف فالبلاد	هذ هي اجود عمارة شفنا
Transliteration	hada huwa akbar moth'af fi-l-ablad	hadi hiya ajwad i'mara chaf-na
Gloss	this it biggest museum in-the-country	this it best building saw-we
English Source	This is the biggest museum in the country	This is the best building we have seen

Table 9: Examples of MD Superlative construction

THE X-ER THE Y-ER Construction (or `covariational conditional') has a unique form in which degree-words are nested into phrases with *the* occurring at the beginning (Goldberg, 2003):

The higher you fly, the harder you fall.
The more you practice, the less you will have to think about it.

The construction conveys the correlation between two variables changing along distinct scales. This construction is another excellent example warranting the development of constructicons, since it is the form alone that conveys this meaning, without any explicit lexical-semantic marking of correlation. In our analysis, we find that English instances of The X-er the Y-er can be translated into at least three distinct construction in MD. The three constructions are given in 5, where each is used as a possible translation for the same English sentence exemplifying The X-er the Y-er. While all plausible translations for The X-er the Y-er, these constructions certainly have distinctions in meaning and usage as well. Further analysis is required to determine those nuances and the extent to which The X-er the Y-er might be an adequate English translation of all three of these constructions. Thus, our analysis of MD translations of English constructions has led to three new potential candidates for a MD constructicon.

6   Related Work

6.1   Moroccan Darija

There are a variety of other recent efforts to create computational resources for MD, not to mention other Arabic dialects. For example, Al-Shargi et al. (2016) create a morphologically annotated corpus of MD, which they use to train an automatic morphological analyzer, and Darwish et al. (2018) leverage a diacritized MD Bible to build a diacritization system for MD. Another area receiving attention from

---

[10]FrameNet Constructicon: http://www.icsi.berkeley.edu/pubs/ai/framenetconstructicon11.pdf

English Source	The less we feed him the more defiant he gets
MD 1	شحال ما نقصنا ليه في الماكلة وهو تيزيد يحيح
Transliteration 1	chh'al ma nqass-na li-h fi al-makla w-huwa t-y-zid y-h'ayah'
Gloss 1	as_much_as that decreased-we to-him in the-food and-he (PRS)-he-increases he-defies
MD 2	ماحدنا نقصو ليه في الماكلة وهو تيزيد يحيح
Transliteration 2	ma-h'ad-na naqss-u li-h fi al-makla w-huwa t-y-zid y-h'ayah'
Gloss 2	as_long_as-we decreased-(PL) to-him in the-food and-he (PRS)-he-increases he-defies
MD 3	كلما نقصنا ليه في الماكلة كلما تيزيد يحيح
Transliteration 3	kul-ma nqass-na li-h fi al-makla kul-ma t-y-zid y-h'ayah'
Gloss 3	all/every-what/that decreased-we to-him in the-food all/every-what/that (PRS)-he-increases he-defies

Table 10: Examples of the-Xer, the-Yer MD constructions

NLP researchers is automatic dialect/language identification, especially for code-switched data, since MD speakers frequently mix MD with other languages such as MSA, French, and English. Samih and Maier (2016a) create a 223,000 token corpus from Moroccan internet discussion forums and blogs and annotate it for use in code-switching detection experiments (Samih and Maier, 2016b).[11] Voss et al. (2014) also build a code-switching detection system for MD, focusing on MD text written in Latin script.

In addition to the aforementioned digital resources, there are a few print dictionaries for Moroccan, including a recent verb dictionary (El Haloui and Bowman, 2011) as well as an older dictionary in Latin script edited by Harrell and Sobelman (1966). The Moroccan Darija Wordnet (MDW) project (Mrini and Bond, 2017) is endeavoring to create a WordNet from the Harrell and Sobelman dictionary and link it with Princeton's WordNet (Fellbaum, 1998). MDW will eventually be released as part of the Open Multilingual Wordnet project (Bond and Foster, 2013).

6.2 Idioms

In the last decade, researchers have turned to the task of automatically detecting idioms in English texts, developing statistical measures that go beyond the tradition of relying on manually identifying expressions in terms of their syntactic and semantic idiosyncrasies; instead, researchers have analyzed a wide range of actual usage patterns in texts (Fazly et al., 2009), and most recently using word embeddings (Peng and Feldman, 2017) and leveraging existing sources of idioms, such as in Wiktionary (Muzny and Zettlemoyer, 2013). Related research in idiom identification in non-English languages is also being conducted by native speakers of those languages, e.g., Hindi (Priyanka and Sinha, 2014), Italian (Vietri, 2014), Russian (Aharodnik et al., 2018), and Japanese (Hashimoto and Kawahara, 2008).

6.3 Constructicons

Though constructicons are intended to be language-specific, they are based on the notion of continuity between the grammar and the lexicon in all languages (Fillmore, 2008). Resources for constructicons that we are aware of (Bäckström et al., 2014; Torrent et al., 2014; Forsberg et al., 2014; Ohara, 2016) take the following approach (similar to our own here): they begin by comparing English constructions to known constructions in another language of choice. Such comparison offers a baseline of constructions that may exist in the language, elucidating equivalent, approximate, and divergent constructions in the process; also, it addresses the possibility of linking constructicon resources in a dictionary-like manner. Backström et al. (2014) elaborate potential Swedish correspondents for Berkeley's English constructicon,[12] noting that full equivalence is difficult between constructions due to their use of content, form, and pragmatic usage combined. In contrast, Torrent et al. (2014) focus on a set of known constructions in Brazilian Portuguese (the *Para Infinitive* family), and through a close study of how to link theses constructions to

---

[11]Per personal communication with the authors, the corpus is not currently being redistributed due to intellectual property right concerns.

[12]https://www1.icsi.berkeley.edu/~kay/bcg/ConGram.html

English constructions as established by Goldberg (2003), they develop guidelines to help future annotators identify valid Brazilian Portuguese constructions. Though these constructions do not find full equivalence between languages, this type of analysis can provide useful diagnostics for identifying cross-linguistic commonalities and innovations alike.

7 Conclusion and Future Work

In this paper, we explore the challenges of building a computational lexicon for Moroccan Darija (MD). Starting from MD source text found online, we report on the construction of a parallel translation corpus of MD-English sentences and the computational lexicon derived in the process with bilingual MD-English entries.[13]

The construction analyses that we have begun, while preliminary, demonstrate that future work in linking constructicons across languages will be useful for translation by revealing places where one construction can be translated into another construction of a relatively similar form (e.g., for English and MD, the Comparative and Superlative), or a construction may be translated into one or more constructions of dissimilar form (e.g., The X-er the Y-er), and places where a construction in one language could only be translated periphrastically in another language (e.g., the English Caused-Motion and Intransitive Motion constructions translate into MD paraphrases). Instead of considering what English constructions may be present in MD, future work in expanding the MD constructicon will consider what unique constructions may exist in MD, which may not be expressed as constructions in other languages like English.

References

Katsiaryna Aharodnik, Anna Feldman, and Jing Peng. 2018. Designing a Russian Idiom-Annotated Corpus. In *Proceedings of the Language Resources and Evaluation Conference (LREC)*.

Monireh Akbari. 2013. Strategies for translating idioms. *Journal of Academic and Applied Studies (Special Issue on Applied Linguistics) Vol*, 3(8):32–41.

Faisal Al-Shargi, Aidan Kaplan, Ramy Eskander, Nizar Habash, and Owen Rambow. 2016. Morphologically Annotated Corpora and Morphological Analyzers for Moroccan and Sanaani Yemeni Arabic. In *Proceedings of the Language Resources and Evaluation Conference (LREC)*.

Linnéa Bäckström, Benjamin Lyngfelt, and Emma Sköldberg. 2014. Towards interlingual constructicography: On correspondence between constructicon resources for english and swedish. *Constructions and Frames*, 6(1):9–33.

Mona Baker. 1992. *In Other Words: A Coursebook on Translation*. Routledge, United Kingdom.

Laura Banarescu, Claire Bonial, Shu Cai, Madalina Georgescu, Kira Griffitt, Ulf Hermjakob, Kevin Knight, Philipp Koehn, Martha Palmer, and Nathan Schneider. 2013. Abstract Meaning Representation for Sembanking. In *Proceedings of the 7th Linguistic Annotation Workshop and Interoperability with Discourse*, page 178–186.

Francis Bond and Ryan Foster. 2013. Linking and extending an open multilingual wordnet. In *Proceedings of the 51st Annual Meeting of the Association for Computational Linguistics (Volume 1: Long Papers)*, volume 1, page 1352–1362.

Claire Bonial, Bianca Badarau, Kira Griffitt, Ulf Hermjakob, Kevin Knight, Tim O'Gorman, Martha Palmer, and Nathan Schneider. 2018. Abstract Meaning Representation of Constructions: The More We Include, the Better the Representation. In *Proceedings of the 2018 Language Resources and Evaluation Conference (LREC)*.

Houda Bouamor, Nizar Habash, and Kemal Oflazer. 2014. The Multidialectal Parallel Corpus of Arabic. In *Proceedings of the Language Resources and Evaluation Conference (LREC)*.

Houda Bouamor, Nizar Habash, Mohammad Salameh, Wajdi Zaghouani, Owen Rambow, Dana Abdurahim, Ossama Obeid, Salam Khalifa, Fadhi Eryani, Alexander Erdmann, and Kemal Oflazer. 2018. The MADAR Arabic Dialect Corpus and Lexicon. In *Proceedings of the Language Resources and Evaluation Conference (LREC)*.

Kristin E. Brustad. 2002. *The Syntax of Spoken Arabic*. Georgetown University Press.

---

[13]We expect to release these resources to the research community, with further documentation in addition to this paper.

William Croft and D. Alan Cruse. 2004. *Cognitive Linguistics*. Cambridge University Press.

Kareem Darwish, Ahmed Abdelali, Hamdy Mubarak, Younes Samih, and Mohammed Attia. 2018. Diacritization of Moroccan and Tunisian Arabic Dialects: A CRF Approach. In *Proceedings of the 3rd Workshop on Open-Source Arabic Corpora and Processing Tools*.

Bonnie Dorr and Clare R. Voss. 2018. The Case for Systematically Derived Spatial Language Usage. In *Proceedings of the NAACL 2018 Workshop on Spatial Language Understanding (SpLU)*.

Abdennebi El Haloui and Steven L. Bowman. 2011. *Moroccan Arabic Verb Dictionary*. Artisanal Treasures.

Afsaneh Fazly, Paul Cook, and Suzanne Stevenson. 2009. Unsupervised Type and Token Identification of Idiomatic Expressions. *Computational Linguistics*, page 61–103.

Christiane Fellbaum, editor. 1998. *WordNet: An Electronic Lexical Database*. MIT Press.

Chitra Fernando. 1996. *Idioms and Idiomaticity*. Oxford University Press. Google-Books-ID: 5lViAAAAMAAJ.

Charles Fillmore, Paul Kay, and Mary Catherine O'connor. 1988. Regularity and idiomaticity in grammatical constructions: The case of let alone. *Language*, page 501–538.

Charles Fillmore, Russell Lee-Goldman, and Russell Rhodes. 2012. The Framenet Constructicon. *Sign-based construction grammar*, page 309–372.

Charles Fillmore. 2008. Border conflicts: Framenet meets construction grammar. In *Proceedings of the XIII EURALEX international congress*, volume 4968.

Markus Forsberg, Richard Johansson, Linnéa Bäckström, Lars Borin, Benjamin Lyngfelt, Joel Olofsson, and Julia Prentice. 2014. From construction candidates to constructicon entries: An experiment using semi-automatic methods for identifying constructions in corpora. *Constructions and Frames*, 6(1):114–135.

Adele Goldberg. 1995. *Constructions: A construction grammar approach to argument structure*. University of Chicago Press.

Adele Goldberg. 2003. Constructions: a new theoretical approach to language. In *TRENDS in Cognitive Sciences*, volume 7(5).

Richard Slade Harrell and Harvey Sobelman, editors. 1966. *A Dictionary of Moroccan Arabic: Moroccan-English English-Moroccan*. Georgetown University Press.

Chikara Hashimoto and Daisuke Kawahara. 2008. Construction of an idiom coprus and its application to idiom identification based on wsd incorporating idiom-specific features. In *Proceedings of the Empirical Methods for Natural Language Processing Conference (EMNLP)*.

Khalil Mrini and Francis Bond. 2017. Building the Moroccan Darija Wordnet (MDW) using Bilingual Resources. In *Proceedings of the International Conference on Natural Language, Signal and Speech Processing (ICNLSSP)*.

Grace Muzny and Luke Zettlemoyer. 2013. Automatic Idiom Identification in Wiktionary. In *Proceedings of the Empirical Methods for Natural Language Processing Conference (EMNLP)*.

Geoffrey Nunberg, Ivan A. Sag, and Thomas Wasow. 1994. Idioms. *Language*, 70(3):491–538.

Kyoko Hirose Ohara. 2016. Toward constructicon building for japanese in japanese framenet. *Revista Veredas*, 17(1).

Jing Peng and Anna Feldman. 2017. Automatic Idiom Recognition with Word Embeddings. In *Proceedings of the Annual International Symposium on Information Management and Big Data*.

Priyanka and R.M.K. Sinha. 2014. A System for Identification of Idioms in Hindi. In *Seventh International Conference on Contemporary Computing (IC3)*.

Ivan A. Sag, Timothy Baldwin, Francis Bond, Ann Copestake, and Dan Flickinger. 2002. "Multiword Expressions: A Pain in the Neck for NLP?". In *Proceedings of the Third International Conference on Computational Linguistics and Intelligent Text Processing (CICLing'02)*.

Younes Samih and Wolfgang Maier. 2016a. An Arabic-Moroccan Darija Code-Switched Corpus. In *Proceedings of the Language Resources and Evaluation Conference (LREC)*.

Younes Samih and Wolfgang Maier. 2016b. Detecting Code-Switching in Moroccan Arabic Social Media. In *SocialNLP Workshop at International Joint Conference on Artificial Intelligence (IJCAI)*.

Amir Shojaei. 2012. Translation of Idioms and Fixed Expressions: Strategies and Difficulties. *Theory and Practice in Language Studies*, 2(6), June.

Gary F. Simons and Charles D. Fennig, editors. 2018. *Ethnologue: Languages of the World, Twenty-first edition*. Online version: http://www.ethnologue.com.

Toshiyuki Takezawa, Genichiro Kikui, Masahide Mizushima, and Eiichiro Sumita. 2007. Multilingual Spoken Language Corpus Development for Communication Research. *International Journal of Computational Linguistics & Chinese Language Processing: Special Issue*, 12(3):303–324.

Leonard Talmy. 1985. Lexicalization patterns: Semantic structure in lexical forms. *Language typology and syntactic description*, 3(99):36–149.

Leonard Talmy. 2000. *Toward a cognitive semantics*, volume 2. MIT press.

Tiago Timponi Torrent, Ludmila Meireles Lage, Thais Fernandes Sampaio, Tatiane da Silva Tavares, and Ely Edison da Silva Matos. 2014. Revisiting border conflicts between FrameNet and Construction Grammar: Annotation policies for the Brazilian Portuguese Constructicon. *Constructions and Frames*, 6(1):34–51.

Simonetta Vietri. 2014. The Lexicon-Grammar of Italian Idioms. In *Proceedings of the International Conference on Computational Linguistics (COLING)*.

Clare R Voss, Stephen Tratz, Jamal Laoudi, and Douglas Briesch. 2014. Finding Romanized Arabic Dialect in Code-Mixed Tweets. In *Proceedings of the Language Resources and Evaluation Conference (LREC)*.

Mohammad Ali Yaghan. 2008. "Arabizi": A Contemporary Style of Arabic Slang. *Design Issues*, 24(2):39–52.

Rabih Zbib, Erika Malchiodi, Jacob Devlin, David Stallard, Spyros Matsoukas, Richard Schwartz, John Makhoul, Omar F. Zaidan, and Chris Callison-Burch. 2012. Machine Translation of Arabic Dialects. In *Proceedings of the 2012 Conference of the North American Chapter of the Association for Computational Linguistics: Human Language Technologies*, NAACL HLT '12, page 49–59, Stroudsburg, PA, USA. Association for Computational Linguistics.

Verbal Multiword Expressions in Basque Corpora

Uxoa Iñurrieta, Itziar Aduriz*, Ainara Estarrona,
Itziar Gonzalez-Dios, Antton Gurrutxaga, Ruben Urizar, Iñaki Alegria**
IXA NLP group, University of the Basque Country
*IXA NLP group, University of Barcelona
**Elhuyar Foundation
usoa.inurrieta@ehu.eus, itziar.aduriz@ub.edu,
ainara.estarrona@ehu.eus, itziar.gonzalezd@ehu.eus,
a.gurrutxaga@elhuyar.eus, ruben.urizar@ehu.eus, i.alegria@ehu.eus

Abstract

This paper presents a Basque corpus where Verbal Multiword Expressions (VMWEs) were annotated following universal guidelines. Information on the annotation is given, and some ideas for discussion upon the guidelines are also proposed. The corpus is useful not only for NLP-related research, but also to draw conclusions on Basque phraseology in comparison with other languages.

1   Introduction

For Natural Language Processing (NLP) tools to produce good-quality results, it is necessary to detect which words need to be treated together (Sag et al., 2002; Savary et al., 2015). However, identifying Multiword Expressions (MWEs) is a challenging task for NLP, and current tools still struggle to do this properly. This is mainly due to the multiple morphosyntactic variants that these kinds of word combinations can have, especially when their syntactic head is a verb.

(1)   *They **made** a **decision**.*

(2)   *They **made** some difficult **decisions**.*

(3)   *The **decisions** they **made** were correct.*

In order to promote research on this topic, the PARSEME Shared Task on Automatic Identification of Verbal Multiword Expressions (VMWEs) was organised (Savary et al., 2017), which holds its second edition this year. One of the outcomes of this initiative is an MWE-annotated corpus including 20 languages. Along with other relevant resources (Losnegaard et al., 2016), this kind of corpus can be helpful to tackle the problems posed by MWEs to NLP. The present paper aims at describing the Basque annotation carried out for this Shared Task (ST), Basque being one of the novel languages included in the new edition.

Comprehensive work has been done on Basque MWEs, not only from a linguistic perspective (Zabala, 2004), but also concerning identification within parsing (Alegria et al., 2004), extraction of VMWEs for lexicographical purposes (Gurrutxaga and Alegria, 2011) and translation (Inurrieta et al., 2017). Nevertheless, this is the first corpus where these kinds of expressions are manually annotated[1].

The paper starts by introducing what resources are used (Section 2), and it goes on to briefly describe how the annotation process was done overall (Section 3). Then, the main confusing issues concerning Basque VMWEs are commented on (Section 4), and a few questions about the guidelines are proposed for future discussion (Section 5). Some remarks about Basque VMWEs are also made based on the annotated corpus (Section 6), and finally, conclusions are drawn (Section 7).

---

[1]Annotation of Verb+Noun MWEs in Basque was carried out by Gurrutxaga and Alegria (2011), but note that this was not done on corpora but on automatically extracted out-of-context word combinations.

Proceedings of the Joint Workshop on
Linguistic Annotation, Multiword Expressions and Constructions (LAW-MWE-CxG-2018), pages 86–95
Santa Fe, New Mexico, USA, August 25-26, 2018.

2   Resources and setup

For the annotation described in this paper, a **Basque corpus** was created by collecting texts from two different sources: (A) 6,621 sentences from the Universal Dependencies treebank for Basque (Aranzabe et al., 2015), that is, the whole UD treebank, and (B) 4,537 sentences taken from the Elhuyar Web Corpora[2]. Thus, in all, the Basque corpus consists of 11,158 sentences (157,807 words).

The UD subcorpus comprises news from Basque media, whereas the Elhuyar subcorpus consists of texts which were automatically extracted from the web. Although only good-quality sources were selected and a cleanup was done before performing the annotation, a few strange sentences can still be found in this part due to automatic extraction (such as sentences missing some words or a few words in languages other than Basque). Scripts made available by the ST organisers[3] were used to prepare the corpus before and after annotation.

Likewise, the **annotation guidelines**[4] created specifically for the ST edition 1.1 were used. The guidelines are intended to be universal and were the result of thoughtful discussions among experts from many different languages (Savary et al., 2018). Six different categories of VMWEs are included in the guidelines, but only two of them are applicable to Basque: Verbal Idioms (VID) and Light Verb Constructions (LVCs), the latter being divided into two subcategories, LVC.full and LVC.cause. All of them are universal categories.

Detailed information about each of the categories can be found in the guidelines, as well as decision trees and specific tests provided in order to make it easier to decide whether/how a given combination should be annotated. As a brief explanation to better follow the content of this paper, categories can be broadly defined as follows.

- **VID:** combinations of a verb and at least another lexicalised component whose meaning is not derivable from the separate meanings of the component words.

    (4)   ***adarra jo***[5]
          horn-the.ABS play
          '(to) trick, (to) pull somebody's leg'

- **LVC.full:** combinations of a verb and a noun phrase (sometimes introduced or followed by an adposition) where the noun denotes an event or state and the verb adds only morphological features but no meaning.

    (5)   ***proba egin***
          test.BARE do
          '(to) try'

- **LVC.cause:** combinations of a verb and a noun phrase (sometimes introduced or followed by an adposition) where the noun denotes an event or state and the verb is causative.

    (6)   ***berri izan***
          news.BARE have
          '(to) know (about), (to) have heard (of)'

As for the **annotation platform**, FLAT[6] was used, which has a very user-friendly interface and greatly simplifies the task of adding, deleting or modifying tags.

---

[2] http://webcorpusak.elhuyar.eus/

[3] https://gitlab.com/parseme/utilities/tree/master/1.1

[4] http://parsemefr.lif.univ-mrs.fr/parseme-st-guidelines/1.1/?page=home

[5] Explanations for glosses in examples: ABS → absolutive case; ADV → adverb; AUX → auxiliary verb; BARE → bare noun; FUT → future; LOC → locative postposition; 1PS/3PS → 1st/3rd person singular; 3PP → 3rd person plural.

[6] http://flat.readthedocs.io/en/latest/

3   The annotation process

The annotation process had several phases. First of all, a few training sessions were organised with a dual objective: on the one hand, to help participants get familiarised with the guidelines and the annotation platform; on the other hand, to identify tricky issues that might arise from annotating Basque VMWEs in corpora. Some decisions were made on problematic cases, which were then collected in an internal document to be used as a reference tool along with the guidelines.

Six experts took part in this annotation task: five linguists and a lexicographer, most of which have broad experience in the field of phraseology. The training sessions will now be briefly described (Section 3.1), and some more details on the final annotated corpus will be given (Section 3.2).

3.1   Training sessions

After receiving explanations about the guidelines and the annotation platform, all participants were asked to annotate the same part of the corpus: 500 sentences in all. At this first attempt, the degree of disagreement was considerably high among annotators, whose number of tags varied from 85 to 170 for the same sentences. The main reason for this was that two oposed positions were adopted: whereas some participants marked everything which showed any kind of similarity with VMWEs, others opted for annotating only the cases they were completely sure of.

All examples which caused disagreements were collected and classified, and three more sessions were organised, where participants tried to reach an agreement on the main problematic cases. A lot of the differently-annotated sentences were quite easy to decide on, as they were due to misunderstandings on basic concepts, either related to general language or to the guidelines. The rest of the cases, however, required further discussion. Decisions made on these cases were collected in an internal document for Basque annotators, so that they knew what criteria they should follow. Details about this document will be given in Section 4.

3.2   Final annotation and Inter-Annotator Agreement

After disagreements were discussed and decided on, each annotator was assigned some texts, and a small part of the corpus was double-annotated as a basis to calculate Inter-Annotator Agreement (IAA). This subcorpus was fully annotated by one participant, and was then split into two parts, so that two more annotators would work on one part each. Following the measurements of the first edition of the ST, the final IAA scores for Basque are sumed up in Table 1[7].

sent	inst-file1	inst-file2	mwe-fscore	kappa	kappa-cat
871	327	355	0.86	0.82	0.86

Table 1: IAA scores

As it can be noticed, scores are noteworthily high for all three measures. This is presumably an outcome of, on the one hand, the clarity of the guidelines and the specific tests provided, and on the other hand, the effectiveness of the training sessions held before starting the real annotation. Additionally, as a further step towards ensuring the unity of all annotations, consistency checks were performed once the main annotations were finished. Considering that before such checks these IAA scores were already much higher than average (comparing to the rest of the languages included in the ST), the good quality of this resource becomes evident beyond doubt.

The final annotated corpus comprises 3,823 VMWE tags of three categories in a total of 11,158 sentences. General data about the annotations is collected in Table 2, and further comments on them will be made in Section 6.

---

[7]Meaning of the table columns: sent = sentence; inst-file1 = instances annotated by one of the annotators; inst-file2 = instances annotated by the other two annotators; mwe-fscore = F score for MWEs; kappa = kappa score for VMWEs annotated; kappa-cat = kappa score for VMWE categories. More details on how scores were calculated are given in (Savary et al., 2018).

sentences	tokens	MWEs	LVC.cause	LVC.full	VID
11,158	157,807	3,823	183	2,866	774

Table 2: Data about the final Basque VMWE corpus

4 Difficult language-dependent cases

As pointed out previously, all the conclusions drawn from the training sessions were collected in an internal document for annotators. The main issues found during the annotation of Basque VMWEs will now be commented on, and the decisions made for each of the issues will be explained. Note that only general questions will be brought here. Individual cases which led to disagreements among annotators will not be included in this section, although a few examples of this kind were also collected.

4.1 Morphological variation of the nouns inside LVCs

In Basque, noun phrases almost always have a determiner, and there are hardly any instances of "bare" nouns (Laka, 1996), that is, nouns with no determiner at all. However, the presence of this kind of noun followed by a (usually light) verb seems to be a common characteristic among VMWEs. More specifically, it is frequent in VMWEs which denote very common actions, usually expressed by single verbs in other languages.

(7) *lo egin*
sleep.BARE do
'(to) sleep', (ES) 'dormir', (FR) 'dormir'

(8) *hitz egin*
word.BARE do
'(to) speak', (ES) 'hablar', (FR) 'parler'

While some of these VMWEs accept almost no morphological modification in the noun phrase, others are also used with determiners and modifiers, as the one shown in Examples (9)-(10). In these cases, the VMWEs display a canonical morphosyntactic variation.

(9) *lan egin*
work.BARE do
'(to) work'

(10) *lana egin*
work-the.ABS do
'(to) work, (to) do some work'

Morphological variants of this kind of LVC caused some trouble to annotators at the beginning, probably because only variants where the noun is "bare" are currently considered MWEs by Basque parsers (Alegria et al., 2004). Although it has sometimes been argued that instances with a determiner should not be treated as VMWEs, they pass all the LVC tests in the guidelines. Thus, our decision was to annotate these kinds of combinations both when they have some determiner and when they do not.

4.2 The future time in LVCs containing the verb *izan*

Izan 'have/be' is one of the most common verbs inside Basque LVCs, but it is also an auxiliary verb, which can be confusing for annotators sometimes. The usage of this verb is somewhat peculiar concerning the future form of LVCs. When we want to express that a given action will happen in the future, the verb participle is inflected by taking the morpheme *-ko/-go* at the end. However, this morpheme does not always follow the verb when an LVC with *izan* is used: in many cases, it can also be attached to the noun inside the VMWE, eliding the verb.

    (11)   **behar dut**
           need.BARE have.1PS.PR
           'I need'

    (12)   **behar izango** *dut*
           need.BARE have-FUT AUX.1PS
           'I will need'

    (13)   **beharko** *dut*
           need-FUT AUX.1PS
           'I will need'

Example (11) shows the VMWE *behar izan* '(to) need' in its present form, while the other examples show two variants of the future form. In Example (12), the *-go* morpheme is attached to the verb as usual, while in Example (13) the verb is elided, and the morpheme *-ko* is added to the noun *behar* instead[8]. Whereas the first two cases must be annotated, there is no VMWE in the third one, as only one lexicalised component is present, *behar*.

The fact that *izan* is also an auxiliary verb makes it easy to mistakenly think that the auxiliary after a word like *beharko* is a lexicalised component of the VMWE. However, this difference is an important detail annotators should always bear in mind. To see this difference, it can be helpful to use a morphological analyzer like Morfeus (Alegria et al., 1996), as it analyses *beharko* as an inflected form of *behar_izan*.

4.3   The blurred limit between adjectives and nouns in Basque VMWEs

All languages have words which can belong to more than one different part of speech. In some Basque VMWEs, it is not always clear if the non-verbal element is a noun or an adjective, and many parsers struggle to get the right tag. For instance, the word *gose* 'hunger/hungry' can be either one or the other depending on the context, even though its usage as an adjective is quite marginal nowadays. In Examples (14)-(15), two VMWEs containing this word and the verb *izan* 'be/have' are shown. Although intuition indicates us that *gose* is an adjective in Example (14) but a noun in (15), it is very common for parsers to tag both instances as nouns.

    (14)   **gose naiz**
           hungry/hunger.BARE be.1PS.PR
           'I am hungry.'

    (15)   **gosea dut**[9]
           hunger-the.ABS have.1PS.PR
           'I am hungry.'

Besides, sometimes, the usage of a word which always holds one category may even suggest that it belongs to a different part of speech within a VMWE. For instance, the first element in the expression *nahi izan* (wish.BARE have → '(to) want') can take the comparative suffix *-ago*, which is used to grade adjectives and adverbs: *nahiago izan* (wish-more have → '(to) prefer'). This usage may suggest that *nahi* is used as an adjective in this expression, even if it is always used as a noun out of it.

For coherence, it was concluded that these kinds of examples should all be grouped equally, and they were classified in the LVC categories. Given that the non-verbal element is sometimes closer to adjectives

---

[8]Note that *-ko* and *-go* are allomorphs of the same morpheme (due to phonemic context).

[9]Example (15) is probably a loan translation, as this is the way the idea of *being hungry* is expressed in Spanish and French, the main languages sharing territory with Basque. This usage is more recent and, according to some speakers, it is not as 'proper' as the first one. However, it is more and more common in real corpora and, thus, it must be considered.

than to nouns, it could be pertinent to add a note in the guidelines along with the one about Hindi, which states "the noun can be replaced by an adjective which is morphologically identical to an eventive noun". Exactly the same could be applied to Basque as well.

(16) ***bizi izan***
      live/life be
      '(to) live'

In fact, as the adjectives of this kind have identical nouns, combinations like the one in Example (16) pass LVC tests with no difficulty, and thus, this is the category they were assigned, regardless of their adjectival nature.

4.4 (Apparently) cranberry words inside LVCs

Some VMWEs which have reached us from a former stage of the language may present some idiosyncrasies from a diachronic perspective, e.g. the lack of determiners in noun phrases (see Section 4.1). They may also contain words which are only used within the context of a given verbal expression. For example, the word *merezi* is almost exclusively used as part of the VMWE *merezi izan* 'to deserve'.

Something similar occurs with *ari* in the verbal expression *ari izan*, which is categorised as a complex aspectual verb in Basque grammars (Etxepare, 2003). It is used in phrases such as *lanean ari izan* 'to be at work' and becomes grammaticalised when used to make the continuous forms of verbs, as in *jaten ari izan* 'to be eating'.

For the vast majority of Basque speakers, it is not a straight-forward assumption that these words are nouns. Nevertheless, if we take a look at the *Orotariko Euskal Hiztegia* (Mitxelena, 1987), the reference historical dictionary created by the Royal Academy of the Basque language, Euskaltzaindia[10], we realise that these words have an entry by themselves and are actually classified as nouns. Futhermore, while speakers might first think that these expressions do not pass test LVC.5, that is, that the verb can be ommitted when a possessive is added to the noun, some examples[11] of this kind can be found in the dictionary:

(17) *Eman diote (...)* ***bere merezia.***
      give AUX.3PP (...) his/her deserved-the.ABS
      'They gave him what he deserved.'

(18) *Ez zuen utzi* ***bere aria.***
      not AUX.3PS leave his/her practice-the.ABS
      'He did not stop doing what he was doing.'

To sum up, although some non-verbal elements in VMWEs might look like cranberry words, it is important to contrast information with reference material, especially when the verb is accompanied by a light verb. For the examples mentioned here, it was clear to us that LVC.full was the category where they fitted best.

5 Discussion on some conceptions in the guidelines

Overall, it is a remarkable point that the most controversial issues during the training sessions were all related to LVCs. This is probably an effect of the very high frequency of this type of VMWE in Basque corpora (more details will be given in Section 6), but it should also be considered that, as far as LVCs are concerned, there are notable differences between the guidelines and the rest of the literature on Basque (and Spanish) phraseology. Therefore, it is very likely that this fact has also conditioned the doubts arisen to participants.

It is an enormous challenge to create universal guidelines in a field like phraseology, where boundaries are never as definite as NLP tools would need. The guidelines created for both PARSEME Shared

---

[10] `www.euskaltzaindia.eus`
[11] For clarity, examples were re-written following current ortographical rules.

Tasks are a really important step towards unifying different conceptions about MWEs, and the clarity of tests simplifies the annotation task greatly. However, some points might still benefit from further consideration, which will be briefly noted here. If these points were problematic in other languages as well, the ideas presented in this section could be used as a starting point for future discussion.

Two main notions will be mentioned here related to the gap existent between the guidelines and our previous conceptions about phraseology: on the one hand, the understanding of collocations as a phenomenon separate from MWEs (Section 5.1), and on the other hand, the fact that LVCs are defined as combinations of a verb and a noun phrase only (Section 5.2).

5.1 Collocations as non-VMWEs

LVCs are usually understood as a subcategory of collocations in the reference literature about Basque phraseology (Urizar, 2012; Gurrutxaga and Alegria, 2013), as well as in that about Spanish phraseology (Corpas Pastor, 1997). However, in the guidelines, collocations are defined as a mere statistical phenomenon, and they are discriminated not only from LVCs but also from VMWEs in general. The line separating ones and others was not always clear, and despite the comprehensive tests, annotators sometimes found it hard not to annotate some instances which, according to them, were clearly related to phraseology somehow.

(19) *deia egin*
call-the.ABS make
'(to) make a call'

(20) *deia jaso*
call-the.ABS receive
'(to) receive a call'

For instance, the guidelines say that, whereas the combination in Example (19) must be annotated, the one in Example (20) must not. The fact that one passes all tests and the other one does not made it relatively easy to let the second example apart. However, it is still not that evident to us that it should not be treated as a VMWE at all, since the noun *deia* 'call' always chooses the verb *jaso* 'receive' to express that meaning. As a matter of fact, it is extremely rare to see it accompanied by other verbs which could equally express that meaning, such as *eduki* 'have'. Similar examples were found quite often in the corpus, so it might be worth examining those cases further for future editions.

5.2 LVCs accepting only noun phrases

On the other hand, according to the guidelines, LVCs can only be composed of a light verb and a noun phrase (except for Hindi, as it is pointed out in Section 4.3). This noun phrases can be preceded by prepositions or followed by postpositions. According to this, VMWEs like the one in Example (21) should not be annotated as LVC.full, as *korrika* is an adverb.

(21) *korrika egin*
running.ADV do
'(to) run'

By definition, LVCs are VMWEs where the verb is void of meaning and the other component carries the whole semantic weight about the event or state the combination denotes. In Basque, many events can be expressed by adverbs, and this definition could equally be applied to constructions of adverbs and light verbs like the one in Example (21).

Furthermore, many of these adverbs are created by attaching a suffix to a noun, often *-ka*, such as *hazka* 'scratching', which comes from *hatz* 'finger' and forms part of the VMWE *hazka egin* (scratching do → '(to) scratch'). Thus, the LVC.full and LVC.cause categories would probably be more coherent if they had a wider scope and this kind of combination was also considered.

6 Information about Basque VMWEs inferred from annotations

As already mentioned, VMWEs from three different categories were annotated in Basque: VID, LVC.full and LVC.cause. Table 2 shows how many tags there are in the corpus, where the number of VMWEs annotated as LVC.full clearly stands out from the rest: 75% of all tags belong to this category. If we add the instances in the LVC.cause group to this number, the whole group of LVCs amounts to almost 80% of all annotations.

This is not surprising, since, as it is pointed out in Section 4.1, it is not strange that very common actions expressed by single verbs in some other languages are denoted by an LVC in Basque. Thus, it was to be expected that the number of instances in this category would be higher in our corpus than in other languages.

Table 3 makes this fact obvious. It collects the ratio of LVCs and VMWEs per sentence in the Basque corpus, as well as the average ratio of the whole ST corpus (20 languages in all) and the ratios for Spanish, French and English corpora[12], the three languages which affect Basque the most. In order to make comparisons properly, only the three universal categories were taken into account, even if all except Basque include other categories as well. From the languages included in the ST, only Farsi and Hindi have a higher number of LVCs per 100 sentences (95 and 40 respectively).

	VMWEs per 100 sentences	LVCs per 100 sentences
Basque	34	27
Average	18	11
French	20	9
Spanish	15	9
English	6	4

Table 3: Average frequencies of tags in Basque, Spanish, French and English

On the other hand, the number of instances annotated as LVC.cause is very low (less than 5% of all tags), and this seems to be quite a common tendency also in other languages. Considering only annotations from the three universal categories, the average percentage of VMWEs classified in this group is only 3% (taking all 20 languages into account). This might be a sign that either: (A) the LVC.cause category would be better merged with the LVC.full one, or (B) maybe it would be a good idea to broaden this category so that it includes combinations that are not yet annotated, such as collocations.

Concerning morphology, the VMWEs in the Basque corpus are mostly combinations of a verb and a noun (94%)[13], which was easy to anticipate considering that LVCs can only be of this kind according to the guidelines. Consistent with other work about VMWEs in dictionaries (Inurrieta et al., 2017), such nouns are mainly found in the absolutive case (85%) in the corpus, and among the rest, the locative is the most frequent postposition, as in Example (22).

> (22) **_jolasean ibili_**
> game-the.LOC be
> '(to) be playing, (to) play'

Something comparable probably happens in other languages as well. In the Spanish corpus, for example, out of the VMWEs where the main constituents are a verb and a noun, only 23% include a preposition.

7 Conclusion

VMWEs were annotated in a 11,158-sentence Basque corpus, following the universal guidelines of edition 1.1 of the PARSEME Shared Task on Automatic Identification of Verbal Multiword Expressions. In

---

[12]Corpora for all languages can be accessed here: `https://gitlab.com/parseme/sharedtask-data/tree/master/1.1`

[13]When calculating this number, non-verbal elements of LVCs which could be either a noun or an adjective (see Section 4.3) were counted as nouns.

all, 3,823 instances were annotated and classified into two main categories: Verbal Idioms and Light Verb Constructions. High Inter-Annotator Agreement scores make it evident that this is a very good-quality resource, which can be useful not only for NLP-related research, but also for future studies on Basque phraseology.

After explaining how the annotation process was organised, the main doubts arisen to Basque annotators while performing this task were commented on in this paper. The decisions taken on language-dependent issues were presented, and some ideas for discussion on the universal guidelines were also proposed. If these ideas are shared by annotators from other languages, it could be interesting to take a further look at them for future editions.

References

Maria Jesus Aranzabe, Aitziber Atutxa, Kepa Bengoetxea, Arantza Díaz de Ilarraza, Koldo Gojenola and Larraitz Uria. 2015. Automatic conversion of the Basque dependency treebank to universal dependencies. In *Proceedings of the Workshop on Treebanks and Linguistic Theories (TLT 2015)*, 233–241.

Iñaki Alegria, Xabier Artola, Kepa Sarasola, and Miriam Urkia. 1996. Automatic morphological analysis of Basque. In *Literary and Linguistic Computing*, 11(4):193–203.

Iñaki Alegria, Olatz Ansa, Xabier Artola, Nerea Ezeiza, Koldo Gojenola and Ruben Urizar. 2004. Representation and treatment of Multiword Expressions in Basque. In *Proceedings of the Workshop on Multiword Expressions: Integrating Processing*, 48–55. Association for Computational Linguistics.

Gloria Corpas Pastor. 1997. Manual de fraseología española. Editorial Gredos.

Ricardo Etxepare. 2003. Valency and argument structure in the Basque verb. In Jose Ignacio Hualde and Jon Ortiz de Urbina (eds.) *A grammar of Basque*. Mouton de Gruyter.

Antton Gurrutxaga and Iñaki Alegria. 2011. Automatic extraction of NV expressions in Basque: basic issues on cooccurrence techniques. In *Proceedings of the Workshop on Multiword Expressions: from parsing and generation to the real world*, 2–7. Association for Computational Linguistics.

Antton Gurrutxaga and Iñaki Alegria. 2013. Combining different features of idiomaticity for the automatic classification of noun+verb expressions in Basque. In *Proceedings of the 9th Workshop on Multiword Expressions*, 116–125. University of the Basque Country.

Uxoa Inurrieta, Itziar Aduriz, Arantza Díaz de Ilarraza, Gorka Labaka and Kepa Sarasola. 2017. Rule-based translation of Spanish Verb-Noun combinations into Basque. In *Proceedings of the 13th Workshop on Multiword Expressions, in EACL 2017*, 149–154. Association for Computational Linguistics.

Uxoa Inurrieta, Itziar Aduriz, Arantza Díaz de Ilarraza, Gorka Labaka and Kepa Sarasola. 2018 (in print). Analysing linguistic information about word combinations for a Spanish-Basque rule-based machine translation system. In Ruslan Mitkov, Johanna Monti, Gloria Corpas Pastor and Violeta Seretan (eds.), *Multiword Units in Machine Translation and Translation Technologies*, 39–60. John Benjamins publishing company.

Koldo Mitxelena. 1987. *Orotariko Euskal Hiztegia*. Euskaltzaindia, the Royal Academy of the Basque language.

Itziar Laka Mugarza. 1996. *A brief grammar of Euskera, the Basque language*. University of the Basque Country.

Gyri Smørdal Losnegaard, Federico Sangati, Carla Parra Escartín, Agata Savary, Sascha Bargmann and Johanna Monti. 2016. PARSEME survey on MWE resources. In *9th International Conference on Language Resources and Evaluation (LREC 2016)*, 2299–2306. European Association for Language Resources.

Ivan A Sag, Timothy Baldwin, Francis Bond, Ann Copestake, and Dan Flickinger. 2002. Multiword expressions: a pain in the neck for NLP. In *International Conference on Intelligent Text Processing and Computational Linguistics*, 1–15. Springer.

Agata Savary, Manfred Sailer, Yannick Parmentier, Michael Rosner, Victoria Rosén, Adam Przepiórkowski, Cvetana Krstev, Veronika Vincze, Beata Wójtowicz, Gyri Smørdal Losnegaard, and others. 2015. PARSEME–PARSing and Multiword Expressions within a European multilingual network. In *7th Language & Technology Conference: Human Language Technologies as a Challenge for Computer Science and Linguistics (LTC 2015)*.

Agata Savary, Carlos Ramisch, Silvio Cordeiro, Federico Sangati, Veronika Vincze, Behrang QasemiZadeh, Marie Candito, Fabienne Cap, Voula Giouli, Ivelina Stoyanova and others. 2017. The PARSEME Shared Task on automatic identification of Verbal Multiword Expressions. In *Proceedings of the 13th Workshop on Multiword Expressions, in EACL 2017*, 31–47. Association for Computational Linguistics.

Agata Savary, Carlos Ramisch, Silvio Cordeiro, Veronika Vincze and others. 2018. Edition 1.1 of the PARSEME Shared Task on automatic identification of Verbal Multiword Expressions. In *Proceedings of the 14th Workshop on Multiword Expressions, in COLING 2018*. Association for Computational Linguistics.

Ruben Urizar. 2012. *Euskal lokuzioen tratamendu konputazionala*. University of the Basque Country.

Igone Zabala Unzalu. 2004. Los predicados complejos en vasco. In *Las fronteras de la composicin en lenguas romnicas y en vasco*, 445–534. Universidad de Deusto.

Annotation of Tense and Aspect Semantics for Sentential AMR

Lucia Donatelli
Georgetown University
led66@georgetown.edu

Michael Regan
University of New Mexico
University of Colorado Boulder
michael.regan@colorado.edu

William Croft
University of New Mexico
wcroft@unm.edu

Nathan Schneider
Georgetown University
nathan.schneider@georgetown.edu

Abstract

Although English grammar encodes a number of semantic contrasts with tense and aspect marking, these semantics are currently ignored by Abstract Meaning Representation (AMR) annotations. This paper extends sentence-level AMR to include a coarse-grained treatment of tense and aspect semantics. The proposed framework augments the representation of finite predications to include a four-way temporal distinction (event time before, up to, at, or after speech time) and several aspectual distinctions (including static vs. dynamic, habitual vs. episodic, and telic vs. atelic). This will enable AMR to be used for NLP tasks and applications that require sophisticated reasoning about time and event structure.

1 Introduction

The Abstract Meaning Representation (AMR) is a readable and compact framework for broad-coverage semantic annotation of English sentences (Banarescu et al., 2013).[1] AMR aims to abstract away from syntactic idiosyncrasies such that sentences with the same basic meaning are represented by the same AMR graph. This paper extends existing AMR to include a coarse-grained representation of tense and aspect. Example (1) shows a sentence with its annotation from the current AMR corpus alongside our proposed additions for tense (in blue) and aspect (in purple):

(1) "Your brother's in the hospital and he's not going to last the night."

```
CURRENT                                           NEW

(a / and
    :op1 (b / be-located-at-91              :stable -     :time (n2 / now)
        :ARG1 (p / person
            :ARG0-of (h / have-rel-role-91
                :ARG1 (y / you)
                :ARG2 (b2 / brother)))
        :ARG2 (h2 / hospital))
    :op2 (l / last-01 :polarity -          :ongoing -
                                           :time (a / after :op1 (n3 / now))
        :ARG1 p
        :ARG2 (d / date-entity
            :dayperiod (n / night))))
```

In AMR, each *concept* (entity or predicate) is tied to a variable which uniquely identifies a graph node. In PENMAN notation (Matthiessen and Bateman, 1991), a slash links a variable to its concept, and names of relations/roles (edges in the graph) are preceded by a colon. PropBank framesets of semantic roles (Palmer et al., 2005) that account for argument structure play a central role in AMR design; sentential AMR additionally includes entity typing and wikification, as well as entity and event coreference within sentences.[2]

---

[1] http://amr.isi.edu/; data released at https://amr.isi.edu/download/amr-bank-struct-v1.6.txt (*Little Prince*) and https://catalog.ldc.upenn.edu/LDC2017T10

[2] *Multi-sentence* AMR is an additional layer developed to indicate cross-sentence coreference links within documents (O'Gorman et al., 2018, https://github.com/timjogorman/Multisentence-AMR-guidelines/blob/master/ms-amr.md).

Proceedings of the Joint Workshop on
Linguistic Annotation, Multiword Expressions and Constructions (LAW-MWE-CxG-2018), pages 96–108
Santa Fe, New Mexico, USA, August 25-26, 2018.

The current annotation in (1) specifies entities and propositional structure[3] but notably omits the present time meaning of the copula and the future meaning of *"going to."* It also does not specify whether these eventualities are stative (temporary or permanent) or dynamic, and if the latter whether they are in progress, progressed to completion, or terminated prematurely. The current AMR in (1) would thus be identical for the sentence *"Your brother **was** in the hospital and **did not** last the night."* The distinction between these two interpretations could have vital importance for practical scenarios in which automated decision-making systems operate, as well as for information extraction applications that involve identifying and situating linguistically described events both in time and in relation to one another.

Excluding semantics expressed by morphosyntactic elements such as inflection and articles has been a deliberate design decision in AMR thus far: to ensure the human annotation process would scale, it was decided that AMR should focus on the semantics of content words and relations between them.[4] Nevertheless, the AMR design leaves room to fold in additional aspects of meaning, and as AMR is refined, we believe that the semantics of tense and aspect can be incorporated at scale by asking annotators to specify key pieces of information about eventualities as explained here.

This paper identifies and formalizes the linguistic phenomena that convey temporal and aspectual information at the sentence level, taking into account both lexical aspect and morphosyntactic cues in finite verbs/predications. Tense and aspect have been widely studied in theoretical and computational linguistics (§2). Here, we synthesize this work and develop an approach that we believe embodies AMR's guiding principles of simplicity and transparency (§3). Finally, we discuss constructions that merit special attention as evidenced through initial pilot annotation work (§4), and we conclude with ongoing troubleshooting and future work to update the annotation scheme (§5).

2   The Case for Tense and Aspect Semantics in AMR

Developing a framework for semantic representation of tense and aspect necessitates striking a balance between the elements that grammatically encode relevant information and the more flexible pragmatic effects that such information may have. There has been a vast amount of research on temporality and aspectuality, both theoretical (Reichenbach, 1947; Vendler, 1957; Comrie, 1976; Comrie, 1985; Langacker, 1982; Dowty, 1986; Hinrichs, 1986; Moens and Steedman, 1988; Klein, 1994; Chang, 1997; Chang et al., 1998; Partee, 1999; Allen et al., 2008; Croft, 2012) and applied to corpora (see §2.2). However, we wish to capture basic distinctions of practical value for NLP applications, and so we must distill this research into a small number of annotation categories.

Here we present elements of existing AMR that relate to the new annotations; we then consider how previous and existing frameworks apart from AMR have attempted to define and specify the temporal nature of eventualities in text. These serve as points of comparison for how to integrate both theoretical and cross-linguistic findings into a versatile, albeit English-centric, annotation design for AMR.

2.1   Tense and Aspect Relevant Semantics in Current AMR

Current AMR does not explicitly formalize the semantics of tense and aspect. However, temporal or aspectual properties of eventualities are represented in the AMR if lexically explicit in the sentence.

AMR uses PropBank framesets of semantic roles as a central part of its overall annotation scheme. Though these framesets may represent eventualities in the syntax, the correspondence is not one-to-one, making it necessary to reference the original sentence for precise event identification.[5] When these frames are specified with lexically overt temporal expressions (typically in the form of prepositional phrases and adverbials, marked using the AMR role :time), event identification is facilitated.[6] Such expressions may imply a specific event time in relation to the discourse, as with adverbials including *yesterday* or

---

[3]This includes both the PropBank frameset last-01 and the AMR-specific frameset be-located-at-91.

[4]Grammatical elements such as mood, modality, and negation were included in AMR 1.0, as they were identified as more "contentful" than other pieces of morphosyntax at the time.

[5]For example, *teacher* is annotated as (p / person :ARG0-of (t2 / teach-01)), where the frame teach-01 is not an identifiable eventuality or suitable for current tense and aspect annotation without morphological decomposition.

[6]:time is used for all temporal location modifiers, however, as in expressions like *former Soviet Union* (:time former) and is not limited to eventualities.

tomorrow; other times, these temporal relations are ambiguous, such as *in June* (in the past or future). The aspectual interpretation of these eventualities remains unspecified, but it may fall out from the participant roles expressed: *"I ran a marathon"* conveys a different aspect than *"I ran for two hours."*

Apart from :time, AMR annotates additional "non-core" roles; these roles may convey temporal or aspectual information, but they crucially depend on the presence of explicit lexical material to be included in the annotation. For example, the role :duration specifies the temporal length of an event; :purpose may specify the future-oriented endpoint of an event; :cause may specify the (typically) past-oriented reason for an event; :condition or the frame have-condition-91 may specify the non-temporal conditional antecedent of an event; :subevent indicates a part-whole event relation; and :frequency indicates how often something may occur. In the absence of explicit lexical material, such non-core roles are accordingly absent in AMR frames though they may exist implicitly in the discourse or via reasoning.

2.2 Related Tense and Aspect Semantic Annotation Frameworks

Temporality and aspectuality have played an important role in several annotation schemes that have been applied to English corpora for NLP.[7]

TimeML. TimeML (Pustejovsky et al., 2003; Pustejovsky, 2017; Pustejovsky et al., 2017), a markup language for temporal and event expressions, is designed to address four key questions in event and temporal expression markup: (i) how to timestamp an event (identify it and anchor it in time); (ii) how to order events with respect to one another (considering both lexical and discourse properties of ordering); (iii) how to reason with contextually underspecified events (e.g. *"last week"* and *"two weeks before"*); and (iv) how to reason about the persistence of events (i.e. how long the event or its outcome lasts). TimeML precisely identifies events and their temporal relations within a text. This ability to reason with contextually underspecified events at the sentence level is a main concern of the current framework.

Situation entity labeling. Friedrich and Palmer (2014) and Friedrich et al. (2016) present a method for automatically identifying the type of a situation entity (SE) using a system of seven SE types (Smith, 2008). The authors assume SEs to be expressed at the clause level: *state, event, report, generic sentence, generalizing sentence, question,* and *imperative.* The labeling of SE types is a non-trivial task even for humans, and the annotation trial encountered many borderline cases—an issue the current framework also deals with. The clause-level focus of annotation is the most similar to the current proposed framework, and the current framework makes reference to a few of the SE types.

Richer Event Description (RED). The RED corpus (O'Gorman et al., 2016) captures coreference, bridging, temporal, causal, and subevent relations in the same annotation; the annotations provide an integrated sense of how the events in a particular document relate to each other with the intent of developing systems that learn rich interactions between events. The annotation scheme itself is based on a fine-grained analysis of aspectual structure combined with an analysis of physical event types following proposals in theoretical linguistics (Vendler, 1957; Croft, 2012). For example, *states* are further specified as (i) transitory, (ii) inherent permanent, (iii) acquired permanent, or (iv) point. By decomposing complex events in a clause, the overall dynamic causal network of entities interacting over time as described in a text may be modeled. Though the RED framework is more fine-grained and discourse-oriented than the current proposed framework, the need to specify event-event relationships for a complete event structure of the sentence is an important takeaway. Challenging areas (event relations conveyed via presupposition, modality, idioms, and/or inference) overlap with challenges for the current guidelines, as well.

Causal and Temporal Relation Scheme (CaTeRS). CaTeRS (Mostafazadeh et al., 2016) is a semantic annotation framework of event-event relations in commonsense stories designed to capture a comprehensive set of causal and temporal relations. The authors define an event to be any lexical entry under the following ontology types in the TRIPS ontology (Allen et al., 2008): Event-of-state; Event-of-change; Event-type; Physical-condition; Occurring; and Natural-phenomenon. Temporal relations are specified between events following the Interval Algebra of (Allen, 1984). Causal relations are further specified

---

[7]Different languages face different hurdles: e.g., tense is not overt in Chinese grammar, which has prompted work on disambiguation using contextual cues (Zhang and Xue, 2014). The approaches listed here assume different stances with regards to their cross-linguistic validity, for which the reader is directed to the original papers.

	States		Dynamic Events
	`:stable +`	`:stable -`	
Episodic	`:time ∎` now if salient *He lives/lived/used to live in Paris.*	`:time ∎` now *He was/is living in Paris.*	`:time ∎` now, `:ongoing +/-/?`, and `:complete +/-` if telic and realized *He went/is going/will go to Paris.* *He has been to Paris (ever, recently).* *He has been touring Paris for the past week.*
Habitual		`:habitual +`, and `:time ∎` now if salient *He is in Paris often.*	`:habitual +`, and `:time ∎` now if salient *He goes to Paris often.*

Table 1: Overview of tense/aspect annotation scheme by stativity and habituality. Aspectual features are in bold. `:time ∎` now is short for one of: `:time now`, `:time before now`, `:time after now`, `:time up-to now`. For habituals and stable states, `:time` is only annotated if there is a clear relation to the present time, e.g. past time expressed by *used to*.

as *cause (before/overlaps)*; *enable (before/overlaps)*; *prevent (before/overlaps)*; and *cause-to-end (before/overlaps/during)*. For example, *"The [famine]$_{e1}$ ended the [war]$_{e2}$"* relates *e1* and *e2* as *cause-to-end (overlap)*; these relations are annotated at both the sentence and discourse levels. CaTeRs is noteworthy for the current paper because, while the ability to describe events as individual units may be relatively straightforward, the intersective temporal and causal relations between events may be less obvious.

Tense Sense Disambiguation. The Tense Sense Disambiguation (TSD) (Reichart and Rappoport, 2010) task addresses the multiple possible semantic senses of English grammatical tense constructions, which are listed in a lexicon. For example, the 'present simple' construction has several possible meanings, including that of a future event at a definite time (viz. *arrives* in *"My brother arrives in the evening"*) and that of a repeated event (*rises* in *"The sun rises in the East"*). We share the philosophy of TSD that grammatical tense constructions are ambiguous, though our approach is less atomic in nature to make fewer distinctions and create semantic tense/aspect categories more amenable to annotators.

3 Annotation Scheme

3.1 Principles of the Annotation Scheme

As AMR is a semantic annotation scheme, we seek an inventory of categories capturing the semantic dimensions of tense and aspect. Labels of *morphosyntactic* tense and aspect categories like PAST PERFECT and SIMPLE PRESENT would be too superficial as these categories are polysemous. For example, "I leave for Paris tomorrow" presents a *future* event in the guise of the SIMPLE PRESENT. A semantic scheme should abstract away from the morphosyntax and mark it as having future time.

Based on the literature on tense and aspect, we propose a set of key semantic contrasts for annotating English sentences. We believe our approach is in the spirit of AMR, striking an effective balance between the complexity of natural language on the one hand, and simplicity and readability in the meaning representation necessary for its scalability to large corpora on the other. As such, we do not claim to cover all possible distinctions in the realm of tense and aspect, though we keep finer-grained nuances of temporal and aspectual meaning in mind for potential future work. Our annotation principles are as follows: (i) We enhance AMR **as it currently exists** to better capture tense and aspect. Where time and event structure are already encoded (e.g., via temporal adverbials), we do not propose major changes. (ii) AMR abstracts away from morphosyntactic particularities of English. Our extensions therefore capture **semantic** distinctions, going deeper than grammatical tense/aspect categories (e.g. morphological past/present, progressive, perfect, etc.), which are polysemous. (iii) Our extensions are mostly **categorical** in nature (e.g. past/present/future time, static vs. dynamic, habitual vs. episodic) rather than a full calculus of timeline points and intervals. (iv) We focus on the semantic contrasts that are important to **English** grammar. Nevertheless, our design decisions are informed by reference to tense and aspect expression in other languages and the possibility of AMR being extended beyond English (Xue et al., 2014; Li et al., 2016; Migueles-Abraira et al., 2018). (v) Our current approach is limited to the semantics of **finite** verbs/predications. (vi) Our current approach is annotated at/below the level of the **individual sentence**. Additional temporal relations in discourse would need to be annotated at the document level. (vii) As AMR prioritizes broad-coverage corpus annotation, we have developed our scheme with reference to

corpus data. This has required us to consider tense/aspect as it intersects with other semantics and constructions, including narrative tense morphology, generics/habituals, conditionals, and modality.

In line with the neo-Davidsonian approach that AMR takes, we treat tense and aspect as non-core roles or variables that modify eventualities (events/states). The annotation for each category follows current AMR guidelines closely so that it may be integrated seamlessly into existing annotations. The basic distinctions are summarized in table 1; we describe them below.

3.2 Annotation Procedure

Annotators are given a set of guidelines that explain how to identify annotation targets (§3.3); how to use table 1 and table 2 and apply labels for tense (§3.4) and aspect (§3.5); and how to address challenging constructions such as modality, certain auxiliary verbs, AMR special frames, and negation (§4). Thus far, annotators have used the online AMR editor, adding new relations presented here to existing AMRs.[8] Several initial pilot annotations with both expert and novice annotators (further detailed in §4) have helped to refine both our annotation procedure and our overall labeling scheme.

3.3 Annotation Targets

To keep the annotation task manageable, we only consider as sites for tense/aspect annotation those concepts in the AMR that correspond to finite predications in the syntax.[9] This restriction is motivated by the understanding that finite clauses explicitly describe eventualities on the temporal dimension, and thus tense-aspect category values are relevant (Langacker, 1987).

We understand eventualities to include all kinds of events: states, activities, achievements, accomplishments, and processes (Bach, 1986). Though labels themselves are annotated on the AMR concept that corresponds to the finite verb, they refer to the event structure denoted by the entire predication as evident in the frameset (which corresponds to the verb's argument structure). Thus, while the sentence *"I read a book last night while sitting"* possesses only one annotation target (read-01), *"I read a book last night while I was sitting"* possesses two targets (read-01, sit-01). Note that a verb's arguments may be relevant to the aspectual annotation on the annotation target: e.g., *"I read a book last night"* is telic whereas *"I read poems last night"* is atelic due to the nature of the complement. All annotation targets receive explicit aspectual labels, and some will additionally receive explicit time labels.

3.4 Time

We annotate the location of an eventuality in time relative to speech time.[10] This may be signaled grammatically with auxiliaries and/or verbal morphology, and/or with temporal adverbials. We annotate this information on an AMR annotation target using the :time role (note that another :time annotation may already be present to reflect temporal information expressed adverbially).

Present Time. The current annotation overtly marks expressions of well-defined semantically present tense when the event time cooccurs with the speech time. Target expressions are verbs in the present form. They are annotated by adding :time (n / now) under the AMR annotation target.[11]

(2) "What are you doing here?"[12]

```
(b / be-located-at-91
    :time (n / now))
```

Future Time. We mark expressions of semantically future tense when the event time occurs after the speech time (disregarding any notions of modality in such constructions). Typical targets are (i) the use of the auxiliary "will" in front of the bare verb; and (ii) the use of the present tense with a future-oriented

---

[8]https://amr.isi.edu/editor.html

[9]As mentioned above, many of the PropBank predicates in AMR correspond to eventualities expressed with nonfinite clauses, deverbal nouns, and so forth. In future work, we will explore extending our annotations to such concepts.

[10]Hence the label "time" instead of "tense."

[11]Aspectual annotations are not shown in this section.

[12]Many sentences provided here come from *The Little Prince*, which has been annotated for English AMR. For purposes of clarity and space, we omit parts of the AMR that are not relevant to the current annotation framework.

temporal adverbial, as *"I leave for Paris tomorrow."* The grammaticalized expression *going to* can also have a future meaning, as in (1). Targets are annotated with `:time (a / after :op1 (n / now))`:

(3)   "I will try to make my portraits."

```
(t / try-01
    :time (a / after
            :op1 (n / now)))
```

Past Time. We mark expressions of semantically past tense when the event time occurs prior to speech time. Typical target expressions are past tense verbs, though not all uses of morphological past tense reflect past time.[13] Targets are annotated with `:time (b / before :op1 (n / now))`.

(4)   "I pondered over the adventures of the jungle."

```
(p / ponder-01
    :time (b / before
            :op1 (n / now)))
```

Continuative Time. The English perfect can indicate that an eventuality has been in effect up to the present moment, without specifying whether it will continue.[14] We represent this with up-to in the AMR (as contrasted with AMR's current until, indicating an endpoint of the eventuality's duration):

(5)   "The wildfire has spread." (to its current size, and may not be done spreading)

```
(s / spread-02
    :time (u / up-to
            :op1 (n / now)))
```

Discourse Time. Often, the time reference of a event is sensitive to the structure of the discourse, which is not fully determined by the grammatical tense of the predicate. In such cases, we omit `:time` annotation and leave the sentence temporally underspecified. This occurs in two primary circumstances:

1. *Sequence of tense / embedded clause environments.* For example, in *"He said the elephant was noisy"*, we annotate the matrix clause frame `say-01` with past time, leaving the embedded clause bare.

2. *Ongoing narrative / discourse.* In the course of discussing a situation that takes place in the past or future, the use of tense may not always signal a contrast with the present, but may simply reflect the frame of reference for the situation. For the sentence sequence, *"There was a book on the table. It was in Russian."* (Klein, 1994), we do not consider the book's being Russian to be limited to the past. Thus, we omit `:time` annotation on the second sentence, letting it fall out from the discourse.[15]

3.5 Aspect

Grammatical aspect may be understood as the *how* of an eventuality, in comparison to the *when* denoted by grammatical tense. Our basic approach to aspect is summarized in table 2. It relies on the following features:[16]

:stable + / - We use this role only to refer to states, capturing the canonical distinction between events and states in our annotation. Examples of `:stable +` states are those that are permanent characteristics of individuals or entities that last a lifetime; acquired states that signal a (mostly) irreversible change; and identity relationships. `:stable +` is also used to mark stative generalizations over kinds (Friedrich et al., 2016). `:stable -` states are likely to change, including transitory states that are bounded in time; point states that are bounded and exist at a single point in time; and descriptions that vary by context or time.[17]

---

[13]Clear examples of these non-past time uses are conditionals (*"If our team lost tomorrow, it would be a disaster"*) and polite requests (*"I wanted to ask you..."*)

[14]The English perfect has additional uses, which we address in §4.

[15]It is often difficult to decide when discourse time is established, how long it is maintained for, and when it needs to be reestablished. We do not have specific guidelines on this point as of now, and look forward to further work on multi-sentence AMR to fully elaborate this standard.

[16]Throughout we cite terminology established by Vendler (1957) and utilized by others in linguistic research (Abusch, 1985; Levin, 1993; Rothstein, 2008; Croft, 2012). Readers are directed to these source for clarification on any linguistic terminology.

[17]Exceptional copula constructions that are not marked as stative are discussed in §4.

	APPLIES TO ANY AND ALL STATIVE EVENTUALITIES.
`:stable +/-`	`:stable +` → inherent/permanent states *Stella **is** French.* `:stable -` → temporary/transitory/non-inherent states *Stella **is** (currently) in France.*
`:ongoing +/-/?`	APPLIES TO EPISODIC EVENTS (BOTH TELIC AND ATELIC). `:ongoing +` → unbounded event / event in progress viewed from interior *I **am looking for** a sheep.* `:ongoing -` → bounded event / event viewed as a whole from exterior *I **walked** all over the city yesterday.* `:ongoing ?` → event that has been in progress and may yet continue *I **have been walking** all over the city today.*
`:complete +/-`	APPLIES ONLY TO REALIZED, TELIC EVENTS IN COMBINATION WITH `:ongoing +/-`. `:complete -` → realized, telic event that is ongoing/in process, or has ended and not reached completion *Lucas **mowed** the lawn for an hour (but did not finish).* `:complete +` → realized, telic event that has ended and reached completion *Lucas **read** the entire book.*
`:habitual +`	APPLIES TO REGULARLY RECURRENT EVENTUALITIES; CANNOT BE USED WITH `:stable +`, `:ongoing`, OR `:complete`. *Boa constrictors **swallow** their prey whole.*

Table 2: Basic annotation for aspectual types. As shown in table 1, the `:stable +/-` annotation applies to states; `:ongoing +/-/?` and `:complete +/-` apply to dynamic episodic events; and `:habitual +` applies to non-episodic eventualities.

As states often possess lasting duration, their temporal nature may be unclear. Below, we annotate `:time` (above) only if there is a clear semantic time for the state; otherwise, we leave time underspecified.

(6) "It was a picture of a boa constrictor."[18]

```
(p / picture :stable +
   :domain (i / it))
```

(7) "He was in Turkish costume."

```
:ARG2 (c / costume-01 :stable -
      :ARG1 (h / he)
      :time (b / before
         :op1 (n / now)))
```

So-called "inactive actions," also known as "progressive states", may be analyzed as either `:stable +/-`. This depends on the nature of the individuals or entities involved in the sentence and the nature of the verb. An example of such a contrast is as follows: *"The Sandia mountains lie to the east of Albuquerque"* `:stable +` versus *"The box is lying/lies on the bed"* `:stable -` (Croft, 2012).

`:ongoing + / - / ?` This role indicates the interior or exterior perspective on the event signaled by the grammatical tense. `:ongoing +`, corresponding to the canonical use of the progressive BE + V-ing with dynamic episodic events,[19] signals that the perspective is from the interior of the event, when it is in progress (Comrie, 1976; Portner, 1998).[20] `:ongoing +` can combine with past, present, or future time to mark the progression of both atelic activities with intransitive predicates (*"He was/is/will be eating"*) and telic activities with transitive predicates (*"He was/is/will be eating a sandwich"*).[21]

(8) "He was looking for a sheep."

---

[18] `:time` is absent from this annotation, as it reflects discourse time; see above.

[19] Other uses of the progressive that are *not* `:ongoing +` include *"The box is lying on the bed"* (`:stable -`; see above) and the present progressive signaling future time, e.g. *"I am leaving for Paris tomorrow"* (aspectually annotated as `:ongoing -`).

[20] This is similar to the imperfective aspect, though imperfective aspect may be understood to include progressives, iteratives, and habituals (Dowty, 1986; Comrie, 1985). We have a special category for the latter; see `:habitual +`. Iteratives are simplified here as atelic events and may be annotated as `:ongoing +`. (*"The light flickers occasionally"*) and `:ongoing -` (*"The light flickered all day"*).

[21] Undirected activities used to describe present disposition (*"He's being a jerk again"*) as well as construals of transitory states (*"Mary's sitting on the sofa"*) are understood here to be stative (Croft, 2012), and are marked accordingly as `:stable -`.

```
(l2 / look-01 :ongoing +
     :time (b / before
          :op1 (n / now)))
```

`:ongoing ?` is used with an episodic event that may continue or not, as in (5); this is signaled in certain constructions using the English perfect (§4). All other episodic events are `:ongoing -`.

:complete + / - We use this role only with episodic, realized, telic events, i.e. directed events that include a measurable change in the status of one of the verb's arguments and that have or are taking place.[22] As such, the annotation `:ongoing +/-/?` is a prerequisite for adding `:complete +/-`. complete + events are commonly associated with English simple past tense constructions for events that have a result state different from the initial state (i.e. prototypical accomplishments and achievements; semelfactives and activities lack marking of `:complete +/-`). Again, as AMR considers tense and aspect at the sentence level, typical activity verbs (such as *jump*, (9)) may be construed as telic depending on their use in the sentence as a whole.

(9) "I jumped to my feet, completely thunderstruck."

```
(j / jump-03 :ongoing - :complete +
     :destination (f / foot)
     :time (b / before
          :op1 (n / now)))
```

Likewise, transitive constructions that typically receive telic interpretations due to the nature of their arguments (*"I read a book last night"*) may be construed as atelic (*"I read poems last night"*). Though rare in corpora, an example of `:ongoing - :complete -` is a sentence of finite temporal duration with a telic verb that has not reached completion: *"I ate lunch for an hour."* Alternatively, a telic event that is in progress is `:ongoing + :complete -`: *"I am eating a sandwich right now."*

:habitual + Most basically, `:habitual +` indicates aggregation of occurrences of events or `:stable -` states, implying they are recurrent.[23] `:habitual +` is used for clauses that contain a lexically dynamic verb and that denote a regular recurrence of an event, whether generic (*"Bears usually eat blueberries"*) or specific (*"I used to make pie daily in summer"*) (Mathew and Katz, 2009). This contrasts with episodic events, which refer to specific finite, irregular events (*"Mary ate oatmeal for breakfast yesterday"*). `:habitual +` also applies to recurring `:stable -` states (*"Mary is always in her seat when the bell rings"*). This contrasts with `:stable +`, which applies to inherent characteristics of kinds or individuals (Friedrich et al., 2016).

4 Challenging Phenomena

Many phenomena related to tense and aspect are noteworthy for their complexity and debated in the literature cited in §2; these phenomena are additionally challenging for annotation frameworks that attempt to distill such phenomena into clean categories and relations (§2.2).

The phenomena discussed here are presented as a result of the challenges our own annotators encountered during initial pilot tasks. In the process of developing the current annotation scheme, we conducted two pilot annotation studies (each using slightly modified annotation roles and guidelines) to validate and update our approach. Two expert annotators individually annotated a total of 200 existing AMRs for *The Little Prince* (the only text written for a non-specialist audience for which AMRs are publicly available), calculated inter-annotator agreement[24] at the overall level and for individual AMRs, and then discussed areas of agreement and disagreement. To address disagreements, we have developed a thorough set of

---

[22]The criteria of 'realized' alludes to a distinction we explain further in §4 for modality. We recognize that this currently does not allow us to specify the telicity of non-realized events, an issue we will address as we further develop the annotation scheme. Telic events may be formally understood as accomplishments or achievements (Vendler, 1957).

[23]The current annotation scheme is unable to capture event quantification intermediary between `:habitual +` and `:ongoing -`, such as *"I ate a an apple every hour for the whole day"*. We leave this work to future developments of the scheme. The reader is directed to more recent work on such matters for reference (Bunt and Pustejovsky, 2010).

[24]We do not present these numbers as the scheme has since evolved on the basis of the disagreements.

annotation guidelines with which to provide annotators. Currently, a larger-scale pilot study is under way with non-expert annotators that will allow us to further evaluate these guidelines and the labels presented here. Some key challenging phenomena are enumerated below.

4.1 The perfect

The semantics of the English (and cross-linguistic) perfect is far from straightforward (Anderson, 1982; Portner, 1998; Croft, 2012). We recognize three semantic categories of the perfect:

(i) CONTINUATIVE casts an eventuality as having lasted up to the present moment, without specifying whether it will continue. In the present perfect, these receive time annotation of :time (u / up-to :op1 (n / now)). In the past and future perfects, the time is specified as before or after now, and if there is an appropriate temporal reference point in the AMR due to an adverbial, time up-to that point is also specified. Aspectual annotation depends on the nature of the eventuality: *"The wildfire has spread"* as in (5) is :ongoing ?; *"Mary has lived in London for five years"* is :stable +; and *"I have been visiting the hospital daily"* is :habitual +.

(ii) EXISTENTIAL, emphasizing that something has happened ever, at least once in the past: *"The Orioles have won three World Series championships"*. Modifying our treatment of past time, we annotate this with :time (b / before :mod (e / ever) :op1 (n / now)). Aspect is annotated as usual.

(iii) RECENT, emphasizing that something has recently happened: *"The Orioles have won!"*, *"I've decided to stay home tonight."* Modifying our treatment of past time, we annotate this with :time (b / before :mod (j / just) :op1 (n / now)). Aspect is annotated as usual.

4.2 Quotations

Currently, we annotate tense/aspect in quotations as if they were independent sentences. A deeper representation would relate the time of the quoted content to the time of the containing sentence, which is better left to discourse-level tense and aspect annotation. We also annotate the speech act predicate in the AMR that corresponds to quotation marks, even in the absence of an explicit speech verb.

4.3 Copula Constructions

Copula constructions are annotated following the guidelines for :stable +/- unless exceptional as described here. Presentational copulas (*"Here is the book you loaned me."*) are only annotated for semantically salient :time. Existential copulas (*"There is a hat on the table."*) are marked for semantically salient :time and as :stable -. Categorical copulas (*"This is a hat."*) are annotated as :stable +; :time is only added if semantically salient. Finally, certain uses of the copula, such as in identificational constructions (*"It is/was John who ate the cake."*), function semantically like auxiliaries to an embedded clause and are left bare in the current annotation scheme.

4.4 Inceptive States

Stative verbs may be coerced to have achievement readings, such as *"He suddenly **knew** the answer"* or *"The students **got bored** in class yesterday."* In such construals, the verb marks the initial boundary of a state and may be understood as *start/begin to* VERB or *become* VERB (Breu, 1994; Croft, 2012). We mark such inceptive states as :ongoing - (:complete +, if realized), although the frames that indicate the completion of inception vary depending on the construction: know-01 itself would be marked as :ongoing - :complete + in the first example, while get-03 would be marked as a special *become* sense of the verb in the second example.[25]

4.5 Negation

AMR currently marks negation cues as :polarity -, without detailing scope, focus, or negated events. No explicit differentiation is made between syntactic, lexical, and morphological negation. We adapt our current annotation scheme to this practice and annotate sentence-level temporal and aspectual information as if :polarity - were not present. For example: *"I never learned to draw anything"* is annotated

---

[25]Cross-linguistic work may elucidate how best to annotate these construals in future work. For example, the inchoative (Finnish, Lithuanian) explicitly marks these and the perfective aspect in Romance changes stative verbs to achievement verbs.

as :polarity - :ongoing - :complete + :time (b / before :op1 (n / now)). Though this will sometimes result in fully labeling unrealized events (contrary to §3.5), AMR's treatment of negation does not differentiate realized events (*"The patient did not test positive"*) from unrealized events (*"The patient was not tested"*).

4.6 Conditionals and modals

Though space does not permit us to outline the entirety of issues raised by modality and conditionals, it is worth making several observations.

(i) AMR does not canonicalize modal meanings expressed verbally. Thus *"You need to leave"*, *"You are required to leave"*, and *"You must leave"* are essentially paraphrases, but the modality is semantically represented as `need-01`, `require-01`, and `obligate-01` (the canonical frame for modal auxiliaries of requirement). Though we hope to address this discrepancy in a future proposal, for now we annotate as follows: Canonical modal frames in AMR (`obligate-01`, `possible-01`, `permit-01`, etc.) do not receive annotation; rather, their embedded verbs receive annotation for both tense and aspect following above guidelines. Auxiliaries that are represented lexically in the AMR (such as `need-01` and `require-01`) are annotated for tense and aspect themselves; their embedded verbs receive no annotation.

(ii) AMR does not in general mark a distinction between realis (realized) and irrealis (future, hypothetical, desired, etc.) eventualities, apart from certain expressions of negation (see above). For example, *"I tried to eat"* and *"I managed to eat"* differ only in the predicate frame for the matrix verb (`try-01` vs. `manage-02`); the PropBank frame lexicon does not mark that the ARG1 of `manage-02` is realis while the ARG1 of `try-01` is irrealis.[26] We do not attempt to fully distinguish realis and irrealis eventualities in assigning tense and aspect to modal/conditional eventualities. However, we allude to future work in this area by only marking :complete +/- on realized events. This decision is driven by the idea that a goal-oriented event cannot be assessed for culmination or completion if it has not occurred.

(iii) Modal auxiliaries and conditionals can be used generically (*"I can eat an entire pizza by myself"*; *"If I am really hungry, I get angry"*) and non-generically (*"I couldn't sleep last night"*; *"If you don't eat that slice, I will"*). While conditional relations in AMR are typically expressed with :condition, this can be reified to `have-condition-91` for adding :habitual + when the conditional as a whole is generic.

(iv) Deontic and related modalities (Palmer, 2001) refer to future but uncertain events. Thus the eventuality in question should be annotated with future time.

5   Conclusions and Future Work

This paper has proposed a framework for enhancing the Abstract Meaning Representation to encode the semantics of tense and aspect in English. As with most complex annotation tasks, many cases are nontrivial to categorize for tense and aspect. Striking a balance between specifying tense and aspect information in detail, while keeping the annotation task realistic and scalable, presents a challenge.

The current framework is coarse-grained and leaves room for further consideration of extensions such as more precise temporal relations between events, and the annotation of tense/aspect phenomena at the discourse level. We plan to examine additional genres, expecting differences in the distribution of temporal and aspectual categories—e.g., we speculate that present time, future time, and progressive aspect will be more common in speech than writing. Finally, since AMR has been adapted to other languages (Xue et al., 2014; Li et al., 2016; Migueles-Abraira et al., 2018), it is worth more fully examining how the expression of tense and aspect in other languages reflects deeper cross-linguistic semantics that AMR could capture.

Acknowledgements

We are grateful to Tim O'Gorman, Lori Levin, James Pustejovsky, Paul Portner, Nancy Chang, and members of the NERT research group at Georgetown for helpful discussions, and to anonymous reviewers for their feedback. Regan and Croft are supported by funding from the Defense Threat Reduction Agency under grant number HDTRA1-15-1-0063. Donatelli's research was partially sponsored by the

---

[26]Though neither embedded verb would receive a label following the current scheme, we provide the example as fodder for future work.

Army Research Laboratory and was accomplished under Cooperative Agreement Number W911NF-18-2-0066. The views and conclusions contained in this document are those of the authors and should not be interpreted as representing the official policies, either expressed or implied, of the Army Research Laboratory or the U.S. Government. The U.S. Government is authorized to reproduce and distribute reprints for Government purposes notwithstanding and copyright notation herein.

References

Dorit Abusch. 1985. *On verbs and time*. Doctoral dissertation. University of Massachusetts, Amherst.

James F. Allen, Mary Swift, and Will de Beaumont. 2008. Deep semantic analysis of text. In *Proc. of the 2008 Conference on Semantics in Text Processing*, STEP '08, pages 343–354, Stroudsburg, PA, USA.

James F. Allen. 1984. Towards a general theory of action and time. *Artificial Intelligence*, 23:123–54.

Lloyd B. Anderson. 1982. The 'perfect' as a universal and as a language-specific category. In Paul J. Hopper, editor, *Tense-aspect: Between semantics and pragmatics*, pages 227–264. John Benjamins, Amsterdam.

Emmon Bach. 1986. The algebra of events. *Linguistics and philosophy*, 9(1):5–16.

Laura Banarescu, Claire Bonial, Shu Cai, Madalina Georgescu, Kira Griffitt, Ulf Hermjakob, Kevin Knight, Philipp Koehn, Martha Palmer, and Nathan Schneider. 2013. Abstract Meaning Representation for sembanking. In *Proc. of the 7th Linguistic Annotation Workshop and Interoperability with Discourse*, pages 178–186, Sofia, Bulgaria, August.

Walter Breu. 1994. Interactions between lexical, temporal and aspectual meanings. *Studies in Language. International Journal sponsored by the Foundation "Foundations of Language"*, 18(1):23–44.

Harry Bunt and James Pustejovsky. 2010. Annotating temporal and event quantification. In *Proc. of 5th ISA Workshop*.

Nancy Chang, Daniel Gildea, and Srini Narayanan. 1998. A dynamic model of aspectual composition. In Morton Ann Gernsbacher and Sharon J. Derry, editors, *Proc. of CogSci*, pages 226–231, Madison, WI, USA, August.

Nancy Chang. 1997. A motor-and image-schematic analysis of aspectual composition. Technical Report TR-97-034, International Computer Science Institute, Berkeley, CA, September.

Bernard Comrie. 1976. *Aspect*. Cambridge University Press, Cambridge MA.

Bernard Comrie. 1985. *Tense*. Cambridge University Press, Cambridge MA.

William Croft. 2012. *Verbs: Aspect and Causal Structure*. Oxford University Press, Oxford, UK, March.

David R. Dowty. 1986. The effects of aspectual class on the temporal structure of discourse: semantics or pragmatics? *Linguistics and Philosophy*, 9(1):37–61.

Annemarie Friedrich and Alexis Palmer. 2014. Automatic prediction of aspectual class of verbs in context. In *Proc. of ACL*, Baltimore, USA.

Annemarie Friedrich, Alexis Palmer, and Manfred Pinkal. 2016. Situation entity types: Automatic classification of clause-level aspect. In *Proc. of ACL*, pages 1757–1768, Berlin, Germany, August.

Erhard Hinrichs. 1986. Temporal anaphora in discourses of English. *Linguistics and philosophy*, 9(1):63–82.

Wolfgang Klein. 1994. *Time in language*. Routledge, London.

Ronald W. Langacker. 1982. Remarks on English aspect. In Paul J. Hopper, editor, *Tense-aspect: Between semantics and pragmatics*, pages 265–304. John Benjamins, Amsterdam.

Ronald W Langacker. 1987. *Foundations of cognitive grammar: Theoretical prerequisites*, volume 1. Stanford University Press.

Beth Levin. 1993. *English verb classes and alternations: A preliminary investigation*. University of Chicago Press.

Bin Li, Yuan Wen, Lijun Bu, Weiguang Qu, and Nianwen Xue. 2016. Annotating The Little Prince with Chinese AMRs. In *Proc. of LAW X – the 10th Linguistic Annotation Workshop*, pages 7–15, Berlin, Germany, August.

Thomas A. Mathew and E. Graham Katz. 2009. Supervised categorization for habitual versus episodic sentences. In *Sixth Midwest Computational Linguistics Colloquium*, Bloomington, Indiana.

Christian Matthiessen and John A. Bateman. 1991. Text generation and systemic-functional linguistics: Experiences from english and japanese.

Noelia Migueles-Abraira, Rodrigo Agerri, and Arantza Diaz de Ilarraza. 2018. Annotating Abstract Meaning Representations for Spanish. In Nicoletta Calzolari, Khalid Choukri, Christopher Cieri, Thierry Declerck, Sara Goggi, Koiti Hasida, Hitoshi Isahara, Bente Maegaard, Joseph Mariani, Hélène Mazo, Asuncion Moreno, Jan Odijk, Stelios Piperidis, and Takenobu Tokunaga, editors, *Proc. of LREC*, pages 3074–3078, Miyazaki, Japan, May.

Marc Moens and Mark Steedman. 1988. Temporal ontology and temporal reference. *Computational Linguistics*, 14(2):15–28.

Nasrin Mostafazadeh, Alyson Grealish, Nathanael Chambers, James Allen, and Lucy Vanderwende. 2016. CaTeRS: Causal and temporal relation scheme for semantic annotation of event structures. In *Proc. of the Fourth Workshop on Events*, pages 51–61, San Diego, California, June. Association for Computational Linguistics.

Tim O'Gorman, Kristin Wright-Bettner, and Martha Palmer. 2016. Richer Event Description: Integrating event coreference with temporal, causal and bridging annotation. In *Proc. of the 2nd Workshop on Computing News Storylines*, pages 47–56, Austin, Texas, USA, November.

Tim O'Gorman, Michael Regan, Kira Griffitt, Ulf Hermjakob, Kevin Knight, and Martha Palmer. 2018. AMR beyond the sentence: the Multi-sentence AMR corpus. In *Proc. of COLING*, Santa Fe, New Mexico, USA, August.

Martha Palmer, Daniel Gildea, and Paul Kingsbury. 2005. The Proposition Bank: An annotated corpus of semantic roles. *Computational Linguistics*, 31(1):71–106, March.

Frank Robert Palmer. 2001. *Mood and modality*. Cambridge University Press.

Barbara H Partee. 1999. Nominal and temporal semantic structure: Aspect and quantification. *Prague Linguistic Circle Papers: Travaux du cercle linguistique de Prague nouvelle série*, 3:91.

Paul Portner. 1998. The progressive in modal semantics. *Language*, 74(4):760, December.

James Pustejovsky, José M. Castaño, Robert Ingria, Roser Saurí, Robert J. Gaizauskas, Andrea Setzer, Graham Katz, and Dragomir R. Radev. 2003. TimeML: Robust specification of event and temporal expressions in text. In *IWCS-5, Fifth International Workshop on Computational Semantics*, Tilburg, Netherlands, January.

James Pustejovsky, Harry Bunt, and Annie Zaenen. 2017. Designing annotation schemes: From theory to model. In *Handbook of Linguistic Annotation*, pages 21–72. Springer.

James Pustejovsky. 2017. ISO-Space: Annotating static and dynamic spatial information. In *Handbook of Linguistic Annotation*, pages 989–1024. Springer.

Roi Reichart and Ari Rappoport. 2010. Tense sense disambiguation: A new syntactic polysemy task. In *Proc. of the 2010 Conference on Empirical Methods in Natural Language Processing*, pages 325–334, Cambridge, MA, October.

Hans Reichenbach. 1947. *Elements of symbolic logic*. The Free Press, New York.

Susan Rothstein. 2008. Telicity, atomicity and the Vendler classification of verbs. *Theoretical and Crosslinguistic Approaches to Aspect*, pages 43–77.

Carlota S. Smith. 2008. Time with and without tense. In *Time and Modality*, Studies in Natural Language and Linguistic Theory, pages 227–249. Springer, Dordrecht.

Zeno Vendler. 1957. Verbs and times. *The Philosophical Review*, 66:143–60.

Nianwen Xue, Ondřej Bojar, Jan Hajič, Martha Palmer, Zdeňka Urešová, and Xiuhong Zhang. 2014. Not an interlingua, but close: comparison of English AMRs to Chinese and Czech. In Nicoletta Calzolari, Khalid Choukri, Thierry Declerck, Hrafn Loftsson, Bente Maegaard, Joseph Mariani, Asuncion Moreno, Jan Odijk, and Stelios Piperidis, editors, *Proc. of LREC*, pages 1765–1772, Reykjavík, Iceland, May.

Yuchen Zhang and Nianwen Xue. 2014. Automatic inference of the tense of Chinese events using implicit linguistic information. In *Proc. of EMNLP*, pages 1902–1911, Doha, Qatar, October.

A Syntax-Based Scheme for the Annotation and Segmentation of German Spoken Language Interactions

Swantje Westpfahl
Institut für Deutsche Sprache
Mannheim, Germany
westpfahl@ids-mannheim.de

Jan Gorisch
Institut für Deutsche Sprache
Mannheim, Germany
gorisch@ids-mannheim.de

Abstract

Unlike corpora of written language where segmentation can mainly be derived from orthographic punctuation marks, the basis for segmenting spoken language corpora is not predetermined by the primary data, but rather has to be established by the corpus compilers. This impedes consistent querying and visualization of such data. Several ways of segmenting have been proposed, some of which are based on syntax. In this study, we developed and evaluated annotation and segmentation guidelines in reference to the topological field model for German. We can show that these guidelines are used consistently across annotators. We also investigated the influence of various interactional settings with a rather simple measure, the word-count per segment and unit-type. We observed that the word count and the distribution of each unit type differ in varying interactional settings and that our developed segmentation and annotation guidelines are used consistently across annotators. In conclusion, our syntax-based segmentations reflect interactional properties that are intrinsic to the social interactions that participants are involved in. This can be used for further analysis of social interaction and opens the possibility for automatic segmentation of transcripts.

1 Introduction

Since the beginning of research on spoken language, many different proposals for the segmentation of spoken language have been proposed. However, there is presently no segmentation system that could be used for large corpora of spoken language, i.e. a system that is linguistically substantiated as well as workable for large scale corpus segmentation. The lack of such a theory-based segmentation impedes the use of the corpora for research on language technology, comparative corpus linguistics as well as analyses in terms of spoken language interaction.

Focusing on the syntactic segmentation of such data has several advantages. Firstly, syntax theory is well understood in its application to written language corpora, so there are many tools for further processing of the data based on the scheme of syntactic units (e.g. POS, parsers, etc.). Secondly, a shallow syntactic segmentation and annotation can be used as a basis for linguistic analyses, also with various syntactic theories, pragmatic or prosodic approaches.

The need for a new segmentation of transcript data is based on the fact that the FOLK corpus (Schmidt, 2014b) in the DGD (data base for spoken German) (Schmidt, 2014a) is currently only segmented according to inter-pausal units, i.e. pauses longer than 0.2 seconds mark the boundary of each segment. This results in either very long sequences of speech when the speakers do not pause, or in segments of only partial structures when speakers make many pauses. This has two major disadvantages: One is the inconsistent visual representation that hinders researchers doing qualitative analyses based on transcripts, as it is common among conversation analysts, for example. The other is the limited value of such transcripts for contextually structured searches on the entire corpus, e.g. "Search for all instances of discourse markers at the beginning of a segment". Figure 1 shows an example of a very long speaker contribution that is merely segmented through pauses. Thus, the goal of a segmentation based on syntactic principles is that users of our corpus will be able to find whatever they are looking for in syntactic units rather than in inter-pausal units.

Proceedings of the Joint Workshop on
Linguistic Annotation, Multiword Expressions and Constructions (LAW-MWE-CxG-2018), pages 109–120
Santa Fe, New Mexico, USA, August 25-26, 2018.

0106 FL   [mit einem]

0107   (0.32)

0108 FL   r radius von zweihundertfünfzig meter für den es eine (.) ausnahmegenehmigung brauch was aber durchaus genehmigungsfähig is °h wo die güterzüge dann noch mit tempo achzig °h fahren könnten °h sie haben dann an beiden enden auch wieder die vorher schon besagten überwerfungsbauwerke da sie diese bahnstrecke °h kreuzungsfrei ausschleifen müssen °h insbesondere im bereich (.) der (.) remstalbahn vor dem (.) bahnhof (.) vor der es bahn haltestelle nürnberger straße °h ham sie dann den zustand dass dies sie die heute (sch) viergleisige trasse °h die in eimen engen einschnitt dort liegt (.) auf (.) sechs gleise aufweiten müssten

0109   (0.21)

0110 FL   °h was mit erheblichen (.) eingriffen in die (randbitter) bauung (.) äh ein einhergehen würde °h sie ham hier dann noch den bereich (.) mit einem gymnasium dem elly heuss knapp (.) gymnasium °h äh wo davon auszugehen wäre dass die überdeckung in diesem bereich des tunnels sehr gering wäre °h wo mer fragen muss ob das gebäude so (.) bestand haben könnte °h oder hinterher dann neu erstellt werden müsste

Figure 1: Example of the inconsistent visual representation of the data because of the current inter-pausal segmentation in the DGD, cf. Transkript FOLK_E_00064_SE_01_T_02_DF_01, 01:03:44.53 - 01:04:38.91.

In our study, we sampled a sub-corpus of various types of interactions. We developed a segmentation and annotation scheme based on the syntactic analysis of topological fields, i.e. the position of the finite verb and the complexity of the depending structures. We segmented and annotated this corpus according to this scheme. We validated the scheme and the reliability of the results with inter-annotator-agreement measures.

The research questions we aim at answering in this paper are: How reliable are segmentations and annotations on this kind of data, and where are the limits of syntax theory with transcripts of spoken language interaction? An additional question that arises naturally from the way we set up our test corpus is: How does syntax differ between interaction types?

2   Related work

As an approach for the descriptive analysis of the surface structure of the German syntax, the topological field model based on Drach (1937) has been widely discussed and further developed, e.g. by Wöllstein (2010; 2014) or Pittner and Berman (2013). In corpus linguistics, this model also has been used for the annotation of written data like the TüBa-D/Z (Telljohann et al., 2006), learner data like the Falco corpus (Reznicek et al., 2012), and to some extent also on transcriptions of spoken language (Andersen, 2008; Stegmann et al., 2000). In these works, the annotation of the topological fields is based on an existent segmentation of the data and is used as a basis for further linguistic analysis such as parsing as demonstrated e.g by Becker and Frank (2002). However, no solutions have been proposed for the annotation of typical spoken language phenomena as described below and thus their schemes for the annotation of topological fields cannot be used as a basis for the segmentation of transcripts of spoken language.

Since the development of oral corpora, the question and the need for a segmentation model of such data has been discussed. To date, segmentation into inter-pausal units is common for spoken language corpora as for example in the Switchboard corpus (Hamaker et al., 1998). However, for the analysis of syntactic structures a segmentation like this is not satisfying. Unlike sentences in written language data, transcripts of spoken interactions contain many features that do not appear in written language syntax. As Deppermann and Proske (2015) point out, many of the strategies for successful communication used by speakers is not sentence-like such as overlapping speech and collaborative turns, disruptions, ellipses and analepses, right and left dislocations, free topics, apokoinu constructions, vocatives and various types of speech particles such as backchannel signals, hesitation markers, and interjections.

Also Auer (2010) highlights the problems of transferring insights from research on written data to the analysis of spoken data and postulates four methodological principles considering the segmentation of corpus data. a) Exhaustiveness, i.e. the segmentation cannot leave out any material; b) Atomism, i.e. the segments must not include other segments of the same type; c) Discreteness, i.e. one element must not be part of more than one segment, e.g. segment boundaries have to be clearly defined; d) Coherence of the linguistic level (Ebenenkonstanz), i.e. the segmentation has to be based on one approach of linguistic description. These principles must be considered in developing an approach for large scale corpus segmentation.

Many of the segmentation approaches proposed so far seem to work for selected examples or for specific types of data but violate at least one of Auer's methodological principles when it comes to the segmentation of entire corpora. However, some schemes have been developed specifically with the aim of corpus segmentation. In a pilot study, we assessed each of the following schemes (GAT2, HIAT, Macrosyntax) using our corpus data. Selting et al. (2009) presents a transcription system called GAT2 (Gesprächsanalytisches Transkriptionssystem) that is widely used in the field of Conversation Analysis (CA) for the representation of CA data extracts. According to GAT2, the segmentation of the data is based on the intonation phrase (IP), i.e. on prosodic cues. Problems with this approach arise from the fact that the definition for those IPs are circular in the GAT2 conventions and its criteria only vaguely defined as, e.g. in Grice and Bauman (2007) resulting in highly subjective interpretative annotations and segmentations. The circularity of these definitions can be explained as follows: the unit is defined by identifying "initial" or "final" movements in the intonation contour, i.e. the unit already has to be defined in order to identify the beginning and ending of it. Second, the definition gives several criteria for the identification of pitch movements pointing out that not all of them are necessary and some of them might be stronger or weaker in their presence. Thus, the definition remains rather vague and it is not clear which criteria must be fulfilled in order to constitute a unit (Selting et al., 2009, 370). We have encountered such problems in a test segmentation scenario in which three colleagues and experts on the field of conversation analysis have segmented the same transcript excerpts. The resulting segmentations turned out to be very different from one another.

With respect to pragmatic segmentation, two influential approaches have been proposed. The Handbook for computer-mediated transcription according to HIAT (Rehbein et al., 2004) relies on a method that translates into semi-interpretative working transcription (Halbinterpretative Arbeitstranskription) (Rehbein et al., 2004). The problem with this segmentation method is already implied in the title. It relies on subjective individual identification and interpretation of speech acts which proves to be problematic for a consistent analysis of the data especially with respect to inter-annotator agreements.

The second pragmatic approach is widely used in the segmentation of French oral corpora "Le protocol de codage macrosyntaxique". Strictly speaking, it is a mix of identifying illocutionary units with the help of the identification of structures according to dependency grammar (Benzitoun et al., 2012). Thus, this approach violates the principle of coherence of the linguistic level (cf. Auer (2010)). Moreover, first experiments on our German data with these guidelines have shown that in various cases the segmentation according to one linguistic level would contradict the other.

With respect to syntactic segmentation, there are two further approaches to be considered. The Analysis of Speech Unit (AS-unit) according to Foster et al. (2000) was developed for the segmentation and interpretation of English as a second language (ESL) and is based on the identification of syntactic structures taking into account typical spoken language phenomena. Yet, guidelines for the segmentation according to this approach are not published and there is no information on its performance with respect to inter-rater-agreements. The approach leaves the option for three levels of segmentation and only one level is supposed to segment the data exhaustively. Finally, it is advised that this kind of analysis should not be performed on data of very interactive interactions (Foster et al., 2000, 370f.).

Another approach for the segmentation according to a syntactic scheme was developed for texts of Early New High German where no punctuation is given and hence the segmentation of the data is necessarily done otherwise (Weiß and Schnelle, 2016). These guidelines describe several phenomena that also appear in transcripts of spoken language, such as parentheses and ellipses (Weiß and Schnelle, 2016). However, the most problematic cases for the segmentation of transcripts of spoken language such as disruptions, repetitions, and reported speech are not considered in that approach.

3 Material and method

3.1 Data and tools

The ultimate aim of our project is to find an approach to segmentation which can be applied on German as well as French and at the same time to analyze the language specific phenomena of each language. In order to be able to analyze various phenomena typical for spoken language interaction, it seems imperative to create a sample of various interaction types, which represent the variety of speech situations in our society (here, France and Germany). Hence, the pilot corpus comprises private interactions (e.g. family table talk) as well as public interactions (e.g. panel discussion or expert talk), informal face-to-face interactions (e.g. discussions with friends), and formal interactions, i.e. strongly governed by institutional rules (e.g. a school lesson or a panel discussion), speech influenced by written language (e.g. expert talk or reading a book to a child), and activity driven interactions (e.g. a cooking interaction or a service encounter), technically mediated communication (e.g. a telephone call between friends), and interactions with longer narrative passages (e.g. a biographical interview). Also, the number of speakers taking part in an interaction may vary from dyadic interactions to up to eleven participants. Moreover, the pilot corpus comprises data from speakers of the north, west, east, and south of Germany with some of them speaking rather standard high German and others speaking German influenced by their dialect. With this sampling we want to make sure that any segmentation scheme we develop is applicable for all of the data of our corpora in the DGD.

In sum, the German part of the pilot corpus that we are working on in this study comprises thirteen excerpts of transcripts from eleven interaction types. This amounts to about 110 minutes of audio material and about 22,150 tokens. The transcription is time-aligned with the audio data. For each transcription excerpt in German, there is an equivalent in French containing data of the same interaction type. The transcripts follow the cGAT transcription scheme (Schmidt et al., 2015) and are stored in the FOLKER format (Schmidt and Schütte, 2010). In order to change the segmentation and annotate the segments, we used the EXMARaLDA Partitur Editor (Schmidt, 2012).

3.2 Annotation and segmentation scheme

For the initial development of the segmentation guidelines we chose two transcripts: the telephone call and the panel discussion. They proved to exhibit many phenomena typical for spoken language interactions and also very different phenomena as the telephone call is a very interactive, private, and colloquial interaction whereas the panel discussion is structured by a moderator and the speakers can build very long and complex turns without anyone interrupting them. This way, we would already be faced with problematic structures typical for the different transcripts of spoken language in the development phase of the syntactic segmentation and annotation scheme.

Our first analyses of the data led to an inventory of segmentation problems, some of which are typical spoken language phenomena, some of them could appear in written language as well and especially so in computer mediated communication such as chat data or WhatsApp group communication. This inventory of segmentation problems can be grouped with respect to

1. specific phenomena on the word level such as discourse particles, hesitation markers, tag questions or vocatives,

2. characteristics of transcriptions themselves, such as transcribed breathing, nonverbal behaviour, vocal communication, pauses or alternative transcriptions, or

3. phenomena on the syntactic level such as disfluencies, disruptions, anacolutha, repairs, parenthesis, reported speech, expansions, lists with varying structures, ellipses, and collaborative turns.

Our syntactic segmentation and annotation scheme is composed of three annotation layers, which hierarchically depend on one another. The first annotation layer (cf. the second tier in Figure 2) is based on the identification of topological fields (Pittner and Berman, 2013; Wöllstein, 2014). The topological field model is based on the analysis of the surface structure of German sentences. One of the key features of the German language is the verb bracket, i.e. the parts of the verb are anchored in two major positions. The left bracket constitutes either the first or the second position of the sentence, i.e. there can only be one constituent before the left bracket is realized. The right bracket is always at the end of the sentence. The topological field model is based on the identification of the verb brackets. The first constituent would then be the pre-field (**VF**, Vorfeld), followed by the left bracket (**LK**, Linke Klammer, e.g. a finite (auxiliary) verb), followed by the middle field (**MF**, Mittelfeld) in which the arguments of the verb and adjuncts are realized, followed by the (optional) right bracket (**RK**, Rechte Klammer, e.g. an infinitive, participle or verb particle). If material is added preceding this structure, which is also related syntactically to the sentence, it is situated in the pre-pre-field (**VVF**, Vor-Vorfeld), e.g. left dislocations, discourse markers, etc. If there is material added following the right bracket, this will be placed either in the post-field (**NF**, Nachfeld) in the case of right dislocations, i.e. material which would usually be placed in the middle field, or in the right outer field (**RAF**, Rechtes Außenfeld), e.g. question tags.

transcription	ja	also	dies	[.]	soll	ein	äh	beispielsatz	sein	weil	man	beispielsätze	braucht	ne	(0.24)	hey
field	KA	VVF	VF	LK		MF			RK	LK	MF		RK	NF		KA
clause	KVS	V2								VL						KVS
maximal unit	C															N
translation	yes	well	this	(pause)	is supposed	an	uhm	example	to be	because	one	examples	needs	right		hey

Figure 2: Exemplary illustration of the segmentation and annotation scheme.

Our annotation scheme contains seven major categories for the annotation of topological fields as described, e.g. by Wöllstein (2010) or Pittner and Berman (2013). However, if the topological field cannot be specified because there is no verb in the utterance, we choose the annotation **KA** (keine Angabe - not specified). We also allow the possibility that the annotation of the topological field might be ambiguous (**AMB**) and that fields can be separated by parentheses in which case the field-annotations are numbered (**...-1/...-2**).

An annotation and segmentation scheme based on this model has several advantages. First, the identification of the syntactic structures relies on the surface structure of the text data, i.e. in the transcript, and explicitly not on characteristics that can only be found in the audio, e.g. prosodic features. This also helps to further process the data with automatic language processing tools that equally rely on the surface structure of the transcribed text. Second, the identification of the topological fields leads to the identification of larger syntactic structures, namely clauses. They also already provide the position of the finite verb and information on the type of clause that they occur in. In German, clauses with the finite verb in the second position are main clauses and mainly declarative sentences. If the finite verb is in the first position, e.g. if there is no pre-field, the clause is either an imperative, a question or sometimes a declarative with subject ellipsis, typical for colloquial speech (Auer, 1993). In German subordinate clauses, the finite verb is always in the last position.

In our annotation scheme, there are four major categories for clauses that contain a finite verb, the second of which has been newly introduced in our annotation scheme (cf. the second annotation layer (3rd tier) in Figure 2): **V1** for verb first clauses, **V1/2** for colloquial verb first clauses (e.g. subject ellipses), **V2** for verb-second clauses, and **VL** for verb-last clauses.

Moreover, we added a category for the typical spoken language phenomenon of apokoinu constructions (**APO**). Yet again, if there is no finite verb in the utterance, an annotation according to the topological field model is not possible. Thus, we added two categories that are based on pragmatic linguistic analyses; The first one is for utterances that are complete in their pragmatic function, yet do not yield a finite verb (**KVS**, Kein Verb aber satzwertig). The second category is for structures that do not contain a finite verb and that do not fulfil the function of a sentence either (**KVN**, Kein Verb und nicht satzwertig), i.e. anacolutha. Also on this layer, the clause might be interrupted by a parenthesis, in which case we number the clause-annotations (**...-1/...-2**). Thus, our annotation scheme allows an exhaustive annotation of the data.

The annotation of the clause types has the advantage that the relation between various clauses can be made visible, yet no information about their content gets lost. The dependencies between the various clauses are accounted for in the third annotation layer (cf. fourth tier in Figure 2), which at the same time represents the final segmentation of the data, i.e. the annotations of the maximal syntactic units. The categorisation of the maximal syntactic units represents the information gathered on the other levels of annotation and results in four categories (**S, C, N**, and **A**), which are specified as follows:

S: The simple sentential unit consists of one and only one V1, V1/2, V2 or in very exceptional cases VL without any dependencies, cf. Figure 3.

C: The complex sentential unit consists of several clauses that are dependent on one another: Main clauses with subordinate clauses or relative clauses, conditional sentences, reported speech, and matrix-clause with sentient-verbs, complex pre-pre-fields with main clause, discontinuous sentences, and coordinated sentences if and only if the second sentence shows subject or verb ellipsis, cf. Figure 2.

N: Non-sentential units are all units that are not structured by a finite verb. On the clause level they are either annotated as KVS or KVN such as: (Sequences of) interjections, responses, or reception signals, words, and phrases without a finite verb, e.g. nominal phrases or prepositional phrases, or vocal communication, non-verbal behaviour, unintelligible utterances or vocatives, respectively, cf. Figure 4.

A: An utterance which is disrupted, i.e. it opens a projection that is not fulfilled in what follows. This is segmented and tagged as abandoned unit (A), cf. Figure 5.

3.3 Segmentation problems and solutions

The categorisation already reflects some of the segmentation problems mentioned above. In addition, our guidelines provide additional rules for the handling of typical spoken language phenomena as well as for phenomena related to the transcription of spoken language. Thus, problems related to the groups (1.) and (2.) specified above, can be handled by simple rules that do not ground on any theory but that are rather formulated bearing in mind the ease of annotation and segmentation for the annotators.

Discourse particles such as interjections, response particles or reception signals always have a pragmatic meaning in context. Hence, they are segmented independently on the field and clause level, however, for matters of representation, they are subsumed on the maximal syntactic unit level as the initial "ja" in Figure 2 shows. Only when they occur surrounded by speaker pauses, they get their own, unspecified segment and are considered as non-sentential units, i.e. receive the tag "N" as the "hey" in Figure 2 shows. The example in Figure 3 illustrates the different handling of the discourse particle *ja* at the beginning and the transcribed breathing *hh°* at the end of the utterance.

EG [tok] [v]	ja	un	dann	ham	wir die feu	erwehr	angerufen	hh°
EG [tok] [Feld]	KA	VVF	VF	LK	MF		RK	
EG [tok] [POV]	KVS	V2						
EG [tok] [Max]	S							

Figure 3: Example for the annotation of discourse particles at the beginning of a turn.

In contrast, hesitation markers, if they co-occur with other parts of an utterance, are always segmented **within the following** segment as the "äh" in Figure 2. If the element is uttered at the end of a turn, it is segmented together with the preceding segment. Again, only when it occurs surrounded by speaker pauses, it gets its own, unspecified segment and is considered as non-sentential unit, i.e. receives the tag "N" as in Figure 4. The same rule holds true for transcribed breathing or micro pauses and any material that does not necessarily bear any semantic or pragmatic content.

Disruptions and self-corrections are a much bigger problem as they quite often result in ambiguous syntactic structures. In many cases, if at all, disambiguation is only possible with the help of context

SF [tok] [v]	äh
SF [tok] [Feld]	KA
SF [tok] [POV]	KVN
SF [tok] [Max]	N

Figure 4: Example for the annotation of hesitation markers surrounded by silence.

	ja	wie	er	das	hat	fallen	lassen	wei	wieso	hast	du	das	paket	eigentlich	fallen	lassen
EG [tok] [v]	ja	wie	er	das	hat	fallen	lassen	wei	wieso	hast	du	das	paket	eigentlich	fallen	lassen
EG [tok] [Feld]	KA	VF						LK	VF	LK	MF				RK	
EG [tok] [POV]	KVS	VL						V2	V2							
EG [tok] [Max]	A							S								
EG [tok] [v]	ja	wie	er	das	hat	fallen	lassen	wei	wieso	hast	du	das	paket	eigentlich	fallen	lassen
EG [tok] [Feld]	KA	VF						KA	VF	LK	MF				RK	
EG [tok] [POV]	KVS	VL						KVN	V2							
EG [tok] [Max]	S							A	S							

Figure 5: Example of an ambiguous case. The annotation guidelines indicate to take the lower option.

knowledge and/or knowledge about the prosody of the utterance as illustrated for the two annotation and segmentation versions of the example in Figure 5. By listening to the audio, one can guess that the disruption *wei* might have been the word *weiß* (know), which would result in the interpretation of a verb second clause preceded by a relative clause (first option). The whole structure would then have to be interpreted as an abandoned unit. If one, on the other hand, assumes that the verb-last clause is an exclamation, it would already constitute a unit for itself (second option). Thus, the abandoned unit would consist of the *wei* only. The solution we propose for this type of problem is parsing the data from the left to the right. If an utterance can be considered complete on the syntactic level, it is annotated as such (second option). This solution bears in mind future work with other language processing tools, most of which follow the same scheme.

3.4 Evaluation methods

We hired two student assistants who segmented and annotated the entire pilot corpus each and independently according to the scheme described above. In order to evaluate the annotation scheme, we measured the inter-annotator-agreement on the two annotated data sets, i.e. we calculated the raw agreement and a modified kappa value with the help of the ELAN tool (Wittenburg et al., 2006). The raw agreement measures the percentage of exactly similar segmentation and annotations. The modified kappa value uses the same basis but takes chance agreement into account. For the evaluation, we excluded the transcript excerpts used for the development of the guidelines, i.e. the telephone call and the panel discussion (cf. Table 4). The results are shown in Table 4.

In order to evaluate the segmented and annotated data, we chose a method proposed by Grabar and Eshkol (2016): we counted the segments and the tokens in each segment. This way we can retrieve information about the annotated segments with respect to (i) their length depending on the annotation (here: label), i.e. the average number of tokens in the segment, (ii) whether the average length of the segments differs with respect to the interaction type, and (iii) whether the annotators chose the same annotations in the same transcript type, i.e. whether the length of the segmentation and their labelling vary significantly. We used a chi-square test to evaluate the amount of syntactic unit types per interactional setting. Further, we used a linear regression model to predict the number of tokens in a segment by its label, the type of interaction, and the annotator (as well as all possible interactions). This model allows to address three questions at once: (a) Do segments differ in the number of tokens with respect to their labels? (b) Do annotators differ in their overall segmentations and labelling? (c) Do the number of tokens in segments of a specific category differ with respect to the annotator? The results of the latter questions also add to the analysis of inter-annotator-agreement.

4 Results and discussion

First, we present the results of the inter-annotator-agreement. As can be seen in Table 4, the results on inter-annotator agreement of topological fields are on average 84% raw agreement and result in a Kappa value of 0.81, indicating almost perfect agreement. The raw agreement on the clause level (pov) and on the maximal unit level (max) is slightly lower, i.e. around 74% and a Kappa value of 0.67, and 78% and a Kappa value of 0.69 respectively, indicating substantial agreement.

Table 1: Inter-Annotator-Agreement calculations (raw agreement and kappa) according to annotation layers (field, pov, max) and various interaction types. Excluded are the telephone call and the panel discussion, as they were the annotation training data.

metric	layer	Reading child	Table talk	Social meeting	Conflictual interac.	Expert talk	School lesson	Interview	Preparing meal	Service encounter	mean
raw agr.	[field]	89.55	82.32	79.36	80.11	79.32	87.97	84.13	89.26	87.33	**84.37**
	[pov]	81.02	72.43	65.53	65.29	71.88	71.69	74.25	83.01	80.80	**73.99**
	[max]	83.80	82.42	80.24	61.69	72.79	79.05	76.49	79.48	85.74	**85.74**
kappa	[field]	0.87	0.78	0.75	0.77	0.75	0.85	0.81	0.87	0.85	**0.81**
	[pov]	0.73	0.63	0.58	0.57	0.67	0.63	0.67	0.78	0.73	**0.67**
	[max]	0.76	0.70	0.68	0.53	0.63	0.69	0.69	0.71	0.71	**0.69**

The individual agreement measures indicate that the conflictual interaction as well as the meeting in the social institution are the most problematic transcript excerpts.

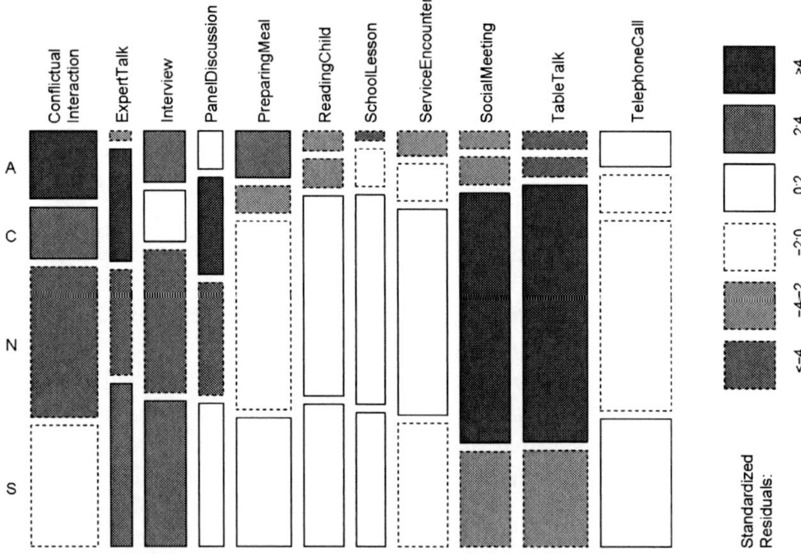

Figure 6: Mosaic plot: standardized residuals from the chi-square test showing the dependencies of the number of segments of a certain category with the interaction type. The height of the tiles represents the relative number of segments of each category in each transcript. The width of the tiles represents the number of segments in the whole transcript compared to the others.

The chi-square test reveals statistically significant differences in the distribution of unit types in the various interaction types. Figure 6 shows a mosaic plot visualizing the residuals of the test. For example, non-sentential units (N) are relatively less frequent in the conflictual interaction, the expert talk, the interview, and the panel discussion, but relatively more frequent in the social meeting and the family table talk. Most interactions mainly consist of non-sentential units (N) and simple sentential units (S) whereas the expert talk and the panel discussion have an increased number of complex sentential units (C) relative to their total number of segments.

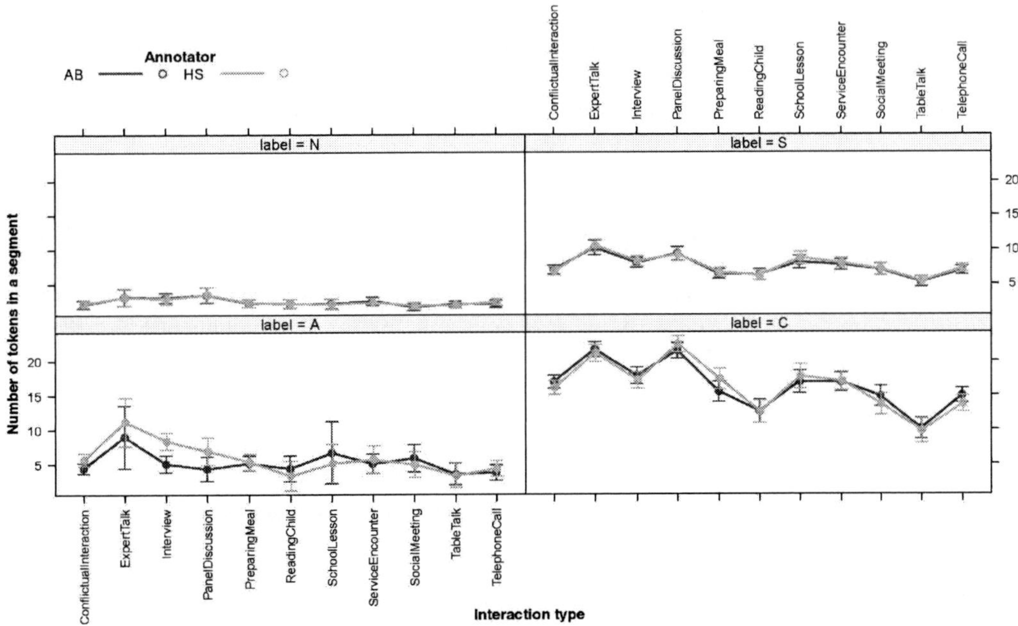

Figure 7: Effect plot: dependencies of the annotated categories (labels), the segment length (number of tokens in a segment along the y-axes), the interaction type (along the x-axes), and the annotators (AB = student assistant 1; HS = student assistant 2).

The linear regression model reveals statistically significant differences relating segment labels (N, S, A, and C), number of tokens, interaction types, and annotators. Figure 7 shows the effect plot. We can see that segments annotated as non-sentential units (N) are shorter in the number of tokens (with an average length of 2.26) than abandoned units (A) (with an average length of 5.09), which are in turn shorter than simple sentential units (S) (with an average length of 7.35 tokens), which are again shorter than complex sentential units (C) (with an average length of 16.84 tokens). These differences in the length of the segments are statistically significant, which implies that the categories we chose actually represent different syntactic phenomena. Moreover, the results show that different interaction types indeed vary significantly in the length of their syntactic units. Complex (C) and simple (S) sentential units are significantly longer in the expert talk than in all other types of interactions except for the panel discussion. In the table talk, the two unit types (C and S) are significantly shorter than in all other interactions except for the reading to the child interaction.

With respect to the annotations of the two annotators, one can see that only in the interview the annotations of the abandoned unit category differ statistically significantly from one another. Hence, one can see that even though we focused on this problem in writing the guidelines, the abandoned units seem to be a greater challenge to segment and annotate than other units. In a detailed qualitative analysis, we found that many cases in which the annotators disagreed with respect to abandoned units result in true structural and syntactic ambiguities. These results imply that we have to improve the guidelines in a way that default rules for ambiguous cases are offered. The segmentation and annotation of the gold standard will include these improvements, which will hopefully resolve the remaining disagreements.

5   Conclusion and perspectives

In this paper, we could show that syntactic units can be segmented and annotated fairly reliably, and that these annotations add valuable information to the data. Our evaluation showed that there are indeed statistically significant differences in the syntax used by speakers in different interactional settings. On the one hand, private interactions generally contain much more speech particles and other non-sentential segments than for example interactions in the public. Also, their sentential units such as simple and complex sentences are generally shorter than in other interactions. On the other hand, one can see that if the speakers have the floor, they tend to make much fewer but more complex and longer syntactic units and even abandoned units are significantly longer than in other interactions.

Generally, abandoned units, e.g. disruptions, self-corrections, and anacolutha are the greatest challenge for the segmentation and annotation of syntactic structures. In contrast to other annotation approaches of topological fields and syntactic structures (Stegmann et al., 2000), we explicitly do not exclude these typical spoken language phenomena from the annotation. Thus, our segmentation and annotation scheme allows for an exhaustive segmentation of the data and also respects the methodological principles of atomism and discreteness described by Auer (2010). It also reflects the coherence of the linguistic level insofar as it is made clear in the guidelines that syntax is the dominating level of analysis and pragmatic knowledge is only used if there is no finite verb for the analysis of syntactic dependencies.

We improved the guidelines and established a reference segmentation for the pilot corpus, which we present as a gold standard and which we will make publicly available at the end of the project. Apart from the syntactic annotations described above, the gold standard also contains additional pragmatic annotations of typical spoken language phenomena such as disruptions, non-verbal behaviour, collaborative turns, vocal communication, vocatives, reported speech, parentheses, and unintelligible utterances.

With the improved guidelines we will segment and annotate a larger pilot corpus of about five hours of transcriptions, consisting of other interaction types as well as similar ones in order to corroborate the findings stated above.

With this study, we could also corroborate findings of conversational analysis that social actions determine the use of the language depending on the conversational situation. Our data can help in designing language processing tools adjusted to varying interaction types.

Due to the large size of spoken language corpora, one of our aims is to automatize their segmentation or at least to be able to reduce manual effort in segmenting the data. A gold standard of segmented data on several syntactic levels can be a valuable help for the development of automated segmentation. We also make use of online annotation experiments (Schmidt and Westpfahl, submitted) for the annotation of the boundary status of pauses of various types. Further parameters such as prosody or non-verbal behaviour, POS-tags or statistics derived from interaction type, speech rate, overall distribution of pauses, etc. could be considered as well. Finally, we hope to take advantage of the outcome of our various annotations in a multi-factorial model.

The solutions presented in this paper are language specific for German and related V2-languages. At a later stage of our project Segmentation of Oral Corpora we aim at finding a shared solution with our French cooperation partners (Interactions, Corpora, Apprentissages, Représentations (ICAR), Université Lyon and Laboratoire Ligérien de Linguistique (LLL), Université Orléans) who work on the segmentation of French spoken corpora. A shared inventory of segmentation problems helps in finding similar means to solve problems and identifies structures for which rules have to be found language specifically. The analyses based on the comparison of a Germanic and a Romance language may reveal structures which are language independent and could be transferred to other languages as well. However, as each language has its own syntax, language specific rules will have to be found in order to do justice to each language.

Acknowledgements

We would like to thank the ANR and DFG for funding this work in the project "Segmentation of oral Corpora" (SegCor, DFG project number 281693063). We are grateful for the collaboration, assistance and support of Thomas Schmidt, Hanna Strub, Anton Borlinghaus, and Robert Owen Jones.

References

Christiane Andersen. 2008. Topologische Felder in einem Korpus der gesprochenen Sprache: Probleme zwischen theoretischem Modell und Annotation. *Göteborger Arbeitspapiere zur Sprachwissenschaft*, 3.

Peter Auer. 1993. Zur Verbspitzenstellung im Gesprochenen Deutsch. *Deutsche Sprache*, 23:193–222.

Peter Auer. 2010. Zum Segmentierungsproblem in der Gesprochenen Sprache. *InLiSt - Interaction and Linguistic Structures*, 49.

Markus Becker and Anette Frank. 2002. A stochastic topological parser for German. In *COLING '02*, Stroudsburg, PA, USA. Association for Computational Linguistics.

Christophe Benzitoun, Frédéric Sabio, Paola Pietrandrea, and Sylvain Kahane. 2012. Protocole de codage macrosyntaxique.

Arnulf Deppermann and Nadine Proske. 2015. Grundeinheiten der Sprache und des Sprechens. In Christa Dürscheid and Jan Georg Schneider, editors, *Handbuch Satz, Äußerung, Schema*, 4, pages 17–47. De Gruyter, Berlin.

Erich Drach. 1937. *Grundgedanken der deutschen Satzlehre*. Diesterweg, Frankfurt am Main.

Pauline Foster, Alan Tonkyn, and Gillian Wigglesworth. 2000. Measuring Spoken Language: A Unit for All Reasons. *Applied Linguistics*, 21(3):354–375.

Natalia Grabar and Iris Eshkol. 2016. Why do we reformulate? Automatic Prediction of Pragmatic Functions. In *HrTAL*, Dubrovnik, Croatia.

Martine Grice and Stefan Baumann. 2007. An introduction to intonation – functions and models. In Jürgen Trouvain and Ulrike Gut, editors, *Non-Native Prosody*, Trends in Linguistics. Studies and Monographs [TiLSM], pages 25–51. De Gruyter, Berlin and New York.

Jonathan Hamaker, Yu Zeng, and Joseph Picone. 1998. Rules and guidelines for transcription and segmentation of the Switchboard large vocabulary conversational speech recognition corpus. Technical Report Version 7.1, Institute for Signal and Information Processing, Mississippi State University.

Karin Pittner and Judith Berman. 2013. *Deutsche Syntax: Ein Arbeitsbuch*. Narr Studienbücher. Narr, Tübingen, 5 edition.

Jochen Rehbein, Thomas Schmidt, Bernd Meyer, Franziska Watzke, and Annette Herkenrath. 2004. Handbuch für das computergestützte Transkribieren nach HIAT. *Arbeiten zur Mehrsprachigkeit*, 56.

Marc Reznicek, Anke Lüdeling, Cedric Krummes, Franziska Schwantuschke, Maik Walter, Karin Schmidt, Hagen Hirschmann, and Torsten Andreas. 2012. Das Falko-Handbuch. Korpusaufbau und Annotationen Version 2.01.

Thomas Schmidt and Wilfried Schütte. 2010. FOLKER: An annotation tool for efficient transcription of natural, multi-party interaction. In *Proceedings of the Seventh conference on International Language Resources and Evaluation (LREC'10)*, pages 2091–2096.

Thomas Schmidt and Swantje Westpfahl. A study on gaps and syntactic boundaries in spoken interaction. (submitted).

Thomas Schmidt, Wilfried Schütte, and Jenny Winterscheid. 2015. cGAT. Konventionen für das computergestützte Transkribieren in Anlehnung an das Gesprächsanalytische Transkriptionssystem 2 (GAT2).

Thomas Schmidt. 2012. EXMARaLDA and the FOLK tools – two toolsets for transcribing and annotating spoken language. In *Proceedings of the Eighth conference on International Language Resources and Evaluation (LREC'12)*, pages 236–240.

Thomas Schmidt. 2014a. The database for spoken german - dgd2. In *Proceedings of the Ninth conference on International Language Resources and Evaluation (LREC'14)*, pages 1451–1457.

Thomas Schmidt. 2014b. The research and teaching corpus of spoken german – folk. In *Proceedings of the Ninth conference on International Language Resources and Evaluation (LREC'14)*, pages 383–387.

Margret Selting, Peter Auer, Dagmar Barth-Weingarten, Jörg Bergmann, Pia Bergmann, Karin Birkner, Elizabeth Couper-Kuhlen, Arnulf Deppermann, Peter Gilles, Susanne Günthner, Martin Hartung, Friederike Kern, Christine Mertzlufft, Christian Meyer, Miriam Morek, Frank Oberzaucher, Jörg Peters, Uta Quasthoff, Wilfried Schütte, Anja Stukenbrock, and Susanne Uhmann. 2009. Gesprächsanalytisches Transkriptionssystem 2 (GAT 2). *Gesprächsforschung*, 10:353–402.

Rosmary Stegmann, Heike Telljohann, and Erhard W Hinrichs. 2000. Stylebook for the German Treebank in VERBMOBIL. Technical report, Technical Report 239, Verbmobil.

Heike Telljohann, Erhard W Hinrichs, Sandra Kübler, Heike Zinsmeister, and Kathrin Beck. 2006. Stylebook for the Tübingen treebank of written German (TüBa-D/Z). In *Seminar fur Sprachwissenschaft, Universitat Tubingen, Tubingen, Germany*.

Zahar Weiß and Gohar Schnelle. 2016. Frühneuhochdeutsche Satzsegmentierung: Annotationsrichtlinien: Version 4.0.

Peter Wittenburg, Hennie Brugman, Albert Russel, Alex Klassmann, and Han Sloetjes. 2006. ELAN: A professional framework for multimodality research. *Proceedings of the Fifth International Conference on Language Resources and Evaluation (LREC 2006)*.

Angelika Wöllstein. 2010. *Topologisches Satzmodell*, volume 8 of *Kurze Einführungen in die germanistische Linguistik*. Winter, Heidelberg.

Angelika Wöllstein. 2014. Topologisches Satzmodell. In Jörg Hagemann, editor, *Syntaxtheorien: Analysen im Vergleich*, Stauffenburg-Einführungen, pages 143–164. Stauffenburg-Verlag, Tübingen.

An Annotated Corpus of Picture Stories Retold by Language Learners

Christine Köhn and Arne Köhn
Natural Lanuguage Systems Group
Department of Informatics
Universität Hamburg
{ckoehn, koehn}@informatik.uni-hamburg.de

Abstract

Corpora with language learner writing usually consist of essays, which are difficult to annotate reliably and to process automatically due to the high degree of freedom and the nature of learner language. We develop a task which mildly constrains learner utterances to facilitate consistent annotation and reliable automatic processing but at the same time does not prime learners with textual information. In this task, learners retell a comic strip. We present the resulting task-based corpus of stories written by learners of German. We designed the corpus to be able to serve multiple purposes: The corpus was manually annotated, including target hypotheses and syntactic structures. We achieve a very high inter-annotator agreement: $\kappa = 0.765$ for the annotation of minimal target hypotheses and $\kappa = 0.507$ for the extended target hypotheses. We attribute this to the design of our task and the annotation guidelines, which are based on those for the Falko corpus (Reznicek et al., 2012).

1 Introduction

Learner corpora are useful for a variety of tasks in natural language processing (NLP) and linguistics, including analyzing learner language, developing and evaluating NLP tools with respect to learner language and building grammatical error correction (GEC) systems. Many learner corpora are available today but they are far from covering the whole spectrum of learner utterances: First, they usually consist of essays, escpecially the large corpora such as ICLE (Granger et al., 2009), NUCLE (Dahlmeier et al., 2013), or Falko (Reznicek et al., 2012; Reznicek et al., 2013), and second, languages other than English are underrepresented.

Writing essays is a common task for students and it is therefore worthwhile to conduct research on student essays. However, the content and form of essays is only marginally constrained, which results in a low agreement between error annotations (e.g. Fitzpatrick and Seegmiller (2004)). To foster reliable interpretation of learner texts, Ott et al. (2012) argue for collecting learner corpora with explicit task contexts. Intuitively, knowing the context of an utterance facilitates interpreting it. Ott et al. (2012) chose reading comprehension as such a task and achieve reasonable inter-annotator agreement for meaning assessment of the responses. Reading comprehension exercises have the advantage that they include questions and texts as contextual information, which can be exploited for automating meaning assessment (e. g. Bailey and Meurers (2008), Hahn and Meurers (2012)). However, the provided texts and prompts influence the learner's choice of words and therefore pure interlanguage cannot be observed.

One task with explicit task context but without providing the students with texts or text fragments which encode the correct answer is picture description. Pictures showing a single activity in isolation constrain the answers to a sensible degree for further processing, e.g. King and Dickinson (2013) achieve 92.3% accuracy for extracting semantic triples of the form *verb(subj,obj)*. The identification of the verb, the subject and the object are crucial parts for content and grammatical assessment and work well for this type of picture description tasks because the resulting sentences are conceptually simple. We strive to move a step further and increase the variance of the learner writing and correspondingly the processing

Proceedings of the Joint Workshop on
Linguistic Annotation, Multiword Expressions and Constructions (LAW-MWE-CxG-2018), pages 121–132
Santa Fe, New Mexico, USA, August 25-26, 2018.

(a) Moral mit Wespen "moral with wasps" by Erich Ohser

Der Sohn will die Wespe töten _ aber
The son wants to the wasp kill but
der Vater haltet er.
the father **hold he**.
'The son wants to kill the wasp, but the father **holds** him'   (text 3nnn_1)

---

*Der Sohn sitzt auf **ein** Hocker neben dem*
The son sits on a stool next to the
Tisch und schwingt ein Handtuch _ um die
table and swings a towel to the
Wespe zu töten.
wasp to kill.
'The son sits on a stool next to the table and swings a towel in order to kill the wasp.'   (text 2mVs_1)

---

*Der Sohn will **es** mit einem Tuch töten.*
The son wants it with a cloth kill.
'The son wants to kill it with a cloth.'   (text ATwN_1)

(b) Examples for image 1, describing the son's actions. Errors in bold, underscores mark missing commas. Verb error in first sentence results in distorted meaning: The learner used *halten* "to hold" instead of *aufhalten* "to stop".

Figure 1: One of the picture stories from the retelling task with example sentences from the descriptions of the first panel of the story.

difficulty while sustaining a strong visual context. Simply increasing the number of items and situations that can be described in a picture is insufficient since this would probably result in descriptions about mainly unrelated actions happening in parallel as if concatenating the descriptions of single actions. The task we designed to obtain a language learner corpus meets the following criteria:

- It has a *strong visual context* which allows human annotators (and machines) to find a clear target hypothesis (in contrast to essay based corpora)
- It *captures real language use* and has no linguistic context in the form of texts, which would contain or influence the expected result (in contrast to question answering)
- It has *free-form answers* (in contrast to fill-the-gap exercises)
- It elicits a *variety of sentence structures*, e.g. encourages to establish causal or temporal links between sentences (in contrast to simple activity descriptions)

We designed a picture story retelling task in which language learners narrate the story shown in a comic strip, which we describe in more detail in Section 2. We name the result **Comic Strips Retold by Learners of German: the ComiGS corpus**. The circumstances of the corpus collection and the type and amount of data collected are reported in Section 3 and 4.

Manual annotation is time-consuming and expensive. Therefore, an annotation serving more than one purpose is desirable and we annotated the corpus in a way that it can be utilized for different tasks. Section 4 explicates the annotations we added to the learners' texts and what they can be used for.

2   Picture Story Retelling Task

In the task, learners retell what they see in a comic strip. In order to meet the criteria mentioned above, the picture story as well as the instructions must be selected carefully. The story must

- not contain text
- provide enough material to write about, especially have more than one actor

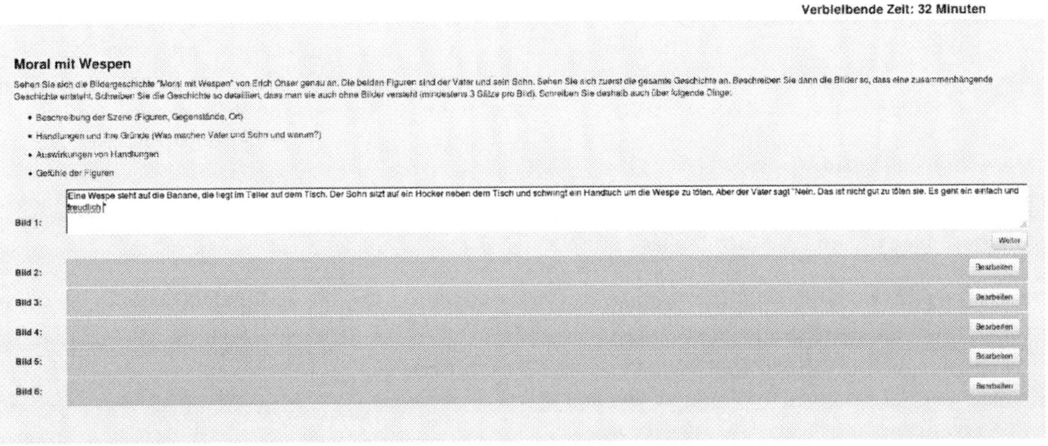

Figure 2: User interface for participants. Top to bottom: Title of the picture story, general task description, input boxes for each picture in the story. Top right: remaining time.

- be easy to understand for learners
- be pleasant enough in order to make the learner comfortable writing about it

Since we wanted to make the results of our corpus collection freely available, we also required that the picture stories can be distributed together with the corpus. We found the numerous *Vater und Sohn* ("father and son") stories by Erich Ohser to be fitting, of which some had already been used for teaching German as a foreign language (da Luz Videira Murta, 1991; Eppert, 2001), and the copyright expired at the end of 2014[1]. We selected five stories, which we regarded as most suitable[2].

The task instructions should prevent the learners from writing short and superficial stories but we did not want to point the learner directly to the events in the story to avoid imposing our interpretation and our choice of words on the learner. Instead, the task instructs the learner to first look carefully at the whole picture story and then write a detailed and coherent story. The learners were required to write at least three sentences per image but we did not enforce this requirement. Then we added a list of things that the learner should include: description of the scene (characters, items, locations), actions and their causes (what do the characters do and why?), consequences of actions, the characters' feelings.

We made one exception to our "no textual influence" policy: We stated the context of the story, i.e. the story's name, the author's name and the family's characters: the father, the mother and the son. One of the titles contains a word which references an important item in the story but it is unlikely that the learners know the word, so we explained it in a few words.

We tested the complete task (instructions and story) on native speakers. Afterwards, we ranked the stories by perceived fit for the task and selected the two best stories for our corpus collection task (see Figure 1a). Then we estimated the difficulty of the task to determine the CEFR[3] level the learners should have in order to do the exercise. We estimated the taskto be suitable for levels A2 (elementary, i.e. upper beginner) and B1 (intermediate). We consulted a German as a foreign language instructor and

---

[1] Erich Ohser was prohibited from working under the Nazi regime and published the father and son comics under a pseudonym. He and Erich Knauf were arrested for making political jokes in 1944. Ohser commited suicide the day before his trial, Knauf was executed. (https://en.wikipedia.org/wiki/E._O._Plauen)

[2] None of the stories contains text, but not all of them are completely devoid of symbols: One of the stories (Der Schmöker "The page-turner") contains two question marks to indicate a vacant chairs.

[3] The Common European Framework of Reference for Languages: Learning, Teaching, Assessment defines three levels of language proficiency for learners, which are each subdivided into two levels: A1/A2 (basic user), B1/B2 (independent user) and C1/C2 (proficient user).

he confirmed our estimation of level and time needed to complete the exercise (90 min for two stories). Therefore, all learners had 90 min for the task but the time limit was not strictly enforced. However, the actual time the participants needed for each picture story is documented. Learners with levels A2 and B1 were given two stories. Learners who had a higher level or who were very fast were given one additional story (the third best story). Learner levels and mother languages are reported in Table 1.

3   Data Collection

The language learners typed their text into a web interface (see Figure 2). Since the task did not provide a vocabulary list, they were asked to bring a dictionary or a dictionary app with them but were not allowed to translate whole sentences using tools such as Google Translate.

The interface showed the exercise text and a text area for each image. This way, each story part was assigned to one image without manual annotation. Naturally, this mapping is rough: A part may reference other pictures (e.g. relating the current situation to a previous one) or it may contain content which is not inferable from the story (e.g. the learners own experience) or is not inferable from one picture alone (e.g. if something changes from one picture to the other and the learner describes the actions to cause the change). Despite these shortcomings, we found the mapping to be very useful when annotating the target hypotheses.

An important question when designing the interface was whether or not to include some kind of spellchecking. Without a spellchecker, the texts would be as if the learner would write them

CEFR level	#	Mother language	#
A2	6	Italian	5
A2/B1	3	Chinese	5
B1	11	Spanish	4
B1/B2	1	Russian	4
B2	5	Portuguese	3
B2/C1	4	English	3
		Persian	2
		Turkish	1
		Romanian	1
		Polish	1
		Korean	1
		Igbo	1
		Armenian	1

Table 1: Learner levels and mother languages represented in the corpus. For each learner, we report the maximum of their certified and self-reported level, as the certification was sometimes outdated. Some learners reported two mother languages (English and another language), in which case we count both.

offline by hand but this would not be a realistic scenario. Most learners would probably use a spellchecker when writing on a computer – at least to avoid typing errors. Furthermore, in the subsequent error annotation, the annotator interprets misspelled words when formulating the target hypothesis. In our opinion, the learners should at least get the chance to correct their error. Therefore, we decided to make the learners aware that they might have typed something wrong: We implemented a compromise between using no spellchecking at all and a full-fledged spellchecker. We used the browser-internal spellchecking which underlines possibly misspelled words but we decided not to provide suggestions on how to correct the error[4]: The main reason for this is that we feared that learners confide too much in the spellchecker and distort their texts, e. g. choose a wrong suggestion over their correctly spelled word.

In the beginning, the learners were instructed by the supervisor. They started with an input test page where they got used to the interface and were made aware of the spellchecker: They were told to regard the spellchecker as an aid to make them aware of possible mistakes but that the spellchecker is imperfect. They were given examples to show that not every misspelled word is underlined and that an underline does not necessarily mean that the word is incorrect. Note that the texts were not part of an exam and the learners were aware that their texts would not be graded. The learners were instructed that they should rather cover the stories' content entirely than to write perfect sentences.

Overall, we collected texts from thirty learners. Twenty wrote texts for two stories and ten wrote texts for three stories. We collected a variety of meta data about each learner and each learner's text, including the background of the language learner and apart from the common data, we also asked for their previous

---

[4]Due to technical problems, some learners used suggestions but we marked these texts.

experience with this kind of task. For most of the learners, we also stored the text and timestamp every time they pressed a key as well as a video capture of their screen. This makes it possible for future work to draw conclusions about the development of the texts. For every learner, we got a certificate, e. g. the completion of a course, about their language level. However, this might not be identical to the actual level on the day of the performance. We therefore noted level, type of certificate and time span between issuing the certificate and the day of the task.

4 Annotations

We wanted to create annotations suitable for a variety of tasks, either directly or as a basis. The tasks which we wanted to cover in particular are: analysis by means of corpus linguistics, grammatical error diagnosis, grammatical error correction (GEC), and the development of NLP tools such as parsers and taggers.

All tasks except GEC[5] either need or profit from syntax annotation and it is therefore essential. Next in importance are Part-of-Speech (PoS) tags. The first three tasks benefit from annotation with error tags, i. e. tags that mark and categorize errors according to an error classification scheme. Lüdeling (2008) argues that error tags should only be used with respect to a reconstructed utterance. Therefore, a reconstruction known as target hypothesis is needed to annotate error tags. There can be a wide range of acceptable target hypotheses for the same sentence and even trained teachers do not agree on the same correction.

Learner utterances can diverge from the target language on several linguistic levels: orthography, morphology, syntax, semantics and pragmatics. Existing corpora annotate corrections on different levels: The EAGLE annotation scheme (Boyd, 2010) considers sentences in isolation and considers them ungrammatical "if there is no context in which the sentence could be uttered". With this definition, a sentences or a corrected sentence which is not semantically or pragmatically appropriate in the actual context may be regarded as correct. Many existing corpora address errors only on the grammatical level. Sakaguchi et al. (2016) argue that corpora for GEC should not aim at grammaticality but at what they call *native-language fluency*: They "consider a text to be *fluent* when it looks and sounds natural to a native-speaking population". Reznicek et al. (2013) propose two target hypotheses with different scopes to cover these differences – a minimal target hypothesis (TH1) and an extended target hypothesis (TH2) – and show that depending on the TH, different phenomena can be studied. Both THs should change the original text as little as possible. TH1 addresses only lower linguistic levels. It changes the original text to make it grammatical without regarding semantics, pragmatics and style. In contrast, TH2 does not ignore these levels. It takes the given context into account and aims at creating a text that is as similar as possible to that of a native speaker (Reznicek et al., 2012). By design, the TH2 may deviate substantially from the original text (Reznicek et al., 2013).

For TH1, there are detailed annotation rules, whereas there are only rough guidelines and annotation examples for the TH2 (Reznicek et al., 2013; Reznicek et al., 2012). An interesting property of TH1 is that it is explicitly designed to serve as a normalization layer suitable for automatic processing, which has proven to be useful in the past (e. g. Rehbein et al. (2012)). In particular, syntax parses of TH1 can be mapped back to the original utterance, obtaining a syntax annotation of the learner utterance (Hirschmann et al., 2013).

Ragheb and Dickinson (2011) argue that annotation schemes for learner language should be specifically tailored for this purpose because comparing it to the target language (or to the L1 of the learner) might obscure properties of the interlanguage. Because of this, Ragheb and Dickinson (2012) developed an annotation scheme for syntax and PoS tags for learner English. Each word is annotated with two PoS tags since a single PoS tag is often not adequate (see Díaz-Negrillo et al. (2010) for a discussion): One captures morphological evidence and one distributional evidence. The syntax annotation includes a subcategorization layer and a dependency layer. The morphosyntactic dependencies are based on the surface forms and morphological evidence and the subcategorization frames represent arguments that are

---

[5]Some approaches for GEC have been shown to benefit from syntactic information, e. g. adding syntactic features to a classifier for agreement errors (Rozovskaya and Roth, 2014). Approaches that treat correction as a machine translation task and are now close to human-level performance (Grundkiewicz and Junczys-Dowmunt, 2018) do not need syntactic information.

required in the target language. This annotation scheme has been shown to achieve good inter-annotator agreement (Ragheb and Dickinson, 2013).

Another approach to annotating learner syntax is to use an existing annotation scheme for the target language and use it on learner language. Ott and Ziai (2010) annotated 109 sentences written by learners of German with the dependency scheme by Foth (2006) because using an annotation scheme specifically for learner language is not suitable for their purpose. They measured an inter-annotator agreement between the three annotators of 88.1% in terms of labeled attachment accuracy. However, for 42 sentences all three annotations (dependencies and labels) differed. For 6 of them this was due to differences on the underlying target hypothesis (though they were not annotated). Therefore, Ott and Ziai (2010) recommend to explicitly annotate target hypotheses as proposed by Lüdeling (2008).

Rosén and De Smedt (2010) and Hirschmann et al. (2013) argue that target hypotheses are necessary for automatic analysis of learner language. Rosén and De Smedt (2010) discuss problems with an early version of Ragheb and Dickinson's annotation scheme (Dickinson and Ragheb, 2009) which we think are still valid for the latest version.

Overall, the best approach for syntactic annotation of our corpus is to annotate target hypotheses and map their syntactic structures back to the original utterances. This way, we obtain corrections of the sentences and syntax annotations.

We annotated our corpus manually with two target hypotheses, a minimal TH and an extended TH, following the guidelines for the Falko corpus (Reznicek et al., 2012; Reznicek et al., 2013). We made a few adaptations which we will explain later. We manually annotated dependencies for the target hypotheses using the well-documented scheme by (Foth, 2006) which has the advantages that it is a genuine dependency scheme and was used for annotating the largest German dependency treebank HDT (Foth et al., 2014). We annotated the target hypotheses manually with lemmas and PoS tags using the STTS tag set (Schiller et al., 1999).

The ComiGS corpus contains 18k tokens. The sentence lengths of the original texts have a relatively even distribution with an average of 12.2 tokens, which is close to the median of 11 tokens (see Table 3). This shows that the learners on average produce more complex sentences than just canonical subject verb object sentences (see example sentences in Figure 1b). For comparison, the answers to the reading comprehension questions in the CREG-109 corpus only have an average sentence length of 8.26 tokens.

Tag	Description
INS	inserted token in TH
DEL	deleted token in TH
CHA	changed token in TH
MOVS	source location of moved token in TH
MOVT	target location of moved token in TH
MERGE	tokens merged in TH
SPLIT	tokens split in TH

Table 2: Automatic error tags from Reznicek et al. (2013), which are used for this corpus

	#orig	#TH1	#TH2
25%	8	8	8
Median	11	12	12
75%	15	16	16
Mean	12.2	12.5	12.6

Table 3: Distribution of sentence lengths (in tokens) in our corpus

4.1 Minimal and Extended Target Hypotheses

The minimal target hypothesis (TH1) and the extended target hypothesis (TH2) reconstruct the original utterance while attempting to minimize the changes to the original text. The TH1 only corrects errors on lower linguistic levels (orthography, morphology and syntax). In contrast, the TH2 aims at creating a reconstructed text which is as similar as possible to a native speaker utterance and, therefore, also considers semantics, pragmatics and information structure (Reznicek et al., 2012).

The rules for the TH1 cover many cases for disambiguating conflicting evidence, e.g. if the verb and the arguments do not match, the verb should be preserved and the arguments adjusted. Consider the examples

ctok	Die	Kind	ist	liegend	[...]
TH2	Das	Kind	liegt		[...]
	The	*child*	*is lying/lies*		[...]

(a) Example where two tokens are corrected into one token. Without explicit alignment it would be impossible to differentiate between deleting "ist" and correcting "liegend" and correcting both into a single word.

ctok	Die	Kind	ist	[...]	liegend
TH2	Das	Kind	liegt	[...]	
tmid			1	[...]	1

(b) Example where two tokens are corrected into one token, with other tokens in between. Same as 3a, but the correspondence has to be established by an additional linking layer.

ctok	Der	Mann	geht	weiter	[...]
TH2	Der	Mann	fährt	fort	[...]
	The	*man*	*walks/goes*	*on*	[...]
tmid			1	1	[...]

(c) Example where two tokens are corrected into two other tokens. The linking layer is used to denote that this is a single correction. Without this additional annotation, independent but neighboring corections could not be distinguished from a single correction.

Figure 3: Examples for alignments in the error annotation. ctok: manually corrected tokenization, TH2: correction layer, tmid: token move id.
Sources: Example 3a from text YRGN_2, Example 3b adapted from 3a, Example 3c from text bsPg_3.

in Figure 1b: The TH1 corrects the verb form error, adds a separable verb prefix to the first sentence and corrects the pronoun (*haltet er → hält ihn auf* "stops him") whereas the TH2 uses a more suitable verb which requires the addition of an adverb (*hält ihn davon ab* "prevents him from doing it"). The TH2 of the third sentence corrects the pronoun *es* "it" to *sie*, a female pronoun, because it references a previously mentioned noun with female gender. The TH1, in contrast, does not change this pronoun as the sentence is grammatically correct but not adequate.

An important feature of the target hypotheses is that they are manually aligned to the original text token by token. This makes it possible to compute automatic error tags in the form of edit tags as has been done for the Falko corpus (Reznicek et al., 2013). We annotated our corpus with the same tags (see Table 2). When searching for patterns in the corpus, these error tags are useful for constraining the search results. Note that an automatically created alignment would not allow to derive all of the error tags: Merged and split tokens could not be identified except for simple cases such as deleting or inserting spaces and an inserted token followed by a deleted token (or a deleted token followed by an inserted token) could not be distinguished from a changed token. If more detailed error tags are needed, e. g. for evaluating GEC systems with respect to error type, error types could be automatically annotated as proposed by Bryant et al. (2017). This approach has the advantage that the same error set can be automatically annotated to different corpora (as long as target hypotheses are available) yielding a unified error annotation.

4.2 Adaptations and Extensions to the Falko scheme

The Falko manual requires that split or merged tokens are annotated as overlapping spans if possible. Tokens from the original text are merged like shown in Figure 3a. While this is a useful feature as it shows when a token with the same function is changed, this information gets lost when the token is moved. Therefore, we added a layer called tokmovid for every TH which assigns a unique identifier (we used numbers) to any number of tokens which would have been annotated as an overlapping span (tmid= tokmovid for TH2), see Figure 3b. Note that this also applies to tokens which are contiguous but cannot be annotated by an overlapping span. This is the case when one set of tokens is changed into another, see Figure 3c. In that example, the learner used *geht weiter* as in "walks on" but this is changed into a separable verb *fährt fort* ("goes on") in TH2. The tokmovid indicates that the words are not replaced in isolation but as a unit. Note that the original learner sentence does not reflect the intention by the learner: "geht weiter" could be literally translated as "goes on", but would describe an actual movement in this context. From the picture story it is evident that the learner wanted to describe that the man continues an action, therefore the text needs to be corrected.

The annotation of the tokmovid layers means an extra annotation effort, but we consider it rather low compared to the result: This information is mostly obvious to human annotators, but it can neither be easily recovered automatically later nor to the same extent. We also use this layer to explicitly annotate every movement of tokens. This way, we ensure that token movements can reliably be identified even if they are changed, e. g. due to spelling correction. For the Falko corpus, automatic identification of token movements was used. This has two disadvantages: A movement where the token was altered in the TH cannot be identified and a deletion of a token t in the original text and an insertion of token t in the TH would automatically be considered as a movement although they might be unrelated, e. g. consider deletion of an article in one noun phrase and insertion of the same article in another noun phrase.

The tokmovid layers do not influence the assignment of automatic error tags, e. g. a token which is moved and changed is tagged as `DEL` at the position where it was moved from and as `INS` at the position where it was moved to. However, the tokmovid can be queried in addition to find out whether the token was actually moved and changed.

We tried to adhere to the Falko annotation manual as far as possible since it already provides a reasonable and detailed rule set. Moreover, we wanted our annotations to be compatible with those of the Falko corpus to make comparison between learners productions in the ComiGS corpus to those of the Falko corpus possible. However, due to the differences between the tasks and language levels between both corpora, some minor changes or extensions to the guidelines were necessary which we documented in our annotation guide. For example, we do not discourage colloquial language for the TH2 in general. All in all, most of our changes can be regarded as an extension or clarification of the original guidelines so that the annotation is mainly compatible to that of the Falko corpus.

4.3 Annotation Process

The annotations were created by two annotators, annotator A and annotator B, using EXMARaLDA (Schmidt, 2004). We split the stories based on the learners into two sets, Set 1 and Set 2. Set 1 was jointly annotated by annotator A and B. Set 2 contains two independent annotations of THs, one by each annotator. The inter-annotator agreement was measured on Set 2 and it can be used as an evaluation set for systems trained on Set 1 as it contains two valid error corrections for each text.

We selected learners for Set 2 randomly but ensured that this set covers different mother languages and proficiency levels and also contains texts for the third story. Set 1 consists of 51 stories from 22 learners, totaling 12.5k tokens. Set 2 consists of 19 stories from 8 learners, totaling 5.4k tokens. The texts were automatically tokenized and segmented into sentences and the tokenization was manually corrected. Annotator A annotated TH1 and TH2 on Set 1 and met regularly with annotator B for discussions. Annotator B checked the annotations of annotator A and in case of disagreement discussed it with annotator A. Both annotators were forced to agree on one annotation. If necessary, the annotation was changed after the discussion. As a result, the annotations of the THs for Set 1 have been agreed upon by both annotators. While annotating Set 1, we developed the adaptation of the annotation guidelines for the THs. After annotating Set 1, both annotators annotated Set 2 independently with THs. The TH1 was annotated twice for measuring inter-annotator agreement and the TH2 was annotated twice for having two independent interpretations of the original learner utterance in Set 2.

Afterwards, one annotator annotated dependency trees including PoS tags and the other checked the annotation. The annotation was performed using the manual annotation interface of jwcdg (Beuck et al., 2013), a parser based on defeasible grammaticality rules. During the manual annotation, rule violations are displayed to highlight potential annotation errors. We did not annotate the same data twice with dependency structures and therefore did not perform an inter-annotator agreement evaluation on the dependency structures. Language learner sentences can be syntactically annotated with high inter-annotator agreement (91.5%) using the HDT annotation scheme even on the uncorrected learner sentences (Köhn et al., 2016). We assume that annotation of the already grammatically corrected sentences with explicit visual context can be annotated even more consistently.

4.4 Inter-annotator Agreement

The rules for TH1 are designed to make the TH1 structurally close to the original utterance. This and a good inter-annotator agreement is important to draw reliable conclusions about the original texts based on the TH1. Therefore, we measured the inter-annotator agreement on the minimal target hypotheses from Set 2 using Cohen's Kappa coefficient (Cohen, 1960). For the computation, token changes are always considered with respect to a token in the original text. A token from the original text is considered changed if there are any tokens on the TH1 layer between the end of the previous (original) token and the end of the current (original) token that differ from the current token[6]. A token is considered unchanged if the token is the same on the original and on the TH1 layer. Note that the κ coefficient does not measure agreement on the type of token change (in terms of Table 2) and that we use the manual alignment for the computation and not an automatic alignment based on extracted texts. The latter means that an insertion of token i followed by a deletion of token d by one annotator and a deletion of token d followed by an insertion of token i are considered as a disagreement although the resulting text is identical. Therefore, the κ values are likely to be an underestimation of agreement with respect to the resulting text.

Of the 5424 tokens in the original texts from Set 2, annotator A changed 1215 tokens and B 1248 while annotating TH1. Much more changes were made for TH2 than for TH1 (A: 2k changes, B: 1.9k changes). For TH1, 273 tokens were changed by one annotator but not by the other. If considering identical changes (agreement on which token to change and the correction) the annotators disagreed on 448 tokens. Overall, the κ coefficient for agreement on which tokens to change is 0.856 and for identical token change 0.765. We consider the agreement exceptionally high given the nature of language learner texts. Obviously, we cannot infer from this how precise the annotators worked because there are no comparable annotations available but the result shows that the clear annotations guidelines of TH1 in conjunction with a task-based corpus result in a reliable annotation.

Even the TH2 level, for which the annotation guidelines are less restrictive, is annotated with high agreement. The κ coefficient for identical token change on TH2 is 0.507 and agreement on which tokens to change is 0.728. For comparison, Dahlmeier et al. (2013) measured an average agreement of 0.3877 for the agreement of token change on the NUCLE corpus.

5 Conclusions and Outlook

We presented a task with a strong visual context which constrains the texts written by language learners without severely restricting their input and without linguistic priming. The task encourages learners to produce complex utterances. Despite this, the intentions of the utterances can be recovered quite well by annotators due to the visual context. This is reflected in the exceptionally high inter-annotator agreement for both the minimal and extended target hypothesis which shows that the annotation is reliable.

The corpus contains several layers of annotations for the texts, including a minimal and an extended target hypotheses and dependency annotations to facilitate different directions of research. The visual context is not only helpful for consistent annotation but could also be used as an additional input for automatic grammatical error detection and correction, e. g. by encoding the information in the picture stories into a knowledge base (cmp. Köhn and Menzel (2015)).

We make this corpus freely available and provide the software and instructions necessary to extend the corpus under `https://nats.gitlab.io/comigs`. We hope that this corpus will be useful for a variety of tasks which need learner data.

Acknowledgements

We are grateful to Inga Kempfert for annotating the corpus together with the first author and for implementing a part of the software for automatic processing and format conversion. We thank Maike Paetzel

---

[6]Additions after the last token are also added to the last token.

for the initial implementation of the data collection software and Robert Schmidt for extending it and for conducting the majority of the data collection. We thank Sven Zimmer for his work on the syntax annotation interface. We thank Wolfgang Menzel for helpful discussions on our data collection effort. We thank Nils Bernstein for his feedback on our task design and the other teachers for German as a Foreign Language at the Sprachenzentrum for forwarding our request to language learners. We thank Sebastian Beschke and the anonymous reviewers for their feedback. We thank the participants for their work.

References

Stacey Bailey and Detmar Meurers. 2008. Diagnosing Meaning Errors in Short Answers to Reading Comprehension Questions. In *Proceedings of the Third Workshop on Innovative Use of NLP for Building Educational Applications*, pages 107–115, Columbus, Ohio, USA, June. Association for Computational Linguistics.

Niels Beuck, Arne Köhn, and Wolfgang Menzel. 2013. Predictive incremental parsing and its evaluation. In Kim Gerdes, Eva Hajičová, and Leo Wanner, editors, *Computational Dependency Theory*, volume 258 of *Frontiers in Artificial Intelligence and Applications*, pages 186 – 206. IOS press.

Adriane Boyd. 2010. EAGLE: an Error-Annotated Corpus of Beginning Learner German. In Nicoletta Calzolari (Conference Chair), Khalid Choukri, Bente Maegaard, Joseph Mariani, Jan Odijk, Stelios Piperidis, Mike Rosner, and Daniel Tapias, editors, *Proceedings of the International Conference on Language Resources and Evaluation*, Valletta, Malta, May. European Language Resources Association (ELRA).

Christopher Bryant, Mariano Felice, and Ted Briscoe. 2017. Automatic Annotation and Evaluation of Error Types for Grammatical Error Correction. In *Proceedings of the 55th Annual Meeting of the Association for Computational Linguistics (Volume 1: Long Papers)*, pages 793–805, Vancouver, Canada, July. Association for Computational Linguistics.

Jacob Cohen. 1960. A coefficient of agreement for nominal scales. *Educational and Psychological Measurement*, 20(1):37–46.

Maria da Luz Videira Murta. 1991. "Vater und Sohn" im Anfängerunterricht: Eine Hörverstehensübung und ein Schreibauftrag. *Fremdsprache Deutsch: Zeitschrift für die Praxis des Deutschunterrichts*, pages 46–47. Issue 5: Das Bild im Unterricht, Klett Edition Deutsch, München, Germany.

Daniel Dahlmeier, Hwee Tou Ng, and Siew Mei Wu. 2013. Building a Large Annotated Corpus of Learner English: The NUS Corpus of Learner English. In *Proceedings of the Eighth Workshop on Innovative Use of NLP for Building Educational Applications*, pages 22–31, Atlanta, Georgia, June. Association for Computational Linguistics.

Markus Dickinson and Marwa Ragheb. 2009. Dependency Annotation for Learner Corpora. In Marco Passarotti, Adam Przepiórkowski, Savina Raynaud, and Frank Van Eynde, editors, *Proceedings of the Eighth Workshop on Treebanks and Linguistic Theories (TLT-8)*, pages 59–70, Milan, Italy, December.

Ana Díaz-Negrillo, Detmar Meurers, Salvador Valera, and Holger Wunsch. 2010. Towards interlanguage POS annotation for effective learner corpora in SLA and FLT. *Language Forum*, 36(1–2):139–154. Special Issue on Corpus Linguistics for Teaching and Learning. In Honour of John Sinclair.

Franz Eppert. 2001. *Deutsch mit Vater und Sohn: 10 Bildgeschichten von E. O. Plauen für den Unterricht Deutsch als Fremdsprache*. Max Hueber Verlag, Ismaning, Germany, 1st edition.

Eileen Fitzpatrick and M.S. Seegmiller. 2004. The Montclair Electronic Language Database Project. In Ulla Connor and Thomas A. Upton, editors, *Language and Computers, Applied Corpus Linguistics. A Multidimensional Perspective*. Rodopi.

Kilian A. Foth, Arne Köhn, Niels Beuck, and Wolfgang Menzel. 2014. Because Size Does Matter: The Hamburg Dependency Treebank. In Nicoletta Calzolari (Conference Chair), Khalid Choukri, Thierry Declerck, Hrafn Loftsson, Bente Maegaard, Joseph Mariani, Asuncion Moreno, Jan Odijk, and Stelios Piperidis, editors, *Proceedings of the Language Resources and Evaluation Conference 2014*, Reykjavik, Iceland, May. European Language Resources Association (ELRA).

Kilian A. Foth, 2006. *Eine umfassende Constraint-Dependenz-Grammatik des Deutschen*. Fachbereich Informatik, Universität Hamburg. URN: urn:nbn:de:gbv:18-228-7-2048.

Sylviane Granger, Estelle Dagneaux, Fanny Meunier, and Magali Paquot, editors. 2009. *International Corpus of Learner English. Version 2. Handbook and CD-Rom*. Presses universitaires de Louvain, Louvain-la-Neuve.

Roman Grundkiewicz and Marcin Junczys-Dowmunt. 2018. Near Human-Level Performance in Grammatical Error Correction with Hybrid Machine Translation. In *Proceedings of the 2018 Conference of the North American Chapter of the Association for Computational Linguistics: Human Language Technologies, Volume 2 (Short Papers)*, pages 284–290. Association for Computational Linguistics.

Michael Hahn and Detmar Meurers. 2012. Evaluating the Meaning of Answers to Reading Comprehension Questions: A Semantics-Based Approach. In *Proceedings of the Seventh Workshop on Building Educational Applications Using NLP*, pages 326–336, Montréal, Canada, June. Association for Computational Linguistics.

Hagen Hirschmann, Anke Lüdeling, Ines Rehbein, Marc Reznicek, and Amir Zeldes. 2013. Underuse of Syntactic Categories in Falko – A Case Study on Modification. In S. Granger, G. Gilquin, and F. Meunier, editors, *Twenty Years of Learner Corpus Research: Looking back, Moving ahead*, Corpora and Language in Use – Proceedings – 1. Presses Universitaires de Louvain.

Levi King and Markus Dickinson. 2013. Shallow semantic analysis of interactive learner sentences. In *Proceedings of the Eighth Workshop on Innovative Use of NLP for Building Educational Applications*, pages 11–21, Atlanta, Georgia, June. Association for Computational Linguistics.

Christine Köhn and Wolfgang Menzel. 2015. Towards parsing language learner utterances in context. In *Proceedings of the International Conference of the German Society for Computational Linguistics and Language Technology (GSCL 2015)*, pages 144–153, University of Duisburg-Essen, Germany.

Christine Köhn, Tobias Staron, and Arne Köhn. 2016. Parsing free-form language learner data: Current state and error analysis. In Stefanie Dipper, Friedrich Neubarth, and Heike Zinsmeister, editors, *Proceedings of the 13th Conference on Natural Language Processing (KONVENS 2016)*, number 16 in Bochumer Linguistische Arbeitsberichte, pages 135–145. Stefanie Dipper, Sprachwissenschaftliches Institut, Ruhr-Universität Bochum, Universitätsstr. 150, 44801 Bochum, Bochum, Germany, September.

Anke Lüdeling. 2008. Mehrdeutigkeiten und Kategorisierung: Probleme bei der Annotation von Lernerkorpora. In Maik Walter Patrick Grommes, editor, *Fortgeschrittene Lernervarietäten*, pages 119–140. Niemeyer.

Niels Ott and Ramon Ziai. 2010. Evaluating Dependency Parsing Performance on German Learner Language. In Markus Dickinson, Kaili Müürisep, and Marco Passarotti, editors, *Proceedings of the Ninth International Workshop on Treebanks and Linguistic Theories*, volume 9 of *NEALT Proceeding Series*, pages 175–186.

Niels Ott, Ramon Ziai, and Detmar Meurers. 2012. Creation and Analysis of a Reading Comprehension Exercise Corpus: Towards Evaluating Meaning in Context. In Thomas Schmidt and Kai Wörner, editors, *Multilingual Corpora and Multilingual Corpus Analysis*, Hamburg Studies in Multilingualism (HSM), pages 47–69. Benjamins, Amsterdam.

Marwa Ragheb and Markus Dickinson. 2011. Avoiding the comparative fallacy in the annotation of learner corpora. In *Selected Proceedings of the 2010 Second Language Research Forum: Reconsidering SLA Research, Dimensions, and Directions*, pages 114–124, Somerville, MA. Cascadilla Proceedings Project.

Marwa Ragheb and Markus Dickinson. 2012. Defining syntax for learner language annotation. In *Proceedings of COLING 2012: Posters*, pages 965–974, Mumbai, India, December.

Marwa Ragheb and Markus Dickinson. 2013. Inter-annotator agreement for dependency annotation of learner language. In *Proceedings of the Eighth Workshop on Innovative Use of NLP for Building Educational Applications*, pages 169–179, Atlanta, Georgia, June. Association for Computational Linguistics.

Ines Rehbein, Hagen Hirschmann, Anke Lüdeling, and Marc Reznicek. 2012. Better tags give better trees – or do they? *Linguistic Issues in Language Technology (LiLT)*, 7(10), 1.

Marc Reznicek, Anke Lüdeling, Cedric Krummes, Franziska Schwantuschke, Maik Walter, Karin Schmidt, Hagen Hirschmann, and Torsten Andreas, 2012. *Das Falko-Handbuch*.

Marc Reznicek, Anke Lüdeling, and Hagen Hirschmann. 2013. Competing target hypotheses in the falko corpus. In Ana Ballier Díaz-Negrillo and Paul Nicolas Thompson, editors, *Automatic Treatment and Analysis of Learner Corpus Data*, pages 101–123. John Benjamins Publishing Company, Amsterdam, NLD.

Victoria Rosén and Koenraad De Smedt. 2010. Syntactic annotation of learner corpora. In K. Johansen, H.; Tenfjord, editor, *Systematisk, variert, men ikke tilfeldig : antologi om norsk som andresspråk i anledning Kari Tenfjords 60-årsdag*, pages 120–132. Novus.

Alla Rozovskaya and Dan Roth. 2014. Building a state-of-the-art grammatical error correction system. *Transactions of the Association for Computational Linguistics*, 2:419–434.

Keisuke Sakaguchi, Courtney Napoles, Matt Post, and Joel Tetreault. 2016. Reassessing the goals of grammatical error correction: Fluency instead of grammaticality. *Transactions of the Association for Computational Linguistics*, 4:169–182.

Anne Schiller, Simone Teufel, Christine Stöckert, and Christine Thielen. 1999. Guidelines für das Tagging deutscher Textcorpora mit STTS. Technical report, Universität Stuttgart / Universität Tübingen.

Thomas Schmidt. 2004. Transcribing and annotating spoken language with EXMARaLDA. In *Proceedings of the LREC-Workshop on XML based richly annotated corpora, Lisbon 2004*. ELRA.

Developing and Evaluating Annotation Procedures for Twitter Data during Hazard Events

Kevin Stowe[1], Martha Palmer[1], Jennings Anderson[1], Leysia Palen[1], Kenneth M. Anderson[1],
Marina Kogan[2],Rebecca Morss[3], Julie Demuth[3], Heather Lazrus[3]
[1]University of Colorado, Boulder, CO, 80309
[2]University of New Mexico, Albuquerque, NM, 87131
[3]National Center for Atmospheric Research (NCAR), Boulder, CO, 80307

Abstract

When a hazard such as a hurricane threatens, people are forced to make a wide variety of decisions, and the information they receive and produce can influence their own and others' actions. As social media grows more popular, an increasing number of people are using social media platforms to obtain and share information about approaching threats and discuss their interpretations of the threat and their protective decisions. This work aims to improve understanding of natural disasters through social media and provide an annotation scheme to identify themes in user's social media behavior and facilitate efforts in supervised machine learning. To that end, this work has three contributions: (1) the creation of an annotation scheme to consistently identify hazard-related themes in Twitter, (2) an overview of agreement rates and difficulties in identifying annotation categories, and (3) a public release of both the dataset and guidelines developed from this scheme.

1 Background

People's responses to hurricane events encompass a variety of factors, including their behavior, attitudes, and perceptions of information. As social media becomes more and more prevalent, analysis of data from platforms such as Twitter offers potential to build understanding of how and why people make different protective decisions as a hazard approaches. This understanding can then be used to help design strategies to enhance hazard risk communication and support protective decision making (Morss et al., 2017).

Ethnographic and qualitative content analyses of Twitter data from recent hazard events indicate that careful analysis of data can reveal new insights about how people interpret different types of information, evaluate and respond to risks, and manage impacts as a hazard approaches and arrives. Such analyses are resource-intensive, however, taking time and computing power both in terms of selecting a suitable sample and in reading and analyzing the data. Automated extraction offers significant potential for helping narrow down the vast volume of Twitter data to that which is likely to be of greatest interest for research focused on different topics, thus supporting in-depth qualitative analyses. Machine learning can also aid the quantitative analysis of macroscale patterns in the data, such as how mentions of different topics evolve over time.

Here, we are interested in what is salient to people who are at risk from a hazard as they gather and process information, assess risks, and decide how to respond as the threat and its impacts evolve. Our qualitative analyses of Twitter narratives to date indicate that these data can help reveal how people use forecasts, evacuation orders, environmental and social cues, and other information to help assess risks. These analyses also reveal that Twitter data contains content related to people's cognitive risk perceptions, their affective responses to the risk and the event's impacts, and their protective and coping behaviors (Anderson et al., 2016; Demuth et al., 2018; Mileti and Sorenson, 1990). Thus, the annotation reported here focuses on identifying these types of topics, as they are represented in the Twitter data.

Proceedings of the Joint Workshop on
Linguistic Annotation, Multiword Expressions and Constructions (LAW-MWE-CxG-2018), pages 133–143
Santa Fe, New Mexico, USA, August 25-26, 2018.

2 Data Collection

Our annotation study is based on Twitterers active during Hurricane Sandy, which made landfall in the US in New Jersey on October 29th, 2012. This event affected millions of people in and around the New York City area. In order to identify and study protective decision making behavior, our annotation is aimed at users rather than individual tweets. Social media studies in a variety of domains tend to focus on individual tweets, but this approach often lacks the depth necessary to properly understand an individual's behavior. Recent work indicates that using data beyond individual tweets is critical to understanding user response during disaster events (Palen and Anderson, 2016; Kogan and Palen, 2018). Without the context of a user's entire stream of tweets, we are often unable to determine which tweets reference particular behaviors. Additionally if we work at the user level, this allows us to mitigate biases accumulated by specific heuristic based methods for tweet collection, which are often based on search terms that miss important tweets and include irrelevant tweets due to alternate uses of the terms.

For these reasons, we annotated based on users. However, finding the most relevant users for this task is difficult. Despite the weakness of collecting on search terms only, our user selection process begins with a set of users that used a Hurricane Sandy related keyword. We then employ multiple other filters. To obtain the first data set annotated, we removed users who tweeted less than 50 times as well as those whose tweets were primarily non-English. Most importantly, we limited our users to those that had at least 3 geo-tagged tweets within a mandatory evacuation zone. This allowed us to leverage Twitter's geo-location feature to refine our selection of users to only those that are likely to have been directly impacted by the storm's physical affects and were required to make a protective decision.

Over the course of developing our annotation scheme, we went through four different variations (referred to as Scheme 1, 2, 3, and 4). Our initial dataset (used for Scheme 1) includes 93 of the nearly 5,000 users that satisfied these requirements. It should be noted that the mandatory evacuation zone included very dense parts of Manhattan, Brooklyn, and Staten Island.

Through coding this first set of users we identified a bias in which types of users are tweeting with location services enabled. Our data had a disproportionate amount of high school aged persons that were not necessarily discussing their protective decisions or actions, but were instead affected by those decisions of their families. Occasionally, we could identify decisions to evacuate or take other protective actions through a user's comments (often complaints) about their family's location.

To improve this sample, rather than use the evacuation zone, we looked for users with "Far Rockaway" listed in their location or used in their tweets. Far Rockaway, located on the east end of the Rockaway Peninsula was under mandatory evacuation and impacted heavily by the storm. Filtering for these users identified 263 users that likely had to take protective action. We further filtered this list down to 53 users local to the area with descriptive tweet content that we could code. From these 53 users, we randomly selected subsets to annotate. This process yielded 12 users for scheme 2, 12 users for scheme 3, and 10 users for scheme 4.

Note that there is still significant bias in this data: Twitter users do not represent the entire population, and our collection methods aimed at identifying those at risk necessarily introduce additional bias into the sample. As we remove users that are not primarily in English, we also lose a substantial portion of users that may have been affected. To address these issues, our team also conducted focus groups with affected populations in New York City, with the goal of identifying risk factors for those who may not have access to Twitter and primarily non-English speaking populations (Lazrus et al., 2017).

Another bias in the collected data is the public visibility of user accounts. Dozens of user accounts have since been marked private or deleted since Hurricane Sandy, so retro-active collection or analysis of their tweets is impossible should researchers allow for participants the right to be forgotten. This highlights just one of many more ethical challenges of using social media data, especially within crisis informatics (Finn and Crawford, 2015). Furthermore, for the hundreds of users whose publicly visible tweets we did collect an analyze, research suggests they are likely unaware of the potential for such research and if asked directly would not give informed consent to being part of such a study (Fiesler and Proferes, 2018). That said, the data is publically available for such purposes. We acknowledge the ethical concerns and release our annotated dataset with usernames redacted and the knowledge that the

Scheme	Total Users	Total Tweets	Tweets/User
1	93	7490	81
2	12	2886	241
3	12	2536	211
4	10	1964	196

Table 1: Tweet and User counts by Scheme

data is now more than five years old. In other investigations, we have reached out to specific users before (re)publishing their public tweets alongside our in-depth analysis of their decisions (Anderson et al., 2016).

3 Annotation Overview

We initially developed a coding scheme via an iterative process, inspecting vulnerable Twitterers and identifying the kinds of protective decisions, attitudes, and information sources they were tweeting about. After determining a general idea of what kind of information users made explicit in tweets, we attempted to devise a scheme that is both exhaustive and mutually exclusive. We then pulled data for new users and applied the coding scheme to those. New users allowed us to identify new tweet categories that weren't covered by previous iterations. This process was repeated until the scheme settled, and no persistent new categories appeared. Our goal was to develop a scheme that covered every possible type of tweet that was of interest, and then narrow down to only those that reflected particularly informative tweets that were also consistently identifiable by non-domain experts.

This process was completed four times. Scheme 1 is multidimensional, including top-level and lower level categories for a broad spectrum of behaviors we found in the data[1]. We then ran three more iterations based on what we could consistently identify in the data. Scheme 2 refined the guidelines and added a small number of categories domain experts found particularly important. Scheme 3 compressed these down into a single layer, using only top-level categories, but still contained a large number of possible annotations. Finally, with Scheme 4, we settled on the 6 most important high level concepts, thus allowing annotation to be done with reasonable agreement while still capturing important behaviors.

The annotation process was done by giving the annotators all of a user's tweets from three weeks before landfall to three weeks after. This allows them to use contextual information to better understand user behavior. Each user was double annotated. Annotators met with members of the research team regularly to better understand the guidelines and help inform decisions about categories that were potentially difficult to distinguish. Annotators all had backgrounds in linguistics, with varying degrees of experience with Twitter. Over the course of the project we employed 5 different annotators. We recognize the possibility that variation in annotators may lead to bias in agreement rates. However, we annotated a handful of the same users using the same guidelines with different pairs and saw no significant difference in agreements, so we believe this concern is minimal.

4 Annotation Categories

Each category has been refined and clarified through the four different schemes. Across all schemes, we first annotated tweets for RELEVANCE. This allowed us to determine, at a high level, what tweets were related to the event and what tweets were not. Beyond relevance, there are a variety of important themes that we attempted to find and classify. For a general overview of high level categories, see Figure 1. These themes fall broadly into the six categories, which will be explored in the follow sections. Each relevant tweet can be annotated as one or more of these categories as many tweets expressed multiple propositions and behaviors. [2]

---

[1]We will use small caps for TOP-LEVEL categories, and *italics* for subcategories. Schemes 3 and 4 include only TOP LEVEL categories.

[2]Due to space constraints, we've refrained from providing examples for each category. Full examples and annotation guidelines will be made publicly available along with the dataset.

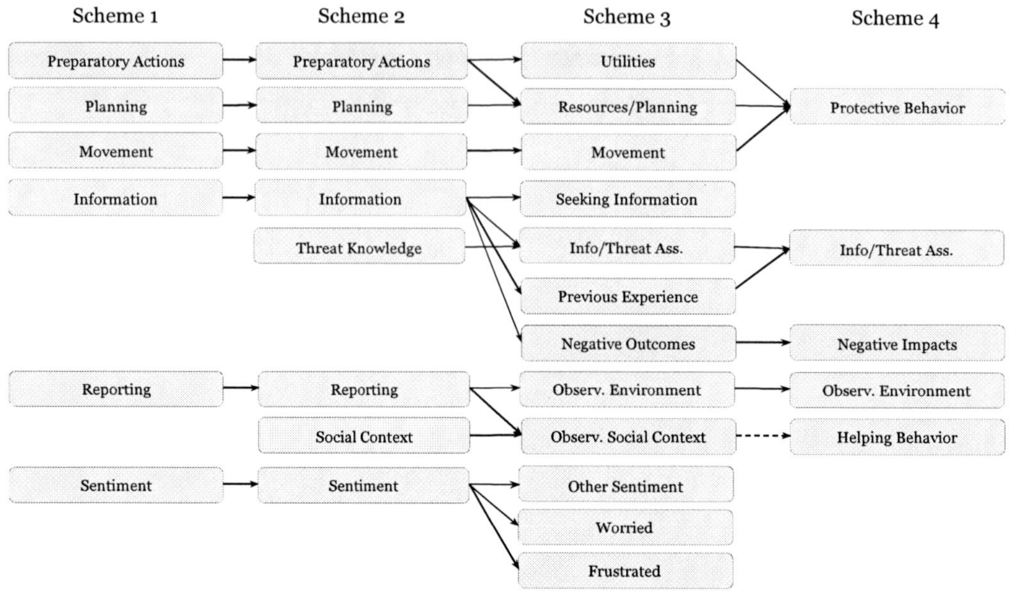

Figure 1: Evolution of the top-level categories. Note that subcategories were significantly shifted in Schemes 1 and 2 to promote coherence, and subsequently dropped for Schemes 3 and 4. Relevance was annotated across all schema. The dashed line indicates that Helping Behavior was only a small part of the original Observ. Social Context category.

Scheme	Count	%	Agreement
1	1662	26.8	.592
2	478	34.8	.920
3	889	29.4	.917
4	440	22.4	.911

Table 2: **Relevance** : Counts and Agreement Rates for annotation of ***relevant*** tweets

4.1 Relevance

Anything referencing the event or its effects was annotated as RELEVANT. This goes beyond the situational awareness annotation of Verma et al (2011), in that it includes tweets that don't exhibit any awareness but still refer to the event, including jokes, retweets, and speculation.

As our goal is to capture all tweets that relevant, we allowed annotators to use the full contextual stream to make decisions about relevant tweets. While this can often disambiguate difficult tweets, it also posed some difficulties in the level of inference possible, which will be explored in Section 5.1.2.

The RELEVANCE category was not changed over the course of the annotation, but the annotation guidelines were updated to include better descriptions and examples as we encountered border cases. This is reflected in agreement rates, which greatly improved from Scheme 1 to Scheme 2 (Table 2). Most difficult are cases of short tweets that contain little information which can not be disambiguated through context.

4.2 Preparatory Action

People exhibit a wide variety of preparatory behavior, much of which is present in their tweets. The goal of this category is to identify actions individuals take to try to protect themselves and their households from the hazard and its impacts. It also includes decisions and planning related to these activities. We identified three core kinds of preparatory action: supplies/electricity, planning, and movement.

4.2.1 Supplies and Electricity

We created a top-level PREPARATORY ACTION category based on material supplies and electricity that is necessarily broad, including various kinds of information. This category contains five subcategories for Schemes 1 and 2:

- *General Electricity* (household power, generators, etc)
- *Electricity for Communication* (electricity preparation specific to communicative devices such as phones and computers)
- *Material Assets and Supplies* (food, flashlights, etc)
- *Drugs and Alcohol*
- *Preparing Home and Property* (actions taken to protect property)

These categories remained the same from Scheme 1 to Scheme 2, but were merged to provide better distinctions in Scheme 3. We combined any mention of electrical power with mentions of other utilities such as sewage, water, and phone service. This became a single UTILITIES category. We then condensed any mention of household resources (such as food, water, and alcohol) along with physical preparation, yielding a single HOUSEHOLD PREPARATION category. The goal of this change is to improve top-level consistency, so removing electricity related tweets from material assets seemed necessary.

4.2.2 Planning

Making plans for the event and possible actions that may be required in the future are both kinds of preparation. For Scheme 1 we attempted to identify four different types of planning: *changing, considering,* and *maintaining* plans, as well as *transportation* planning. However these subcategories were found to be less important and hard to identify, and were lumped into a single PLANNING top-level category for Scheme 2. For Scheme 3 these were lumped into the HOUSEHOLD RESOURCES AND PLANNING category.

4.2.3 Movement

A critical user behavior is movement: either evacuating, deliberately sheltering in place, or returning from an evacuation. For Schemes 1 and 2, we included MOVEMENT as a top-level category, with *evacuation, sheltering in place,* and *returning from evacuation* as fine-grained subcategories. Our goal was to differentiate different types of movement because the different behaviors plausibly represent different risk and vulnerability profiles that are interesting for examination, both here and across different weather hazards. However, they are sparse in the data, and for scheme 3, these were collapsed. We rely on only the top-level MOVEMENT category, and for Scheme 4 these were included in the broad PREPARATORY ACTION category.

Agreement for MOVEMENT tweets is difficult, largely because they are so infrequent. Most users don't reference their positional behavior, either as evacuation or protective sheltering. This leads to difficulty in finding good examples, and also limits the potential of using supervised machine learning to identify movement tweets, as training data will likely be insufficient.

Due to persistent difficulty in distinguishing various preparatory behaviors, for Scheme 4 all three of the subcategories were included in a single PREPARATORY ACTION category, including any mention of household resources, electricity or other utilities, household preparation, and any movement-related behavior.

4.3 Information

The question of how people acquire and distribute information from social media is critical to the analysis of the roles different types of information play in protective decision making. We began with a top level INFORMATION category, with subcategories for *passing on information*, including retweets, direct quotes, and paraphrases, as well as any tweets *seeking information* from outside sources.

For Scheme 2, we included a handful of subcategories deemed particularly useful for evaluating tweeter's information sources. We categorized any references to weather *forecasts* (or forecasters), as well as any *public officials*, or announcements from public officials. This was intended to capture knowledge of people's use of information from official sources. We also added three new categories:

- *evacuation factors*, which indicates references to specific factors affecting the user's ability to evacuate, such as pets or immobile family members
- *threat knowledge*, which includes information from any sources about their perceptions of the level of severity of the approaching event
- *previous experience*, which includes mentions of their responses and opinions about previous hurricane events.

For Scheme 3 we collapsed these three items along with *forecasts* and *public officials* into a single category, INFORMATION AND THREAT ASSESSMENT. We also split out ASKING QUESTIONS, as it doesn't directly reflect a person's threat information and appeared relatively easy to classify separately. The *pass on information* category was dropped.

For Scheme 4, we added previous experience to the INFORMATION AND THREAT ASSESSMENT category, with significant guideline clarifications, ensuring that the category captures any mention of future damage from the event. We dropped the ASKING QUESTIONS category as it was deemed not critical to capture.

4.4 Environment Observations

People's first-hand reports of their surrounding environment are critical for assessing their risk and vulnerability. For Scheme 1 and Scheme 2, the REPORTING category captures these reports. It includes subcategories for reports of *natural environment* (including weather and flooding), reports of *built environment* (road and structure damage), reports of *immediate personal environment* (including direct observations of the person's current location), and reports of *what other people are doing*, later folded into the social context themes covered in Section 4.5.

These categories proved somewhat confusing for annotators and contained significant overlap, so for Scheme 3 they were condensed into one key observation category : ENVIRONMENT OBSERVATIONS (including natural, built, and personal). A key difficulty in identifying observations of environment is the distinction between a tweeter's own observations and those of others - it is often unclear whether they are directly reporting or relaying the reports of others. This was clarified to allow only direct observations in Scheme 3, with indirect reports being a type of threat assessment, and thus falling in the INFORMATION AND THREAT ASSESSMENT category.

For Scheme 4, all observations of any impacts, including weather, physical damage, and other environmental factors, are included in the same ENVIRONMENT OBSERVATIONS category. We also relaxed the guidelines to include any mention of environment observation regardless of source. This allows for a broader and easier to define category that still captures the necessary tweets.

4.5 Social Observations

Along with observations of their physical environment, people's observations of social context are strong indicators of their ability to prepare for and cope with disaster. Additionally, observations of other people taking preparatory actions may influence a user's own decisions.

For Scheme 1, social observations are captured only through a subcategory of REPORTING, *what others are doing*. This was difficult to annotate, perhaps due to its potentially vague or ambiguous nature. In order to better capture the full extent of observations relating to social context, a new top level category was created for Scheme 2: SOCIAL CONTEXT. Fine-grained categories for this top-level category are mentions of the user's *social network*, which indicates ability to lower one's risk and/or vulnerability, mentions of *community organizations*, and mentions of *sensitive populations*: those that may be disadvantaged in preparing for or responding to the event.

For Scheme 3, all of these codes were condensed into one top level code, SOCIAL CONTEXT, as distinguishing between them proved difficult. Scheme 3 also included the *what others are doing* subcategory of REPORTING in the new SOCIAL CONTEXT category.

Due to inconsistency in annotation, for Scheme 4 most of what was included in this category was dropped. We included a new category, HELPING BEHAVIOR, to include any mentions of relief provided by the user or others, which was determined to be more important, more prevalent, and easier to identify.

Scheme	Relevance	Negative Outcomes	Helping Behavior	Preparatory Action				Information					Env. Obs.			Social Context			Sentiment		
				Planning	Material Supplies	Electricity/Utilities	Movement	Passing on Info.	Seeking Info.	Evac. Factors	Threat Knowledge	Previous Experience	Natural Environment	Built Environment	Personal Environment	Social Networks	Community Orgs.	Sensitive Populations/Inequality	Worried	Frustrated	Other
1	.59	-	-	.39	.40	.50	.47	.12	-	-	-	-	.47	.46	.29	-	-	-	.43	.39	.24
2	**.92**	.23	-	.50	.48	.71	.46	.53	.63	0	.46	.56	.29	.58	.40	.23	.41	.48	.56	.73	.43
3	**.92**	.36	-	.27		.65	.56	-	.37	.53		.57	.61			.47			.51	.56	.62
4	**.91**	.54	**.76**	.58				-	-	.52			**.79**			-			-		

Table 3: Inter-annotator Agreement as F1 across Schema. Bold numbers are those that showed agreement over .75.

4.6 Negative Social and Economic Outcomes

Particularly important to researchers studying the effects of hazard events are the negative outcomes that follow. This category is specifically designed to capture indirect effects - lifestyle disruption, personal loss (of jobs, wellbeing, etc.), and damages to mental and physical health (physical or emotional suffering, loss of life, injury, illness, etc.). Introduced as a subcategory of INFORMATION in Scheme 2, it was pulled out into its own category in Schemes 3 and 4, along with substantial clarifications to the guidelines. This category is hard to consistently annotate, as it is broad and not very frequent, but we've maintained it due to its importance to the understanding of hazard events.

4.7 Sentiment

SENTIMENT is the most traditional category of annotation, having received a large amount of treatment for social media (see Barnes et al (2017) for a recent review of sentiment models and tasks). Our goal was ambitious - we aimed to capture a large set of diverse sentiments, rather than simply positive/negative. For Schemes 1 and 2, we included 8 different subcategories of sentiment. These are *awe, boredom, excitement, humor, frustration, positive coping, worry,* and being *settled*.

For Scheme 3, we removed categories that were rare (*awe, boredom, settled, excitement*), as well as those with very low agreement rates (*positive coping, humor*). We kept three different sentiment categories as top level categories : WORRY, FRUSTRATION, and an OTHER category which is used for any of the other sentiments. This allows us to capture the most common sentiments as well as those that are relevant to people's decision making. It also allows us to capture any other sentiment at a general level, and this data can be further analyzed to find specific themes.

In annotating these sentiment categories, we encountered numerous problems. First, we were largely unable to consistently distinguish between the fine-grained categories. There were a large number of instances that annotators did not agree on the correct sentiment even after discussion. This was particularly prevalent for categories like *humor*, where the subjective nature of the emotion makes it difficult to obtain reliable agreement, and in differentiating WORRY and FRUSTRATION which are indistinguishable in many cases. Second, most of the fine-grained categories showed fairly sparse results, making them impractical to use for machine learning.

For these reasons in Scheme 4 we decided to drop sentiment from our annotation. Given the inability to consistently annotate across the spectrum of possible sentiments and the sparseness of the data, we believe that using available sentiment classification tools is a practical alternative.

5 Analysis

Inter-annotator agreement for each category over time are shown in Figure 3. Agreement was calculated as F1 between annotators, as the distribution is highly skewed. We considered agreement rates over .75 to be "good", and preliminary results show this evaluation roughly matches "good" arguments calculated scores via Cohen's kappa.

With clarification, guideline improvements, and merging of difficult themes, some categories became clearer and better defined. Others remained difficult despite category compression and clarification. Relevance agreement was greater than .90 from Scheme 2 to Scheme 4, showing that it can be reliably coded across users. With the clarification of ENVIRONMENT OBSERVATIONS, agreement reached .79 in Scheme 4, also showing that it can be reliably captured. The new category HELPING BEHAVIOR also achieved an agreement rate over .75. The NEGATIVE OUTCOMES, PREPARATORY ACTION, and THREAT ASSESSMENT categories all proved much more difficult, showing agreement rights between .5 and .6.

The release of this data will include all of the relevance annotation as agreement is generally good, as well as all of the data annotated for the most current guideline, Scheme 4. The data annotated for this research will be made available in compliance with Twitter's terms of service, meaning that tweets that have been deleted or made private by their owners will not be retrievable. The contextual streams we annotated are available through Twitter, and thus this process can be replicated (provided these users allow their tweets to remain public) and applied to new users. We will also release the guidelines for the current version of Scheme 4, with the knowledge that some categories can be consistently annotated while others require further improvement.

We observed a variety of challenges in the disagreements that demonstrate difficulties in these annotations.

5.1 Disagreements

Two related, dependent properties are present in a large number of disagreements. One is that the level of inferencing deemed possible given only a short text varies between annotators. The other is that there often isn't sufficient content in a tweet to allow interpretation. These factors are related - short tweets often allow for varying levels of interpretation. However, they aren't always the same - there are tweets that contain a full amount of content that still pose inference problems, and there are short tweets that are unambiguous.

5.1.1 Inference

The key problem for most of the disagreements is the degree to which the annotators made inferences from the text. While there are many cases where users exhibit a clear behavior from their tweet, there are many more that yield some insight into what they are experiencing but are unclear as to the exact extent that they are affected.

We found it difficult to restrict annotators to a specific level of inference. While it may be possible to only allow them to use information directly present in a single tweet, this will lead to the omission of a large amount of data that does indicate relevant and important behavior but requires world knowledge to understand the user's intent. The inferencing problem, where annotators disagreed on how much to read into a particular tweet, is primarily caused by three factors: insufficient context, insufficient content, and the modality of the information.

5.1.2 Insufficient Context

An important factor in identifying user behavior is the context of their tweets. While Twitter research often focuses on isolated tweets collected via keyword searches, our data indicates that knowledge of a user's stream and their behavior in context is critical to determining their situation within events. For this reason, we encourage annotators to read through the user's contextual tweets before and after the target tweet in order to understand the context that influences it. Consider the following stream of tweets from a user:

1. The news goes to the blocks that always flood and sit out here like oh no it's flooded..Lol
2. @user_2 nah stop watching the news.../they full of shit

In this example, tweet 2 is ambiguous without context: it could refer to hurricane or non-hurricane related news. However, their previous tweet 1 is about the untrustworthiness of news broadcasters during disaster events, so it seems reasonable to infer that tweet 2 is also about the hurricane. This doesn't always clarify matters, however, especially with regard to tweets that are short and contain minimal context and content:

1. Im extremely bored!
2. 👍 😈..... #nvm
3. I've never heard that but it makes so much sense. Lol

In this context, these tweets are all still indeterminate, showing the difficulty of assessing user's behavior given the limited nature of the text produced. While we tend to mark these as irrelevant, it can be difficult to tell which tweets play a part in their decisions and which are irrelevant, and annotators often disagreed about how to interpret contextual information.

5.1.3 Content

From the data we observed that there are numerous tweets that contain very little content. These are difficult to annotate with any category, and require extensive inferencing from context to determine the user's experience. For this reason, we instructed annotators to mark tweets that appeared lacking in content as irrelevant. Many of these cases are straightforward:

1. @user1 lmaooo
2. Got real quick

Our guidelines indicate that tweets with this extreme deficit of content can be marked as irrelevant. However, there are also cases where a small amount of content is present, and it becomes difficult to determine if the content is relevant or indicative of a particular behavior.

1. Turn on the light!
2. @user2 u can come here :)
3. Store run

These cases are indeterminate without context, and even within user streams they are difficult to assess. While we attempted to decipher the users' situations from their contextual stream, in many cases the context is also sparse and we theorized that the lack of content may lead to disagreement.

As an experiment, we removed tweets that contained less than a given number of words from the data and then reassessed agreement rates. The results for change of agreement rates without these short tweets, as well as the percentage of tweets removed, are displayed in Figure 2.

This analysis shows that removing only very short tweets yields no significant result in terms of annotator agreement. Most short tweets aren't relevant, the percentage of short tweets removed increases slower. Removing tweets up to 14 words improves agreement performance by only 1.5%, requiring the removal of 40% of the data (over 10% of the relevant tweets). Thus only minimal gain is achieved while sacrificing large amounts of data. This shows the danger in trimming Twitter data based on word count, as large of amounts of data may be removed without improving the quality of the dataset. This can also introduce extra biases in the data, and compounding this with the biases already present in Twitter data will yield a final dataset with extensive sampling issues.

5.1.4 Modality

Another common theme in annotator disagreement is when user's tweets indicate either a lack of knowledge or uncertainty about future or present events. These tweets are difficult to handle because we are often unable to determine the user's actual intent or situation, and thus their protective decision making behavior is unclear.

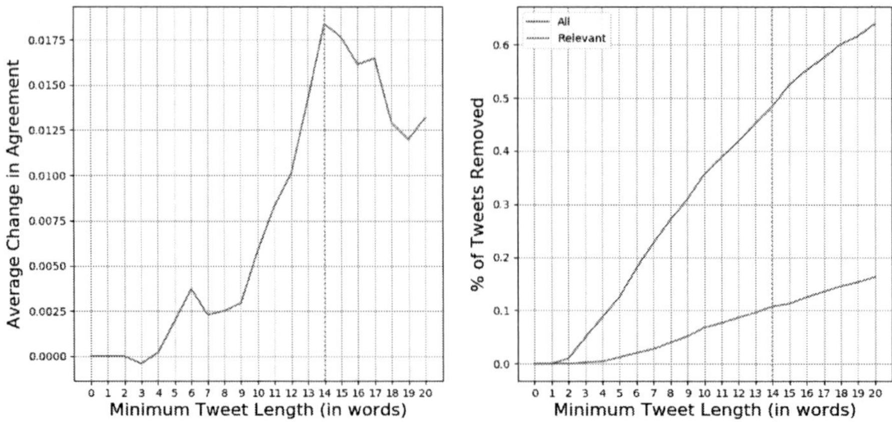

Figure 2: Agreement rates and data size after removing tweets below a certain word count.

1. @user2 did you evacuate?

2. Tight I'm not getting any of these emergency alerts on my phone

3. How Siri can't tell me where sandy is at tho? Siri is really good for nothing

In 1, the user is asking a friend if they evacuated. Were it a first person reference, we could assume protective decision making behavior. That not being the case, annotators disagreed on how far to infer. If she knows people are considering evacuation, does that also reflect her evacuation decision? In 2 and 3, the user lacks information about the threat due to technical problems. Does their demonstrating that they lack knowledge indicate that they consider the threat to be more serious, or that they should take some decision? Lack of context and level of inference both cause this kind of tweet to be difficult to consistently annotate.

6 Future Work

Although our initial development and testing of the annotation scheme reported here uses Twitter data from Hurricane Sandy, the scheme was developed using knowledge about the factors that affect decision making for hurricanes and other weather-related hazards (e.g., tornadoes, floods) based on the body of existing literature on these topics that has been developed using other research methods (e.g., (Brotzge and Donner, 2013), (Gladwin, 2007), (Lindell and Perry, 2012), (Ruin et al., 2014), (Morss et al., 2017)). Thus, we anticipate that with minor modifications based on the context, the approach discussed here will also be applicable for studying other hurricanes that threaten the US, and other types of weather hazards. Our ongoing research will be testing the utility of the approach for Hurricane Matthew, which occurred in 2016, and tornado events.

Tornadoes are rapid-onset, spatially localized hazards as compared to hurricanes. Thus, they represent information, risk assessment, and response behaviors that are similar to hurricanes but that are time-compressed and plausibly different in other ways. We aim to apply the coding scheme developed here to such events as a test of its external validity and use these events to refine the scheme so that it can be more broadly useful for other hazards.

Acknowledgements

We would like to thank all of our collaborators in CHIME: Communicating Hazard Information in the Modern Environment, the larger research effort that supported this work, as well as the University of Colorado.

References

Jennings Anderson, Marina Kogan, Leysia Palen, Kenneth Anderson, Kevin Stowe, Rebecca Morss, Julie Demuth, Heather Lazrus, Olga Wilhelmi, and Jennifer Henderson. 2016. Far far away in far rockaway: Responses to risks and impacts during hurricane sandy through first-person social media narratives. In *Proceedings of the Information Systems for Crisis Response and Management (ISCRAM) Conference.*

Jeremy Barnes, Roman Klinger, and Sabine Schulte im Walde. 2017. Assessing state-of-the-art sentiment models on state-of-the-art sentiment datasets. In *Proceedings of the 8th Workshop on Computational Approaches to Subjectivity, Sentiment and Social Media Analysis*, pages 2–12, Copenhagen, Denmark, September. Association for Computational Linguistics.

J. Brotzge and W. Donner. 2013. The tornado warning process: A review of current research, challenges, and opportunities. *Bulletin of the American Meteorological Society*, 94(11):1715–1733.

Julie Demuth, Rebecca Morss, Leysia Palen, Kenneth Anderson, Jennings Anderson, Marina Kogan, Kevin Stowe, Melissa Bica, Heather Lazrus, Olga Wilhelmi, and Jen Henderson. 2018. "sometimes da #beachlife ain't always da wave": Understanding people's evolving risk assessments and responses during hurricane sandy using twitter (in press). *Weather, Climate and Society.*

C. Fiesler and N. Proferes. 2018. "Participant" perceptions of twitter research ethics. *Social Media + Society*, 4(1).

M. Finn and K. Crawford. 2015. The limits of crisis data: analytical and ethical challenges of using social and mobile data to understand disasters. *GeoJournal*, 80(4):491–502.

Nicole Dash Hugh Gladwin. 2007. Evacuation decision making and behavioral responses: Individual and household. *Natural Hazards Review*, 8(3):69–77.

Marina Kogan and Leysia Palen. 2018. Conversations in the eye of the storm: At-scale features of conversational structure in a high-tempo, high-stakes microblogging environment. In *Proceedings of the 2018 CHI Conference on Human Factors in Computing Systems*, CHI '18, pages 84:1–84:13, New York, NY, USA. ACM.

H. Lazrus, O. Wilhelmi, J. Henderson, R. E. Morss, and A. Dietrich. 2017. Information as intervention: How can hurricane risk communication reduce vulnerability?

Michael K. Lindell and Ronald W. Perry. 2012. The protective action decision model: Theoretical modifications and additional evidence. *Risk Analysis*, 32(4):616–632.

D.S. Mileti and J.H. Sorenson. 1990. *Communication of Emergency Public Warnings: A Social Science Perspective and State-of-the-ART Assessment.* Oak Ridge National Laboratory Rep. ORNL-6609.

Rebecca E. Morss, Julie L. Demuth, Heather Lazrus, Leysia Palen, C. Michael Barton, Christopher A. Davis, Chris Snyder, Olga V. Wilhelmi, Kenneth M. Anderson, David A. Ahijevych, Jennings Anderson, Melissa Bica, Kathryn R. Fossell, Jennifer Henderson, Marina Kogan, Kevin Stowe, and Joshua Watts. 2017. Hazardous weather prediction and communication in the modern information environment. *Bulletin of the American Meteorological Society*, 98(12):2653–2674.

Leysia Palen and Ken M. Anderson. 2016. Crisis informatics: New data for extraordinary times. *Science*, 353(6296):224–225.

Isabelle Ruin, Cline Lutoff, Brice Boudevillain, Jean-Dominique Creutin, S. Anquetin, M. Bertran Rojo, L. Boissier, L. Bonnifait, M. Borga, L. Colbeau-Justin, L. Creton-Cazanave, G. Delrieu, J. Douvinet, E. Gaume, E. Gruntfest, J.-P. Naulin, O. Payrastre, and O. Vannier. 2014. Social and hydrological responses to extreme precipitations: An interdisciplinary strategy for postflood investigation. *Weather, Climate, and Society*, 6(1):135–153.

Sudha Verma, Sarah Vieweg, William Corvey, Leysia Palen, James Martin, Martha Palmer, Aaron Schram, and Kenneth Anderson. 2011. Natural language processing to the rescue? extracting "situational awareness" tweets during mass emergency.

A Treebank for the Healthcare Domain

Oinam Nganthoibi
Computational Linguist
ezDI Inc. Kentucky
oinam.n@ezdi.us

Diwakar Mishra
Computational Linguist
ezDI Inc. Kentucky
diwakar.m@ezdi.us

Pinal Patel
Team Lead, Research
ezDI Inc. Kentucky
pinal.p@ezdi.us

Narayan Choudhary
Lecturer cum Junior Research Officer
CIIL, Mysore
choudharynarayan@gmail.com

Hitesh Desai
Research Engineer
ezDI Inc. Kentucky
hitesh.d@ezdi.us

Abstract

This paper presents a treebank for the healthcare domain developed at ezDI. The treebank is created from a wide array of clinical health record documents across hospitals. The data has been de-identified and annotated for constituent syntactic structure. The treebank contains a total of 52053 sentences that have been sampled for subdomains as well as linguistic variations. The paper outlines the sampling process followed to ensure a better domain representation in the corpus, the annotation process and challenges, and corpus statistics. The Penn Treebank tagset and guidelines were largely followed, but there were many syntactic contexts that warranted adaptation of the guidelines. The treebank created was used to re-train the Berkeley parser and the Stanford parser. These parsers were also trained with the GENIA treebank for comparative quality assessment. Our treebank yielded greater accuracy on both parsers. Berkeley parser performed better on our treebank with an average F1 measure of 91 across 5-folds. This was a significant jump from the out-of-the-box F1 score of 70 on Berkeley parser's default grammar.

1 Introduction

There is severe paucity of data in healthcare due to the confidentiality regulations entailed. However, the importance of domain specific training data cannot be denied. It is a well acknowledged fact that systems trained on the general domain do not perform well in highly specialized domains like healthcare (Jiang et al., 2015; Zhang et al., 2015; Ferraro et al., 2013). The research is further hindered for tasks that require a large volume of annotated data such as syntactic parsing.

Parsing is one of the complex natural language processing (NLP) tasks. Its complexity is inherited from syntax. Syntactic annotation is based on phrase structure grammar which posits a universal framework based on well-formedness conditions (Chomsky, 1965, 1993, 1995). However, these frameworks are modeled on formal language and therefore fail to account for ungrammaticality or variations in style. A universal syntactic framework even for a well-studied language like English is not established due to these reasons. Clinical healthcare data is an apposite example. It is populated with ungrammatical fragments and domain specific idiosyncrasies that cannot be accounted by standard grammatical rules. Therefore, the annotation task involves a high level of complexity and subjectivity. This paper showcases specific examples that justified adoption of new rules that are not postulated under the Penn Treebank guidelines (Bies et al., 1995). This is domain specific annotation. This approach has been rewarding. The Berkeley parser (Petrov et al., 2006) trained on this domain specific treebank gave a high F1 score of 91.58 using ParsEval (Harrison et al., 1991) method of evaluation. This is a remarkable improvement from the F1 of 70 that was attained on the parser's default grammar model.

Proceedings of the Joint Workshop on
Linguistic Annotation, Multiword Expressions and Constructions (LAW-MWE-CxG-2018), pages 144–155
Santa Fe, New Mexico, USA, August 25-26, 2018.

2   Related work

There are various types of corpora available in the field of clinical/medical NLP research. Good examples of raw text corpora include Stockholm corpus (Dalianis et al., 2012) which contains over a million patient record documents; Mayo Clinic clinical notes, referred in Wu et al. (2012) which contains 51 million documents, and a public repository of medical documents available at ClinicalTrials.gov (Hao et al., 2014). Zweigenbauma et al. (2001) also created a balanced raw text corpus annotated with meta-information to represent the medical domain sub-language.

Some corpora are annotated for part-of-speech (PoS), such as GENIA corpus (Tateisi and Tsujii, 2004) and the corpus of Pakhomov et al., (2006) while others are annotated and trained for named entity recognition (NER) such as Orgen et al. (2007), who have created a medical NER evaluation corpus that contains 160 clinical notes, 1556 annotations of 658 concept codes from SNOMED CT. Wang (2009) also reports training an NER system on a corpus of Intensive Care Service documents, containing >15000 medical entities of 11 types.

Alnazzawi et al. (2014), GENIA corpus version 3.0 (Kim et al., 2003) and CLEF corpus (Roberts et al., 2009) are examples of semantically annotated corpora. The source of GENIA corpus is 2000 research abstracts from MEDLINE database and is limited to specific type of documents while Alnazzawi's (2014) corpus is limited to covering only congestive heart and renal failure. BioScope corpus (Vinczer et al., 2008) is annotated for uncertainty, negation and their scope; THYME corpus (Styler et al., 2014) is annotated for temporal ordering using THYME-TimeML guidelines, an extension of ISO-TimeML; and Chapman et al. (2012) have annotated a corpus of 180 clinical reports for all anaphora-antecedent pairs. Xia and Yetisgen-Yildiz (2012) describe 3 clinical domain corpora, in which, the first corpus is annotated at the sentence level; the second corpus is annotated at the document level, for presence of pneumonia and infection score in X-ray reports; and the third corpus is annotated for pneumonia detection per patient in ICU reports. Some researchers have combined parse trees and multiword entities for specific tasks such as multiword entity recognition (Finkel and Manning, 2009) and entity relation identification (Shi et al., 2007). Cohen et al. (2005) list and classify six publically available biomedical corpora, namely, PDG, Wisconsin, GENIA, MEDSTRACT, Yapex and GENETAG, according to various corpus design features and characteristics.

Apart of these, work such as Pathak et al. (2015), have customized Unified Medical Language System (UMLS) thesaurus for concept unique identifier (CUI) detection as part of disorder detection.

In literature closely related to the work presented here, there are treebanks (syntactically annotated corpora) that use customized or original Penn Treebank guidelines (Bies et al., 1995). Albright et al. (2013) have annotated 13091 sentences of MiPECQ corpus for syntactic structure, predicate-argument structure and UMLS based semantic information. Fan et al. (2013) have customized Penn parsing guidelines to handle ill-formed sentences and have annotated 1100 sentences for syntactic structure. A subset of GENIA corpus, 500 abstracts, is also annotated for syntactic structure (Tateisi et al., 2005) using GENIA corpus manual (Kim et al., 2006). This is further extended to 1999 abstracts (GENIA project website). These three treebanks have sentences annotated for constituency structure. There are also treebanks annotated with dependency structure such as The Prague Dependency Treebank (Hajic, 1998).

As evident from the work listed above, there has not been any attempt of corpus creation to the expanse of the project presented here. Our corpus exceeds in quantity with 52053 sentences covering a variety of sentence structures from various document types and sources. Our work also differs in the corpus sampling process. MiPACQ corpus consists of randomly selected clinical notes and pathology notes from Mayo Clinic related to colon cancer. GENIA corpus is a set of abstracts from MEDLINE database that contain specific keywords. We have followed a sampling procedure that takes into consideration sentence patterns and domain representation. Our corpus sampling method covers the clinical domain on a large scale by giving representation to a variety of hospitals, specialties and document types. A more detailed comparison of corpus structure between our work and the GENIA Treebank (biomedical domain) and Wall Street Journal section of Penn Treebank (general domain) is shown in Section 4.

3 Creation of the Treebank

The task of treebank creation can be divided into two major parts - data sampling and annotation/bracketing. Section 3.1 describes how the data was sampled from clinical documents of different hospitals and specialty clinics. Section 3.2 discusses special cases of annotation that are peculiar to this domain.

3.1 Data Sampling

The current corpus has been assembled over time from different databases. The first set was extracted from an internal database of 237,100 documents from 10 hospitals in the US from the year 2012-2013. These hospitals were selected due to the fact that they were large establishments housing variety of specialties and therefore a good resource for different types of documents. These documents were classified into different work types, service lines and section heads, based on which, 10,000 representative documents were manually selected. A graph-based string similarity algorithm was used to find similar sentences which resulted in a collection of unique patterns. A sentence clustering algorithm was then used to narrow them down into pattern heads that were representative of all the unique patterns. The final corpus was selected by giving proportional weight to each pattern head. A detailed discussion of the methodology is found in Choudhary et al., (2014). This set was created for the development of a part-of-speech (PoS) tagger. 38,000 sentences from this dataset were used as the base for this parsing project as well. The Table 1 below shows the sub-domains included in this dataset.

IM_After Hours Care	IM_Endocrinology	Pathology	IM_Oncology
Vascular and Thoracic Surgery	Emergency Medicine	IM_Occupational Medicine	IM_Internal Medicine General
Obstetrics	Psychiatry	Anesthesiology	Neurosurgery
IM_Pain Management	Family Medicine	Urology	Opthalmology
IM_Physical Medicine and Rehabilitation	IM_General Medicine	IM_Physician Assistant	Nurse Practitioner
IM_Nephrology	IM_Hematology	IM_Pediatrics	Otorhinolaryngology
IM_Gastroenterology	IM_Neurology	IM_Geriatrics	Radiology
IM_Infectious Diseases	IM_Rheumatology	Hospitalist	Orthopedics
Obstetrics & Gynecology	IM_Cardiology	Oncology	Unclassified
Podiatry	Surgery		

Table 1: Subdomains included in Dataset 1 from Database 1

The second dataset was sampled from a different database of 3 hospitals in the US containing 1,473 documents dated April to September, 2016. This database was used to update the corpus with current clinical data. The need to update arose from the observation that the style of electronic health record documentation has changed significantly between 2012 and 2016. It is evident by the relative proportion of S nodes (well-formed sentences/clauses) and FRAG nodes (fragments) between the two datasets. Dataset 1 contains 29435 S nodes and 15118 FRAG nodes (S-FRAG ratio of 1:0.513), while Dataset 2 contains 2786 S nodes and 12102 FRAG nodes (S-FRAG ratio of 1:4.343).

The 1,473 documents from these three hospitals were categorized according to their work types. It contained 535 documents of 25 work types from hospital A, 93 documents of 20 work types from hospital B, and 845 documents of 14 work types from hospital C. These work types were grouped into three broader categories – Admission, Progress and Discharge. So, for example, worktypes "History and Physical" and "ER Physician Document" were kept under the 'Admission' category; "Preprocedure Checklist" and "Anesthesia postoperative Note" were kept in 'Progress' category, and so on. Then, a certain number of documents were manually selected from each of the three categories, keeping in mind a balanced ratio of the original work types. The following Table 2 shows the number of documents selected from each hospital from each category.

Hospitals	Admission	Progress	Discharge	Total
A	8 / 36	42 / 457	10 / 42	60 / 535
B	4 / 16	20 / 57	8 / 20	32 / 93
C	6 / 26	50 / 775	8 / 44	64 / 845
All Hospitals	18 / 78	112 / 1289	26 / 106	156 / **1473**

Table 2: Number and type of documents from each category included in Dataset 2 from Database 2

After a simple algorithm to remove duplicate sentences, this process resulted in a dataset of 19,011 unique sentences. 12,000 sentences were eventually selected from this source.

The third sampling stage was done on the basis of 'rare syntactic pattern'. Low frequency patterns were extracted from the corpus compiled so far. These patterns were identified based on grammatical categories, keywords and subject to human judgment in the background of extended interaction with the domain. These patterns were then converted to regular expressions, which was used to extract similar sentences from Database 1 and 2. For example, sentences with wh-questions have a low distribution in clinical texts and were therefore left out during the sampling methods employed so far. These were added. Low frequency closed grammatical categories like prepositions were also added to the corpus. This method contributed to around 2,000 sentences. The Table 3 below is a summary of the corpus creation in the three steps.

Source	No. of Hospitals	Dated	Method	Dataset
Database 1	10	2012-13	sub-domain selection + sentence clustering	(1) 38,000 sents
Database 2	3	2016	sub-domain selection + duplicate removal	(2) 12,000 sents
Database 1 + 2	13	2012-16	rare syntactic pattern + regular expression	(3) 20,53 sents
Total corpus				**52053 sents**

Table 3: Source databases, methods and resulting datasets

3.2 Challenges in annotation

The corpus was annotated for phrase structure following a customized version of the Penn Treebank guidelines (Bies et al., 1995). Null elements and function tags have not been incorporated at this point. This section discusses the data structures where deliberate and novel guidelines were adopted.

3.2.1 Binary branching vs Tertiary branching

Binary branching was adopted in post phrase structure syntactic theories viz. Government and Binding (Chomsky, 1993) and Minimalist Program (Chomsky, 1995). In the binary structure, the relations between parts of the sentences are expressed through hierarchy. This hierarchy is also crucial for the linear ordering of the sentence. However, there were many instances where binary branching could not be adopted. For example, there is no hierarchy in conjunction and therefore conjunctive phrases/clauses/sentences or multiple elements inside the NP were kept in multiple branches, which extended beyond 3 tokens or more. For example, Figure (1) has four phrase branches because there are four different fragments conjoined by commas and a conjunctive word. Each branch has a composite meaning that does not have a hierarchical relationship with the others. The same is true for elements inside the noun phrase (NP). In clinical texts, an NP can have a token span of up to 5 and more. There is, again, no hierarchical relationship between NP internal elements. Figure (2) shows a typical NP in the clinical domain which contains numerals and symbols as part of the NP.

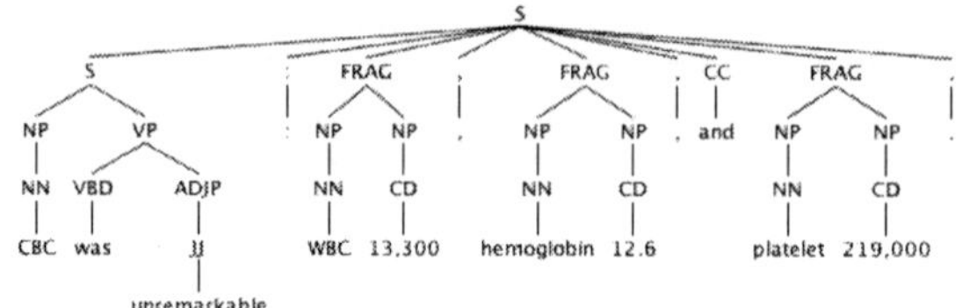 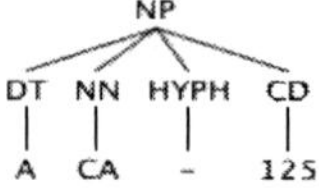

Figure 1: Multiple branch at the clause level   Figure 2: Tertiary branch inside an NP

Tertiary branching is also adopted for moved elements such as sentential adverbs and prepositional adjuncts that are topicalized. Other such data include section heads and list symbols that appear at the front of the phrase as shown in Figure (3)

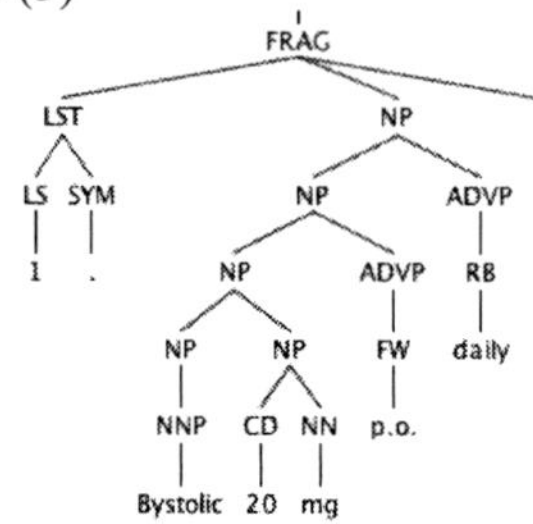

Figure 3: Tertiary branch in list items

This shows that multiple branching is present at the highest clausal/sentential level as well as at the lowest phrase internal elements. Given that there is no theoretical limit to conjunction or NP internal elements (especially within this domain), there is no limit to the number of branches as well.

3.2.2   Ambiguous categories

Clinical text contains Latin abbreviations indicating manner of medical dosage or manner of action. We adopted a principle to annotate the abbreviation based on the syntactic category of its translation or the full-form. For example, 'q. 8 h' stands for 'every 8 hours' and therefore annotated as an NP. 'IV' is tagged as JJ (adjectival token) and does not have a maximal projection when it functions as an adjective in a phrase like 'IV (intravenous) fluid'. However, it has a maximal projection ADVP (adverbial phrase) when it modifies a verb as in Figure (4). Beyond abbreviations, clinical texts also contain phrases like 'x 3' which stands for 'times 3' in the context of the test results such as 'test is negative/positive x 3' or in the context of a patient's condition as in 'the patient is oriented x 3'. Such phrases that have an adverbial flavor but do not explicitly function as adverbs are kept under NP. Such NPs are however post-modifiers of the preceding category and therefore they also form a maximal projection of their own as shown in Figure (5).

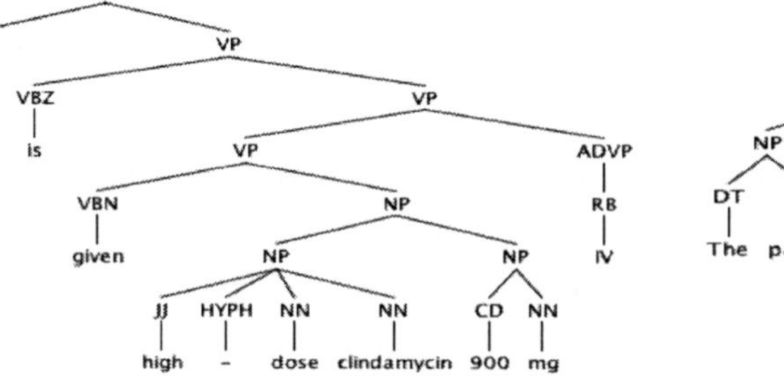

Figure 4: 'IV' forms an ADVP node   Figure 5: 'x 3' labelled as NP

Another form of ambiguity in category arises in clinical texts due to a practice of omitting the head of the phrase. This creates a mismatch between the rightmost PoS tag (the head of the phrase) and the maximal category. This violates the 'projection principle' which states that 'lexical structure must be represented categorically at every syntactic level' (Chomsky, 1986). However, this mismatch is deliberately maintained in our annotation for accuracy at the phrase level. For example, in Figure (6) 'celiac' stands for 'celiac artery' but the token 'artery' is absent. So, rightmost tag is JJ but the phrase label is kept as an NP.

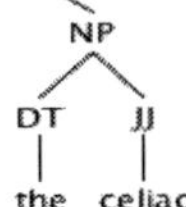

Figure 6: Mismatch between PoS and phrase labels

3.2.3 Multi-level NPs

Clinical data contains instances of multiple NPs modifying one another. We used right C-adjunction to account for these kinds of data. C-adjunction is a syntactic operation in which an element is added to the constituent of a category X by moving the element and adjoining it to a mother node above category X. Multi-level NP is peculiar to, as well as widely distributed in this domain. It is found mostly in the documentation of medical dosages. Each modifier such as the duration, manner or quantity is adjoined to the first NP as shown in Figure (7) below.

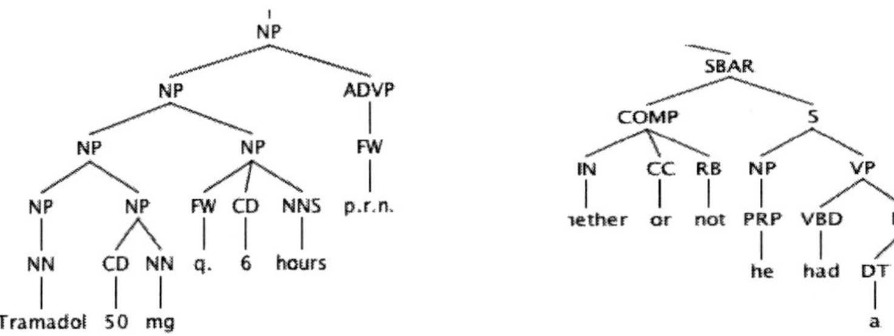

Figure 7: Multi-level NP   Figure 8: Multi-word complementizer under COMP

3.2.4 Multi-word Complementizer

Complementizers/subordinators can be multi-words. This is a phenomenon not peculiar to the clinical domain but nevertheless inadequately addressed in theoretical syntax or annotation literature. Some examples of multi-word complementizers are 'Even if', 'Whether or not', 'So that', 'As if', 'If and when', 'Should if' etc. To handle such words, we introduced the phrase label COMP which stands for Complemtizer Phrase, a commonly used in generative syntax. This phrase layer is necessary for accurate representation of syntactic objects and syntactic relations. Projection principle (Chomsky, 1986) allows only one head to project. Without the COMP layer, it would appear that both lexical categories in a multi-word complementizer are projecting to be the head of the SBAR. The COMP layer enables only one head to project at the phrase level.

3.2.5 FRAG

FRAG is the label used for fragmented sentences/clauses that arise due to transcription errors, grammatical errors or shorthand documentation. Its abundant occurrence in clinical health data creates much unwanted variation within the domain itself. The fragments however fall within identifiable patterns as follows:

- Isolated phrases: These are instances of medical dosage, description of patient status etc. written in shorthand. It can be any phrase, although, the majority present in this domain are NPs. (Figure 9)
- Copula dropped sentences: These are sentences where the copula 'is' or 'are' are missing. (Figure 10)
- Subject-less sentences: Existential subjects such as 'It is' as well as nominal subjects like 'He/She/Patient' are omitted from these sentences. (Figure 11)
- Irregular conjunctive phrases: These are sentences where two syntactically different objects are conjoined using punctuations. (Figure 12)
- Template data: These are sentences where the left token denotes a disease/condition and the right token gives value such as 'present/absent', 'yes/no' etc. (Figure 13)
- Incomplete sentences: These sentences are incomplete due to line break or transcription error. (Figure 14)

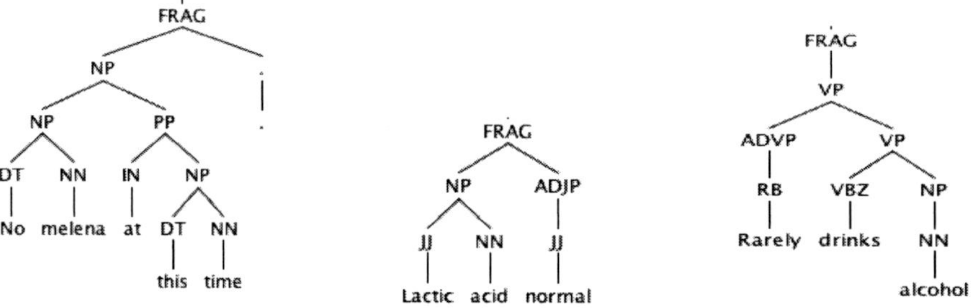

Figure 9: Isolated phrases   Figure 10: Copula drop   Figure 11: Subject less sentence

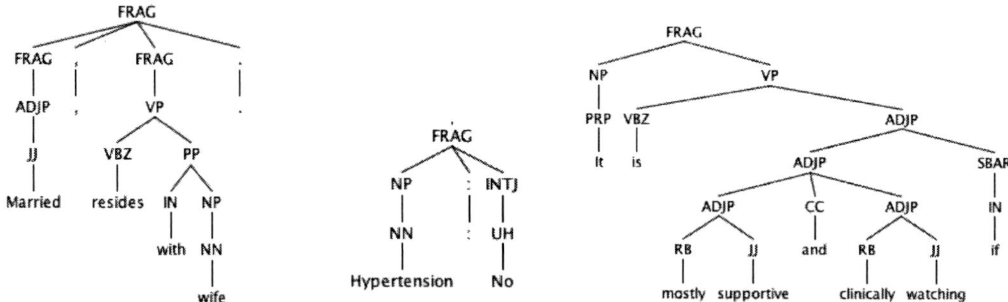

Figure 12: Irregular conjunction   Figure 13: Template   Figure 14: Incomplete sentences

These types of FRAGs can occur at the top sentential level as well as deep within the clause.

3.2.6   XXP

Missing data in this case does not mean ellipses (which are a part of syntactic transformation rules). These are data missing due to the de-identification process or incomplete transcription. In such cases, XXP is used to represent a placeholder node which can be computed in relation to other categories in the tree.

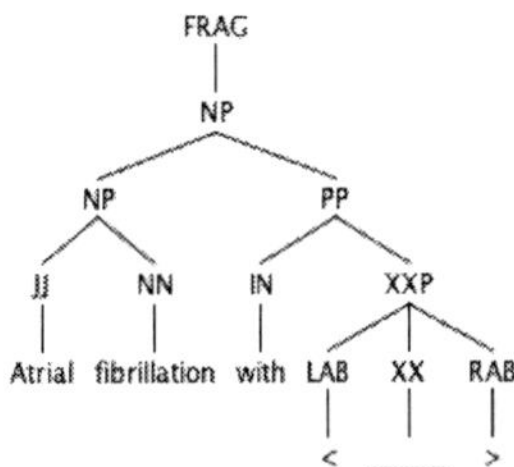

Figure 15: 'XX' and 'XXP' denoting missing elements

3.3 Inter-annotator agreement

The corpus was annotated by four linguistics students and reviewed by 2 in-house linguists. The students were first trained on clinical language annotation with 1000 sentences for one month to establish familiarity with the domain. Each annotator was then provided with sets of 50 PoS tagged sentences. PoS tagged sentences were provided to facilitate a better understanding of the meaning of the sentence. The annotated file was reviewed by two expert linguists. The annotators were instructed to follow the Penn Treebank guidelines (Bies et al., 1995). Given the anomalistic nature of the data as described in the previous sections, there were significant disagreements among the annotators. Weekly discussions were held to resolve the ambiguities and doubts. New rules were adopted based on these discussions. The annotator-reviewer disagreement is an indicator of the complexity of the task. Table 4 shows the inter-annotator agreement among the annotators and the two reviewers. The agreement between the four annotators was calculated using ParsEval (Harrison et al., 1991) F1 score on 500 sentences from each annotator. The inter-annotator agreement (IAA) between the two reviewers responsible for finalizing the corpus was 98.2%, based on 2000 sentences. Table 5 shows a comparative study with other treebanks. The IAA for GENIA corpus is reported to be 96.7% and 97.4% for two annotators respectively, as measured on 108 sentences, compared against 'gold standard' (Tateisi et al., 2005). The IAA for MiPACQ treebank is reported to be 0.926 (92.6%) (Albright et al., 2013).

	Reviewer1	Reviewer2	Reviewer1- Reviewer2
Annotator1	86.53	86.22	98.07
Annotator2	88.88	88.29	98.72
Annotator3	86.31	85.39	98.11
Annotator4	87.16	87.84	97.92

Table 4: Inter-annotator agreement calculated on 500 sentences from each annotator

	Method	Evaluated sentences	IAA
ezDI treebank	ParsEval F1	2000	98.2%
GENIA	Manual comparison against gold standard	108	96.7%, 97.4%
MiPACQ	EvalB F1	8% of total data	92.6%

Table 5: Comparison of inter-annotator agreement for various treebanks

4 Corpus Statistics

A treebank can be interpreted as a set of context free grammar (CFG) rules in the form of 'A $\rightarrow$ B C', where A is the higher node that branches into two lower nodes viz. B and C. For instance, our treebank has 5580 unique CFG rules which is an indication of the size of the grammar model. A detailed examination of the nodes and labels and the relative frequency of these rules is also an indicator of the data structure contained in the corpus.

Table 6 is a comparison of the percentage of non-terminal nodes (phrase and clause labels) in our treebank, GENIA Treebank and Wall Street Journal (WSJ) section of the Penn Treebank. The most notable difference is the proportion of FRAG which is more than 100 times higher than the other two treebanks. This shows that ill-formedness in clinical texts is a norm rather than an exception. Other significant differences are in lower proportion of the WH-phrases (WHNP, WHPP, WHADVP) and PP (prepositional phrase), and higher proportion of LST (list marker), and UCP (unlike coordinated phrase). There is also a higher proportion of ROOT node in our treebank, which signifies less average sentence length. The table also shows that there is a high frequency of NP nodes in our treebank on par with the other two treebanks. In our case however, this may be an indication of the number of hierarchical noun phrases created due to multiple adjunctions of the type discussed in Section 3.2.3 (Figure 7).

Node name	ezDI tree-bank	GENIA	WSJ (PTB)		Node name	ezDI tree-bank	GENIA	WSJ (PTB)
-NONE-	--	--	7.15		ROOT/S1	10.23	4.55	4.44
ADJP	2.60	2.91	1.62		RRC	--	0.00024	0.005
ADVP	3.04	2.06	2.50		S	8.24	8.899	11.16
COMP	0.016	--	--		SBAR	2.02	2.18	3.41
CONJP	0.02	0.17	0.03		SBARQ	0.026	0.0017	0.026
FRAG	6.55	0.03	0.06		SINV	0.0019	0.012	0.233
INTJ	0.05	--	0.01		SQ	0.047	0.004	0.04
LST	0.167	0.061	0.006		UCP	0.112	0.059	0.053
NAC	0.002	--	0.049		VP	16.71	13.47	16.31
NP	40.97	47.96	39.09		WHADJP	--	0.0007	0.0059
NX	--	--	0.15		WHADVP	0.078	0.114	0.294
PP	8.64	15.19	10.64		WHNP	0.249	0.689	1.012
PRN	--	1.28	0.27		WHPP	0.009	0.073	0.043
PRT	0.13	0.009	0.29		XXP	0.036	--	--
QP	--	0.23	1.03					

Table 6: Comparative percentage of non-terminal nodes in three treebanks

5 Discussion

As expected, the out-of-the-box performance of open source parsers did not perform well when tested on our treebank. Berkeley parser (Petrov et al., 2006) gave an F1 score of 70 on its default grammar. For a comparative study, Stanford parser (Manning et al., 2014) and Berkeley parser (Petrov et al., 2006) were trained with our treebank. Training took place in two stages to assess the quality of the treebank and the parser. We also did a comparative study with Penn Treebank (PTB) style version of GENIA corpus distributed by McClosky (2009). The GENIA Treebank consisted of 18541 sentences while our treebank consisted of 52053 sentences. Both the corpora were divided into 20% test data and 80% training data. The performance of the parsers was evaluated with ParsEval (Harrison et al., 1991) method across 5 folds. The training results show that our treebank performs better on both the Stanford parser and Berkeley parser. The F1 score of 85.32 and 91.58 are also significantly higher than the original Berkeley score of 70.

Treebank → Parser ↓	GENIA TB	ezDI TB 30k	ezDI TB 52k
Test Sentences	3708	6011	10411
Stanford F1	83.36	87.65	85.32
Berkeley F1	87.38	92.69	91.58

Table 7: Comparison of treebanks trained on different parsers. Results in F1 score using ParsEval

Albright et al. (2013) have shown the importance of in-domain annotation. Even a small amount of in-domain annotated data can enhance the performance of different NLP components down the pipeline. They also suggest that more divergent data will result in less improvement. The same is also reflected in our training results. The accuracy on both parsers came down by an average of 2 percent when the corpus size increased from 30+k to 52+k. As noted in Section 3.1, more variety of sentences were added in Datasets 2 and 3, which were not part of Dataset 1. An open source parser trained with this treebank is being currently used to enhance the performance of systems like information extraction which ultimately improves the performance of the end products like computer assisted coding (CAC) and clinical document improvement (CDI). The treebank is not publicly available, but a parser trained with this treebank will be made available as a part of a clinical NLP service

6 Conclusion

This paper showed the processes entailed in the development of a representative treebank for clinical healthcare. An elaborate and meticulous data sampling is an important first step towards creating a treebank. Next, the annotation has to be domain specific in the sense that grammatical principles have to be adapted to tackle the variety of linguistic structures present in the domain. This also means that the resulting structures should follow a pattern that is not far removed from theoretical principles of phrase structure rules. This will create a grammar that can generate domain specific structures. Finally, the need for domain specific treebank is validated by the high performance of Stanford and Berkeley parsers. Further research should focus on automation of the annotation task and optimal use of the parser for various NLP tasks.

Acknowledgements

We acknowledge the contribution of the linguists at JNU, New Delhi, namely, Srishti Singh, Arushi Uniyal, Sakshi Kalra and Azzam Obaid. We also acknowledge the help of Dr. Binni Shah and Disha Dave in understanding domain specific concepts and expressions. We would also like to thank Prof. Pushpak Bhattacharya and Prof. Girish Nath Jha for their advice.

References

Angus Roberts, Robert Gaizauskas, Mark Hepple, George Demetriou, Yikun Guo, Ian Roberts and Andrea Setzer. 2009. Building a semantically annotated corpus of clinical texts. *Journal of Biomedical Informatics*, 42(5):950-966.

Ann Bies, Mark Ferguson, Karen Katz, and Robert MacIntyre. 1995. *Bracketing guidelines for Treebank II Style Penn Treebank project*. University of Pennsylvania. Retrieved, February 2015, from https://catalog.ldc.upenn.edu/docs/LDC99T42/prsguid1.pdf.

Christopher D. Manning, Surdeanu, Mihai, Bauer, John, Finkel, Jenny, Bethard, Steven J., and David McClosky. 2014. The Stanford CoreNLP Natural Language Processing Toolkit. *Proceedings of 52nd Annual Meeting of the Association for Computational Linguistics: System Demonstrations*:55-60.

Daniel Albright, Arrick Lanfranchi, Anwen Fredriksen, William F. Styler IV, Colin Warner, Jena D. Hwang, Jinho D. Choi, Dmitriy Dligach, Rodney D. Nielsen, James Martin, Wayne Ward, Martha Palmer and Guergana K. Savova. 2013. Towards comprehensive syntactic and semantic annotations of the clinical narrative. *Journal of the American Medical Informatics Association*, 20(5):922-930.

David McClosky. 2009. Self-trained biomedical parsing. Retrieved March 8, 2018, from https://nlp.stanford.edu/~mcclosky/biomedical.html.

GENIA Project website. Retrieved March 8, 2018, from http://www.geniaproject.org/genia-corpus/treebank.

Fei Xia and Meliha Yetisgen-Yildiz. 2012. Clinical Corpus Annotation: Challenges and Strategies. *Proceedings of the Third Workshop on Building and Evaluating Resources for Biomedical Text Mining (BioTxtM'2012) under LREC-2012.*

Hercules Dalianis, Martin Hassel, Aron Henriksson and Maria Skeppstedt. 2012. Stockholm EPR Corpus: A Clinical Database Used to Improve Health Care. *Proceedings of Swedish Language Technology Conference*:17-18.

Jeffrey P Ferraro, Hal Daume III, Scott L Du Vall, Wendy W. Chapman, Henk Harkema and Peter J Haug. 2013. Improving Performance of Natural Language Processing Part-of-Speech Tagging on Clinical Narratives through Domain Adaptation. *Journal of the American Medical Informatics Association*, 20:931–939.

Jenny Rose Finkel and Christopher D. Manning. 2009. Joint Parsing and Named Entity Recognition. *Proceedings of Human Language Technology: 2009 Conference of the North American Chapter of the Association of Computational Linguistics*:326-334.

Jin-Dong Kim, Tomoko Ohta, Yuka Tateisi and Jun'ichi Tsujii. 2003. GENIA corpus – A semantically annotated corpus for bio-text mining. *Bioinformatics*, 19(1):i180-i182.

Jin-Dong Kim, Tomoko Ohta, Yuka Teteisi and Jun'ichi Tsujii. 2006. *GENIA Corpus Manual - Encoding schemes for the corpus and annotation.* Technical Report (TR-NLP-UT-2006-1). Tsujii Laboratory, University of Tokyo.

Jung-wei Fan, Elly W. Yang, Min Jiang, Rashmi Prasad, Richard M. Loomis, Daniel S. Zisook, Josh C. Denny, Hua Xu and Yang Huang. 2013. Syntactic parsing of clinical text: guideline and corpus development with handling ill-formed sentences. *Journal of the American Medical Informatics Association*, 20(6):1168-1177.

Kevin Bretonnel Cohen, Philip V. Ogren, Lynne Fox and Lawrence Hunter. 2005. Corpus design for biomedical natural language processing. *Proceedings of the ACL-ISMB Workshop on Linking Biological Literature, Ontologies and Databases: Mining Biological Semantics*:38-45.

Min Jiang, Yang Huang, Jung-Wei Fan, Buzhou Tang, Joshua C. Denny and Hua Xu. 2015 Parsing clinical text: how good are the state-of-the-art parsers? *BMC Medical Informatics and Decision Making*, 15(1):S2.

Mitchell P. Marcus, Beatrice Santorin i and Mary Ann Marcinkiewicz. 1993. Building a Large Annotated Corpus of English: The Penn Treebank. Computational Linguistics 19: 313–330

Narayan Choudhary, Parth Pathak, Pinal Patel, Vishal Panchal. 2014. Annotating a Large Representative Corpus of Clinical Notes for Parts of Speech. *Proceedings of 8th Linguistic Annotation Workshop*:87-92

Noam Chomsky. 1965. *Aspects of the theory of syntax.* MIT Press, Cambridge, Massachusetts.

Noam Chomsky. 1993. *Lectures on government and binding: the Pisa lectures.* 7th edition (1st edition, 1981). Mouton de Gruyter, Berlin and New York.

Noam Chomsky. 1995. *The minimalist program.* MIT Press, Cambridge, Massachusetts and London.

Noha Alnazzawi, Paul Thompson and Sophia Ananiadou. 2014. Building a semantically annotated corpus for congestive heart and renal failure from clinical records and the literature. *Proceedings of the 5th International Workshop on Health Text Mining and Information Analysis*:69-74.

Parth Pathak, Pinal Patel, Vishal Panchal, Sagar Soni, Kinjal Dani, Amrish Patel, and Narayan Choudhary. 2015. *ezDI: A supervised NLP system for clinical narrative analysis.* Proceedings of the 9th International Workshop on Semantic Evaluation (SemEval 2015):412-416.

Philip Harrison, Steven Abney, Ezra Black, Dan Flickinger, Claudia Gdaniec, Ralph Grishman, Donald Hindle, Robert Ingria, Mitch Marcus, Beatrice Santorini, Tomek Strzalkowski. 1991. Evaluating syntax performance of parser/grammars. *Proceedings of the Natural Language Processing Systems Evaluation Workshop, Berkeley (Rome Laboratory Technical Report, RL-TR-91-362).*

Philip V. Orgen, Guergana K. Savova and Christopher G. Chute. 2007. Constructing Evaluation Corpora for Automated Clinical Named Entity Recognition. *Proceedings of the 12th World Congress on Health (Medical) Informatics*:3143-3150.

Pierre Zweigenbauma, Pierre Jacquemarta, Natalia Grabara and Benoît Habert. 2001. Building a Text Corpus for Representing the Variety of Medical Language. *Studies in health technology and informatics*, 84(1):290-294.

Serguei V. Pakhomov, Anni Coden and Christopher G. Chute. 2006. Developing a corpus of clinical notes manually annotated for part-of-speech. *International Journal of Medical Informatics*, 75(6):418-429.

Slav Petrov, Leon Barrett, Romain Thibaux and Dan Klein. 2006. Learning accurate, compact, and interpretable tree annotation. *Proceedings of the 21st International conference on computational linguistics and the 44th annual meeting of the Association for Computational Linguistics*:443–440.

Stephen T. Wu, Hongfang Liu, Dingcheng Li, Cui Tao, Mark A. Musen, Christopher G. Chute and Nigam H. Shah. 2012. Unified Medical Language System term occurrences in clinical notes: a large-scale corpus analysis. *Journal of the American Medical Informatics Association*, 19(e1):e149-e156.

Tianyong Hao, Alexander Rusanov, Mary Regina Boland and Chunhua Weng. 2014. Clustering clinical trials with similar eligibility criteria features. *Journal of Biomedical Informatics*, 52:112-120.

Veronika Vinczer, György Szarvas, Richárd Farkas, György Móra and János Csirik. 2008. The BioScope corpus: biomedical texts annotated for uncertainty, negation and their scopes. *Proceedings of the Workshop on Current Trends in Biomedical Natural Language Processing*:38-45.

Wendy W. Chapman, Guergana K. Savova, Jiaping Zheng, Melissa Tharp and Rebecca Crowley. 2012. Anaphoric reference in clinical reports: Characteristics of an annotated corpus. *Journal of Biomedical Informatics*, 45(3):507-521.

William F. Styler IV, Steven Bethard, Sean Finan, Martha Palmer, Sameer Pradhan, Piet C. de Groen and Brad Erickson, Timothy Miller, Chen Lin, Guergana Savova and James. 2012. Temporal Annotation in the Clinical Domain. *Transactions of the Association for Computational Linguistics*, 2:143-154.

Yefeng Wang. 2009. Annotating and recognising named entities in clinical notes. *Proceedings of the ACL-IJCNLP 2009 Student Research Workshop*:18-26.

Yuka Tateisi, Akane Yakushiji, Tomoko Ohta and Jun'ichi Tsujii. 2005. Syntax annotation for the GENIA corpus. *Companion Volume to the Proceedings of Second international joint conference on natural language processing*:220-225.

Yuka Tateisi and Jun-ichi Tsujii. 2004. Part-of-Speech Annotation of Biology Research Abstracts. *Proceedings of 4th International Conference on Language Resources and Evaluation (LREC 2004)*:1267-1270.

Yusuke Oda, Graham Neubig, Sakriani Sakti, Tomoki Toda and Satoshi Nakamura. 2015. Ckylark: A more robust PCFG-LA parser. *Proceedings of the 2015 Conference of the North American Chapter of the Association for Computational Linguistics*:41-45.

Zhongmin Shi, Anoop Sarkar and Fred Popowich. 2007. Simultaneous Identification of Biomedical Named-Entity and Functional Relations Using Statistical Parsing Techniques. *Proceedings of Human Language Technology: 2007 Conference of the North American Chapter of the Association of Computational Linguistics*:161-164.

The RST Spanish-Chinese Treebank

Shuyuan Cao
Universitat Pompeu Fabra (UPF)
shuyuan.cao@hotmail.com

Iria da Cunha
Universidad Nacional de Educación a Distancia (UNED)
iriad@flog.uned.es

Mikel Iruskieta
University of Basque Country (UPV-EHU)
mikel.iruskieta@ehu.eus

Abstract

Discourse analysis is necessary for different tasks of Natural Language Processing (NLP). As two of the most spoken languages in the world, discourse analysis between Spanish and Chinese is important for NLP research. This paper aims to present the first open Spanish-Chinese parallel corpus annotated with discourse information, whose theoretical framework is based on the Rhetorical Structure Theory (RST). We have evaluated and harmonized each annotation part to obtain a high annotated-quality corpus. The corpus is already available to the public.

1 Introduction

Spanish and Chinese are two of the most spoken languages in the world; the language pair occupies an important position in the Natural Language Processing (NLP) research world. Recently, discourse analysis has called much attention as an unsolved problem and is crucial for many NLP tasks (Zhou et al., 2014). The great language distance causes a great number of discourse differences between Spanish and Chinese. Comparative or contrastive studies of discourse structures reveal information to identify properly equivalent discourse elements in a language pair (Cao and Gete, 2018). Here we give an example to show the discourse similarity and difference between the two languages.

Ex.1[1]:
1.1 Sp: Aunque aún no contamos con resultados, intuimos que el modelo será más amplio que el del sintagma nominal.

[Aunque aún no contamos con resultados,]Unit$_1$ [intuimos que el modelo sera mas amplio que el del sintagma nominal.]Unit$_2$

[DM[2] still no get results,] [we consider that the model will more extensive than the sentence group nominal.][3]

1.2 Sp: Intuimos que el modelo será más amplio que el del sintagma nominal, aunque aún no contamos con resultados.

[Intuimos que el modelo será más amplio que el del sintagma nominal,]Unit$_1$ [aunque aún no contamos con resultados.]Unit$_2$

[We consider that the model will more extensive than the sentence group nominal,] [DM still no get results.]

1.3 Ch: 尽管还没有取得最终结果，但是我们认为该模型已囊括了语段模型涉及的内容。

---

[1] The examples have been extracted from the corpus.

[2] DM means discourse marker. In this work, we use the definition of DM by Eckle-Kohler, Kluge and Gurevych (2015). DMs are used to signal discourse relations in a text segment. Specially, the DMs in our work are traditional markers and markers including verbal structures, as da Cunha indicates (2013).

[3] In this work, we give an English literal translation for both Spanish and Chinese examples in order to make the readers understand the content better.

Proceedings of the Joint Workshop on
Linguistic Annotation, Multiword Expressions and Constructions (LAW-MWE-CxG-2018), pages 156–166
Santa Fe, New Mexico, USA, August 25-26, 2018.

[尽管还没有取得最终结果，]Unit₁ [但是我们认为该模型已囊括了语段模型涉及的内容。]Unit₂

    [DM1 still no get results,] [DM2 we consider that the model contains the sentence group nominal.]

1.4 Eng: Although we haven't got the results yet, we consider that the model will be more extensive than the nominal sentence group.

In Example 1, we can see that the Spanish passage has a similar discourse structure to the Chinese passage. Both passages start the text with a discourse marker in the first unit. However, the usage of discourse markers in both languages is different. To show same meaning, in Chinese, it is mandatory to include two discourse markers: one marker is "*jinguan*" (尽管), at the beginning of the first unit, and another marker is "*danshi*" (但是), at the beginning of the second unit. These two discourse markers are equivalent to the English discourse marker 'although'. By contrast, in Spanish, just one discourse marker "*aunque*" is being used at the beginning of the first unit, and this discourse marker is also equivalent to the English discourse marker *although*. Moreover, the order of the discourse units in the Spanish passage can be changed and it makes sense syntactically, but the order cannot be changed in the Chinese passage, because neither syntactically nor grammatically makes sense.

Additionally, as a large electronic library, a corpus can provide a large amount of linguistic information (Wu, 2014). Therefore, this paper aims to present the first open Spanish-Chinese parallel corpus with annotated discourse information under the Rhetorical Structure Theory (RST) (Mann and Thompson, 1988).

In the second section, we present the theoretical framework of this study. In the third section, we talk about some related works. In the fourth section, we give detailed information about the research corpus. In the fifth section, we discuss how we carry out the study by introducing different annotation steps. In the sixth section, we evaluate the annotation results and give the qualitative analysis about the annotation quality. In the last section, we conclude our work and look ahead at our future work.

2   Theoretical framework

The Rhetorical Structure Theory (RST) (Mann and Thompson, 1988) is a theory that was created especially for discourse analysis. RST addresses both hierarchical and relational aspects of text structures for discourse analysis. Elementary Discourse Units (EDUs) (Marcu, 2000) and coherence relations are established in RST. Relations are recursive in RST and are held between EDUs, which can be Nuclei or Satellites, denoted by N and S. Satellites offer additional information about nuclei. EDUs can be linked among them holding a nucleus-satellite (e.g. CAUSE, JUSTIFY, EVIDENCE) function or a multinuclear (e.g. CONJUNCTION, LIST, SEQUENCE) function. As relations are recursive, all the discourse units of the text have a function in a treelike structure, if and only if the text is coherent.

Comparing to other discourse theory, the Penn Discourse Treebank (PDTB) (Prasad et al., 2008), RST focuses on the hierarchical structure of a whole text, where discourse relations can be annotated within a sentence (intra-sentence style) and between sentences (inter-sentence style). The intra-sentence annotation and inter-sentence annotation styles help to inform how discourse elements are being expressed in a language.

3   State of the art

3.1 Comparative discourse study

Some previous research using RST for comparative discourse has compared Chinese and English. Cui (1986) presents some aspects regarding discourse relations between Chinese and English; Kong (1998) compares Chinese and English business letters; Guy (2000, 2001) compares Chinese and English journalistic news texts. The only work that compares Spanish and Chinese using RST is by Cao, da Cunha and Bel (2016). They explore sentences that contain the Spanish discourse marker *aunque* ('although') and their Chinese parallel sentences in the UN subcorpus.

3.2 RST Treebanks for different languages

With the development of discourse analysis, annotated corpora with relational discourse structure under the RST exist for several languages: (i) for English, the RST Discourse Treebank (Carlson, Marcu and Okurowski, 2001)[4] and the Discourse Relations Reference Corpus (Taboada and Renkema, 2008)[5]; (ii) for German, the Potsdam Commentary Corpus (Stede and Neumann, 2014)[6]; (iii) for Spanish, the RST Spanish Treebank (da Cunha, Torres-Moreno and Sierra, 2011; da Cunha et al., 2011)[7]; (iv) for Basque, the RST Basque Treebank (Iruskieta et al., 2013[8]; (v) for Portuguese, the CorpusTCC (Pardo, Nunes and Rino, 2008) and *Rhetalho* (Pardo and Seno, 2005)[9]; (vi) for Russian, the Russian RST Treebank (Toldova et al., 2017)[10].

Bilingual and multilingual RST Treebanks are not common; Iruskieta, da Cunha and Taboada, (2015) create one of the few with the Multilingual RST Treebank[11] for Spanish, Basque and English. For Basque and Spanish, Imaz and Iruskieta (2017) establish the RST Basque-Spanish DELIB Treebank[12]. To our knowledge, our corpus is the first bilingual corpus serves for the discourse analysis between Spanish and Chinese under the RST.

4   Research corpus

There are currently few parallel Spanish-Chinese corpora. the already existing parallel corpora are: (i) The Holy Bible (Resnik, Olsen & Diab, 1999), (ii) The United Nations Multilingual Corpus (UN) (Rafalovitch and Dale, 2009) and (iii) Sina Weibo Parallel Corpus (Wang et al., 2013). Cao, da Cunha and Iruskieta (2017) indicate the three corpora contain their own limitations for Spanish-Chinese comparative discourse analysis. To carry out our work, we develop a new Spanish-Chinese parallel corpus.

Complexity of discourse structure and heterogeneity are the main characteristics taken into account for corpus development. The specific considerations are the following: (a) texts with different sizes (between 100 and 2,000 words), (b) specialized texts and non-specialized texts, (c) texts from different domains, (d) texts from different genres, (e) texts from different original publications, and (f) texts from different authors.

Based on the mentioned aspects, finally, we selected 100 texts to form our research corpus[13]. The genres of the texts are the following: (a) abstracts of research papers, (b) news, (c) advertisements, and (d) announcements. The longest text of the corpus contains 1,774 words and the shortest one contains 111 words.

The sources of these texts are: (a) International Conference about Terminology (1997), (b) Shanghai Miguel Cervantes Library, (c) Chamber of Commerce and Investment of China in Spain, (d) Spain Embassy in Beijing, (e) Spain-China Council Foundation, (f) Confucius Institute Foundation in Barcelona, (g) Beijing Cervantes Institute and (h) Granada Confucius Institute.

The corpus includes texts related to seven domains: (a) terminology (30 texts), (b) culture (12 texts), (c) language (16 texts), (d) economy (14 texts), (e) education (8 texts), (f) art (10 texts), and (g) international affairs (10 texts).

The corpus was enriched automatically with POS information by using the Stanford parser (Levy and Manning, 2003) for Chinese.

Finally, we created an online interface to access the research corpus: `http://ixa2.si.ehu.es/rst/zh/`. Users can search POS information, discourse segments, key information and discourse structure of each text in the research corpus. Moreover, users can also download the texts of the corpus.

---

[4] https://catalog.ldc.upenn.edu/LDC2002T07 [Last consulted: 06 of July of 2017]

[5] http://www.sfu.ca/rst/06tools/discourse_relations_corpus.html [Last consulted: 06 of July of 2017]

[6] http://angcl.ling.uni-potsdam.de/resources/pcc.html [Last consulted: 06 of July of 2017]

[7] http://corpus.iingen.unam.mx/rst/citar.html [Last consulted: 06 of July of 2017]

[8] http://ixa2.si.ehu.es/diskurtsoa/en/ [Last consulted: 06 of July of 2016]

[9] http://www.icmc.usp.br/~taspardo/projects.htm [Last consulted: 06 of July of 2017]

[10] https://github.com/nasedkinav/rst_corpus_rus [Last consulted: 06 of July of 2017]

[11] http://ixa2.si.ehu.es/rst/ [Last consulted: 06 of July of 2017]

[12] http://ixa2.si.ehu.es/diskurtsoa/rstfilo/ [Last consulted: 06 of July of 2017]

[13] Due to the limited resources that guarantee the complexity of discourse structure and heterogeneity, finally, we choose 50 Spanish texts and their translated Chinese texts (50 texts) to form the corpus.

5   Methodology

In this work, firstly, we elaborate some criteria to segment the corpus. Secondly, we annotate the Central Unit (CU) for each text following Iruskieta et al. (2014). Lastly, we annotate the discourse structure for each text in the corpus following Pardo (2005).

5.1 Segmentation annotation

Segmentation affects the discourse annotation quality; this makes it a crucial step for RST study. Two notable works for Spanish segmentation from the discourse level are mentioned previously: the RST Spanish Treebank (da Cunha, Torres-Moreno and Sierra, 2011; da Cunha et al., 2011) and the Multilingual RST Treebank (Iruskieta, da Cunha and Taboada, 2015). Few works focus on the Chinese segmentation from the discourse level under RST. There are three works that use form-based criteria that use punctuation marks to elaborate segmentation rules for Chinese (Yue, 2006; Qiu, 2010; Li, Feng and Zhou, 2013).

In our work, we elaborate the discourse segmentation criteria proposal for both Spanish and Chinese based on linguistic function (the function of the syntactic components) and linguistic form (punctuation category and verbs). We have not considered the meaning (of any coherence relation between propositions) to segment EDUs to avoid circularity in the annotation process. For the function and form perspective, we adopt the segmentation criteria from Iruskieta, da Cunha and Taboada (2015). A Spanish-Chinese bilingual linguists and two Spanish linguists are in charge of the segmentation for the Spanish subcorpus while the bilingual linguists and a Chinese linguists carry out the segmentation task for the Chinese subcorpus[14]. The segmentation tool is the RSTTool (O'Donnell, 2000). Table 1 shows the segmentation criteria[15].

Criteria to form an EDU	Non EDU criteria
Every EDU should have an adjunct verb clause	Relative, modifying and appositive clauses
Paragraphs with line breaks (titles)	Reported speech
Period and question exclamation marks	Truncated EDUs (same-unit)
Comma + adjunct verb clause	
Semicolon + adjunct verb clause	
Colon + adjunct verb clause	
Parenthetical & dash + adjunct verb clause	
Coordination with two subordinate verb clauses	

Table 1: The segmentation criteria

5.2 Central Unit (CU) annotation

Under RST, for each segmented text, among the EDUs, there is an EDU called Central Unit (CU) that contains the key information of the text (Iruskieta, Labaka and Desiderato, 2016).

According to van Dijk (1980), language users are able to summarize discourses, expressing the main topics of the summarized discourse. For our work, for all the segmented texts, the annotators decide which EDUs represent the main idea of the text. Table 2 shows the statistical information of the segmented texts and the annotated CUs in the corpus.

---

[14] The bilingual expert annotates all the 100 texts, each of the two Spanish experts annotate 25 Spanish texts. The Chinese expert annotate all the 50 Chinese texts.

[15] For the examples of the segmentation criteria, consult Cao et al (2017).

Corpus part	EDUs	CUs
Spanish	840	76
Chinese	953	81

Table 2: Statistical information of EDUs and CUs in the corpus

A Spanish-Chinese bilingual linguist and a Spanish linguist annotate the CUs for all the Spanish texts. The bilingual linguist and a Chinese linguist selected the CUs for all the Chinese texts.

5.3 Discourse structure annotation

Discourse structure annotation is one of the most difficult challenges for annotation works (Hovy and Lavid, 2010). Our study adopts the intra-sentence annotation and inter-sentence annotation styles. Figure 1 shows an annotated parallel Spanish-Chinese text[16].

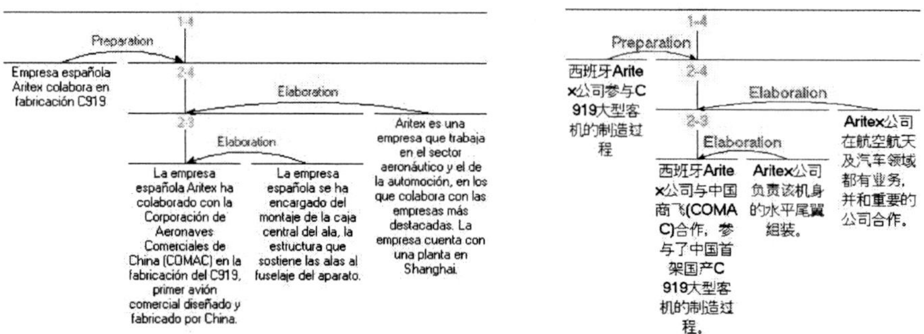

Figure 1: Example of the annotated parallel text (EEP1)

The selected discourse relations are presented in the Table 3. The annotation tool we use is the RSTTool (O'Donnell, 2000). All the annotation results are saved by the rstWeb (Zeldes, 2016).

N-S		N-N
Antithesis	Background	Conjunction
Circumstance	Cause	Contrast
Condition	Concession	Disjunction
Enablement	Elaboration	List
Evaluation	Evidence	Sequence
Justify	Interpretation	
Motivation	Means	
Purpose	Otherwise	
Restatement	Preparation	
Solutionhood	Result	
Summary		

Table 3: Selected relations for the discourse annotation[17]

---

[16] English translation of the text EEP1: [Spanish company Aritex collaborates in manufacturing C919] [The Spanish company Aritex has collaborated with the Commercial Aircraft Corporation of China (COMAC) in the manufacture of the C919, the first commercial aircraft designed and manufactured by China.] [The Spanish company has been responsible for the assembly of the central wing box, the structure that holds the wings to the fuselage of the aircraft.] [Aritex is a company that works in the aeronautical and automotive sectors, in which it collaborates with the most outstanding companies. The company has a plant in Shanghai.]

[17] The selected relations are extracted from the RST webpage: http://www.sfu.ca/rst/02analyses/index.html [Last consulted: 06 of July of 2017]. The selected relations are the common used ones for RST studies.

6 Evaluation result

6.1 Segmentation annotation evaluation

In this annotation level, we use Cohen Kappa to measure inter-annotator agreement of the segmented discourse units[18]. Kappa calculates the agreement between annotators as:

$$K = \frac{P(A) - P(E)}{1 - P(E)}$$

where (A) represents the current observed agreement, and P(E) represents chance agreement. Kappa was calculated by considering titles, parentheses, and verbs, as EDUs candidates. Table 4 includes the agreement between the annotators for the Spanish subcorpus and the Chinese subcorpus.

Corpus Source	Kappa Agreement	
	Spanish	Chinese
ICT	0.895	0.815
SMCL	0.945	0.719
CCICS	0.855	0.744
SEB	0.786	0.711
SCCF	0.828	0.711
CIFB	0.716	0.616
BCI	0.863	0.759
GCI	0.873	0.705
Total	0.87	0.76

Table 4: Segmentation annotation agreement of the entire corpus

From Table 4, we can see that, for the Spanish subcorpus, the highest agreement between the annotators is 0.945, and the lowest agreement is 0.716. The agreement for the whole Spanish subcorpus is 0.87. The highest agreement result for the Chinese subcorpus is 0.815, and the lowest agreement result is 0.616. The agreement for the entire Chinese subcorpus is 0.76. The annotation results prove the segmentation criteria are reliable for the language pair. Based on the results, we analyze the segmentation errors to improve the segmentation annotation quality.

6.2 Central Unit (CU) annotation evaluation

Same as the segmentation evaluation, we also use Kappa to measure the CU annotation agreement for exact match. Table 5 shows the evaluation results of the Spanish subcorpus and Table 6 reflects the agreement of the Chinese subcorpus.

From Table 5, we can see that for the Spanish subcorpus, the agreement is 0.961 and the agreement is 0.977 for the Chinese subcorpus (see Table 6). The results show that the CU annotation for the whole corpus is almost perfect.

A1	A2		Total	Kappa
	Yes	No		
Yes	61	16	77	
No	13	750	763	0.961
Total	74	766	840	

Table 5: CU annotation evaluation result of the Spanish subcorpus

[18] For all the annotation steps, the Spanish-Chinese bilingual annotator is assigned as A1, the two Spanish annotators are assigned as A2 (considering as one annotator) and the Chinese annotator is assigned as A3. The agreement are measured between A1 and A2, A1 and A3.

A1	A2		Total	Kappa
	Yes	No		
Yes	55	13	68	
No	7	878	885	0.977
Total	62	881	953	

Table 6: CU annotation evaluation result of the Chinese subcorpus

Based on the annotation results, the annotators discuss the disagreements to confirm the correct CUs for each text in the corpus.

6.3 Discourse structure annotation evaluation

For the discourse structure annotation evaluation, we follow a newly created qualitative method by Iruskieta, da Cunha and Taboada (2015). Under this qualitative method, four elements are being examined by using F-measure: Nuclearity (N), Relation (R), Composition (C) and Attachment (A). In addition, to use this method for the discourse evaluation between two or more languages, the comparison parts must be aligned and must contain the same number of EDUs, to avoid confusing analysis disagreement and segmentation disagreement. The following example explains how we follow this comparison rule by using our corpus:

Ex.2: Text name: CCICE3_ESP & CCICE3_CHN
Sp: [El jueves, el Tesoro volverá a los mercados con una subbasta de bonos y obligaciones en la que intentará colocar entre 3.000 y 4.000 millones.]
  [On Thursday, the Treasury will return to the markets with a subbase of bonds and obligations in which it will try place between 3,000 and 4,000 million.]
Ch: [另外，财政部将在本周四再次回到市场拍卖中长期国债，] [欲拍卖 30 亿至 40 亿欧元。]
  [In addition, the Ministry of Finance will on Thursday again return to the markets to auction of medium-term and long-term treasury bonds,] [to auction 3 billion to 4 billion euros.]
Eng: On Thursday, the Treasury will return to the markets with a sub-base of bonds and obligations in which it will try to place between 3,000 and 4,000 million.

From the above example, we can see the Spanish message is an interdependent EDU and its parallel Chinese message contains three EDUs. For the qualitative comparison, Iruskieta, da Cunha and Taboada (2015) suggest a simple rule, which is to erase the segmentation differences and get the same number of EDUs for the parallel content. Therefore, we combine three Chinese EDUs as a discourse unit (DU) or text span. Although the harmonization process erases some rhetorical relations, the higher level of RS-Tree structure is not affected.

Table 7 shows the evaluation results of the original Spanish subcorpus and the original Chinese subcorpus, meanwhile Table 8 shows the qualitative evaluation of the harmonized corpus.

From Table 7, we can conclude that in the Spanish subcorpus, the agreement of the Nuclearity is from 0.761 to 1, the agreement of the Relation is from 0.641 to 1, the agreement of the Composition is from 0.761 to 0.947, and the agreement of the Attachment is from 0.731 to 0.933. The annotation evaluation results of the Chinese subcorpus shows the agreement of the Nuclearity is from 0.864 to 0.978, the agreement of the Relation is from 0.727 to 0.844, the agreement of the Composition is from 0.864 to 0.978, and the agreement of the Attachment is from 0.84 to 0.978. The evaluation results prove that the annotation of the Spanish subcorpus and the annotation of the Chinese subcorpus are reliable. Two aspects explain why we have the good annotation results: (i) the annotation guideline has been discussed many times and (ii) some texts in the corpus are general publications and the discourse structure of these texts are more simple than others.

Table 8 informs that in the harmonized corpus, the agreement of the Nuclearity is from 0.855 to 1, the agreement of the Relation is from 0.794 to 0.923, the agreement of the Composition is from 0.855 to 1, and the agreement of the Attachment is from 0.855 to 1.The evaluation results of the harmonized corpus are better than the original corpus because of the removal of the annotation disagreements during the harmonized process for both Spanish subcorpus and Chinese subcorpus.

The qualitative analysis and quantitative evaluation results of the harmonized corpus demonstrate the reliability of the annotation quality. The reason that we get the good results is because of: (i)

Before carrying out the annotation work, we elaborate the annotation guideline, which requires the same inter-sentence annotation process and intra-sentence annotation process, and (ii) comparing to other annotation campaigns and texts (news, argumentation texts, scientific texts and abstracts), some texts have a simpler discourse structure.

Source	Corpus	Nuclearity		Relation		Composition		Attachment	
		Match	F	Match	F	Match	F	Match	F
ICT	Spanish	290/315	0.921	268/315	0.851	290/315	0.921	288/315	0.914
	Chinese	313/357	0.877	278/357	0.779	313/357	0.877	312/357	0.874
SMCL	Spanish	51/67	0.761	43/67	0.641	51/67	0.761	49/67	0.731
	Chinese	66/72	0.917	58/72	0.806	66/72	0.917	66/72	0.917
CCICS	Spanish	37/41	0.902	30/41	0.732	36/41	0.878	37/41	0.902
	Chinese	44/45	0.978	38/45	0.844	44/45	0.978	44/45	0.978
SEB	Spanish	54/57	0.947	50/57	0.877	54/57	0.947	53/57	0.930
	Chinese	60/64	0.938	54/64	0.844	60/64	0.938	60/64	0.938
SCCF	Spanish	46/50	0.92	37/50	0.74	46/50	0.92	45/50	0.90
	Chinese	62/65	0.954	51/65	0.785	62/65	0.954	62/65	0.954
CIFB	Spanish	39/44	0.886	34/44	0.773	39/44	0.886	38/44	0.864
	Chinese	44/50	0.88	41/50	0.82	44/50	0.88	42/50	0.84
BCI	Spanish	96/108	0.889	83/108	0.769	96/108	0.889	96/108	0.889
	Chinese	122/134	0.910	110/134	0.821	122/134	0.910	122/134	0.910
GCI	Spanish	15/15	1	15/15	1	14/15	0.933	14/15	0.933
	Chinese	19/22	0.864	16/22	0.727	19/22	0.864	19/22	0.864

Table 7: Qualitative evaluation of the Spanish annotation and Chinese annotation

Source	Nuclearity		Relation		Composition		Attachment	
	Match	F	Match	F	Match	F	Match	F
ICT	275/285	0.965	242/285	0.846	274/285	0.961	274/285	0.961
SMCL	59/69	0.855	55/69	0.797	59/69	0.855	59/69	0.855
CCICS	34/34	1	27/34	0.794	31/34	0.912	31/34	0.912
SEB	46/48	0.958	41/48	0.854	45/48	0.938	45/48	0.938
SCCF	40/42	0.952	35/42	0.833	40/42	0.952	40/42	0.952
CIFB	29/31	0.935	28/31	0.82	29/31	0.935	29/31	0.935
BCI	99/103	0.961	95/103	0.922	97/103	0.942	97/103	0.942
GCI	13/13	1	12/13	0.923	13/13	1	13/13	1

Table 8: Qualitative evaluation of the harmonized corpus between Spanish and Chinese

7 Conclusion

In this work, we present the first RST Spanish-Chinese Treebank with open access. We annotate the discourse information for all the 100 texts by using the RSTTool. We use Kappa to evaluate the annotation quality. The evaluation results for each annotation step show that we get an annotated corpus with high quality. Our corpus fills an important gap for Spanish-Chinese discourse analysis. Moreover, the corpus texts can be downloaded online. The POS information, discourse segments, CU information and the annotations of discourse structure can also be found online.

The corpus can be used for different NLP tasks, for instance, Spanish-Chinese language learning, evaluation of the machine translation (MT) between the two languages from the discourse level, information retrieval, etc. In the future, we will select and annotate more Spanish-Chinese parallel texts and will develop a protocol to help the MT for the language pair.

Acknowledgments

We thank the anonymous reviewers for their comments and suggestions on this work. Iria da Cunha is funded by a Ramón y Cajal contract (RYC-2014-16935) associated with the National Distance Education University (UNED) in Spain. Mikel Iruskieta is funded by the TUNER project (TIN2015-65308-C5-5-R, MINECO/FEDER, UE).

References

Cao Shuyuan, Xue Nianwen, da Cunha Iria, Iruskieta Mikel, and Wang Chuan. 2017. Discourse Segmentation for Building a RST Chinese Treebank. In *Proceedings of the 6th Workshop Recent Advances in RST and Related Formalisms*, 73-81.

Cao Shuyuan, da Cunha Iria, and Iruskieta Mikel. 2016. A Corpus-based Approach for Spanish-Chinese Language Learning. In *Proceedings of the 3rd Workshop on Natural Language Processing Techniques for Educational Applications (NLP-TEA3)*, 97-106.

Cao Shuyuan, da Cunha Iria, and Bel Nuria. 2016. An analysis of the Concession relation based on the Spanish discourse marker aunque in a Spanish-Chinese parallel corpus. *Procesamiento del Lenguaje Natural*, 56: 81-88.

Cao Shuyuan, da Cunha Iria, and Iruskieta Mikel. 2017. Toward the Elaboration of a Spanish-Chinese Parallel Annotated Corpus. *EPiC Series of Language and Linguistics*, 2: 315-324.

Cao Shuyuan, and Gete Harritxu. 2018. Using Discourse Information for Education with a Spanish-Chinese Parallel Corpus. In *Proceedings of the 11th edition of the Language Resources and Evaluation Conference (LREC'2018)*, 2254-2261.

Carlson Lynn, Marcu Daniel, and Okurowski Mary Ellen. 2001. Building a Discourse-Tagged Corpus in the Framework of Rhetorical Structure Theory. In *Proceedings of the 2nd SIGDIAL Workshop on Discourse Dialogue*, 1-10.

Cui Songren. 1985. *Comparing Structures of Essays in Chinese and English*. Master thesis. Los Angeles: University of California.

da Cunha Iria. 2013. A Symbolic Corpus-based Approach to Detect and Solve the Ambiguity of Discourse Markers. *Research in Computing Science*, 70: 95-106.

da Cunha Iria, and Iruskieta Mikel. 2010. Comparing rhetorical structures of different languages: The influence of translation strategies. *Discourse Studies*, 12(5): 563-598.

da Cunha Iria, SanJuan Eric, Torres-Moreno Juan-Manuel, Lloberes Marina, and Castellón Irene. 2012. DiSeg 1.0: The First System for Spanish Discourse Segmentation. *Expert Systems with Applications (ESWA)*, 39(2): 1671-1678.

da Cunha Iria, Torres-Moreno Juan-Manuel, and Sierra, Gerardo. 2011. On the Development of the RST Spanish Treebank. In *Proceedings of the 5th Linguistic Annotation Workshop*, 1-10.

da Cunha Iria, Torres-Moreno Juan-Manuel, Sierra Gerardo; Cabrera-Diego Luis Adrián; Castro Rolón Brenda Gabriela; and Rolland Bartilotti Juan Miguel. 2011. The RST Spanish Treebank On-line Interface. In *Proceedings of Recent Advances in Natural Language Processing (RANLP'2011)*, 698-703.

Eckle-Kohler Judith, Kluge Roland., and Gurevych Iryna. 2015. On the Role of Discourse Markers for Discriming Claims and Premises in Argumentative Discourse. In *Proceedings of the 2015 Conference on Empirical Methods in Natural Language Processing (EMNLP'2015)*, 2236-2242.

Guy Ramsay. 2000. Linearity in Rhetorical Organisation: A Comparative Cross-cultural Analysis of Newstext from the People's Republic of China and Australia. *International Journal of Applied Linguistics*, 10(2): 241-58.

Guy Ramsay. 2001. What Are They Getting At? Placement of Important Ideas in Chinese Newstext: A Contrastive Analysis with Australian Newstext. *Australian Review of Applied Linguistics*, 24(2): 17-34.

Hovy Eduard, and Lavid Julia. 2010. Toward a 'Science' of Corpus Annotation: A New Methodology Challenges for Corpus Linguistics. *International Journal of Translation*, 22(1): 13-36.

Imaz Oier, and Iruskieta Mikel. 2017. Deliberation as Genre: Mapping Argumentation through Relational Discourse Structure. In *Proceedings of the 6th Workshop Recent Advances and Related Formalisms*, 1-10.

Iruskieta Mikel, Aranzabe María Jesús, Diaz de Ilarraza Arantza, Gonzalez-Dios Itziar, Lersundi Mikel, and Lopez de Lacalle Oier. 2013. The RST Basque TreeBank: an online search interface to check rhetorical relations. In *Proceedings of IV Workshop A RST e os Estudos do Texto*, 40-49.

Iruskieta Mikel, Díaz de Ilarraza Arantza, and Lersundi Mikel. 2014. The annotation of the Central Unit in Rhetorical Structure Trees: A Key Step in Annotating Rhetorical Relations. In *Proceedings of COLING 2014, the 25th International Conference on Computational Linguistics: Technical Papers*, 466-475.

Iruskieta Mikel, da Cunha Iria, and Taboada Maite. 2015. A Qualitative Comparison Method for Rhetorical Structures: Identifying different discourse structures in multilingual corpora. *Language resources and evaluation*, 49(2): 263-309.

Iruskieta Mikel, Labaka Gorka, and Desiderato Juliano. 2016. Detecting the central units in two different genres and languages: a preliminary study of Brazilian Portuguese and Basque texts. *Procesamiento de Lenguaje Natural*, 56: 65-72.

Li Yancui, Feng Wenhe, and Zhou Guodong. 2012. Elementary Discourse Unit in Chinese Dsicourse Structure Analysis. *Chinese Lexical Semantics*, 7717: 186-198.

Mann William C. and Thompson Sandra A. 1988. Rhetorical Structure Theory: Toward a functional theory of text organization. *Text&Talk*, 8(3): 243-281.

Marcu Daniel. 2000. The rhetorical parsing of unrestricted texts: A surface-based approach. *Computational Linguistics*, 26(3): 395-448.

O'Donnell Michael. 2000. RSTTool 2.4 – A Markup Tool For Rhetorical Structure Theory. In *Proceedings of First International Conference on Natural Language Generation (INLG'2000)*, 253-256.

Pardo Thiago Alexandre Salgueiro. 2005. *Software vai melhorar compreensão de textos em computadores*. PhD thesis. São Paulo, University of São Paulo.

Pardo Thiago Alexandre Salgueiro, Nunes Maria Maria das Graças V., and Rino Lucia H. M. 2008. Dizer: An Automatic Discourse Analyzer for Brazilian Portuguese. *Lecture Notes in Artificial Intelligence*, 3171:224-234.

Pardo Thiago Alexandre Salgueiro, and Seno Eloize R. M. 2005. Rhetalho: um corpus dereferência anotado retoricamente. *Anais do V Encontro de Corpora*. São Carlos-SP, Brasil.

Prasad Rashmi, Dinesh Nikhil, Lee Alan, Miltsakaki Eleni, Robaldo Livio, Joshi Aravind, and Webber Bonnie. 2008. The Penn Discourse Treebank 2.0. In *Proceedings of the 6th International Conference on Language Resources and Evaluation (LREC'2008)*, 2961-2968.

Qiu Wusong. 2010. *Jiyu xiucijiegoulilun de hanyuxinwenpinglun yupianjiegou yanjiu* (基于修辞结构理论的汉语新闻评论语篇研究 *[Analysis of Discourse Structure in Chinese News Commentaries under Rhetorical Structure Theory]*). Master thesis. Nanjing: Nanjing Normal University.

Rafalovitch Alexandre, and Dale Robert. 2009. United Nations general assembly resolutions: A six-languages parallel corpus, In *Proceedings of Machine Translation Summit XII*, 292-299.

Resnik Philip, Olsen Mari Broman, and Diab Mona. 1999. The Bible as a Parallel Corpus: Annotating the 'Book of 2000 Tongues'. *Computers and the Humanities*, 33(1-2): 129-153.

Stede Manfred, and Neumann Arne. 2014. Potsdam Commentary Corpus 2.0: Annotation for Discourse Research. In *Proceedings of the International Conference on Language Resources and Evaluation (LREC'2014)*, 925-929.

Taboada Maite, and Renkema Jan. 2008. *Discourse Relations Reference Corpus* [Corpus]. Simon Fraser University and Tilburg University.

Toldova Svetlana, Pisarevskaya DIna, Ananyeva Margarita, Kobozeva Maria, Nasedkin Alexander, Nikiforova Sofia, Pavlova Irina, and Shelepov Alexey. 2017. Rhetorical relation markers in Russian RST Treebank. In *Proceedings of 6th Workshop Recent Advances in RST and Related Formalisms*, 29-33.

van Dijk Teun A. 1980. *MACROSTRUCTURES: AnInterdisciplinary Study of Global Structures in Discourse, Interaction, and Cognition*. New Jersey: Lawrence Erlbaum Associations.

Wang Ling, Guang Xiang, Dyer Chris, Black Alan, and Trancoso Isabel. 2013. Mircoblogs as Parallel Corpora. In *Proceedings of the 51st Annual Meeting of the Association for Computational Linguistics (ACL' 2013)*, 176-186.

Wu Shangyi. 2014. On Application of computer-based corpora in translation. In *Proceedings of 2nd International Conference on Computer, Electrical, and Systems Sciences, and Engineering (CESSE' 2014)*, 173-178.

Yue Ming. 2006. Discursive Usage of Six Chinese Punctuation Marks. In *Proceedings of the COLING/ACL 2006 Student Research Workshop*, 43-48.

Zhou Lanjun, Li Binyang, Wei Zhongyu, and Wong Kam-Fai. 2014. The CUHK Discourse Treebank for Chinese: Annotating Explicit Discourse Connectives for the Chinese Treebank. In *Proceedings of the International Conference on Language Resources and Evaluation (LREC'2014)*, 942-949.

Zeldes Amir. 2016. rstWeb - A Browser-based Annotation Interface for Rhetorical Structure Theory and Discourse Relations. In *Proceedings of NAACL-HLT 2016 System Demonstrations*, 1-5.

All Roads Lead to UD: Converting Stanford and Penn Parses to English Universal Dependencies with Multilayer Annotations

Siyao Peng
Department of Linguistics
Georgetown University
sp1184@georgetown.edu

Amir Zeldes
Department of Linguistics
Georgetown University
amir.zeldes@georgetown.edu

Abstract

We describe and evaluate different approaches to the conversion of gold standard corpus data from Stanford Typed Dependencies (SD) and Penn-style constituent trees to the latest English Universal Dependencies representation (UD 2.2). Our results indicate that pure SD to UD conversion is highly accurate across multiple genres, resulting in around 1.5% errors, but can be improved further to fewer than 0.5% errors given access to annotations beyond the pure syntax tree, such as entity types and coreference resolution, which are necessary for correct generation of several UD relations. We show that constituent-based conversion using CoreNLP (with automatic NER) performs substantially worse in all genres, including when using gold constituent trees, primarily due to underspecification of phrasal grammatical functions.

1 Introduction

In the past two years, the Universal Dependencies project (UD, Nivre et al. 2017), offering freely available dependency treebanks with a unified annotation scheme in over 50 languages, has grown rapidly, allowing for cross-linguistic comparison and computational linguistics applications. At the same time, because of its rapid growth and the need to negotiate annotation schemes across languages, annotating large resources from scratch in the latest UD standard is challenging, not only because of the annotation effort, but also because guidelines may change mid-way, and data and annotator training must be revisited to match the latest developments. Instead, a large number of projects within UD capitalize on existing treebanks converted from constituent treebanks (in English usually using CoreNLP, Manning et al. 2014) or other dependency schemes, meaning that for those projects that are not annotated directly in UD, changes to the UD guidelines generally mean adapting an existing converter framework.

In this paper, we concentrate on English dependency treebanking, which has been dominated by data converted from Penn Treebank-style constituent trees (cf. Bies et al. 1995). We compare results of constituent treebank conversions with results from converting English dependency data annotated using the older (and by now frozen) Stanford Typed Depenendencies (hence SD, de Marneffe and Manning 2013). Specifically, we will be working with the freely available Georgetown University Multilayer corpus (GUM, http://corpling.uis.georgetown.edu/gum/), which we have converted to the latest UD standard (as of UD version 2.2). The paper has several goals:

1. To describe and evaluate the accuracy of gold standard SD to UD conversion (SD2UD)

2. To explore the necessary layers of annotation for generating gold UD from gold SD data, including information that is not strictly present in the syntactic parse

3. Comparing conversions from SD source data and constituent tree source data

4. Making a substantial new English resource, with over 85,000 tokens in 8 genres, available in UD

*Proceedings of the Joint Workshop on
Linguistic Annotation, Multiword Expressions and Constructions (LAW-MWE-CxG-2018), pages 167–177
Santa Fe, New Mexico, USA, August 25-26, 2018.*

We will show that while rule-based SD to UD conversion is already highly accurate, it must also rely on multiple annotation layers outside of the parse proper if the full range of dependencies is targeted. For the third goal in particular, our evaluation of the converted UD product reveals that 'native' dependency data in English differs from converted constituents in several ways, including the presence of some rare labels and the proportion of non-projective dependencies.

2   Corpora

The main corpus used in this paper is the Georgetown University Multilayer corpus (GUM, Zeldes 2017), a freely available corpus covering data from eight English genres: news, interviews, how-to guides, travel guides, academic writing, biographies, fiction and web forum discussions. The corpus is annotated by students at Georgetown University[1] and currently contains 101 documents, with over 85,000 tokens, annotated for:

- Multiple POS tags (Penn tags, Santorini 1990, TreeTagger tags and CLAWS5 tags, Garside and Smith 1997), as well as lemmatization

- Sentence segmentation and rough speech act (based on SPAAC, Leech et al. 2003)

- Document structure (paragraphs, headings, etc.), ISO date/time annotations and speaker information

- Gold SD dependencies and automatic constituent parses based on gold POS tags

- Information status (given, accessible and new, based on Dipper et al. 2007)

- Entity and coreference annotation, including bridging anaphora

- Discourse parses in Rhetorical Structure Theory (Mann and Thompson 1988)

A second English corpus we will be comparing this data to in Section 4.4 is the English Web Treebank (Bies et al. 2012, Silveira et al. 2014), containing over 1,170 documents with over 250,000 tokens in five genres: blog posts, e-mails, newsgroup discussions, online answer forums and online reviews. This corpus was originally annotated using Penn-style constituent trees and converted to UD using CoreNLP (Schuster and Manning 2016), with subsequent scripts and manual corrections producing the version now available in UD V2.2.

3   Method

In this section we focus on describing our approach to converting SD parses to UD with and without supplemental information from further layers of annotation. The evaluation in Section 4 will compare these scenarios with several conversion scenarios from constituent trees.

3.1   SD conversion rules

Our conversion process comprises three parts:

1. a preprocessing step pulling in information from annotation layers outside of the syntax tree proper

2. the main rule-based conversion

3. a postprocessing step in which punctuation is attached using the freely available udapi API (Popel et al. 2017)

This section concentrates on the main, syntactic rule-based conversion, while the next section focuses on information brought in from other annotation layers.

---

[1] For an analysis of annotation quality and genre differences within the corpus, see Zeldes and Simonson (2016)

attributes	relations	actions
func=/dobj/	none	#1:func=obj
func=/.*/;func=/^cc\$/;func=/^conj\$/	#1>#2;#1>#3	#3>#2
func=/prep/;pos=/^W.*/;func=/pcomp/	#1>#3;#3>#2	#2:func=pobj;#1>#2;#2>#3;#3:func=rcmod

Table 1: Examples of DepEdit rules

The main step uses a configurable rule-based converter called DepEdit[2] which allows the definition of conversion rules, each having three components: 1. a set of key-value pairs denoting regular expressions matching targeted token properties; 2. a set of relations which must hold between these tokens; and 3. instructions on how to alter token properties when the rule is matched. Some example rules are given in Table 1.

The first example illustrates a trivial renaming rule, in which the SD label *dobj* is renamed to UD *obj*: the definition in the first column matches any token with a function label matching `/dobj/`, no relations are imposed (`none`), and the action specifies that the first (and only) token in the definition, #1, should have its function label set to *obj*. Similar rules are used to create Universal POS tags, which is almost trivial, since the corpus already contains gold Penn Treebank-style POS tags and lemmas. However, in some cases, dependency relations must be consulted too, e.g. the verb 'be' must be given the AUX tag as a copula or auxiliary, and otherwise VERB; determiners (e.g. *that*) become DET when modifying nouns, but are PRON when used independently; etc.

The second example in Table 1 is more complex and changes the graph in Figure 1 from the coordinating conjunction 'and' being governed by the first conjunct (SD guidelines) to being governed by the second (UD V2.2 guidelines). The attribute definitions first specify 'any function' (`func=/.*/`), then for a second token (separated by ';') that its function must be *cc* (coordinating conjunction), followed by a third token labeled *conj*. The relations column then specifies that token #1 governs #2 and that it also governs #3. Finally the actions column specifies that #3 should now govern #2, leaving unchanged the fact that #1 governs #3. The process of applying these two rules is shown for a fragment in Figure 1, where the source (SD) graph is rendered above the tokens, and the result (UD) below, rendered in blue.

The third rule handles free relative clauses, and targets WH pronouns governed by a preposition and *pcomp*, in constructions such as "an expectation of$_{\#1}$ what$_{\#2}$ to do$_{\#3}$", which should be converted to a relative clause (in SD, *rcmod*). Note that since this rule occurs before conversion of prepositions to the UD label *case* and relatives to *acl*, SD labels are still used in this rule. POS substitutions are also cascaded, meaning rules can initially refer to Penn tags, and later on to UPOS tags.[3]

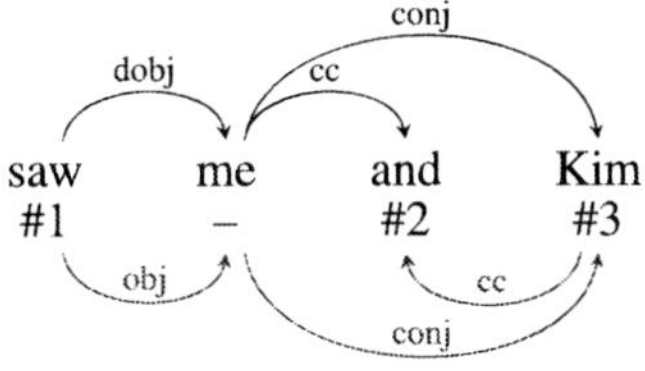

Figure 1: Converting coordination from SD to UD

The most current set of conversion rules, numbering nearly 100 items, can be found along with conversion utilities is freely available online.[4]

---

[2] Available at `https://corpling.uis.georgetown.edu/depedit/` and via PyPI (`pip install depedit`).
[3] Morphological features, by contrast, are generated at the end of the process using CoreNLP, as is the case for EWT. Their accuracy is not evaluated in this paper.
[4] `https://github.com/amir-zeldes/gum/blob/dev/_build/utils/stan2uni.ini`

3.2 Using multilayer annotations

The availability of several kinds of non-syntactic gold annotations in GUM allows us to refine the conversion process further. While it could be argued that syntax trees should not contain non-syntactic information to begin with, UD parses do in fact integrate information which seems to be not completely syntactic, and more so than SD: specifically, as we will see below, factors such as ontological entity types, coreference information and presence of errors or disfluencies all affect the analysis in UD. This can be viewed as an advantage of UD trees once the information is available, but also as an unfair requirement from parsers and converters attempting to generate data in the UD scheme.

One of the most widespread changes not recognizable from pure SD dependencies is the conversion of SD *nn* (noun modified noun) into one of two structures: *compound* for nominal compounds with internal syntactic structure and *flat* for headless multi-word expressions that are not part of the closed list receiving the label *fixed*. In practice, the *flat* label in English usually translates to proper nouns supplying names.

The large majority of *flat* cases correspond to names of persons, while most named non-persons retain a syntactic head (usually on the right).[5] This means that knowing entity types can be crucial. For example, knowing that *World Bank* is an *organization* in Figure 2 induces the *compound* relation between the two tokens; by contrast, in Figure 3, *Frank Bank*, annotated as a *person* entity on another annotation layer results in a *flat* UD annotation.[6] The preprocessing step reads entity annotation information from parallel files and flags the (SD) head of each entity mention with its entity type, which is then used in the DepEdit conversion rules. The entity's head token is matched by finding a token in the entity span which is either the sentence root, or is governed by a non-punctuation parent from outside the span.

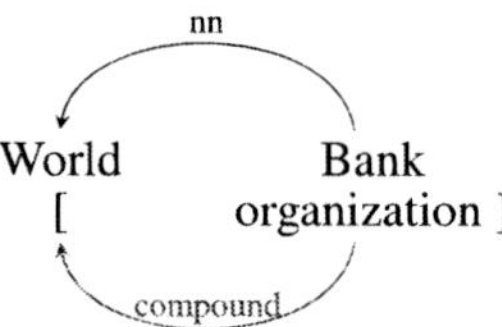

Figure 2: Converting 'World Bank' (organization)

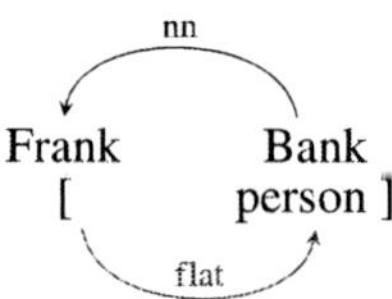

Figure 3: Converting 'Frank Bank' (person)

However, the mapping between dependencies and entity types is not one-to-one, meaning some errors are inevitable even with gold entity information. For example, some company names arguably do not exhibit internal syntactic structure and should be annotated as *flat* in UD, for example *Wells Fargo* in Figure 4. Currently, our automatic conversion will erroneously label such cases as *compound* (see Section 4.3 for error analysis).

---

[5] The other main category containing *flat* names is place names, but the majority of multi-word place names are nevertheless headed, and therefore labeled *compound*. A discussion on whether or not proper names such as 'Kim King' should be treated as non-headed, or arbitrarily annotated as head-initial, is beyond the scope of this paper.

[6] An anonymous reviewer has remarked that the difference between Frank Bank and World Bank is arguably only a convention. This is certainly a valid point in general, but there is also some reason to consider differences between the structures, as codified in UD: while *World Bank* is without a doubt a kind of 'bank', the decision whether *Frank Bank* is a kind of 'Frank' or 'Bank' is more arbitrary. This becomes more crucial when nested compounds are considered, since multi-part names can be seen as truly flat, but compounds like *World Bank Federation* are recursive and right-headed.

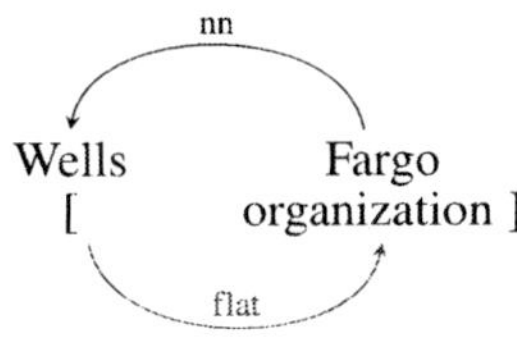

Figure 4: Analysis of 'Wells Fargo' (organization)

A second type of information is required by the introduction of the label *dislocated* in UD. Although dislocation, shown in (1), is ostensibly a syntactic operation, it appears very much like any kind of topicalization, as shown in (2). Both types are annotated as *dep* in the GUM SD annotations, for lack of a better label.

(1)   We like pets. [**My neighbors**$_{dislocated}$], their pets drive [**them**$_{obj}$] nuts

(2)   We like [**canned foods**]. My neighbors$_{dep}$, their pets eat [**them**$_{obj}$] every day

The semantic criterion distinguishing these two examples is that the dislocated node must be coreferential with a dependent of the verb ('them'='neighbors').[7] Because GUM has gold coreference annotations available, the preprocessing step again introduces a feature into the SD data which indicates a coreference ID for each coreferent nominal head, and nodes with the same coreference ID and syntactic head are changed from *dep* to *dislocated*.

Another type of information that may be seen as not purely syntactic is the presence of disfluencies. Though rare in written data, UD reserves a label for repairs in disfluencies or false starts, which can be used for both spoken and written data. The guidelines apply the label *reparandum* to the head of the 'aborted' part of the sentence, which is attached to the repair. The SD annotations in GUM follow the same structure, but apply the default label *dep*, meaning that the presence of the disfluency needs to be detected. This is accomplished in the preprocessing step by checking GUM's TEI XML annotations that denote all types of errors in the corpus with <sic> tags. Although these tags do not indicate the nature of the error or the repair, any occurrences of the *dep* label inside an error and governed from outside of it are converted into *reparandum*, as shown for the false start in Figure 5.

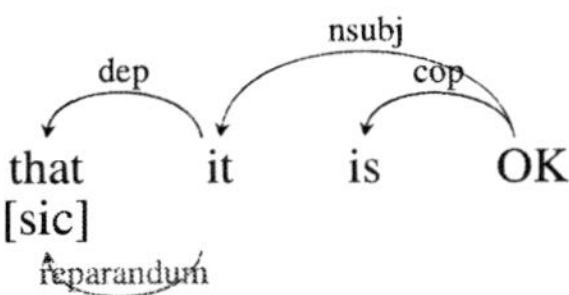

Figure 5: labeling errors as *reparandum*

We also use the <sic> annotations to create a feature in the MISC column defined by the CoNLL-U format with the value Typo=Yes, as used to denote errors in other UD treebanks. These are not necessarily always cases of repair, but also cases of unusual or non-standard grammatical constructions or even orthographic anomalies such as non-matching quotation marks, as in (3).

(3)   so quite a few fans <sic>**known**</sic> about the "Mets Poet<sic>'</sic>

---

[7]One anonymous reviewer has suggested that *dislocated* should be used for all fronted dependents, even if they are not realized a second time, citing a Japanese example from the UD guidelines. While we believe that marking fronting in general is interesting, and could perhaps be done using sublabels (e.g. *obj:front*), we feel that marking fronted English arguments, as in "him, I like" with *dislocated* is counter-intuitive, since it makes a verb such as 'like' appear to be missing an object. The practice in other English corpora, and specifically in EWT, has been to only mark *dislocated* in the presence of a second realization of the argument. The difference in the practice for Japanese may be due to the fact that in that language a second mention as a pronoun is usually omitted, and the closest equivalent of such a pronoun is therefore a zero-mention.

The same MISC column is also used to indicate whether tokens are followed by spaces using the feature `SpaceAfter=No`. The latter feature is also derived from the TEI annotations, where the presence of the tag `<w>` indicates multiple tokens spelled together as one orthographic word.

4 Evaluation

4.1 Experimental setup

We compare UD conversions from SD and constituent annotations in several scenarios on a total of 8,300 tokens, comprising just over 1,000 tokens from each genre in GUM, or about 10% of the corpus, for which we created manually checked gold UD parses. To evaluate constituent to UD ('C2UD') conversion accuracy, we created three constituent parsed versions of the same data using the Stanford Parser: one based on gold-tokenized plain text, one from data with gold POS tags, and the third, also parsed from gold POS tags, but then manually corrected for errors. The manually corrected constituent parses do not introduce empty categories such as PRO or traces, but do use function labels that may be critical for conversion, such as S-TPC (for fronted direct speech, common e.g. in fiction) and NP-VOC, NP-TMP and NP-ADV for vocative, temporal and other adverbial NPs.[8] C2UD conversion was carried out using CoreNLP 3.9.1, which uses built-in NER and heuristic time expression recognition, but is not completely up-to-date with the current UD standard. We therefore apply trivial renaming of labels where needed and two heuristic corrections: all coordinating conjunctions (labeled *cc*) are attached to the original target of the *conj* relation, so that they point right to left; and all nominal modifiers of verbs (labeled *nmod*) are re-labeled as *obl*.

In scoring correct conversion we focus on two metrics: attachment accuracy ignoring punctuation tokens (since punctuation is automatically attached using udapi, Popel et al. 2017, and errors are therefore by-products of other attachment errors), and label accuracy, including punctuation (since some punctuation symbols are occasionally used for non-punctuation functions). Because there are some differences in the label subtypes produced by CoreNLP and GUM (e.g. *obl:tmod*, *nmod:npmod*), we ignore subtypes for the evaluation and focus on main label types.

4.2 Results

Figure 6 shows boxplots for the range of error rates across documents from different genres in five scenarios (tokenwise micro-averaged global means are given in blue diamonds), each splits into two metrics: head and label accuracy.

In the best scenario, converting SD to UD with parallel multilayer information, conversion errors are very few, at 0.45%/0.42% of tokens (head/label errors). When multilayer annotations are removed, accuracy suffers somewhat, but is still rather good, with under 1.73%/1.38% errors. The more difficult genres for pure SD conversion are news and biographies, though only by a little: since these genres contain many multi-token proper names, correct conversion relies more on entity types, which cannot be recognized in the pure DepEdit conversion, but are available to the multilayer conversion.

Comparing SD with constituent conversions, error rates become more substantial. Errors in the 'plain text' scenario are just under 20%; keeping in mind that the Stanford parser is trained on Wall Street Journal data, this is in line with previous results on parsing accuracy for out-of-domain constituent to dependency conversion (Choi and Palmer, 2010).

The not much better results for gold POS and gold constituents, by contrast, may seem surprising initially, since in general, constituents do identify the main argument structure relations, such as subjects and objects. However, a range of decisions cannot be made deterministically without semantic knowledge. Some of these might be avoided more reliably in datasets containing empty categories (traces, pro-forms) and more category sub-labels (e.g. PP-CLR, etc. see Bies et al. 1995), but the GUM constituents, even in their cleanest form, are based on CoreNLP constituent parses, which do not contain these.

Outliers in the 'plain text' scenario correspond to fiction texts, which frequently contained different Unicode quotation marks that are mistagged by CoreNLP. Gold POS tags remove the issue, as

---

[8]The data used for the evaluation, including different versions of constituent parses, is available at `https://github.com/gucorpling/GUM_UD_LAW2018`.

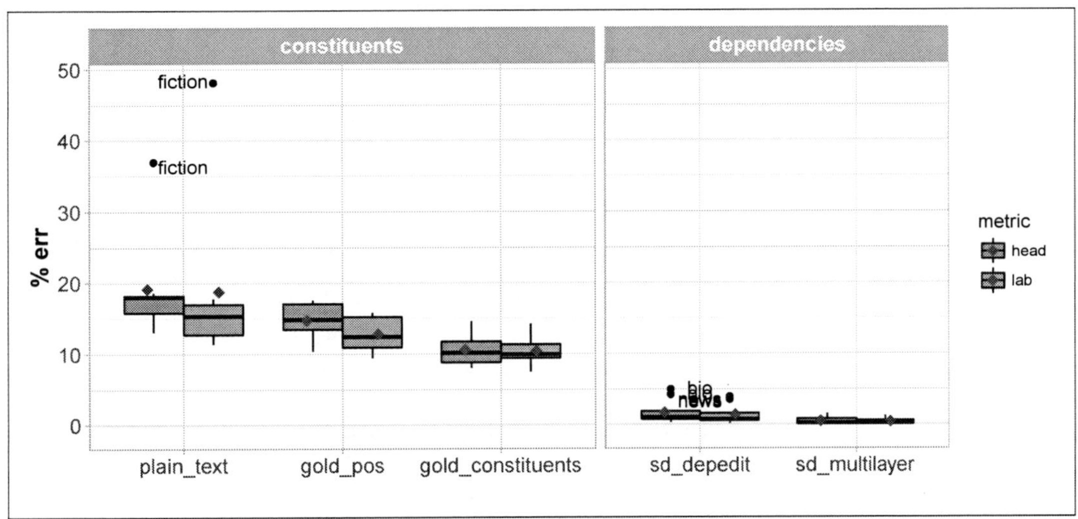

Figure 6: Error rates

the 'gold pos' scenario shows. Nevertheless, even with gold constituents, mean error rates remain at 10.62%/10.44%. To understand the limitations of both constituent and SD to UD conversions, we examine some specific error patterns in the next section.

4.3 Error analysis

To understand what conversion errors need to be avoided, we first consider the difficulties in C2UD conversion. Table 2 shows the top 3 most frequent gold labels causing attachment and labeling errors for gold constituents, pure SD, and multilayer SD conversion.

scenario	head errs		lab errs	
C2UD	84	nsubj	130	obl
(gold)	82	nmod	74	nmod
	71	conj	62	conj
SD	37	flat	37	flat
(pure)	10	nmod	8	obl
	8	appos	7	nsubj
SD	8	compound	9	compound
(multi)	6	nmod	7	obl
	6	flat	6	nmod

Table 2: Top 3 gold labels showing head and label errors in three scenarios

In C2UD, even given gold constituents, many pure phrase labels are highly ambiguous with respect to their exact function. This is especially true for fronted NPs without function labels, which can be fronted arguments (*dislocated, obj, iobj*), a spatio-temporal adverbial (*advmod:npmod*), a vocative (*vocative*) and more. These are sometimes misidentified as subjects, leading to true gold subjects being misrecognized (objects are not as susceptible due to their position inside VPs). Conversely, the label *obl* is most often mislabeled, usually in cases where prepositional modifiers of nominal or adjectival predicates are not recognized and labeled *nmod*. In general, whenever phrases are extraposed, their attachment site cannot be predicted accurately in the absence of trace annotations, and these are most often labeled *nmod* and *obl*.

In third place, coordination is the next most problematic construction, due to the fact that PTB brackets do not explicitly mark coordination (except for Unlike Coordinate Phrases, labeled UCP). As a result, some non-standard but frequent types of coordination are missed, such as using '/' for 'or' (common in web data), 'et al.' (common in academic data) and unmarked coordination or lists using commas, which can look like appositions in constituent trees. All of these distinctions are represented directly in SD, which is conceptually much closer to UD, and thus these errors are virtually absent in the SD scenarios.

The errors in the Pure SD scenario are dominated by missing *flat* relations in proper names, due to the lack of entity recognition; guessing that all SD *nn* relations are UD *compound* is the safer choice. The confusion of *obl* and *nmod* features here as well, but is much less frequent, due to gold attachment data in the SD parses which is usually trivial to convert to UD. Errors in appositions and subject relations are almost only by-products of incorrect name conversions, since the head token of the entire name is wrongly selected. In the Multilayer SD scenario, we see the over-generation errors in producing *compound* relations for non-person names – these are cases like 'Well Fargo', which should in fact be *flat* as well.

Additionally we note that the conversion from constituents is qualitatively missing some rare labels. These include cases that require the extra-syntactic knowledge described in section 3.2, such as *dislocated* and *reparandum*, but also the label *goeswith*, which indicates multiple tokens belonging to one 'word' but spelled apart, and the *vocative* label, which could hypothetically be guessed or derived directly if constituents include the NP-VOC subtype. While all of these labels represent rare phenomena, their exclusion from the constituent conversion output is problematic.

Finally we wish to point out one label that is currently not generated by any of our scenarios: the label *orphan*, which indicates promotion of a token to dominate the child of a missing coordinate parent. The construction, shown in Figure 7, is not directly expressible using SD relations and as such has been annotated somewhat unfaithfully by reference to the non-elliptical parent in the example.

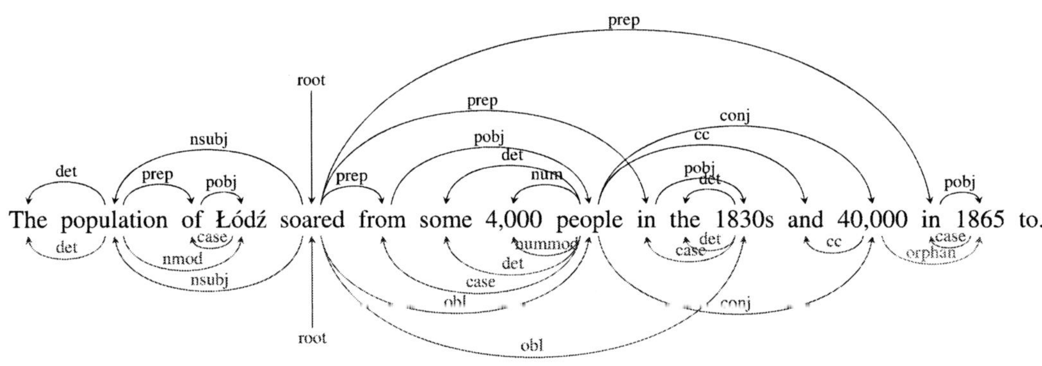

Figure 7: Example showing the *orphan* relation, not represented in SD

In the SD original (black edges), the population of Lodz is said to have soared from 4,000 people in the 1830s (two prepositional modifiers of 'soared'), and from 40,000 in 1865, to some other number. The inclusion of both the '1830s' and the '1865' as modifiers of 'soared' makes it seem as if both years apply at the same time. UD adds the relation *orphan* to express a second elliptical 'soared', which would have connected '40,000' and '1865' ("and [soared from] 40,000 in 1865..."). Though the UD solution seems clearly superior to the SD one, it is difficult to derive automatically without further annotations indicating the semantic structure, or using labels other than those found in SD.[9]

---

[9]One reviewer has suggested that a better analysis of Figure 7 is to treat the two phrases after 'from' as a coordination, making the years part of the same constituents as the numbers of people, i.e.: "[from [[some 4000 people in the 1830s] and [40000 in 1865]]]...". However this solution incorrectly groups together the years and numbers, despite the fact that '4000 people in the 1830s' is not a constituent. Although the UD analysis with *orphan* is imperfect in not explicitly duplicating the node corresponding to 'soar', such an explicit analysis could be made using the optional Enhanced UD representation, which includes

4.4 Comparison with other corpora

Aside from the accuracy of the conversion, we would like to suggest that there are some qualitative and quantitative differences between UD English data from 'native dependencies' and 'native constituents'. Qualitatively, some UD labels cannot be reliably produced via conversion, and are therefore absent in the initial C2UD result. This applies as noted above to the labels *dislocated* and *reparandum*, as well as *vocative* if conversion from NP-VOC is not used, though these labels can be reintroduced manually, as has been done in subsequent corrections to the EWT, for example.

Quantitatively, we note that non-projective dependencies, which are generally rare in English, are more frequent in SD2UD conversion than in C2UD. Table 3 shows frequencies for non-projective dependencies, excluding punctuation cases, across the entire EWT and GUM corpora in two scenarios: first, automatic C2UD conversion with CoreNLP is compared for both corpora. Then the current, partially manually corrected UD EWT V2.2 is compared with the multilayer conversion from SD for GUM, and the proportion of non-projectivity in the original gold SD data is given for comparison.

	C2UD	**UD V2.2 (corrected)**	
EWT	0.34%	0.46%	
	C2UD	**UD V2.2 (from SD multi)**	**original SD**
GUM	0.29%	0.79%	0.63%

Table 3: Non-projectivity in GUM and EWT.

The table shows that C2UD conversion creates less non-projectivity than human corrected or SD converted data, which is perhaps unsurprising. A more surprising result is that the manually corrected EWT contains substantially less non-projectivity than the SD2UD version of GUM. This could be due to genre differences, though the difference is rather substantial (almost double). If the numbers in EWT in fact under-represent the actual non-projectivity in the data, then this may be an indication that the less projective nature of the 'native constituents' EWT is shining through to the end result in the current UD version of the data. Finally we note that, at least for GUM, the conversion from gold SD to UD introduces further non-projectivity when compared to the original. A preliminary inspection of the constructions responsible for this suggests that coordinating conjunctions (the label *cc*) pointing backwards in UD instead of forwards in SD is responsible for the largest increase in cases of non-projectivity, but further study is needed to understand the extent and distribution of non-projective constructions generated by each scheme.

5 Discussion and outlook

The approach taken in this paper confirms that SD annotations are conceptually quite close to UD, making a purely rule-based conversion highly accurate. At the same time, we have shown that for some less frequent labels, information from annotation layers beyond the pure syntax tree is needed, and this reduces error rates from around 1.5% to closer to 0.4%. By contrast, conversion from constituent trees, even when these are manually checked, still results in around 10% errors (excluding punctuation).

An advantage of the present approach is the relative ease of the ability to change rules quickly as UD guidelines evolve: because the SD inventory is frozen, information that is derivable from the parse tree and further layers of annotation can be harnessed to produce the latest UD annotation scheme. It is also conceivable that retaining both SD and UD parses of the corpus can offer complementary information in some cases where UD collapses distinctions, e.g. between verbal modifiers labeled *vmod* in SD and other adverbial clauses labeled *advcl*.

One of the main limitations of the SD scheme with respect to producing the current UD standard is the lack of a function corresponding to *orphan*. This relation is also difficult for parsers to analyze correctly (see Schuster et al. 2018 for recent progress), meaning on the one hand that it is difficult to recognize

---

'copy nodes'.

automatically, and on the other, that it is desirable to include it in treebanks precisely in order to improve the availability of training data for such constructions.

In the future we would like to harness even more information from other layers in the corpus, both to enrich UD annotations with data in the MISC field and to validate annotation correctness. For example, using RST discourse parses available in GUM, we can draw on knowledge that certain clauses are *purpose* clauses to distinguish controlled to-infinitives (*xcomp*) from infinitival adverbial clauses (*advcl*). We are currently considering which other annotations can be used to enrich and improve the quality of UD corpora for which other concurrent annotations are available.

Acknowledgments

We would like to thank the reviewers, Nathan Schneider, and the UD community, for valuable comments on previous versions of this work, and the growing GUM annotation team for making their annotations available in the corpus – this resource could not have been created without their contributions. For the latest list of GUM contributors, please see the corpus website at http://corpling.uis.georgetown.edu/gum/.

References

Ann Bies, Mark Ferguson, Karen Katz, and Robert MacIntyre. 1995. Bracketing guidelines for Treebank II style. Penn Treebank Project. CIS Technical Report MS-CIS-95-06, University of Pennsylvania.

Ann Bies, Justin Mott, Colin Warner, and Seth Kulick. 2012. English Web Treebank. LDC2012T13, Linguistic Data Consortium, Philadelphia, PA.

Jinho D. Choi and Martha Palmer. 2010. Robust constituent-to-dependency conversion for English. In *Proceedings of the 9th International Workshop on Treebanks and Linguistic Theories (TLT 2010)*, pages 55–66, Tartu, Estonia.

Marie-Catherine de Marneffe and Christopher D. Manning. 2013. Stanford typed dependencies manual. Technical report, Stanford University.

Stefanie Dipper, Michael Götze, and Stavros Skopeteas. 2007. Information structure in cross-linguistic corpora: Annotation guidelines for phonology, morphology, syntax, semantics, and information structure. *Interdisciplinary Studies on Information Structure*, 7.

Roger Garside and Nicholas Smith. 1997. A hybrid grammatical tagger: CLAWS4. In Roger Garside, Geoffrey Leech, and Anthony McEnery, editors, *Corpus Annotation: Linguistic Information from Computer Text Corpora*, pages 102–121. Longman, London.

Geoffrey Leech, Tony McEnery, and Martin Weisser. 2003. 3PAAC speech-act annotation scheme. Technical report, Lancaster University.

William C. Mann and Sandra A. Thompson. 1988. Rhetorical Structure Theory: Toward a functional theory of text organization. *Text*, 8(3):243–281.

Christopher D. Manning, Mihai Surdeanu, John Bauer, Jenny Finkel, Steven J. Bethard, and Davide McClosky. 2014. The Stanford CoreNLP natural language processing toolkit. In *Proceedings of ACL 2014: System Demonstrations*, pages 55–60, Baltimore, MD.

Joakim Nivre, Željko Agić, Lars Ahrenberg, Maria Jesus Aranzabe, Masayuki Asahara, Aitziber Atutxa, Miguel Ballesteros, John Bauer, Kepa Bengoetxea, Riyaz Ahmad Bhat, Eckhard Bick, Cristina Bosco, Gosse Bouma, Sam Bowman, Marie Candito, Gülşen Cebiroğlu Eryiğit, Giuseppe G. A. Celano, Fabricio Chalub, Jinho Choi, Çağrı Çöltekin, Miriam Connor, Elizabeth Davidson, Marie-Catherine de Marneffe, Valeria de Paiva, Arantza Diaz de Ilarraza, Kaja Dobrovoljc, Timothy Dozat, Kira Droganova, Puneet Dwivedi, Marhaba Eli, Tomaž Erjavec, Richárd Farkas, Jennifer Foster, Cláudia Freitas, Katarína Gajdošová, Daniel Galbraith, Marcos Garcia, Filip Ginter, Iakes Goenaga, Koldo Gojenola, Memduh Gökırmak, Yoav Goldberg, Xavier Gómez Guinovart, Berta Gonzáles Saavedra, Matias Grioni, Normunds Grūzītis, Bruno Guillaume, Nizar Habash, Jan Hajič, Linh Hà Mỹ, Dag Haug, Barbora Hladká, Petter Hohle, Radu Ion, Elena Irimia, Anders Johannsen, Fredrik Jørgensen, Hüner Kaşıkara, Hiroshi Kanayama, Jenna Kanerva, Natalia Kotsyba, Simon Krek, Veronika Laippala, Lê Hồng, Alessandro Lenci, Nikola Ljubešić, Olga Lyashevskaya, Teresa Lynn, Aibek Makazhanov, Christopher Manning, Cătălina Mărănduc, David Mareček, Héctor Martínez Alonso, André Martins, Jan Mašek,

Yuji Matsumoto, Ryan McDonald, Anna Missilä, Verginica Mititelu, Yusuke Miyao, Simonetta Montemagni, Amir More, Shunsuke Mori, Bohdan Moskalevskyi, Kadri Muischnek, Nina Mustafina, Kaili Müürisep, Luong Nguyễn Thị, Huyền Nguyễn Thị Minh, Vitaly Nikolaev, Hanna Nurmi, Stina Ojala, Petya Osenova, Lilja Øvrelid, Elena Pascual, Marco Passarotti, Cenel-Augusto Perez, Guy Perrier, Slav Petrov, Jussi Piitulainen, Barbara Plank, Martin Popel, Lauma Pretkalniņa, Prokopis Prokopidis, Tiina Puolakainen, Sampo Pyysalo, Alexandre Rademaker, Loganathan Ramasamy, Livy Real, Laura Rituma, Rudolf Rosa, Shadi Saleh, Manuela Sanguinetti, Baiba Saulīte, Sebastian Schuster, Djamé Seddah, Wolfgang Seeker, Mojgan Seraji, Lena Shakurova, Mo Shen, Dmitry Sichinava, Natalia Silveira, Maria Simi, Radu Simionescu, Katalin Simkó, Mária Šimková, Kiril Simov, Aaron Smith, Alane Suhr, Umut Sulubacak, Zsolt Szántó, Dima Taji, Takaaki Tanaka, Reut Tsarfaty, Francis Tyers, Sumire Uematsu, Larraitz Uria, Gertjan van Noord, Viktor Varga, Veronika Vincze, Jonathan North Washington, Zdeněk Žabokrtský, Amir Zeldes, Daniel Zeman, and Hanzhi Zhu. 2017. Universal dependencies 2.0. Technical report, LINDAT/CLARIN digital library at the Institute of Formal and Applied Linguistics (ÚFAL), Faculty of Mathematics and Physics, Charles University.

Martin Popel, Zdenek Zabokrtský, and Martin Vojtek. 2017. Udapi: Universal API for Universal Dependencies. In *Universal Dependencies Workshop at NoDaLiDa 2017*, Gothenburg.

Beatrice Santorini. 1990. Part-of-speech tagging guidelines for the Penn Treebank project (3rd revision). Technical report, University of Pennsylvania, University of Pennsylvania.

Sebastian Schuster and Christopher D. Manning. 2016. Enhanced English Universal Dependencies: An improved representation for natural language understanding tasks. In *Proceedings of LREC 2016*, pages 2371–2378, Portorož, Slovenia.

Sebastian Schuster, Joakim Nivre, and Christopher D. Manning. 2018. Sentences with gapping: Parsing and reconstructing elided predicates. In *Proceedings of NAACL 2018*, pages 1156–1168, New Orleans, LA.

Natalia Silveira, Timothy Dozat, Marie-Catherine de Marneffe, Samuel R. Bowman, Miriam Connor, John Bauery, and Christopher D. Manning. 2014. A gold standard dependency corpus for English. In *Proceedings of the Ninth International Conference on Language Resources and Evaluation (LREC-2014)*, pages 2897–2904, Reykjavik, Iceland.

Amir Zeldes and Dan Simonson. 2016. Different flavors of GUM: Evaluating genre and sentence type effects on multilayer corpus annotation quality. In *Proceedings of LAW X The 10th Linguistic Annotation Workshop*, pages 68–78, Berlin.

Amir Zeldes. 2017. The GUM Corpus: Creating multilayer resources in the classroom. *Language Resources and Evaluation*, 51(3):581–612.

The Other Side of the Coin: Unsupervised Disambiguation of Potentially Idiomatic Expressions by Contrasting Senses

Hessel Haagsma, Malvina Nissim, Johan Bos
Centre for Language and Cognition, University of Groningen
The Netherlands
{hessel.haagsma, m.nissim, johan.bos}@rug.nl

Abstract

Disambiguation of potentially idiomatic expressions involves determining the sense of a potentially idiomatic expression in a given context, e.g. determining that *make hay* in 'Investment banks *made hay* while takeovers shone.' is used in a figurative sense. This enables automatic interpretation of idiomatic expressions, which is important for applications like machine translation and sentiment analysis. In this work, we present an unsupervised approach for English that makes use of literalisations of idiom senses to improve disambiguation, which is based on the lexical cohesion graph-based method by Sporleder and Li (2009). Experimental results show that, while literalisation carries novel information, its performance falls short of that of state-of-the-art unsupervised methods.

1 Introduction

Interpreting potentially idiomatic expressions (PIEs, for short) is the task of determining the meaning of PIEs in context.[1] In its most basic form, it consists of distinguishing between the figurative and literal usage of a given expression, as illustrated by *hit the wall* in Examples (1) and (2), respectively.

(1)   Melanie *hit the wall* so familiar to British youth: not successful enough to manage, but too successful for help. (British National Corpus (BNC; Burnard, 2007) - doc. ACP - sent. 1209)

(2)   There was still a dark blob, where it might have *hit the wall*. (BNC - doc. B2E - sent. 1531)

Distinguishing literal and figurative uses is a crucial step towards being able to automatically interpret the meaning of a text containing idiomatic expressions. It has been shown that idiomatic expressions pose a challenge for various NLP applications (Sag et al., 2002), including sentiment analysis (Williams et al., 2015) and machine translation (Salton et al., 2014a; Isabelle et al., 2017). For the latter, it has also been shown that being able to interpret idioms indeed improves performance (Salton et al., 2014b).

In this work, we use a method for unsupervised disambiguation that exploits semantic cohesion between the PIE and its context, based on the lexical cohesion approach pioneered by Sporleder and Li (2009). We extend this method and evaluate it on English data in a comprehensive evaluation framework, in order to answer the following research question: Do contexts enriched with literalisations of idioms provide a useful new signal for disambiguation?

2 Approach

The disambiguation systems presented here[2] are based on the original lexical cohesion graph classifier developed by Sporleder and Li (2009). Their classifier is based on the idea that the words in a PIE will be more cohesive with the words in the surrounding context when used in a literal sense than when used

---

[1]The task is also known as *token-based idiom detection*.

[2]The code and refined definitions used for implementing these systems are available at https://github.com/hslh/pie-detection.

Proceedings of the Joint Workshop on
Linguistic Annotation, Multiword Expressions and Constructions (LAW-MWE-CxG-2018), pages 178–184
Santa Fe, New Mexico, USA, August 25-26, 2018.

in a figurative sense. This classifier builds cohesion graphs, i.e. graphs of content word tokens in the PIE and its context, where each pair of words is connected by an edge weighted by the semantic similarity between the two words. If the average similarity of the complete graph is higher than within the context, the PIE component words add to overall cohesiveness and thus imply a literal sense for the PIE. If it is lower, the PIE component words decrease cohesiveness and thus imply a figurative sense. An example of these graphs is shown in Figure 1.

In the original approach, though, it is only tested whether the literal sense fits or not, by comparing the full and pruned graph. However, this does not measure whether the figurative sense fits. Ideally, we would like to compare the fit of the literal and figurative senses directly. We do this by introducing and using *idiom literalisations* (Section 2.2).

2.1 Basic Lexical Cohesion Graph

We reimplement the original lexical cohesion graph method with one major modification: instead of Normalized Google Distance we use cosine similarity between 300-dimensional GloVe word embeddings (Pennington et al., 2014). Furthermore, we adapt specifics of the classifier to optimise performance on the development set. We use only nouns to build the contexts, where the part-of-speech of words is determined automatically using the spaCy PoS-tagger[3], instead of both nouns and verbs. As a context window, we use two sentences of additional context on either side of the sentence containing the PIE. We also remove edges between two PIE component words, since those are the same for all instances of the same type and thus uninformative. Finally, PIEs are only classified as *literal* if average similarity of the pruned graph is 0.0005 higher than that of the whole graph, in order to compensate for overprediction of the *literal* class.

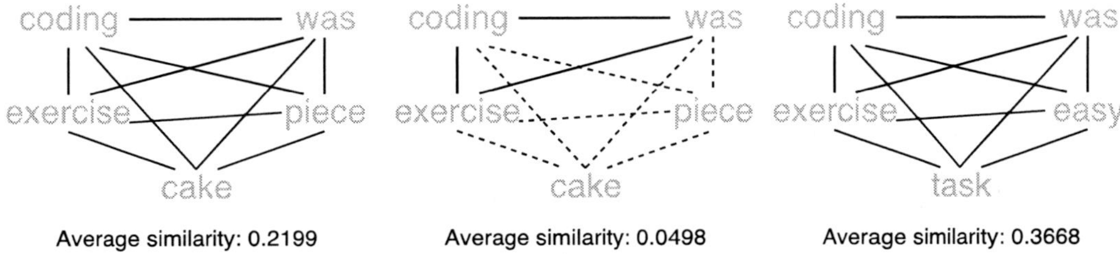

Figure 1: Three lexical cohesion graphs for the sentence 'That coding exercise was a piece of cake', with their average similarity score. The leftmost figure represents the full graph for the original method, the middle figure the pruned graph, and the right figure the graph containing the idiom literalisation.

2.2 Idiom Literalisation

Idiom literalisations are literal representations of the PIE's figurative sense, similar to dictionary definitions of an idiom's meaning. For example, a possible literalisation of *a piece of cake* is 'a very easy task'. This provides the possibility of building two graphs: one with the original PIE component words, and one with the original PIE replaced with the literalisation of its idiomatic sense. In this way, we can contrast lexical cohesion with a representation of the literal sense to lexical cohesion with a representation of the figurative sense. If the latter is more cohesive, the classifier will label the PIE as idiomatic, and vice versa. Figure 1 illustrates this process; the rightmost graph containing the literalisation has higher cohesion than the original graph, leading to the correct classification of *idiomatic*. Generally, the change in average similarity will be small, since the context words (which stay the same) greatly outnumber the changed PIE component words. However, since we compare the original and the literalised graph directly, only the direction of the similarity change matters and the size of the change is irrelevant.

In this work, we rely on definitions extracted from idiom dictionaries which were manually refined in order to make them more concise. For example, the definition 'Permanently fixed or firmly established;

---

[3]`https://spacy.io`

not subject to any amendment or alteration.' for the idiom *etched in stone* is refined to 'permanently fixed or established', in order to represent the figurative meaning of the idiom more concisely.

3 Experiments

Our research question asks whether literalisations of figurative senses are a useful source of information for improved disambiguation of PIEs. To provide an answer, we test our lexical cohesion graph with and without literalisation on a collection of existing datasets (Section 3.1), and evaluate performance using both micro- and macro-accuracy (Section 3.2).

3.1 Data

In order to provide a comprehensive evaluation dataset, we make use of four sizeable corpora containing sense-annotated PIEs:[4] the VNC-Tokens Dataset (Cook et al., 2008), the IDIX Corpus (Sporleder et al., 2010), the SemEval-2013 Task 5b dataset (Korkontzelos et al., 2013), and the PIE Corpus.[5] An overview of these datasets is provided in Table 1.

	# Types	# Instances	# Sense labels	Source Corpus
VNC-Tokens	53	2,984	3	BNC
IDIX	52	4,022	6	BNC
SemEval-2013 Task 5b	65	4,350	4	ukWaC
PIE Corpus	278	1,050	3	BNC
Combined (development)	299	8,235	2	BNC & ukWaC
Combined (test)	146	3,073	2	BNC & ukWaC

Table 1: Overview of existing corpora of sense-annotated PIEs. The source corpus indicates the corpora from which the PIE instances were selected, either the British National Corpus (Burnard, 2007) or ukWaC (Ferraresi et al., 2008).

Each corpus has slightly different benefits and downsides: VNC-Tokens only contains verb-noun combinations (e.g. *hit the road*) and contains some types which we would not consider idioms (e.g. *have a future*); the IDIX corpus covers various syntactic types and has a large number of instances per PIE type, but is partly singly-annotated; the SemEval dataset is large and varied, but the base corpus, ukWaC (Ferraresi et al., 2008), is noisy; the PIE Corpus covers a very wide range of PIE types, but has only few instances per type and is partly singly-annotated. We combine these four datasets in order to create a more well-rounded dataset. All labels are normalised to a binary sense label. For PIEs with senses which do not fit the binary split, such as *meta-linguistic*, no binary sense label is defined, and we discard those instances. The same goes for false extractions, i.e. sentences included in the corpus not containing any PIEs at all. The combined dataset is split into development and test sets using existing splits of the original datasets. We use the test sets of the original corpora to build the combined test set, which thus consists of: VNC-Test, IDIX-Double, SemEval-*-Test, and PIE-Test. The remaining subsets, including both training and development sets, make up the development set.

3.2 Evaluation

Performance is judged by three evaluation measures: macro-averaged accuracy ('macro-accuracy'), micro-averaged accuracy ('micro-accuracy'), and the harmonic mean of the two. Micro-accuracy reflects how good the disambiguation system is doing overall. Macro-accuracy serves to ensure that we do not just optimise on the most frequent types, since some PIE types are much more frequent than others. By using the harmonic mean of the two, we can rely on a single value to indicate balanced performance.

---

[4] We do not include the Gigaword-based corpus of Sporleder and Li (2009), since we currently do not have a license for Gigaword.

[5] Corpus available at https://github.com/hslh/pie-annotation

3.3 Results & Discussion

The results on the development set are displayed in Table 2. Note that the optimal settings for the literalisation method differ somewhat from those for the original method, as the optimal context window is 5 words on each side, instead of 2 sentences, and the optimal threshold value is $+0.005$, rather than $+0.0005$. These values were optimised by evaluating a range of settings: 0–3 sentences and 1–8 words of context and threshold values from the set $\{-0.05, -0.01, -0.005, +0.0001, +0.0005, +0.001, +0.005, +0.01, +0.05\}$. We also compare to a most frequent sense baseline.

	Macro-Accuracy (%)	Micro-Accuracy (%)	Harmonic Mean (%)
most frequent sense	73.25	57.89	64.67
original	72.74	63.78	67.97
literalisation	71.21	64.94	67.93

Table 2: Results of the original and literalisation-extended cohesion graph classifiers on the combined development set. Accuracy scores are micro- and macro-averages over PIE types, in addition to the harmonic mean of the two.

The graph including literalisations achieves an almost identical score to the original method. It has higher micro-accuracy, but lower macro-accuracy, indicating that it performs better on frequent types than the original classifier. It underpredicts the idiomatic sense quite strongly, which we compensate for by using a higher threshold value.

Although both classifiers show similar performance scores, they make the same judgement in only 5,737 ($\approx 70\%$) of 8,235 instances in the dataset. Additionally, in only $\approx 49\%$ of cases both classifiers are correct, while in $\approx 15\%$ of cases only the original classifier gets it right, and in $\approx 16\%$ of cases, the literalisation classifier predicts the right label. This indicates that the classifiers have at least some partially complementary performances, as they use different information sources, yielding potential for combination; in $\approx 79\%$ of PIE instances, at least one of the classifiers is right.

We combine the classifiers by using the difference in similarity between the two graphs as a confidence value and selecting the classification with the highest confidence value. Rather than improving over the scores of the individual classifiers, this yields a macro-accuracy score of 71.88% and a micro-accuracy of 64.07%, which is squarely in between the scores of the two classifiers. Although the potential for combination is still there, we can conclude that similarity differences do not make reliable confidence values, since larger similarity differences do not correlate with more accurate classifications. As such, the current combination setup yields an average of the two systems, rather than a selection of the best classifications from each system.

By looking at examples with different classifications, we get additional insight into the differences between the two classifiers. In some cases, the differences between the average similarity of the pruned graph, original graph, and the literalised graph are tiny, and any resulting differences are close to random. In other cases, however, both the advantages and disadvantages of using the literalisations come through much more clearly and strongly. Example (3) shows a sentence for which the literalisation graph (3-b) yields the correct classification (idiomatic) and the original graph (3-a) does not. Here, the literalisation is much more cohesive with the context (*feeling-confidence*, 0.69; *feeling-situation*, 0.67) than the idiom (*feeling-feet*, 0.37). Conversely, Example (4) is a case for which only the original gets the correct classification (idiomatic), because of the high similarity between *waste* and *disaster* (0.57), which is lost in the literalisation. The problem here is both related to this specific literalisation, as well as to the more general issue of idioms which are relatively semantically transparent, since those have higher similarity between the context and the component words (in this case, *waste*).

(3)   a.   In just a couple of days you'll *find your feet* and get that special feeling that you belong in your Club.

    b.   In just a couple of days you'll *grow in confidence in a new situation* and get that special feeling that you belong in your Club.

(4)   a.   These figures move slowly around a terrain apparently *laid waste* by some great disaster.

        b.   These figures move slowly around a terrain apparently *ravage* (sic) by some great disaster.

Splitting out performance by subcorpus shows that the original classifier does better on the VNC-Skewed dataset with a 13% higher score. Conversely, the classifier using literalisations performs about 10 percentage points better on PIE-Train and SemEval-Unknown-Phrases-Dev. The difference on the VNC-Skewed dataset is likely caused by the fact that it contains several frequent types which we would not consider PIEs, such as *catch (someone's) attention* and *have (a) future*.[6] For these items, there is no clear idiomatic sense, so adding literalisations hurts, rather than helps, performance.

Since the graph-based classifiers are optimised on the development set and we report results on that same set, the risk of overfitting exists. Therefore, we evaluate on the unseen combined test set as well. Results in Table 3 indicate that our models generalise well. In absolute terms, performance is very similar to that on the development set. Relative to the most frequent sense baseline, the models do better on the test set than on the development set. In contrast to the identical performance on the development set, the literalisation classifier does better than the original on the test set.

	Macro-Accuracy (%)	Micro-Accuracy (%)	Harmonic Mean (%)
most frequent sense	70.22	55.47	61.98
original	69.68	65.66	67.61
literalisation	69.80	69.18	69.49

Table 3: Results of the original and literalisation classifiers on the combined test set, compared to a most frequent sense baseline. Accuracy scores are micro- and macro-averages over PIE types, in addition to the harmonic mean of the two.

4   Comparison to Related Work

Ideally, we would be able to compare approaches from different papers directly, but this is often impossible. The lack of an established evaluation framework means that reported results for PIE disambiguation are often on different (splits of) datasets, obtained in different ways (cross-validation, leave-one-out) using a range of different metrics (micro- and macro-averaged accuracy and F1-score). For example, Sporleder and Li (2009) report micro-accuracy and micro-F1 scores on the Gigaword corpus, whereas Fazly et al. (2009) report macro-accuracy scores on the VNC-Tokens dataset. A potential solution to this problem was provided by SemEval-2013 Task 5b on PIE disambiguation (Korkontzelos et al., 2013), as results from different participants could be directly compared. However, this dataset does not seem to have been used by the community since.

Nevertheless, we compare to two other unsupervised approaches, the canonical form classifier (CForm) by Fazly et al. (2009), and the k-means clustering approach (KMeans) of Gharbieh et al. (2016). The CForm classifier is based on the assumption that idiomatic PIEs show less variability than literal ones. It uses a set of canonical forms for each idiom (e.g. *make a mark*, *make one's mark*), and labels all PIEs occurring in a canonical form as idiomatic, and literal otherwise. The KMeans classifier builds vector representations of both the PIE and its immediate context based on word embeddings, and clusters those using the k-means algorithm. It then uses the CForm classifier to label the clusters, and propagates the majority label for each cluster to all PIEs in that cluster. Both are evaluated on the test set of the VNC dataset using macro-accuracy by Gharbieh et al. (2016), so we do the same with our system to facilitate comparison.

---

[6]Both items are not in the Oxford Dictionary of English Idioms (Ayto, 2009), nor in Wiktionary (`https://en.wiktionary.org/wiki/Category:English_idioms`), which is a lot less stringent.

On VNC-Test, the original classifier scores 66.11% macro-accuracy and the literalisation classifier scores 64.67%, compared to 73.7% for CForm and 78.1% for KMeans. As such, our classifiers are outperformed by existing systems. One possible explanation is that our classifiers are optimised on a combination of both macro- and micro-accuracy, whereas previous work focuses only on the macro-averaged score. In addition, Gharbieh et al. (2016) optimise their classifier on the test set, whereas it was completely unseen in our case. Nevertheless, even using development set parameter values, their method achieves a macro-accuracy of 76.5%, which is still clearly higher.

5   Conclusion

In this work, we reimplemented and optimised the original lexical cohesion graph classifier for disambiguation of potentially idiomatic expressions and extended it to make use of literalisations of PIE's figurative senses. By evaluating the systems in a comprehensive evaluation setup, we aimed to answer questions about the contribution of literalisations as an information source.

We have found that the current approach comparing the cohesion of PIEs and their literalisations by itself is not enough to outperform the original lexical cohesion graph classifier. However, both classifiers do well on different subsets of the data, meaning that literalisations are a complementary novel information source and that there is potential for combining the two types of classification to achieve better performance. Using average similarity differences as confidence values to pick one classifier over the other for a particular instance proved ineffective, but a more advanced setup combining the features of the two classifiers could yield a more effective combination.

Moreover, literalisations are cheap to acquire and are available for many PIE types and for any language for which an idiom dictionary exists. Although we use manually created definitions, these can also be acquired and refined automatically, as done by Liu and Hwa (2016). A side benefit of considering both figurative and literal senses is that separate scores can be assigned for both senses. This could be used for detecting difficult cases like dual meanings or puns, since those cases would get high scores for both senses.

In future work, our aim is to further improve these cohesion graph-based classifiers by exploring different similarity measures, such as those tested by Ehren (2017) for German. Another promising avenue is to use more compositional representations of contexts and literalisations (see also Gharbieh et al., 2016). This would also allow us to use the information from verbs and modifiers more effectively, as in its current form our method relies on word-to-word comparisons and only nouns contribute to performance. Finally, we find that, for evaluation, using both micro- and macro-averaged metrics is an important way of ensuring balanced performance on both infrequent and frequent PIE types, in addition to using a wide range of corpora.

Acknowledgements

This work was funded by the NWO-VICI grant "Lost in Translation – Found in Meaning" (288-89-003). We would also like to thank the anonymous reviewers for their useful comments, which helped to significantly improve this paper.

References

John Ayto, editor. 2009. *From the horse's mouth: Oxford dictionary of English Idioms*. Oxford University Press, Oxford; New York, 3rd edition.

Lou Burnard. 2007. Reference guide for the British National Corpus (XML edition).

Paul Cook, Afsaneh Fazly, and Suzanne Stevenson. 2008. The VNC-Tokens dataset. In *Proceedings of the LREC workshop towards a shared task for Multiword Expressions*, pages 19–22.

Rafael Ehren. 2017. Literal or idiomatic? Identifying the reading of single occurrences of German multiword expressions using word embeddings. In *Proceedings of the Student Research Workshop at the 15th Conference of the European Chapter of the Association for Computational Linguistics*, pages 103–112.

Afsaneh Fazly, Paul Cook, and Suzanne Stevenson. 2009. Unsupervised type and token identification of idiomatic expressions. *Computational Linguistics*, 35(1):61–103.

Adriano Ferraresi, Eros Zanchetta, Marco Baroni, and Silvia Bernardini. 2008. Introducing and evaluating uk-WaC, a very large web-derived corpus of English. In *Proceedings of LREC*, pages 47–54.

Waseem Gharbieh, Virendra C. Bhavsar, and Paul Cook. 2016. A word embedding approach to identifying verb-noun idiomatic combinations. In *Proceedings of the 12th Workshop on Multiword Expressions*, pages 112–118.

Pierre Isabelle, Colin Cherry, and George Foster. 2017. A challenge set approach to evaluating machine translation. In *Proceedings of the 2017 Conference on Empirical Methods in Natural Language Processing (EMNLP)*, pages 2476–2486. Association for Computational Linguistics.

Ioannis Korkontzelos, Torsten Zesch, Fabio Massimo Zanzotto, and Chris Biemann. 2013. SemEval-2013 task 5: Evaluating phrasal semantics. In *Proceedings of SemEval*, pages 39–47.

Changsheng Liu and Rebecca Hwa. 2016. Phrasal substitution of idiomatic expressions. In *Proceedings of NAACL*, pages 363–373.

Jeffrey Pennington, Richard Socher, and Christopher D. Manning. 2014. GloVe: Global vectors for word representation. In *Proceedings of EMNLP 2014*, pages 1532–1543.

Ivan A. Sag, Timothy Baldwin, Francis Bond, Ann Copestake, and Dan Flickinger. 2002. Multiword expressions: A pain in the neck for NLP. In *Proceedings of CICLING*, pages 1–15.

Giancarlo D. Salton, Robert J. Ross, and John D. Kelleher. 2014a. An empirical study of the impact of idioms on phrase based statistical machine translation of English to Brazilian-Portuguese. In *Proceedings of the 3rd Workshop on Hybrid Approaches to Translation (HyTra)*, pages 36–41.

Giancarlo D. Salton, Robert J. Ross, and John D. Kelleher. 2014b. Evaluation of a substitution method for idiom transformation in statistical machine translation. In *Proceedings of the 10th Workshop on Multiword Expressions*, pages 38–42.

Caroline Sporleder and Linlin Li. 2009. Unsupervised recognition of literal and non-literal use of idiomatic expressions. In *Proceedings of EACL*, pages 754–762.

Caroline Sporleder, Linlin Li, Philip John Gorinski, and Xaver Koch. 2010. Idioms in context: The IDIX corpus. In *Proceedings of LREC*, pages 639–646.

Lowri Williams, Christian Bannister, Michael Arribas-Ayllon, Alun Preece, and Irena Spasić. 2015. The role of idioms in sentiment analysis. *Expert Systems with Applications*, 42(21):7375–7385.

Do Character-Level Neural Network Language Models Capture Knowledge of Multiword Expression Compositionality?

Ali Hakimi Parizi and **Paul Cook**
Faculty of Computer Science, University of New Brunswick
Fredericton, NB E3B 5A3 Canada
ahakimi@unb.ca, paul.cook@unb.ca

Abstract

In this paper we propose the first model for multiword expression (MWE) compositionality prediction based on character-level neural network language models. Experimental results on two kinds of MWEs (noun compounds and verb-particle constructions) and two languages (English and German) suggest that character-level neural network language models capture knowledge of multiword expression compositionality, in particular for English noun compounds and the particle component of English verb-particle constructions. In contrast to many other approaches to MWE compositionality prediction, this character-level approach does not require token-level identification of MWEs in a training corpus, and can potentially predict the compositionality of out-of-vocabulary MWEs.

1   Introduction

Multiword expressions (MWEs) are lexical items that are composed of multiple words, and exhibit some degree of idiomaticity (Baldwin and Kim, 2010), for example semantic idiomaticity, in which the meaning of an MWE is not entirely transparent from the meanings of its component words, as in *spill the beans*, which has an idiomatic meaning of 'reveal a secret'. Compositionality is the degree to which the meaning of an MWE is predictable from the meanings of its component words. It is typically viewed as lying on a continuum, with expressions such as *speed limit* and *gravy train* lying towards the compositional and non-compositional ends of the spectrum, respectively, and expressions such as *rush hour* and *fine line* falling somewhere in between as semi-compositional.[1] Compositionality can also be viewed with respect to an individual component word of an MWE, where an MWE component word is compositional if its meaning is reflected in the meaning of the expression. For example, in *spelling bee* and *grandfather clock*, the first and second component words, respectively, are compositional, while the others are not.

Knowledge of multiword expressions is important for natural language processing (NLP) tasks such as parsing (Korkontzelos and Manandhar, 2010) and machine translation (Carpuat and Diab, 2010). In the case of translation, compositionality is particularly important because a word-for-word translation would typically be incorrect for a non-compositional expression. Much research has therefore focused on compositionality prediction of MWEs, primarily at the type level. One common approach to measuring compositionality is to compare distributional representations of an MWE and its component words (e.g., Schone and Jurafsky, 2001; Baldwin et al., 2003; Katz and Giesbrecht, 2006; Reddy et al., 2011; Schulte im Walde et al., 2013; Salehi et al., 2015). The hypothesis behind this line of work is that the representation of a compositional MWE will be more similar to the representations of its component words than the representation of a non-compositional MWE will be to those of its component words. One issue faced by such approaches is that token-level instances of MWEs must be identified in a corpus in order to form distributional representations of them. Token-level MWE identification has been studied for specific types of MWEs such as verb-particle constructions (e.g., Kim and Baldwin, 2010) and

---

[1]These expressions and compositionality judgements are taken from Reddy et al. (2011).

Proceedings of the Joint Workshop on
Linguistic Annotation, Multiword Expressions and Constructions (LAW-MWE-CxG-2018), pages 185–192
Santa Fe, New Mexico, USA, August 25-26, 2018.

verb–noun idioms (e.g., Salton et al., 2016). Broad coverage MWE identification has also been studied, and remains a challenge (Schneider et al., 2014; Gharbieh et al., 2017).

Language models are common throughout NLP in tasks including machine translation (Brants et al., 2007), speech recognition (Collins et al., 2005), and question answering (Chen et al., 2006). Although word-level language models are widely used, and their performance can be higher than character-level language models, character-level models have the advantage that they can model out-of-vocabulary words (Mikolov et al., 2012). Owing to this advantage, character-level language models have been applied in a range of NLP tasks, including authorship attribution, (Peng et al., 2003), part-of-speech tagging (Santos and Zadrozny, 2014), case restoration (Susanto et al., 2016), and stock price prediction (dos Santos Pinheiro and Dras, 2017). Moreover, character-level information can be composed to form representations of words (Ling et al., 2015).

In this paper we consider whether character-level neural network language models capture knowledge of MWE compositionality. We train character-level language models based on recurrent neural networks — including long short-term memory (LSTM, Hochreiter and Schmidhuber, 1997) and gated recurrent unit (GRU, Cho et al., 2014). We then use these language models to form continuous vector representations of MWEs and their component words. Following prior work, we then use these representations to predict the compositionality of MWEs. This method overcomes the limitation of previous work in this vein of having to identify token instances of MWEs in a corpus in order to form a distributional representation of them. Moreover, this approach could potentially be applied to predict the compositionality of out-of-vocabulary expressions that were not seen in the corpus on which the language model was trained. To the best of our knowledge, this is the first work to apply character-level neural network language models to predict MWE compositionality. Our experiments on two kinds of MWEs (noun compounds and verb-particle constructions) and two languages (English and German) produce mixed results, but suggest that character-level neural network language models do indeed capture some knowledge of multiword expression compositionality, in particular for English noun compounds and the particle component of English verb-particle constructions.

2   A Character-level Model for MWE Compositionality

If an MWE is compositional, it is expected to be similar in meaning to its component words. Since the vector representation of a word/MWE is taken as a proxy for its meaning, we expect the vector representation of a compositional MWE to be similar to its component words' vectors. In order to obtain vectors representing each of an MWE and its component words through a character-level neural network language model, each of the MWE and its component words are considered as a sequence of characters. Each of these character sequences includes a special end-of-sequence character. In the case of an MWE, the character sequence includes a space character between the component words. For example, the MWE *ivory tower* is represented as the sequence $< i, v, o, r, y, \ , t, o, w, e, r, \text{END} >$. These character sequences are fed to the neural network language model, and the hidden state of the neural network at the end of the sequence is taken as the vector representation for that sequence.[2]

Once vector representations of an MWE and its component words are obtained, following Salehi et al. (2015), the following equations are then used to compute the compositionality of an MWE:

$$\text{comp}_1(\text{MWE}) = \alpha \, sim(\text{MWE}, \text{C}_1) + (1 - \alpha) sim(\text{MWE}, \text{C}_2) \tag{1}$$

$$\text{comp}_2(\text{MWE}) = sim(\text{MWE}, \text{C}_1 + \text{C}_2) \tag{2}$$

where MWE is the vector representation of the MWE, and C_1 and C_2 are vector representations for the

---

[2]This approach does have the limitation that it is not immediately clear how to input a "gappy" MWE, such as *give X a chance*, to the language model. A possible solution would be to attempt to select a prototypical slot filler. However, this issue does not arise in this study because the evaluation datasets used — English and German noun compounds, and English verb-particle constructions — do not consist of gappy expressions. (Although English verb-particle constructions can appear in the split configuration, we input them to the language model in the joined configuration.)

Language	Number of Characters	Number of Tokens	Size
English	102M	16.5M	103 MB
German	102M	14.2M	102 MB

Table 1: The size of the English and German training corpora in terms of characters, tokens, and megabytes.

first and second components of the MWE, respectively.[3] In both cases, we use cosine as the similarity measure. $comp_1$ is based on Reddy et al. (2011). As shown in equation (1), the compositionality of an MWE is computed based on measuring the similarity of the MWE and each of its component words, and then combining these two similarities into an overall compositionality score. $comp_2$ is based on Mitchell and Lapata (2010) and measures compositionality by considering the similarity between the MWE and the summation of its component words' vectors.

3   Materials and Methods

In this section, we describe the language model and corpus it was trained on, as well as the evaluation dataset and methodology.

3.1   Language Model

We use a publicly available TensorFlow implementation of a character-level RNN language model.[4] We use the following parameter settings as defaults: a two-layer LSTM with one-hot character embeddings and a hidden layer size of 128 dimensions. The batch size, learning rate, and dropout are set 20, 0.002, and 0, respectively.[5] We consider some alternative parameter settings to these defaults in section §4.

3.2   Training Corpus

We train language models over a portion of English and German Wikipedia dumps — following Salehi et al. (2015) — from 20 January 2018. The raw dumps are preprocessed using WP2TXT[6] to remove wikimarkup, metadata, and XML and HTML tags.

The text from Wikipedia contains many characters that are not typically found in MWEs, for example, non-ASCII characters. Such characters drastically increase the size of the vocabulary of the language model, which leads to very long training times. We therefore remove all non-ASCII characters from the English dump, and all non-ASCII characters other than *ä, Ä, ö, Ö, ü, Ü, ß* from the German dump.

Training the character-level language model over the Wikipedia dumps in their entirety would take a prohibitively long time due to their size. We therefore instead carry out experiments training on a 1% sample of the English dump, and a 2% sample of the German dump (to give a corpus of similar size to the English one). Details of the resulting training corpora are provided in table 1.

3.3   Evaluation Data

The proposed model is evaluated over the same three datasets as Salehi et al. (2015), which cover two languages (English and German) and two kinds of MWEs (noun compounds and verb-particle constructions).

ENC This dataset contains 90 English noun compounds (e.g., *game plan*, *gravy train*) which are annotated on a scale of [0,5] for both their overall compositionality, and the compositionality of each of their component words (Reddy et al., 2011).

---

[3]Although $comp_1$ and $comp_2$ are formulated for MWEs with two component words, they could be extended to handle MWEs with more than two component words.

[4]https://github.com/crazydonkey200/tensorflow-char-rnn

[5]These settings were used for a pre-trained language model that is distributed with this implementation, and so we adopted them as our defaults.

[6]https://github.com/yohasebe/wp2txt

Dataset	Comp_1	Comp_2	Salehi et al. (2015)
ENC	*0.239	*0.286	0.717
EVPC: verb	0.012	0.019	0.289
EVPC: particle	*0.313	*0.301	-
GNC	−0.033	−0.096	0.400

Table 2: Pearson's correlation (r) for each dataset, using comp$_1$ and comp$_2$. Significant correlations ($p < 0.05$) are indicated with *. The best results from Salehi et al. (2015) using comp$_1$ with representations of the MWE and component words obtained from word2vec (Mikolov et al., 2013), are also shown.

EVPC This dataset consists of 160 English verb-particle constructions (e.g., *add up*, *figure out*) which are rated on a binary scale for the compositionality of each of the verb and particle component words (Bannard, 2006) by multiple annotators; no ratings for the overall compositionality of MWEs are provided in this dataset. The binary compositionality judgements are converted to continuous values as in Salehi et al. (2015) by dividing the number of judgements that an expression is compositional by the total number of judgements.

GNC This dataset contains 244 German noun compounds (e.g., *Ahornblatt* 'maple leaf', *Knoblauch* 'garlic') which are annotated on a scale of [1,7] for their overall compositionality, and the compositionality of each component word (von der Heide and Borgwaldt, 2009).

3.4 Evaluation Methodology

We evaluate our proposed approach following Salehi et al. (2015) by computing Pearson's correlation between the predicted compositionality (i.e., from either comp$_1$ or comp$_2$) and human ratings for overall compositionality. For EVPC, no overall compositionality ratings are provided. In this case we report the correlation between the predicted compositionality scores and both the verb and particle compositionality judgements.[7]

4 Results

We begin by considering results using the default settings (described in section §3.1) using both comp$_1$ and comp$_2$. For comp$_1$, we set α to 0.7 for ENC and GNC following Salehi et al. (2015); for EVPC we set α to 0.5. Results are shown in table 2. For ENC, and the particle component of EVPC, both comp$_1$ and comp$_2$ achieve significant correlations (i.e., $p < 0.05$). However, for GNC, and the verb component of EVPC, neither approach to predicting compositionality gives significant correlations. These correlations are well below those of previous work. For example, using comp$_1$ with representations of the MWE and component words obtained from word2vec (Mikolov et al., 2013), Salehi et al. (2015) achieve correlations of 0.717, 0.289, and 0.400 for ENC, the verb component of EVPC, and GNC, respectively.[8] Nevertheless, the results in table 2, and in particular the significant correlations for ENC and the particle component of EVPC, indicate that character-level neural network language models do capture some information about the compositionality of MWEs, at least for certain types of expressions.

We now consider the compositionality of individual component words. Because of the low correlations on GNC in the previous experiments, we do not consider it further here. In this case, we compute the compositionality of a specific component word as below, where C is the vector representation of a component word.

$$\text{comp}(C) = sim(\text{MWE}, C) \tag{3}$$

Note that this corresponds to comp$_1$ with $\alpha = 1$ or 0, in the case of the first and second component words, respectively. We compare these compositionality predictions with the human judgements for

---

[7]In this case Salehi et al. (2015) took the verb compositionality as a proxy for the overall compositionality, and did not consider particle compositionality.

[8]Salehi et al. (2015) did not consider the compositionality of the particle component for EVPC.

Dataset	word 1	word 2
ENC	0.135	*0.335
EVPC	0.019	*0.200

Table 3: Pearson's correlation (r) for the ENC and EVPC datasets for each of component word 1 and 2. Significant correlations ($p < 0.05$) are indicated with *.

Dataset		Number of MWEs	$Comp_1$	$Comp_2$
ENC	Attested	66	*0.296	*0.372
	Unattested	24	0.040	0.049
EVPC: verb	Attested	147	0.019	0.010
	Unattested	13	0.034	*−0.208
EVPC: particle	Attested	147	*0.313	*0.286
	Unattested	13	0.366	0.385
GNC	Attested	167	0.009	−0.067
	Unattested	77	−0.110	−0.154

Table 4: Pearson's correlation (r) for MWEs that are attested, and unattested, in each dataset, using $comp_1$ and $comp_2$. Significant correlations ($p < 0.05$) are indicated with *. The number of attested and unattested MWEs in each dataset is also shown.

the compositionality of the corresponding component word. Results are shown in table 3. For EVPC, the results are perhaps not surprising given the previous findings, with a significant correlation being achieved for the particle (word 2) but not the verb (word 1). In the case of ENC, a significant correlation is also achieved for the second component word, but not the first.

The above results suggests that the model is better able to predict the compositionality of the second component word of an MWE than the first. To determine whether there is a relationship between the directionality of a character-level language model and the compositionality information it can capture, we also consider a backward LSTM that was trained by reversing the training corpus. The MWE and its component words were then reversed when computing compositionality. However, none of the correlations from this approach were significant.

One interesting aspect of our proposed model is that it can potentially predict the compositionality of out-of-vocabulary expressions that are not observed in the training corpus. In table 4 we present results for each dataset, in the same setup as for table 2, but computing the correlation separately for MWEs that are attested, and unattested, in the training corpus. For ENC, both compositionality measures achieve significant correlations for attested expressions, but not for unattested ones, suggesting that the model cannot predict the compositionality of unseen expressions. In the case of the compositionality of the particle component of EVPC, for both $comp_1$ and $comp_2$, the correlations for the unattested expressions are higher than for the attested ones, although for unattested expressions the correlations are not significant. The relatively small number of unattested expressions in EVPC (13) could play a role in this finding. To further investigate this, we focused on expressions in EVPC with less than 5 usages in the training corpus. There are 71 such expressions. For the compositionality of the particle component, $comp_1$ and $comp_2$ achieve correlations of 0.327 and 0.308, respectively. These correlations are significant ($p < 0.05$). Word embedding models — such as that used in the approach to predicting compositionality of Salehi et al. (2015) — typically do not learn representations for low frequency items.[9] These results demonstrate that the proposed model is able to predict the compositionality for low frequency items, that would not typically be in-vocabulary for word embedding models, and for which compositionality models based only on word embeddings would not be able to make predictions.[10] For GNC, and the verb component

---

[9]Salehi et al. (2015) used a minimum frequency of 15, for example.

[10]Note, however, that Salehi et al. (2015) were able to make predictions for all items in EVPC because they trained on a larger corpus (full Wikipedia dumps, as opposed to samples of them) and all items in this dataset were sufficiently frequent in

of EVPC, in line with the previous results over the entire dataset, neither compositionality measure gives significant correlations, with the exception of the verb component of EVPC using $comp_2$ for unattested expressions, although again the number of expressions here is relatively small.

In an effort to improve on the default setup we considered a range of model variations. In particular we considered an RNN and GRU (instead of an LSTM), character embeddings of size 25 and 50 (instead of a one-hot representation), increasing the batch size to 100 (from 20), using dropout between 0.2–0.6, and using a bi-directional LSTM. None of these variations led to consistent improvements over the default setup.

5 Conclusions

In this paper we proposed an approach to predicting the compositionality of multiword expressions based on a character-level neural network language model. To the best of our knowledge, this is the first work to consider such character-level models for this task. Our proposed character-level approach has an advantage over prior approaches to compositionality prediction based on distributed representations of words in that we do not require token-level identification of MWEs in order to form representations of them. Our proposed approach can furthermore potentially predict the compositionality of out-of-vocabulary MWEs that are not observed in the training corpus. We carried out experiments over three compositionality datasets: English and German noun compounds, and English verb-particle constructions. Our experimental results indicate that character-level neural network models do capture knowledge of multiword expression compositionality, at least in the case of English noun compounds and the particle component of English verb-particle constructions. We further find that our proposed model captures knowledge of the compositionality of the particle component of English verb-particle constructions that are low frequency or not observed in the training corpus, but not of the compositionality of unobserved English noun compounds.

In future work we intend to further explore the various parameter settings of the language model — such as the batch size, learning rate, and dropout — to better understand their impact on MWE compositionality prediction. We also intend to train the language model on larger corpora. Finally, we intend to combine our character-level approach to compositionality prediction with approaches based on other sources of information, for example distributed representations of words and knowledge from translation dictionaries (Salehi et al., 2014). Specifically, we intend to determine whether the compositionality information from character-level neural network language models is complementary to that in these other approaches.

References

Timothy Baldwin, Colin Bannard, Takaaki Tanaka, and Dominic Widdows. 2003. An empirical model of multiword expression decomposability. In *Proceedings of the ACL 2003 Workshop on Multiword Expressions: Analysis, Acquisition and Treatment*. Association for Computational Linguistics, Sapporo, Japan, pages 89–96.

Timothy Baldwin and Su Nam Kim. 2010. Multiword expressions. *Handbook of natural language processing* 2:267–292.

Colin James Bannard. 2006. *Acquiring phrasal lexicons from corpora*. Ph.D. thesis, University of Edinburgh.

Thorsten Brants, Ashok C Popat, Peng Xu, Franz J Och, and Jeffrey Dean. 2007. Large language models in machine translation. In *Proceedings of the 2007 Joint Conference on Empirical Methods in Natural Language Processing and Computational Natural Language Learning (EMNLP-CoNLL)*.

Marine Carpuat and Mona Diab. 2010. Task-based evaluation of multiword expressions: a pilot study in statistical machine translation. In *Human Language Technologies: The 2010 Annual Conference of the North American Chapter of the Association for Computational Linguistics*. Los Angeles, California, pages 242–245.

their training corpus.

Yi Chen, Ming Zhou, and Shilong Wang. 2006. Reranking answers for definitional qa using language modeling. In *Proceedings of the 21st International Conference on Computational Linguistics and the 44th annual meeting of the Association for Computational Linguistics*. Association for Computational Linguistics, pages 1081–1088.

Kyunghyun Cho, Bart Van Merriënboer, Caglar Gulcehre, Dzmitry Bahdanau, Fethi Bougares, Holger Schwenk, and Yoshua Bengio. 2014. Learning phrase representations using rnn encoder-decoder for statistical machine translation. *arXiv preprint arXiv:1406.1078* .

Michael Collins, Brian Roark, and Murat Saraclar. 2005. Discriminative syntactic language modeling for speech recognition. In *Proceedings of the 43rd Annual Meeting on Association for Computational Linguistics*. Association for Computational Linguistics, pages 507–514.

Leonardo dos Santos Pinheiro and Mark Dras. 2017. Stock market prediction with deep learning: A character-based neural language model for event-based trading. In *Proceedings of the Australasian Language Technology Association Workshop 2017*. pages 6–15.

Waseem Gharbieh, Virendrakumar Bhavsar, and Paul Cook. 2017. Deep learning models for multiword expression identification. In *Proceedings of the 6th Joint Conference on Lexical and Computational Semantics (*SEM 2017)*. Association for Computational Linguistics, Vancouver, Canada, pages 54–64.

Sepp Hochreiter and Jürgen Schmidhuber. 1997. Long short-term memory. *Neural computation* 9(8):1735–1780.

Graham Katz and Eugenie Giesbrecht. 2006. Automatic identification of non-compositional multi-word expressions using latent semantic analysis. In *Proceedings of the Workshop on Multiword Expressions: Identifying and Exploiting Underlying Properties*. Sydney, Australia, pages 12–19.

Su Nam Kim and Timothy Baldwin. 2010. How to pick out token instances of english verb-particle constructions. *Language Resources and Evaluation* 44(1–2):97–113.

Ioannis Korkontzelos and Suresh Manandhar. 2010. Can recognising multiword expressions improve shallow parsing? In *Human Language Technologies: The 2010 Annual Conference of the North American Chapter of the Association for Computational Linguistics*. Association for Computational Linguistics, Los Angeles, California, pages 636–644.

Wang Ling, Chris Dyer, Alan W Black, Isabel Trancoso, Ramon Fermandez, Silvio Amir, Luis Marujo, and Tiago Luis. 2015. Finding function in form: Compositional character models for open vocabulary word representation. In *Proceedings of the 2015 Conference on Empirical Methods in Natural Language Processing*. Association for Computational Linguistics, Lisbon, Portugal, pages 1520–1530.

Tomas Mikolov, Kai Chen, Greg Corrado, and Jeffrey Dean. 2013. Efficient estimation of word representations in vector space. In *Proceedings of Workshop at the International Conference on Learning Representations, 2013*. Scottsdale, USA.

Tomáš Mikolov, Ilya Sutskever, Anoop Deoras, Hai-Son Le, Stefan Kombrink, and Jan Cernocky. 2012. Subword language modeling with neural networks. *preprint (http://www. fit. vutbr. cz/imikolov/rnnlm/char. pdf)* .

Jeff Mitchell and Mirella Lapata. 2010. Composition in distributional models of semantics. *Cognitive science* 34(8):1388–1429.

Fuchun Peng, Dale Schuurmans, Shaojun Wang, and Vlado Keselj. 2003. Language independent authorship attribution using character level language models. In *Proceedings of the tenth conference on European chapter of the Association for Computational Linguistics-Volume 1*. Association for Computational Linguistics, pages 267–274.

Siva Reddy, Diana McCarthy, and Suresh Manandhar. 2011. An empirical study on compositionality in compound nouns. In *Proceedings of 5th International Joint Conference on Natural Language Processing*. pages 210–218.

Bahar Salehi, Paul Cook, and Timothy Baldwin. 2014. Using distributional similarity of multi-way translations to predict multiword expression compositionality. In *Proceedings of the 14th Conference of the EACL (EACL 2014)*. Gothenburg, Sweden, pages 472–481.

Bahar Salehi, Paul Cook, and Timothy Baldwin. 2015. A word embedding approach to predicting the compositionality of multiword expressions. In *Proceedings of the 2015 Conference of the North American Chapter of the Association for Computational Linguistics: Human Language Technologies*. Denver, Colorado, pages 977–983.

Giancarlo Salton, Robert Ross, and John Kelleher. 2016. Idiom token classification using sentential distributed semantics. In *Proceedings of the 54th Annual Meeting of the Association for Computational Linguistics (Volume 1: Long Papers)*. Association for Computational Linguistics, Berlin, Germany, pages 194–204.

Cicero D Santos and Bianca Zadrozny. 2014. Learning character-level representations for part-of-speech tagging. In *Proceedings of the 31st International Conference on Machine Learning (ICML-14)*. pages 1818–1826.

Nathan Schneider, Emily Danchik, Chris Dyer, and Noah A. Smith. 2014. Discriminative lexical semantic segmentation with gaps: Running the mwe gamut. *Transactions of the Association of Computational Linguistics* 2:193–206.

Patrick Schone and Daniel Jurafsky. 2001. Is knowledge-free induction of multiword unit dictionary headwords a solved problem? In *Proceedings of the 6th Conference on Empirical Methods in Natural Language Processing (EMNLP 2001)*. Hong Kong, China, pages 100–108.

Sabine Schulte im Walde, Stefan Müller, and Stefan Roller. 2013. Exploring vector space models to predict the compositionality of German noun-noun compounds. In *Second Joint Conference on Lexical and Computational Semantics (*SEM), Volume 1: Proceedings of the Main Conference and the Shared Task: Semantic Textual Similarity*. Atlanta, GA, pages 255–265.

Raymond Hendy Susanto, Hai Leong Chieu, and Wei Lu. 2016. Learning to capitalize with character-level recurrent neural networks: An empirical study. In *Proceedings of the 2016 Conference on Empirical Methods in Natural Language Processing*. pages 2090–2095.

Claudia von der Heide and Susanne Borgwaldt. 2009. Assoziationen zu unter-, basis-und oberbegriffen. eine explorative studie. In *Proceedings of the 9th Norddeutsches Linguistisches Kolloquium*. pages 51–74.

Constructing an Annotated Corpus of Verbal MWEs for English

Abigail Walsh
ADAPT Centre
Dublin City University
abigail.walsh@adaptcentre.ie

Claire Bonial
U.S. Army Research Laboratory
claire.n.bonial.civ@mail.mil

Kristina Geeraert
University of Alberta
geeraert@ualberta.ca

John P. McCrae
Insight Centre for Data Analytics
National University of Ireland Galway
john.mccrae@insight-centre.org

Nathan Schneider   Clarissa Somers
Georgetown University
nathan.schneider@georgetown.edu

Abstract

This paper describes the construction and annotation of a corpus of verbal MWEs for English as part of the PARSEME Shared Task 1.1 on automatic identification of verbal MWEs. The criteria for corpus selection, the categories of MWEs used, and the training process are discussed, along with the particular issues that led to revisions in edition 1.1 of the annotation guidelines. Finally, an overview of the characteristics of the final annotated corpus is presented, as well as some discussion on inter-annotator agreement.

1   Introduction

Multiword expressions (MWE) present a challenge in Natural Language Processing (NLP) due to their idiosyncrasy, which necessitates an interpretation of these expressions that is distinct from that of compositional phrases (literal, non-idiosyncratic word combinations) that may be similar or identical in their surface forms (Sag et al., 2002). MWEs are extremely prevalent in our lexicon; up to half of our lexicon is composed of MWEs (Ramisch, 2015). Understanding MWEs can aid in a variety of NLP tasks, ranging from syntactic disambiguation, to conceptual understanding, to semantic tagging, to word alignment (Baldwin and Kim, 2010). Given the critical nature of identifying and interpreting MWEs correctly, MWEs have been the main item on the agenda of several working groups, including PARSEME, which aims to improve cross-linguistic understanding of MWEs through the development of manually annotated data and shared tasks focused on automatic MWE identification (Constant et al., 2017).

This paper describes the construction and annotation of a corpus of English verbal MWEs (VMWEs) for the second edition of the PARSEME Shared Task (Shared Task 1.1). The term MWE frequently encompasses a wide variety of linguistic phenomena such as idioms, compound nouns, verb particle constructions, institutionalized phrases, etc. Although the precise definition can differ depending upon the community of interest (Constant et al., 2017), the annotation guidelines for the PARSEME shared task[1] define MWEs as continuous or discontinuous sequences of words with the following properties:

- Some degree of idiosyncrasy in respect to grammar (statistical idiosyncrasy[2] is not considered here)
- Their component words include a head and at least one other syntactically dependent word
- At least two of the components are lexicalised

PARSEME is focused on VMWEs, which are MWEs whose syntactic head is a verb in its prototypical form.

After providing some background on the past PARSEME shared task, we will describe the data and annotation procedures, including some of the annotation challenges, of the 2018 English corpus. We provide a quantitative overview of the characteristics of the corpus, as well as inter-annotator agreement figures.

---

[1]http://parsemefr.lif.univ-mrs.fr/parseme-st-guidelines/1.1/?page=010_Definitions_and_scope/020_Verbal_multiword_expressions

[2](Farahmand and Nivre, 2015)

Proceedings of the Joint Workshop on
Linguistic Annotation, Multiword Expressions and Constructions (LAW-MWE-CxG-2018), pages 193–200
Santa Fe, New Mexico, USA, August 25-26, 2018.

1.1 Background: The PARSEME Shared Task 1.0

The Shared Task 1.1 (Ramisch et al., 2018) is based on a similar Shared Task 1.0 that took place in 2017 (Savary et al., 2017). The aim of the shared task is to identify VMWEs in running texts across a variety of languages, and to establish a consistent set of guidelines for the annotation of these VMWEs. The 1.0 task and data encompassed 18 languages. English, the focus of this paper, is one of the five languages added to this new edition of the shared task, along with Arabic, Basque, Croatian, and Hindi. The guidelines have evolved from version 1.0 to accommodate these new languages. Specifically, two of the categories (VPC and LVC) have now been extended to allow for more fine-grained categorisation (see section 3.1 for more information on categories).

2 Data

There were several considerations when selecting appropriate text for inclusion in this corpus. This section describes the selection criteria, followed by a description of the annotation tool used. The suggestions for selecting an appropriate source of data were provided by PARSEME in the language leader guidelines, and were informed by version 1.0 of the shared task. Of those suggestions, the following criteria were deemed to be of the highest priority:

1. The corpus should be available under an open licence

2. The text must be originally written in English

3. The text should be annotated for morphosyntactic information

4. The size of the corpus should allow for at least 3,500 MWE annotations

5. The language must be of sufficiently high quality

There were several corpora considered for selection, including the DiMSUM corpus (Schneider et al., 2016), the UP/TAP corpus,[3] Wikidata parallel text (Vrandečić and Krötzsch, 2014) and the Universal Dependencies (UD) treebanks.[4] Three corpora from the UD treebanks for English were ultimately selected as a source of data, as they alone fulfilled the criteria mentioned above: text was selected from the English-EWT corpus (Silveira et al., 2014),[5] the LinES parallel corpus (Ahrenberg, 2007) and the Parallel Universal Dependencies (PUD) treebank (Zeman et al., 2017).[6] The files were extracted in CoNLL-U format and converted to FoLiA XML format (see section 3) for annotating. The training, development and testing datasets for each treebank were concatenated, and then split into files of 201 sentences for annotation.

3 Annotation

During the data preparation period, annotators were trained in the use of the FoLiA Linguistic Annotation Tool (FLAT). FLAT is an open-source web-based environment,[7] using the XML-based FoLiA format. In order to aid annotators in annotating only verbal MWEs, FLAT highlights verbs using POS information taken from the CoNLL-U file. Figure 1 shows a screenshot of the FLAT platform, demonstrating how the selecting and annotating of lexicalised components works. Annotators were also trained to recognize and categorise VMWEs of different types, detailed in the sections to follow.

The annotation team was comprised of volunteers who had experience with or interest in annotating multiword expressions, and were all native speakers of English. Four dialects of English were represented: Irish English, British English, American English and Canadian English.

---

[3]Documentation for UP/TAP: https://www.l2f.inesc-id.pt/~thomas/metashare/report-UP-TAP.pdf

[4]Documentation for UD: http://universaldependencies.org

[5]Originally sourced from the English Web Treebank (Bies et al., 2012)

[6]Though not a part of the task dataset, we have also fully annotated the Reviews portion of the UD English-EWT corpus by adding VMWE types to the existing VMWEs in STREUSLE (Schneider et al., 2014; Schneider and Smith, 2015, https://github.com/nert-gu/streusle/); they were previously uncategorized. STREUSLE as of version 4.1 comprises 3812 sentences and 871 VMWE instances (121 IAV, 12 LVC.cause, 123 LVC.full, 310 VID, 206 VPC.full, 99 VPC.semi).

[7]http://flat.readthedocs.io/en/latest/

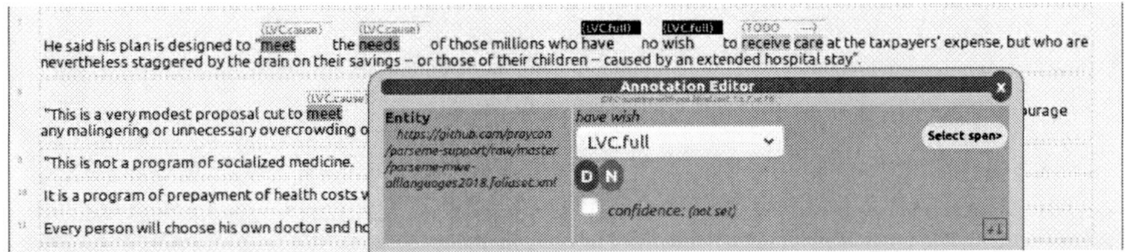

Figure 1: Screenshot of the FLAT Platform

3.1 Categories of VMWE

Seven categories of VMWE were used in the English annotation task: Verbal Idioms (VID), Verb-Particle Constructions (VPC.full and VPC.semi),[8] Light-Verb Constructions (LVC.full and LVC.cause),[8] Multi-Verb Constructions (MVC) and Inherently Adpositional Verbs (IAV). The categories are divided into universal categories (valid for all participating languages), quasi-universal categories (valid for some language groups or languages), and an experimental category (which may be optionally considered for some languages).

Verbal idioms (VIDs) and the **Light-Verb Constructions** (LVCs) constitute universal categories. VIDs have at least two lexicalised components, including a head and at least one dependent. Dependents can be of different grammatical roles and parts of speech, meaning VIDs may be confused with other categories of VMWEs, such as LVCs. VIDs also include sentential expressions with no open slots, such as proverbs.

> **VID:** *to **take** something **with a pinch of salt***: VMWE with an adverbial complement

LVCs are formed by a verb and a single or compound dependent noun. The noun must be abstract and predicative. The verb can be of two types: a 'light' verb, which arguably contributes no extra semantics to the expression beyond the semantics denoted by the predicative noun (annotated as LVC.full), and a 'causative' verb, which contributes only the semantics of causation, as the subject of the verb is the cause or source of the event or state expressed by the dependent noun (annotated as LVC.cause).

> **LVC.full:** *to **make** a **decision***: verb adds nothing substantive to the semantics of 'decision'
> **LVC.cause:** *to **give** a **headache***: the subject of 'give' is the cause of the headache

Verb-Particle Constructions (VPCs) and **Multi-Verb Constructions** (MVCs) are quasi-universal categories that are applicable to English. VPCs are formed by a verb and a dependent particle. The verb can be either fully non-compositional, where the addition of the particle changes the meaning of the verb significantly (annotated as VPC.full), or semi-non-compositional where the particle adds a partially predictable but non-spatial meaning to the verb (annotated as VPC.semi).

> **VPC.full:** *to **check in** upon arrival*: omitting 'in' leads to very different meaning
> **VPC.semi:** *to **eat** the cookies **up***: 'up' adds a sense of completion, but not a spatial meaning

MVCs are composed of two adjacent verbs, one of which is a governing verb and the other a dependent verb; together they function as a single predicate. The test for this category in English involves replacing the dependent verb with another verb from the same semantic class. If this leads to ungrammaticality or an unexpected change in meaning, the expression is categorised as MVC.

> **MVC:** *to **let go***: replacing 'go' with 'depart', 'move', etc. changes the meaning significantly

Inherently Adpositional Verbs (IAVs) constitute an experimental category that has been included in the English annotation. IAVs consist of a verb and an adposition that is integral to the meaning of the expression. The guidelines include a test to differentiate between adpositions and particles, the former of which are exclusively used in IAVs.[9]

---

[8] New categories added to edition 1.1 of the shared task

[9] Adpositions are fixed in occurring exclusively before a noun phrase, unlike particles, which either modify an intransitive

IAV: *to **come across*** *something*: omitting adposition 'across' leads to very different meaning

IAVs may also contain particles: e.g. *to **put up with*** *something* (verb+particle+preposition) means to endure it, and cannot have this meaning absent *up* or *with*.

3.2   Pilot Annotation Tasks

Three pilot annotation tasks were held to allow annotators to familiarize themselves with FLAT and the guidelines, as well as raise any potential issues and disagreements concerning the categorisation of VMWEs in English. Two small corpora were used for the first two pilot annotations, consisting of 200 sentences taken from the Brown corpus.[10]

Pilot annotation 1 was held in the beginning of June 2017, using version 1.0 of the guidelines. Following a discussion of this task, many disagreements seemed to stem from LVC tests that were difficult to apply and did not cover all cases. For example:

*The grand jury **took** a **swipe** at the State Welfare Department...*: While annotators felt this should be categorised as LVC, the original tests for LVC state that the noun must be used in one of its original senses, i.e. non-idiomatic use of the word, which would cause this expression to fail as an LVC. In response, the noun requirements within LVCs were generalized such that the noun must only be predicative, but need not retain one of its senses used outside of LVCs.

Annotators came across cases of LVCs that were fairly straightforward because the verb quite clearly adds little semantics beyond that of the predicative noun (e.g., *She has a terrible headache*). However, variant expressions with a different light verb were not clearly LVCs, given a minimal amount of causative semantics contributed by the verb (e.g., *The buzzing radio gave him a headache*). Such cases were another source of disagreement in LVC annotations. To accommodate both types of LVCs while maintaining an acknowledgment of the causative semantics, it was decided after discussion to provide a distinction in the guideline tests between a fully light verb (LVC.full) and a causative light verb construction (LVC.cause). Causative light verbs, unlike fully light verbs, contribute the semantics of causation to the expression by licensing an outside causer or agent semantic role assigned to the verb's subject.

Other disagreements centered around unclear tests for particles, particularly particles which contribute aspectual or other subtle information, but do not significantly alter the meaning of the verb, leading to inconsistencies in VPC annotation. For example:

*...the Senate **passed** the bill **on** to the House*: Here the verb keeps its meaning but the particle contributes non-compositionally. Like LVCs, it was decided to subdivide the VPC category into the VPC.full and VPC.semi categories described above; thus improving agreement on borderline VPC.semi examples like this instance.

Pilot annotation 2 took place towards the end of November 2017, following the rewriting of the guidelines into version 1.1. In discussing the new annotation guidelines, some issues were raised. Many of these again centered around LVCs, including the productive nature of candidates in the new LVC.cause category (such productivity runs somewhat counter to the expectations of idiosyncrasy and lexicalisation for all VMWEs), as well as disagreements surrounding nouns categorized as either concrete or abstract (nouns within LVCs must be abstract and predicative). For example:

*A certain **vagueness** may also be **caused** by tactical appreciation of the fact...*: Here, and in all cases of *cause* in combination with an abstract/predicative noun, it was debated as to whether these should be considered LVC.cause. *Cause* expressions seemed to defy the normative expectations of idiosyncracy and lexicalization put forth for all VMWEs given that, unlike other light verbs, *cause* seems to combine productively with any predicative noun and the resulting expression is felicitous while maintaining its purely compositional semantics. After discussion, it was decided that such cases should be included as LVC.cause; however, a note that these cases do not exhibit some of the hallmarks of other LVCs and MWEs was added to the guidelines.

*The scholarship plan would **provide** federal **contributions** to each medical and dental school equal to $1500...*: It is unclear here if the noun *contributions* should be understood as abstract and

---

verb (***check in***) or are mobile with respect to full noun phrase complements (***eat** the cookies **up**/**eat up** the cookies*).

[10] Access the Brown Corpus Manual here: http://clu.uni.no/icame/manuals/BROWN/INDEX.HTM

predicative, or if it refers to the concrete contribution of the specific sum of money mentioned later in the sentence. If the noun is understood as abstract and predicative, then the expression could be considered a case of LVC.cause, given that presumably the *scholarship plan* is an outsider causer of the contribution, while *federal* likely refers to the actual contributer. Additional guidance on distinguishing abstract and concrete nouns was added in response.

Related to distinguishing IAVs from VPCs, annotators also expressed confusion regarding the difference between particles and adpositions (and the recently added test to differentiate). For example:

*...to **set aside** the privilege resolution*: The categorisation of this expression was controversial because of uncertainty as to whether 'aside' could be considered a particle, and thus, belonging to a VPC. Following this confusion, tests for differentiating between adpositions and particles were featured more prominently as part of the decision tree for categorising VPCs.

After clarifying some of the intended interpretations and tests in the guidelines, it was decided to hold a third round of pilot annotations for English, reusing the corpus from the second pilot task, during the month of December 2017. **Pilot annotation 3** led to a more informed, robust discussion of the previous issues, and concluded with amendments to the guidelines, including notes regarding the productive characteristic of many LVC.cause VMWEs and additional pointers for distinguishing IAVs with adpositions from VPCs with particles.

Table 1 in Section 4 shows the number of VMWEs that were annotated during each pilot task, and the breakdown of categories that were annotated. Note that the categories VPC.full and LVC.full represent VPC and LVC respectively for Pilot 1, as the fine-grained labels did not exist in version 1.0 of the guidelines. Similarly, the optional category IAV was not considered for the first pilot task.

After iteration throughout piloting, the 1.1 edition of the guidelines were finalized for all languages. Several of the changes to the guidelines came about due to challenges with annotation of English VMWEs during the pilot annotation task, namely the subdivision of the LVC and VPC categories.

4   Corpus Annotation and Results

The annotation of the final corpus took place between the start of January 2018 and the end of February 2018. During this period, a total of 7437 sentences (124,202 tokens) were annotated. 4221 of these sentences were from the English Web Treebank, 3015 were from the LinES parallel corpus, and the remaining 201 sentences were from the PUD treebank. Out of a total of 14,121 verbs, 832 were annotated as VMWEs. Table 1 displays the categories of VMWE that were annotated. The most commonly annotated category of English VMWE is full Verb-Particle Constructions, followed by full Light-Verb Constructions.

Following the end of the annotation period, the corpus was prepared for release. The annotated files were downloaded from FLAT in FoLiA XML format and aligned with the original CoNLL-U files. The annotated data from each annotator was consolidated, and a consistency check was performed to ensure that VMWEs were consistently annotated across all the data. Following this stage, the FoLiA files were then merged with the aligned CoNLL-U files to be converted into PARSEME TSV format, which is the format of the released data.[11]

Following the release of the annotated corpus, a portion of the corpus (804 sentences) was selected for annotation by all four annotators, in order to measure the quality of the corpus. The categorisation of VMWE types is shown in table 2. The table shows the greatest level of disagreement in the categorisation of LVCs, particularly the LVC.cause category. Despite having provided additional guidance on the subject in the guidelines, the general VMWE definitional requirement of idiosyncrasy may have affected the categorisation of LVC.cause, as many instances of LVC.cause appear regular, and thus annotators may find it counter-intuitive to label these candidates as VMWEs.

The IAA scores between all the pairs of annotators are given in Table 3. The agreement between annotators is fair, showing moderate agreement when calculating the span of annotation (*F-score* and *Kappa*), and substantial agreement when calculating the agreement of categorisation only (*Kappa-cat*).

---

[11]The full PARSEME shared task data can be found at: `https://gitlab.com/parseme/sharedtask-data/tree/master/1.1`

Category	Pilot 1	Pilot 2	Pilot 3	Final
VPC.full	40	33	49	297
VPC.semi	0	25	25	45
LVC.full	37	43	82	244
LVC.cause	0	21	44	43
VID	38	19	30	139
MVC	0	2	1	4
IAV	0	15	34	60
Total	**115**	**158**	**265**	**832**

Table 1: Number of annotations per category.

Category	A1	A2	A3	A4
VPC.full	27	41	62	41
VPC.semi	17	3	9	23
LVC.full	77	32	43	42
LVC.cause	28	2	5	11
VID	13	14	25	41
MVC	4	0	0	1
IAV	22	9	9	17
Total	**188**	**101**	**153**	**176**

Table 2: VMWEs in doubly annotated corpus.

We see from the table that the agreement between the two annotators who completed all three pilot tasks (A3 and A4) is higher than the agreement between the two annotators who did not participate in the three pilot tasks (A1 and A2), in as far as annotating the span of the VMWEs (*F-score* and *Kappa*). This is not the case when only the category of the VMWE is considered (*Kappa-cat*).

Pair	#X	#Y	*F-score*	*Kappa*	*Kappa-cat*
1x2	188	101	0.436	0.396	0.661
1x3	188	153	0.452	0.402	0.647
1x4	188	176	0.478	0.427	0.635
2x3	101	153	0.480	0.446	0.773
2x4	101	176	0.513	0.479	0.636
3x4	153	176	0.529	0.487	0.625

Table 3: IAA scores between annotator pairs (X and Y) for a subset (804 sentences) of the corpus. *F-score* is the F-measure between annotators, and is an optimistic measure that ignores agreement due to chance. The kappa scores used for *Kappa* and *Kappa-cat* are variants of 2-raters Cohen's kappa. *Kappa* is a calculation of the rate of agreement of annotation for all verbs in the corpus, while *Kappa-cat* takes into account only those VMWEs where both annotators agreed on the span, and measures the agreement of categorisation for these VMWEs.

4.1 Conclusions & Future Work

The development of manually annotated training data and support of shared tasks facilitating automatic identification of MWEs is critical for enabling the idiosyncratic interpretation required of these prevalent, but often ignored, elements of natural language. The challenging nature of this task for automatic systems is made evident by how challenging consistent VMWE identification and categorization can be, even for trained human annotators. The results of the pilot tasks in Section 3.2 demonstrate that MWE categorisation is a task requiring specialised training and clear guidelines. The IAA scores in Section 4 indicate that even with specialised training, disagreements in labelling VMWEs is to be expected. The process of annotating VMWEs in English led to some interesting discussion surrounding the categorisation of light-verb constructions and verb-particle constructions in particular. We look forward to the results of the second edition of the PARSEME shared-task, which may highlight English annotation gaps and inconsistencies to be addressed in the future.

5 Acknowledgements

The first author's work is funded by the Irish Government Department of Culture, Heritage and the Gaeltacht under the GaelTech Project, and is also supported by Science Foundation Ireland in the ADAPT Centre (Grant 13/RC/2106) (http://www.adaptcentre.ie) at Dublin City University.

References

Lars Ahrenberg. 2007. LinES: An English-Swedish parallel treebank. In *Proc. of NODALIDA*, pages 270–273, Tartu, Estonia, May.

Timothy Baldwin and Su Nam Kim. 2010. Multiword expressions. In Nitin Indurkhya and Fred J. Damerau, editors, *Handbook of Natural Language Processing, Second Edition*, pages 267–292. CRC Press, Taylor and Francis Group, Boca Raton, FL.

Ann Bies, Justin Mott, Colin Warner, and Seth Kulick. 2012. English Web Treebank. Technical Report LDC2012T13, Linguistic Data Consortium, Philadelphia, PA.

Mathieu Constant, Gülşen Eryiğit, Johanna Monti, Lonneke van der Plas, Carlos Ramisch, Michael Rosner, and Amalia Todirascu. 2017. Multiword expression processing: a survey. *Computational Linguistics*, 43(4):837–892, December.

Meghdad Farahmand and Joakim Nivre. 2015. Modeling the statistical idiosyncrasy of multiword expressions. In *Proc. of the 11th Workshop on Multiword Expressions*, pages 34–38, Denver, Colorado, June.

Carlos Ramisch, Silvio Ricardo Cordeiro, Agata Savary, Veronika Vincze, Verginica Barbu Mititelu, Archna Bhatia, Maja Buljan, Marie Candito, Polona Gantar, Voula Giouli, Tunga Güngör, Abdelati Hawwari, Uxoa Iñurrieta, Jolanta Kovalevskaitė, Simon Krek, Timm Lichte, Chaya Liebeskind, Johanna Monti, Carla Parra Escartín, Behrang QasemiZadeh, Renata Ramisch, Nathan Schneider, Ivelina Stoyanova, Ashwini Vaidya, and Abigail Walsh. 2018. Edition 1.1 of the PARSEME Shared Task on Automatic Identification of Verbal Multiword Expressions. In *Proc. of the Joint Workshop on Linguistic Annotation, Multiword Expressions and Constructions (LAW-MWE-CxG-2018)*, Santa Fe, New Mexico, USA, August.

Carlos Ramisch. 2015. *Multiword Expressions Acquisition: A Generic and Open Framework*. Theory and Applications of Natural Language Processing. Springer.

Ivan Sag, Timothy Baldwin, Francis Bond, Ann Copestake, and Dan Flickinger. 2002. Multiword expressions: a pain in the neck for NLP. In Alexander Gelbukh, editor, *Computational Linguistics and Intelligent Text Processing*, volume 2276 of *Lecture Notes in Computer Science*, pages 189–206. Springer, Berlin.

Agata Savary, Carlos Ramisch, Silvio Ricardo Cordeiro, Federico Sangati, Veronika Vincze, Behrang QasemiZadeh, Marie Candito, Fabienne Cap, Voula Giouli, Ivelina Stoyanova, and Antoine Doucet. 2017. The PARSEME Shared Task on Automatic Identification of Verbal Multiword Expressions. In *Proc. of the 13th Workshop on Multiword Expressions (MWE 2017)*, pages 31–47, Valencia, Spain, April.

Nathan Schneider and Noah A. Smith. 2015. A corpus and model integrating multiword expressions and supersenses. In *Proc. of NAACL-HLT*, pages 1537–1547, Denver, Colorado, June.

Nathan Schneider, Spencer Onuffer, Nora Kazour, Emily Danchik, Michael T. Mordowanec, Henrietta Conrad, and Noah A. Smith. 2014. Comprehensive annotation of multiword expressions in a social web corpus. In Nicoletta Calzolari, Khalid Choukri, Thierry Declerck, Hrafn Loftsson, Bente Maegaard, Joseph Mariani, Asuncion Moreno, Jan Odijk, and Stelios Piperidis, editors, *Proc. of LREC*, pages 455–461, Reykjavík, Iceland, May.

Nathan Schneider, Dirk Hovy, Anders Johannsen, and Marine Carpuat. 2016. SemEval-2016 Task 10: Detecting Minimal Semantic Units and their Meanings (DiMSUM). In *Proc. of SemEval*, pages 546–559, San Diego, California, USA, June.

Natalia Silveira, Timothy Dozat, Marie-Catherine De Marneffe, Samuel R. Bowman, Miriam Connor, John Bauer, and Christopher D. Manning. 2014. A gold standard dependency corpus for English. In Nicoletta Calzolari, Khalid Choukri, Thierry Declerck, Hrafn Loftsson, Bente Maegaard, Joseph Mariani, Asuncion Moreno, Jan Odijk, and Stelios Piperidis, editors, *Proc. of LREC*, pages 2897–2904, Reykjavík, Iceland, May.

Denny Vrandečić and Markus Krötzsch. 2014. Wikidata: A free collaborative knowledgebase. *Communications of the ACM*, 57(10):78–85, September.

Daniel Zeman, Martin Popel, Milan Straka, Jan Hajič, Joakim Nivre, Filip Ginter, Juhani Luotolahti, Sampo Pyysalo, Slav Petrov, Martin Potthast, Francis Tyers, Elena Badmaeva, Memduh Gökirmak, Anna Nedoluzhko, Silvie Cinková, Jan Hajič Jr., Jaroslava Hlaváčová, Václava Kettnerová, Zdeňka Urešová, Jenna Kanerva, Stina Ojala, Anna Missilä, Christopher D. Manning, Sebastian Schuster, Siva Reddy, Dima Taji, Nizar Habash, Herman Leung, Marie-Catherine de Marneffe, Manuela Sanguinetti, Maria Simi, Hiroshi Kanayama, Valeria de Paiva, Kira Droganova, Héctor Martínez Alonso, Çağrı Çöltekin, Umut Sulubacak, Hans Uszkoreit, Vivien Macketanz, Aljoscha Burchardt, Kim Harris, Katrin Marheinecke, Georg Rehm, Tolga Kayadelen, Mohammed

Attia, Ali Elkahky, Zhuoran Yu, Emily Pitler, Saran Lertpradit, Michael Mandl, Jesse Kirchner, Hector Fernandez Alcalde, Jana Strnadová, Esha Banerjee, Ruli Manurung, Antonio Stella, Atsuko Shimada, Sookyoung Kwak, Gustavo Mendonça, Tatiana Lando, Rattima Nitisaroj, and Josie Li. 2017. CoNLL 2017 Shared Task: Multilingual Parsing from Raw Text to Universal Dependencies. In *Proc. of the CoNLL 2017 Shared Task: Multilingual Parsing from Raw Text to Universal Dependencies*, pages 1–19, Vancouver, Canada, August.

Cooperating Tools for MWE Lexicon Management and Corpus Annotation

Yuji Matsumoto
Nara Institute of Science & Technology
`matsu@is.naist.jp`

Akihiko Kato
Nara Institute of Science & Technology
`kato.akihiko.ju6@is.naist.jp`

Hiroyuki Shindo
Nara Institute of Science & Technology
`shindo@is.naist.jp`

Toshio Morita
Sowa Giken
`morita@sowa.com`

Abstract

We present tools for lexicon and corpus management that offer cooperating functionality in corpus annotation. The former, named Cradle, stores a set of words and expressions where multi-word expressions are defined with their own part-of-speech information and internal syntactic structures. The latter, named ChaKi, manages text corpora with part-of-speech (POS) and syntactic dependency structure annotations. Those two tools cooperate so that the words and multi-word expressions stored in Cradle are directly referred to by ChaKi in conducting corpus annotation, and the words and expressions annotated in ChaKi can be output as a list of lexical entities that are to be stored in Cradle.

1 Introduction

This paper presents tools for corpus and lexicon management, especially based on syntactic dependency structures. Annotating multi-word expressions (MWEs) in POS-tagged and/or syntactically analyzed corpora pose a number of problems. Out of three dependency relations for MWE annotations defined in Universal Dependency (UD) (Nivre et al., 2016) [1], only the `compound` relation can define internal syntactic structures, whereas the other two, `fixed` and `flat`, annotate MWEs with flat structures. Some issues of MWE annotation in UD are discussed in (Kahane et al., 2017). Since some MWEs have clear internal structure and they themselves interact with other words in the sentence with their own syntactic functionality, representing all their information solely in a dependency structure is not easy, or even possible. An MWE may be included in another flexible MWE. While an extended hierarchical BIO annotation scheme was proposed in (Schneider et al, 2002), it still cannot represent nested interaction of more than two MWEs.

In this paper, we do not discuss these issues in detail since the annotation standards are changing and there can be several standards for MWE annotation. We rather introduce two annotation tools that we are developing that are adaptable to various annotation standards as far as they are based on dependency syntax. The examples we show in this paper adopt the Stanford Typed Dependency (de Marneffe et al., 2008). One tool is a dictionary management tool named Cradle, which allows for the representation of the internal structures of MWEs, and stores them as a lexical resource. The other is an annotated corpus management tool called ChaKi, which communicates with Cradle and uses the stored lexical information during the corpus annotation process. While both tools are language independent and are currently used to develop English, Japanese, and Chinese dictionaries and corpora, we use English to explain how these tools cooperate in handling MWEs in corpus annotation.

2 Dictionary Management Tool: Cradle

The tool called Cradle was developed to maintain multi-lingual dictionaries. It stores words (including multi-word expressions), their part-of-speech labels, and additional information (such as inflection types, lemma forms, and internal structures for MWEs). Other than the information about individual

---

[1] Universal Dependency version 2: http://universaldependencies.org/

Proceedings of the Joint Workshop on
Linguistic Annotation, Multiword Expressions and Constructions (LAW-MWE-CxG-2018), pages 201–206
Santa Fe, New Mexico, USA, August 25-26, 2018.

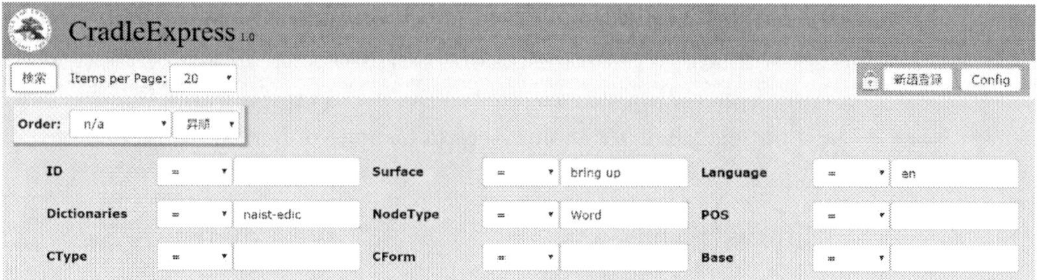

Figure 1: Snapshot of Cradle's start page

words/expressions, it retains the derivation relation between a base word and its derived forms (for now only inflected forms of verbs, nouns, adjectives, and adverbs) and the translation relation between pairs of translated words in two or more languages.

In this paper, we focus in particular on how MWEs are represented in the system. MWEs are categorized into fixed expressions, semi-fixed expressions, syntactically-flexible expressions, and institutional phrases (Sag et al, 2002). While all those types of MWEs can be handled in Cradle, we mainly focus on the first three types of English MWEs in this paper.

Figure 1 shows a snapshot of the start page of Cradle. When retrieving words or expressions, the user can optionally specify the language and the name of the dictionary. MWEs are defined as entries that include more than one word. Regular expressions can be used for retrieving words/expressions. In Figure 1, POS means part-of-speech and CType means the type of conjugation (or inflection). In the case of English, it is either "regular" or "irregular" and is only defined for verbs, nouns, adjectives, and adverbs. Figure 2 shows the word information pane that shows the basic information of the retrieved word (in this case "bring up"), its part-of-speech (POS), conjugation type (CType), and lemma form (Base). In the case of MWEs, we can specify not only their basic information like POS, CType, and lemma form, but also their internal dependency structures.

Examples of fixed multi-word expressions are "with respect to" and "lots of," which behave as single lexical entries with their respective parts-of-speech. The former behaves as a preposition and the latter behaves as a determiner as a whole. Semi-fixed and syntactically-flexible expressions may have modifiers within them or allow for syntactic variations. For example, while "a number of" behaves as a determiner, it has some variations such as "a small number of" or "a large number of," and both behave as a determiner with additional meaning. Another flexible expression "take into account" behaves as a transitive verb associated with a direct object, but is often used as "take *something* into account," taking a direct object within the

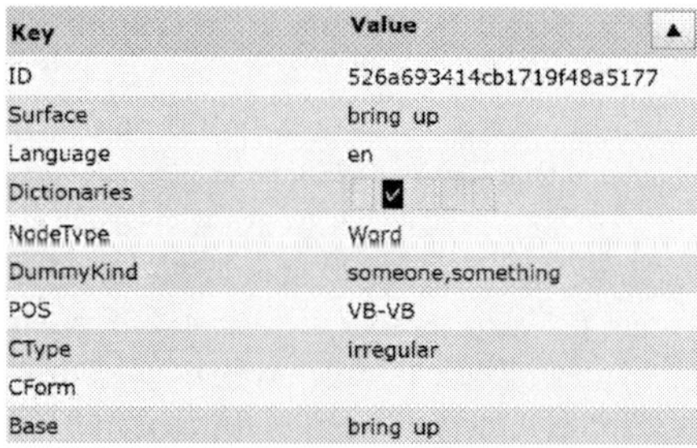

Figure 2: Word information

expression. Figure 3 explains how the dependency structures of such MWEs are defined in Cradle. In the figure, an asterisk defines a "placeholder" that matches any word. While it is not visible on this screen, the POS tag information can be specified on the placeholder as a constraint. In the case of "a * number of *," the first placeholder stands for an adjective and the second stands for a noun. In the case of "take * into account," the placeholder stands for a noun. The rightmost box without any word or asterisk is a dummy box for pointing to the head word. The reason that the words are depicted as sequences of characters is for handling non-segmented languages like Japanese and Chinese, in which annotators need to segment a sequence of characters into words when they first define the structure of MWEs.

In our English dictionary, we define an extended version of the POS tag set of PennTreebank (Marcus et al., 1993). All the POS tags are define by two tag layers. For example, the POS tags of singular and plural nouns "NN" and "NNS" are defined as "NN-NN" and "NN-NNS," respectively. Similarly, "VBP" and "VBD" are defined as "VB-VBP" and "VB-VBD" so that the second layer corresponds exactly to the PTB POS tags and the first layer defines the coarse-grained tag groups. An adjective, a noun, and a verb (in any form) are defined as "JJ-*," "NN-*," and "VB-*." Moreover, "a * number of *" and "take * into account" are defined as a determiner and a verb for their own parts-of-speech.

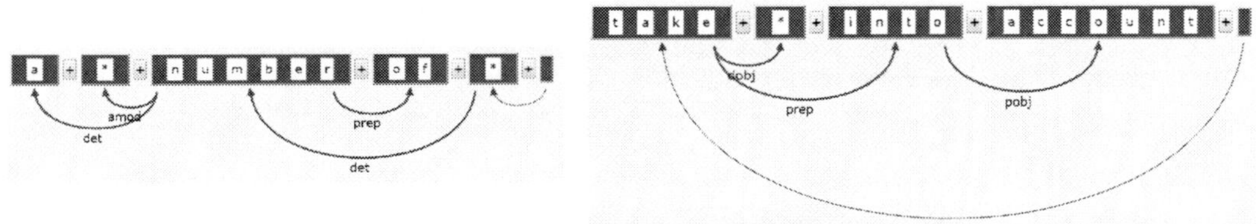

Figure 3: Dependency annotation of MWEs in Cradle

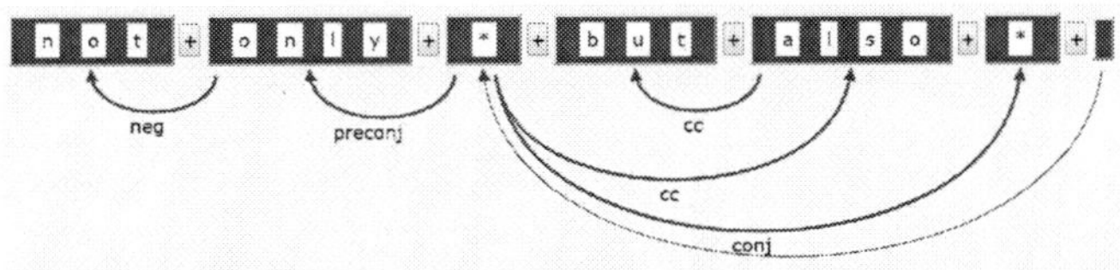

Figure 4: Dependency annotation of "not only ⋯ but also ⋯"

There are some MWEs that do not have an appropriate POS tag of their own. Our English dictionary includes flexible MWEs that do not stand for a single POS tag but define a complex syntactic structure. One such example is "not only ⋯ but also ⋯," which constitutes a coordination. Figure 4 shows the dependency structure associated with this expression. The two placeholders are the heads of the conjuncts connected by this MWE. While they should share a common syntactic property such as a common POS, the current Cradle does not provide such a functionality (equivalence relation between POS tags).

3   Corpus Management Tool: ChaKi

This section introduces a tool called ChaKi, which helps to annotate corpora with POS and dependency information. It also offers flexible search operations for sentences using character sequences, words with various lexical properties, and dependency relations. Other than POS and word dependency annotation, ChaKi is equipped with segment and group annotation functions. A sequence of words are put together in a segment, and two or more segments are related in a group. A segment can be used to define named entities or fixed/flat multi-word expressions. Two or more segments are related to form a group.

Figure 5 shows a snapshot of ChaKi when a user retrieves sentences that include the expression "but also." The top box shows the pattern of the sentence retrieval, and the middle window shows three sentences that include this expression. The lowest window, the dependency pane, shows a part of the dependency tree of the first sentence. There are two groups as shown in this sentence: The first corresponds to "not only ⋯ but also ⋯" (green boxes labeled by "1:MWE"), and the second corresponds to the coordination structure conjoined by this MWE (orange boxes labeled with "2:Parallel"). Segment and group annotation as well as other annotation such as the POS tag and dependency edge correction/modification can be done via mouse operations on this interface.

When we annotate MWEs that have specific syntactic functions like determiners or adverbs, it is not only their internal dependency structure but also their dependency relation with other words in the sentence that may need to be modified. For example, Figure 6 shows how the dependency annotation should be changed after an expression is found as an MWE. The left-hand side shows the original dependency tree. Note that the syntactic head of the noun phrase "a number of southern states" is "number" in this tree. When "a number of" in this sentence is found as an MWE that functions as a determiner, they are to

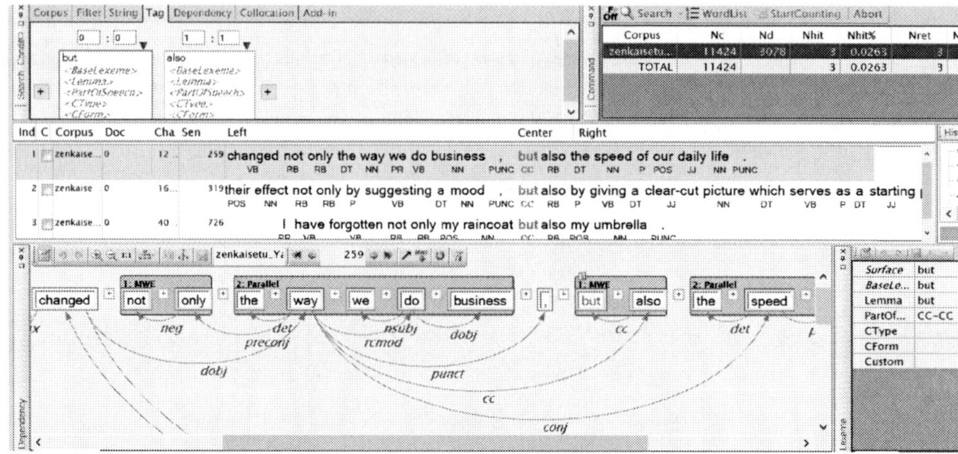

Figure 5: Snapshot of ChaKi in retrieving "but also"

be annotated in a group (shown by a green box) as shown on the right-hand side. Simultaneously, since it is regarded as a single determiner, the head of the noun phrase should be "states" and the dependency relations need to be corrected as shown in the figure.

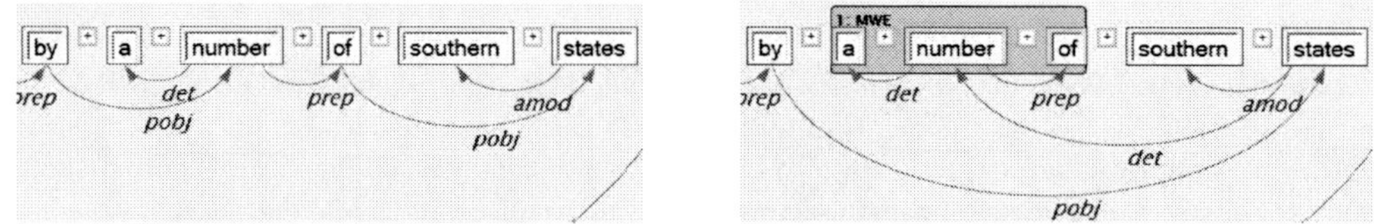

Figure 6: Bare annotation and MWE-aware annotation of "a number of"

While ChaKi offers intuitive mouse operations to annotate segments and groups and to modify dependency edges, it is very tiresome to do the same operation when the same MWEs appear repeatedly in a corpus. This is why we implemented the close cooperation of the above two tools, which is described in the next section.

4   Cooperation between Cradle and ChaKi

To maintain the internal structures and other lexical information of MWEs and to utilize them for efficient corpus annotation, we implemented cooperation functions that connect Cradle and ChaKi. ChaKi can refer to the information in Cradle in the annotation process. Suppose an annotator is working on POS and dependency structure annotation or on the correction of the following sentence:

"Currently, a great number of electric cars are operating on Japanese streets."

By pressing the MWE button, ChaKi presents a list of all possible MWEs and their positions in the sentence by consulting the dictionary in Cradle; the MWEs and their positions are shown in Figure 7. There appears a flexible MWE, "a great number of," in this sentence, and the list shows all possible matching positions of this MWE. Note that it is defined as "a (JJ-∗) number of (NN-∗)" in Cradle. Each line in Figure 7 corresponds to an MWE, its position. For example, the second line indicates that "a (great) number of (cars)" matches with an MWE. The column "WordPositions" shows the word positions of the MWE in the sentence, meaning that the position of "a" is at 2, and that of "number" is at 4, etc. When a user selects a line by clicking the button on the "Apply" column, the dependency structure of the

MWE is tentatively shown on the dependency pane. The user then presses the apply button (not shown on the figure) to effect the annotation.

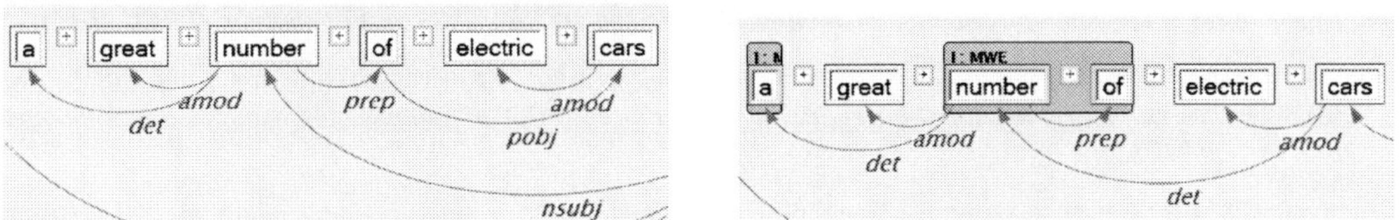

	Apply	Surface		WordPositions
▶	■	a number of		2,4,5
	☐	a (great) number of (streets)		2,3,4,5,12
	☐	a (great) number of (cars)		2,3,4,5,7

Figure 7: List of possible MWEs included in the current sentence

The left-hand side of Figure 8 shows the original dependency structure of the sentence before MWE annotation. After checking the MWE list shown in Figure 7 and applying the second line, the annotation on the right-hand side of Figure 8 is obtained automatically.

Figure 8: Before and after MWE annotation of "a great number of"

Currently, ChaKi can consult the dictionary defined in Cradle and conduct efficient annotation of MWEs (as well as other lexical entries) as explained above. If the user does not find any definition of an MWE in Cradle, he/she can group the words together to form an MWE group, modify the dependency structure, and output the result. The output format is based on the CoNLL-U format [2] with some additional information for MWE groups and their POS tags. The dictionary manager needs to examine which MWEs are to be registered in Cradle, and may need to add additional information like POS constrains on placeholders and modify the dependency structures if necessary.

5   Conclusion

This paper presented our tools for managing dictionaries and (POS and dependency) annotated corpora. The system for dictionary management, Cradle, stores words and multi-word expressions together with their POS and syntactic dependency structure information. The system for corpus annotation, ChaKi, deals with POS and dependency annotated corpora to retrieve sentences and to modify or correct annotations including MWE annotation. We presented the main functions of those two tools and introduced the cooperation between them that is especially effective for MWE annotation by simply selecting possible MWEs defined in the dictionary.

There are several dependency annotation schemes in many languages, such as Universal dependency and CoNLL dependency. Initially, our dependency definition adopted the CoNLL dependency and then the Stanford dependency. Since MWEs often cause problematic cases of syntactic annotation, our framework of managing MWEs and their syntactic information in a dictionary provides an easy and consistent way of coping with definition changes or transferring one scheme to another.

Currently, Cradle is not publicly available, but is available on request. ChaKi is available from the following site:

https://ja.osdn.net/projects/chaki/

Acknowledgements

This work was partially supported by JST CREST Grant Number JPMJCR1513, Japan.

---

[2]http://universaldependencies.org/format.html

References

Marie-Catherine de Marneffe and Manning, C.D. 2008. Stanford Typed Dependencies Manual (revised in 2016). Stanford University.

Marie-Catherine de Marneffe, M-C., Dozat, T., Silveira, N., Haverinen, K., Ginter, F., Nivre, J. and Manning, C. 2014. Universal Stanford dependencies: A cross-linguistic typology. *Proceedings of the Ninth International Conference on Language Resources and Evaluation (LREC'14)*, 4585–4592, Reykjavik, Iceland.

Kahane, S., Courtin, M. and Gerdes, K. 2017. Multi-word annotation in Syntactic treebanks: Proposition for Universal Dependency. *Proceedings of the 16th International Workshop on Treebanks and Linguistic Theories*, 181–189, Prague, Czech Republic.

Marcus, M. et al. 1993. Building a Large Annotated Corpus of English: The Penn Treebank, *Computational Linguistics*, 19(2):313–330.

Nivre, J., de Marneffe, M-C., Ginter, F., Goldberg, Y., Hajic, J., Manning, C., McDonald, R., Petrov, S., Pyysalo, S., Silveira, N., Tsarfaty, R. and Zeman, D. 2016. Universal Dependencies v1: A Multilingual Treebank Collection. *Proceedings of the Tenth International Conference on Language Resources and Evaluation (LREC 2016)*.

Sag, I., Baldwin, T., Bond, F., Copestake, A. and Flickinger, D. 2002. Multiword expressions: A pain in the neck for NLP. *Proceedings of the Third International Conference on Computational Linguistics and Intelligent Text Processing. CICLing*, Springer-Verlag, 1–15.

Schneider, N., Onuffer, S., Kazour, N., Danchik, E., Mordowanec, M., Conrad, H. and Smith, N. 2014. Comprehensive annotation of multiword expressions in a social web corpus. *Proceedings of the Ninth International Conference on Language Resources and Evaluation (LREC 14)*, 455–461, Reykjavik, Iceland.

"Fingers in the Nose":
Evaluating Speakers' Identification of Multi-Word Expressions Using a Slightly Gamified Crowdsourcing Platform

Karën Fort
Sorbonne Université, STIH EA 4509
28, rue Serpente 75006 Paris, France
karen.fort@sorbonne-universite.fr

Bruno Guillaume
Université de Lorraine, CNRS,
Inria, LORIA, 54000 Nancy, France
bruno.guillaume@inria.fr

Matthieu Constant
Université de Lorraine, CNRS, ATILF
54000 Nancy, France
Mathieu.Constant@univ-lorraine.fr

Nicolas Lefèbvre
Université de Lorraine, CNRS,
Inria, LORIA, 54000 Nancy, France
nicolas.lefebvre@inria.fr

Yann-Alan Pilatte
Sorbonne Université
28, rue Serpente 75006 Paris, France
yann-alan.pilatte@etu.sorbonne-universite.fr

Abstract

This article presents the results we obtained in crowdsourcing French speakers' intuition concerning multi-work expressions (MWEs). We developed a slightly gamified crowdsourcing platform, part of which is designed to test users' ability to identify MWEs with no prior training. The participants perform relatively well at the task, with a recall reaching 65% for MWEs that do not behave as function words.

1 Introduction and State of the Art

The identification of multi-word expressions (MWEs) is crucial in natural language processing (NLP) (Constant et al., 2017). Significant efforts have been made in recent years on the subject, in particular though the PARSEME international network (Savary et al., 2015). However, although some collective expert-based annotation initiatives have been successfully undertaken (Schneider et al., 2016; Savary et al., 2017), language resources are still limited in coverage and the need remains to identify newly-created MWEs. One potential solution is to exploit the so-called "wisdom of the crowd".

There have been several research papers on the interpretation of MWEs by native speakers, in particular by Gibbs (Gibbs, 1992; Gibbs et al., 1997). More recently, Ramisch et al. (2016) involved microworking crowdsourcing on Amazon Mechanical Turk. Finally, the experiment described in Krstev and Savary (2018) involves a gamified interface allowing MWE researchers to guess the meaning of opaque MWEs in other languages.

However, we could find no publication concerned with evaluating human ability to identify MWEs in a text, without taking their interpretation into account.

On the other hand, voluntary crowdsourcing, especially in the form of Games with a Purpose (GWAPs), has proven effective in terms of both the quantity and quality of the data produced. Successful examples of such platforms include JeuxDeMots (Lafourcade, 2007), Phrase Detectives (Poesio et al., 2013), and ZombiLingo (Guillaume et al., 2016).

We created a gamified platform named RigorMortis[1] (see Figure 1), the first of its kind, for MWEs annotation in French[2]. This platform includes a task enabling evaluation of the participants' intuition concerning MWEs, the results of which we present here.

---

[1]See: rigor-mortis.org

[2]We believe it is adaptable to any language.

Proceedings of the Joint Workshop on
Linguistic Annotation, Multiword Expressions and Constructions (LAW-MWE-CxG-2018), pages 207–213
Santa Fe, New Mexico, USA, August 25-26, 2018.

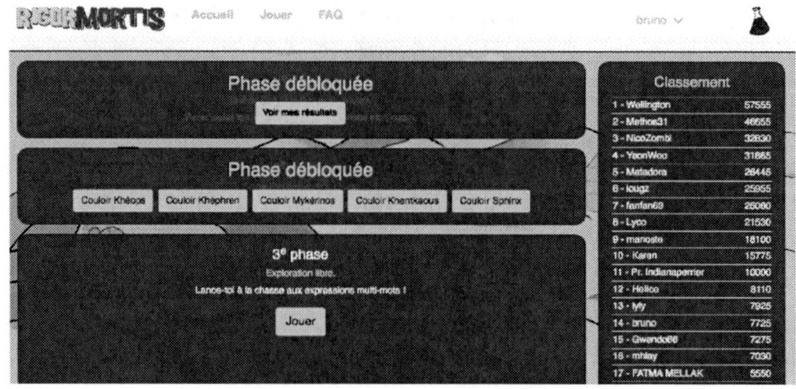

Figure 1: Interface for game selection.

For non-francophones, the phrase "Fingers in the nose" refers to the French idiom "Les doigts dans le nez" which means "without any difficulty", "with both hands behind one's back", etc.

2 Description of the Experiment

2.1 Reference corpus

As the participants are volunteers, we had to keep the intuition task short. We therefore created a rather small reference corpus. It is composed of ten sentences taken from articles on French political scandals from the French Wikipédia. Although their number is small, they were carefully selected to include MWEs corresponding to distinct identification criteria. The corpus was annotated and adjudicated in MWEs by experts. It contains 16 MWEs. One sentence, however contains no MWEs (see Table 1).

This reference corpus has been built following precise annotation guidelines inspired by those of the PARSEME shared task on verbal MWEs (Savary et al., 2017), which includes a French dataset (Candito et al., 2017). The criteria used for identifying MWEs, and in particular for detecting their morphosyntactic, syntactic and semantic idiosyncrasies are purely formal: for instance, no possible lexical substitution of a component by a synonym, presence of a "cranberry" word, no possible insertion of plausible material. We therefore discard semantically and syntactically compositional expressions that display statistical idiosyncrasy: for instance, institutionalized phrases in the sense of (Sag et al., 2001), like *traffic light*. Further, only fixed lexical components of the expressions are annotated, so final prepositions in MWEs that can be considered part of the MWE valency frame (like simple verbs) are not annotated. For instance, only *en raison* (because) is annotated in *en raison de* (because of) where *de* (of) is a preposition. Such subtlety is unknown and not natural for participants. This is why we took both variants into account when evaluating the task.

The reference MWEs can be divided into two subtypes: MWEs that behave as function words (later called *functional MWEs*) and MWEs that do not. In French, functional MWEs are mainly fixed in the sense of Sag et al. (2001). Such fully lexicalized expressions are immutable: they can undergo neither morphosyntactic nor syntactic variations, and insertion of plausible material is impossible. Notice that not all fixed expressions are necessarily functional MWEs: *dommages et intérêts* (damages), for example, functions as a noun. Furthermore, some of the functional MWEs that we consider are not entirely fixed: for instance, **aux yeux** *des enfants* (**in the eyes** of the children) = *à leurs yeux* (in their eyes). In our corpus, 7 MWEs are functional and 9 MWEs are not.

Our notion of functional MWEs can also be related to the category of fixed MWEs defined in the Universal Dependencies (Nivre et al., 2016) where the guidelines state that: *"[A fixed MWE] is used for certain fixed grammaticized expressions that behave like function words or short adverbials."*

MWEs	Glosses	Translations
se voiler la face	to cover one's face	to bury one's head in the sand
file d'attente	queue of waiting	waiting line
dommages et intérêts	damages and interests	damages
mode de vie	way of life	way of life
le président de la République	the President of the Republic	the President of the Republic
ministre des finances	Minister of finances	Secretary of the Treasury
extrême droite	extreme right	far right (political)
chef d'État	chief of state	head of the State
mettre aux voix	put to the voices	put to the vote
entre autre	between other	among others
au-delà	further	beyond
en raison (de)	in reason (of)	because (of)
peut-être	may-be	maybe
aux yeux (de X)	at the eyes of X	in X's view
d'ailleurs	from elsewhere	by the way
dans le but (de)	in the goal (of)	in order to

Table 1: Glosses and translations of the MWEs of the experiment.

2.2 Crowdsourcing platform

We ask the participants to find "expressions multi-mots" (multi-word expressions) and give them a couple of examples, explaining that MWEs are non-compositional. We also mention that more "functional" expressions can also be MWEs and should be annotated. The participants are then directly asked to identify the MWEs in the sentences we propose, without any prior training.

The interface, inspired by that of `TileAttack` (Madge et al., 2017), allows users to annotate multiple and discontinuous MWEs (see Figure 2). It should be noted that the intuition task is part of a larger gamified platform and that, while the participants did not gain points in this phase, they did in the other phases (see Figure 1).

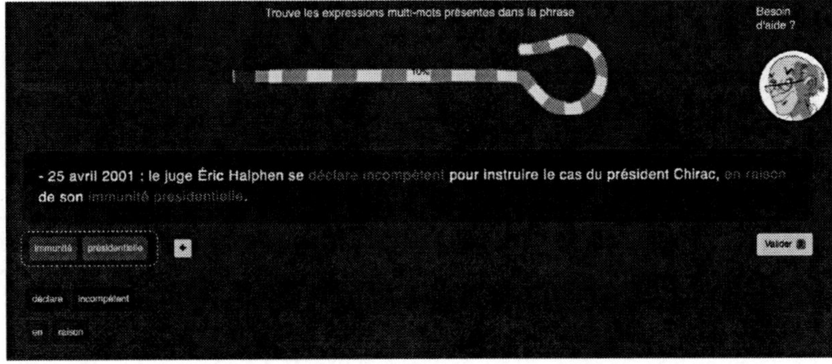

Figure 2: Interface for the annotation of the MWEs.

It is important that, during this phase, we give no feedback to the participants on their annotations. They can see feedback concerning their results only once they are finished annotating all ten sentences (see Figure 3), so that they are not biased.

The crowdsourcing interface was publicized mainly on social networks and natural language processing lists.

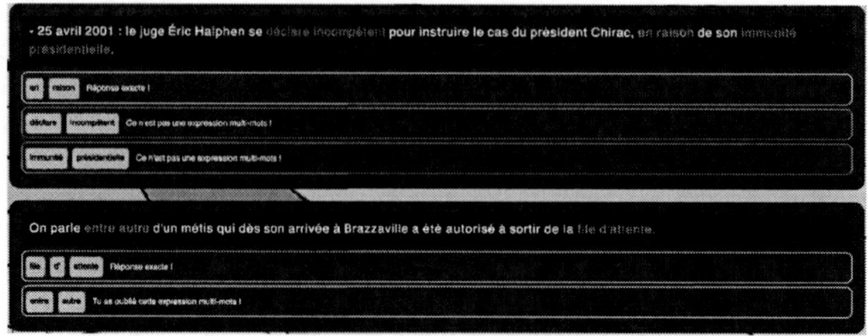

Figure 3: Feedback given to the participant *after* the intuition phase.

3   Results Obtained

3.1   Global Results

The ten reference sentences were played by 65 to 68 players (66.8 participants on average)[3].

Table 2 shows the precision, recall and F-measure for the whole annotation with two settings:

- **Perfect** match: the player selected exactly the same tokens as in the reference;

- **Approximate** match: the difference between the selection of the player and the reference includes only function words; for instance, [*président+République*] is accepted for [*président+de+la+République*], as *de* (of) is a preposition and *la* (the) is a determiner.

	Precision	Recall	F-measure
Perfect	48.13	41.22	44.41
Approximate	58.22	49.86	53.72

Table 2: Global results.

It should be noted that 40 out of 68 participants (i.e. 58.82%) correctly annotated the sentence which contains no MWE.

These global results show that when the participants identify an MWE, they are often right (in 58.22% of the cases), but that they are less good at finding them all (less than 50% were found).

3.2   Results for Individual MWEs: the Impact of Functional MWEs

To determine if an MWE is more or less easy to find, we computed the recall for each MWE separately (see Figure 4).

Again, we show the two values: i) perfect (dark blue) and ii) approximate (light blue) match.

We observe in Figure 4 that there is a significant difference between the subset of *functional* MWEs (on the left) and that of *none-functional* MWEs (on the right).

Table 3 gives the recall value for these two subsets. The last column gives the overall value (already given above) for comparison. The recall for non functional MWEs reaches 65.05, which is more than twice that of functional ones (30.41).

In our own experience (and that of some participants), this difference in the identification of functional MWEs arises because we are so accustomed to them (they are so familiar) that we simply do not "see" them and forget to annotate them.

These results are encouraging, as they show that the participants can be rather efficient at identifying at least some types of MWE.

---

[3]We removed from this analysis four participants who are experts in the MWE subdomain.However, we kept the participants from the more general NLP and linguistics domains.

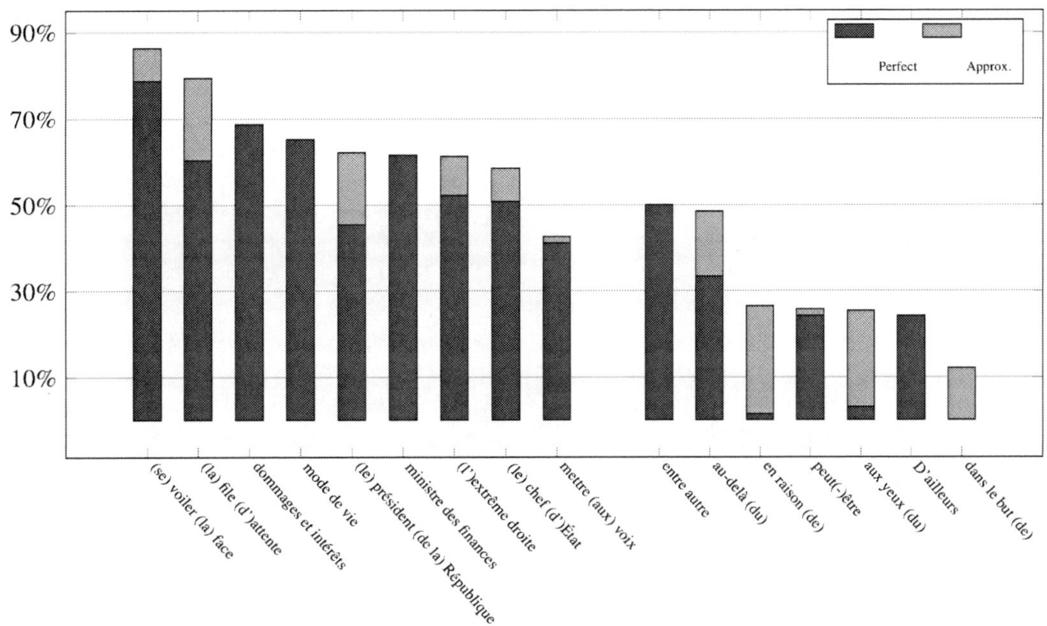

Figure 4: Recall of the participants on each MWE (left: non-functional; right: functional).

	non-functional	*functional*	All
Perfect	58.19	19.48	41.22
Approximate	65.05	30.41	49.86

Table 3: Recall for functional and non-functional MWEs.

3.3 Analysis of the Noise Produced

Table 4 lists the ten expressions that were identified by more than 10% of the participants and which are not in the reference.

Note that we reserve the term collocation to refer to any statistically significant co-occurrence, including all forms of MWEs as described above and compositional phrases which are predictably frequent

It shows that, unsurprisingly, the participants had difficulty distinguishing between MWEs and compositional expressions exhibiting statistical idiosyncrasy (in six cases). This can be explained by the fact that our definition of MWEs partially overlaps with the notion of collocation, as defined in (Sag et al., 2001). Collocations refer to "any statistically significant co-occurrence", that includes both syntactically/semantically compositional and non-compositional expressions.

Other mistakes include boundary errors (two cases) and common civilities annotated as MWEs (two cases). These could probably be avoided if the participants were properly trained.

4 Conclusion and perspectives

Although it was carried out on a small corpus[4], this experiment gathered results from a satisfying number of participants and showed that volunteers with no prior training can help identify at least some MWEs in texts. It is encouraging that the most difficult MWEs to find are the functional ones, as these are usually the first to be listed and are the least prone to neologism.

However, while the participants' intuition proves valuable, it should be complemented by proper training, using at least some of the tests defined by the PARSEME network.

---

[4]A way to increase the size of the corpus without making the task longer could be to randomize the sentences proposed to the participants.

Noisy expressions	% of participants	Comment
immunité présidentielle (presidential immunity)	55.88%	collocation (not a MWE)
élection présidentielle (presidential election)	34.85%	collocation (not a MWE)
aux yeux du public (to the eye of the public)	28.36%	boundary error
destin tragique (tragic faith)	23.88%	collocation (not a MWE)
Monsieur le Président (Mister President)	19.70%	common civilities
affaire politique (political scandal)	15.38%	collocation (not a MWE)
chers collègues (dear colleagues)	15.15%	common civilities
instruire le cas (investigate the case)	14.71%	collocation (not a MWE)
se déclare incompétent (withdraw from the case)	11.76%	collocation (not a MWE)
aux voix (to the vote)	10.29%	boundary error

Table 4: Identified expressions which were not in the reference.

A complementary experiment on the subject is work in progress, as the platform also enables researchers to train participants and collect annotations from them.

The reference corpus is freely available under a CC BY-SA license, on the platform itself.

References

Marie Candito, Mathieu Constant, Carlos Ramisch, Agata Savary, Yannick Parmentier, Caroline Pasquer, and Jean-Yves Antoine. 2017. Annotation d'expressions polylexicales verbales en français. In *Proceedings of Traitement Automatique des Langues Naturelles (TALN)*, pages 1–9, Orléans, France, June.

Mathieu Constant, Gülşen Eryiğit, Johanna Monti, Lonneke van der Plas, Carlos Ramisch, Michael Rosner, and Amalia Todirascu. 2017. Multiword expression processing: A survey. *Computational Linguistics*, 43(4):837–892.

Raymond W. Gibbs, Josephine M. Bogdanovich, Jeffrey R. Sykes, and Dale J. Barr. 1997. Metaphor in idiom comprehension. *Journal of Memory and Language*, 37:141–154.

Raymond W Gibbs. 1992. What do idioms really mean? *Journal of Memory and Language*, 31(4):485 – 506.

Bruno Guillaume, Karën Fort, and Nicolas Lefebvre. 2016. Crowdsourcing complex language resources: Playing to annotate dependency syntax. In *Proceedings of the 26th International Conference on Computational Linguistics (COLING): Technical Papers*, pages 3041–3052, Osaka, Japan, December.

Cvetana Krstev and Agata Savary. 2018. Games on multiword expressions for community building. *INFOtheca: Journal of Information and Library Science*, February

Mathieu Lafourcade. 2007. Making people play for lexical acquisition. In *Proceedings of the 7th Symposium on Natural Language Processing (SNLP 2007)*, Pattaya, Thailand, December.

Chris Madge, Jon Chamberlain, Udo Kruschwitz, and Massimo Poesio. 2017. Experiment-driven development of a gwap for marking segments in text. In *Extended Abstracts Publication of the Annual Symposium on Computer-Human Interaction in Play*, pages 397–404. ACM.

Joakim Nivre, Marie-Catherine de Marneffe, Filip Ginter, Yoav Goldberg, Jan Hajic, Christopher D. Manning, Ryan McDonald, Slav Petrov, Sampo Pyysalo, Natalia Silveira, Reut Tsarfaty, and Daniel Zeman. 2016. Universal dependencies v1: A multilingual treebank collection. In *Proceedings of the Tenth International Conference on Language Resources and Evaluation (LREC 2016)*, Portoroz, Slovenia, May. European Language Resources Association (ELRA).

Massimo Poesio, Jon Chamberlain, Udo Kruschwitz, Livio Robaldo, and Luca Ducceschi. 2013. Phrase detectives: Utilizing collective intelligence for internet-scale language resource creation. *ACM Trans. Interact. Intell. Syst.*, 3(1):3:1–3:44.

Carlos Ramisch, Silvio Cordeiro, Leonardo Zilio, Marco Idiart, Aline Villavicencio, and Rodrigo Wilkens. 2016. How naked is the naked truth? a multilingual lexicon of nominal compound compositionality. In *Proceedings of the 54th Annual Meeting of the Association for Computational Linguistics (Volume 2: Short Papers)*, pages 156–161, Berlin, Germany. Association for Computational Linguistics.

Ivan A. Sag, Timothy Baldwin, Francis Bond, Ann Copestake, and Dan Flickinger. 2001. Multiword Expressions: A Pain in the Neck for NLP. In *In Proc. of the 3rd International Conference on Intelligent Text Processing and Computational Linguistics (CICLing-2002*, pages 1–15.

Agata Savary, Manfred Sailer, Yannick Parmentier, Michael Rosner, Victoria Rosén, Adam Przepiórkowski, Cvetana Krstev, Veronika Vincze, Beata Wójtowicz, Gyri Smørdal Losnegaard, Carla Parra Escartín, Jakub Waszczuk, Matthieu Constant, Petya Osenova, and Federico Sangati. 2015. PARSEME – PARSing and Multiword Expressions within a European multilingual network. In *7th Language & Technology Conference: Human Language Technologies as a Challenge for Computer Science and Linguistics (LTC 2015)*, Poznan, Poland, November.

Agata Savary, Carlos Ramisch, Silvio Cordeiro, Federico Sangati, Veronika Vincze, Behrang QasemiZadeh, Marie Candito, Fabienne Cap, Voula Giouli, Ivelina Stoyanova, and Antoine Doucet. 2017. The parseme shared task on automatic identification of verbal multiword expressions. In *Proceedings of the 13th Workshop on Multiword Expressions (MWE 2017)*, pages 31–47, Valencia, Spain, April. Association for Computational Linguistics.

Nathan Schneider, Dirk Hovy, Anders Johannsen, and Marine Carpuat. 2016. SemEval-2016 Task 10: Detecting Minimal Semantic Units and their Meanings (DiMSUM). In *Proceedings of SemEval*, San Diego, California, USA, June.

Improving Domain Independent Question Parsing
with Synthetic Treebanks

Halim-Antoine Boukaram, Nizar Habash,[†] Micheline Ziadee, and Majd Sakr[‡]
American University of Science and Technology, Lebanon
[†]New York University Abu Dhabi, UAE
[‡]Carnegie Mellon University, USA
{hboukaram,mziadee}@aust.edu.lb, nizar.habash@nyu.edu, msakr@cs.cmu.edu

Abstract

Automatic syntactic parsing for question constructions is a challenging task due to the paucity of training examples in most treebanks. The near absence of question constructions is due to the dominance of the news domain in treebanking efforts. In this paper, we compare two synthetic low-cost question treebank creation methods with a conventional manual high-cost annotation method in the context of three domains (news questions, political talk shows, and chatbots) for Modern Standard Arabic, a language with relatively low resources and rich morphology. Our results show that synthetic methods can be effective at significantly reducing parsing errors for a target domain without having to invest large resources on manual annotation; and the combination of manual and synthetic methods is our best domain-independent performer.

1 Introduction

Automatic syntactic parsing for questions is a challenging task since most treebanks are built from news domain articles that contain few questions (Hermjakob, 2001). Consequently, parsers can have difficulty with parsing questions (Hara et al., 2011; Gayo, 2011). This is a problem, especially in low resource languages like Arabic where the main gold standard treebank, the Penn Arabic TreeBank (PATB) (Maamouri et al., 2004), contains only 428 questions out of 12k annotated sentences (PATB Part 3).

In addition to the issue of sparse question data, parsing accuracy is further affected by the difference between the training data domain and the test data domain (Sekine, 1997; Haddow and Koehn, 2012; Van der Wees et al., 2015). The cost of manually building and labeling a treebank can be prohibitive; so different methods to maximize the impact of available human resources are utilized. One of these methods is model adaptation through using the output of a model trained on one domain (e.g., news) to annotate data from a different target domain (e.g., science fiction) (Su and Yan, 2017; Petrov et al., 2010). The automatically annotated data is then used to train a new model that has improved accuracy in the target domain. There are published efforts that deal specifically with adapting models for question parsing (Judge et al., 2006; Petrov et al., 2010; Seddah and Candito, 2016).

In this paper, we evaluate the efficacy of two low-cost synthetic treebank generation methods at improving the parsing accuracy of questions for Arabic in a number of domains. One of the methods we use relies on existing treebanks and uses phrase structure transformations to create questions from statements. The second method elicits generic unlexicalized templates from human users of a specific application. Another contribution of this paper is the creation of a manually annotated treebank of 988 questions (5.3k words) in two question-heavy domains to allow us to evaluate the three methods.

2 Methodology

Our basic approach is to train a syntactic parser with different combinations of treebanks (synthetic and manual) on top of a baseline of a commonly used treebank (PATB). We will evaluate the parser with a number of data sets from different domains with a high proportion of question constructions.

Proceedings of the Joint Workshop on
Linguistic Annotation, Multiword Expressions and Constructions (LAW-MWE-CxG-2018), pages 214–221
Santa Fe, New Mexico, USA, August 25-26, 2018.

We created three treebanks using three different methods: one manually validated, and two synthetically constructed. The manual treebank covers two domains: talk shows and chatbots. The first synthetic question treebank is generated automatically from PATB using a number of manual question generation rules. The second is created from manual unlexicalized annotated question templates. Each synthetic corpus covers one domain of questions. We present next the different treebanks we created.

2.1 The Manual Treebank

We acquired the data used to build the manual treebank from two domains. This resulted in two sub-treebanks, TalkShow and Chatbot, described in the next subsections. The raw data was automatically parsed using the Stanford parser (Klein and Manning, 2003; Green and Manning, 2010) with a model built from the PATB. The output (POS and syntactic structure) was validated by a human before being integrated into our manual treebank.

2.1.1 The TalkShow Treebank

We annotated 687 questions from the transcripts of a political TV talk show. After the initial automatic parsing, 54% of the questions were accepted without modification. We corrected 18% of the questions, and entirely re-annotated 28% of the questions when the automated process failed to produce reasonable results Although its domain is close to that of the PATB (news) there were some specific constructions in the TalkShow treebank which include: (a) Declarative questions; (b) Non-sentential utterances, e.g., 'Which state?'; (c) Questions where the question word is at the end of the phrase rather than the beginning, e.g.,'That state supports you, why?'; (d) Questions with vocative elements; and (e) Questions with topicalization, e.g., 'The problem, who caused it?'

2.1.2 The Chatbot Treebank

We annotated 162 questions from the CMUQ Hala logs. Hala (Makatchev et al., 2010), a roboceptionist that was deployed at the CMU Qatar campus, would answer users' typed questions in Arabic and English. These questions consisted of a high proportion of simple *where* questions (e.g., 'where is the bathroom?', due to user priming). In order to extend this conversational treebank, we ran a survey among Arabic speaking university students asking them what questions they have asked or would ask a university receptionist. This gave us an additional 139 questions for a total of 301 university-related questions. As with the TalkShow treebank, this treebank was annotated either by using the unmodified parser output (62% of questions), correcting the parser output (26%), or annotating manually (12%). Unlike TalkShow whose source is spoken language, Chatbot's source is written language.

2.2 The QGen$_{PATB}$ Synthetic Treebank

We decided to increase the number of annotated questions available to the model in order to increase its familiarity with interrogative structures. We implemented an automatic procedure to generate annotated questions similar to the latter stages of the work by Ali et al. (2010) and Heilman and Smith (2010) who used the parsed output of raw English data. Our procedure took as input an annotated PATB sentence, to which we added some extra gender, number, and rationality information (GNR) (Alkuhlani and Habash, 2011), and produced a set of annotated questions, following 21 question generators. Multiple question trees could be generated from each PATB tree. All questions began with a question word since this is the most common type of question.[1]

Each question-generating procedure worked by examining the semantic dash-tags available in the input PATB tree. The dash-tags used are: -SBJ (subject), -OBJ (object), -PRD (predicate), -DIR (direction), -LOC (locative), -TMP (temporal), and -CLR (closely related). The question generators implemented grammatical tree conversion rules on the input elements (Subject, Verb, etc.) to create questions with correct morphological agreement in terms of gender, number, and verb tense. Figure 1 shows some examples of automatically generated question structures.

---

[1]93% of TalkShow questions and 100% of Chatbot questions begin with a question word (ignoring any sentence-initial conjunctions and interjections).

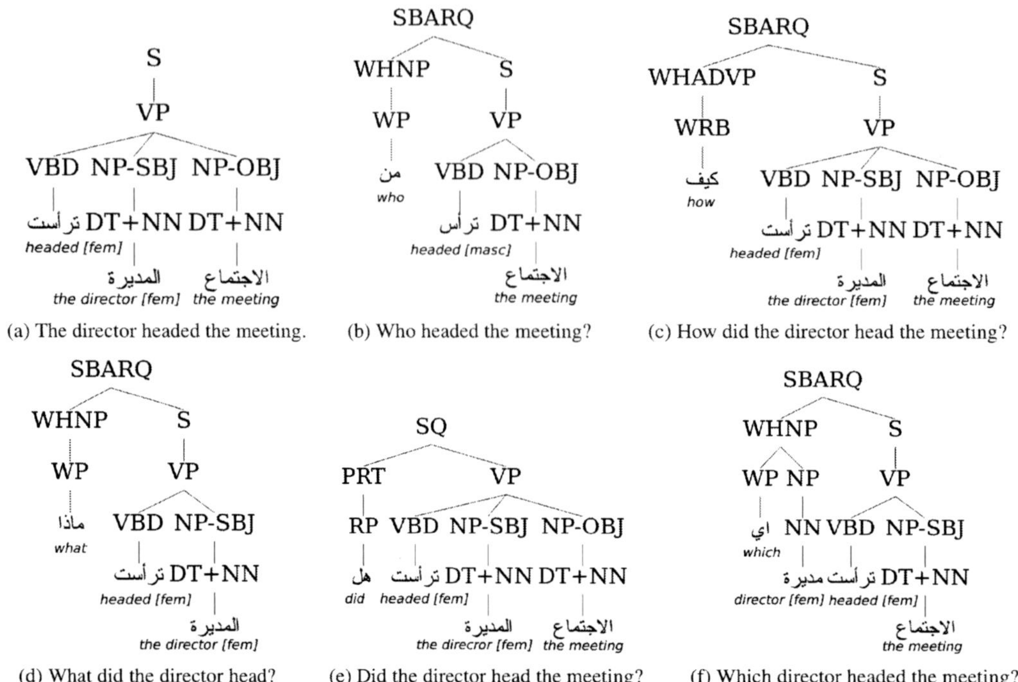

Figure 1: Example questions in QGen$_{PATB}$ (b,c,d,e,f) generated from original tree (a).

Some questions have sub variations to account for optional elements in the input sentence or the output question. For example, in Arabic, the subject can be inferred from the conjugation of the verb, so some pronouns can be added/removed from the sentence without affecting its meaning. Other variations take into consideration synonymous Arabic question words, e.g., ما mA[2] and ماذا $mAðA$ 'what'; لم $limA$ and لماذا $limAðA$ 'why'; and أ $Â$ and هل hal 'is it true that'.

Arabic has two types of sentences, verbal and nominal (Habash, 2010). Table 1 lists some question generators for the two types of sentences with optional elements encapsulated in square braces.

	Input Form	Output Form	Input Sentence		Output Question	
Verbal	Verb [Subj] Obj	Who Verb Obj	He took a flag	أخذ علما	Who took a flag ?	من أخذ علما؟
	Verb [Subj] Obj	What Verb [Subj]	He took a flag	أخذ علما	What did he take ?	ماذا أخذ؟
	Verb Obj Subj	Which Subj Verb Obj	Iran's ambassador attended the meeting	حضر اللّقاء سفير إيران	Which ambassador attended the meeting?	أي سفير حضر اللقاء؟
	Verb [Subj] PP	Prep What Verb [Subj]	He is looking into the case	يبحث في القضية	Into what is he looking?	في ماذا يبحث؟
Nominal	Subj Pred	Who Pred	They (dual) are honest (dual)	انهما صادقان	Who is honest (singular)?	من صادق؟
	Subj Pred	What Pred	Its repercussions are negative	إنعكاساته سلبية	What is negative?	ماذا سلبي؟
	Subj Pred	Is Subj Pred	They are present	هم حاضرون	Are they present?	هل هم حاضرون؟
	Subj Pred	Is Subj Pred	He is outside	هو في الخارج	Is he outside?	أهو في الخارج؟

Table 1: Example questions of QGen$_{PATB}$.

The limitation of this synthetic technique is its dependence on an existing annotated treebank. However, its main advantage is that it can be easily reused to generate many question trees from any new non-question treebank in another domain with no added cost.

---

[2] Arabic script transliteration is presented in the Habash-Soudi-Buckwalter transliteration scheme (Habash et al., 2007).

2.3 The QTemp Synthetic Treebank

To address the lack of raw data in our desired domain (conversational), we tasked an in-house team with the generation of questions that they would ask a university receptionist. The tasks were divided into topics. The topics included *place questions* such as asking for directions, *process questions* such as obtaining academic transcripts, *event questions* such as graduations and expositions, and *degree questions* such as available majors. The questions were written as templates similar to Serban et al. (2016). Each question template (e.g., Where is %place%?) included a token (e.g., %place%) that could be replaced with real values (e.g., cafeteria, reception). Table 2 shows an example of an annotated question template and some generated questions for the place topic. In order to maximize coverage, we asked several team members to generate questions on the same topics.

Template: (SBARQ (WHADVP (WRB أين 'where')) (S (NP **%place%**)) (PUNC ?))
(SBARQ (WHADVP (WRB أين 'where')) (S (NP **(DT+NN** المدخل **'the entrance'**))) (PUNC ?))
(SBARQ (WHADVP (WRB أين 'where')) (S (NP **(DT+NNS** الصفوف **'the classrooms'**))) (PUNC ?))
(SBARQ (WHADVP (WRB أين 'where')) (S (NP (NN مكتب **'office'**) (NP **(DT+NN** العميد **'the dean'**))))(PUNC ?))

Table 2: Example of question generation for %place% question template.

Each question template was annotated by three in-house independent annotators with an average agreement rate of 92%. The differences were discussed and resolved resulting in a single annotation. When combining the annotated question templates with the annotated values of the tokens, care was taken to match for number, gender and case. Table 3 lists the number of templates and values annotated per topic. The number of generated questions per topic equals the number of question templates times the number of token values.

Topic	Place	Process	Event	Degree
# Templates	65	137	188	187
# Token Values	86	41	43	22

Table 3: Number of annotated templates and values.

One difference between QTemp and the PATB is the prevalence of first and second person singular verbs and pronouns in the former versus third person plural verbs and pronouns in the latter.

3 Experimental Setup

For all evaluations, the Stanford parser (Version 3.8.0) was used to train models for various combinations of train sets which were evaluated against all test sets. The parser's command-line *maxLength* argument was set to 30 so as to exclude longer sentences. All other configuration variables were left to default. Given the complexity of evaluating both segmentation and syntactic parsing together (Marton et al., 2013; Tsarfaty et al., 2012), we used the gold segmentation but the POS tags were predicted. Table 4 shows the distribution of treebanks between train and test sets, which are explained in the next subsections.

Treebank	Domain	Train # Sentences (# Words)	Test # Sentences (# Words)
ATB	News articles	10,836 (320,998)	794 (12,884)
ATBQ	News articles	N/A	67 (1,054)
TalkShow	Political talk show	544 (2,691)	143 (692)
Chatbot	Conversational	239 (1,505)	62 (441)
QGen$_{PATB}$	News articles (Synthetic)	962 (8,140)	N/A
QTemp	Conversational (Synthetic)	1,607 (13,099)	N/A

Table 4: The various treebanks used in terms of domain, training and testing sizes.

3.1 Train Sets

The Baseline The PATB is made up of 3 parts. Our baseline model was trained using the PATB (part 3) train dataset (PATB3.train) as defined by Diab et al. (2013).

The Manual Treebank Our manual treebank train set consisted of randomly selecting 80% of each of the TalkShow and Chatbot treebanks (783 questions). These two train sets were merged since their individual impact on their own test set is generally understood.

QGen$_{PATB}$ For QGen$_{PATB}$, 91k questions were generated from 10k trees in the PATB3.train set. Testing against the PATB3 development set (PATB3.dev), we found that using the entire QGen$_{PATB}$ treebank reduced accuracy due to the imbalance in question and non-question trees. All generated questions had the question word at the start of the phrase so the parser was biased against being able to detect the PATB questions that didn't begin with question words. This lead to an increase of SBARQs and SQs being tagged as SBARs and Ss respectively. To avoid the imbalance, the number of questions incorporated into the train set was empirically optimized by tuning against the PATB3.dev set, forming a random subset of QGen$_{PATB}$ with 962 questions.

QTemp QTemp consisted of a total of 23k questions. As with QGen$_{PATB}$, QTemp was tuned against PATB3.dev resulting in a random subset of 1.6k questions being used.

3.2 Test Sets

We report our results on four test sets. First is the standard PATB3 test set (Diab et al., 2013) which has only a small proportion of questions. Second is a question rich test set (PATBQ) created by merging trees with question structures (SBARQ, SQ) from PATB (parts 1 and 2), and PATB3.test (Diab et al., 2013). Third and fourth are the 20% (non-train) of the TalkShow and Chatbot treebanks, respectively. We obviously do not report on test portions from the synthetic treebanks because they are not manually validated.

4 Results

The parsing scores for different combinations (C1-C6) of train sets (shown in the second column) are shown in Table 5. The *Average Q* row is a macro average of the three question test sets (PATBQ, TalkShow, and Chatbot).

	Corpus	Baseline	C1	C2	C3	C4	C5	C6	All	CQ	Error Reduction All over Baseline	Error Reduction Synthetic (C5) over Baseline
Train	**PATB**	✓	✓	✓	✓	✓	✓	✓	✓			
	QGen$_{PATB}$ (Synthetic)		✓		✓		✓		✓	✓		
	QTemp (Synthetic)					✓	✓	✓	✓	✓		
	TalkShow+Chatbot			✓	✓			✓	✓	✓		
Test	**PATB**	80.6	80.6	80.6	80.7	80.7	80.6	80.8	**80.9**	43.0	1%	1.2%
	PATBQ	73.8	74.1	74.9	74.9	73.8	74.0	75.8	**75.9**	53.1	8%	4.1%
	TalkShow	88.2	88.2	91.4	92.1	87.5	87.3	92.7	**92.9**	83.2	38%	-8.2%
	Chatbot	90.5	90.7	93.3	93.0	93.6	93.6	**94.1**	**94.1**	86.7	40%	32.3%
	Average Q	84.2	84.3	86.5	86.7	85.0	84.9	87.5	**87.6**	74.3	22%	4.9%

Table 5: F-scores for Baseline to All models. C1-C6 and CQ represent the different combination of training sets which are shown in the second column.

The TalkShow+Chatbot treebank data was the best single addition to the baseline (C2 in Table 5), but is also the most costly and most difficult to build. In experiments not shown here, we found that excluding Chatbot or TalkShow from C2 reduces the performance on the TalkShow and Chatbot tests, respectively, which clearly shows that the two training sets boosted each other's test set.

The positive impact of the synthetic QTemp (C4) train set on the Chatbot test set was similar to that of the TalkShow+Chatbot train set (C2). However, QTemp had a negative impact on the TalkShow test set due to the domain specific properties mentioned in 2.1.1. This suggests that synthetic data (if used alone) is beneficial for in-domain cases; but may have a negligible to negative effect on out-of-domain tests. For similar reasons, QGen_{PATB} (C1) primarily had a positive impact on the PATBQ test set.

The cumulative model (All in Table 5), which includes all manual and synthetic train sets, was the most accurate suggesting added value for a combination of techniques. However, The model trained with only the question train sets (CQ in Table 5), suffered due to reduced coverage thereby justifying why PATB should always be part of the training data.

We used a two-tailed paired t-Test to evaluate the significance of the error reduction exhibited by the cumulative model over the baseline. The p-values were 0.0039 for PATB, 0.086 for PATBQ, 8×10^{-5} for TalkShow, and 0.031 for Chatbot. Only the results of the PATBQ were not significant due to the small test size and the relatively small error reduction.

5   Related Work

There is a large body of literature on automatic parsing for English and other languages (Charniak, 1997; Steedman et al., 2003; Judge et al., 2006; Kübler et al., 2009; Green and Manning, 2010; Petrov et al., 2010; Zaki et al., 2016). Some of these efforts dealt with the issue of automatic training data enrichment to boost parsing accuracy. Steedman et al. (2003) showed that self training, i.e., using the output of a parser on raw text as additional training data, did not do as well as co-training, i.e., iteratively retraining two (or more) parsers on each other's output. We do not report here on self training experiments that we did because they gave negative results. Petrov et al. (2010) showed that training with the output of a different parser can increase accuracy. In this paper, we only worked with one parser.

Our work is more closely related to the work by Judge et al. (2006) on the English Question Bank. They obtained a 51.7% reduction in the error rate of parsing questions by adding manually annotated questions to their train set. In our case, using only the synthetic QTemp treebank, we achieved a 32.3% on the Chatbot test set. Also similar to Judge et al. (2006), was the result of training only on the question sets which gave reduced parsing accuracy across all test sets (particularly the statement-rich test set).

In regards to work on Arabic parsing, we use similar but not directly comparable data sets and parameters to Green and Manning (2010). Our baseline is similar to what they achieved. There is a growing body of research on Arabic dependency parsing (Habash and Roth, 2009; Marton et al., 2013; Taji et al., 2017; Taji et al., 2018). Most recently, Taji et al. (2018) introduced a travel domain treebank that had a very high proportion of question constructions (40% of the trees).

The annotation speeds reported by Habash and Roth (2009) were between 540 and 715 tokens/hour. They also reported annotation speeds of 250-300 tokens/hour for the PATB and around 75 tokens/hour for the Prague Arabic Dependancy Treebank (PADT) (Smrž and Hajic, 2006). Our annotation speeds for QTemp are not directly comparable given the difference in the tasks, but they were around 4.2 templates/hour which included the time taken for the three annotators to discuss any differences.

6   Conclusion and Future Work

In this paper, we have shown that low-cost methods to produce synthetic domain-specific training data can greatly improve syntactic parsing accuracy for in-domain tests. Using synthetic training data, we achieved an error reduction rate that was comparable to that achieved with manually annotated data (in-domain). However, the synthetic data was found to have a negligible to negative effect on out-of-domain tests. The resulting synthetic and manual data is useful for other researchers working in Arabic computational linguistics especially with regards to analyzing questions.

In the future, we plan to write additional question-generating procedures targeting particular question constructions such as 'how much/many' and 'which' that are sparse in the current QGen_{PATB}. Inspired by Petrov et al. (2010), we plan to evaluate other parsers against our test sets to identify which parser would be best suited to provide automatic training data. We will also test whether the synthetic approach is generalizable to other languages. Finally, we will investigate how the improvement in syntactic parsing affects a question answering task and compare that against a pure grammar rule-based approach.

References

Husam Ali, Yllias Chali, and Sadid A Hasan. 2010. Automation of question generation from sentences. In *Proceedings of QG2010: The Third Workshop on Question Generation*, pages 58–67.

Sarah Alkuhlani and Nizar Habash. 2011. A corpus for modeling morpho-syntactic agreement in Arabic: gender, number and rationality. In *Proceedings of the 49th Annual Meeting of the Association for Computational Linguistics: Human Language Technologies: short papers-Volume 2*, pages 357–362. Association for Computational Linguistics.

Eugene Charniak. 1997. Statistical parsing with a context-free grammar and word statistics. *AAAI/IAAI*, 2005(598-603):18.

Mona Diab, Nizar Habash, Owen Rambow, and Ryan Roth. 2013. LDC Arabic treebanks and associated corpora: Data divisions manual. *arXiv preprint arXiv:1309.5652*.

Iria Gayo. 2011. Question parsing for QA in Spanish. In *Proceedings of the Second Student Research Workshop associated with RANLP 2011*, pages 73–78.

Spence Green and Christopher D Manning. 2010. Better Arabic parsing: Baselines, evaluations, and analysis. In *Proceedings of the 23rd International Conference on Computational Linguistics*, pages 394–402. Association for Computational Linguistics.

Nizar Habash and Ryan M Roth. 2009. CATiB: The Columbia Arabic treebank. In *Proceedings of the ACL-IJCNLP 2009 conference short papers*, pages 221–224. Association for Computational Linguistics.

Nizar Habash, Abdelhadi Soudi, and Tim Buckwalter. 2007. On Arabic Transliteration. In A. van den Bosch and A. Soudi, editors, *Arabic Computational Morphology: Knowledge-based and Empirical Methods*. Springer.

Nizar Y Habash. 2010. Introduction to Arabic natural language processing. *Synthesis Lectures on Human Language Technologies*, 3(1):1–187.

Barry Haddow and Philipp Koehn. 2012. Analysing the effect of out-of-domain data on SMT systems. In *Proceedings of the Seventh Workshop on Statistical Machine Translation*, pages 422–432. Association for Computational Linguistics.

Tadayoshi Hara, Takuya Matsuzaki, Yusuke Miyao, and Jun'ichi Tsujii. 2011. Exploring difficulties in parsing imperatives and questions. In *Proceedings of 5th International Joint Conference on Natural Language Processing*, pages 749–757.

Michael Heilman and Noah A Smith. 2010. Good question! statistical ranking for question generation. In *Human Language Technologies: The 2010 Annual Conference of the North American Chapter of the Association for Computational Linguistics*, pages 609–617. Association for Computational Linguistics.

Ulf Hermjakob. 2001. Parsing and question classification for question answering. In *Proceedings of the workshop on Open-domain question answering-Volume 12*, pages 1–6. Association for Computational Linguistics.

John Judge, Aoife Cahill, and Josef Van Genabith. 2006. Questionbank: Creating a corpus of parse-annotated questions. In *Proceedings of the 21st International Conference on Computational Linguistics and the 44th annual meeting of the Association for Computational Linguistics*, pages 497–504. Association for Computational Linguistics.

Dan Klein and Christopher D Manning. 2003. Fast exact inference with a factored model for natural language parsing. In *Advances in neural information processing systems*, pages 3–10.

Sandra Kübler, Ryan McDonald, and Joakim Nivre. 2009. Dependency parsing. *Synthesis Lectures on Human Language Technologies*, 1(1):1–127.

Mohamed Maamouri, Ann Bies, Tim Buckwalter, and Wigdan Mekki. 2004. The Penn Arabic Treebank: Building a large-scale annotated Arabic corpus. In *NEMLAR conference on Arabic language resources and tools*, volume 27, pages 466–467. Cairo.

Maxim Makatchev, Imran Fanaswala, Ameer Abdulsalam, Brett Browning, Wael Ghazzawi, Majd Sakr, and Reid Simmons. 2010. Dialogue patterns of an Arabic robot receptionist. In *Human-Robot Interaction (HRI), 2010 5th ACM/IEEE International Conference on*, pages 167–168. IEEE.

Yuval Marton, Nizar Habash, and Owen Rambow. 2013. Dependency parsing of modern standard Arabic with lexical and inflectional features. *Computational Linguistics*, 39(1):161–194.

Slav Petrov, Pi-Chuan Chang, Michael Ringgaard, and Hiyan Alshawi. 2010. Uptraining for accurate deterministic question parsing. In *Proceedings of the 2010 Conference on Empirical Methods in Natural Language Processing*, EMNLP '10, pages 705–713, Stroudsburg, PA, USA. Association for Computational Linguistics.

Djamé Seddah and Marie Candito. 2016. Hard time parsing questions: Building a questionbank for French. In *Tenth International Conference on Language Resources and Evaluation (LREC 2016)*.

Satoshi Sekine. 1997. The domain dependence of parsing. ANLC '97, pages 96–102, Stroudsburg, PA, USA. Association for Computational Linguistics.

Iulian Vlad Serban, Alberto García-Durán, Caglar Gulcehre, Sungjin Ahn, Sarath Chandar, Aaron Courville, and Yoshua Bengio. 2016. Generating factoid questions with recurrent neural networks: The 30m factoid question-answer corpus. *arXiv preprint arXiv:1603.06807*.

Otakar Smrž and Jan Hajic. 2006. The other Arabic treebank: Prague dependencies and functions. *Arabic computational linguistics: Current implementations. CSLI Publications*, 104.

Mark Steedman, Miles Osborne, Anoop Sarkar, Stephen Clark, Rebecca Hwa, Julia Hockenmaier, Paul Ruhlen, Steven Baker, and Jeremiah Crim. 2003. Bootstrapping statistical parsers from small datasets. In *Proceedings of the tenth conference on European chapter of the Association for Computational Linguistics-Volume 1*, pages 331–338. Association for Computational Linguistics.

Yu Su and Xifeng Yan. 2017. Cross-domain semantic parsing via paraphrasing. *CoRR*, abs/1704.05974.

Dima Taji, Nizar Habash, and Daniel Zeman. 2017. Universal dependencies for Arabic. In *Proceedings of the Third Arabic Natural Language Processing Workshop*, pages 166–176.

Dima Taji, Jamila El Gizuli, and Nizar Habash. 2018. An Arabic dependency treebank in the travel domain. In *Proceedings of the 3rd Workshop on Open-Source Arabic Corpora and Processing Tools*, Miyazaki, Japan.

Reut Tsarfaty, Joakim Nivre, and Evelina Andersson. 2012. Joint evaluation of morphological segmentation and syntactic parsing. In *Proceedings of the 50th Annual Meeting of the Association for Computational Linguistics: Short Papers-Volume 2*, pages 6–10. Association for Computational Linguistics.

Marlies Van der Wees, Arianna Bisazza, Wouter Weerkamp, and Christof Monz. 2015. What's in a domain? analyzing genre and topic differences in statistical machine translation. In *Proceedings of the 53rd Annual Meeting of the Association for Computational Linguistics and the 7th International Joint Conference on Natural Language Processing (Volume 2: Short Papers)*, volume 2, pages 560–566.

Youssef Zaki, Haisam Hajjar, Mohamad Hajjar, and Gilles Bernard. 2016. A survey of syntactic parsers of Arabic language. In *Proceedings of the International Conference on Big Data and Advanced Wireless Technologies*, page 31. ACM.

Edition 1.1 of the PARSEME Shared Task on Automatic Identification of Verbal Multiword Expressions

Carlos Ramisch
Aix Marseille
University, France

Silvio Ricardo Cordeiro
Aix Marseille
University, France

Agata Savary
University of Tours,
France

Veronika Vincze
University of Szeged,
Hungary

Verginica Barbu Mititelu
Romanian Academy,
Romania

Archna Bhatia
Florida IHMC,
USA

Maja Buljan
University of Stuttgart,
Germany

Marie Candito,
Paris Diderot University,
France

Polona Gantar
Faculty of Arts,
Slovenia

Voula Giouli
Athena Research Center,
Greece

Tunga Güngör
Boğaziçi University,
Turkey

Abdelati Hawwari
George Washington
University, USA

Uxoa Iñurrieta
University of the Basque
Country, Spain

Jolanta Kovalevskaitė
Vytautas Magnus
University, Lithuania

Simon Krek
Jožef Stefan Institute,
Slovenia

Timm Lichte
University of Düsseldorf,
Germany

Chaya Liebeskind
Jerusalem College
of Technology, Israel

Johanna Monti
"L'Orientale" University
of Naples, Italy

Carla Parra Escartín
Dublin City University,
Ireland

Behrang QasemiZadeh
University of Düsseldorf,
Germany

Renata Ramisch
Interinstitutional Center
for Computational Linguistics, Brazil

Nathan Schneider
Georgetown University,
USA

Ivelina Stoyanova
Bulgarian Academy of Sciences,
Bulgaria

Ashwini Vaidya
IIT Delhi,
India

Abigail Walsh
Dublin City University,
Ireland

Abstract

This paper describes the PARSEME Shared Task 1.1 on automatic identification of verbal multiword expressions. We present the annotation methodology, focusing on changes from last year's shared task. Novel aspects include enhanced annotation guidelines, additional annotated data for most languages, corpora for some new languages, and new evaluation settings. Corpora were created for 20 languages, which are also briefly discussed. We report organizational principles behind the shared task and the evaluation metrics employed for ranking. The 17 participating systems, their methods and obtained results are also presented and analysed.

1 Introduction

Across languages, multiword expressions (MWEs) are widely recognized as a significant challenge for natural language processing (NLP) (Sag et al., 2002; Baldwin and Kim, 2010). An international and highly multilingual research community, forged via regular workshops and initiatives such as the PARSEME network (Savary et al., 2015), has rallied around the goals of characterizing MWEs in lexicons, grammars and corpora and enabling systems to process them. Recent shared tasks, namely DiM-SUM (Schneider et al., 2016) and the first edition of the PARSEME Shared Task on automatic identification of verbal multiword expressions in 2017 (Savary et al., 2017), have helped drive MWE research forward, yielding new corpora and testbeds for MWEs identification systems.

Proceedings of the Joint Workshop on
Linguistic Annotation, Multiword Expressions and Constructions (LAW-MWE-CxG-2018), pages 222–240
Santa Fe, New Mexico, USA, August 25-26, 2018.

This paper describes edition 1.1 of the PARSEME Shared Task, which builds on this momentum. We amalgamated organizational experience from last year's task, a more polished version of the annotation methodology and an extended set of linguistic data, yielding an event that attracted 12 teams from 9 countries. Novel aspects in this year's task include additional annotated data for most of the languages, some new languages with annotated datasets and enhanced annotation guidelines.

The structure of the paper is the following. First, related work is presented, then details on the annotation methodology are described, focusing on changes from last year's shared task. We have annotated corpora for 20 languages, which are briefly discussed. Main organizational principles behind the shared task, as well as the evaluation metrics are reported next. Finally, participating systems are introduced and their results are discussed before we draw our conclusions.

2 Related Work

In the last few years, there have been several evaluation campaigns for MWE identification. First, the 2008 MWE workshop contained an MWE-targeted shared task. However, the goal of participants was to rank the provided MWE candidates instead of identifying them in raw texts. The recent DiMSUM 2016 shared task (Schneider et al., 2016) challenged participants to label English sentences in tweets, user reviews of services, and TED talks both with MWEs and supersenses for nouns and verbs. Last, the 1.0 edition of the PARSEME Shared Task in 2017 (Savary et al., 2017) provided annotated datasets for 18 languages, where the goal was to identify verbal MWEs in context. Our current shared task is similar in vein to the previous edition. However, the annotation methodology has been enhanced (see Section 3) and the set of languages covered has also been changed.

Rosén et al. (2015) reports on a survey of MWE annotation in 17 treebanks for 15 languages, collaboratively documented according to common guidelines. They highlight the heterogeneity of MWE annotation practices. Similar conclusions have been drawn for Universal Dependencies (McDonald et al., 2013). With regard to these conclusions, we intended to provide unified guidelines for all the participating languages, in order to avoid heterogeneous, hence incomparable, datasets.

MWE identification in syntactic parsing has also gained some popularity in recent years. While often treated as a pre-processing step for parsing, both tasks are now more and more integrated (Finkel and Manning, 2009; Green et al., 2011; Green et al., 2013; Candito and Constant, 2014; Le Roux et al., 2014; Nasr et al., 2015; Constant and Nivre, 2016). Although fewer works deal with verbal MWEs, there are some notable exceptions (Wehrli et al., 2010; Vincze et al., 2013; Wehrli, 2014; Waszczuk et al., 2016). Some systems that participated in edition 1.0 of the PARSEME Shared Task are also based on parsing (Al Saied et al., 2017; Nerima et al., 2017; Simkó et al., 2017). Other approaches to MWE identification include sequence labeling using CRFs (Boroş et al., 2017; Maldonado et al., 2017) and neural networks (Klyueva et al., 2017).

3 Enhanced Annotation Methodology

The first PARSEME annotation campaign (Savary et al., forthcoming) generated a rich feedback from annotators and language team leaders. It also attracted the interest of new teams, working on languages not covered by the previous version of the PARSEME corpora. About 80 issues were raised and discussed among dozens of contributors.[1] This boosted our efforts towards a better understanding of VMWE-related phenomena, and towards a better synergy of terminologies across languages and linguistic traditions. The annotation guidelines were gradually enhanced, so as to achieve more clear-cut distinctions among categories, and make the decision process easier and more reliable. As a result, we expected higher-quality annotated corpora and better VMWE identification systems learned on them.

3.1 Definitions

We maintain all major definitions (unified across languages) introduced in edition 1.0 of the annotation campaign (Savary et al., forthcoming, Sec. 2). In particular, we understand *multiword expressions*

---

[1] The issues can be found at Gitlab: `https://gitlab.com/parseme/sharedtask-guidelines/issues`

as expressions with at least two *lexicalized components* (i.e. always realised by the same lexemes), including a head word and at least one other syntactically related word. Thus, lexicalized components of MWEs must form a connected dependency graph. Such expressions must display some degree of lexical, morphological, syntactic and/or semantic idiosyncrasy, formalised by the annotation procedures.

As previously, syntactic variants of MWE candidates are normalised to their least marked form (called the *canonical form*) maintaining the idiomatic reading, before it is submitted to linguistic tests. A *verbal MWE* is defined as a MWE whose head in a canonical form is a verb, and which functions as a verbal phrase, unlike e.g. FR *peut-être* 'may-be' ⇒ 'maybe' (which is always an adverbial). As in edition 1.0, we account for single-token VMWEs with multiword variants, e.g. ES ***hacerse*** 'make-self' ⇒ 'become' vs. ***se hace*** 'self makes' ⇒ 'becomes'.

3.2 Typology

Major changes in the annotation guidelines between edition 1.0 and 1.1 include redesigning the VMWE typology, which is now defined as follows:[2]

1. Two *universal* categories, that is, valid for all languages participating in the task:
   (a) LIGHT VERB CONSTRUCTIONS (LVC), divided into two subcategories:
       i. LVCs in which the verb is semantically totally bleached (LVC.full), DE *eine **Rede halten*** 'hold a speech' ⇒ 'give a speech',
       ii. LVCs in which the verb adds a causative meaning to the noun (LVC.cause),[3] e.g. PL ***narazić na straty*** 'expose to losses'
   (b) VERBAL IDIOMS (VID),[4] grouping all VMWEs not belonging to other categories, and most often having a relatively high degree of semantic non-compositionality, e.g. LT *našta **gula ant** savivaldybių **pečių*** 'the burden lies on the shoulders of the municipality' ⇒ 'the municipality is in charge of the burden'

2. Three *quasi-universal* categories, valid for some language groups or languages, but not all:
   (a) INHERENTLY REFLEXIVE VERBS (IRV)[5] – pervasive in Romance and Slavic languages, and present in Hungarian and German – in which the reflexive clitic (REFL) either always co-occurs with a given verb, or markedly changes its meaning or subcategorisation frame, e.g. PT ***se formar*** 'REFL form' ⇒ 'graduate'
   (b) VERB-PARTICLE CONSTRUCTIONS (VPC) – pervasive in Germanic languages and Hungarian, rare in Romance and absent in Slavic languages – with two subcategories:
       i. fully non-compositional VPCs (VPC.full),[6] in which the particle totally changes the meaning of the verb, e.g. HU ***berúg*** 'in-kick' ⇒ 'get drunk'
       ii. semi non-compositional VPCs (VPC.semi),[7] in which the particle adds a partly predictable but non-spatial meaning to the verb, e.g. EN ***wake up***
   (c) MULTI-VERB CONSTRUCTIONS (MVC)[8] – close to semantically non-compositional serial verbs in Asian languages like Chinese, Hindi, Indonesian and Japanese (but also attested in Spanish), e.g. HI ***kar le*** 'do take' ⇒ 'do (for one's own benefit)', ***kar de*** 'do give' ⇒ 'do (for other's benefit)'

3. One *language-specific* category, introduced for Italian:

---

[2]In-line examples contain a two-letter language code, a literal translation into English, and an idiomatic translation. The lexicalized components are highlighted in bold.

[3]This subcategory is new in edition 1.1. It absorbs some verb-noun combinations previously annotated as IDs, but also includes many previously non-annotated ones.

[4]This category largely overlaps with IDs introduced in edition 1.0. Major changes include: (i) shifting some verb+noun combinations into the LVC.cause category, (ii) absorbing the previously used OTH category (covering verbs not having a single verbal head) due to its very restricted use.

[5]In edition 1.0 the acronym IReflV was used for this category. It was changed to IRV for easier pronunciation.

[6]This subcategory corresponds to the VPC category from edition 1.0.

[7]This subcategory is new in edition 1.1.

[8]This subcategory is new in edition 1.1. It absorbs some rare cases of previously annotated verb-verb combinations like FR ***laisser tomber*** 'let fall' ⇒ 'abandon'.

(a) INHERENTLY CLITIC VERBS (LS.ICV),[9] in which at least one non-reflexive clitic (CLI) either always accompanies a given verb or markedly changes its meaning or its subcategorisation frame, e.g. IT *prenderle* 'take-them'⇒'get beaten up'

4. One *optional experimental* category, to be considered in the post-annotation step:

(a) INHERENTLY ADPOSITIONAL VERBS (IAV) - they include idiomatic combinations of verbs with prepositions or post-positions, depending on the language, e.g. HR *ne dode do* uspora-vanja 'it will not come to delay'⇒'no delay will occur'[10]

3.3 Decision tree for annotation

Edition 1.0 featured a two-stage annotation process, according to which VMWEs were supposed to be first identified in a category-neutral fashion, then classified into one of the VMWE categories. Since the annotation practice showed that VMWE identification is virtually always done in a category-specific way, for this year's task we constructed a unified decision tree, shown in Fig. 1.[11] Note that the first 4 tests are structural. They first hypothesize as VIDs those candidates which: (S.1) do not have a unique verb as head, e.g. HE *britanya nas'a ve-natna* 'im micrayim 'Britain carried and gave with Egypt'⇒'Britain negotiated with Egypt', (S.2) have more than one lexicalized dependent of the head verb, EL ρίχνω λάδι στη φωτιά 'pour oil to-the-fire'⇒'make a bad or negative situation feel worse', (S.3) have a lexicalized subject, e.g. EU *deabruak eraman* 'devil-the.ERG[12] take'⇒'be taken by the devil, go to hell'. The remaining candidates, i.e. those having exactly one head verb and one lexicalized non-subject dependent, trigger category specific tests depending on the part-of-speech of this dependent (S.4).

```
↳ Apply test S.1 - [1HEAD: Unique verb as functional syntactic head of the whole?]
    ↳ NO ⇒ Apply the VID-specific tests ⇒ VID tests positive?
        ↳ YES ⇒ Annotate as a VMWE of category VID
        ↳ NO ⇒ It is not a VMWE, exit
    ↳ YES ⇒ Apply test S.2 - [1DEP: Verb v has exactly one lexicalized dependent d?]
        ↳ NO ⇒ Apply the VID-specific tests ⇒ VID tests positive?
            ↳ YES ⇒ Annotate as a VMWE of category VID
            ↳ NO ⇒ It is not a VMWE, exit
        ↳ YES ⇒ Apply test S.3 - [LEX-SUBJ: Lexicalized subject?]
            ↳ YES ⇒ Apply the VID-specific tests ⇒ VID tests positive?
                ↳ YES ⇒ Annotate as a VMWE of category VID
                ↳ NO ⇒ It is not a VMWE, exit
            ↳ NO ⇒ Apply test S.4 - [CATEG: What is the morphosyntactic category of d?]
                ↳ Reflexive clitic ⇒ Apply IRV-specific tests ⇒ IRV tests positive?
                    ↳ YES ⇒ Annotate as a VMWE of category IRV
                    ↳ NO ⇒ It is not a VMWE, exit
                ↳ Particle ⇒ Apply VPC-specific tests ⇒ VPC tests positive?
                    ↳ YES ⇒ Annotate as a VMWE of category VPC.full or VPC.semi
                    ↳ NO ⇒ It is not a VMWE, exit
                ↳ Verb with no lexicalized dependent ⇒ Apply MVC-specific tests ⇒ MVC tests positive?
                    ↳ YES ⇒ Annotate as a VMWE of category MVC
                    ↳ NO ⇒ Apply the VID-specific tests ⇒ VID tests positive?
                        ↳ YES ⇒ Annotate as a VMWE of category VID
                        ↳ NO ⇒ It is not a VMWE, exit
                ↳ Extended NP ⇒ Apply LVC-specific decision tree ⇒ LVC tests positive?
                    ↳ YES ⇒ Annotate as a VMWE of category LVC
                    ↳ NO ⇒ Apply the VID-specific tests ⇒ VID tests positive?
                        ↳ YES ⇒ Annotate as a VMWE of category VID
                        ↳ NO ⇒ It is not a VMWE, exit
                ↳ Another category ⇒ Apply the VID-specific tests ⇒ VID tests positive?
                    ↳ YES ⇒ Annotate as a VMWE of category VID
                    ↳ NO ⇒ It is not a VMWE, exit
```

Figure 1: Decision tree for joint VMWE identification and classification.

---

[9]This subcategory is new in edition 1.1. It absorbs some cases of previously annotated IDs in Italian.

[10]This category is considered experimental since, so far, we did not manage to come up with satisfactory tests clearly distinguishing such cases from regular verbal valency.

[11]For Italian and Hindi, this tree is slightly modified to account for: (i) the Italian-specific LS.ICV category, (ii) Hindi MVCs in which an adjective is morphologically identical to an eventive noun.

[12]ERG: ergative case, which is generally attached to the subject of transitive verbs in Basque.

3.4 Consistency checks

Due to manpower constraints, we could not perform double annotation followed by adjudication. For most languages, only small fractions of the corresponding corpus were double-annotated (Sec. 4.2). Therefore, in order to increase the consistency of the annotations, we applied the consistency checking tool developed for edition 1.0 (Savary et al., forthcoming, Sec. 5.4). The tool provides an "orthogonal" view of the corpus, where all annotations of the same VMWE are grouped and can be corrected interactively. Previous experience showed that the use of this tool greatly reduced noise and silence errors. This year, almost all language teams completed the consistency check phase (with the exception of Arabic).

4 Corpora

For edition 1.1, we prepared annotated corpora for 20 languages divided into four groups:
- Germanic languages: German (DE), English (EN)
- Romance languages: Spanish (ES), French (FR), Italian (IT), Portuguese (PT), Romanian (RO)
- Balto-Slavic languages: Bulgarian (BG), Croatian (HR), Lithuanian (LT), Polish (PL), Slovene (SL)
- Other languages: Arabic (AR), Greek (EL), Basque (EU), Farsi (FA), Hebrew (HE), Hindi (HI), Hungarian (HU), Turkish (TR)

Arabic, Basque, Croatian, English and Hindi were additional languages, compared to the first edition of the shared task. However, the Czech, Maltese and Swedish corpora were not updated and hence were not included in edition 1.1 of the shared task. The Basque corpus comprises texts from the whole UD corpus (Aranzabe et al., 2015) and part of the Elhuyar Web Corpora.[13] The Bulgarian corpus comprises news articles from the Bulgarian National Corpus (Koeva et al., 2012). The Croatian corpus contains sentences from the Croatian version of the *SETimes* corpora: mostly running text but also selected fragments, such as introductory blurbs and image descriptions characteristic of newswire text. The English corpus consists of 7,437 sentences taken from three of the UD: the Gold Standard Universal Dependencies Corpus for English, the LinES parallel corpus and the Parallel Universal Dependencies treebank. The Farsi corpus is built on top of the MULTEXT-East corpora (QasemiZadeh and Rahimi, 2006) and VMWE annotations are added to a portion of Orwell's 1984 novel. The French corpus contains the Sequoia corpus (Candito and Seddah, 2012) converted to UD, the GDS French UD treebank, the French part of the Partut corpus, and part of the Parallel UD (PUD) corpus. The German corpus contains shuffled sentences crawled from online news, reviews and wikis, derived from the WMT16 shared task data (Bojar et al., 2016), and Universal Dependencies v2.0. The Greek corpus comprises Wikipedia articles and newswire texts from various on-line newspaper editions and news portals. The Hebrew corpus contains news and articles from *Arutz 7* and *HaAretz* news websites, collected by the MILA Knowledge Center for Processing Hebrew. The Hindi corpus represents the news genre sentences selected from the test section of the Hindi Treebank (Bhat et al., 2015). The Hungarian corpus contains legal texts from the Szeged Treebank (Csendes et al., 2005). The Italian corpus is a selection of texts from the PAISÁ corpus of web texts (Lyding et al., 2014), including Wikibooks, Wikinews, Wikiversity, and blog services. The Lithuanian corpus contains articles from a Lithuanian news portal DELFI. The Polish corpus builds on top of the National Corpus of Polish (Przepiórkowski et al., 2011) and the Polish Coreference Corpus (Ogrodniczuk et al., 2015). These are balanced corpora, from which we selected mainly daily and periodical press extracts. The Portuguese corpus contains sentences from the informal Brazilian newspaper *Diário Gaúcho* and from the training set of the *UD_Portuguese-GSD* v2.1 treebank. The Romanian corpus is a collection of articles from the concatenated editions of the *Agenda* newspaper. The Slovenian corpus contains parts of the ssj500k 2.0 training corpus (Krek et al., 2017), which consists of sampled paragraphs from the Slovenian reference FidaPLUS corpus (Arhar Holdt et al., 2007), including literary novels, daily newspapers, web blogs and social media. The Spanish corpus consists of newspaper texts from the the Ancora corpus (Taulé et al., 2016), the UD version of Ancora, a corpus compiled by the IXA group in the University of the Basque country, and parts of the training set of the UD v2.0 treebank. The Turkish corpus consists of 18,611 sentences of newswire texts in several genres.

---

[13] http://webcorpusak.elhuyar.eus/

As shown in Table 2, most languages provided corpora containing several thousand VMWEs, totalling 79,326 VMWEs across all languages. The smallest corpus is in English, containing around 7,437 sentences and 832 VMWEs, and the largest one is in Hungarian, with 7,760 VMWEs. All corpora, except the Arabic one, are available under different flavours of the Creative Common license.[14]

4.1 Format

Edition 1.1 of the shared task saw a major evolution of the data format, motivated by a quest for synergies between PARSEME (Savary et al., forthcoming) and Universal Dependencies (Nivre et al., 2016), two complementary multilingual initiatives aiming at unified terminologies and methodologies. The new format called `cupt`, combines in one file the `conllu` format[15] and the `parsemetsv` format[16], both used in the previous edition of this shared task.

```
# global.columns = ID FORM LEMMA UPOS XPOS FEATS HEAD DEPREL DEPS MISC PARSEME:MWE
# source_sent_id = . . corola-35693
# text = Lidia se stingea pe picioare.
1 Lidia    Lidia  NOUN   Ncfsry          Case=Acc|Definite=Def...    3 nsubj   _ _               *
2 se       sine   PRON   Px3-a———w       Case=Acc|Person=3l...       3 expl:pv _ _               1:IRV;2:VID
3 stingea  stinge VERB   Vmii3s          Mood=Ind|Number=Singl...    0 root    _ _               1;2
4 pe       pe     ADP    Spsa            AdpType=Prep|Case=Acc       5 case    _ _               2
5 picioare picior NOUN   Ncfp-n          Definite=Ind|Gender=Feml... 3 obl     _ SpaceAfter=No   2
6 .        .      PUNCT  PERIOD          _                           3 punct   _ _               *
```

Figure 2: First sentence of a corpus, with a nested VMWE, in the `cupt` format: RO *Lidia **se stingea pe picioare*** 'Lidia Refl.Cl.3.Sg.Acc. was_extinguishing on legs' ⇒ 'Lidia was going into decline'.

As seen in Fig. 2, each token in a sentence is now represented by 11 columns: the 10 columns compatible with the `conllu` specification (notably: rank, token, lemma, part-of-speech, morphological features, and syntactic dependencies), and the 11th column containing the VMWE annotations, according to the same conventions as `parsemetsv` but with the updated set of categories (cf. Sec. 3.2). Note the presence of an IRV (tokens 2–3) embedded in a VID (tokens 2–5). The underscore '_', when it occurs alone in a field, is reserved for underspecified annotations. It can be used in incomplete annotations or in blind versions of the annotated files. The star '*', when it occurs alone in a field, is reserved for empty annotations, which are different from underspecified. This concerns sporadic annotations, typical for VMWEs (where not necessarily all words receive an annotation, as opposed to e.g. part-of-speech tags).

Besides adding a new column to `conllu`, `cupt` also introduces additional conventions concerning comments (lines starting with '#'). The first line of each file must indicate the ordered list of columns (with standardized names) that this file contains, i.e. the same format can be used for any subset of standard columns, in any order. Each sentence is then preceded by the identifier of the source sentence (`source_sent_id`) which consists of three fields: (i) the persistent URI of the original corpus (e.g. of a UD treebank), (ii) the path of the source file in the original corpus, (iii) the sentence identifier, unique within the whole corpus. Items (i) and (ii) contain '.' if there is no external source corpus, as in the example of Figure 2. The following comment line contains the text of the current sentence. Validation scripts and converters were developed for `cupt`, and published before the shared task.

4.2 Inter-Annotator Agreement

Contrary to standard practice in corpus annotation, most corpora were not double-annotated due to lack of human resources. Nonetheless, each language team has double-annotated a sample containing at least 100 annotated VMWEs.[17] The number of sentences (S), number of VMWEs annotated by the first (A_1) and by the second annotator (A_2) are shown in Table 1. The last three columns report two measures to assess span agreement (tokens belonging to a VMWE) and one measure to assess the agreement on

---

[14]At `https://gitlab.com/parseme/sharedtask-data/tree/master/1.1`.

[15]`http://universaldependencies.org/format.html`

[16]`https://typo.uni-konstanz.de/parseme/index.php/2-general/184-parseme-shared-task-format-of-the-final-annotation`

[17]The Lithuanian team double-annotated a sample from the Lithuanian Treebank ALKSNIS.

	S	A_1	A_2	F_{span}	κ_{span}	κ_{cat}		S	A_1	A_2	F_{span}	κ_{span}	κ_{cat}
AR	200	205	207	0.961	0.923	1.000	**HI**	300	188	162	0.634	0.553	0.766
BG	1237	472	459	0.917	0.899	0.957	**HR**	272	270	204	0.515	0.359	0.792
DE	696	305	265	0.673	0.601	0.604	**HU**	308	274	329	0.892	0.831	1.000
EL	1617	428	462	0.694	0.665	0.673	**IT**	1000	341	379	0.586	0.550	0.882
EN	804	153	176	0.529	0.487	0.625	**LT**	2343	157	103	0.469	0.460	0.788
ES	1508	197	103	0.253	0.227	0.573	**PL**	2079	759	707	0.619	0.568	0.882
EU	871	327	355	0.859	0.820	0.859	**PT**	1000	275	241	0.713	0.684	0.837
FA	402	416	336	0.606	0.470	1.000	**RO**	2503	529	556	0.533	0.491	0.823
FR	803	329	363	0.766	0.729	0.960	**SL**	800	214	220	0.811	0.795	0.982
HE	1800	290	291	0.806	0.794	0.932	**TR**	187	154	150	0.987	0.984	0.955

Table 1: Per-language inter-annotator agreement on a sample of S sentences, with A_1 and A_2 VMWEs annotated by each annotator. F_{span} is the F-measure between annotators, κ_{span} is the agreement on the annotation span and κ_{cat} is the agreement on the VMWE category. EL, EN and HI provided corpora annotated by more than 2 annotators. We report the highest scores among all possible annotator pairs.

VMWE categories (Sec. 3.2). The F_{span} score is the MWE-based F-measure when considering that one of the annotators tries to predict the other one's annotations.[18] This is identical to the F1-MWE score used to evaluate participating systems (Sec. 6). F_{span} is an optimistic estimator which ignores chance agreement. On the other hand, κ_{span} and κ_{cat} estimate to what extent the observed agreement P_O exceeds the expected agreement P_E, that is, $\kappa = \frac{P_O - P_E}{1 - P_E}$.

Observed and expected agreement for κ_{span} are based on the number of verbs V in the sample, assuming that a simplification of the task consists of deciding whether each verb belongs to a VMWE or not.[19] If annotators perfectly agree on $A_{1=2}$ annotated VMWEs, then we estimate that they agree on $N = V - A_1 - A_2 + A_{1=2}$ verbs <u>not</u> belonging to a VMWE, so $P_O = \frac{A_{1=2} + N}{V}$ and $P_E = \frac{A_1}{V} \times \frac{A_2}{V}$. As for κ_{cat}, we consider only the $A_{1=2}$ VMWEs on which both annotators agree on the span, and calculate P_O and P_E based on the proportion of times both annotators agree on the VMWE's category label.

Inter-annotator agreement scores can give an idea of the quality of the guidelines and of the training procedures for annotators. We observe a high variability among languages, especially for determining the span of VMWEs, with κ_{span} ranging from 0.227 for Spanish to 0.984 for Turkish. Macro-averaged κ_{span} is 0.691, which is superior to the macro-averaged κ_{unit} reported in 2017, which was of 0.58 (Savary et al., 2017).[20] Categorization agreement results are much more homogeneous, with a macro-average κ_{cat} of 0.836, which is also slightly higher than the one obtained in 2017, which was of 0.819.

The variable agreement values observed could be explained by language and corpus characteristics (e.g. web texts are harder to annotate than newspapers). They could also be explained by the fact that the double-annotated samples are quite small. Finally, they could indicate that the guidelines are still vague and that annotators do not always receive appropriate training. In reality, probably a mixture of all these factors explains the low agreement observed for some languages. In short, Table 1 strongly suggests that there is still room for improvement in (a) guidelines, (b) annotator training, and (c) annotation team management, best practices, and methodology. It should also be noted that lower agreement values may correlate with the results obtained by participants: the lower the IAA for a given language (i.e. the more difficult the task is for humans), the lower the results of automatic MWE identification. Nevertheless, we believe that the systematic use of our in-house consistency checks tool helped homogenizing some of these annotation disagreements (Sec. 3.4).

5 Shared Task Organization

Each language in the shared task was handled by a team that was responsible for the choice of sub-corpora and for the annotation of VMWEs, in a similar setting as in the previous edition. For each

---

[18] Every annotator annotated at least one VMWE, as attested by A_1 and A_2.

[19] When no POS information was available (i.e. for AR), we approximated V as the number of sentences S, i.e. $V \approx S$.

[20] Notice that in 2017, the $V \approx S$ approximation was used for all languages, so both scores are not directly comparable.

language, we then split its corpus into training, test and development sets (train/test/dev), as follows:

- If the corpus has less than 550 VMWEs: Take sentences containing 90% of the VMWEs as test, and the other 10% as a small training corpus.
- If the corpus has between 550 and 1500 VMWEs: Take sentences containing 500 VMWEs as test, and take the rest for training.
- If the corpus has between 1,500 and 5,000 VMWEs: Take sentences containing 500 VMWEs as test, take sentences containing 500 VMWEs as dev, and take the rest for training.
- If the corpus has more than 5,000 VMWEs: Take sentences containing 10% of the VMWEs as test, take sentences containing 10% of the VMWEs as dev, and take the remaining 80% for training.

As in edition 1.0, participants could submit their systems to two tracks: open and closed. Systems in the closed track were only allowed to train their models on the train and dev files provided.

In this edition, we distinguished sentences based on their origin, so as to make sure that the fraction of each sub-corpus is the same in all splits for each language. For example, around 59% of all Basque sentences came from UD, while the other 41% came from the sub-corpus Elhuyar. We have made sure that similar percentages also applied to test/train/dev when taken in isolation. Due to this balancing act, for most languages, we could not keep the VMWEs in the same split as in edition 1.0.

6 Evaluation Measures

The goal of the evaluation measures is to represent the quality of system predictions when compared to the human-annotated gold standard for a given language. As in edition 1.0, we define two types of evaluation measures: a strict *per-VMWE* score (in which each VMWE in gold is either deemed predicted or not, in a binary fashion); and a fuzzy *per-token* score (which takes partial matches into account). For each of these two, we can calculate precision (P), recall (R) and F_1-scores (F).

Orthogonally to the type of measure, there is the choice of what subset of VMWEs to take into account from gold and system predictions. As in the previous edition, we calculate a general category-agnostic measure (both per-VMWE and per-token) based on the totality of VMWEs in both gold and system predictions — this measure only considers whether each VMWE has been properly predicted, regardless of category. We also calculate category-specific measures (both per-VMWE and per-token), where we consider only the subset of VMWEs associated with a given category.

We additionally consider the following phenomenon-specific measures, which focus on some of the challenging phenomena specifically relevant to MWEs (Constant et al., 2017):

- *MWE continuity*: We calculate per-VMWE scores for two different subsets: continuous e.g. [TR] *is-tifa edecek* 'resignation will-do'⇒'he/she will resign', and discontinuous VMWEs e.g. [SL] *imajo investicijske načrte* 'they-have investment plans'⇒'they have investment plans'.
- *MWE length*: We calculate per-VMWE scores for two different subsets: single-token, e.g. [DE] *an-fangen* 'at-catch'⇒'begin', [ES] *abstenerse* 'abstain-REFL'⇒'abstain', and multi-token VMWEs e.g. [FA] چشم انداختن 'eye throw'⇒'to look at'.
- *MWE novelty*: We calculate per-VMWE scores for two subsets: seen and unseen VMWEs. We consider a VMWE in the (gold or prediction) test corpus as seen if a VMWE with the same multiset of lemmas is annotated at least once in the training corpus. Other VMWEs are deemed unseen. For instance, given the occurrence of [EN] *has a new look* in the training corpus, the occurrence of [EN] *had a look* of innocence and of [EN] *having a look* at this report in the test corpus would be considered seen and unseen, respectively.
- *MWE variability*: We calculate per-VMWE scores for the subset of VMWEs that are variants of VMWEs from the training corpus. A VMWE is considered a variant if: (i) it is deemed as a seen VMWE, as defined above, and (2) it is not identical to another VMWE, i.e. the training corpus does not contain the sequence of surface-form tokens as seen in this VMWE (including non-lexicalized components in between, in the case of discontinuous VMWEs). E.g., [BG] накриво ли беше стъпил is a variant of стъпя накриво 'to step to the side'⇒'to lose (one's) footing'.

Systems may predict VMWEs for all languages in the shared task, and the aforementioned measures are independently calculated for each language. Additionally, we calculate a macro-average score based on all of the predictions. In this case, the precision P for a given measure (e.g. for continuous VMWEs) is the average of the precisions for all 19 languages. Arabic is not considered due to delays in the corpus release. Missing system predictions are assumed to have P = R = 0. The recall R is averaged in the same manner, and the average F score is calculated from these averaged P and R scores.

7 System Results

For the 2018 edition of the PARSEME Shared Task, 12 teams submitted 17 system results: 13 to the closed track and 4 to the open track. No team submitted system results for all 20 languages of the shared task, but 11 teams covered 19 languages (all except Arabic). Detailed result tables are reported on the shared task website.[21] In the tables, systems are referred to by anonymous nicknames. System authors and their affiliations are available in the system description papers published in these proceedings.

Most of the systems (Deep-BGT, GBD-NER-standard, GBD-NER-resplit, mumpitz, mumpitz-preinit, SHOMA, TRAPACC, TRAPACC-S and Veyn) exploited neural networks. Syntactic trees and parsing methods were employed in other systems (Milos, MWETreeC and TRAVERSAL) while CRF-DepTree-categ and CRF-Seq-noncateg are based on a tree-structured CRF. Polirem-basic and Polirem-rich use statistical methods and association measures whereas varIDE relies on a Naive Bayes classifier.

As for the best performing systems, TRAPACC and TRAVERSAL were ranked first for 8 languages and 7 language, respectively. TRAVERSAL is more effective in Slavic and Romance languages, whereas TRAPACC works well for German and English. In the "Other" language group, GDB-NER achieved the best results for Farsi and Turkish, and CRF approaches proved to be the best for Hindi. The best results for Bulgarian were obtained by varIDE, based on a Naive Bayes classifier.

Results per language show that, Hungarian and Romanian were the "easiest" languages for the systems, with best MWE-based F-scores of 90.31 and 85.28, respectively. Hebrew, English and Lithuanian show the lowest MWE-based F-scores, not exceeding 23.28, 32.88 and 32.17, respectively. This is likely due to the amount of annotated training data: Hungarian had the highest, whikle English and Lithuanian the lowest, number of VMWEs in the training data. A notable exception to this tendency is Hindi, where good results (an F-score of 72.98) could be achieved building on a small amount of training data. This is probably due to the high number of multi-verb constructions (MVCs) in Hindi, which are usually formed by a sequence of two verbs, hence relatively easily identified by relying on POS tags.

Table 12 shows the effectiveness of MWE identification with regard to MWE categories. The highest F-scores were achieved for IRVs (especially for Balto-Slavic languages). This might be due to the fact that the IRVs tend to be continuous and must contain a reflexive pronoun/clitic, therefore the presence of such a pronoun in the immediate neighborhood of a verb is a strong predictor for IRVs. The LVC.full category is present in all languages. Interestingly, they are most effectively identified in the "Other" language group. Idioms occur in the test corpora of almost all languages (except Farsi), and they can be identified to the greatest extent in Romance languages. VPCs seem to be the easiest to find in Hungarian.

In regards to phenomenon-specific macro-average results (Tables 4 to 11), let us have a closer look at the F_1-MWE measure of the 11 systems which submitted results to all 19 languages, except MWE-TreeC (whose results are hard to interpret). The differences are: (i) from 13 to 28 points (17 points on average) for continuous vs. discontinuous VMWEs, (ii) from 14 to 43 points (27 points on average) for multitoken vs. single-token VMWEs, (iii) from 45 to 56 points (50 points on average) for seen-in-train vs. unseen-in-train VMWEs, and (iv) from 13 to 27 points (20 points on average) for identical-to-train vs. variant-of-train VMWEs. These results confirm that the phenomena they focus on are major challenges in the VMWE identification task, and we suggest that the corresponding measures should be systematically used for future evaluation. The hardest challenge is the one of identifying unseen-in-train VMWEs. This result is not a suprise since MWE-hood is, by nature, a lexical phenomenon, that is, a particular idiomatic reading is available only in presence of a combination of particular lexical units. Replacing one of them by a semantically close lexeme usually leads to the loss of idiomatic reading, e.g. **force** one's **hand** 'compel someone to act against her will' is an idiom, while *force one's arm* can only be understood literally. Few other, non-lexical, hints are given to distinguish a particular VMWE

---

[21] http://multiword.sourceforge.net/sharedtaskresults2018

occurrence from a literal expression, because a VMWE usually takes syntactically regular forms. Morphosyntactic idiosyncrasy (e.g. the fact that a given VMWE allows some and blocks some other regular syntactic transformations) is a property of types rather than tokens. We expect, therefore, satisfactory unseen-in-train VMWE identification results mostly from systems using large-scale VMWE lexicons or semi/unsupervised methods and very large corpora.

8 Conclusions and Future Work

We reported on edition 1.1 of the PARSEME Shared Task aiming at identifying verbal MWEs in texts in 20 languages. We described our corpus annotation methodology, the data provided to the participants, the shared task modalities and evaluation measures. The official results of the shared task were also presented and briefly discussed. The outputs of individual systems[22] should be compared more thoroughly in the future, so as to see how systems with different architectures cope with different phenomena. For instance, it would be interesting to check if, as expected, discontinuous VMWEs are handled better by parsing-based methods vs. sequential taggers, or by LSTMs vs. other neural network architectures.

Compared to the first edition in 2017, we attracted a larger number of participants (17 vs. 7), with 11 of the submissions covering 19 languages. We expect that this growing interest in modeling and computational treatment of verbal MWEs will motivate teams working on corpus annotation, especially from new language families, to join the initiative. We expect to maintain and continuously increase the quality and the size of the existing annotated corpora. For instance, we have identified weaknesses in the guidelines for MVCs that will require enhancements. Furthermore, we need to collect feedback about the IAV experimental category, and decide whether we consolidate its annotation guidelines.

Our ambitious goal for a future shared task is to extend annotation to other MWE categories, not only verbal ones. We are aware of corpora and guidelines for individual languages (e.g. English or French) and/or MWE categories (e.g. noun-noun compounds). However, a considerable effort will be required to design and apply universal annotation guidelines for the annotation of new MWE categories. We strongly believe that the large community and collective expertise gathered in the PARSEME initiative will allow us to take on this challenge. We definitely hope that this initiative will continue in the next years, yielding available multilingual annotated corpora that can foster MWE research in computational linguistics, as well as in linguistics and translation studies.

Acknowledgments

This work was supported by the IC1207 PARSEME COST action[23], and national funded projects: LD-PARSEME[24] (LD14117) in the Czech Republic, and PARSEME-FR[25] (ANR-14-CERA-0001) in France. Carla Parra Escartín is funded by the European Union's Horizon 2020 programme under the Marie Skłodowska-Curie grant agreement No 713567, and Science Foundation Ireland in the ADAPT Centre (Grant 13/RC/2106) at Dublin City University. Behrang QasemiZadeh and Timm Lichte are funded by the Deutsche Forschungsgemeinschaft (DFG) within the CRC 991 "The Structure of Representations in Language, Cognition, and Science". Veronika Vincze was supported by the UNKP-17-4 New National Excellence Program of the Ministry of Human Capacities, Hungary. The Slovenian team was supported by the Slovenian Research Agency via New grammar of contemporary standard Slovene: sources and methods (J6-8256 project). Ashwini Vaidya was supported by the DST-CSRI (Dept of Science and Technology, Govt. of India, Cognitive Science Research Initiative) fellowship. The Turkish team was supported by Boğaziçi University Research Fund Grant Number 14420. We are grateful to Maarten van Gompel for his help with adapting the FLAT annotation platform to our needs. Our thanks go also to all language leaders (LLs) and annotators, listed in Appendix A, for their their feedback on the annotation guidelines and preparing the annotated corpora.

---

[22] Available at `https://gitlab.com/parseme/sharedtask-data/tree/master/1.1/system-results`.

[23] `http://www.parseme.eu`

[24] https://ufal.mff.cuni.cz/grants/ld-parseme

[25] `http://parsemefr.lif.univ-mrs.fr/`

References

Hazem Al Saied, Matthieu Constant, and Marie Candito. 2017. The ATILF-LLF system for Parseme shared task: a transition-based verbal multiword expression tagger. In *Proceedings of the 13th Workshop on Multiword Expressions (MWE 2017)*, pages 127–132, Valencia, Spain, April. Association for Computational Linguistics.

Maria Jesús Aranzabe, Aitziber Atutxa, Kepa Bengoetxea, Arantza Diaz de Ilarraza, Iakes Goenaga, Koldo Gojenola, and Larraitz Uria. 2015. Automatic conversion of the Basque dependency treebank to Universal Dependencies. In Markus Dickinsons, Erhard Hinrichs, Agnieszka Patejuk, and Adam Przepiórkowski, editors, *Proceedings of the Fourteenth International Workshop on Treebanks an Linguistic Theories (TLT14)*, pages 233–241. Warszawa, Poland. Institute of Computer Science of the Polish Academy of Sciences.

Špela Arhar Holdt, Vojko Gorjanc, and Simon Krek. 2007. FidaPLUS corpus of Slovenian: the new generation of the Slovenian reference corpus: its design and tools. In *Proceedings of the Corpus Linguistics Conference, CL2007*, Birmingham.

Timothy Baldwin and Su Nam Kim. 2010. Multiword expressions. In Nitin Indurkhya and Fred J. Damerau, editors, *Handbook of Natural Language Processing, Second Edition*, pages 267–292. CRC Press, Taylor and Francis Group, Boca Raton, FL. ISBN 978-1420085921.

Riyaz Ahmad Bhat, Rajesh Bhatt, Annahita Farudi, Prescott Klassen, Bhuvana Narasimhan, Martha Palmer, Owen Rambow, Dipti Misra Sharma, Ashwini Vaidya, Sri Ramagurumurthy Vishnu, and Fei Xia, 2015. *The Hindi/Urdu Treebank Project*. Springer Press.

Ondrej Bojar, Rajen Chatterjee, Christian Federmann, Yvette Graham, Barry Haddow, Matthias Huck, Antonio Jimeno Yepes, Philipp Koehn, Varvara Logacheva, Christof Monz, Matteo Negri, Aurelie Neveol, Mariana Neves, Martin Popel, Matt Post, Raphael Rubino, Carolina Scarton, Lucia Specia, Marco Turchi, Karin Verspoor, and Marcos Zampieri. 2016. Findings of the 2016 Conference on Machine Translation (WMT16). In *Proceedings of the First Conference on Machine Translation (WMT16), Volume 2: Shared Task Papers*, pages 131–198.

Tiberiu Boroş, Sonia Pipa, Verginica Barbu Mititelu, and Dan Tufiş. 2017. A data-driven approach to verbal multiword expression detection. PARSEME Shared Task system description paper. In *Proceedings of the 13th Workshop on Multiword Expressions (MWE 2017)*, pages 121–126, Valencia, Spain, April. Association for Computational Linguistics.

Marie Candito and Matthieu Constant. 2014. Strategies for contiguous multiword expression analysis and dependency parsing. In *Proceedings of the 52nd Annual Meeting of the Association for Computational Linguistics (Volume 1: Long Papers)*, pages 743–753, Baltimore, Maryland, June. Association for Computational Linguistics.

Marie Candito and Djamé Seddah. 2012. Le corpus sequoia : annotation syntaxique et exploitation pour l'adaptation d'analyseur par pont lexical. In *Proceedings of TALN 2012 (in French)*, Grenoble, France, June.

Matthieu Constant and Joakim Nivre. 2016. A transition-based system for joint lexical and syntactic analysis. In *Proceedings of the 54th Annual Meeting of the Association for Computational Linguistics (Volume 1: Long Papers)*, pages 161–171, Berlin, Germany, August. Association for Computational Linguistics.

Mathieu Constant, Gülşen Eryiğit, Johanna Monti, Lonneke van der Plas, Carlos Ramisch, Michael Rosner, and Amalia Todirascu. 2017. Multiword expression processing: A survey. *Computational Linguistics*, 43(4):837–892.

Dóra Csendes, János Csirik, Tibor Gyimóthy, and András Kocsor. 2005. The Szeged TreeBank. In Václav Matousek, Pavel Mautner, and Tomás Pavelka, editors, *Proceedings of the 8th International Conference on Text, Speech and Dialogue, TSD 2005*, Lecture Notes in Computer Science, pages 123–132, Berlin / Heidelberg, September. Springer.

Jenny Rose Finkel and Christopher D. Manning. 2009. Joint parsing and named entity recognition. In *HLT-NAACL*, pages 326–334. The Association for Computational Linguistics.

Spence Green, Marie-Catherine de Marneffe, John Bauer, and Christopher D. Manning. 2011. Multiword expression identification with tree substitution grammars: A parsing tour de force with French. In *Proceedings of the 2011 Conference on Empirical Methods in Natural Language Processing*, pages 725–735, Edinburgh, Scotland, UK., July. Association for Computational Linguistics.

Spence Green, Marie-Catherine de Marneffe, and Christopher D. Manning. 2013. Parsing models for identifying multiword expressions. *Computational Linguistics*, 39(1):195–227.

Natalia Klyueva, Antoine Doucet, and Milan Straka. 2017. Neural networks for multi-word expression detection. In *Proceedings of the 13th Workshop on Multiword Expressions (MWE 2017)*, pages 60–65, Valencia, Spain, April. Association for Computational Linguistics.

Svetla Koeva, Ivelina Stoyanova, Svetlozara Leseva, Rositsa Dekova, Tsvetana Dimitrova, and Ekaterina Tarpomanova. 2012. The Bulgarian National Corpus: Theory and practice in corpus design. *Journal of Language Modelling*, 0(1):65–110.

Simon Krek, Kaja Dobrovoljc, Tomaž Erjavec, Sara Može, Nina Ledinek, Nanika Holz, Katja Zupan, Polona Gantar, and Taja Kuzman. 2017. Training corpus ssj500k 2.0. Slovenian language resource repository CLARIN.SI, http://hdl.handle.net/11356/1165.

Joseph Le Roux, Antoine Rozenknop, and Matthieu Constant. 2014. Syntactic parsing and compound recognition via dual decomposition: Application to French. In *Proceedings of COLING 2014, the 25th International Conference on Computational Linguistics: Technical Papers*, pages 1875–1885, Dublin, Ireland, August. Dublin City University and Association for Computational Linguistics.

Verena Lyding, Egon Stemle, Claudia Borghetti, Marco Brunello, Sara Castagnoli, Felice Dell'Orletta, Henrik Dittmann, Alessandro Lenci, and Vito Pirrelli. 2014. The PAISÀ Corpus of Italian Web Texts. In *Proceedings of the 9th Web as Corpus Workshop (WaC-9)*, pages 36–43, Gothenburg, Sweden, April. Association for Computational Linguistics.

Alfredo Maldonado, Lifeng Han, Erwan Moreau, Ashjan Alsulaimani, Koel Dutta Chowdhury, Carl Vogel, and Qun Liu. 2017. Detection of verbal multi-word expressions via conditional random fields with syntactic dependency features and semantic re-ranking. In *Proceedings of the 13th Workshop on Multiword Expressions (MWE 2017)*, pages 114–120, Valencia, Spain, April. Association for Computational Linguistics.

Ryan McDonald, Joakim Nivre, Yvonne Quirmbach-Brundage, Yoav Goldberg, Dipanjan Das, Kuzman Ganchev, Keith Hall, Slav Petrov, Hao Zhang, Oscar Täckström, Claudia Bedini, Núria Bertomeu Castelló, and Jungmee Lee. 2013. Universal dependency annotation for multilingual parsing. In *Proceedings of the 51st Annual Meeting of the Association for Computational Linguistics (Volume 2: Short Papers)*, pages 92–97, Sofia, Bulgaria, August. Association for Computational Linguistics.

Alexis Nasr, Carlos Ramisch, José Deulofeu, and André Valli. 2015. Joint dependency parsing and multiword expression tokenization. In *Proceedings of the 53rd Annual Meeting of the Association for Computational Linguistics and the 7th International Joint Conference on Natural Language Processing (Volume 1: Long Papers)*, pages 1116–1126, Beijing, China, July. Association for Computational Linguistics.

Luka Nerima, Vasiliki Foufi, and Eric Wehrli. 2017. Parsing and MWE detection: Fips at the PARSEME shared task. In *Proceedings of the 13th Workshop on Multiword Expressions (MWE 2017)*, pages 54–59, Valencia, Spain, April. Association for Computational Linguistics.

Joakim Nivre, Marie-Catherine de Marneffe, Filip Ginter, Yoav Goldberg, Jan Hajič, Christopher D. Manning, Ryan McDonald, Slav Petrov, Sampo Pyysalo, Natalia Silveira, Reut Tsarfaty, and Daniel Zeman. 2016. Universal Dependencies v1: a multilingual treebank collection. In Nicoletta Calzolari, Khalid Choukri, Thierry Declerck, Marko Grobelnik, Bente Maegaard, Joseph Mariani, Asuncion Moreno, Jan Odijk, and Stelios Piperidis, editors, *Proceedings of the Tenth International Conference on Language Resources and Evaluation*, pages 1659–1666, Portorož, Slovenia, May.

Maciej Ogrodniczuk, Katarzyna Głowińska, Mateusz Kopeć, Agata Savary, and Magdalena Zawisławska. 2015. *Coreference in Polish: Annotation, Resolution and Evaluation*. Walter De Gruyter.

Adam Przepiórkowski, Mirosław Bańko, Rafał L. Górski, Barbara Lewandowska-Tomaszczyk, Marek Łaziński, and Piotr Pęzik. 2011. National Corpus of Polish. In Zygmunt Vetulani, editor, *Proceedings of the 5th Language & Technology Conference: Human Language Technologies as a Challenge for Computer Science and Linguistics*, pages 259–263, Poznań, Poland.

Behrang QasemiZadeh and Saeed Rahimi. 2006. Persian in MULTEXT-East framework. In Tapio Salakoski, Filip Ginter, Sampo Pyysalo, and Tapio Pahikkala, editors, *Advances in Natural Language Processing*, pages 541–551, Berlin, Heidelberg. Springer Berlin Heidelberg.

Victoria Rosén, Gyri Smørdal Losnegaard, Koenraad De Smedt, Eduard Bejček, Agata Savary, Adam Przepiórkowski, Petya Osenova, and Verginica Barbu Mitetelu. 2015. A survey of multiword expressions in treebanks. In *Proceedings of the 14th International Workshop on Treebanks & Linguistic Theories conference*, Warsaw, Poland, December.

Ivan A. Sag, Timothy Baldwin, Francis Bond, Ann Copestake, and Dan Flickinger. 2002. Multiword Expressions: A Pain in the Neck for NLP. In *Proceedings of the 3rd International Conference on Intelligent Text Processing and Computational Linguistics (CICLing-2002)*, pages 1–15, Mexico City, Mexico.

Agata Savary, Manfred Sailer, Yannick Parmentier, Michael Rosner, Victoria Rosén, Adam Przepiórkowski, Cvetana Krstev, Veronika Vincze, Beata Wójtowicz, Gyri Smørdal Losnegaard, Carla Parra Escartín, Jakub Waszczuk, Matthieu Constant, Petya Osenova, and Federico Sangati. 2015. PARSEME – PARSing and Multiword Expressions within a European multilingual network. In *7th Language & Technology Conference: Human Language Technologies as a Challenge for Computer Science and Linguistics (LTC 2015)*, Poznań, Poland, November.

Agata Savary, Carlos Ramisch, Silvio Cordeiro, Federico Sangati, Veronika Vincze, Behrang QasemiZadeh, Marie Candito, Fabienne Cap, Voula Giouli, Ivelina Stoyanova, and Antoine Doucet. 2017. The PARSEME shared task on automatic identification of verbal multiword expressions. In *Proceedings of the 13th Workshop on Multiword Expressions (MWE 2017)*, pages 31–47, Valencia, Spain, April. Association for Computational Linguistics.

Agata Savary, Marie Candito, Verginica Barbu Mititelu, Eduard Bejček, Fabienne Cap, Slavomír Čéplö, Silvio Ricardo Cordeiro, Gülşen Eryiğit, Voula Giouli, Maarten van Gompel, Yaakov HaCohen-Kerner, Jolanta Kovalevskaitė, Simon Krek, Chaya Liebes kind, Johanna Monti, Carla Parra Escartín, Lonneke van der Plas, Behrang QasemiZadeh, Carlos Ramisch, Federico Sangati, Ivelina Stoyanova, and Veronika Vincze. forthcoming. PARSEME multilingual corpus of verbal multiword expressions. In Stella Markantonatou, Carlos Ramisch, Agata Savary, and Veronika Vincze, editors, *Multiword expressions at length and in depth. Extended papers from the MWE 2017 workshop*. Language Science Press, Berlin, Germany.

Nathan Schneider, Dirk Hovy, Anders Johannsen, and Marine Carpuat. 2016. SemEval-2016 Task 10: Detecting Minimal Semantic Units and their Meanings (DiMSUM). In *Proceedings of the 10th International Workshop on Semantic Evaluation (SemEval-2016)*, pages 546–559, San Diego, California, June. Association for Computational Linguistics.

Katalin Ilona Simkó, Viktória Kovács, and Veronika Vincze. 2017. USzeged: Identifying verbal multiword expressions with POS tagging and parsing techniques. In *Proceedings of the 13th Workshop on Multiword Expressions (MWE 2017)*, pages 48–53, Valencia, Spain, April. Association for Computational Linguistics.

Mariona Taulé, Aina Peris, and Horacio Rodríguez. 2016. Iarg-AnCora: Spanish corpus annotated with implicit arguments. *Language Resources and Evaluation*, 50(3):549–584, Sep.

Veronika Vincze, János Zsibrita, and István Nagy T. 2013. Dependency parsing for identifying Hungarian light verb constructions. In *Proceedings of the Sixth International Joint Conference on Natural Language Processing*, pages 207–215, Nagoya, Japan, October. Asian Federation of Natural Language Processing.

Jakub Waszczuk, Agata Savary, and Yannick Parmentier. 2016. Promoting multiword expressions in A* TAG parsing. In Nicoletta Calzolari, Yuji Matsumoto, and Rashmi Prasad, editors, *COLING 2016, 26th International Conference on Computational Linguistics, Proceedings of the Conference: Technical Papers, December 11-16, 2016, Osaka, Japan*, pages 429–439. ACL.

Eric Wehrli, Violeta Seretan, and Luka Nerima. 2010. Sentence analysis and collocation identification. In *Proceedings of the Workshop on Multiword Expressions: from Theory to Applications (MWE 2010)*, pages 27–35, Beijing, China, August. Association for Computational Linguistics.

Eric Wehrli. 2014. The relevance of collocations for parsing. In *Proceedings of the 10th Workshop on Multiword Expressions (MWE)*, pages 26–32, Gothenburg, Sweden, April. Association for Computational Linguistics.

Appendix A: Composition of the corpus anotation teams

Balto-Slavic languages: (BG) Ivelina Stoyanova (LL), Tsvetana Dimitrova, Svetlozara Leseva, Valentina Stefanova, Maria Todorova; (HR) Maja Buljan (LL), Goranka Blagus, Ivo-Pavao Jazbec, Kristina Kocijan, Nikola Ljubešić, Ivana Matas, Jan Šnajder; (LT) Jolanta Kovalevskaitė (LL), Agnė Bielinskienė, Loic Boizou; (PL) Agata Savary (LL), Emilia Palka-Binkiewicz; (SL): Polona Gantar (LL), Simon Krek (LL), Špela Arhar Holdt, Jaka Čibej, Teja Kavčič, Taja Kuzman.

Germanic languages: (DE) Timm Lichte (LL), Rafael Ehren; (EN) Abigail Walsh (LL), Claire Bonial, Paul Cook, Kristina Geeraert, John McCrae, Nathan Schneider, Clarissa Somers.

Romance languages: (ES) Carla Parra Escartín (LL), Cristina Aceta, Héctor Martínez Alonso; (FR) Marie Candito (LL), Matthieu Constant, Carlos Ramisch, Caroline Pasquer, Yannick Parmentier, Jean-Yves Antoine, Agata Savary; (IT) Johanna Monti (LL), Valeria Caruso, Maria Pia di Buono, Antonio Pascucci, Annalisa Raffone, Anna Riccio; (RO) Verginica Barbu Mititelu (LL), Mihaela Onofrei, Mihaela Ionescu; (PT) Renata Ramisch (LL), Aline Villavicencio, Carlos Ramisch, Helena de Medeiros Caseli, Leonardo Zilio, Silvio Ricardo Cordeiro.

Other languages: (AR) Abdelati Hawwari (LL), Mona Diab, Mohamed Elbadrashiny, Rehab Ibrahim; (EU) Uxoa Inurrieta (LL), Itziar Aduriz, Ainara Estarrona, Itziar Gonzalez, Antton Gurrutxaga, Ruben Urizar; (EL) Voula Giouli (LL), Vassiliki Foufi, Aggeliki Fotopoulou, Stella Markantonatou, Stella Papadelli; (FA) Behrang QasemiZadeh (LL), Shiva Taslimipoor; (HE) Chaya Liebeskind (LL), Yaakov Ha-Cohen Kerner (LL), Hevi Elyovich, Ruth Malka; (HI) Archna Bhatia (LL), Ashwini Vaidya (LL), Kanishka Jain, Vandana Puri, Shraddha Ratori, Vishakha Shukla, Shubham Srivastava; (HU) Veronika Vincze (LL), Katalin Simkó, Viktória Kovács; (TR) Tunga Güngör (LL), Gözde Berk, Berna Erden.

Appendix B: Shared task results

Lang-split	Sent.	Tok.	Sent. length	VMWE	VID	IRV	LVC full	LVC cause	VPC full	VPC semi	IAV	MVC ICV	LS
AR-train	2370	231030	97.4	3219	1272	17	940	0	957	0	0	33	0
AR-dev	387	16252	41.9	500	17	0	419	0	64	0	0	0	0
AR-test	380	17962	47.2	500	31	0	410	0	59	0	0	0	0
AR-Total	3137	265244	84.5	4219	1320	17	1769	0	1080	0	0	33	
BG-train	17813	399173	22.4	5364	1005	2729	1421	135	0	0	74	0	0
BG-dev	1954	42020	21.5	670	173	240	214	35	0	0	8	0	0
BG-test	1832	39220	21.4	670	82	254	274	52	0	0	8	0	0
BG-Total	21599	480413	22.2	6704	1260	3240	1909	222	0	0	90	0	0
DE-train	6734	130588	19.3	2820	977	220	218	28	1264	113	0	0	0
DE-dev	1184	22146	18.7	503	181	48	34	2	221	17	0	0	0
DE-test	1078	20559	19	500	183	40	42	2	210	23	0	0	0
DE-Total	8996	173293	19.2	3823	1341	3548	294	32	1695	153	0	0	0
EL-train	4427	122458	27.6	1404	395	0	938	44	19	0	0	8	0
EL-dev	2562	66431	25.9	500	81	0	376	34	8	0	0	1	0
EL-test	1261	35873	28.4	501	169	0	308	11	11	0	0	2	0
EL-Total	8250	224762	27.2	2405	645	3548	1622	89	38	0	0	11	0
EN-train	3471	53201	15.3	331	60	0	78	7	151	19	16	0	0
EN-test	3965	71002	17.9	501	79	0	166	36	146	26	44	4	0
EN-Total	7436	124203	16.7	832	139	3548	244	43	297	45	60	4	0
ES-train	2771	96521	34.8	1739	167	479	223	36	0	0	360	474	0
ES-dev	698	26220	37.5	500	65	114	84	17	0	0	87	133	0
ES-test	2046	59623	29.1	500	95	121	85	28	1	0	64	106	0
ES-Total	5515	182364	33	2739	327	4262	392	81	1	0	511	713	0
EU-train	8254	117165	14.1	2823	597	0	2074	152	0	0	0	0	0
EU-dev	1500	21604	14.4	500	104	0	382	14	0	0	0	0	0
EU-test	1404	19038	13.5	500	73	0	410	17	0	0	0	0	0
EU-Total	11158	157807	14.1	3823	774	4262	2866	183	0	0	0	0	0
FA-train	2784	45153	16.2	2451	17	1	2433	0	0	0	0	0	0
FA-dev	474	8923	18.8	501	0	0	501	0	0	0	0	0	0
FA-test	359	7492	20.8	501	0	0	501	0	0	0	0	0	0
FA-Total	3617	61568	17	3453	17	4263	3435	0	0	0	0	0	0

Continued on next page.

Lang-split	Sent.	Tok.	Sent. length	VMWE	VID	IRV full	LVC cause	LVC full	VPC semi	VPC	IAV	MVC ICV	LS
FR-train	17225	432389	25.1	4550	1746	1247	1470	68	0	0	0	19	0
FR-dev	2236	56254	25.1	629	207	154	252	15	0	0	0	1	0
FR-test	1606	39489	24.5	498	212	108	160	14	0	0	0	4	0
FR-Total	21067	528132	25	5677	2165	5772	1882	97	0	0	0	24	0
HE-train	12106	237472	19.6	1236	519	0	545	113	59	0	0	0	0
HE-dev	3385	65843	19.4	501	258	0	148	61	34	0	0	0	0
HE-test	3209	65698	20.4	502	182	0	211	49	60	0	0	0	0
HE-Total	18700	369013	19.7	2239	959	5772	904	223	153	0	0	0	0
HI-train	856	17850	20.8	534	23	0	321	14	0	0	0	176	0
HI-test	828	17580	21.2	500	38	0	320	12	0	0	0	130	0
HI-Total	1684	35430	21	1034	61	5772	641	26	0	0	0	306	0
HR-train	2295	53486	23.3	1450	113	468	303	45	0	0	521	0	0
HR-dev	834	19621	23.5	500	34	139	143	26	1	0	157	0	0
HR-test	708	16429	23.2	501	33	118	131	31	0	0	188	0	0
HR-Total	3837	89536	23.3	2451	180	6497	577	102	1	0	866	0	0
HU-train	4803	120013	24.9	6205	84	0	892	363	4131	735	0	0	0
HU-dev	601	15564	25.8	779	10	0	85	10	539	135	0	0	0
HU-test	755	20759	27.4	776	10	0	166	28	486	86	0	0	0
HU-Total	6159	156336	25.3	7760	104	6497	1143	401	5156	956	0	0	0
IT-train	13555	360883	26.6	3254	1098	942	544	147	66	0	414	23	20
IT-dev	917	32613	35.5	500	197	106	100	19	17	2	44	6	9
IT-test	1256	37293	29.6	503	201	96	104	25	23	0	41	5	8
IT-Total	15728	430789	27.3	4257	1496	7641	748	191	106	2	499	34	37
LT-train	4895	90110	18.4	312	106	0	195	11	0	0	0	0	0
LT-test	6209	118402	19	500	202	0	284	14	0	0	0	0	0
LT-Total	11104	208512	18.7	812	308	7641	479	25	0	0	0	0	0
PL-train	13058	220465	16.8	4122	373	1785	1531	180	0	0	253	0	0
PL-dev	1763	26030	14.7	515	57	245	153	33	0	0	27	0	0
PL-test	1300	27823	21.4	515	73	249	149	15	0	0	29	0	0
PL-Total	16121	274318	17	5152	503	9920	1833	228	0	0	309	0	0
PT-train	22017	506773	23	4430	882	689	2775	84	0	0	0	0	0
PT-dev	3117	68581	22	553	130	83	337	3	0	0	0	0	0
PT-test	2770	62648	22.6	553	118	91	337	7	0	0	0	0	0
PT-Total	27904	638002	22.8	5536	1130	10783	3449	94	0	0	0	0	0
RO-train	42704	781968	18.3	4713	1269	3048	250	146	0	0	0	0	0
RO-dev	7065	118658	16.7	589	169	373	29	18	0	0	0	0	0
RO-test	6934	114997	16.5	589	173	363	34	19	0	0	0	0	0
RO-Total	56703	1015623	17.9	5891	1611	14567	313	183	0	0	0	0	0
SL-train	9567	201853	21	2378	500	1162	176	40	0	0	500	0	0
SL-dev	1950	38146	19.5	500	121	224	30	12	0	0	113	0	0
SL-test	1994	40523	20.3	500	106	245	35	13	0	0	101	0	0
SL-Total	13511	280522	20.7	3378	727	16198	241	65	0	0	714	0	0
TR-train	16715	334880	20	6125	3172	0	2952	0	0	0	0	1	0
TR-dev	1320	27196	20.6	510	285	0	225	0	0	0	0	0	0
TR-test	577	14388	24.9	506	233	0	272	0	0	0	0	1	0
TR-Total	18612	376464	20.2	7141	3690	16198	3449	0	0	0	0	2	0
Total	280838	6072331	21.6	79326	18757	16198	28190	2285	8527	1156	3049	1127	37

Table 2: Statistics on the training (train), development (dev), and test corpora. Number of sentences (Sent.), number of tokens (Tok.), average sentence length in number of tokens (Sent. length), total number of annotated VMWEs (VMWE), and number of annotated VMWEs broken down by category (VID, IRV, ...)

System	Track	#Langs	P MWE	R MWE	F1 MWE	Rank MWE	P Tok	R Tok	F1 Tok	Rank Tok
TRAVERSAL	closed	19/19	67.58	44.97	54	1	77.41	48.55	59.67	1
TRAPACC_S	closed	19/19	62.28	41.4	49.74	2	68.54	42.06	52.13	4
TRAPACC	closed	19/19	55.68	44.67	49.57	3	62.1	46.37	53.09	3
CRF-Seq-nocategs	closed	19/19	56.13	39.12	46.11	4	73.44	43.49	54.63	2
varIDE	closed	19/19	61.49	36.71	45.97	5	64.13	37.63	47.43	6
CRF-DepTree-categs	closed	19/19	52.33	37.83	43.91	6	64.65	41.56	50.6	5
GBD-NER-standard	closed	19/19	36.56	48.3	41.62	7	41.11	52.21	46	7
GBD-NER-resplit	closed	19/19	30.26	52.95	38.51	8	33.83	58.03	42.74	9
Veyn	closed	19/19	42.76	32.51	36.94	9	58.13	36.57	44.9	8
mumpitz	closed	7/19	17.14	13.03	14.81	10	24.95	15.5	19.12	11
Polirem-rich	closed	3/19	10.9	2.87	4.54	11	13.07	3.89	6	12
Polirem-basic	closed	3/19	10.78	0.65	1.23	12	11.33	0.68	1.28	13
MWETreeC	closed	19/19	0.21	3.72	0.4	13	23.5	24.78	24.12	10
SHOMA	open	19/19	66.08	51.82	58.09	1	76.22	54.27	63.4	1
Deep-BGT	open	10/19	33.41	25.29	28.79	2	39.77	26.47	31.78	2
Milos	open	4/19	9.17	7.87	8.47	3	11.5	8.25	9.61	3
mumpitz-preinit	open	1/19	2.28	1.9	2.07	4	3.71	2.35	2.88	4

Table 3: General results.

System	Track	#Langs	P-MWE	R-MWE	F1-MWE	Rank-MWE
TRAVERSAL	closed	19/19	68.19	49.78	57.55	1
TRAPACC_S	closed	19/19	65.12	48.18	55.38	2
TRAPACC	closed	19/19	59.09	51.99	55.31	3
CRF-Seq-nocategs	closed	19/19	54.99	49.84	52.29	4
varIDE	closed	19/19	78.03	37.98	51.09	5
CRF-DepTree-categs	closed	19/19	52.8	42.44	47.06	6
GBD-NER-standard	closed	19/19	38.76	55.2	45.54	7
GBD-NER-resplit	closed	19/19	33.5	57.92	42.45	8
Veyn	closed	19/19	41.76	37.76	39.66	9
mumpitz	closed	7/19	16.83	15.32	16.04	10
Polirem-rich	closed	3/19	10.9	4.78	6.65	11
Polirem-basic	closed	3/19	10.78	1.09	1.98	12
MWETreeC	closed	19/19	0.21	4.21	0.4	13
SHOMA	open	19/19	66.07	59.73	62.74	1
Deep-BGT	open	10/19	36.05	27.54	31.23	2
Milos	open	4/19	9.42	9.49	9.45	3
mumpitz-preinit	open	1/19	1.97	2.31	2.13	4

Table 4: Results for continuous MWEs.

System	Track	#Langs	P-MWE	R-MWE	F1-MWE	Rank-MWE
TRAVERSAL	closed	19/19	61.14	34.81	44.36	1
varIDE	closed	19/19	44.53	32.24	37.4	2
CRF-DepTree-categs	closed	19/19	48.8	26.4	34.26	3
TRAPACC_S	closed	19/19	53.23	24.88	33.91	4
TRAPACC	closed	19/19	43.29	27.3	33.48	5
GBD-NER-standard	closed	19/19	29.32	33.69	31.35	6
GBD-NER-resplit	closed	19/19	23.22	41.41	29.76	7
Veyn	closed	19/19	40.53	19.07	25.94	8
CRF-Seq-nocategs	closed	19/19	54.2	15.48	24.08	9
mumpitz	closed	7/19	18.34	8.71	11.81	10
Polirem-rich	closed	3/19	3.51	0.06	0.12	11
Polirem-basic	closed	3/19	0	0	0	n/a
MWETreeC	closed	19/19	0	0	0	n/a
SHOMA	open	19/19	62.95	32.87	43.19	1
Deep-BGT	open	10/19	28.83	19.4	23.19	2
Milos	open	4/19	9.37	5.79	7.16	3
mumpitz-preinit	open	1/19	3.25	1.44	2	4

Table 5: Results for discontinuous MWEs.

System	Track	#Langs	P-MWE	R-MWE	F1-MWE	Rank-MWE
TRAVERSAL	closed	19/19	74.66	44.59	55.83	1
TRAPACC	closed	19/19	57.23	43.42	49.38	2
TRAPACC_S	closed	19/19	63.6	39.97	49.09	3
CRF-Seq-nocategs	closed	19/19	66.16	38.23	48.46	4
CRF-DepTree-categs	closed	19/19	60.52	37.21	46.09	5
varIDE	closed	19/19	61.49	36.18	45.56	6
GBD-NER-standard	closed	19/19	36.56	51.05	42.61	7
GBD-NER-resplit	closed	19/19	30.26	55.86	39.26	8
Veyn	closed	19/19	52.16	30.33	38.36	9
mumpitz	closed	7/19	22.23	12.47	15.98	10
Polirem-rich	closed	3/19	10.9	2.87	4.54	11
Polirem-basic	closed	3/19	10.78	0.65	1.23	12
MWETreeC	closed	19/19	0	0	0	n/a
SHOMA	open	19/19	73.37	50.65	59.93	1
Deep-BGT	open	10/19	35.04	25.09	29.24	2
Milos	open	4/19	10.37	6.89	8.28	3
mumpitz-preinit	open	1/19	3	1.61	2.1	4

Table 6: Results for multi-token MWEs.

System	Track	#Langs	P-MWE	R-MWE	F1-MWE	Rank-MWE
TRAPACC	closed	5/5	35.13	30.8	32.82	1
TRAPACC_S	closed	5/5	34.64	30.49	32.43	2
TRAVERSAL	closed	5/5	30.7	22.49	25.96	3
CRF-DepTree-categs	closed	5/5	28.49	21.81	24.71	4
Veyn	closed	5/5	22.91	25.76	24.25	5
CRF-Seq-nocategs	closed	5/5	24.95	22.69	23.77	6
varIDE	closed	5/5	36.47	6.43	10.93	7
mumpitz	closed	1/5	4.87	12.62	7.03	8
MWETreeC	closed	5/5	0.79	61.8	1.56	9
Polirem-rich	closed	0/5	0	0	0	n/a
Polirem-basic	closed	0/5	0	0	0	n/a
GBD-NER-standard	closed	5/5	0	0	0	n/a
GBD-NER-resplit	closed	5/5	0	0	0	n/a
SHOMA	open	5/5	27.77	28.9	28.32	1
Deep-BGT	open	3/5	27.61	24.33	25.87	2
Milos	open	2/5	12.23	15.84	13.8	3
mumpitz-preinit	open	1/5	6.43	9.8	7.77	4

Table 7: Results for single-token MWEs.

System	Track	#Langs	P-MWE	R-MWE	F1-MWE	Rank-MWE
TRAVERSAL	closed	19/19	86.54	63	72.92	1
GBD-NER-resplit	closed	19/19	82.76	63.82	72.07	2
TRAPACC	closed	19/19	82.72	61.41	70.49	3
GBD-NER-standard	closed	19/19	82.92	60.74	70.12	4
TRAPACC_S	closed	19/19	82.04	57.06	67.31	5
CRF-Seq-nocategs	closed	19/19	78.27	52.71	63	6
CRF-DepTree-categs	closed	19/19	83.23	50.03	62.49	7
varIDE	closed	19/19	62.8	56.2	59.32	8
Veyn	closed	19/19	76.6	43.7	55.65	9
mumpitz	closed	7/19	30.69	17.81	22.54	10
Polirem-rich	closed	3/19	14.98	4.44	6.85	11
MWETreeC	closed	19/19	13.16	3.99	6.12	12
Polirem-basic	closed	3/19	15.79	1.16	2.16	13
SHOMA	open	19/19	89	66.78	76.31	1
Deep-BGT	open	10/19	46.25	30.36	36.66	2
Milos	open	4/19	16.46	10.4	12.75	3
mumpitz-preinit	open	1/19	4.34	3.07	3.6	4

Table 8: Results for seen-in-train MWEs.

System	Track	#Langs	P-MWE	R-MWE	F1-MWE	Rank-MWE
GBD-NER-standard	closed	19/19	14.33	31.54	19.71	1
GBD-NER-resplit	closed	19/19	12.74	37.66	19.04	2
TRAVERSAL	closed	19/19	23.94	13.61	17.35	3
CRF-DepTree-categs	closed	19/19	18.71	15.58	17	4
TRAPACC	closed	19/19	19.19	14.52	16.53	5
TRAPACC_S	closed	19/19	24.07	12.47	16.43	6
CRF-Seq-nocategs	closed	19/19	20.49	13.63	16.37	7
Veyn	closed	19/19	11.57	10.58	11.05	8
mumpitz	closed	7/19	5.5	5.92	5.7	9
varIDE	closed	19/19	14.61	3.31	5.4	10
Polirem-rich	closed	3/19	1.76	0.36	0.6	11
MWETreeC	closed	19/19	0.02	1.99	0.04	12
Polirem-basic	closed	3/19	0	0	0	n/a
SHOMA	open	19/19	31.73	25.8	28.46	1
Deep-BGT	open	10/19	12.99	13	12.99	2
Milos	open	4/19	5.56	5.89	5.72	3
mumpitz-preinit	open	1/19	0.75	0.72	0.73	4

Table 9: Results for unseen-in-train MWEs.

System	Track	#Langs	P-MWE	R-MWE	F1-MWE	Rank-MWE
TRAPACC	closed	19/19	90.44	77.94	83.73	1
TRAVERSAL	closed	19/19	89.15	75.71	81.88	2
TRAPACC_S	closed	19/19	85.56	73.04	78.81	3
GBD-NER-resplit	closed	19/19	87.27	71.18	78.41	4
GBD-NER-standard	closed	19/19	87.39	69.44	77.39	5
CRF-Seq-nocategs	closed	19/19	80.32	70.54	75.11	6
CRF-DepTree-categs	closed	19/19	85.85	60.25	70.81	7
varIDE	closed	19/19	82.23	57.52	67.69	8
Veyn	closed	19/19	81.15	53.37	64.39	9
mumpitz	closed	7/19	31.57	22.25	26.1	10
Polirem-rich	closed	3/19	15.31	5.99	8.61	11
MWETreeC	closed	19/19	13.16	4.69	6.92	12
Polirem-basic	closed	3/19	15.79	2.03	3.6	13
SHOMA	open	19/19	90.26	85.15	87.63	1
Deep-BGT	open	10/19	46.45	36.71	41.01	2
Milos	open	4/19	17.2	11	13.42	3
mumpitz-preinit	open	1/19	4.25	3.66	3.93	4

Table 10: Results for identical-to-train MWEs.

System	Track	#Langs	P-MWE	R-MWE	F1-MWE	Rank-MWE
GBD-NER-resplit	closed	19/19	76.6	56.48	65.02	1
TRAVERSAL	closed	19/19	83.22	50.82	63.1	2
GBD-NER-standard	closed	19/19	76.63	52.16	62.07	3
TRAPACC	closed	19/19	74.73	47.22	57.87	4
TRAPACC_S	closed	19/19	76.22	43.11	55.07	5
varIDE	closed	19/19	52.7	53.97	53.33	6
CRF-DepTree-categs	closed	19/19	78.29	39.01	52.07	7
CRF-Seq-nocategs	closed	19/19	73.17	35.48	47.79	8
Veyn	closed	19/19	70.65	34.62	46.47	9
mumpitz	closed	7/19	29.96	13.77	18.87	10
Polirem-rich	closed	3/19	14.51	3.21	5.26	11
MWETreeC	closed	19/19	7.89	2.16	3.39	12
Polirem-basic	closed	3/19	10.53	0.48	0.92	13
SHOMA	open	19/19	85.95	50.03	63.25	1
Deep-BGT	open	10/19	45.04	22.42	29.94	2
Milos	open	4/19	15.96	9.97	12.27	3
mumpitz-preinit	open	1/19	4.44	2.67	3.33	4

Table 11: Results for variant-of-train MWEs.

	IAV		IRV		LVC.cause		LVC.full		MVC		VID		VPC.full		VPC.semi		LS.IVC	
	MF	TF	MF	TF	MF	TF	MF	TF	MF	TF	MF	TF	MF	TF	MF	TF	MF	TF
BG	0.00	0.92	65.56	66.20	13.82	14.19	36.67	37.57			22.68	25.70						
HR	31.61	45.03	42.34	48.00	9.17	10.32	19.16	21.11			4.83	6.40						
LT					18.31	19.74	17.05	21.61			5.20	5.77						
PL	34.89	44.17	58.36	64.16	9.13	10.80	34.01	38.12			13.34	19.64						
SL	33.38	37.60	48.95	50.97	7.78	13.42	15.09	17.38			12.03	16.10						
AV	24.97	31.93	53.80	57.33	11.64	13.69	24.40	27.16			11.61	14.72						
ES	17.23	23.24	27.62	30.35	3.29	4.24	12.89	16.54	19.72	26.29	10.16	13.53	0.00	0.00				
FR			46.73	50.27	2.91	3.37	30.55	35.50	7.28	7.28	34.31	42.88						
IT	20.69	26.41	31.08	33.30	17.58	20.21	24.16	26.05	9.52	9.66	16.58	20.66	19.93	21.02			4.93	7.31
PT			49.70	50.45	11.09	14.82	43.80	46.55			31.73	35.64						
RO			69.34	74.46	65.56	77.74	52.26	55.88			62.96	68.24						
AV	18.96	24.83	44.89	47.76	20.09	24.08	32.73	36.10	12.17	14.41	31.15	36.19	9.97	10.51			4.93	7.31
DE			20.75	32.05	5.56	4.76	5.69	7.94			18.99	25.15	45.47	49.11	10.77	11.64		
EN	7.92	8.75			0.00	0.00	10.15	11.25	0.00	0.00	3.68	3.70	28.16	30.22	2.79	5.06		
AV	7.92	8.75	20.75	32.05	2.78	2.38	7.92	9.60	0.00	0.00	11.33	14.43	36.82	39.66	6.78	8.35		
EL					2.03	3.05	38.36	46.37	12.12	14.14	21.36	27.88	7.68	12.66				
EU					19.19	20.03	57.24	59.82			28.37	30.03						
FA							62.07	70.10										
HE					15.77	20.03	19.13	23.29			13.54	18.40	0.00	0.00				
HI					7.57	8.69	57.01	63.02	68.95	73.68	7.21	6.30						
HU					49.91	52.33	45.68	50.75			47.36	56.09	61.47	64.04	58.74	58.54		
TR							25.13	27.83	0.00	0.00	19.33	22.21						
AV					23.11	25.27	44.38	49.13	34.48	36.84	23.16	26.61	30.73	32.02	58.74	58.54		
MA	19.76	25.16	44.61	49.03	15.06	17.29	31.11	34.72	16.42	18.23	20.50	24.37	24.02	25.92	27.57	28.43	4.93	7.31

Table 12: Average F1-scores per category for each language and language group. MF: MWE-based F1-score, TF: token-based F1-score, AV: average, MA: macro-average.

CRF-Seq and CRF-DepTree at PARSEME Shared Task 2018: Detecting Verbal MWEs Using Sequential and Dependency-Based Approaches

Erwan Moreau
Adapt Centre
Trinity College Dublin
erwan.moreau@adaptcentre.ie

Ashjan Alsulaimani
School of Computer Science and Statistics
Trinity College Dublin
alsulaia@tcd.ie

Alfredo Maldonado
Adapt Centre
Trinity College Dublin
alfredo.maldonado@adaptcentre.ie

Carl Vogel
Trinity Centre for Computing
and Language Studies
Trinity College Dublin
vogel@scss.tcd.ie

Abstract

This paper describes two systems for detecting Verbal Multiword Expressions (VMWEs) which both competed in the closed track at the PARSEME VMWE Shared Task 2018. *CRF-DepTree-categs* implements an approach based on the dependency tree, intended to exploit the syntactic and semantic relations between tokens; *CRF-Seq-nocategs* implements a robust sequential method which requires only lemmas and morphosyntactic tags. Both systems ranked in the top half of the ranking, the latter ranking second for token-based evaluation. The code for both systems is published under the GNU General Public License version 3.0[1] and is available at http://github.com/erwanm/adapt-vmwe18.

1 Introduction

This paper describes two systems for identifying verbal multiword expressions (VMWEs). This work builds on the authors' previous attempt at the same task (Maldonado et al., 2017; Moreau et al., 2018). The two systems were designed and developed in the context of the 2018 edition of the PARSEME VMWE Shared Task, in which training data annotated with VMWEs is provided for 20 different languages (Ramisch et al., 2018). This setting naturally leads to considering the task as a supervised learning problem.[2]

In this edition of the PARSEME shared task, we attempted an approach which focuses on leveraging the syntactic and semantic dependency relations between tokens; the aim is to take into account the phrase structure of the expressions in order to improve their identification. We expect this to be useful especially in the case of discontinuous VMWEs, which can be hard to identify using sequential approaches. In §2.1 we motivate this approach with a detailed analysis of the expressions found in the data; the rest of §2 describes the design and implementation of our first and main system, called *CRF-DepTree-categs*.

Comparatively, the second system *CRF-Seq-nocategs* (described in §3) is very simple and was originally intended as a baseline and/or a fallback option. It relies on a method inspired from the one presented in (Moreau and Vogel, 2018) to optimize a sequential CRF model. To our surprise, the system performed better than *CRF-DepTree-categs* with most datasets. A brief comparative analysis of the results of the two systems is provided in §5, which validates our initial assumption that, despite its weaknesses, *CRF-DepTree-categs* is better at identifying discontinuous VMWEs.

---

[1] https://www.gnu.org/licenses/gpl-3.0.en.html. Last verified: May 2018.

[2] It is worth noticing that this view also entails a complete dependency on the annotations with respect to what is defined as a VMWE. In particular, there can be differences between datasets in the number, diversity and syntactic or semantic complexity of the annotated expressions (Maldonado et al., 2017).

Proceedings of the Joint Workshop on
Linguistic Annotation, Multiword Expressions and Constructions (LAW-MWE-CxG-2018), pages 241–247
Santa Fe, New Mexico, USA, August 25-26, 2018.

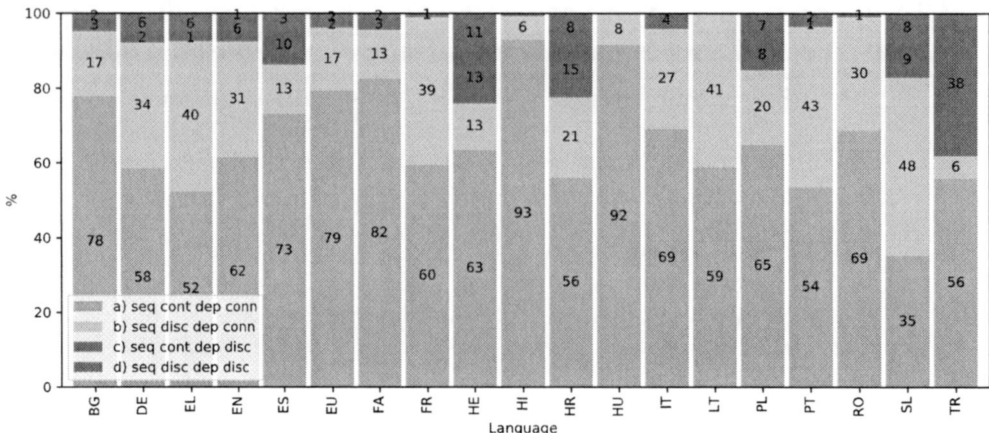

Figure 1: Proportion of a) sequentially-continuous and dependency-connected VMWEs (seq cont dep conn), b) sequentially-discontinous but dependency-connected VMWEs (seq disc dep conn), c) sequentially-continuous but dependency-disconnected VMWEs (seq cont dep disc) and d) sequentially-discontinuous and dependency-disconnected VMWEs (seq disc dep disc), for each language in the 2018 training dataset.[4]

The full implementation of the two systems is published under the GNU GPL License v 3.0 and available at `http://github.com/erwanm/adapt-vmwe18`.

2 Dependency Tree Approach

2.1 Motivations

The previous edition of this shared task (Savary et al., 2017) found that a significant minority of VMWEs in most language datasets were discontinuous, that is, VMWEs whose individual tokens did not necessarily occur as an uninterrupted sequence within a sentence (e.g. *take something into account*). Therefore, a system able to handle discontinuities could potentially make significant gains in performance. For a sequential tagging method to be able to handle these discontinuities, sufficiently large word windows would need to be considered. However, it can be difficult to determine an ideal word window size that can cover a majority of cases and yet be tractable.

Nevertheless, we hypothesise that tokens in a VMWE should be directly connected to each other via their syntactic dependency links, even if they are not sequentially continuous. We expect that most VMWEs in a given language would tend to be fully dependency-connected, regardless of whether they are sequentially continuous or not. If this is the case indeed, then a tree-based tagging method that exploits these direct dependency links should perform well, even in sequentially-discontinuous VMWEs.

To estimate the potential gains to be made through such a dependency tree-based tagging method, we counted the proportion of VMWEs in each language that are sequentially continuous/discontinuous and dependency-connnected/not fully dependency-connected. Figure 1 shows the proportions of each continuity and connectedness combination in each language. For the purposes of this figure, a VMWE is deemed to be sequentially continuous if each of its member tokens appear in a sentence sequentially with no tokens foreign to the VMWE breaking this continuity. Analogously, a VMWE is deemed to be dependency connected if its member tokens are fully connected via their syntactic dependency links. That is, all member tokens of a dependency-connected VMWE, depend on another member with the exception of at most one member, which depends on a non-member token (i.e. the head for the whole VMWE). We also consider a VMWE to be dependency connected if it has more than one member depending on the same non-member token. But if at least two members depend on two different non-member tokens, then the VMWE is deemed to be dependency disconnected for our purposes.

```
<Feature xsi:type="Current-Parent" name="example">
  <Ycur xsi:type="Label" value="label_O"/>
  <Ypar xsi:type="Label" value="label_I"/>
  <TestX value="self::TOKEN[@upos=='P']"/>
  <TestX value="ancestor::TOKEN[@upos=='V']"/>
</Feature>
```

Figure 2: Example of an XCRF feature generated from the French training set. The value of this feature is true if and only if the current node is labeled O, its parent node is labeled I,[8] the attribute *upos* of the current node has value *P* and the current node has an ancestor containing value *V* for its attribute *upos*.

Not surprisingly for most languages, the majority of VMWEs are both sequentially continuous and dependency connected (a in Figure 1), but the proportion of sequentially discontinuous but dependency connected VMWEs (b) is quite significant. In fact, the vast majority of the VMWEs in all languages are dependency connected (a + b), confirming that there are significant gains in performance to be made by developing a method that is able to exploit the connectedness of dependency trees. The other two combinations, (c and d), tend to be a minority in most languages. In some cases they are negligible (less than 10%), but in others they are relatively significant (in particular for Turkish). We do not propose strategies to deal with these combinations in this paper and leave their further analysis for future work.

2.2 Tree-Structured Dependencies in Conditional Random Fields

Conditional Random Fields (CRFs) can in theory handle dependencies of any level of complexity between variables (Lafferty et al., 2001; Sutton and McCallum, 2012).[5] In practice, however, most applications where CRF proved sucessful are based on the most simple kind of dependency network, which takes only sequential dependencies into account; this is largely due to the high computational cost of adding dependency relations between variables for training a CRF model. Nonetheless, there are several CRF software tools which are able to handle non-sequential dependencies; in this work we chose XCRF, a Java library for labeling XML trees (Jousse et al., 2006; Jousse, 2007).[6]

Based on the analysis presented in §2.1, our approach relies on the dependency tree structure of a sentence, provided in the Shared Task data for most languages (see §4). XCRF can deal with three kinds of dependency relations between nodes in a tree; a group of inter-dependent nodes is called a *clique*, and the different kinds of cliques, called the *clique levels*, are:

- Level 1: the label of the current node does not depend on any other label;

- Level 2: the label of the current node depends on its parent label;

- Level 3: the label of the current node depends on its parent label as well as on the label of its next sibling.

2.3 Implementation

2.3.1 Feature Generation

The XCRF software requires boolean features which consist of two parts: the *clique* is the set of classes for the current node (level 1), possibly with its parent (level 2) and possibly with its next sibling (level 3); the second part is a set of *tests* expressed as XPath expressions over the XML tree. Figure 2 shows an example of such a feature.

After converting the *cupt* dataset to a set of XML tree, the system iterates through the data in order to collect and count all the existing combinations of *cliques* and *tests*. Atomic tests are based on a triple $\langle Neighbourhood, Attribute, Value \rangle$, where: $Neighbourhood$ describes a set of target nodes,

---

[4]In the case of Lithuanian (LT) the dependency structure was not provided; in this particular case, VMWEs are arbitrarily represented as fully dependency-connected in figure 1.

[5]Here the word *dependency* refers to the probabilistic concept of conditional independence.

[6]http://treecrf.gforge.inria.fr/. Last verified: May 2018.

[8]The labeling scheme is explained in §4.

which can be: the node itself, its parent, its children its preceding siblings or its following siblings; *Attribute* specifies the attribute to test: the lemma, the Part-of-Speech tag (*upos*) or the dependency relation (*deprel*); *Value* is the value of the attribute. Additionally, conjunctions of a pair of tests are generated by cartesian product for each node. All the possible features for XCRF are generated by combining each test with the actual cliques that this node belongs to: for example, if the node has a parent, each of the tests is counted at both clique levels one and two. Finally, the collected frequencies (by clique, by clique level, by test and by combination clique+test) are used to calculate the probabilities used for feature selection.

2.3.2   Feature Selection

In order to select the most relevant features but also to avoid memory issues with XCRF, we implemented three different feature selection methods; the maximum number of features is a parameter (we used 25,000 for most languages). The number of features are shared equally between the atomic tests and the multi-tests, as well as between the different clique levels. Thus for every clique level, we reduce the number of features depending on the method, as explained below.

- Clique-blind: This method assumes that features with a similar proportion of true and false cases are more likely to help predict the clique. To this end, for every feature we take the minimum frequency difference between the case where the test is true and where it is false, and select the features for which this value is the highest. This method is based on the frequency of the test only, without taking into account the relation between the test and the clique within a feature.

- Binary Split: with this method, we select the tests which behave the most differently when occuring with the default clique versus with another clique. The default clique is defined as the one which contains only the default class (i.e. the class for the tokens which are not part of an expression). More precisely, we select the tests which maximize $|p(test = T|dc = T) - p(test = T|dc = F)|$, where dc is the default clique.

- Conditional entropy: $H(Y|X) = \sum_{x \in X} \sum_{y \in Y} p(x, y) \log \frac{p(x)}{p(x, y)}$, where Y is the set of cliques and X is the boolean test. The features which have the lowest conditional entropy are selected.

Additionally, a boolean option specifies whether to use the probability of the clique as a weight. That is, by not using a clique prior, it is assumed that all the cliques are equally important, even though this is not representative of the actual clique distribution.

3   Sequential Approach

3.1   Motivations

The sequential CRF approach was originally implemented as a simple and robust alternative to the dependency-tree approach (see §2). It uses only the lemma and the POS tag as features, so that it can be applied to a dataset even if no syntactic information is provided.[9] This can be useful in particular in the case of languages for which no (good) parser exists.

As explained in §2.1, the majority of the VMWEs are continuous in almost every language. Thus sequential CRFs are potentially capable of identifying most VMWEs, even though they are not well equipped to capture discontinuous VMWEs (at least when the VMWE components are distant from each other). Moreover, the efficiency of sequential CRFs implementations makes it possible to optimize the parameters of the model, in particular the length of the window of tokens to consider around the target token. Using this method, we expect the system to achieve a high performance on the continuous cases.

---

[9]In fact, the original intention was to use the sequential approach only for Lithuanian and Slovenian (see §2.2); the high level of performance achieved by this method motivated its application to all the datasets.

3.2 Implementation

To train a CRF model, we use the Wapiti sequence labelling toolkit (Lavergne et al., 2010).[10] As in most sequence labelling software tools, the features to be used in the model are specified as a list of patterns in a template file; each pattern describes the observations to use as features for predicting the current token.

The *CRF-Seq-nocategs* system implements a simple brute-force method to optimize the sequential CRF model, similar to the one used in (Moreau and Vogel, 2018): for every dataset, we generate a large set of templates by varying the use of a column or not (lemma, POS or both), the maximum length of the window (i.e. the number of tokens before and after the target token), and the maximum size n of n-grams to use in the representation of the sequence of tokens. During the development stage, a model is trained using every template, and each such model is evaluated against the development set; then we simply select the model which achieves the highest performance.

4 Data and Training Process

For both systems, the data is first converted to a sequential labelling scheme which can be any of the following options:

- IO: a token which belongs to a VMWE is labelled *I*, any other is labelled *O*;

- BIO: IO with an additional label *B* for the first token in a VMWE;

- BILOU: BIO with label *L* for the last token in a VMWE and label *U* for a single token span.

Embedded and overlapping VMWEs cannot be represented adequately in any of these labelling schemes. Additionally, three options control how categories are handled: the default *joint* preserves categories by suffixing a label with the category name, e.g. *I_IAV*; in the *independent* mode, a distinct version of the data is created for every category which contains only the expressions belonging to this category, and an independent model is trained for each category; finally the *ignore* mode does not take categories into account. The *CRF-DepTree-categs* system uses the best of the first two options by language, while *CRF-Seq-nocategs* uses the last option.

The *CRF-DepTree-categs* system also requires converting the sentences to XML dependency trees. The Shared Task data files are provided in *.cupt* format, and include a column *HEAD* which contains the id of the parent for every token.[11] Due to the complexity of the training process and memory issues with the XCRF library, we had to reduce the size of the training set to a maximum 8,000 sentences.[12]

For every of the 19 datasets, the two systems have been trained using the training set provided; various parameters were tuned using the development set if provided, or a 20% subset of the training set if not. For *CRF-DepTree-categs* (resp. *CRF-Seq-nocategs*) we selected the model which achieves the highest performance for the MWE-based evaluation (resp. token-based evaluation).

5 Results and Discussion

Table 1 gives a brief summary of the performance of our two systems in the PARSEME VMWE Shared Task 2018.[13] The two systems performed rather consistently across the 19 languages compared to other participant systems: *CRF-Seq-nocategs* ranked from position 1 to 6 for all but one language, and *CRF-DepTree-categs* ranked from position 2 to 7 for all but two languages (according to the token-based evaluation). Both performed particularly well for Hindi, quite bad for Hebrew and especially bad for Lithuanian, but overall the two methods work fairly well independently from the language.

---

[10] `https://wapiti.limsi.fr/`. Last verified: May 2018.

[11] This information is provided in full for 17 languages out of 19, excluding Lithuanian (no information in the *HEAD* column) and Slovenian (incomplete information in the *HEAD* column); for these two languages the predictions made by *CRF-Seq-nocategs* are used. For several languages, the dependency tree can have multiple roots (DE, EU, HU, IT, PL, TR).

[12] Thus the *CRF-DepTree-categs* system does not use the full training set for the following datasets: BG, EU, FR, HE, IT, PL, RO, SL.

[13] The results cannot be detailed and analyzed fully in this paper, because there are many categories of evaluation and languages; for more details, see the overview paper (Ramisch et al., 2018) and the full official results at `http://multiword.sourceforge.net/PHITE.php?sitesig=CONF&page=CONF_04_LAW-MWE-CxG_2018&subpage=CONF_50_Shared_task_results`.

System	MWE-based evaluation				Token-based evaluation			
	Precision	Recall	F1-score	Rank	Precision	Recall	F1-score	Rank
Best system (TRAVERSAL)	67.58	44.97	54.00	1	77.41	48.55	59.67	1
CRF-Seq-nocategs	56.13	39.12	46.11	4	73.44	43.49	54.63	2
CRF-DepTree-categs	52.33	37.83	43.91	6	64.65	41.56	50.60	5
Median system (GBD-NER-standard)	36.56	48.30	41.62	7	41.11	52.21	46.00	7

Table 1: Performance and ranking of the two systems at the PARSEME VMWE Shared Task 2018 (closed track, 13 participant systems, macro-average scores).

Lang.	Percentage of **continuous** expressions found by system:				Percentage of **non-continuous** expressions found by system:			
	none	both	*CRF-Seq*	*CRF-DepTree*	none	both	*CRF-Seq*	*CRF-DepTree*
BG	32.56	42.65	**18.07**	6.72	75.26	12.89	4.12	**7.73**
DE	60.30	23.22	**8.99**	7.49	67.38	8.15	4.29	**19.31**
EL	39.64	37.45	**16.73**	6.18	62.83	7.52	5.75	**23.89**
EN	60.34	18.31	**16.27**	5.08	87.86	0.00	0.00	**12.14**
ES	39.55	23.40	**25.35**	11.70	86.52	0.71	2.84	**9.93**
EU	20.39	62.90	**12.78**	3.93	79.57	5.38	0.00	**15.05**
FA	19.60	63.82	**12.31**	4.27	74.76	8.74	7.77	**8.74**
FR	44.48	36.65	**13.52**	5.34	61.75	12.44	5.53	**20.28**
HE	88.80	0.00	0.00	**11.20**	95.76	0.00	0.00	**4.24**
HI	23.66	59.78	6.88	**9.68**	42.86	31.43	0.00	**25.71**
HR	52.22	17.06	**17.41**	12.63	79.81	2.88	3.85	**12.98**
HU	14.06	71.73	**9.99**	4.22	38.46	24.62	12.31	**24.62**
IT	51.34	20.00	**19.40**	8.06	77.98	1.19	0.00	**19.05**
PL	24.93	36.57	**25.21**	13.30	64.29	7.79	3.90	**24.03**
PT	34.50	33.87	**24.60**	7.03	58.33	4.58	0.42	**36.67**
RO	12.98	57.76	**26.46**	2.80	20.92	56.63	**13.78**	8.67
TR	46.63	35.10	**12.02**	6.25	71.14	15.10	**7.05**	6.71

Table 2: Percentage of continuous and non-continuous expressions found by (1) none of the two systems, (2) both of them, (3) *CRF-DepTree-categs* only and (4) *CRF-Seq-nocategs* only.[16] The percentage is based on the number of expressions according to the gold-standard labels, therefore these figures do not take false positive cases into account (thus are akin to recall statistics: the recall measure for a given system corresponds to the sum of the percentage for this system and the one for both). For every case, the highest of the two values between (3) and (4) is displayed in bold.

Although the simple sequential approach significantly outperforms the more sophisticated dependency tree-based one, there are indications that the latter might be able to deal with more complex cases: in the special evaluation categories for discontinuous VMWEs and unseen-in-train VMWEs, *CRF-DepTree-categs* ranks respectively 3rd and 4th, i.e. comparatively better than in the other evaluation categories.[14] This suggests that despite its moderate success at detecting VMWEs in general, the method might be good at capturing some of the hardest cases; in order to confirm this interpretation, we analyze the predictions made by both systems by contrasting the continuous and discontinuous cases: table 2 unambiguously shows that even if both systems are able to identify both kinds of expressions, each system tends to specialize on a specific kind; for most languages, *CRF-Seq-nocategs* identifies significantly more continuous expressions than *CRF-DepTree-categs*, but the latter identifies significantly more discontinuous expressions than the former.

6   Conclusion and Future Work

In this paper we presented two CRF-based systems for detecting VMWEs: *CRF-DepTree-categs* which exploits the dependency structure of the sentence, and *CRF-Seq-nocategs* which implements a simple sequential approach. While the latter achieved better performance in the PARSEME VMWE Shared Task 2018, our analysis shows that the two methods are complementary: *CRF-Seq-nocategs* identifies contin-

---

[14]For the sake of comparison, *CRF-Seq-nocategs* ranks 9th for discontinuous VMWEs and 7th for unseen VMWEs.

[16]Language with no dependency information (Lithuanian and Slovenian) are excluded; see §4.

uous VMWEs better, while conversely *CRF-DepTree-categs* identifies discontinous VMWEs better. As a consequence, combining the two approaches into a single system seems a very promising direction for future work.

Acknowledgements

The ADAPT Centre for Digital Content Technology is funded under the SFI Research Centres Programme (Grant 13/RC/2106) and is co-funded under the European Regional Development Fund.

References

Florent Jousse, Rémi Gilleron, Isabelle Tellier, and Marc Tommasi. 2006. Conditional Random Fields for XML Trees. In *Proceedings of the ECML Workshop on Mining and Learning in Graphs*.

Florent Jousse. 2007. *XML Tree Transformations with Probabilistic Models*. Theses, Université Charles de Gaulle - Lille III, October.

John D. Lafferty, Andrew McCallum, and Fernando C. N. Pereira. 2001. Conditional random fields: Probabilistic models for segmenting and labeling sequence data. In *Proceedings of the Eighteenth International Conference on Machine Learning*, ICML '01, pages 282–289, San Francisco, CA, USA. Morgan Kaufmann Publishers Inc.

Thomas Lavergne, Olivier Cappé, and François Yvon. 2010. Practical very large scale CRFs. In *Proceedings the 48th Annual Meeting of the Association for Computational Linguistics (ACL)*, pages 504–513. Association for Computational Linguistics, July.

Alfredo Maldonado, Lifeng Han, Erwan Moreau, Ashjan Alsulaimani, Koel Dutta Chowdhury, Carl Vogel, and Qun Liu. 2017. Detection of Verbal Multi-Word Expressions via Conditional Random Fields with Syntactic Dependency Features and Semantic Re-Ranking. In Agata Savary Stella Markantonatou, Carlos Ramisch and Veronika Vincze, editors, *Proceedings of the 13th Workshop on Multiword Expressions (MWE 2017)*, pages 114–120, Valencia, Spain, April. Association for Computational Linguistics.

Erwan Moreau and Carl Vogel. 2018. Multilingual Word Segmentation: Training Many Language-Specific Tokenizers Smoothly Thanks to the Universal Dependencies Corpus. In Nicoletta Calzolari (Conference chair), Khalid Choukri, Christopher Cieri, Thierry Declerck, Sara Goggi, Koiti Hasida, Hitoshi Isahara, Bente Maegaard, Joseph Mariani, Hélène Mazo, Asuncion Moreno, Jan Odijk, Stelios Piperidis, and Takenobu Tokunaga, editors, *Proceedings of the Eleventh International Conference on Language Resources and Evaluation (LREC 2018)*, Miyazaki, Japan, May 7-12, 2018. European Language Resources Association (ELRA).

Erwan Moreau, Ashjan Alsulaimani, Alfredo Maldonado, Lifeng Han, Carl Vogel, and Koel Dutta Chowdhury. 2018. Semantic Re-Ranking of CRF Label Sequences for Verbal Multiword Expression Identification. In Stella Markantonatou, Carlos Ramisch, Agata Savary, Veronika Vincze, editor, *to appear*. Language Science Press.

Carlos Ramisch, Silvio Ricardo Cordeiro, Agata Savary, Veronika Vincze, Verginica Barbu Mititelu, Archna Bhatia, Maja Buljan, Marie Candito, Polona Gantar, Voula Giouli, Tunga Güngör, Abdelati Hawwari, Uxoa Iñurrieta, Jolanta Kovalevskaitė, Simon Krek, Timm Lichte, Chaya Liebeskind, Johanna Monti, Carla Parra Escartín, Behrang QasemiZadeh, Renata Ramisch, Nathan Schneider, Ivelina Stoyanova, Ashwini Vaidya, and Abigail Walsh. 2018. Edition 1.1 of the PARSEME Shared Task on Automatic Identification of Verbal Multiword Expressions. In *Proceedings of the Joint Workshop on Linguistic Annotation, Multiword Expressions and Constructions (LAW-MWE-CxG 2018)*, Santa Fe, New Mexico, USA, August. Association for Computational Linguistics.

Agata Savary, Carlos Ramisch, Silvio Ricardo Cordeiro, Federico Sangati, Veronika Vincze, Behrang QasemiZadeh, Marie Candito, Fabienne Cap, Voula Giouli, Ivelina Stoyanova, and Antoine Doucet. 2017. The PARSEME Shared Task on Automatic Identification of Verbal Multiword Expressions. In *Proceedings of The 13th Workshop on Multiword Expressions*, pages 31–47, Valencia.

Charles Sutton and Andrew McCallum. 2012. An Introduction to Conditional Random Fields. *Found. Trends Mach. Learn.*, 4(4):267–373, April.

Deep-BGT at PARSEME Shared Task 2018: Bidirectional LSTM-CRF Model for Verbal Multiword Expression Identification

Gözde Berk, Berna Erden and Tunga Güngör
Boğaziçi University
Department of Computer Engineering
34342 Bebek, Istanbul, Turkey
{gozde.berk, berna.erden, gungort}@boun.edu.tr

Abstract

This paper describes the Deep-BGT system that participated to the PARSEME shared task 2018 on automatic identification of verbal multiword expressions (VMWEs). Our system is language-independent and uses the bidirectional Long Short-Term Memory model with a Conditional Random Field layer on top (bidirectional LSTM-CRF). To the best of our knowledge, this paper is the first one that employs the bidirectional LSTM-CRF model for VMWE identification. Furthermore, the gappy 1-level tagging scheme is used for discontiguity and overlaps. Our system was evaluated on 10 languages in the open track and it was ranked the second in terms of the general ranking metric.

1 Introduction

Baldwin and Kim (2010) define multiword expressions (MWE) as lexical items that have properties that cannot be derived from their component items at the lexical, syntactic, semantic, pragmatic, and/or statistical levels. Moreover, they consider the process of identification of MWEs as the determination of individual occurrences of MWEs in running text.

In this paper, we describe the Deep-BGT system developed for the second edition of the PARSEME shared task on automatic identification of verbal MWEs (VMWE) which covers 20 languages. The corpora provided are in cupt [1] format and include annotations of VMWEs consisting of categories defined and annotated according to the guidelines provided by Ramisch et al. (2018). The categories of VMWEs are light verb constructions with two subcategories (LVC.full and LVC.cause), verbal idioms (VID), inherently reflexive verbs (IRV), verb-particle constructions with two subcategories (VPC.full and VPC.semi), multi-verb constructions (MVC), inherently adpositional verbs (IAV) and inherently clitic verbs (LS.ICV).

2 Related Work

There are several studies related to identification of multiword expressions. Constant et al. (2017) outline the challenges in the MWE identification task as discontiguity, overlaps, ambiguity, and variability. The flexible nature of these expressions allows reordering or inserting tokens within the MWE components, which results in discontiguity. Discontiguity also poses overlaps such that the gaps in a discontiguous MWE can contain other MWEs. Additionally, it was stated that the MWE identification problem can be addressed using sequence tagging methods with the BIO tagging scheme.

Schneider et al. (2014) describe new tagging schemes that are variants of BIO tagging for MWE identification. One of these, the gappy (discontinuous) 1-level tagging, introduces additional tags to encode gappy MWEs. Huang et al. (2015) propose a bidirectional LSTM-CRF model to solve the sequence tagging problem. While the bidirectional LSTM (Long Short-Term Memory) components consider both the past and future features (Graves et al., 2013), the CRF (Conditional Random Field) component uses

[1] http://multiword.sourceforge.net/PHITE.php?sitesig=CONF&page=CONF_04_LAW-MWE-CxG_2018___lb__COLING__rb__&subpage=CONF_45_Format_specification

Proceedings of the Joint Workshop on
Linguistic Annotation, Multiword Expressions and Constructions (LAW-MWE-CxG-2018), pages 248–253
Santa Fe, New Mexico, USA, August 25-26, 2018.

sentence level tag information (Lafferty et al., 2001). Although the bidirectional LSTM-CRF delivers similar performance to stochastic models using external resources in natural language processing benchmark sequence tagging data sets, its performance does not depend on handcrafted features as in stochastic models. Therefore, the bidirectional LSTM-CRF model is a good option to use as both a non-linear and a statistical approach without relying on hand-crafted features.

Klyueva et al. (2017) implement a supervised approach based on recurrent neural networks to identify VMWEs. The feature set is formed of the concatenation of the embeddings of the tokens surface form, lemma, and POS tag. Legrand and Collobert (2016) present a neural network model that uses the IOBES tagging scheme in order to perform MWE identification.

3 System Description

In this paper, we consider the MWE identification task as a sequence tagging problem. We develop a language-independent system based on the bidirectional LSTM-CRF model provided by Huang et al. (2015). In addition, the gappy 1-level tagging scheme is used which was proposed by Schneider et al. (2014). The architecture of the system is shown in Figure 1.

In the training phase, the training set and the development set provided in the cupt format are merged and then preprocessed by applying the tagging format and getting rid of problematic MWEs. Then, the bidirectional LSTM-CRF model runs. In the test phase, the test set is again preprocessed and is executed on the trained model. Afterwards, post processing is applied to convert the output to the cupt format.

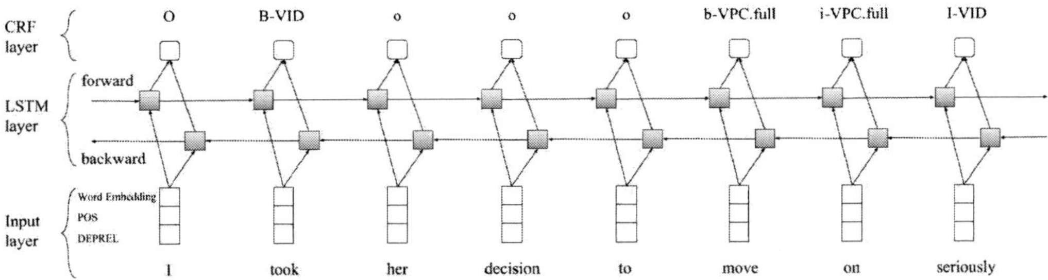

Figure 1: Our Bidirectional LSTM-CRF Model.

3.1 Tagging Scheme

For sequence tagging problems, generally the BIO tagging scheme and its variants are used. To overcome the problems of discontiguity and overlaps in MWE identification, the gappy 1-level tagging scheme was proposed by Schneider et al. (2014). In this scheme there are six types of tags, which are B, I, O, b, i, and o. The uppercase tags are similar to the ones in the simple BIO encoding. **B** denotes a token at the beginning of a chunk, **I** is used for a token belonging to the remaining part of the chunk, and **O** represents a token outside of any chunk. The lowercase labels have similar meanings for gappy chunks. **b** corresponds to a token at the beginning of a nested chunk which is within a gap, **i** denotes a token in the remaining part of the nested chunk, and **o** represents a token outside of any chunk within a gap. Since we identify the VMWEs according to their categories in this work, we use the tags B-*category*, I-*category*, b-*category*, i-*category* (for each category), O, and o. Figure 1 shows two VMWEs, which are "took seriously" of type VID and "move on" of type VPC.full.

Since the gaps in the MWEs can be represented by lowercase tags, the gappy 1-level tagging scheme solves the discontiguity problem. In the case of overlaps, there are two different problems. The first one is nesting and it is solved by the b and i tags. Since the tagging scheme is 1-level, we can handle 1-level nesting. Fortunately, more level of nesting is not frequent in practice. An example of nested MWEs can be seen in Figure 1. The other problem is that MWEs can share tokens. The tagging method we use cannot solve the shared token problem. In this case, we follow a simple strategy in the sense that we preserve only one of the MWEs and remove the other MWE(s) during preprocessing. Thus, our model cannot take into account shared MWEs. In fact, the number of such cases is quite limited in the corpora.

3.2 Proposed Model

As shown in Figure 1, the bidirectional LSTM-CRF model consists of three layers. The inputs are word embeddings along with the POS (part-of-speech) and DEPREL (dependency relation) tags provided in the cupt files. Each input vector is represented as a concatenation of the embeddings of word, POS, and DEPREL. We chose the DEPREL tag as a feature in order to capture dependencies at sentence level. We use pre-trained word embeddings released by fastText (Grave et al., 2018), which were trained on Common Crawl and Wikipedia. The vocabulary size of the embeddings is 2M words and the embedding vector dimension is 300.

The input layer passes features to the LSTM layer. The bidirectional LSTM network takes into account both past and future features. On the one side, the forward LSTM units process the sequence from left to right so that they use past information. On the other side, the backward LSTM units process the sequence from right to left so that they use future information. The outputs of the LSTM units are fed into the CRF layer in order to decode the sequence labels. In this way, both non-linear and statistical models are applied to the sequence tagging problem with no extra data engineering.

We use Keras (Chollet and others, 2015) with Tensorflow backend (Abadi et al., 2015) to implement the neural network architecture. Since tuning parameters of the neural network is time intensive, we follow the evaluated network configurations by Reimers and Gurevych (2017). They state that Nadam optimization converges faster than other optimization methods on average after nine epochs, and variational dropout performs better than both naive dropout and no-dropout. They also claim that mini batch sizes between 8 and 32 are good for large training sets, but batch sizes past 64 decrease performance of the network. We chose parameters of the neural network based on these suggestions. Consequently, we apply a fixed dropout rate of 0.1 for all the bidirectional LSTM layers throughout all the experiments. We set batch sizes of 32 for BG, FR, PT, RO and batch sizes of 16 for DE, ES, HU, IT, PL and SL, with regard to the size of the training sets. We trained the model for 12, 15, 15, 12, 15, 12, 12, 12, 12, 12 epochs for, respectively, the languages BG, DE, ES, FR, HU, IT, PL, PT, RO, SL. We set the node size of the network to 20 for each language.

4   Results

Table 1 shows the cross-lingual macro average results of the Deep-BGT system over 19 languages in the 2018 edition of the PARSEME shared task. The results are given in terms of MWE-based F-measure (F1). Each row in the table represents a metric, including the general metrics and metrics focusing on specific phenomena.

Metrics	Official Results on 19 Languages	Unofficial Results on 10 Languages
General ranking	28.79	54.70
Continuous VMWEs	31.23	59.34
Discontinuous VMWEs	23.19	44.06
Multi-token VMWEs	29.24	55.56
Single-token VMWEs	25.87	43.12
Seen-in-train VMWEs	36.66	69.65
Unseen-in-train VMWEs	12.99	24.68
Variant-of-train VMWEs	29.94	56.89
Identical-to-train VMWEs	41.01	77.92

Table 1: The Macro-averaged Results of Deep-BGT.

We participated the shared task for 10 languages. The official shared task results (second column in

Table 1) are obtained by averaging the success rates for 19 languages, independent of the number of submitted results. In order to reflect the performance of the Deep-BGT system better, we also show the cross-lingual macro averages over the 10 languages covered (third column in Table 1).

PARSEME shared task allows not only multi-token VMWEs but also single-token ones (*abstenerse* in Spanish, *aufmachen* in German). Our system can handle single-token VMWEs by means of the gappy 1-level tagging scheme but the performance of the system regarding single-token VMWEs is lower than multi-token ones. The performance of the system for VMWEs unseen in the train data is lower compared to those that occur in both train and test data because it is more troublesome to detect unseen-in-train VMWEs compared to seen-in-train ones. With respect to the variability of the expressions, we see that the success rate for the identical-to-train VMWEs is higher than the variant-of-train VMWEs. Finally, the performance of discontinuous VMWEs is lower than that of continuous VMWEs, as expected.

Five of the languages we covered in the shared task are the Romance languages, which are Spanish (ES), French (FR), Italian (IT), Brazilian Portuguese (PT), and Romanian (RO). We chose the other languages based on two criteria. Since our system learns better with more data, we considered such languages. Also, we favored languages with higher occurring frequency of VMWEs. The frequencies were calculated from the statistics provided along with the corpora. So, we included the languages Bulgarian (BG), German (DE), Hungarian (HU), Polish (PL), and Slovenian (SL) in the experiments. We did not cover Turkish (TR) not to introduce a bias to system evaluation because we were in the Turkish annotation team.

Table 2 gives the results of Deep-BGT for each language separately. MWE-based and Token-based precision (P), recall (R), F-measure (F1), and rankings in the open-track are presented. According to the shared task results, Deep-BGT was ranked first in Bulgarian (BG) in terms of both MWE-based and Token-based F-measure, and was ranked first in German (DE) in terms of MWE-based F-measure. Constant et al. (2017) state that discontiguity is common in Germanic languages. Therefore, the MWE-based results obtained in German adds to the value of Deep-BGT. In French (FR) and Polish (PL), Deep-BGT was ranked first regarding the Token-based F-measure. Overall, in general ranking, our system was ranked second among the open-track systems participated in the shared task.

Languages	MWE-based				Token-based			
	P	R	F1	Rank	P	R	F1	Rank
BG	85.96	52.99	65.56	1	91.00	52.82	66.85	1
DE	60.94	36.35	45.53	1	77.92	37.64	50.76	3
ES	24.50	34.20	28.55	2	33.13	38.61	35.66	2
FR	57.81	49.80	53.51	2	78.88	56.45	65.80	1
HU	78.00	71.26	74.48	2	80.71	73.11	76.72	2
IT	45.52	25.60	32.77	2	70.00	27.63	39.62	2
PL	70.87	56.70	63.00	2	80.23	57.85	67.23	1
PT	72.44	46.11	56.35	2	79.40	44.83	57.30	2
RO	79.80	69.10	74.07	2	92.11	73.66	81.86	2
SL	58.90	38.40	46.49	2	72.19	40.34	51.76	2

Table 2: The Language-specific Results of Deep-BGT.

MWE-based and Token-based F1 scores per VMWE category of Deep-BGT are given in Table 3 and Table 4. The mark "-" denotes that the language does not have the corresponding category in the test set. Table 5 displays the number of VMWEs per category in the training and the development set. When we take a look at the MWE-based and Token-based F1 scores per VMWE category in Table 3 and Table 4 and the number of VMWEs per category in Table 5, we observe that the figures are correlated. In general, F1 scores increase as the number of VMWEs increases since the system learns better with more examples. Our system copes well with the IRV category. IRVs do not only have a large percentage in the data set, but they also appear in specific forms such as together with reflexive pronouns.

	LVC.full	LVC.cause	VID	IRV	VPC.full	VPC.semi	MVC	IAV	LS.ICV
BG	50.65	26.67	24.14	87.32	-	-	-	0.00	-
DE	4.17	0.00	24.35	33.77	63.47	0.00	-	-	-
ES	18.03	0.00	6.94	39.22	0.00	-	23.40	31.06	-
FR	61.38	0.00	32.26	78.70	-	-	0.00	-	-
HU	60.00	61.02	62.50	-	74.06	90.24	-	-	-
IT	31.71	20.51	9.59	51.14	57.89	-	33.33	28.07	0.00
PL	53.72	15.38	3.42	82.40	-	-	-	61.90	-
PT	66.56	0.00	21.94	50.70	-	-	-	-	-
RO	68.97	4.65	56.86	85.26	-	-	-	-	-
SL	16.33	0.00	10.11	65.61	-	-	-	44.60	-

Table 3: MWE-based F1 scores per VMWE category of Deep-BGT.

	LVC.full	LVC.cause	VID	IRV	VPC.full	VPC.semi	MVC	IAV	LS.ICV
BG	51.45	26.25	31.73	87.53	-	-	-	0.00	-
DE	9.43	0.00	36.62	48.19	67.44	6.25	-	-	-
ES	21.10	0.00	11.05	39.78	0.00	-	33.50	30.86	-
FR	62.67	0.00	59.92	79.35	-	-	0.00	-	-
HU	65.82	66.07	78.57	-	76.27	89.16	-	-	-
IT	37.39	26.67	21.13	52.72	58.23	-	30.77	33.85	0.00
PL	55.90	15.69	32.87	83.25	-	-	-	57.78	-
PT	67.60	0.00	28.77	50.35	-	-	-	-	-
RO	67.23	75.25	73.45	85.69	-	-	-	-	-
SL	21.05	22.22	25.64	66.97	-	-	-	43.77	-

Table 4: Token-based F1 scores per VMWE category of Deep-BGT.

	LVC.full	LVC.cause	VID	IRV	VPC.full	VPC.semi	MVC	IAV	LS.ICV
BG	1635	170	1178	2969	0	0	0	82	0
DE	252	30	1158	268	1485	130	0	0	0
ES	307	53	232	593	0	0	607	447	0
FR	1722	83	1953	1401	0	0	20	0	0
HU	977	373	94	0	4670	870	0	0	0
IT	644	166	1295	1048	83	2	29	458	29
PL	1684	213	430	2030	0	0	0	280	0
PT	3112	87	1012	772	0	0	0	0	0
RO	279	164	1438	3421	0	0	0	0	0
SL	206	52	621	1386	0	0	0	613	0

Table 5: Number of VMWEs per VMWE category in the training and the development set.

5 Conclusion

In this paper, we presented the Deep-BGT system that has participated to PARSEME Shared Task Edition 1.1. We followed the sequence tagging approach for VMWE identification. Based on this approach, the gappy 1-level tagging scheme, which is a variant of the BIO scheme, was used. We attempted to solve the discontiguity problem and the nested MWE problem by the proposed model.

Deep-BGT is a hybrid system which uses the bidirectional LSTM-CRF model. To the best of our knowledge, the bidirectional LSTM-CRF model was not used before in the VMWE identification task.

Due to the fact that Deep-BGT makes use of deep learning architectures, the more training data is available, the more the system learns. Also, the occurrence frequency of VMWEs in the data plays an important role. So, results for 10 languages following these criteria were submitted. According to the Shared Task results, the system ranked second in the open track and we conclude that the proposed system obtained successful results.

Acknowledgements

This research was supported by Boğaziçi University Research Fund Grant Number 14420.

References

Martín Abadi, Ashish Agarwal, Paul Barham, Eugene Brevdo, Zhifeng Chen, Craig Citro, Greg S. Corrado, Andy Davis, Jeffrey Dean, Matthieu Devin, Sanjay Ghemawat, Ian Goodfellow, Andrew Harp, Geoffrey Irving, Michael Isard, Yangqing Jia, Rafal Jozefowicz, Lukasz Kaiser, Manjunath Kudlur, Josh Levenberg, Dandelion Mané, Rajat Monga, Sherry Moore, Derek Murray, Chris Olah, Mike Schuster, Jonathon Shlens, Benoit Steiner, Ilya Sutskever, Kunal Talwar, Paul Tucker, Vincent Vanhoucke, Vijay Vasudevan, Fernanda Viégas, Oriol Vinyals, Pete Warden, Martin Wattenberg, Martin Wicke, Yuan Yu, and Xiaoqiang Zheng. 2015. TensorFlow: Large-Scale Machine Learning on Heterogeneous Systems. Software available from tensorflow.org.

Timothy Baldwin and Su Nam Kim. 2010. Multiword expressions. *Handbook of natural language processing*, 2:267–292.

François Chollet et al. 2015. Keras. `https://keras.io`.

Mathieu Constant, Gülşen Eryiğit, Johanna Monti, Lonneke Van Der 2017. Multiword expression processing: a survey. *Computational Linguistics*, 43(4):837–892.

Edouard Grave, Piotr Bojanowski, Prakhar Gupta, Armand Joulin, and Tomas Mikolov. 2018. Learning Word Vectors for 157 Languages. In *Proceedings of the International Conference on Language Resources and Evaluation (LREC 2018)*.

Alex Graves, Abdel-rahman Mohamed, and Geoffrey Hinton. 2013. Speech recognition with deep recurrent neural networks. In *Acoustics, speech and signal processing (icassp), 2013 ieee international conference on*, pages 6645–6649. IEEE.

Zhiheng Huang, Wei Xu, and Kai Yu. 2015. Bidirectional LSTM-CRF models for sequence tagging. *arXiv preprint arXiv:1508.01991*.

Natalia Klyueva, Antoine Doucet, and Milan Straka. 2017. Neural Networks for Multi-Word Expression Detection. *MWE 2017*, page 60.

John Lafferty, Andrew McCallum, and Fernando CN Pereira. 2001. Conditional random fields: Probabilistic models for segmenting and labeling sequence data.

Joël Legrand and Ronan Collobert. 2016. Phrase representations for multiword expressions. In *Proceedings of the 12th Workshop on Multiword Expressions*, number EPFL-CONF-219842.

Carlos Ramisch, Silvio Ricardo Cordeiro, Agata Savary, Veronika Vincze, Verginica Barbu Mititelu, Archna Bhatia, Maja Buljan, Marie Candito, Polona Gantar, Voula Giouli, Tunga Güngör, Abdelati Hawwari, Uxoa Iñurrieta, Jolanta Kovalevskaitė, Simon Krek, Timm Lichte, Chaya Liebeskind, Johanna Monti, Carla Parra Escartín, Behrang QasemiZadeh, Renata Ramisch, Nathan Schneider, Ivelina Stoyanova, Ashwini Vaidya, and Abigail Walsh. 2018. Edition 1.1 of the PARSEME Shared Task on Automatic Identification of Verbal Multiword Expressions. In *Proceedings of the Joint Workshop on Linguistic Annotation, Multiword Expressions and Constructions (LAW-MWE-CxG 2018)*, Santa Fe, New Mexico, USA, August. Association for Computational Linguistics.

Nils Reimers and Iryna Gurevych. 2017. Reporting score distributions makes a difference: Performance study of lstm-networks for sequence tagging. *arXiv preprint arXiv:1707.09861*.

Nathan Schneider, Emily Danchik, Chris Dyer, and Noah A Smith. 2014. Discriminative lexical semantic segmentation with gaps: running the MWE gamut. *Transactions of the Association for Computational Linguistics*, 2:193–206.

GBD-NER at PARSEME Shared Task 2018: Multiword Expression Detection Using Bidirectional Long-Short-Term Memory Networks and Graph-Based Decoding

Tiberiu Boros
Adobe Romania
boros@adobe.com

Ruxandra Burtica
Adobe Romania
burtica@adobe.com

Abstract

This paper addresses the issue of multiword expression (MWE) detection by employing a new decoding strategy inspired after graph-based parsing. We show that this architecture achieves state-of-the-art results with minimum feature-engineering, just by relying on lexicalized and morphological attributes. We validate our approach in a multilingual setting, using standard MWE corpora supplied in the PARSEME Shared Task.

1 Introduction

Multiword expression (MWE) detection is a challenging Natural Language Processing (NLP) task that consists in finding isolated tokens or sequences of tokens that form high-level structures (i.e. multiword expressions). Naively, this can be regarded as a sequence labeling task, which in fact influenced legacy methods for MWE detection to use this strategy. In fact, this is not far fetched, since this approach has yielded highly accurate results so far. However, we have to point a couple of task-specific details:

- **Sparsity**: Inside an utterance there are only a couple of tokens that must be labeled as named entities or multiword expressions. This actually yields data sparsity and could bias the model towards not identifying any of the tokens as part of a multiword expression;

- **Overlapping**: MWE corpora contains many examples where high-level entities share tokens among each other. There are several ways in which this issue can be mitigated, for instance training several different classifiers for each type of label;

- **Long spans**: It is often the case that MWE tokens are distantly distributed across a single utterance. Classical classifiers and even modern LSTM-based approaches are unable to detect such long range dependencies (though the later mentioned approach should), mainly because these cases are rare inside the training data and there is insufficient statistical evidence to support them.

In what follows, we propose a new methodology for learning dependencies within MWE tokens which mitigates the impact of the previously mentioned issues. Particularly, we use Bidirectional Long-Short-Term Memory (BDLSTM) (Graves and others, 2012) networks, but we do not employ a naive tagging approach as it is done in similar related work (see section 2). Instead, we use a strategy inspired by the graph-based parser of Kiperwasser and Goldberg (2016), with the following major differences: (a) the network is trained to produce fully connected subgraphs (not parsing trees); (b) we use a different graph-decoding strategy that is tailored for MWEs; (c) our feature-set is composed of morphological and lexicalized features and we apply a two-tier dropout methodology (explained in Section 3) in order to increase the generalization capability of our models.

The proposed methodology was evaluated during the PARSEME Shared Task on Verbal Multiword Expression Detection (Ramisch et al., 2018) and the full evaluation details for all languages are available in our blog[1].

---

[1] http://opensource.adobe.com/NLP-Cube/blog/posts/1-gbd/results.html

Proceedings of the Joint Workshop on
Linguistic Annotation, Multiword Expressions and Constructions (LAW-MWE-CxG-2018), pages 254–260
Santa Fe, New Mexico, USA, August 25-26, 2018.

2 Related work

There is a strong resemblance between NER and MWE detection, and we feel that the related work section should cover both tasks, whenever the underlying methodology and results can be shared between the two. Aside from classical approaches to NER and MWE detection that employ Conditional Random Fields (CRFs), Support Vector Machines (SVMs), Hidden Markov Models (HMMs), Perceptrons etc., there are several neural inspired methods, on which we will currently focus, given that we also use a deep learning approach.

Chiu and Nichols (2015) introduce a NER system that uses stacked BDLSTM layers over word-encodings that are obtained by concatenating word-embeddings with manually engineered word-lever features. The character level embeddings that are computed using convolutional neural networks (CNNs). Their system is trained to distinguish between "PERSON", "ORGANIZATION", "LOCA-TION" and "MISC" entity types and they employ a classical BIOES tagging strategy (Begining, Inside, Outside, Ending and Single)

Shao et al. (2016) compare (a) a "window-based" feed-forward network, (b) a standard BDLSTM network and (c) a "window-based" BDLSTM network. They use word embeddings combined with word-level features as input for their networks and they also rely on IOB labeling strategy. As expected, the feed-forward neural network is easier to train but it is outperformed in accuracy by the standard BDLSTM model; (b) the "window-based" BDLSTM is robust whenever fewer features are employed, but it is outperformed by other BDLSTM models, such as the one presented in Chiu and Nichols (2015).

(Lample et al., 2016) present two network architectures for NER: the CRF-LSTM architecture and the transition-based LSTM strategy, which, just like our strategy, is also inspired after parsing. The input features are based on word-embeddings and character-level embeddings and the results show that, in most cases, the two network architectures obtain similar results, with the CRF-LSTM model always a bit more accurate.

The transition-based strategy is also exploited by Al Saied et al. (2017), but this time for multiword expression detection using SVMs. They evaluate their system during the PARSEME Shared Task (Savary et al., 2017) and, according to the official results, this methodology achieves state-of-the-art results.

3 Proposed methodology

3.1 Graph-based encoding with neural networks

As opposed to (a) local classifiers which work by statically estimating the output label (t_i) probability from localized features (f_i): $P(t_i|f_i)$ and from (b) graph or sequence classical classifiers which work by using a localized set of features (f_i) and by performing decoding using limited-context dependencies : $argmax(P(t_i|\{t_j \in \{dependencies\}\}, f_i))$, Long-Short-Term Memory (LSTM) networks are way better at computing each word's label (t_i) based on features extracted from the entire sentence: $P(t_i|f_{i=\overline{1,n}})$.

This could in theory mean that, if we are not dealing with overlapping expression, one could employ LSTM models for sequence labeling, regardless of the span between the tokens that are part of the same high-level entity. The capacity of the model to detect long-range dependencies is bound to the number of stacked LSTM layers and the number of LSTM cells inside each layer. However, adding more layers and increasing the number of cells is also a recipe for over-fitting the training data, and there is a limit of the extent to which mechanisms to prevent over-fitting mechanisms are able to help.

As such, we propose a graph-based encoding/decoding strategy that is able to cope with overlapping high-level entities and large spans between tokens, by **forcing the model to focus** on the dependencies between tokens that belong to the same expression.

Figure 1 contains a rolled-out version of our network architecture. We start off with a sequence of words as input, and convert it into a sequence of fixed-sized vectors (details will follow). After this, we use two stacked Bidirectional LSTM (BDLSTM) layers (Graves and Schmidhuber, 2009), obtaining a list of vector embeddings for each word inside the original sequence. Next, we take each vector from the internal representation and we split it using three parallel $tanh$ layers into 3 separate "projections".

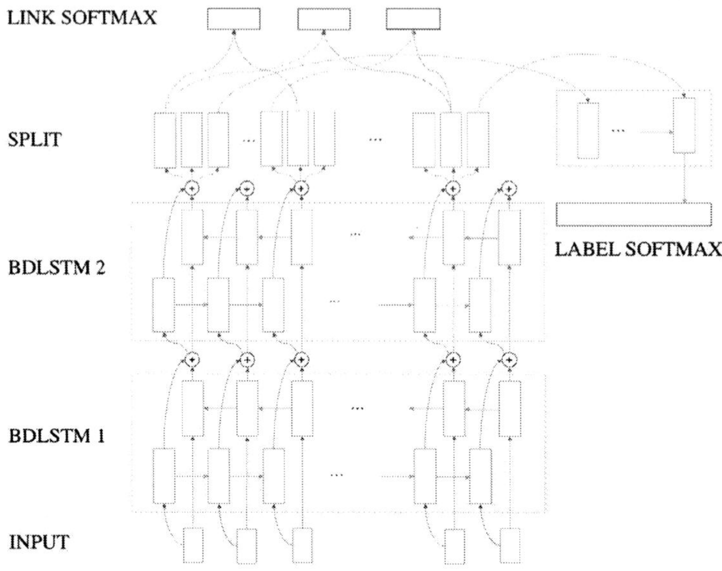

Figure 1: The rolled-out sparse tagging network

Until now, this architecture is similar to the one described in Kiperwasser and Goldberg (2016), except that we use 3 projections instead of one. As such, for each word w_i, we obtain three vectors which we will refer to as v_i^0, v_i^1 and v_i^2. Finally, for every pair of words w_i and w_j with $i \neq j$ we use single unit sigmoid activation, outputting the probability of the two words being part of the same high-level expression or not. The input for the sigmoid unit is obtained by concatenating the first vector from the split operation for word w_i (i.e. v_i^0) with the second vector of the split operation for word w_j (i.e. v_j^1). We store the resulting values in an "adjacency matrix" a (Equation 3).

$$a_{i,j} = \sigma(W_s \cdot (v_i^0 \oplus v_j^1) + b_s) \tag{1}$$

During training, we establish if words w_i and w_j are part of the same high-level entity and, for every pair (i, j) we infer as loss $-\log a_{i,j}$ if the words are constituents of the same expression or $-log(1.0 -$

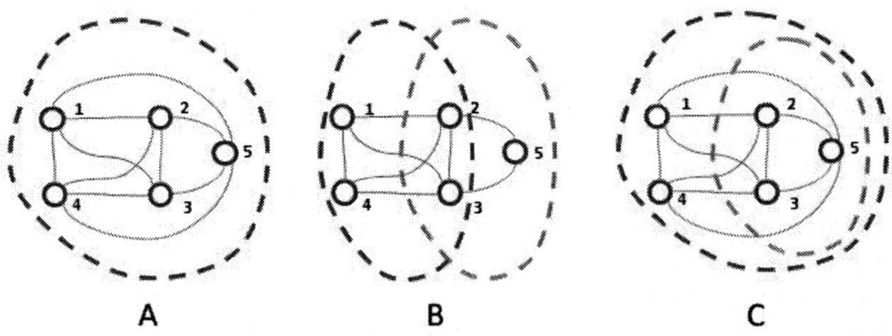

Figure 2: Hard decoding cases in entity extraction

$a_{i,j}$) otherwise.

Because a is an adjacency matrix, we expect it to be symmetrical on the main diagonal and reduce the number of computational steps by adding the condition $j > i$, when we compute the loss. Also, when training, we perform back-propagation and parameter update only after we compute and sum all individual losses.

The feature-set used in our approach is composed of the concatenation of two vectors, one for lexicalized features and the other for morphological features. The lexicalized feature vector is obtained by adding two specialized embeddings, one for the surface-form and one for the word's lemma[2] . Morphological features are obtained by adding three vectors representing embeddings for the three morphological tiers provided as input (see McDonald et al. (2013) for more details): universal part-of-speech (UPOS), language-specific part-of-speech (XPOS) and attributes (ATTRS).

$$a_{i,j} = \frac{\exp(y_{i,j}^0))}{\sum_{k=0}^1 \exp(y_{i,j}^k))}, y_{i,j}^k \in Y_{i,j} \tag{2}$$

$$Y_{i,j} = w \cdot (v_i^0 \oplus v_j^1) + b \tag{3}$$

During training, we use a two-tier dropout methodology: (a) independently drop embedding vectors for word, lemma, UPOS, XPOS and ATTRS, scaling the other vectors to cope with missing values and (b) independently drop one of the lexical or morphological vectors, also using scaling. Given word w_i with its corresponding lemma (l_i), UPOS (u_i), XPOS (x_i) and ATTRS (t_i), we define the input vector for the BDLSTM (Equation 4).

$$f(w_i, l_i, u_i, x_i, t_i) = (((E_{w_i} + E_{l_i}) \cdot s_{1_l}) \oplus (E_{u_i} + E_{x_i} + E_{t_i}) \cdot s_{1_m})) \cdot s_2 \tag{4}$$

where E is used to generically represent an embeddings lookup table and s_{1_l}, s_{1_m} and s_2 are scalars used as scaling factors in the two-tier dropout technique.

Notes:

1. We observed that **character-level features are better suited for standard NER tasks and not for MWE detection**. Likely, this is related to the fact that character-level features such as casing, letter n-grams or appurtenance to the symbol and/or number class are useful in identifying proper names, dates, location etc., but they are not informative for semantics (at least not for most languages);

2. External word embeddings would have rendered our system into the "open" track, which we did not consider in our evaluation, but future development plans include this option.

3.2 Expression decoding and label selection

The first part of the algorithm trains the network to output half of an adjacency matrix inside an undirected graph. Whenever two or more words form a high-level entity we expect them to project into a complete subgraph, because the model is taught that all words inside that entity are adjacent in the graph structure. In order to extract the entities, we use an algorithm to compute all complete subgraphs from the adjacency matrix.

In our experiments we used backtracking to perform the extraction of complete subgraphs. The algorithm starts by building a mini-graph with two nodes that are adjacent. Then, it recursively adds new nodes that satisfy the property of being adjacent with all the nodes already inside the subgraph. Whenever no new nodes can be added to a subgraph, the subgraph is added to the solution list and the recursion is stopped. Partial solutions are ignored and, at the end of the process, we remove duplicates inside the solution list. This naive backtracking implementation works for us mainly because high-level entities only contain a few tokens and the $O(2^n)$ complexity is actually manageable.

To select the correct output label for every sequence of words inside an high-level entity. Let E^k be a detected entity and I_l^k the ordered set of word indices belonging to this entity. In order to predict the

---

[2]We only compute embeddings for frequently-occurring words and lemmas – we used ($f_{tok} \geq 2$)

L	MWE			#	Tok			#	L	MWE			#	Tok			#
	P	R	F		P	R	F			P	R	F		P	R	F	
BG	79.41	56.42	65.97	1	82.10	55.72	66.39	1	HR	51.52	37.35	43.31	4	64.41	42.22	50.69	2
DE	44.13	33.94	38.37	4	64.24	43.49	51.87	1	HU	85.47	76.55	80.76	5	90.54	77.09	83.27	6
EL	64.74	49.10	55.85	1	74.02	52.22	61.24	1	IT	49.52	41.73	45.30	2	62.46	45.59	52.71	2
EN	10.52	57.68	17.79	8	11.86	60.81	19.85	8	LT	07.11	44.80	12.27	4	08.63	49.60	14.70	4
ES	22.22	36.80	27.71	5	30.38	46.17	36.65	7	PL	75.06	62.52	68.22	1	78.30	62.18	69.32	1
EU	82.07	71.40	76.36	1	83.12	71.79	77.14	1	PT	66.59	55.88	60.77	3	69.78	57.58	63.09	2
FA	81.96	75.25	78.46	1	88.60	77.54	82.70	1	RO	88.35	83.70	85.96	1	89.52	83.52	86.41	1
FR	72.76	42.37	53.55	2	81.85	44.66	57.79	2	SL	61.07	52.40	56.40	2	68.57	55.08	61.09	2
HE	74.19	09.16	16.31	7	75.76	08.66	15.54	10	TR	68.07	54.35	60.44	1	70.06	54.64	61.40	1
HI	61.90	72.80	66.91	5	65.18	71.38	68.14	6	**AVG**	**60.36**	**53.38**	**56.65**	**1**	**66.28**	**55.78**	**60.57**	**1**

Table 1: Results obtained on the PARSEME VMWE identification Shared Task

label for this entity we build the corresponding list of internal embeddings vectors from the third split $v^3_{I^k_l}$. We fed the list in natural order into a single layer LSTM trained in a many-to-one fashion and use output of the final state as input for a Softmax layer trained to output the correct label for the sequence.

For clarity, we have included a couple of decoding examples (Figure 2) which we will further discuss. Note that the indexes used for the nodes have nothing to do with the actual indexes of the words that form the graph. We only marked them with numbers from 1 to 5, to be able to easily reference them.

The simplest **Case (A)** shows 5 interconnected graph nodes, which form a single high-level entity. Most of training data contains only this type of example, where we have to mark all the discovered tokens with the same label.

Case (B) is more complex, as we have two overlapping high-level entities which share nodes 2 and 3. As such, the decoding algorithm can still easily spot the two distinct complete subgraphs, [1, 2, 3, 4] and [2, 3, 5] and mark them as two distinct entities (even if they are, or not, of the same type).

Case (C) is by far the hardest. Here we have two distinct entities, with one entity [1, 2, 3, 4, 5] completely including the second entity [2, 3, 5]. We have not encountered this case in any of the training data but we feel obliged to discuss it as well. Obviously, given that the input data is correct, the decoding algorithm will always find a single entity, because all the nodes are adjacent and there is no reason to perform a split into two subgraphs. One solution to this issue is to check if any partial subgraph yields a different label from the full subgraph. This solution is only valid for entities which belong to different classes, but we feel that the two expressions sharing the same label would be highly unlikely to overlap. However, this solution may not always hold, and in the absence of real data to support Case (C).

Finally, we need to select the correct output label for every sequence of words inside an high-level entity. Let E^k be an detected entity and I^k_l the ordered set of word indices belonging to this entity. In order to predict the label for this entity we build the corresponding list of internal embeddings vectors from the third split $v^3_{I^k_l}$. We keep the list in natural order, meaning the order in which the words appear inside the utterance. This list is sequentially feed into a single layer LSTM trained in a many-to-one fashion. This means that we only use the final state of the cells as input for a Softmax layer. The Softmax layer is designed to output the probability distribution over all possible labels. During training we only compute loss for detected entities that are inside the gold standard and we do this even if the algorithm did not detect them correctly at that state. We did not use a bidirectional layer or attention mainly because the input list is usually short and a larger model could easily over-fit the training data.

4 Experimental validation

We validated our approach using the multilingual corpora provided by the PARSEME corpus. The data covers 19 languages and comes in CUPT format. The CUPT format is similar to CONLLU, but adds a new annotation layer for VMWE expressions. For each entry inside a sentence contains the word, it's lemma, UPOS, XPOS and ATTRs, which are automatically labeled using UDPipe (Straka et al., 2016). Table 1 summarizes the results. The "AVG" entry refers to the macro-average computed over all languages. This means that the precision and recall are computed for all languages and then F-score is recalculated using the standard equation. For every language, as well as for the overall result, we include the absolute ranking ('#') of our system based on the results from the official runs. During the official runs. our software was affected by a bug that caused it to ignore any lexical information in the CUPT files. The results shown in the table refer to the corrected version of our system and we do provide full access to the source-code[3] for anyone interested.

As shown, this methodology achieves overall higher results, but it does not always produce state-of-the-art results for certain languages. The lower scores for languages such as EN, HE and LT can be explained by the fact that those languages were only provided with small training sets and no development data. It is somewhat expected that deep learning methods require a critical mass of input data in order to provide good generalization. Also, the proportion of MWEs that were previously unseen in the training data for EN is 92%, 37% for HE and 94% for LT. Without using external data such as word embeddings our intuition is that it is hard to learn patterns that have to do with "word semantics" (the case of MWEs) with so few training examples.

Also, we have to mention that some training sets contained "single token" multiword expressions, which, as the name suggests, means that a multiword expression contained only one token. Our algorithm was originally designed to work by detecting dependencies between each pair of tokens inside a MWE, which is not the case here because the MWEs only contain one word. In order to do this, we adapted our algorithm by introducing a virtual "ROOT" in every sentence. During training we modified the system to output links between all MWE tokens and the ROOT. This solved the issue with single-token MWEs, but biased the model for multiword tokens. For instance, the single token MWE proportion for HU is 74%, and our f-score on this type of expressions is 84.17% using this tweak. However, if we compare the new f-score for multiword MWEs we get an absolute drop of 7%.

5 Conclusions and future work

We have described a new methodology of extracting MWEs using Bidirectional LSTMS and a graph-based representation. Our code is freely available on GitHub and we plan to later integrated it in our NLP processing framework (NLP-Cube)[4].

In the near future we plan to explore and answer a couple of questions, such as:

1. How externally computed word embeddings influence the performance of this methodology on MWE detection;

2. Will this graph-based decoding strategy have a positive impact on standard or domain-specific NER;

3. What is the source for lower f-scores on languages such as Hungarian, Deutsch and Hindi. that, at first glance, have enough training data to support our approach;

4. How will this method work for other NLP tasks which involve sparse and long-range dependencies between words, one good example being co-reference resolution.

Regarding MWE identification, parsing information could help reduce the ambiguities in classification, given that to our knowledge, in the Universal Dependencies Corpus words that form MWEs are marked using the "fixed" subordination dependency, at least for some languages. Whether or not parsing accuracy is sufficient enough to support MWE identification is a different question. Also, given that our system is inspired from parsing, our intuition is that parsing will not enhance results.

On a related note, NLP-Cube has end-2-end raw text processing to UD format processing capabilities. This means that it can be used for MWE detection without requiring external CUPT files. Anyone interested can check the end-2-end raw text processing capacity of NLP-Cube on this year's shared task on universal dependencies parsing[5].

---

[3]https://github.com/adobe/NLP-Cube/tree/dev.gbd-ner

[4]https://github.com/adobe/NLP-Cube

[5]http://universaldependencies.org/conll18/

References

Hazem Al Saied, Matthieu Constant, and Marie Candito. 2017. The atilf-llf system for parseme shared task: a transition-based verbal multiword expression tagger. In *Proceedings of the 13th Workshop on Multiword Expressions (MWE 2017)*, pages 127–132.

Jason PC Chiu and Eric Nichols. 2015. Named entity recognition with bidirectional lstm-cnns. *arXiv preprint arXiv:1511.08308*.

Alex Graves et al. 2012. *Supervised sequence labelling with recurrent neural networks*, volume 385. Springer.

Alex Graves and Jürgen Schmidhuber. 2009. Offline handwriting recognition with multidimensional recurrent neural networks. In *Advances in neural information processing systems*, pages 545–552.

Eliyahu Kiperwasser and Yoav Goldberg. 2016. Simple and accurate dependency parsing using bidirectional lstm feature representations. *arXiv preprint arXiv:1603.04351*.

Guillaume Lample, Miguel Ballesteros, Sandeep Subramanian, Kazuya Kawakami, and Chris Dyer. 2016. Neural architectures for named entity recognition. *arXiv preprint arXiv:1603.01360*.

Ryan McDonald, Joakim Nivre, Yvonne Quirmbach-Brundage, Yoav Goldberg, Dipanjan Das, Kuzman Ganchev, Keith Hall, Slav Petrov, Hao Zhang, Oscar Täckström, et al. 2013. Universal dependency annotation for multilingual parsing. In *Proceedings of the 51st Annual Meeting of the Association for Computational Linguistics (Volume 2: Short Papers)*, volume 2, pages 92–97.

Carlos Ramisch, Silvio Ricardo Cordeiro, Agata Savary, Veronika Vincze, Verginica Barbu Mititelu, Archna Bhatia, Maja Buljan, Marie Candito, Polona Gantar, Voula Giouli, Tunga Güngör, Abdelati Hawwari, Uxoa Iñurrieta, Jolanta Kovalevskaitė, Simon Krek, Timm Lichte, Chaya Liebeskind, Johanna Monti, Carla Parra Escartín, Behrang QasemiZadeh, Renata Ramisch, Nathan Schneider, Ivelina Stoyanova, Ashwini Vaidya, and Abigail Walsh. 2018. Edition 1.1 of the parseme shared task on automatic identification of verbal multiword expressions. In *Proceedings of the Joint Workshop on Linguistic Annotation, Multiword Expressions and Constructions (LAW-MWE-CxG-2018)*, Santa Fe, USA, August. Association for Computational Linguistics.

Agata Savary, Carlos Ramisch, Silvio Cordeiro, Federico Sangati, Veronika Vincze, Behrang Qasemizadeh, Marie Candito, Fabienne Cap, Voula Giouli, Ivelina Stoyanova, et al. 2017. The parseme shared task on automatic identification of verbal multiword expressions. In *Proceedings of the 13th Workshop on Multiword Expressions (MWE 2017)*, pages 31–47.

Yan Shao, Christian Hardmeier, and Joakim Nivre. 2016. Multilingual named entity recognition using hybrid neural networks. In *The Sixth Swedish Language Technology Conference (SLTC)*.

Milan Straka, Jan Hajic, and Jana Straková. 2016. Udpipe: Trainable pipeline for processing conll-u files performing tokenization, morphological analysis, pos tagging and parsing. In *Language Resources and Evaluation Conference*.

Mumpitz at PARSEME Shared Task 2018: A Bidirectional LSTM for the Identification of Verbal Multiword Expressions

Rafael Ehren
Dept. of Comp. Linguistics
Heinrich Heine University
Duesseldorf, Germany
ehren@phil.hhu.de

Timm Lichte
Dept. of Comp. Linguistics
Heinrich Heine University
Duesseldorf, Germany
lichte@phil.hhu.de

Younes Samih
Dept. of Comp. Linguistics
Heinrich Heine University
Duesseldorf, Germany
samih@phil.hhu.de

Abstract

In this paper, we describe Mumpitz, the system we submitted to the PARSEME Shared Task on automatic identification of verbal multiword expressions (VMWEs). Mumpitz consists of a Bidirectional Recurrent Neural Network (BRNN) with Long Short-Term Memory (LSTM) units and a heuristic that leverages the dependency information provided in the PARSEME corpus data to differentiate VMWEs in a sentence. We submitted results for seven languages in the closed track of the task and for one language in the open track. For the open track we used the same system, but with pretrained instead of randomly initialized word embeddings to improve the system performance.

1 Introduction

Multiword Expressions (MWEs) are linguistic expressions that consist of multiple lexemes and exhibit some form of idiomaticity. The term idiomaticity denotes the fact that the properties of the whole cannot (fully) be predicted by the properties of the components. Idiomaticity can surface on the lexical, syntactic, semantic, pragmatic and/or statistical level (Baldwin and Kim, 2010) and it is a reason why MWEs manifest a well-known challenge for natural language processing (NLP) tasks as parsing and machine translation.

The PARSEME shared task (ST) focuses only on a subset of MWEs, namely verbal multiword expressions (VMWEs), since their attributes like discontinuity (i.e. non-adjacency of the VMWEs' components) and semantic or syntactic ambiguity, make them especially challenging for automatic processing (Ramisch et al., 2018). The goal of the ST is the identification of VMWEs in running text. Besides extraction, which is the process of finding new MWE types, identification of MWE tokens in running text is the most important task with regard to MWE processing. In the context of the ST VMWEs are categorized into types like verb-particle constructions (VPC), light verb constructions (LVC), idioms (VID), inherently reflexive verbs (IRV) or multi-verb constructions (MVC). The ST is multilingual, i.e. the PARSEME organizers provide annotated corpora in 20 different languages which are split in train, dev and test sets. Competing teams can choose to only incorporate the features provided in these data sets or use external features such as MWE lexicons, word embeddings, etc. Systems solely based on preexisting features compete in the closed track, systems that also use external data in the open track of the ST.

Our system, Mumpitz, is a bidirectional recurrent neural network (BRNN) with long short-term memory (LSTM) units coupled with a heuristic that distinguishes different VMWEs in a sentence. We submitted results for 7 of the 20 languages to the closed track and for one language to the open track. In the next section we will provide an overview over last year's entries to the ST, before we will describe Mumpitz in detail. Subsequently, we will present the results and discuss the performance of the system as well as its possibilities for improvement.

Proceedings of the Joint Workshop on
Linguistic Annotation, Multiword Expressions and Constructions (LAW-MWE-CxG-2018), pages 261–267
Santa Fe, New Mexico, USA, August 25-26, 2018.

2   Related Work

In this section, we will focus on the system description papers that were submitted to the PARSEME shared task 1.0.

The only (official) entry to the open track of last year's edition of the shared task came from Nerima et al. (2017) who employed a multilingual constituency parser that consists of a generic parsing module that can be adapted to the needs of different languages. The key component for the identification task is its manually built lexicon that contains information about collocations, i.e., a relational database.[1] During the parsing process the input is matched against entries in the database to identify VMWEs. Another parsing approach that in contrast does not rely on external resources and thus was submitted to the closed track stems from Simkó et al. (2017). They trained a dependency parser by merging the training MWE annotation into its dependency annotation. A further parsing-based system came from Al Saied et al. (2017) who used a transition-based dependency parser.

Boroş et al. (2017) entered the shared task with a Conditional Random Fields (CRF) classifier. This classifier decides for every word in an input sequence (sentence) if it is part of a VMWE or not with the help of lemma and part-of-speech features for a certain window of words around it. More precisely, they did this in two steps. First the classifier labeled the head of the VMWE, the verb, and then, in a second step, the words that link to the head were identified. A strategy that resulted in an increase in precision according to the authors. Maldonado et al. (2017) also employed a CRF model but instead of only one set of features they used several – one for every broad language family. In addition to the official results of the CRF classifier, they implemented a postprocessing step that would have been submitted to the open track if the results had been achieved in time. In this step, a re-ranking of the 10 most likely output sequences of the CRF classifier was conducted by calculating context vectors using a third-party corpus. Then those vectors were used to calculate new features that were in turn fed to a supervised regression algorithm.

Since they also used a Bidirectional Recurrent Neural Network (BRNN), the most similar approach to ours came from Klyueva et al. (2017). The main differences (except for the hyperparameters) are the use of gated recurrent units (GRU) instead of Long Short-Term Memory (LSTM) units and randomly initialized word embeddings instead of pretrained word embeddings in their network.

3   System Description

3.1   Why a BRNN with LSTM units?

Mumpitz is a Bidirectional Recurrent Neural Network (BRNN) with Long Short-Term Memory (LSTM) units coupled with a heuristic that leverages the dependency information provided in the PARSEME corpus data to differentiate VMWEs in a sentence. Since, in recent years, RNNs have proved to be very efficient on sequence processing tasks like POS tagging (Labeau et al., 2015) or named entity recognition (NER) (Chiu and Nichols, 2016) and the identification of MWEs can be seen as a sequence labeling task, this choice was quite natural. The great advantage of RNNs over vanilla neural networks is that they are able to draw on an entire history of inputs and not just the most recent input. The following shows a forward propagation step of a simple RNN where g is an activation function like tanh or ReLU, h_t is the hidden state at time step t, x_t is the input at time step t, b_h is the bias vector and W_{hh} and W_{hx} are weight matrices:

$$h_t = g(W_{hh}h_{t-1} + W_{hx}x_t + b_h) \tag{1}$$

The important thing to notice is that the hidden state of the previous time step, h_{t-1}, influences the hidden state of the current time step. Consider the following example from the English train set of the ST:

(1)   The Knight of the Sad Countenance does not give up his obsessions.

---

[1] While collocations are (and were) not considered MWEs according to the PARSEME annotation guidelines, they ironically refer to VMWE categories of the shared task as "verbal collocations". Just another instance of how differently the term is used.

At time step $t = 10$, when the network reads the word *up*, it will have remembered that it read *give* shortly before and thus it could infer that the preposition is part of the VPC *give up*. This example also illustrates a shortcoming of simple RNNs: Just as the co-occurrence of *give* is an indication for *up* being part of a VPC, the co-occurrence of *up* is also an indication for *give* being a part of a VPC. But because the RNN only uses the information of the inputs from the previous and not from future time steps, it cannot use the information that *up* follows *give*. That's why bidirectional RNNs are used for such tasks. As the name suggests, BRNNs read the input from left to right and from right to left and use the hidden states from both passes to make a prediction:

$$\overrightarrow{h}_t = g(\overrightarrow{W}_{hh}\,\overrightarrow{h}_{t-1} + \overrightarrow{W}_{hx}x_t + \overrightarrow{b}_h) \tag{2}$$

$$\overleftarrow{h}_t = g(\overleftarrow{W}_{hh}\,\overleftarrow{h}_{t+1} + \overleftarrow{W}_{hx}x_t + \overleftarrow{b}_h) \tag{3}$$

But also BRNNs have the well known problem of not being awfully good at learning long distance dependencies, because of vanishing/exploding gradients. This is especially problematic for some VMWEs as the following example from the German training sentences illustrates:

(2)   Es scheiden die Vertreter   von Ruanda, Argentinien, Oman, Nigeria und Tschechiens aus.
       it drop   the representatives of Rwanda, Argentine, Oman, Nigeria and Czechia   out.
       'The representatives of Rwanda, Argentine, Oman, Nigeria and Czechia drop out.'

The German VPC *ausscheiden* ('drop out') can occur in split word order, where the particle *aus* can be very far apart from the base word *scheiden* – in the sentence above there are nine words in between them. These long distance dependencies are not unusual for VMWEs and are one of the main challenges in their processing.

LSTM units (Hochreiter and Schmidhuber, 1997) can be employed to tackle this problem. The structure of LSTMs allows them to "forget" certain features, while "remembering" others. For the example above this means that in theory the LSTM could remember that it has seen *scheiden* when it comes to *aus* and thus label it a VMWE.

3.2   Experimental setup for the closed track

We used Keras with TensorFlow as back-end to build our network (Chollet and others, 2015). Keras is a deep learning API written in Python that makes it very convenient to write complex neural network architectures in just a few lines of code. The back-end, TensorFlow, is an open source software library developed by Google Brain (Abadi et al., 2015) that is optimized for large-scale machine learning applications. This is achieved by defining the models as computational graphs which then can be split to distribute them across different servers.

The model we employed for the identification task is a BRNN with 100 LSTM units. The features that were fed as input to the BRNN were mapped to embeddings and concatenated. Of all the features that were provided in the train and test files, combinations of the following were tested as input for the neural network: word form (WF), lemma (L), universal POS (UP), language specific POS (LP), head of the current word (H) and the dependency relation to the head (D). The combination of features that achieved the highest F1 score on the German dev set consisted of L, LP and D and it was subsequently used for the predictions on the test sets for all the languages. Of course, it would have made more sense to choose the best performing set of features for every language or language family (as Maldonado et al. (2017) did), but we chose this course of action because we did not have the time to do so and we were mostly interested in the German data set. One of the reasons for this focus is the fact that two of the authors did some annotation work on the German corpus of this year's edition of the ST and we were eager to see how well a deep learning algorithm would do at this challenging data set.

To form the input for the network the lemmas were mapped to randomly initialized embeddings of dimensionality 50, while the embeddings for LP and D both had 20 dimensions. Thus, the concatenated feature vectors were of size 90 and every sentence was represented by a certain number of those feature vectors. Because Keras requires all input sequences to have the same length, this number had to be fixed.

This was achieved by padding all the feature sequences to the length of the longest sentence (which, for example, was 100 words long in the German corpus) with an arbitrary value of L, LP or D. Hence, every sentence was represented by a matrix of shape *maximum-sentence-length* $\times$ 90 (e.g. 100×90 for German).

To avoid overfitting, we applied a Dropout of 0.1 to the LSTM layer. Dropout is a regularization method that randomly deletes a specific number of nodes (in our case 10% of the nodes) during the training process. This basically has the effect that the network is inhibited from "memorizing" the training data too well which in turn prevents overfitting. We experimented with different dropout rates and found that the performance of the model decreased when using larger rates, so we maintained a rate of 0.1 for all the experiments.

The last part of the model is a softmax layer that returns the probability distribution over the tags. The focus was exclusively on the identification of VMWEs. The classifier did only decide if a certain word was part of a VMWE or not, that is, the classifier did not consider any of the VMWE type labels. One problem that arises by applying this strategy is that the different VMWEs in an sentence are not distinguished, because every word that belongs to a VMWE has the same label, even if they do not belong to the same expression.

Differentiating the words tagged as VMWEs in an sentence was the purpose of the heuristic mentioned above which worked in different steps: first, it identified all the words in a sentence that were labeled as VMWEs and had the universal POS-tag "VERB" and enumerated them. In the next step, every word that was a dependent of an enumerated verb received the same number as this verb. Finally, every verb not labeled as a VMWE by the classifier that had a dependent labeled as such, also got the VMWE label.

To summarize, here is how the classification proceeded: Every sentence was fed into the BRNN one word at a time, i.e. one feature vector at a time. At every time step the hidden states of the LSTM units[2] were passed on to the softmax layer to compute a prediction for the current word that included the information from all the time steps before and all the time steps after. For example, if a sequence of 100 words (feature vectors) was fed to the network, the output was a 100×2 matrix, i.e. the probabilities for every word if it belonged to a VMWE or not. The training was not conducted with a fixed set of epochs, but the loss of a cross validation set (10% of the train set) was monitored and the training was stopped when it did not decrease anymore for two consecutive epochs. The convergence was relatively fast, usually it took between 4 and 7 epochs to train. The loss was computed with binary cross-entropy while the optimization algorithm used was RMSProp. After the network made its predictions the heuristic differentiated the annotated VMWEs as described above.

3.3 Experimental setup for the open track

The model for the open track is essentially the same as for the closed track. The only difference is that we didn't use randomly initialized embeddings, but pretrained word embeddings. We used the word2vec implementation (more precisely the skip-gram model) of the python package gensim to create the word embeddings (Řehůřek and Sojka, 2010). The word vectors were trained on the DECOW16 corpus (Schäfer and Bildhauer, 2012) which is a German web corpus that comes in two variants: one with 20 billion tokens and full documents and one with 11 billion tokens and shuffled sentences. The latter was used for the training. The word embeddings have dimensionality 100 and represent lemmas, not the word surface forms. Besides the embeddings we trained ourselves, we also tested pretrained embeddings that were trained on Wikipedia with fastText (Bojanowski et al., 2016), an extension of word2vec.[3] After evaluation on the dev set we opted for the selftrained embeddings, as they performed considerably better then those pretrained with fastText. And since the training of embeddings on a very large corpus like DECOW16[4] is somewhat time-consuming, we only managed to submit results for the German dataset in time for the open track.

---

[2] The hidden states were activated with the hyperbolic tangent and the gates with the hard sigmoid function.

[3] Pretrained word vectors for 294 languages can be found here: `https://github.com/facebookresearch/fastText/blob/master/pretrained-vectors.md`

[4] Which of course has to exist in the first place for a specific language.

Ahead of the training process every lemma in the vocabulary was mapped to its respective word2vec embedding to form an embeddings matrix which was then used instead of the random instantiations. For some words such an embedding did not exist (because it did not appear often enough in DECOW16), so in these cases the words were mapped to zero vectors. Like the random instantiations the pretrained word embeddings were concatenated with the (still randomly initialized) embeddings for LP and D which resulted in feature vectors of 140 dimensions to represent the words in the sentences. Everything else stayed exactly the same as for the setup of the closed track.

4 Results

Because the general ranking of the shared task seems to depend on the average performance over 19 languages and we only submitted results for 7 languages, it may not be a good indicator for Mumpitz' performance. Therefore we will concentrate on the language-specific evaluation. As already evident from the system description, Mumpitz did not make any predictions for the VMWE type, so we will also skip this part of the evaluation.

The language-specific results for the closed and the open track can be seen in Table 1. Since the selection of the features was conducted on the basis of how well it performed on the German dev set, it is not particularly surprising that Mumpitz achieved its highest rankings on the German test set and considerably lower rankings on other languages. For the closed track it ranks 5th (of 11) in the MWE-based and first (of 11) in the token-based evaluation. For the open track it ranks last (of 4) in the MWE-based, and again first (of 4) in the token-based evaluation. Furthermore Mumpitz ranks relatively high for Bulgarian (4th of 10), French (5th of 13) and Portuguese (4th of 13) in the token-based evaluation, but except for German it ranks quite low in the MWE-based evaluation.

System	Track	Language	MWE-based				Token-based			
			P	R	F1	Rank	P	R	F1	Rank
Mumpitz	closed	BG	75.12	46.42	57.38	6/9	86.99	48.16	62	4/10
Mumpitz	closed	DE	32.15	38.35	34.98	5/11	55.91	48	51.66	1/11
Mumpitz	closed	EL	45	30.54	36.39	8/10	73.21	36.82	49	6/11
Mumpitz	closed	ES	9.66	13	11.08	10/10	31.83	28.87	30.28	6/10
Mumpitz	closed	FR	56.8	33.53	42.17	7/12	81.25	38.86	52.57	5/13
Mumpitz	closed	PL	62.07	38.45	47.48	8/10	80.92	41.34	54.72	8/11
Mumpitz	closed	PT	44.77	47.2	45.95	7/12	63.96	52.37	57.58	4/13
Mumpitz-preinit	open	DE	43.37	36.14	39.43	4/4	70.5	44.62	54.65	1/4

Table 1: Language-specific results

For us, the most interesting part of the evaluation is the comparison of Mumpitz and Mumpitz-preinit, i.e. the comparison of the systems that were completely equal except for the fact that the former was fed randomly initialized word embeddings, while the latter was given pretrained word embeddings. The results seen in Table 1 were achieved with the word embeddings we trained ourselves on the DECOW16 corpus. We used the selftrained embeddings for the test set predictions, rather then the fastText embeddings, because the selftrained embeddings outperformed the fastText word vectors on the dev set. For both evaluation schemes, the precision was increased substantially (11.22 for MWE-based, 14,59 for token-based), while the recall decreased (2.21 for MWE-based, 3,38 for token-based). But since the increase in precision outweighed the decrease, the F1-Score in turn was increased by 4.51 percentage points for the MWE-based, and by 2.99 for the token-based evaluation.

When looking further into the evaluation, it shows that Mumpitz-preinit outperforms Mumpitz in almost every aspect of the continuity and number of tokens metrics (see Table 2 and 3).[5]

---

[5] VMWEs with adjacent components are continuous, VMWEs with non-adjacent components are discontinuous. The number of tokens refers to how many components a VMWE has.

System	Continuous VMWEs			Discontinuous VMWEs		
	MWE-based			MWE-based		
	P	R	F1	P	R	F1
Mumpitz	27.62	48.31	35.15	48.82	26.84	34.64
Mumpitz-preinit	37.38	43.82	40.31	61.76	27.27	37.84

Table 2: Continuity (DE)

System	Multi-token VMWEs			Single-token VMWEs		
	MWE-based			MWE-based		
	P	R	F1	P	R	F1
Mumpitz	46.63	27.79	34.83	24.35	63.09	35.14
Mumpitz-preinit	56.91	30.66	39.85	32.16	48.99	38.83

Table 3: Number of tokens (DE)

5   Conclusion and future work

Mumpitz treats MWE identification as sequence tagging problem using a BRNN with LSTM units. We tried to remain as faithful as possible to this neural approach, leaving orthogonal pre- or post-processing steps aside. The features used are lemma, language-specific POS-tag and the dependency relation to the head; feature selection was conducted based on German, for which Mumpitz also obtained the highest F1 measure as to token-based classification compared to competing systems. The heuristic used to detect the span of MWEs was deliberately kept simple and only consisted in adding MWE-classified tokens to the span of the governing verb. Within the open track, we used pretrained embeddings, which lead to considerable improvements.

There are several possibilities of improving Mumpitz that are worth exploring. One of the most obvious is to choose language-specific (or language family-specific) features instead of optimizing a feature set for one language and then use it for all the others. Furthermore it is unsatisfactory to rely on a heuristic for the differentiation of VMWEs appearing in a single sentence, rather than having the classifier do it. Connected to this issue is the categorization of the VMWE candidates into the different VMWEs types which Mumpitz is unable to do so. For example, if the classifier would assign different labels to different VMWEs in a sentence, that would already automatically distinguish them. Another possibility for improvement would be the usage of character-level embeddings as features. They could improve the performance of the network as well as the word embeddings did.

References

Martín Abadi, Ashish Agarwal, Paul Barham, Eugene Brevdo, Zhifeng Chen, Craig Citro, Greg S. Corrado, Andy Davis, Jeffrey Dean, Matthieu Devin, Sanjay Ghemawat, Ian Goodfellow, Andrew Harp, Geoffrey Irving, Michael Isard, Yangqing Jia, Rafal Jozefowicz, Lukasz Kaiser, Manjunath Kudlur, Josh Levenberg, Dandelion Mané, Rajat Monga, Sherry Moore, Derek Murray, Chris Olah, Mike Schuster, Jonathon Shlens, Benoit Steiner, Ilya Sutskever, Kunal Talwar, Paul Tucker, Vincent Vanhoucke, Vijay Vasudevan, Fernanda Viégas, Oriol Vinyals, Pete Warden, Martin Wattenberg, Martin Wicke, Yuan Yu, and Xiaoqiang Zheng. 2015. TensorFlow: Large-scale machine learning on heterogeneous systems. Software available from tensorflow.org.

Hazem Al Saied, Matthieu Constant, and Marie Candito. 2017. The atilf-llf system for parseme shared task: a transition-based verbal multiword expression tagger. In *Proceedings of the 13th Workshop on Multiword Expressions (MWE 2017)*, pages 127–132, Valencia, Spain, April. Association for Computational Linguistics.

Timothy Baldwin and Su Nam Kim. 2010. Multiword expressions. *Handbook of natural language processing*, 2:267–292.

Piotr Bojanowski, Edouard Grave, Armand Joulin, and Tomas Mikolov. 2016. Enriching word vectors with subword information. *arXiv preprint arXiv:1607.04606*.

Tiberiu Boroş, Sonia Pipa, Verginica Barbu Mititelu, and Dan Tufiş. 2017. A data-driven approach to verbal multiword expression detection. parseme shared task system description paper. In *Proceedings of the 13th Workshop on Multiword Expressions (MWE 2017)*, pages 121–126, Valencia, Spain, April. Association for Computational Linguistics.

Jason Chiu and Eric Nichols. 2016. Named entity recognition with bidirectional lstm-cnns. *Transactions of the Association for Computational Linguistics*, 4:357–370.

François Chollet et al. 2015. Keras. https://keras.io.

Sepp Hochreiter and Jürgen Schmidhuber. 1997. Long short-term memory. *Neural computation*, 9(8):1735–1780.

Natalia Klyueva, Antoine Doucet, and Milan Straka. 2017. Neural networks for multi-word expression detection. In *Proceedings of the 13th Workshop on Multiword Expressions (MWE 2017)*, pages 60–65, Valencia, Spain, April. Association for Computational Linguistics.

Matthieu Labeau, Kevin Löser, and Alexandre Allauzen. 2015. Non-lexical neural architecture for fine-grained pos tagging. In *Proceedings of the 2015 Conference on Empirical Methods in Natural Language Processing*, pages 232–237, Lisbon, Portugal, September. Association for Computational Linguistics.

Alfredo Maldonado, Lifeng Han, Erwan Moreau, Ashjan Alsulaimani, Koel Dutta Chowdhury, Carl Vogel, and Qun Liu. 2017. Detection of verbal multi-word expressions via conditional random fields with syntactic dependency features and semantic re-ranking. In *Proceedings of the 13th Workshop on Multiword Expressions (MWE 2017)*, pages 114–120, Valencia, Spain, April. Association for Computational Linguistics.

Luka Nerima, Vasiliki Foufi, and Eric Wehrli. 2017. Parsing and mwe detection: Fips at the parseme shared task. In *Proceedings of the 13th Workshop on Multiword Expressions (MWE 2017)*, pages 54–59, Valencia, Spain, April. Association for Computational Linguistics.

Carlos Ramisch, Silvio Ricardo Cordeiro, Agata Savary, Veronika Vincze, Verginica Barbu Mititelu, Archna Bhatia, Maja Buljan, Marie Candito, Polona Gantar, Voula Giouli, Tunga Güngör, Abdelati Hawwari, Uxoa Iñurrieta, Jolanta Kovalevskaitė, Simon Krek, Timm Lichte, Chaya Liebeskind, Johanna Monti, Carla Parra Escartín, Behrang QasemiZadeh, Renata Ramisch, Nathan Schneider, Ivelina Stoyanova, Ashwini Vaidya, and Abigail Walsh. 2018. Edition 1.1 of the PARSEME Shared Task on Automatic Identification of Verbal Multiword Expressions. In *Proceedings of the Joint Workshop on Linguistic Annotation, Multiword Expressions and Constructions (LAW-MWE-CxG 2018)*, Santa Fe, New Mexico, USA, August. Association for Computational Linguistics.

Radim Řehůřek and Petr Sojka. 2010. Software Framework for Topic Modelling with Large Corpora. In *Proceedings of the LREC 2010 Workshop on New Challenges for NLP Frameworks*, pages 45–50, Valletta, Malta, May. ELRA. http://is.muni.cz/publication/884893/en.

Roland Schäfer and Felix Bildhauer. 2012. Building large corpora from the web using a new efficient tool chain. In Nicoletta Calzolari, Khalid Choukri, Thierry Declerck, Mehmet Uğur Doğan, Bente Maegaard, Joseph Mariani, Jan Odijk, and Stelios Piperidis, editors, *Proceedings of the Eighth International Conference on Language Resources and Evaluation (LREC-2012)*, pages 486–493, Istanbul, Turkey, May. European Language Resources Association (ELRA). ACL Anthology Identifier: L12-1497.

Katalin Ilona Simkó, Viktória Kovács, and Veronika Vincze. 2017. Uszeged: Identifying verbal multiword expressions with pos tagging and parsing techniques. In *Proceedings of the 13th Workshop on Multiword Expressions (MWE 2017)*, pages 48–53, Valencia, Spain, April. Association for Computational Linguistics.

TraPacc and TraPacc$_S$ at PARSEME Shared Task 2018: Neural Transition Tagging of Verbal Multiword Expressions

Regina Stodden
Heinrich Heine University
Düsseldorf, Germany
regina.stodden@hhu.de

Behrang QasemiZadeh
Heinrich Heine University
Düsseldorf, Germany
zadeh@phil.hhu.de

Laura Kallmeyer
Heinrich Heine University
Düsseldorf, Germany
kallmeyer@phil.hhu.de

Abstract

We describe the TraPacc system and its variant TraPacc$_S$ that participated in the closed track of the PARSEME Shared Task 2018 on labeling verbal multiword expressions (VMWEs). TraPacc is a modified arc-standard transition system based on Constant and Nivre's (2016) model of joint syntactic and lexical analysis in which the oracle is approximated using a classifier. For TraPacc, the classifier consists of a data-independent dimension reduction and a convolutional neural network (CNN) for learning and labelling transitions. TraPacc$_S$ extends TraPacc by replacing the softmax layer of the CNN with a support vector machine (SVM). We report the results obtained for 19 languages, for 8 of which our system yields the best results compared to other participating systems in the closed-track of the shared task.

1 Introduction

The PARSEME shared task on VMWE identification (Savary et al., 2017) is an initiative aiming at improving automatic methods for VMWE identification in a highly multilingual context. To foster this initiative, the 2018 shared task provides test and training corpora, annotated with VMWEs in 19 different languages[1], and a framework to evaluate supervised methods for identifying VMWEs (Ramisch et al., 2018). In this paper, we present TraPacc and its variant TraPacc$_S$ that address the VMWE identification task using a neural transition system.

The general idea behind TraPacc has been motivated by observations from the first edition of the shared task: Saied et al. (2017) showed that the *modified arc-standard transition* method by Constant and Nivre (2016) (hereinafter MAST) can be employed to outperform other systems in which VMWE identification is modeled as a sequence labeling task disregarding of their employed learning model, e.g., conditional random fields (CRFs) (Maldonado et al., 2017), and bidirectional recurrent neural networks (Klyueva et al., 2017). Accordingly, we adapt MAST for the purpose of the PARSEME shared task; but, in contrast to Saied et al. (2017), instead of using a linear SVM for learning and predicting transitions, we use a CNN preceded by a dimension reduction proposed in (QasemiZadeh and Kallmeyer, 2016; QasemiZadeh et al., 2017). Furthermore, TraPacc$_S$ extends the TraPacc system by replacing the *output softmax layer* of the CNN with a kernel SVM. The latter is motivated by research, such as Razavian et al. (2014) and Poria et al. (2015), that suggests using CNN combined with a more elaborate classifier (i.e., to use CNN only as a feature selection method) is likely to improve prediction performance.

The remainder of this paper is structured as follows: We describe our method in Section 2, we report results from the experiment and discuss them in Section 3. Section 4 concludes this paper.

2 Method and System Description

The backbone of TraPacc (and subsequently TraPacc$_S$) is the idea behind the MAST proposed by Constant and Nivre (2016). MAST jointly predicts syntactic dependencies and MWEs in a sentence by

---

[1] Besides Arabic.

Proceedings of the Joint Workshop on
Linguistic Annotation, Multiword Expressions and Constructions (LAW-MWE-CxG-2018), pages 268–274
Santa Fe, New Mexico, USA, August 25-26, 2018.

introducing a new *lexical stack* (and, accordingly a number of transitions specific to this lexical stack) to the arc-standard incremental dependency parsing (Nivre, 2004; Kubler et al., 2009). Since we are only concerned with the identification of MWEs, the *quintuple* model of MAST is reduced to a triple consisting of a) a buffer B of input tokens to be parsed, b) a stack S of lexical units that are partially processed, and c) a set of processed lexical units P. In effect, the identification of VMWEs becomes very simple with only four general types of transitions (apart from initialize and terminate):

- *Shift*: pushes the head of the buffer B to the stack S;

- *Merge*: reduces the top two elements of the stack S to one element in the stack;

- *Reduce*: is a pop operation, i.e., it removes the element on top of the stack S and adds it to the set of processed elements P;

- *Complete-MWE**: is, similar to the reduce transition, a pop operation, except that it additionally marks the removed element from the stack S as an MWE of the type *. In practice, Complete-MWE* is decomposed to several transitions: each transition is labelled by a specific type of VMWE category derived from the training corpora, e.g., Complete-MWE-*VPC.full*, Complete-MWE-*LVC.cause*, and so on.

Additional details and examples about the transition system can be found in Saied et al. (2017). Simply put, the VMWE identification problem is boiled down to finding relationships between words that form VMWEs. When using the modified arc-standard transition approach, the identification of VMWEs in a sentence of length n tokens requires solving $2 \times n$ classification subproblems (without removing the chance of finding most VMWEs in the sentence). However, in other methods, e.g., in a graph-based approach, the number of classification sub-tasks can soar to $n \times (n - 1)$. We assume that the overall VMWE identification problem can be done faster and with a higher accuracy because of the reduced number of classification subproblems in the MAST method.

During the training time, each of the above listed transitions will be converted to a training record, i.e., a labeled feature vector, with its label being the type of the transition and the features being the vector that shows the current state of the system. Each lexical unit in the buffer B and the stack S is accompanied by a set of annotations, e.g., its word form, lemma, part-of-speech-tag, and so on (i.e., whatever is asserted and provided as annotation in the training corpora). These annotations are transformed to (mostly) a set of binary features and (together with a number of other attributes such as the history of the transition system) constitute a feature vectors for each state of the transition system. In our implementation, we use all the features proposed in Saied et al. (2017) and add the following features to them:

- Besides the number of elements in the stack, we use the size of the buffer (i.e. the number of elements that it contains at any time) as an additional feature to take the length of input sentences into account.

- We add the length of tokens as an additional feature, which we believe can be helpful for identifying long single-token VMWEs—e.g., single-token VMWEs in German such as "freigesprochen" (lit: free spoken; to acquit so. of sth., VPC:full).

- In a few languages (e.g., EL, DE, IT), more than 5% of the VMWEs consist of more than three tokens; hence, we use four-grams generated from the elements in the stack and the buffer as additional features to bigram and trigrams used by Saied et al. (2017).

- Given the availability of additional annotations in this year's shared task, compared to Saied et al. (2017), we could use more linguistic features such as universal part of speech tags and morphological information for a larger number of languages.

From this point, the task is to approximate a so-called static oracle using a supervised multi-way classifier to determine the 'best' next transition for the given states of the system. Our method for modelling the oracle differs from Saied et al. (2017) with respect to the classification model that we employ to model the oracle, i.e., instead of classifying high-dimensional and extremely sparse feature vectors using a SVM, we classify feature vectors of reduced dimension using CNN.

The resulting feature vectors from the above-mentioned feature extraction process are of high dimensionality, e.g., in the scale of millions depending on the size of the training corpus and the lexical and morphosynatic diversity of it. These vectors are also highly sparse (i.e., most components of the vector are zero and only a few are non-zero). For classification under these conditions, a linear SVM is usually a fast and reliable choice (Fan et al., 2008) but still overfitting and poor generalization is possible. Given the availability of GPU accelerated computing and in light of the recent advances in deep learning, we replace a classic classifier such as linear SVM—as used by Saied et al. (2017)—or a Perceptron classifier—as used by Constant and Nivre (2016)—with a simple multi-layer CNN.

Usually, when using a deep neural network, the above-stated feature extraction process is altered by using embeddings and particularly pre-trained word embeddings instead of binary-encoded lexical features—e.g., see Chen and Manning (2014). Since the use of pre-trained word embeddings is not an option for systems that participate in the closed track of the shared task[2], we use a data-independent dimensionality reduction method based on random projections. The usage of this dimension reduction method removes engineering issues associated with the use of high-dimensional sparse vectors as input for deep learning methods, e.g., by reducing the memory required to fit the batch of vectors used during training and by decreasing the training time (specially for large corpora).

Our dimension reduction method is based on the positive-only random projections proposed by QasemiZadeh and Kallmeyer (2016). Put simply, an n-dimensional feature space consisting of p training records, represented by a matrix $\mathbf{M}_{p \times n}$, is mapped to an m-dimensional space $\mathbf{M}'_{p \times m}$ ($m \ll n$) by multiplying $\mathbf{M}_{p \times n}$ to a randomly devised projection matrix (of certain characteristics) $\mathbf{P}_{n \times m}$; i.e., $\mathbf{M}'_{p \times m} = \mathbf{M}_{p \times n} \times \mathbf{P}_{n \times m}$. In the method proposed by QasemiZadeh and Kallmeyer (2016), $\mathbf{P}_{n \times m}$ is a randomly-generated matrix in which only a few elements of each row and column of $\mathbf{P}$ have the value 1 and the remaining are 0. As shown in (QasemiZadeh et al., 2017; QasemiZadeh and Kallmeyer, 2017), the matrix multiplication $\mathbf{M}_{p \times n} \times \mathbf{P}_{n \times m}$ can be efficiently computed using a hash function and a number of addition operations: Given an n-dimensional feature vector $\vec{v}$ that represents a state of the transition system, the corresponding m-dimensional vector $\vec{v'}$ is given by computing

$$\forall i \in \{1, \ldots, n\}, \quad \vec{v'}[|i\%m|] + = \vec{v}[i],$$

in which $\vec{v}[i]$ and analogously $\vec{v'}[i]$ denotes the ith component of $\vec{v}$ and $\vec{v'}$, $|x|$ gives the absolute value of its input number x, and $\%$ is the modulo operator that gives the remainder after the division of i by m.

Once these vectors of the reduced dimension m are built, they are fed to our CNN model trained with respect to *categorical cross-entropy loss* using an *ADAM optimizer*. The CNN architecture is straightforward as shown in Figure 1. An input feature vector of the reduced dimension m (we use $m = 500$) is fed to a convolutional layer and it is transformed to a kernel of size 500×128, which is downsampled to a 250×128 kernel using max-pooling. The generated kernel is flattened and mapped to a densely-connected layer of size 512 where a *rectified linear unit* (ReLU) is used as activation function; this is followed by a small drop-out of rate 0.025. For TRAPACC, the last dense layer gives the predicted classes using a *softmax* activation function.

TRAPACC_S slightly differs from TRAPACC in the way that it predicts class labels. As shown in Figure 1, after training the CNN model, TRAPACC_S takes the intermediate dense layer of the CNN and uses it as an input feature vector to a Kernel SVM (we use a *radial basis function* (RBF) kernel). Hence, for TRAPACC_S, the CNN model is effectively reduced to a supervised feature extraction system. For implementation, we alter the Python code of Saied et al. (2017) and implement our CNN using *Keras* (Chollet and others, 2015) with TensorFlow as its backend.[3]

---

[2] The use of any NLP resource or process other than the provided training corpora is not allowed.

[3] Available for download from `https://github.com/rstodden/verbal-multiword-expression-stll`.

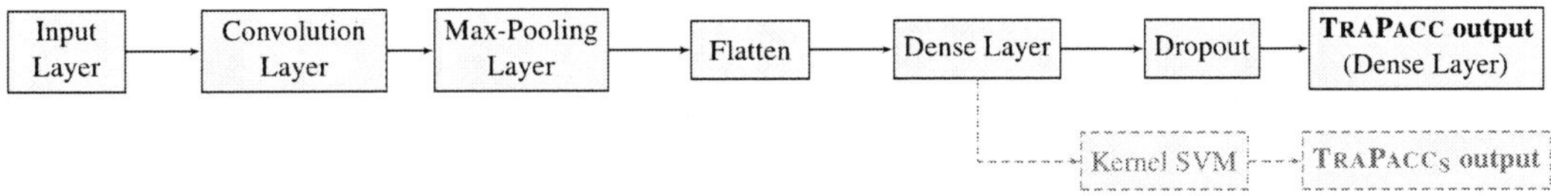

Figure 1: The classification model employed in TRAPACC and TRAPACC_S. In both systems the CNN model shown above is employed. CNN is used directly to generate the output of TRAPACC; but in TRAPACC_S (drawn with dashed red lines), the intermediate dense layer of the CNN model is used as input feature vector for a kernel SVM classifier.

3 Result and Discussion

As implied in the previous section, we use a network of the same architecture for developing prediction models for all the languages in the shared task. During the development, the fixed parameters of our CNN model (e.g., the dropout rate) are decided by trial and error over the development set of DE (German) and FA (Farsi). For training, we use both the train and the development sets so that we decrease the chance of unseen VMWEs when testing the system. As mentioned earlier, we participate in the closed track of the shared task so features used in training and test are limited to those that are made available by organizers in the `.cupt` files (hence, some features, e.g., dependency parses, morphological information, and so on are missing for some languages).

Table 1 reports the official shared task results and ranks per language for both systems. Overall, based on our official submissions, with respect to the MWE-based F1 metric, TRAPACC and TRAPACC_S rank third and second, respectively. In particular, compared to other participating systems, our TRAPACC and TRAPACC_S show the best performance for 8 languages including RO (Romanian), HU (Hungarian), and EN (English); and on the contrary, they perform poorly for SL (Slovenian), PT (Portuguese), FR (French), HR (Croatian) and IT (Italian). For TR (Turkish), neither TRAPACC nor TRAPACC_S converge and the obtained results are unusually bad (near to zero).

Concerning the comparison of TRAPACC and TRAPACC_S, the performance obtained from both systems remains very similar. At first sight, on the basis of per language comparison, TRAPACC seems to perform better than TRAPACC_S for most languages; and, it is only for DE (German), EL (Greek), LT (Lithuanian), and SL that TRAPACC_S yields better results than TRAPACC. However, using a rank correlation metric such as Spearman's ρ for comparing TRAPACC and TRAPACC_S (where results are sorted by language), we observe a high correlation between the results obtained by the two systems—i.e. $\rho = 98.07$ (for MWE-based F1) and $\rho = 97.89$ (for Token-based F1)—compare it, for instance, to $\rho = 81.40$ when comparing MWE-based F1 scores between TRAPACC and *TRAVERSAL*, another participating system in the shared task. This observation suggests that our attempt (i.e., using RBF-SVM instead of softmax layer for classification) to enhance results has not been as effective as we expected it. This can be due to several reasons: E.g., we trained RBF-SVM only using its preset default parameter values whereas we know tuning the parameters of SVM can enhance results to a certain extent; similarly, we would achieve better results using a different kernel. These remain as unanswered research questions for our future investigations.

Concerning TR, the performance gap between TRAPACC (as well as TRAPACC_S) and other participating systems is apparent. Simply put, we failed to deliver any meaningful result for TR. Initially, we associate this failure to the presence of very long sentences, particularly in TR test and train corpora[4] (this is also the case for SL). However, analyzing sentence length in other corpora such as ES (which also contains long sentences but our systems perform relatively well for them) as well additional experiments (i.e., by removing very long sentences from train and test corpora and repeating experiments) ruled out the aforementioned hypothesis (i.e., the long sentence length aggravates poor performance). In our second hypothesis, we related this problem to the inconsistent lemmatization and tagging of the TR corpus, e.g., in a sentence only a few tokens are tagged with their part-of-speech (only 27.6% of the tokens in

---

[4]Some appear to be due to some mistakes.

| Lang | Corpus #VMWEs | | TRAPACC Results MWE-based | | Tok-based | | TRAPACC$_S$ Results MWE-based | | Tok-based | | Best Using TRAPACC | |
	Train+	Test	F1	Rank	F1	Rank	F1	Rank	F1	Rank	F1 MWE	F1 Token
BG	6,034	670	60.83	2/9	62.35	2/10	52.57	8/9	53.47	8/10	61.05	64.18
DE	3,323	500	44.05	2/11	48.37	4/11	45.27	1/11	49.97	3/11	45.14	48.09
EL	1,904	501	46.43	3/10	49.14	5/11	49.76	1/10	53.1	3/11	50.6	52.73
EN	331	501	32.88	1/10	34.37	1/10	30.28	3/10	30.23	2/10	32.88	34.37
ES	2,239	500	31.64	3/10	38.04	4/11	33.98	1/10	39.75	2/11	32.33	38.47
EU	3,323	500	73.23	2/9	74.4	3/10	75.8	1/9	76.83	1/10	73.23	74.4
FA	2,951	501	75.48	3/9	78.12	4/10	74.23	4/9	77.03	5/10	75.48	78.12
FR	5,179	498	46.97	3/12	52.93	4/13	45.96	6/12	50.12	7/13	48.28	53.86
HE	1,737	502	20.37	3/8	24.26	4/10	16.95	6/8	18.97	6/10	21.97	26.08
HI	534	500	69.38	3/7	71.22	3/8	68.39	4/8	68.31	5/8	69.38	71.22
HR	1,950	501	43.39	3/9	49.97	2/10	44.27	2/9	47.95	4/10	47.94	52.39
HU	6,984	776	90.31	1/10	88	1/10	90.12	2/10	87.25	2/10	90.31	88
IT	3,754	503	38.52	2/11	40.64	4/12	33.33	4/11	34.02	8/12	39.7	41.45
LT	312	500	30.82	2/7	34.43	1/10	32.17	1/7	34.1	2/10	33.63	36
PL	4,637	515	60.54	2/10	63.68	3/11	59.86	4/10	61.51	6/11	62.50	65.05
PT	4,983	553	52.73	4/12	59.96	5/13	52.29	5/12	54.51	7/13	56.96	59.35
RO	5,302	589	85.28	1/9	85.69	1/10	83.36	2/9	83.45	5/10	85.28	85.69
SL	2,878	500	23.04	9/9	34.72	9/10	31.36	7/9	38.33	7/10	36.63	44.74
TR	6,635	506	1.61	8/9	4.68	9/10	0.78	9/9	3.01	10/10	39.34	44.09
			49.57	3/13	53.09	3/13	49.74	2/13	52.13	4/13	53.28	56.42

Table 1: Results and rankings for TRAPACC and TRAPACC$_S$ from official submission together with the best results we obtained using TRAPACC after an additional adjustment of our system's parameters/features. The denominators in the rank column show the number of submitted systems per language. Train+ denotes the number of VMWE instances in both training and development set.

the TR training corpus has a POS tag), and it seems as if lemmas appear in wrong places, e.g., as shown in Table 2. Table 2 shows the annotations for a sentence in the TR training corpus: only a few tokens of the sentence are tagged with their part-of-speech (5th column). Moreover, for many tokens in the TR corpus, the lemmas seem to appear in the wrong places such as the case for the word "göstermek" (in line/position 11) for which its lemma (göster) is asserted wrongly in line/position 10.

Hence, we retrained our systems using only word forms and those that can be extracted from them (e.g., suffix, prefix, bigrams, etc.). As shown in Table 1 for the TRAPACC system, the MWE-based F1 score increases from almost zero to 39.34. This leads us to another observation that despite our expectations, our CNN-based method is vulnerable to the presence of noise. Similar to TR, we observe that for PT, only 40.05% of the part-of-speech tags in the training data are available. When we removed features based on part-of-speech tags, the MWE-based F-Score increase by 4.23. For FR, only 4.6% of

ID	WORD FORM	LEMMA	UPOS	XPOS	FEATS	HEAD	DEPREL	DEPS	MISC	MWE
1	_	ülke	Noun	_	A3sg|Loc|P1pl	2	DERIV	_	_	*
2	Ülkemizdeki	_	Adj	Rel	_	4	MODIFIER	_	_	*
3	KOBİ	Kobi	Noun	Prop	A3sg|Nom|Pnon	4	POSSESSOR	_	_	*
4	potansiyelini	potansiyel	Noun	_	A3sg|Acc|P3sg	5	OBJECT	_	_	*
5	_	kullan	Verb	_	Able|Pos	6	DERIV	_	_	*
6	kullanabilmek	_	Noun	Infl	A3sg|Nom|Pnon	7	ARGUMENT	_	_	*
7	için	için	Postp	PCNom	_	10	MODIFIER	_	_	*
8	bu	bu	Det	_	_	9	DETERMINER	_	_	*
9	çabayı	çaba	Noun	_	A3sg|Acc|Pnon	10	OBJECT	_	_	1:LVC.full
10	_	göster	Verb	_	Pos	11	DERIV	_	_	*
11	göstermek	_	Noun	Infl	A3sg|Nom|Pnon	12	SUBJECT	_	_	1
12	şart	şart	Noun	_	A3sg|Nom|Pnon	0	PREDICATE	_	_	*
13	.	.	Punc	_	_	12	PUNCTUATION	_	_	*

Table 2: An example of untypical lemmatization and missing part-of-speech tags in sentences from the train set for TR.

the part-of-speech tags in the train data are available. Likewise TR and PT, removing features related to them leads to an increase of 1.31 in the MWE-based F1-Score. We add to this the observation that the linear-SVM+high-dimensional-sparse-vectors generalize better than CNN over the noisy input. This can be due to the network architecture that we use, criteria used when training, the employed dimension reduction method, or a combination of them. For instance, a slight change in the training procedure (i.e., the use of different conditions for terminating training) leads to an increase of 13.59 in the MWE-based F1-score for SL (the over-fitting problem).[5] The effect of these factors must be investigated further in our future work.

Last but not least, after slight modifications in the original implementation of Saied et al. (2017) and a careful feature selection process, we observe that modeling oracle using high dimensional sparse feature vectors and linear SVM (or multilayer perceptron) can be equally effective as TRAPACC; in other words, the gain from using a deep learning model instead of simpler models such as linear SVM is negligible in the closed track. However, the deep learning modules of TRAPACC and TRAPACC$_S$ permit the use of features such as word embeddings. These features are not easily accessible (and supposedly effective) to simpler learning methods such as linear SVM. As a result, using TRAPACC and TRAPACC$_S$ in the open track and exploiting more complex unsupervised features for their training remain questions for our future work.

4   Conclusion and Future Work

We report the results obtained from our methods TRAPACC and TRAPACC$_S$ for identifying VMWEs in the closed track of the PARSEME shared task. Among 13 participating systems in the closed track of the shared task, TRAPACC ranks and TRAPACC$_S$ ranks third in the official shared task results.

This research is a work in progress and it can be extended in several ways. Firstly, we can improve our results by removing limitations due to partaking in the closed track of the shared task. For instance, we could use word vectors and various association measures such as PMI and χ^2 that are obtained directly from large corpora in order to improve results. Similarly, the availability of large corpora would permit us to look into features that capture 'structural' properties of words and tokens that are inherently a strong cue of the presence of VMWEs, e.g. as seen for DE in which many single-token VMWEs are expected to appear also as multi-token VMWEs.

Our employed learning method is novel in the sense that it combines a data-independent dimension reduction with CNNs. However, it can be changed and improved in several ways, too. For instance, we are currently extending our input feature vectors to matrices, in which a vector replaces the scalar values currently used to represent the value of a feature. Comparing different dimension reduction methods, even removing them from the classification model, is another research avenue. The identification of VMWEs in our current models TRAPACC and TRAPACC$_S$ is carried out per VMWE category; instead, this can be replaced by a two-step process. I.e., we could use a binary classifier for detecting VMWEs disregarding of their category, followed by a category classification process. Similarly, we could utilize a better informed strategy for the training and parameter setting of our models. For example, instead of a language-agnostic method for setting parameters of CNNs (such as layer size and drop-out rate), we could adapt a language-wise methodology.

Acknowledgements

This work was supported by the CRC 991 "The Structure of Representations in Language, Cognition, and Science" funded by the German Research Foundation (DFG). We gratefully acknowledge the support of NVIDIA Corporation with the donation of the Titan Xp GPU used for this research.

---

[5]With these improvements, TRAPACC outperforms the TRAVERSAL system and it ranks first with respect to the average MWE-based F1 scores.

References

Danqi Chen and Christopher Manning. 2014. A fast and accurate dependency parser using neural networks. In *Proceedings of the 2014 Conference on Empirical Methods in Natural Language Processing (EMNLP)*, pages 740–750, Doha, Qatar, October. Association for Computational Linguistics.

François Chollet et al. 2015. Keras. `https://keras.io`.

Matthieu Constant and Joakim Nivre. 2016. A transition-based system for joint lexical and syntactic analysis. In *Proceedings of the 54th Annual Meeting of the Association for Computational Linguistics (Volume 1: Long Papers)*, pages 161–171. Association for Computational Linguistics.

Rong-En Fan, Kai-Wei Chang, Cho-Jui Hsieh, Xiang-Rui Wang, and Chih-Jen Lin. 2008. Liblinear: A library for large linear classification. *Journal of machine learning research*, 9(Aug):1871–1874.

Natalia Klyueva, Antoine Doucet, and Milan Straka. 2017. Neural networks for multi-word expression detection. In *Proceedings of the 13th Workshop on Multiword Expressions, MWE@EACL 2017, Valencia, Spain, April 4, 2017*, pages 60–65.

Sandra Kubler, Ryan McDonald, Joakim Nivre, and Graeme Hirst. 2009. *Dependency Parsing*. Morgan and Claypool Publishers.

Alfredo Maldonado, Lifeng Han, Erwan Moreau, Ashjan Alsulaimani, Koel Dutta Chowdhury, Carl Vogel, and Qun Liu. 2017. Detection of verbal multi-word expressions via conditional random fields with syntactic dependency features and semantic re-ranking. In *Proceedings of the 13th Workshop on Multiword Expressions (MWE 2017)*, pages 114–120, Valencia, Spain, April. Association for Computational Linguistics.

Joakim Nivre. 2004. Incrementality in deterministic dependency parsing. In Frank Keller, Stephen Clark, Matthew Crocker, and Mark Steedman, editors, *Proceedings of the ACL Workshop Incremental Parsing: Bringing Engineering and Cognition Together*, pages 50–57, Barcelona, Spain, July. Association for Computational Linguistics.

Soujanya Poria, Erik Cambria, and Alexander Gelbukh. 2015. Deep convolutional neural network textual features and multiple kernel learning for utterance-level multimodal sentiment analysis. In *Proceedings of the 2015 Conference on Empirical Methods in Natural Language Processing*, pages 2539–2544, Lisbon, Portugal, September. Association for Computational Linguistics.

Behrang QasemiZadeh and Laura Kallmeyer. 2016. Random positive-only projections: Ppmi-enabled incremental semantic space construction. In *Proceedings of the Fifth Joint Conference on Lexical and Computational Semantics*, pages 189–198, Berlin, Germany, August. Association for Computational Linguistics.

Behrang QasemiZadeh and Laura Kallmeyer. 2017. HHU at SemEval-2017 task 2: Fast hash-based embeddings for semantic word similarity assessment. In *Proceedings of the 11th International Workshop on Semantic Evaluation (SemEval-2017)*. Association for Computational Linguistics.

Behrang QasemiZadeh, Laura Kallmeyer, and Peyman Passban. 2017. Sketching word vectors through hashing. *CoRR*, abs/1705.04253.

Carlos Ramisch, Silvio Ricardo Cordeiro, Agata Savary, Veronika Vincze, Verginica Barbu Mititelu, Archna Bhatia, Maja Buljan, Marie Candito, Polona Gantar, Voula Giouli, Tunga Güngör, Abdelati Hawwari, Uxoa Iñurrieta, Jolanta Kovalevskaitė, Simon Krek, Timm Lichte, Chaya Liebeskind, Johanna Monti, Carla Parra Escartín, Behrang QasemiZadeh, Renata Ramisch, Nathan Schneider, Ivelina Stoyanova, Ashwini Vaidya, and Abigail Walsh. 2018. Edition 1.1 of the PARSEME Shared Task on Automatic Identification of Verbal Multiword Expressions. In *Proceedings of the Joint Workshop on Linguistic Annotation, Multiword Expressions and Constructions (LAW-MWE-CxG 2018)*, Santa Fe, New Mexico, USA, August. Association for Computational Linguistics.

Ali Sharif Razavian, Hossein Azizpour, Josephine Sullivan, and Stefan Carlsson. 2014. Cnn features off-the-shelf: An astounding baseline for recognition. In *Proceedings of the 2014 IEEE Conference on Computer Vision and Pattern Recognition Workshops*, CVPRW '14, pages 512–519, Washington, DC, USA. IEEE Computer Society.

Hazem Al Saied, Matthieu Constant, and Marie Candito. 2017. The ATILF-LLF system for parseme shared task: a transition-based verbal multiword expression tagger. In *Proceedings of the 13th Workshop on Multiword Expressions, MWE@EACL 2017, Valencia, Spain, April 4, 2017*, pages 127–132.

Agata Savary, Carlos Ramisch, Silvio Cordeiro, Federico Sangati, Veronika Vincze, Behrang QasemiZadeh, Marie Candito, Fabienne Cap, Voula Giouli, Ivelina Stoyanova, and Antoine Doucet. 2017. The parseme shared task on automatic identification of verbal multiword expressions. In *Proceedings of the 13th Workshop on Multiword Expressions (MWE 2017)*, pages 31–47, Valencia, Spain, April. Association for Computational Linguistics.

TRAVERSAL at PARSEME Shared Task 2018: Identification of Verbal Multiword Expressions Using a Discriminative Tree-Structured Model

Jakub Waszczuk
Heinrich Heine University
Düsseldorf, Germany
`waszczuk@phil.hhu.de`

Abstract

This paper describes a system submitted to the closed track of the PARSEME shared task (edition 1.1) on automatic identification of verbal multiword expressions (VMWEs). The system represents VMWE identification as a labeling task where one of two labels (MWE or not-MWE) must be predicted for each node in the dependency tree based on local context, including adjacent nodes and their labels. The system relies on multiclass logistic regression to determine the globally optimal labeling of a tree. The system ranked 1st in the general cross-lingual ranking of the closed track systems, according to both official evaluation measures: MWE-based F_1 and token-based F_1.

1 Introduction

In this paper we give a description of TRAVERSAL,[1] a system submitted to the edition 1.1 of the PARSEME shared task on automatic identification of VMWEs (Ramisch et al., 2018). The task was multilingual (treebanks annotated with VMWEs were provided for 20 languages) and its aim was to automatically identify VMWEs of several categories: light-verb constructions, idioms, inherently reflexive verbs, verb-particle constructions, multi-verb constructions, and inherently adpositional verbs.

TRAVERSAL relies on the assumption that MWEs form connected syntactic components, i.e., that lexical elements of a single MWE occurrence should be adjacent in the dependency analysis of the underlying sentence. Based on this assumption, TRAVERSAL represents the task of MWE identification as a labeling task where one of two labels (`MWE` or `not-MWE`) must be predicted for each node in the dependency tree based on local contextual information: dependency labels, word forms, lemmas, POS tags, etc., as well as the `MWE/not-MWE` labels assigned to adjacent nodes.

In order to capture such properties, our system encodes labelings of dependency trees as tree traversals such that each traversal corresponds to a distinct labeling of the input dependency tree. The task of MWE labeling is then reduced to finding the best traversal of the dependency tree. TRAVERSAL relies on multiclass logistic regression to discriminate between plausible and implausible traversals.

Labeling alone is not sufficient to predict MWEs since it doesn't tell us where the individual MWE occurrences start and end, a sub-task which we refer to as MWE segmentation. TRAVERSAL relies on a rather rudimentary solution to this problem – by default, all adjacent dependency nodes marked as `MWE`s of the same category are assumed to form a single MWE occurrence.

This paper is structured as follows. In Sec. 2 we give information about related work. In Sec. 3 we describe our system. In Sec. 4 we describe the experiments performed to determine an optimal setup for the shared task, and in Sec. 5 we summarize the results obtained by our system with this setup. Finally, we conclude in Sec. 6 and outline the possible directions for future work.

2 Related work

A notable example of a dependency treebank in which MWEs are annotated as connected syntactic components (subtrees) is the Prague Dependency Treebank (Bejček et al., 2012), in which named entities

[1]Available at `https://github.com/kawu/traversal` under the 2-clause BSD license.

Proceedings of the Joint Workshop on
Linguistic Annotation, Multiword Expressions and Constructions (LAW-MWE-CxG-2018), pages 275–282
Santa Fe, New Mexico, USA, August 25-26, 2018.

and VMWEs are both annotated on top of the tectogrammatical (deep syntactic/shallow semantic) layer. Treatment of MWEs as connected syntactic components is also adopted by Abeillé and Schabes (1989) within the framework of tree-adjoining grammars (Joshi and Schabes, 1997). In their approach, MWEs are modeled as families of multi-anchored elementary trees.

Two broad strategies of identifying verbal MWEs can be distinguished depending on whether MWE identification takes place during (Vincze et al., 2013; Green et al., 2013; Candito and Constant, 2014; Le Roux et al., 2014; Nasr et al., 2015; Waszczuk et al., 2016; Constant and Nivre, 2016) or after (Constant et al., 2012; Nagy T. and Vincze, 2014) syntactic parsing.[2] The former approach is based on the intuition that both tasks can benefit from each other and, therefore, should be performed jointly. The latter approach is simpler conceptually and can benefit from the significantly restricted solution space in comparison with the joint methods. TRAVERSAL requires that dependency trees are already constructed and, thus, adopts the latter strategy.

The method implemented in TRAVERSAL can be seen as an extension of sequential conditional random fields (CRFs) to tree structures. CRFs were applied to the task of MWE identification by Constant et al. (2012), Scholivet and Ramisch (2017), and Maldonado et al. (2017), among others. However, sequential CRFs are best applied to identification of continuous entities, while verbal MWEs are often discontinuous. The issue of discontinuity is handled in TRAVERSAL transparently since it assumes that input takes the form of a (dependency) tree and not a sequence. Otherwise, it relies on the same statistical backbone as CRFs – multiclass logistic regression (Sutton et al., 2012).

Another family of approaches related to the method used in TRAVERSAL is that of the graph-based approaches to dependency parsing (Kübler et al., 2009). The 2-order extension of Eisner's algorithm, for instance, adopts similar factorization as TRAVERSAL in that it captures relations between the nodes, their parents, and their siblings (McDonald and Pereira, 2006). This algorithm, however, is restricted to projective dependency trees only. Exact non-projective parsing with such a 2-order model is intractable (McDonald and Satta, 2007). The method implemented in TRAVERSAL (which is already 2-order) can be extended to capture higher-order relations without becoming intractable and can be used in combination with non-projective trees. This is possible because TRAVERSAL labels the nodes but considers the input dependency structure as fixed.

3   System description

In this section, we describe the details of the implemented system. In Sec. 3.1, we summarize the types of features the system is able to incorporate. In Sec. 3.2, we explain how to encode the possible tree labelings as tree traversals, and we formalize the notion of traversals themselves. In Sec. 3.3, we describe the multiclass logistic regression model used to score the traversals.

3.1   Feature types

In order to discriminate the "good" from the "bad" labelings, TRAVERSAL relies on the following types of features, restricted in their scope to adjacent nodes and their labels:

- Unary features, restricted to the context of a single node

- Binary parent-child features, restricted to the context of a node and its parent

- Binary sibling features, restricted to the context of a node and its closest sibling[3] on the left

- Ternary features, giving access to the node, its parent, and its closest left sibling node

In our experiments we only relied on unary and binary features, assuming that ternary features might lead to overfitting. Using ternary features is nevertheless a feasible option as it does not change the computational cost of labeling in this model.

---

[2]Another approach would be to identify MWEs before parsing, but we posit it is not very well adapted to verbal MWEs.
[3]We say that node v is a sibling of node w if both have the same parent in the dependency tree.

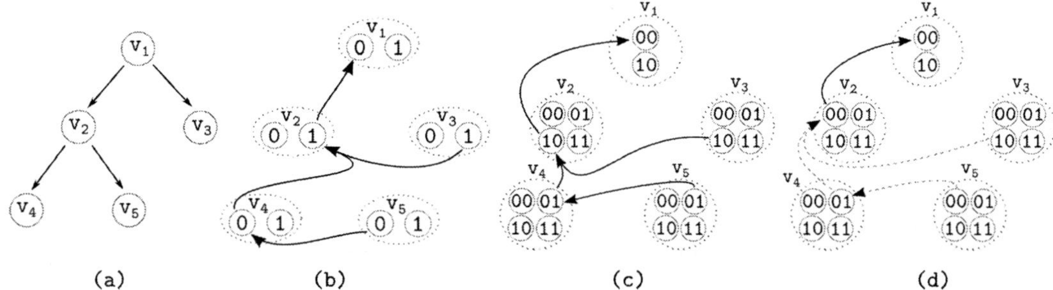

Figure 1: (a) Dependency tree with five lexical nodes. (b) A hyperpath corresponding to the labeling where only v_2 and v_3 are considered as MWEs. (c) A hyperpath with copying of parent labels, corresponding the same labeling as (b). (d) An invalid hyperpath, not encoded in the hypergraph (because of the red dashed hyperarcs – for instance, the hyperarc between v_5 and v_4 connects two hypernodes with different parent labels, even though v_5 and v_4 are siblings).

3.2 Encoding

Encoding consists in constructing a compact representation of all traversals of the given dependency tree. Formally, the resulting structure is a hypergraph (Gallo et al., 1993; Klein and Manning, 2001), and each traversal of the dependency tree is represented by a distinct hyperpath in this hypergraph.

Consider the dependency tree depicted in Fig. 1 (a). Its hypergraph encoding contains two hypernodes for each node in the dependency tree, one labeled with 0 (not-MWE), the other labeled with 1 (MWE). Furthermore, the hypergraph is populated with hyperarcs in such a way that it contains one hyperpath per each possible labeling of the nodes. For instance, the hyperpath shown in Fig. 1 (b) represents the labeling where v_2 and v_3 are both considered as MWEs (the hyperpath traverses these nodes via hypernodes labeled with 1), while the other nodes are not-MWEs.

Hyperacs determine the scope of the features we can define. However, certain relations we want to capture are not available in this hypergraph representation yet. For instance, there is no hyperarc between v_3 and v_1 in Fig. 1 (b), which prevents us from using binary parent/child features. To solve this issue, we copy the labels of parents to their children, as shown in Fig. 1 (c). Namely, each node is now represented by 4 hypernodes encoding the node's label as well as the label of its parent: 00 means that both nodes are not-MWEs, 10 that the node is a MWE but the parent is not, 01 that the parent is a MWE but the node is not, and 11 that both are MWEs. When populating the hypergraph with hyperarcs, we make sure that only valid combinations of hypernodes are connected – invalid hyperpaths such as the one shown in Fig. 1 (d) are thus not encoded.

3.3 Model

Let $\mathcal{H}(d)$ be the set of hyperpaths encoded in the hypergraph for a given dependency tree d. The task of labeling is reduced to the task of finding the best-score hyperpath $h \in \mathcal{H}(d)$. To solve the latter problem, we rely on a multiclass logistic regression model in which each hyperpath h is reduced to a vector of features f^h of a fixed length n, where n is the number of features. More precisely, (i) each hyperarc a is represented as a binary feature vector f^a such that $f_k^a = 1$ iff the k-th feature of the model holds within the context of a, and (ii) $f^h = \sum_{a \in h} f^a$.

Let θ be a vector of real-valued model parameters of length n. The conditional probability of a particular hyperpath $h \in \mathcal{H}(d)$ given dependency tree d is defined as:

$$p_\theta(h|d) = \exp(\theta \cdot f^h) \,/\, \sum_{h' \in \mathcal{H}(d)} \exp(\theta \cdot f^{h'}), \tag{1}$$

where $\cdot$ is a dot product. Determining the highest-probability hyperpath, as well as determining the marginal probabilities of the individual hyperarcs (important for parameter estimation), can be performed efficiently using the inside-outside algorithm. For parameter learning, we rely on the maximum likelihood estimates (w.r.t. training data T) with normal priors over θ. The log-likelihood takes the form:

$$\ell(\theta) = \sum_{(d,h) \in T} \log p_\theta(h|d) - \sum_{k=1}^{n} \frac{\theta_k^2}{2\sigma^2}, \tag{2}$$

where the regularization parameter $1/2\sigma^2$ determines the strength of the penalty on high parameter values. The maximum likelihood estimates are then approximated using stochastic gradient descent with momentum (Qian, 1999; Ruder, 2016).

4   Experimental setup

In this section we describe how the system detailed in Sec. 3 was adapted to the shared task. In Sec. 4.1, we explain the process used to determine the set of feature templates. In Sec. 4.2 we describe the pre-processing steps used to facilitate MWE prediction for the individual languages. In Sec. 4.3 we return to the problem of MWE segmentation and outline the heuristics used to solve it. Finally, in Sec. 4.4, we give some details on how training of our system was performed.

4.1   Features templates

We used the Polish and French DEV datasets to determine a reasonable set of feature templates for our system. We started with a small set and incrementally augmented it with new templates as long as this led to better results on one or both languages. After a couple of iterations we ended up with the following set of templates, where v is the current node, w is its sibling or parent, l_u is the u's lemma, m_u is the u's MWE label, p_u is the u's universal POS tag, d_u is the dependency label of the arc incoming to u, Sib-prefixed templates apply to sibling relations, Par-prefixed templates apply to parent-child relations, and Bin-prefixed templates apply to both types of binary relations:

- Lem: (l_v, m_v)
- SibMwe and ParMwe: (m_v, m_w)
- SibLem and ParLem: (l_v, l_w, m_v, m_w)
- BinLem: unordered pair $\{(l_v, m_v), (l_w, m_w)\}$
- ParMweDep: (m_v, m_w, d_v)

- SibMweDep: (m_v, m_w, d_v, d_w)
- ParLemPosDep: $(l_v, p_w, m_v, m_w, d_v)$
- SibLemPos: (l_v, p_w, m_v, m_w)
- ParPosLemDep: $(p_v, l_w, m_v, m_w, d_v)$
- SibPosLem: (p_v, l_w, m_v, m_w)

We used the above set of templates consistently for all languages and for all VMWE categories, except for Lithuanian – dependency trees were not available for this language. We therefore converted each sentence in the LT dataset to a pseudo-dependency tree in which (i) the first token is the root, (ii) every other token is the child of the preceding token, thus obtaining a model equivalent to a 2-order sequential CRF. We also adapted the default set of templates to Lithuanian by replacing the sibling templates with selected grandparent-related templates (possible due to the structure of pseudo-dependency trees).

4.2   Pre-processing

We applied various pre-processing procedures to 9 datasets in order to facilitate prediction of MWE labels. The pre-processing method most often applied, case lifting, consisted in reattaching case dependents to their grandparents so as to make MWEs of certain categories – notably, inherently adpositional verbs – connected.[4] We applied it to BG, DE, EN, ES, HI, HR, PL, and SL datasets. For Turkish, we removed tokens marked as DERIVs (with unspecified word form, and never marked as MWEs in training data) and copied word forms to lemmas where the latter were not present. In case of Slovak, we relied on language-specific POS tags rather than universal tags, since the latter were not provided, and assumed

---

[4]Consider the expression *based on data*, with the underlined words annotated as an inherently adpositional verb in the EN dataset. Case lifting changes the set of its internal dependency arcs from {based $\rightarrow$ data, on $\leftarrow$ data} to {based $\rightarrow$ on, based $\rightarrow$ data}, thus making *based* and *on* adjacent in the resulting dependency structure.

| | Corpus | | | | | | TRAVERSAL results | | | | | | | | | | |
| | #VMWE | | | %VMWE$_{(train+dev)}$ | | | MWE-based | | | | | Token-based | | | | |
	Train	Dev	Test	Con	Con$_p$	Iso$_p$	P	R	**F1**	Rank	Delta	P	R	**F1**	Rank	Delta
BG	5364	670	670	95.0	97.34	93.42	75.59	47.61	**58.42**	4/11	-4.1	82.36	49.79	**62.06**	3/11	-1.8
DE*	2820	503	500	90.76	93.17	87.69	62.93	32.73	**43.06**	3/11	-2.21	76.17	38.36	**51.02**	2/11	-0.64
EL	1404	500	501		92.86	84.66	65.7	36.33	**46.79**	2/11	-2.97	82.16	42.01	**55.59**	1/11	1.89
EN**	331	0	501	91.84	98.19	95.17	55.5	21.16	**30.64**	2/10	-2.24	58.31	20.33	**30.15**	3/10	-4.22
ES	1739	500	500	76.55	90.13	84.59	28.84	33.4	**30.95**	4/11	-3.03	39.91	40.26	**40.09**	1/11	0.34
EU*	2823	500	500		95.28	84.38	78.28	58.4	**66.9**	4/10	-8.9	83.42	65.01	**73.07**	4/10	-3.76
FA*	2451	501	501		94.48	57.83	73.8	58.48	**65.26**	7/10	-12.57	90.19	65.23	**75.7**	6/10	-5.58
FR**	4550	629	498		98.17	92.62	77.19	44.18	**56.19**	1/13	5.65	84.72	48.76	**61.9**	1/13	6.18
HE	1236	501	502		76.45	73.69	50.33	15.14	**23.28**	1/10	0.59	74.64	18.1	**29.13**	2/10	-0.52
HI	534	0	500	98.5	98.88	85.58	66.3	60.6	**63.32**	5/10	-9.66	73.15	67.12	**70**	4/10	-3.35
HR	1450	500	501	63.38	96.56	87.03	68.04	46.59	**55.3**	1/10	11.03	78.14	50.73	**61.52**	1/10	11.55
HU**	6205	779	776		99.53	90.35	88.01	74.74	**80.84**	4/10	-9.47	89.91	79.61	**84.45**	4/10	-3.55
IT	3254	500	503		94.62	88.12	63.09	40.32	**49.2**	1/12	10.68	74.42	42.11	**53.78**	1/12	7.27
LT†	312	0	500		58.33	58.33	29.61	13.8	**18.83**	3/10	-13.34	55.56	16.92	**25.94**	3/10	-8.49
PL*	4122	515	515	80.87	86.09	82.42	77.02	59.22	**66.96**	1/11	6.42	81.85	59.03	**68.59**	1/11	3.67
PT*	4430	553	553		95.54	90.01	76.8	52.08	**62.07**	1/13	1.23	85.14	54.69	**66.6**	1/13	4.22
RO	4713	589	589		98.64	95.38	86.06	79.63	**82.72**	3/10	-2.56	88.84	82.26	**85.42**	2/10	-0.27
SL*	2378	500	500	71.61	88.12	86.14	79.41	54	**64.29**	1/10	21.95	83.61	54.54	**66.01**	1/10	14.04
TR	6125	510	506	55.54	98.21	91.08	81.48	26.09	**39.52**	5/10	-5.72	88.38	27.66	**42.13**	5/10	-10.89
AVG							*67.58*	*44.97*	*54*	*1/13*	*4.26*	*77.41*	*48.55*	*59.67*	*1/13*	*5.04*

Table 1: Detailed results of TRAVERSAL for 19 languages (identified by their ISO 639-1 codes)

that tokens with an unspecified dependency head are attached to the artificial root node (with ID=0). The same pre-processing steps were applied to TRAIN, DEV, and (blind) TEST data.

4.3 Segmentation

Once the labeling of a given dependency tree is determined, we need to determine the boundaries of the detected MWEs. To this end, we considered two heuristics: (i) all adjacent nodes marked as MWEs of the same category are considered as a single MWE occurrence, and (ii) if a group of adjacent nodes is marked as MWEs but it contains two (or more) verbs, the group is divided into two (or more) distinct MWEs. We applied the first heuristic for all languages except Farsi, where the second heuristic yielded better results, notably due to a relatively high frequency of neighboring MWEs in the FA dataset.

4.4 Training

We trained the models over the combined TRAIN+DEV datasets with $\sigma^2 = 10$ (see Sec. 3.3). For a given language, we trained one model per MWE category so as to handle the phenomenon of overlapping MWEs of different categories, often occurring in the provided annotated datasets.

5 Results

TRAVERSAL ranked 1st in the general ranking among the systems submitted to the closed track, according to both official evaluation measures: MWE-based F_1 and token-based F_1. Table 1 summarizes the performance of our system across 19 languages of the shared task (all except Arabic). For each language, the MWE-based and token-based precision (P), recall (R), and F_1 (F1) scores are reported, as well as the rank (Rank) of our system, and the difference (Delta) between the TRAVERSAL's F_1 score and the score of the other best closed-track system. The datasets with dependencies annotated manually, partially manually, or not at all, are marked with **, *, or †, respectively. For the other datasets/sentences, dependencies were obtained automatically. Con is the % of connected (via parental or sibling relation) VMWEs in the TRAIN+DEV dataset (no value $\implies$ Con=Con$_p$), and Con$_p$ is the same measure after pre-processing. Finally, Iso$_p$ is the % of connected and isolated (with no adjacent VMWEs of the same category) VMWEs after pre-processing, for which the baseline segmentation heuristic is sufficient.

Language-wise, our system performed particularly well for Slavic and Romance languages, which is likely related to our choice of Polish and French for feature template engineering. FA was the most

	Continuous	Discont.	Multi-token	Single-token	Seen	Unseen	Variant	Identical
F1	57.55	44.36	55.83	25.96	72.92	17.35	63.1	81.88
Delta	2.17	6.96	6.45	-6.86	0.85	-2.36	-1.92	-1.85

Table 2: Macro-average MWE-based F_1-scores for different specialized phenomena

	IAV	IRV	LVC.cause	LVC.full	MVC	VID	VPC.full	VPC.semi	LS.ICV
F1	44.31	68.07	23.81	46.03	17.65	34.45	34.84	42.70	30.77
Delta	8.89	8.51	-8.34	6.30	-11.39	8.01	2.07	2.2	10.77

Table 3: Macro-average MWE-based F_1-scores for different MWE categories[5]

challenging dataset for our system, which is clearly due to the low % of isolated VMWEs in this dataset and, consequently, low effectiveness of the implemented segmentation heuristics. TRAVERSAL performed well on datasets with both manually annotated (`FR`) and automatically obtained (`IT`, `HR`, `EL`) dependencies, thus showing robustness w.r.t. the quality of dependency annotations.

Concerning specialized phenomena (see Table 2), TRAVERSAL performed particularly well on discontinuous MWEs. This might be related to the view on MWEs adopted in our system, where continuous and discontinuous MWEs are not really distinguished – both are "continuous" in dependency trees. TRAVERSAL proved better in handling multi-token VMWEs than single-token (e.g. *to pretty-print*) VMWEs (outperformed by TRAPACC and TRAPACC_S in case of the latter) and exhibited certain preference for VMWEs already seen during training (outperformed by GBD-NER-standard and GBD-NER-resplit in case of unseen VMWEs). Besides, TRAVESAL turned out less efficient in identifying identical VMWEs and variants of VMWEs seen during trainig than TRAPACC and GBD-NER-resplit, respectively, even though it outperformed the two systems for the class of seen VMWEs in general.

Category-wise (see Table 3), TRAVERSAL was quite successful in identifying inherently adpositional verbs (IAV), which suggests that the pre-processing strategy of re-attaching case markers was effective. It also performed very well for inherently reflexive verbs (IRV), verbal idioms (VID), light-verb constructions (LVC.full), and inherently clitic verbs (LS.ICV, occurring only in the IT dataset). In case of "causative" LVCs (LVC.cause), TRAVERSAL was outperformed by varIDE, and in case of multi-verb constructions (MVC) – by TRAPACC and CRF-DepTree-categs.

6   Conclusions and future work

This paper presents a system dedicated to identification of verbal MWEs based on the explicit assumption that MWEs form connected components in dependency trees. It divides the task of MWE identification into two subsequent sub-tasks: (i) tree labeling (with two possible labels: `MWE` and `not-MWE`), and (ii) MWE segmentation (determining the boundaries of MWEs). For the former task, it relies on the multiclass logistic regression model in order to find the globally optimal labeling for a given tree. The system ranked 1st in the closed track of the PARSEME shared task, thus showing the viability of applying CRF-like models to identification of verbal – in particular, discontinuous – MWEs.

For future work, we consider improving the MWE segmentation component of our system. In particular, we would like to explore the idea of enriching labels with information about MWE boundaries so as to perform MWE segmentation jointly with MWE labeling. Another direction for future work would be to see to what extent external resources (MWE dictionaries, word embeddings) could be incorporated in our system. We could also explore usefulness of ternary features, so far ignored in our experiments. Finally, we plan to perform a more fine-grained error analysis, so as to get better insight into the advantages and limitations of the implemented method.

Acknowledgements

The author thanks Behrang QasemiZadeh and the anonymous reviewers for their valuable comments.

---

[5]In Tab. 1 and Tab. 2, macro-average F_1 is calculated based on macro-average precision and recall. In Tab. 3, macro-average F_1 is calculated directly as the mean of the relevant F_1-scores obtained for the individual languages.

References

Anne Abeillé and Yves Schabes. 1989. Parsing Idioms in Lexicalized TAGs. In *Proceedings of the Fourth Conference on European Chapter of the Association for Computational Linguistics*, EACL '89, pages 1–9, Stroudsburg, PA, USA. Association for Computational Linguistics.

Eduard Bejček, Jarmila Panevová, Jan Popelka, Pavel Straňák, Magda Ševčíková, Jan Štěpánek, and Zdeněk Žabokrtský. 2012. Prague dependency treebank 2.5 – a revisited version of pdt 2.0. In *In Proceedings of the 24th International Conference on Computational Linguistics (Coling 2012)*, pages 231–246.

Marie Candito and Matthieu Constant. 2014. Strategies for Contiguous Multiword Expression Analysis and Dependency Parsing. In *Proceedings of the 52nd Annual Meeting of the Association for Computational Linguistics (Volume 1: Long Papers)*, pages 743–753. Association for Computational Linguistics.

Matthieu Constant and Joakim Nivre. 2016. A Transition-Based System for Joint Lexical and Syntactic Analysis. In *Proceedings of the 54th Annual Meeting of the Association for Computational Linguistics (Volume 1: Long Papers)*, pages 161–171. Association for Computational Linguistics.

Matthieu Constant, Anthony Sigogne, and Patrick Watrin. 2012. Discriminative Strategies to Integrate Multiword Expression Recognition and Parsing. In *Proceedings of the 50th Annual Meeting of the Association for Computational Linguistics (Volume 1: Long Papers)*, pages 204–212. Association for Computational Linguistics.

Giorgio Gallo, Giustino Longo, Stefano Pallottino, and Sang Nguyen. 1993. Directed Hypergraphs and Applications. *Discrete Appl. Math.*, 42(2-3):177–201, April.

Spence Green, Marie-Catherine de Marneffe, and Christopher D. Manning. 2013. Parsing Models for Identifying Multiword Expressions. *Computational Linguistics*, 39(1).

Aravind K Joshi and Yves Schabes. 1997. Tree-Adjoining Grammars. In Grzegorz Rozenberg and Arto Salomaa, editors, *Handbook of Formal Languages*, pages 69–123. Springer Berlin Heidelberg.

Dan Klein and Christopher D. Manning. 2001. Parsing and Hypergraphs. In *Seventh International Workshop on Parsing Technologies (IWPT-2001)*, October.

Sandra Kübler, Ryan McDonald, and Joakim Nivre. 2009. Dependency parsing. *Synthesis Lectures on Human Language Technologies*, 1(1):1–127.

Joseph Le Roux, Antoine Rozenknop, and Matthieu Constant. 2014. Syntactic Parsing and Compound Recognition via Dual Decomposition: Application to French. In *Proceedings of COLING 2014, the 25th International Conference on Computational Linguistics: Technical Papers*, pages 1875–1885. Dublin City University and Association for Computational Linguistics.

Alfredo Maldonado, Lifeng Han, Erwan Moreau, Ashjan Alsulaimani, Koel Dutta Chowdhury, Carl Vogel, and Qun Liu. 2017. Detection of Verbal Multi-Word Expressions via Conditional Random Fields with Syntactic Dependency Features and Semantic Re-Ranking. In *Proceedings of the 13th Workshop on Multiword Expressions (MWE 2017)*, pages 114–120. Association for Computational Linguistics.

Ryan McDonald and Fernando Pereira. 2006. Online learning of approximate dependency parsing algorithms. In *11th Conference of the European Chapter of the Association for Computational Linguistics*.

Ryan McDonald and Giorgio Satta. 2007. On the complexity of non-projective data-driven dependency parsing. In *Proceedings of the Tenth International Conference on Parsing Technologies*, pages 121–132. Association for Computational Linguistics.

István Nagy T. and Veronika Vincze. 2014. VPCTagger: Detecting Verb-Particle Constructions With Syntax-Based Methods. In *Proceedings of the 10th Workshop on Multiword Expressions (MWE)*, pages 17–25, Gothenburg, Sweden, April. Association for Computational Linguistics.

Alexis Nasr, Carlos Ramisch, José Deulofeu, and André Valli. 2015. Joint Dependency Parsing and Multiword Expression Tokenization. In *Proceedings of the 53rd Annual Meeting of the Association for Computational Linguistics and the 7th International Joint Conference on Natural Language Processing (Volume 1: Long Papers)*, pages 1116–1126. Association for Computational Linguistics.

Ning Qian. 1999. On the momentum term in gradient descent learning algorithms. *Neural networks*, 12(1):145–151.

Carlos Ramisch, Silvio Ricardo Cordeiro, Agata Savary, Veronika Vincze, Verginica Barbu Mititelu, Archna Bhatia, Maja Buljan, Marie Candito, Polona Gantar, Voula Giouli, Tunga Güngör, Abdelati Hawwari, Uxoa Iñurrieta, Jolanta Kovalevskaitė, Simon Krek, Timm Lichte, Chaya Liebeskind, Johanna Monti, Carla Parra Escartín, Behrang QasemiZadeh, Renata Ramisch, Nathan Schneider, Ivelina Stoyanova, Ashwini Vaidya, and Abigail Walsh. 2018. Edition 1.1 of the PARSEME Shared Task on Automatic Identification of Verbal Multiword Expressions. In *Proceedings of the Joint Workshop on Linguistic Annotation, Multiword Expressions and Constructions (LAW-MWE-CxG 2018)*, Santa Fe, New Mexico, USA, August. Association for Computational Linguistics.

Sebastian Ruder. 2016. An overview of gradient descent optimization algorithms. *CoRR*, abs/1609.04747.

Manon Scholivet and Carlos Ramisch. 2017. Identification of Ambiguous Multiword Expressions Using Sequence Models and Lexical Resources. In *Proceedings of the 13th Workshop on Multiword Expressions (MWE 2017)*, pages 167–175. Association for Computational Linguistics.

Charles Sutton, Andrew McCallum, et al. 2012. An introduction to conditional random fields. *Foundations and Trends® in Machine Learning*, 4(4):267–373.

Veronika Vincze, István Nagy T., and János Zsibrita. 2013. Learning to Detect English and Hungarian Light Verb Constructions. *ACM Trans. Speech Lang. Process.*, 10(2):6:1–6:25, June.

Jakub Waszczuk, Agata Savary, and Yannick Parmentier. 2016. Promoting multiword expressions in A* TAG parsing. In *Proceedings of COLING 2016, the 26th International Conference on Computational Linguistics: Technical Papers*, pages 429–439. The COLING 2016 Organizing Committee.

VarIDE at PARSEME Shared Task 2018:
Are Variants Really *as Alike as Two Peas in a Pod?*

Caroline Pasquer
University of Tours
France

Carlos Ramisch
Aix Marseille Univ,
Université de Toulon,
CNRS, LIS, Marseille, France

Agata Savary
University of Tours
France

Jean-Yves Antoine
University of Tours
France

`first.last@(univ-tours|lis-lab).fr`

Abstract

We describe the *VarIDE* system (standing for *Variant IDEntification*) which participated in edition 1.1 of the PARSEME shared task on automatic identification of verbal multiword expressions (VMWEs). Our system focuses on the task of VMWE variant identification by using morphosyntactic information in the training data to predict if candidates extracted from the test corpus could be idiomatic, thanks to a naive Bayes classifier. We report results for 19 languages.

1 Introduction

Identifying multiword expressions (MWEs) such as *to **make ends meet*** and *to **give up*** in running text is a challenging problem (Baldwin and Kim, 2010; Constant et al., 2017). This is especially true for verbal MWEs (VMWEs), which, like verbs together with their subcategorization frames, are subject to complex morphological and syntactic transformations. As a consequence, VMWEs may occur under various forms, and it is especially important to identify expressions which are variants of each other.

Our system VarIDE, submitted to the PARSEME shared task 2018, focuses on the specific problem of variant identification. Shared task organizers provided training, development and test corpora (hereafter TRAIN, DEV, and TEST) manually annotated for VMWEs.[1] Given a VMWE (e.g. *to **have look*** 'to have appearance') that appears in TRAIN under a certain form as in ex. (1), VarIDE aims at identifying the different uses of this VMWE in the corresponding DEV and TEST corpora whatever their surface form, either identical – i.e. with the same sequence of words between the first and last lexicalized component[2] as in (4),(5) or (6) – or not – as in (2) or (3). Even though identifying the former may not seem challenging, especially for (4) that is completely identical to (1), it should be pointed out that (7), despite its apparent similarity, cannot be considered a valid variant because of the additional lexicalized determiner which characterizes a different VMWE (*to **have** a **look*** 'to examine'). Moreover, the other examples teach us that the VMWE ***have look*** tolerates the imperative in (5) or adverbial modifiers (advmod), adverbial clauses (advcl) and inflection for person in (6). With such a knowledge, we can establish the profile of the allowed morphosyntactic transformations for this VMWE, which should be useful when it appears with different surface form, as in (2). Therefore, VarIDE is based on the hypothesis that the variability phenomenon has to take into account the widest range of use of any VMWE, so that we consider all examples from (2) to (6) as *variants* (from now, this term will exclusively refer to this definition) of (1).

However, within the context of the shared task, a more restrictive definition is adopted: among all the occurrences in DEV/TEST corresponding to an annotated VMWE in TRAIN (called *Seen-in-train* VMWEs), only (2) and (3) are called *Variants-of-train*.[3] They exhibit differences within the lexicalized components (verbal inflection) and the insertions (e.g. a negation), contrary to the examples (4), (5) and (6) (called *Identical-to-train* VMWEs). In other words, what we call variants in this work corresponds to the Seen-in-train VMWEs in the shared task.

---

[1] `http://multiword.sourceforge.net/sharedtask2018/`

[2] The lexicalized components of the VMWE, i.e. those always realized by same lexemes, appear in bold.

[3] See details at `http://multiword.sourceforge.net/sharedtaskresults2018`.

Proceedings of the Joint Workshop on
Linguistic Annotation, Multiword Expressions and Constructions (LAW-MWE-CxG-2018), pages 283–289
Santa Fe, New Mexico, USA, August 25-26, 2018.

(1)   *Rooms **have**.Ind.Pres.3rd a personalized **look** with curtains* 'Rooms have a personalized appearance' (TRAIN)

(2)   *This room **has**.Ind.Pres.3rd not a personalized **look*** (TEST)

(3)   *He **has** a **look** of innocence* (TEST)

(4)   *Rooms **have**.Ind.Pres.3rd a personalized **look** with curtains* (TEST)

(5)   *Please **have**.Imp a personalized **look** today* (TEST)

(6)   *You always.advmod **have** a personalized **look** by using.advcl this color* (TEST)

(7)   *Applicants **have a** personalized **look** at their resume* 'Applicants examine their resume in a personalized way' (TEST)

On average, Seen-in-train VMWEs represent 59.8% of all VMWEs in TEST, and, therefore, deserve dedicated analysis and processing. To this aim, our system first extracts a large set of candidates to cover a large proportion of annotated VMWEs (but also a considerable amount of noise). This extraction is based on the most frequent POS patterns of annotated VMWEs in TRAIN. Then, we extract features for VMWE classification based on the morphological and syntactic characteristics of candidates. Finally, we train a naive Bayes classifier which tries to predict, given these features, whether extracted candidates are true VMWEs or ordinary word combinations. VarIDE is a generic multilingual system for VMWE identification. It was evaluated on 19 of the 20 shared task languages. This paper describes the submitted system (Sec. 2) with the variant identification understood as above and analyzes its results (Sec. 3).

2   System description: variant identification

VarIDE is designed to identify variants of VMWEs observed in the training data. It relies on the hypothesis that the more a candidate expression c is similar to at least one annotated VMWE occurrence e, the higher the probability that c and e are variants of the same VMWE. We estimate this similarity by comparing features exhibited by c and e. These features are then used by a classifier to determine whether c is a true VMWE (that is, a variant of an observed one) or an ordinary word combination. We describe the classifier training (Sec. 2.1), and then the variant prediction and categorization on TEST (Sec. 2.2).

2.1   Training data

To train the binary classifier, we need both positive (IDIOMATIC) and negative (LITERAL) examples of VMWEs. Only the former are provided in TRAIN. Therefore, we extract VMWEs and candidates by searching for co-occurrences of the same lemmas as in annotated VMWEs, according to certain patterns. We specify the patterns to be respected since (i) this reduces noise with respect to free lemma co-occurrences, and (ii) features strongly depend on c and e's syntactic patterns. Among the steps described below for TRAIN, candidate and feature extraction will also be applied on TEST for the prediction phase.

2.1.1   Normalization and pattern generation

We aim at obtaining the most frequent patterns of annotated VMWEs in each language. Therefore, two normalization steps are required to accommodate for POS tag variability and morphological inflection.

POS sequence normalization   A given VMWE annotated in TRAIN, e.g. *they **build** a **bridge*** 'they create a relationship', can be represented as a sequence of POS tags of its lexicalized components, here: ⟨VERB,NOUN⟩. The same VMWE may exhibit other POS sequences because of syntactic transformations (e.g. ⟨NOUN,VERB⟩ for *the **bridges** that were **built***). We define the *normalized POS sequence* (hereafter *POSnorm*) as the lexicographically sorted sequence of POS tags of the lexicalized components of a VMWE, e.g. the two occurrences of *to **build** a **bridge*** above have the same *POSnorm* ⟨NOUN,VERB⟩.

Lemma sequence normalization   Inflection and word order should also be neutralized so as to consider e.g. both *builds a bridge* and *bridges built* as variants of the same VMWE. We, thus, define the *normalized lemmatized form* (hereafter *LemmNorm*) as the sequence of lexicographically ordered lemmas (e.g. ⟨bridge,build⟩). Although this form could potentially conflate distinct VMWEs sharing the same *LemmNorm*, such spurious conflation was rarely observed in practice upon inspection of a sample.

Pattern generation Candidate extraction is based on *LemmNorm*, hence we keep the correspondence between a *LemmNorm* and its observed/allowed lemma sequences. However, VMWEs may not exhibit their whole range of possible lemma sequences in TRAIN. Therefore, we apply an extrapolation procedure to avoid missing VMWEs with low frequency or unobserved variants in TRAIN, as exemplified in Table 1. The *LemmNorm* of each VMWE in TRAIN is associated with all its observed POS sequences and their frequencies, and with its *POSnorm*. When the same *LemmNorm* is associated with more than one *POSnorm* (e.g. due to annotation errors), only the most frequent one is kept like for $\langle out, turn \rangle$ in Table 1. When the table is read from left to right, this leads to a list of allowed permutations for each VMWE sharing the same *POSnorm*. For instance, VMWEs associated to the *POSnorm* $\langle$NOUN,VERB$\rangle$ (e.g. **make decisions**) may occur in both orders VERB-NOUN and NOUN-VERB, as opposed to those associated with the *POSnorm* $\langle$PRON,VERB$\rangle$ (e.g. **take it**), which only appears in the VERB-PRON order. As a consequence, the *LemmNorm* $\langle$adjustment,make$\rangle$ will be associated with the POS sequence NOUN-VERB, even if this order (e.g. **adjustments** *which were* **made**) was never observed. This enlarges the possible word-order combinations to be searched during candidate extraction, but does not mean that the full set of POS permutations is allowed by all VMWEs sharing the same *POSnorm*.

2.1.2 Extraction of positive and negative VMWE examples

To be extracted, a candidate must respect one of the POS sequences allowed by its *POSnorm*. For instance, this condition is not fulfilled by *Tower Bridge built*[4] (PROPN instead of NOUN) or by *it takes* (PRON-VERB order instead of VERB-PRON). We select the 10 most frequent *POSnorms* for each language and their associated POS sequences. For each *LemmNorm* in TRAIN whose *POSnorm* belongs to this top-10 list, we generate all allowed permutations of lemmas and search them in the corpus allowing for discontinuities. Given that candidate extraction relies on the *LemmNorm*, we can never find candidates whose lemma sequence never occurs in TRAIN, i.e. we focus on Seen-in-train VMWEs, as explained in Sec. 1. To further limit the quantity of spurious candidates in some languages (e.g. because of sentence segmentation errors), we limit the number of words that can occur between the the first and last components of an extracted candidate to 20. This constraint is referred to as *Filter20*. Moreover, a post-processing script checks whether all annotated VMWEs within the top-10 *POSnorms* were actually extracted as candidates, and adds them automatically if missing (which could occur because of lemmatization errors). To develop the training set for the classifier, the extracted candidates in TRAIN are labeled IDIOMATIC if they were manually annotated as VMWEs, and LITERAL otherwise.

LemmNorm	Occurrence (freq.)	Observed POS sequence	*POSnorm*	Most frequent *POSnorm*	Allowed POS sequences
$\langle$decision,make$\rangle$	*decisions made* (1) *make decisions* (1)	NOUN-VERB VERB-NOUN	$\langle$NOUN,VERB$\rangle$	$\langle$NOUN,VERB$\rangle$	NOUN-VERB VERB-NOUN
$\langle$adjustment,make$\rangle$	*make an adjustment* (2) *make adjustments* (2) *make the Adjustments* (1)	VERB-NOUN VERB-PROPN	$\langle$NOUN,VERB$\rangle$ $\langle$PROPN,VERB$\rangle$	$\langle$NOUN,VERB$\rangle$	
$\langle$take,vote$\rangle$	*the vote will be taken* (1)	NOUN-VERB	$\langle$NOUN,VERB$\rangle$	$\langle$NOUN,VERB$\rangle$	
$\langle$it,take$\rangle$	*we can take it* (1) *take it from me* (1)	VERB-PRON	$\langle$PRON,VERB$\rangle$	$\langle$PRON,VERB$\rangle$	VERB-PRON
$\langle$it,make$\rangle$	*He made it* (1)	VERB-PRON	$\langle$PRON,VERB$\rangle$	$\langle$PRON,VERB$\rangle$	
$\langle$out,turn$\rangle$	*The pics turned out ok* (1) *It turns out* [...] *is fine* (1) *It turns out that* (1)	VERB-ADP VERB-ADV	$\langle$ADP,VERB$\rangle$ $\langle$ADV,VERB$\rangle$	$\langle$ADP,VERB$\rangle$	VERB-ADP

Table 1: Example of VMWEs, their *LemmNorm*, list of POS sequences, and *POSnorm*.

2.1.3 Features

Language-adaptable features We describe each candidate VMWE using a set of feature-value pairs. For that purpose, we adapt the methodology presented for French in (Pasquer et al., 2018) to a multilingual scale. Its main principle is that a *feature* is defined as a named property (e.g. the UD verbal form VERBFORM) which is associated with a value taken from a set of possible values (e.g. *Inf, Ger, Conv*).

---

[4]Wavy underlining means a non-VMWE.

However, we cannot define a fixed set of features and values due to language specificities (e.g. VERB-FORM=*Conv(erb)* exists in Croatian but not in English). Such specificities occur in the POS tagsets, dependency relations, and morphological features. Therefore, we first scan the corpora to list all features and their possible values for each language. As a result, all existing features for each language are considered for all candidates, even if some of them are irrelevant, like the gender of an invariable token. When a feature is irrelevant for a candidate, its value is set to *-1*.

Features represent morphological[5] and syntactic properties, thanks to information available in the shared task corpora in the *.cupt* format. Syntactic features involve both insertions and outgoing dependency relations when available. For the elements inserted between the VMWE components, we disregard adjacency and only consider their POS (e.g. ADV-PRON in *They believed that genuine democracy **was** now.ADV **on** its.PRON **way***). Features can be classified into two classes: absolute and relative.

Absolute (ABS) vs. relative (REL) features For a given candidate, which can be either positive or negative VMWE, ABS features are obtained directly, based on its local properties and on the properties of its component words. For instance, in ex. (8a), the noun is singular, hence the feature ABS_morph_NOUN_Number = *singular*. On the other hand, REL features are obtained by comparing a candidate with all annotated VMWEs in TRAIN that share the same *LemmNorm* (except itself). These features aim at capturing the similarity of a candidate with annotated VMWEs. REL features can take three values: *false*, if no equivalence with any annotated VMWE was found, *true* if at least one equivalence was found[6] , or *-1* if comparison is impossible (e.g. for hapaxes). In other words, this similarity relies on the most similar annotated VMWE (i.e. the REL values are assigned after all the VMWEs in TRAIN have been scanned) even though the considered properties are only observed once. For instance, to obtain the REL feature-values for the VMWE $\langle photo, take \rangle$ in ex. (8a), we compare it with the annotated occurrences (8b) and (8c). First, as synthesized in Table 2 cell (5,4), one determiner (*a, some*) is inserted in both (8a) and (8b), so that the REL_insert_DET value is *true* whatever the insertions in (8c). Second, (8a) and (8b) differ regarding the mood/tense of the verb (imperative vs. preterite) but the imperative is also used in (8c) so that REL_morph_*VERB*_Mood is *true*. Third, the number inflection of the noun *photo* differs from (8b) or (8c), hence REL_morph_*NOUN*_Number = *false* – cf. cell (13,5).

Features can refer to the whole VMWE candidate (e.g. *LemmNorm*) or to its individual tokens. In the latter case, each token is identified by its POS, hence the three cases in Table 2: no duplicated POS so each component can be identified by its POS (Case 1, illustrated by the examples 8a-8b-8c); duplicated POS that can be distinguished by the tokens' incoming dependencies (Case 2, ex. 9a-9b); duplicated POS that cannot be distinguished by the tokens' incoming dependencies (Case 3, ex. 10a-10b).

(8) CASE 1
- a. ***Take**.VERB a.DET **photo**.NOUN of a very light plain subject* [...]
- b. *I **took**.VERB some.DET **photos**.NOUN of my model girlfriend* [ ]
- c. *Please **take**.VERB four.NUM new.ADJ **photos**.NOUN*

(9) CASE 2
- a. *we'll **let**.VERB.root you **know**.VERB.xcomp*
- b. ***Let**.VERB.root me **know**.VERB.xcomp*[...]

(10) CASE 3
- a. ***It's raining cats**.NOUN.obj **and dogs**.NOUN.obj*
- b. ***It was** sometimes.ADV **raining cats**.NOUN.obj **and dogs**.NOUN.obj*

2.2 VMWE prediction and category assignment

Once the training is complete, in the prediction phase we extract candidates from TEST following the procedure described in Sec. 2.1.2, except that we do not know whether they are negative or positive. Absolute feature-values are obtained as described for the candidate extraction in the TRAIN corpus. As for the relative feature-values, they are obtained by comparison with all VMWEs in TRAIN with the same *LemmNorm*: for any given feature, if the same absolute value is found at least once in TEST as in TRAIN, then the Boolean relative feature is set to *true*, and *false* otherwise.

---

[5]Inflection and typology e.g. NUMTYPE $\in$ {*Ord(inal), Card(inal)*}

[6]For instance, as shown in Table 2, similarities are found between the variants (8a) and (8b) whether the presence of an inserted determiner or the absence of an inserted verb.

Feature description	Feature name (without the ABS/REL prefix)	ABSolute and RELative feature-values					
		CASE 1		CASE 2		CASE 3	
		ABS (8a)	REL (8a) vs. (8b/c)	ABS (9a)	REL (9a) vs. (9b)	ABS (10a)	REL (10a) vs. (10b)
Normalized lemma sequence	*LemmNorm*	⟨photo,take⟩	n/a	⟨know,let⟩	n/a	⟨and,be,cat, dog,it,rain⟩	n/a
VMWE category	typeMWE	*LVC.full*	n/a	*VID*	n/a	*VID*	n/a
POS insertions	insertALL	*DET*	*true*	*PRON*	*true*		*false*
All existing POS per language (value=*true* if present, *false* otherwise)	insert_*DET*	*true*	*true*	*false*	*true*	*false*	*true*
	insert_*VERB*	*false*	*true*	*false*	*true*	*false*	*true*
Number of inserted elements between VMWE components in tree	distSyn_VerbNoun	*0*	*true*	*-1*	*true*	*-1*	*true*
Syntactic distance iff two components in the VMWE	distSyn_2elts	*0*	*true*	*0*	*true*	*-1*	*true*
Type of syntactic relation: *direct* (parent-child),*serial* (indirect ancestor) or *parallel* (shared ancestor)	typeSyn_VerbNoun	*direct*	*true*	*-1*	*true*	*-1*	*true*
Type of syntactic distance	typedistSyn_2elts	*direct*	*true*	*direct*	*true*	*-1*	*true*
Lemma of each component	lemma_*NOUN*	*photo*	n/a	*-1*	n/a	*-1*	n/a
	lemma_*VERB*_xcomp	*-1*	*-1*	*know*	*true*	*-1*	*-1*
Morphological features per component (*-1* if irrelevant)	morph_*VERB*_VerbForm	*Fin*	*true*	*-1*	*-1*	*-1*	*-1*
	morph_*VERB*_Mood	*Imp*	*true*	*-1*	*-1*	*-1*	*-1*
	morph_*VERB*_Gender	*-1*	*true*	*-1*	*-1*	*-1*	*-1*
	morph_*NOUN*_Number	*singular*	*false*	*-1*	*-1*	*-1*	*-1*
	morph_*VERB*_xcomp_VerbForm	*-1*	*-1*	*Inf*	*true*	*-1*	*-1*
Outgoing dependencies per component (*1* if satisfied at least once)	depSyn_*NOUN*_obj	*1*	*true*	*-1*	*-1*	*-1*	*-1*
	depSyn_*NOUN*_punct	*0*	*true*	*-1*	*-1*	*-1*	*-1*
	depSyn_*VERB*_xcomp_advcl	*-1*	*-1*	*0*	*true*	*-1*	*-1*

Table 2: Absolute and relative features for examples 8a (RELative to 8b/c), 9a (RELative to 9b), and 10a (RELative to 10b). The table should be read by compositing the ABS or REL prefix with the feature names from column 3, e.g. the cells in line 4 and columns 4 and 5 represent the feature-value pairs ABS_insertALL=*DET* and REL_insertALL=*true*.

Second, we use the NLTK's naive Bayes classifier[7] to classify candidates as negative/positive on the basis of their features. After binary classification, the VMWE category of the predicted candidate is obtained thanks to the most frequent category associated to its *LemmNorm* in TRAIN.

3   Results

Recall that VarIDE aims at identifying VMWEs occurrences which correspond to the Seen-in-train category of the shared task. Therefore, Unseen-in-train VMWEs were not expected to be identified. However, VarIDE achieves a non-zero recall for Unseen-in-train (R = 3.31), which can be due, in French, to language-specific lemma homogenization for reflexive clitics (e.g. *nous* 'us' can be lemmatized either as *nous* 'us' or as *se* 'oneself').

Table 3 shows the number of true and false VMWEs, called IDIOMATIC (ID) and LITERAL (LIT), respectively, extracted from TRAIN to train the classifier, with the ratio of IDIOMATIC (% ID) examples. Recall (R) for Variant-of-train before classification (i.e. after candidate extraction) and after classification is also presented. The comparison between the global and the Variant-of-train F1-score in Table 3 shows to what extent our variant-centered identification system specifically performs on identifying Variant-of-train occurrences, which is a narrower and more challenging task than the Seen-in-train identification.

Candidate extraction   We notice that we obtain satisfactory coverage of the top-10 *POSnorm*, with R > 0.8 for 17 languages (0.62 and 0.75 for IT and DE). Moreover, extraction recall on Variants-of-train depends on their proportion in corpora which varies from 12% (RO) to 83% (LT). Despite few Variants-of-train in RO, global F1 is satisfactory due to well identified Identical-to-train occurrences.

Candidate classification   Variant-of-train classification performance (F1 and R) is sensitive to the reliability of the annotated corpora, being affected by both false positives (e.g. *UV lights*.NOUN *up*.VERB *the temperature* was falsely annotated, probably by analogy to *to **light**.VERB **up**.ADP*) and false nega-

---

| Lang. | Candidates from TRAIN for classifier training | | | Var-of-t % | Var-of-t extraction | Var-of-t classif. | Global F1 MWE | Seen-in-train F1 | Var-of-t F1 MWE | UD tags | dep syn | *Filter 20* |
	# ID	# LIT	% ID	TEST	Recall	Recall	-based	MWE-based	-based			
ES	1580	3414	32	52%	0.8966	0.8345	0.253	0.2854	0.1883	x	x	x
FR	4303	5089	46	50%	0.9286	0.8968	0.5054	0.7003	0.5722	x	x	
IT	2755	5721	32	62%	0.625	0.5707	0.325	0.4024	0.3226		x	x
PT	4171	4014	51	59%	0.9442	0.7082	0.6084	0.728	0.6574	x	x	x
RO	4636	5501	46	12%	0.9692	0.8923	0.7115	0.7243	0.2613	x	x	x
DE	2437	1114	69	59%	0.7568	0.1554	0.153	0.2809	0.2614	x	x	
EN	316	336	48	53%	0.9474	0.5526	0.2417	0.5609	0.525	x	x	x
BG	5031	6637	43	36%	0.9625	0.8562	0.6252	0.7495	0.5842	x	x	x
HR	1381	843	62	73%	0.9698	0.1457	0.1257	0.2152	0.2447	x	x	
LT	301	**96**	**76**	83%	0.9946	0.0269	0.0196	0.0427	0.0515	x		x
PL	3954	2119	65	60%	0.9507	0.1256	0.1125	0.1523	0.2205	x	x	
SL	2281	13330	15	73%	0.9812	0.9624	0.4234	0.4612	0.3908		x	x
EL	1270	1341	49	68%	0.9239	0.3299	0.3477	0.523	0.4676	x	x	
EU	2499	5147	33	39%	0.9451	0.9268	0.5231	0.5527	0.3482		x	x
FA	2437	1707	59	53%	1	0.4311	0.4495	0.6274	0.5806	x	x	
HE	932	820	53	41%	0.8472	0.1528	0.1862	0.4082	0.2157	x	x	
HI	526	463	53	49%	0.95	0.6786	0.568	0.7948	0.7224	x	x	x
HU	6187	516	**92**	21%	1	0.0336	0.1869	0.2041	0.0649		x	
TR	5802	**156652**	**4**	60%	0.9733	0.9733	0.0787	0.3595	0.2598		x	x

Table 3: VarIDE results, with a focus on Variant-of-train (Var-of-t) identification.

tives. Imbalance between IDIOMATIC and LITERAL, i.e. either an over-representation of LITERAL, as in Turkish (96%) or the contrary, as in Hungarian (8%), may also have a detrimental impact. Not only percentages should be considered: in Lithuanian, only 96 candidates are classified as LITERAL. In this case, the classifier may not have enough counter-examples to learn from the features. Finally, after classification, 8 languages remain at R>0.7, but only 3 with F1>0.5: FR, PT, and BG. Features should therefore be improved to optimize both classification recall and precision.

Other problems are non-UD tagsets (which required adjustments for a few languages), sentence segmentation errors (handled with *Filter20*) and missing lemmatization (e.g. in Turkish). Other parameters may also influence the results: despite similarities between FR and ES (both are Romance languages, exhibit similar % of Variants-of-train in Table 3, and similar recall of Variants-of-train after classification) F1 is significantly lower for ES (0.57 vs. 0.19) due to lower precision. A thorough analysis might explain those results and determine whether language families share properties about the alikeness of variants of VMWEs. We believe that the similarity between variants cannot be only evaluated by the visual similarity between strings but also by taking their morphosyntactic properties into account .

4   Conclusions and future work

Our VarIDE system classifies VMWE candidates as VMWEs[8] on the basis of their morphosyntactic features by comparison with annotated VMWEs. After candidate classification, F1 for the Variants-of-train is higher than 0.5 for 6 languages (FR, PT, EN, BG, FA, HI) whereas it does not exceed 0.2 for 3 languages (ES, LT, HU). For Lithuanian or Hungarian, this low performance can be explained by the imbalance in the TRAIN data, but such explanation is not valid for Spanish. A more detailed analysis should be therefore conducted to explain the discrepancies between the observed performances for the 19 languages. For that purpose, we should look more precisely at the most informative features found in TRAIN. For instance, for Hindi, for which the system presents the best Seen-in-train and Variant-of-train performances (respectively, F1 = 0.79 and F1 = 0.72), the insertion of an auxiliary or a verb appears as a determining factor for LITERAL labels. In Basque, Farsi or Italian, the insertion of punctuation also appears among the first features that favor the LITERAL label.

Furthermore, we could also evaluate other classifiers such as a linear SVM or a multilayer perceptron. Finally, we aim at correlating the absolute and relative features used during the classification task with linguistic justifications in order to define a more task-independent variability profile of any VMWE.

---

[8] Input data, scripts and metrics are available at: `https://gitlab.com/cpasquer/SharedTask2018_varIDE`

Acknowledgments

This work was supported by the IC1207 PARSEME COST action[9] and by the PARSEME-FR project (ANR-14-CERA-0001).[10]

References

[Baldwin and Kim2010] Timothy Baldwin and Su Nam Kim. 2010. Multiword expressions. In Nitin Indurkhya and Fred J. Damerau, editors, *Handbook of Natural Language Processing*, pages 267–292. CRC Press, Taylor and Francis Group, Boca Raton, FL, USA, 2 edition.

[Constant et al.2017] Mathieu Constant, Gülşen Eryiğit, Johanna Monti, Lonneke van der Plas, Carlos Ramisch, Michael Rosner, and Amalia Todirascu. 2017. Multiword expression processing: A survey. *Computational Linguistics*, 43(4):837–892.

[Pasquer et al.2018] Caroline Pasquer, Agata Savary, Carlos Ramisch, and Jean-Yves Antoine. 2018. If you've seen some, you've seen them all: Identifying variants of multiword expressions. In *Proceedings of COLING 2018, the 27th International Conference on Computational Linguistics*. The COLING 2018 Organizing Committee.

---

[9] http://www.parseme.eu
[10] http://parsemefr.lif.univ-mrs.fr/

Veyn at PARSEME Shared Task 2018:
Recurrent Neural Networks for VMWE Identification

Nicolas Zampieri and **Manon Scholivet** and **Carlos Ramisch** and **Benoit Favre**
Aix-Marseille Univ, Université de Toulon, CNRS, LIS, Marseille, France
`nicolas.zampieri@etu.univ-amu.fr` and `first.last@lis-lab.fr`

Abstract

This paper describes the Veyn system, submitted to the closed track of the PARSEME Shared Task 2018 on automatic identification of verbal multiword expressions (VMWEs). Veyn is based on a sequence tagger using recurrent neural networks. We represent VMWEs using a variant of the begin-inside-outside encoding scheme combined with the VMWE category tag. In addition to the system description, we present development experiments to determine the best tagging scheme. Veyn is freely available, covers 19 languages, and was ranked ninth (MWE-based) and eight (Token-based) among 13 submissions, considering macro-averaged F1 across languages.

1 Introduction

Multiword expressions (MWEs) pose problem for NLP systems such as machine translation. For instance, in English *there are plenty more fish in the sea* would be translated into French as *une de perdu, dix de retrouvées* (lit. *one lost, ten found*) and not word-by-word as *il y a plus de poissons dans la mer*. To be able to translate MWEs correctly, however, we have to first identify them. Automatic identification of MWEs, and in particular of verbal MWEs (VMWEs), is the topic of this paper.

The PARSEME shared task 2018 is an evaluation campaign of systems for the identification of VMWEs (Ramisch et al., 2018).[1] This task presents many challenges, such as the presence of variants, discontinuous and ambiguous MWEs (Constant et al., 2017). Our system "Veyn" is based on a sequence tagger using recurrent neural networks (RNNs). We represent VMWEs using a variant of the standard begin-inside-outside (BIO) encoding scheme. Moreover, we achieve VMWE categorization by combining the VMWE category with BIO tags. The goal of the RNN is to predict the correct BIO+category tag for each token. We use no external corpus or word embeddings to train our system, hence we participated in the closed track. Veyn is freely available,[2] and covers 19 of the 20 languages of the shared task (all except Arabic, which required a special license).

Sequence taggers were successfully employed by many systems for MWE identification in the past. Most existing models and systems, however, represent features as discrete values taken from finite sets instead of continuous vectors. Examples of such systems employ conditional random fields (Constant and Sigogne, 2011; Riedl and Biemann, 2016; Maldonado et al., 2017; Scholivet and Ramisch, 2017) and structured perceptron (Schneider et al., 2014). Most recent NLP systems for sequence tagging, however, are based on RNNs. Our system follows this trend by adapting an RNN model successful in other tagging tasks to VMWE identification.

Our system is similar to MUMULS, submitted to the previous PARSEME shared task, edition 1.0 (Klyueva et al., 2017). MUMULS was evaluated on fifteen languages with variable results. Our system differs from MUMULS in the hyper-parameter configuration, the tag encoding scheme (IO for MU-MULS, BIO for Veyn), the use of pre-initialized embeddings (not used by MUMULS) and the number of recurrent layers (1 in MUMULS, 2 in Veyn). In the remainder of this paper, we describe the system

---

[1]`http://multiword.sourceforge.net/sharedtask2018`

[2]`https://github.com/zamp13/Veyn`. The version described in this paper corresponds to commit `845f33a`

Proceedings of the Joint Workshop on
Linguistic Annotation, Multiword Expressions and Constructions (LAW-MWE-CxG-2018), pages 290–296
Santa Fe, New Mexico, USA, August 25-26, 2018.

	La	musique	n'	adoucit	pas	toujours	les	mœurs	.
BIO	B	I	g	I	g	g	I	I	O
IO+cat	IVID	IVID	g	IVID	g	g	IVID	IVID	O
BIO+cat	BVID	IVID	g	IVID	g	g	IVID	IVID	O

Figure 1: Three tagging schemes for an example sentence in French: BIO, IO+cat and BIO+cat.

architecture (Sec. 2), the tuning experiments on the development data (Sec. 3), and the results at the shared task (Sec. 4), before concluding (Sec. 5).

2 System Description

We use CoNLL-U's LEMMA and UPOS fields as input features (falling back to FORM and XPOS, respectively, if the former are absent).[3] Each token's LEMMA and UPOS are converted into one-hot vectors, which are then transformed into embeddings and concatenated. Input LEMMA and UPOS embeddings are pre-initialized on the shared task training corpora, but fine-tuned during the training phase. These embeddings are then forwarded to a double bidirectional recurrent layer using gated recurrent units (GRU). Finally, each BIO label prediction is based on a softmax layer that takes as input the concatenation of the GRU cell outputs in both directions for each token. VMWEs annotations are reconstructed on the output based on heuristic rules that group together 'B' and 'I' tags with the same category.

BIO encoding   For all our experiments, we used a variant of the BIO scheme (Ramshaw and Marcus, 1995). In the original BIO scheme, every token is tagged 'B', 'I' or 'O'. If the tag is 'B', it means that the token is the at the beginning of a VMWE. The tag 'I' means the token is inside a VMWE. Finally, if the token's tag is 'O', it means the token does not belong to an VMWE. Since BIO was originally designed for continuous sequences, a special label (lowercase 'g') is used for tokens not belonging to an expression, but occurring in between words that belong to an expression (Schneider et al., 2014). BIO allows abstracting away the order of VMWEs in the sentence. However, it does not allow representing overlaps, that is, tokens belonging to more than one VMWE at the same time. These are quite rare, corresponding to 3,293 out of 982,155 tokens that are part of a VMWE (0.34%) in the training, development and test corpora. We deal with overlaps simply by repeating the sentence and adding one VMWE annotation to each copy of the sentence.

Figure 1 shows different tagging schemes used to tune our system on a French discontinuous VMWE of the verbal idiom (VID) category.[4] The first one is BIO: *La* is tagged B to indicate where the VID begins, ***musique***, ***adoucit***, ***les***, and ***moeurs*** are inside the expression, *n'*, *pas*, and *toujours* do not belong to the expression, but occur in between words that belong to the expression, and the period is outside of the expression. Notice that the system must identify the precise words that are part of the VMWE, and not its span, thus the need for a special tag 'g' to indicate intermediate tokens.

During system development, one of our goals was to evaluate different tagging schemes and choose the best one based on the development corpus performances. Therefore, in addition to the extended BIO scheme, we also tested an adaptation that includes category labels (BIO+cat). 'B' and 'I' tags are thus concatenated with the provided VMWE's category labels (IRV, LVC.full, VID, etc). The idea is that categories present quite heterogeneous characteristics, so it may be a good idea to model/learn them separately in the neural network. This is illustrated in the last row of Figure 1. Finally, We have also evaluated our system using an inside-outside scheme similar to the one used in MUMULs (Klyueva et al., 2017). This scheme does not distinguish the token that begins an expression from the others (IO+cat).[5]

---

[3] http://universaldependencies.org/format.html

[4] Categories are described at http://parsemefr.lif.univ-mrs.fr/parseme-st-guidelines/1.1

[5] Though both are not fully comparable because MUMULS does not use a special label (lowercase 'g') for intervening

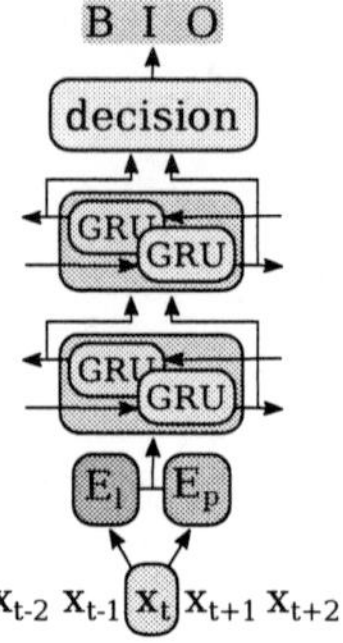

Figure 2: Veyn's architecture, with two layers of bidirectional GRU based on lemma (E_l) and POS (E_p) embeddings, Source: (Scholivet et al., 2018).

Given the performance of these tagging schemes (Sec. 3), we decided not experiment with IO tags, as they were not considered as a promising representation choice.

MWE tagger Veyn is based on a recurrent neural network. Figure 2 shows the architecture of our system. It uses as inputs LEMMA and UPOS (falling back to FORM and XPOS, respectively, if the former are absent). Because of limitations of the library used to implement the system, we must set a fixed length for all sentences in the corpus. Therefore, we considered that each sentence contains 128 tokens. If the sentence is shorter, we pad it with zeros until we reach 128 tokens. If it is longer, we crop it and ignore all remaining tokens. Padding should not pose problems, as the network should easily learn that zeroes are always tagged using a special padding label. Cropping, on the other hand, affects 400 out of 317,816 sentences (0.13%) in the training, development and test corpora, especially in Romanian (148 sentences), Turkish (125 sentences) and Italian (85 sentences). Raising the sentence length above 128 could avoid cropping sentences at the expense of significantly slowing down the RNN training.

Each token's LEMMA and UPOS, represented as one-hot vectors, are transformed into dense vectors of dimension 250 by the first trainable layer of the model, represented by E_l and E_p in Figure 2. In the submitted system, we have pre-initialized these embeddings using word2vec on the training corpus itself.[6] Since pre-initialized embeddings are learned on lemmas and POS tags rather than surface forms, the reduced size of the training corpus does not prevent us from generating useful representations in the form of 250-dimensional vectors.

The first recurrent layer takes as input the concatenation of the embeddings layers E_l and E_p. The second recurrent layer takes as input the concatenation of the forward and backward vectors of the previous one. Both are composed of identical gated recurrent units (GRU), a variant of long short-term memory units (LSTMs). Each recurrent layer is bidirectional, and contains 512 neurons per input position. We use two recurrent layers because preliminary experiments indicated that models using one or three recurrent layers presented lower performance. We have used no regularization or drop-out, but we believe that this could further improve the performance of our system in the future.

For the decision, the activation layer takes the output of the forward and backward units of the second recurrent layer, and use a softmax function to transform results into probabilities for each possible tag. We then choose the tag with the highest probability. Finally, the predicted tags use the BIO scheme provided in the training data. We used heuristics to recognize which tokens are part of the same expression, that is, to transform all tags from the BIO format into the required `cupt` format.

These heuristics will first convert all 'O' and 'g' tags into an asterisk, indicating that the token is not part of a VMWE.[7] Then, for every token tagged with a 'B', we assign it a new VMWE identifier. Furthermore, when BIO+cat or IO+cat are used, we categorize the token according to the predicted

---

tokens.

[6] Word2vec parameters for pre-initialized embeddings: Skip-gram, 5-word window, 10 negative samples, downsampling rate of 1e-3, minimum count of 1, no hierarchical softmax, 15 iterations.

[7] `http://multiword.sourceforge.net/cupt-format`

	BG	DE	EL	ES	EU	FA	FR	HE	HR	HU	IT	PL	PT	RO	SL	TR	avg
							MWE-based										
BIO	48.60	17.60	16.89	18.55	50.70	65.04	58.68	10.06	18.00	84.60	24.13	56.94	53.17	72.60	39.20	45.09	**38.96**
BIO+cat	47.60	25.91	16.15	7.80	57.05	67.46	49.95	11.53	19.46	85.37	18.76	62.79	51.79	75.58	40.88	48.18	**41.56**
IO+cat	48.51	22.74	17.46	7.80	38.70	58.72	45.44	9.34	13.98	74.37	16.98	53.32	18.87	69.96	30.16	31.17	**35.44**
BIO+cat+PI	46.29	29.27	23.65	20.27	60.18	65.30	53.07	15.95	22.44	86.75	33.87	62.31	55.41	80.10	43.29	42.73	**46.31**
							Token-based										
BIO	53.76	42.63	44.53	37.41	62.76	78.25	65.83	22.91	40.69	87.16	36.58	65.68	60.32	78.78	53.37	51.21	**53.90**
BIO+cat	57.83	42.90	32.39	19.48	66.15	75.99	58.89	14.68	31.01	87.36	30.65	69.05	58.49	80.65	52.64	54.03	**50.88**
IO+cat	58.52	44.23	44.12	19.48	59.65	76.61	60.62	23.10	40.02	79.9	38.22	67.29	39.87	78.14	49.38	71.72	**52.13**
BIO+cat+PI	53.88	44.51	42.41	33.74	66.26	73.72	65.32	24.56	41.43	88.38	42.44	68.31	57.36	82.94	52.68	47.43	**55.34**

Table 1: Performance of tested tagging schemes on the development corpus, according to MWE-based and Token-based F1. PI stands for pre-initialized embeddings layer.

category. All subsequent 'I' tokens are associated to the VMWE identifier of the closest preceding 'B', as long as both have the same category. Given that the RNN does not have hard constraints on allowed label sequences, a token can be labelled 'I' even if there is no preceding token labelled 'B'. In this case, we treat the 'I' token as a 'B' starting a new VMWE. For example, in the Spanish sentence *Gracias a Dios vamos conociendo un poquito mas de lo que podria ser un gobierno [...]*, the tokens *vamos* and *conociendo* are respectively tagged 'B+MVC' and 'I+MVC', and so are the tokens *podria* and *ser*. Our heuristics will thus identify a first VMWE *vamos conociendo* and a second one *podria ser*.

All parameters other than the input vectors are initialized randomly.[8] We used `train.cupt` files to train our models for all languages, `dev.cupt` to find the optimal tag encoding scheme, and `test.blind.cupt` to obtain the predicted results for submission. We used the Python library Keras to implement our system, using Tensorflow as backend. We use `sparse_categorical_crossentropy` as loss function, Nadam as optimizer, training takes 10 epochs, and batches are of size 128.

3 Tuning the system

In section 2 we discussed several tagging schemes that could be used to represent VMWEs. To choose which one we would submit to the shared task, we have searched the best tagging scheme on all languages based on their performance on the development corpus. We have tuned our system only on the languages for which we have a training and a development corpus (that is, EN, LT and HI are not considered).

Table 1 shows the results of our experiments to tune our system with different tagging schemes on the development corpus. Each column represents a language code (e.g. BG for Bulgarian, DE for German, etc.) and the last column contains the macro-average over all languages. Two F1 scores were considered: MWE-based performs strict per-MWE comparison, whereas Token-based F1 is a fuzzy score, taking partial matches into account (Savary et al., 2017; Ramisch et al., 2018).

When BIO tags are compared with BIO+cat tags, we noticed that the results depend on the training corpus size. For example, the Romanian corpus is much larger than the Spanish corpus. In Romanian, using category labels in BIO+cat seems to increase performance, whereas in Spanish it seems to degrade performance. These results indicate that the size of the training corpus is important to determine the tagging scheme. Other factors that may affect the quality of predictions include the quality of the corpus, which can be estimated as the inter-annotator agreement. For instance, inter-annotator agreement is lower for Spanish than for Romanian (Ramisch et al., 2018).

When we compare the BIO+cat and BIO schemes on average, BIO+cat scores are higher on the MWE-based evaluation (41.56 for BIO+cat vs. 38.96 for BIO) and BIO scores are higher on the Token-based evaluation (50.88 for BIO+cat vs. 53.90 for BIO). A similar trend is observed when comparing IO+car and BIO+cat, with IO+cat performing better than BIO+cat on the Token-based evaluation (52.13 for IO+car vs. 50.88 for BIO+cat). Both BIO and IO+cat use reduced tagsets with respect to BIO+cat, and

---

[8]As a consequence, the results reported in this paper are not fully reproducible and may oscillate because of random initialization. This has been corrected in the latest version of the system, after the submission.

		avg F1 on dev	avg F1 on test
General	MWE-based	46.68	36.94
	TOK-based	56.32	44.9
Continuous	MWE-based	**49.75**	39.66
Discontinuous	MWE-based	34.23	25.94
Multi-token	MWE-based	48.58	28.96
Single-token	MWE-based	9.23	24.25
Seen-in-train	MWE-based	**69.71**	**55.65**
Unseen-in-train	MWE-based	10.55	11.05
Variant-of-train	MWE-based	**60.16**	46.47
Identical-to-train	MWE-based	**65.49**	**64.36**

Table 2: Average (avg) of characteristics and categories on the development corpus and on the test corpus.

this helps in recognizing words that are parts of an expression. However, these tagsets are not accurate enough to represent full expressions, especially after the use of heuristics to reconstruct the VMWE annotation from the predicted tags. Therefore, we chose BIO+cat as our submission tagging scheme for all languages, assuming that MWE-based evaluation has priority over Token-based evaluation.

Furthermore, the performance of the model depends on the initialization of the RNN. Therefore, we tried to pre-initialize (PI) the input layer with embeddings pre-trained on the training corpus for LEMMA and UPOS. On average, this considerably improves the model performance. However, for some languages such as Farsi, Polish, Portuguese and Turkish, BIO+cat scores are higher than BIO+cat+PI. This outlier behaviour should be investigated in the future to improve our system for these languages.

4   Results and analysis

Sixteen languages (listed in Table 1) contain a development file, whereas three languages are too small to have a development file. Table 2 shows the average F1 scores on the development corpora (16 languages) and on the test corpora (19 languages), both in general and according to linguistic characteristics of the VMWEs reported by the evaluation script.

If we focus on the average performance on the development corpus, we can see that Veyn is better at recognising continuous expressions (49.75%) than discontinuous expressions (34.23%). In fact, discontinuous expressions are more difficult to tag even if we have a special tag to identify tokens not belonging but occurring in the middle of an expression. More sophisticated models (e.g. tree-based or graph-based) would be required to represent discontinuous VMWEs more accurately.

Our system has better scores when it has seen a VMWE or its variants in the training corpus, rather than when VMWEs are unseen in the training corpus. It is indeed unlikely that, by training the system on the training corpus only, we could tag an expression which it has not been seen in the training corpus at all. Nonetheless, if it saw one token which is part of an expression, we may succeed to tag this token. This is why we have a non-zero score of 10.55% MWE-based F1 on expressions which are unseen in the training corpus. Most expressions are formed by several tokens. Therefore, Veyn has higher F1 scores for multi-token expressions (48.58%) than for single-token ones (9.23%).

Table 2 shows that the system obtains an F1 score which is about 10% higher on the development corpus than on the test corpus. The global results on the test corpus are 36.94%($\leq$ 46.68%) for general MWE-based evaluation and 44.9%($\leq$ 56.32%) for Token-based evaluation. Veyn performed better on the test corpus than on the development corpus for Single-token VMWEs. Only expressions identical to training corpus are stable: 65.49% for the development corpus and 64.36% for the test corpus.

These discrepancies could be explained by the low performance for the three languages for which no development set was available, which were also the languages with the smallest training corpora in terms of number of annotated VMWEs. Moreover, our system could not predict any correct VMWE for Bulgarian, whereas the MWE-based F1 score on the development corpus was 46.29. By observing the learning curves of the system, we do not believe that this is due to overfitting. Instead, we think that it can be related to the random initialization of parameters, associated with an insufficient number of training epochs, which led to lower F1 scores on the test corpus than on the development corpus. Our system was ranked ninth (eighth) on the average MWE-based (Toekn-based) F1 score on the official shared task 2018 ranking.

As for the prediction of different categories, the main factor influencing performance seems to be category frequency. While we do admit that some categories are probably harder to identify than others, we have observed that Veyn could not identify most VMWEs that appeared rarely in the training corpus. For instance, in French, only 2% of the VMWEs are tagged as LVC.cause in the development corpus, and 1% in the training corpus. Therefore, our system did not identify any LVC.cause correctly. On the other hand, IRVs correspond to 27% of the VMWEs in the training corpus in French. As a result, our system identified them with an F1 score of 0.72 in the development corpus.

Upon inspection of a sample of predictions for the French data, we have noticed some interesting facts. First, Veyn was capable of correctly identifying some VMWEs that were never observed in the training corpus. For example, Veyn tagged the VMWE ***donner résultat*** (*give result*) as LVC.full in the sentence *Les obligations de parité prévues par la loi ont **donné des résultats*** (dev). In the training corpus, the verb *donner* (*give*) is often annotated as part of an LVC.full, and the noun *résultat* (*result*) was also seen as part of the LVC.full ***produire résultat*** (*produce result*) and ***avoir pour résultat*** (*have as result*). We hypothesize that the RNN was able to combine information from several training instances to be able to tag a new, unseen VMWE.

On the other hand, some seen VMWEs such as ***mener réflexion*** (*carry out reflection*) were missed, as in the sentence *Une **réflexion** commune est **menée** aves les enseignants [...]* (dev). This probably happens because this VMWE only occurs in the training corpus in active voice, with its components in reversed order. The RNN was not able to handle long-distance discontinuity and order change.

Finally, the transformation heuristics used to "glue" the BIO tags into a VMWE in the `cupt` sometimes led to errors. For instance, a sentence may start with two consecutive VMWEs, such as ***Il faut tenir compte*** *de [...]* (dev). Here, ***il faut*** (*One must*) is the first expression and ***tenir compte*** (*take [into] account*) is the second one, both categorized as VID. Our system tagged both as a single VID composed of 4 tokens. This shows that the heuristics could probably be improved if they took POS and syntactic dependencies into account.

One particular limitation of our system is that it cannot tag a single token with several VMWE tags, but we can have sentences containing tokens that belong to several VMWEs. For example, *Il devrait comparaître dans les prochains jours pour indiquer s'il **plaide coupable** ou **non coupable** [...]* (train) contains two expressions which involve the same token: ***plaide coupable*** (*plead guilty*) is the first VID, and ***plaide non coupable*** (*plead non guilty*) is the second one. Our system cannot recognize these two expressions because it can only predict one tag per token.

5 Conclusions and future work

We have presented the Veyn system for the automatic identification of verbal multiword expressions. The system is based on a sequence tagger using an RNN over an extended BIO scheme enriched with category labels. The system has participated in the PARSEME shared task 2018 on the closed track, obtaining reasonably good results. It was ranked ninth and eighth considering the cross-lingual macro-averaged MWE-based and Token-based F1 scores. It performed better on VMWEs seen in the training corpus (identical or variants). It was fifth at the shared task ranking for single-token VMWEs.

Veyn can be improved in several points, especially to deal with expressions never seen in the training corpora. We would like to train our system using embeddings already pre-initialized on larger non-annotated corpora, beyond those provided for the shared task. Moreover, we believe that integrating external lexical resources could improve the system's coverage. A second point for future work concerns the initialization of the RNN, to make it more robust and performing. The initialization of the RNN is currently random, but sometimes the system training procedure fails and predicts no tag at all. These runs were simply manually detected and discarded for the moment. We would like to study why this happens, and find automatic ways to prevent it. A third idea for future work would be to achieve representing overlapping VMWEs. This is quite rare in general, but does occur in many languages, such as English or French. Our system does not handle these cases.

Acknowledgments

This work was supported by the IC1207 PARSEME COST action[9] and by the PARSEME-FR project (ANR-14-CERA-0001).[10]

References

Matthieu Constant and Anthony Sigogne. 2011. MWU-aware part-of-speech tagging with a CRF model and lexical resources. In *Proceedings of the ALC Workshop on Multiword Expressions: From Parsing and Generation to the Real World*, MWE 2011, pages 49–56. Association for Computational Linguistics.

Mathieu Constant, Gülşen Eryiğit, Johanna Monti, Lonneke van der Plas, Carlos Ramisch, Michael Rosner, and Amalia Todirascu. 2017. Multiword expression processing: A survey. *Computational Linguistics*, 43(4):837–892.

Natalia Klyueva, Antoine Doucet, and Milan Straka. 2017. Neural networks for multi-word expression detection. In *Proceedings of the 13th Workshop on Multiword Expressions (MWE 2017)*, pages 60–65, Valencia, Spain, April. Association for Computational Linguistics.

Alfredo Maldonado, Lifeng Han, Erwan Moreau, Ashjan Alsulaimani, Koel Dutta Chowdhury, Carl Vogel, and Qun Liu. 2017. Detection of verbal multi-word expressions via conditional random fields with syntactic dependency features and semantic re-ranking. In *Proceedings of the 13th Workshop on Multiword Expressions* , MWE '17, pages 114–120. Association for Computational Linguistics, April.

Carlos Ramisch, Silvio Ricardo Cordeiro, Agata Savary, Veronika Vincze, Verginica Barbu Mititelu, Archna Bhatia, Maja Buljan, Marie Candito, Polona Gantar, Voula Giouli, Tunga Güngör, Abdelati Hawwari, Uxoa Iñurrieta, Jolanta Kovalevskaitė, Simon Krek, Timm Lichte, Chaya Liebeskind, Johanna Monti, Carla Parra Escartín, Behrang QasemiZadeh, Renata Ramisch, Nathan Schneider, Ivelina Stoyanova, Ashwini Vaidya, and Abigail Walsh. 2018. Edition 1.1 of the PARSEME Shared Task on Automatic Identification of Verbal Multiword Expressions. In *Proceedings of the Joint Workshop on Linguistic Annotation, Multiword Expressions and Constructions (LAW-MWE-CxG 2018)*, Santa Fe, New Mexico, USA, August. Association for Computational Linguistics.

Lance Ramshaw and Mitch Marcus. 1995. Text chunking using transformation-based learning. In *3rd Workshop on Very Large Corpora*, pages 82–94.

Martin Riedl and Chris Biemann. 2016. Impact of MWE resources on multiword recognition. In *Proceedings of the 12th Workshop on Multiword Expressions* , MWE '16, pages 107–111. Association for Computational Linguistics.

Agata Savary, Carlos Ramisch, Silvio Cordeiro, Federico Sangati, Veronika Vincze, Behrang QasemiZadeh, Marie Candito, Fabienne Cap, Voula Giouli, Ivelina Stoyanova, and Antoine Doucet. 2017. The PARSEME Shared Task on Automatic Identification of Verbal Multiword Expressions. In *Proceedings of the 13th Workshop on Multiword Expressions (MWE 2017)*, pages 31–47, Valencia, Spain, April. Association for Computational Linguistics.

Nathan Schneider, Emily Danchik, Chris Dyer, and Noah A. Smith. 2014. Discriminative lexical semantic segmentation with gaps: Running the MWE gamut. *Transactions of the Association for Computational Linguistics*, 2(1):193–206.

Manon Scholivet and Carlos Ramisch. 2017. Identification of ambiguous multiword expressions using sequence models and lexical resources. In *Proceedings of the 13th Workshop on Multiword Expressions*, MWE '17, pages 167–175. Association for Computational Linguistics, April.

Manon Scholivet, Carlos Ramisch, and Benoit Favre. 2018. Identification d'expressions polylexicales avec réseaux de neurones récurrents. *Traitement Automatique des Langues*. (submitted).

---

[9] http://www.parseme.eu
[10] http://parsemefr.lif.univ-mrs.fr/

Author Index

Association for Computational Linguistics
209 N. Eighth Street
Stroudsburg, Pennsylvania 18360

ISBN 978-1-5108-6913-4